# INTERNATIONAL SYSTEMS IN WORLD HISTORY

## REMAKING THE STUDY OF INTERNATIONAL RELATIONS

# INTERNATIONAL SYSTEMS IN WORLD HISTORY

## REMAKING THE STUDY OF INTERNATIONAL RELATIONS

---

## BARRY BUZAN AND RICHARD LITTLE

OXFORD
UNIVERSITY PRESS

# OXFORD

UNIVERSITY PRESS

Great Clarendon Street, Oxford OX2 6DP

Oxford University Press is a department of the University of Oxford.
It furthers the University's objective of excellence in research, scholarship,
and education by publishing worldwide in

Oxford New York

Athens Auckland Bangkok Bogotá Buenos Aires Calcutta
Cape Town Chennai Dar es Salaam Delhi Florence Hong Kong Istanbul
Karachi Kuala Lumpur Madrid Melbourne Mexico City Mumbai
Nairobi Paris São Paulo Singapore Taipei Tokyo Toronto Warsaw

with associated companies in Berlin Ibadan

Oxford is a registered trade mark of Oxford University Press
in the UK and in certain other countries

Published in the United States
by Oxford University Press Inc., New York

British Library Cataloguing in Publication Data

Data available

Library of Congress Cataloging in Publication Data

Data available

ISBN 0-19-878065-6

1 3 5 7 9 10 8 6 4 2

Typeset by RefineCatch Limited, Bungay, Suffolk
Printed in Great Britain by
TJ International Ltd., Padstow, Cornwall

*To Adam Watson*

# PREFACE

This book has had a rather long and complicated gestation. It began when first Henry Hardy and then Tim Barton raised the possibility with Richard Little of writing an IR textbook for Oxford University Press. On the second occasion, Richard Little agreed provided that Barry Buzan was willing to collaborate. This was in 1992 and the two of us, along with Charles Jones, had just completed the final version of *The Logic of Anarchy*. We had very much enjoyed working together and found that our thoughts were running along similar tracks. In particular, we wanted to pursue the synthesis of IR theory and world history that we had begun in the earlier book. Only in this way, we thought, could the concept of international system be adequately conveyed, and our central idea was that international system was the key to the whole subject of international relations. We also thought that such a synthesis would have great potential for a novel approach to IR, and in this expectation we have not (at least from our perspective) been disappointed.

Our ambition was not to write a standard text around the current orthodoxies and debates in the study of international relations. Rather, we wanted to take the main threads of international relations theory, marry them to a fairly orthodox view of world history, and use the fusion to throw light on both. Our purpose in this book is thus to comprehend the whole of the international system in both its historical and its social science aspects. Our assumption is that there can be no systematic or coherent development of grand theory in International Relations unless it incorporates both the systemic and the historical dimensions of the subject. That is where we think theory in our discipline should start from, and the aim of this book is to introduce the subject in that theoretically and methodologically pluralist form, giving overviews of both the subject matter, and the ways in which it can be studied. The book combines a highly generalized world historical account of international systems with a toolkit of mainstream IR theory. Our position is a synthesizing one: history and theory need each other, just as change and continuity cannot be understood apart.

We were fully aware from an early point that we would have to restrain our natural inclination as theorists to pursue fascinating, but arcane and difficult, lines of enquiry. Some of these we handled by developing them as spinoff papers, and the refrain 'remember that this is supposed to be a textbook' became a regular part of our correspondence. Although our ambition remained constant throughout the project, we did experience much more difficulty than expected in finding the right mix of theory and history. Too much theory meant that the analysis got hopelessly complicated and drifted towards a rather mechanical presentation. Too much history meant that length spun quickly out of control. Since both of us came to the project better equipped with theory than with history, there was also a danger that we would be seduced into the endless fascinations of the human story, and never finish our research. In the event, we had to go through two failed drafts before we had learned enough to find a way of doing it. This text is thus the result of a long and rather steep learning curve. It contains much from the earlier drafts, but in this version Buzan did the first drafts of Chapters 4–5 and 8–17, and Little the first drafts of the Introduction, Chapters 1–3, 6–7, and 18–19. We then shuttled the chapters back and forth with each writing extensively into the other's text. We have managed to reconcile all of our major disagreements, and we present this as a truly joint text.

We owe thanks to many people and institutions who helped us along the way. The Economic and Social Research Council (ESRC) provided us with a grant that enabled Little to buy a year of study leave, funded six months of research assistance, and helped with travel costs. The University of Bristol also provided him with a four-month study leave at the end of 1998 which enabled him to complete the penultimate draft of the book. The Copenhagen Peace Research Institute (COPRI) provided both some additional weeks of research assistance, and a sounding board off which we could bounce drafts at various stages. The University of Westminster allowed Buzan leave of absence for the academic year 1995–6, and for half of the academic year 1997–8. The Swedish Council for Research in the Humanities and Social Sciences (HSFR) did Buzan the honour of appointing him Olof Palme visiting professor for 1997. This enabled him to spend six months in the congenial and stimulating environment of the Department of Peace and Development Research in Gothenburg University (PADRIGU), where he had the freedom to focus hard on writing the first drafts of Chapters 8–16.

At what turned out to be an early phase of the project, our first research assistants, Wolf Hassdorf and June Ishikawa, provided us with a steady and invaluable stream of sources, statistical material, and historical sketches on various topics without which it would have taken us much longer to get a grip on world history. Our second research assistant, Jesper Sigurdsson, came in during the final stage, and did a remarkably quick and effective search for a range of mostly statistical data that we needed to fill in the remaining gaps in our story. To all three of these we give our warmest thanks for being dedicated, efficient, and a pleasure to work with.

Many people have read and commented on all or part of this book. At COPRI, Thomas Diez, Lene Hansen, Pertti Joenniemi, Ole Wæver, and Jaap de Wilde made extremely helpful comments on earlier drafts. Tim Dunne, Yale Ferguson, Barry Gills, Martin Hall, Beatrice Heuser, Charles Jones, and an anonymous referee for OUP all helped us to steer the penultimate draft towards the final version. We must also thank Tim Barton for his endless patience; he must have wondered at times if this book was ever going to appear.

Barry Buzan would also like to thank Gerry Segal, with whom he worked on *Anticipating the Future* in parallel with this project, and from which collaboration there was much fruitful spillover into this one.

Both of us would like to give special thanks to Adam Watson, to whom we dedicate this book. His work stimulated our interest by demonstrating some of the possibilities of marrying IR theory and world history. That he has remained so active in promoting the English school since its early days testifies to the wisdom of the school's founding fathers in mixing academics and practitioners. He has helped to inspire our own interest in developing the English school tradition.

And last, but by no means least, we would like to thank our wives. Deborah Buzan not only tolerated the long absence of Barry in Sweden, but also put up with more than the average amount of 'fascinating' information about matters far removed from her interests. Christine Stratford-Little sometimes thought that Richard might just as well have been in Sweden for all she saw of him, and had to extend all her professional counselling skills to maintain tranquillity at home when the going on the book got rough.

*London*                                                                        B.B.
*Bristol*                                                                       R.L.
*July 1999*

# OUTLINE CONTENTS

# DETAILED CONTENTS

# LIST OF FIGURES

# LIST OF MAPS

# LIST OF TABLES

# ABBREVIATIONS

| | |
|---|---|
| ASEAN | Association of Southeast Asian Nations |
| EU | European Union |
| FDI | foreign direct investment |
| GATT | General Agreement on Tariffs and Trade |
| HGB | hunter-gatherer band |
| IAEA | International Atomic Energy Agency |
| IBRD | International Bank for Reconstruction and Development, a.k.a. World Bank |
| ICJ | International Court of Justice |
| ICSU | International Council of Scientific Unions |
| IGO | international governmental organization |
| IMF | International Monetary Fund |
| INGO | international non-governmental organization |
| INTELSAT | International Telecommunications Satellite programme |
| IPE | international political economy |
| IR | international relations (the discipline) |
| ITU | International Telecommunications Union |
| IUCN | International Union for the Conservation of Nature and Natural Resources |
| MFN | Most Favoured Nation |
| MOP | Mode of Production |
| NAFTA | North American Free Trade Association |
| NATO | North Atlantic Treaty Organization |
| NIC | newly industrialized country |
| NPT | non-proliferation treaty |
| OAU | Organization of African Unity |
| OECD | Organization for Economic Cooperation and Development |
| OPEC | Organization of Petroleum Exporting Countries |
| TNC | transnational corporation |
| UN | United Nations |
| UNCTAD | United Nations Conference on Trade and Development |
| UNEP | United Nations Environment Programme |
| WHO | World Health Organization |
| WTO | World Trade Organization |
| YMCA | Young Men's Christian Association |

# INTRODUCTION

This book seeks to remake the study of international relations by viewing international systems from a world historical perspective. It is aimed both at students working in the field of International Relations (hereafter identified as IR), and at others interested in examining the social sciences and history in macro or holistic terms. In a sense it is a textbook, and written as such: for example we include an extensive glossary of the key terms used in the text (pp. 440–2). But it is not the usual type of textbook that presents how a discipline currently sees itself and introduces its subject matter to beginners. We want to use the marriage of theory and history to change what IR understands as its subject matter, and how it sees its mainstream theories relating to each other. Moreover, it is not just designed for an IR audience; we hope to attract interest and comment from historical sociologists, archaeologists, world historians, and anyone else trying to understand humankind as a whole. The book is designed to be accessible to anyone who has mastered a standard undergraduate course on international relations and our hope is that everyone who reads this book will find themselves looking at international relations from a more holistic, more integrated, and more historically contextualized perspective than the one they had before.

Perhaps the biggest difference between this and other IR texts is that instead of tracing the history of the contemporary international system back 350 years to the Treaty of Westphalia in 1648, the date conventionally used in mainstream IR to mark the origins of this system, we examine the whole history of the multiple international systems that have formed over a period of more than five millennia. Our starting point is 3500 BC when the Sumerian city-states began to interact in the area between the Tigris and the Euphrates that now forms part of modern Iraq. From our perspective, it was these city-states that constituted the first known fully-fledged international system. But we also find it both fruitful and necessary to investigate the pre-international systems that evolved during several tens of thousands of years before the rise of city-states. These systems not only provided the precursors for international systems, but existed alongside them right down to the twentieth century. Pre-international systems provide the backdrop to an era of five millennia when a range of very different international systems came into existence around the world. These international systems have been largely ignored within mainstream IR, in part because of the assumption fostered, especially in neorealism, that they can be accounted for by established theory. It is presupposed that there is little purpose to be served by investigating them, because although they provide additional historical depth, they give no extra theoretical purchase on the understanding of international systems. We fundamentally disagree with this position.

From our perspective, existing frameworks in IR are seriously crippled by their failure to build on a long view of history. And because mainstream IR theories are derived almost exclusively from the model of the Westphalian international system established in the seventeenth century, they inadvertently, but effectively, isolate the whole discourse of IR from the wider debates about world history. IR theorists have largely failed to follow the English school injunction that history requires 'the elucidation of the unlikeness between past and present' (Butterfield 1949: 10). On the contrary, to the extent that IR theorists have turned their attention to world history, they have been mainly impressed by how similar previous international systems have been to our own.This position reflects a long-standing tradition of thought in Europe. Nearly 200 years ago, Heeren (1819) produced a Manual charting the history of the European 'states-system'. In outlining his theoretical framework, Heeren observed how similar the European states-system was to the Greek and Italian city-states, as well as the Diadochi Empires, formed after the collapse of Alexander the Great's empire. It has taken a historical sociologist to observe, albeit controversially, that the emergence of international relations is 'coeval with the origins of nation-states' and thus at least to imply that Europe provides the first, and only, example of an international system (Giddens 1985: 4). Like Giddens, we think that there is something very distinctive about the international system that formed in Europe after 1500. But we disagree strongly that the modern European system is the only relevant case, and we want to paint our picture of international systems on a much broader historical canvas. In doing so, we eschew the route followed by Heeren, as well as many contemporary IR theorists, who focus exclusively on the limited number of international systems in world history that appear, superficially, to resemble the contemporary international system. We are intrigued by Wight's (1979: 24) remark that the 'political kaleidoscope of the Greek and Hellenistic ages looks modern to our eyes, while the immense majesty of the Roman peace, and the Christian unity of the medieval world, seem remote and alien'. Do the Greek and Hellenistic ages really look modern? And is the Roman peace and medieval world as 'remote and alien' as Wight makes out? Just as important, can we characterize these very different political arenas as international systems?

To develop a really effective world history of international systems it is necessary to rethink entirely how to approach the conceptualization of the international system. There are two problems with existing mainstream conceptualizations. First, because they are so closely modelled on the Westphalian international system, they are unable to capture the huge swaths of world history where international systems have taken a radically different form. Second, earlier international systems are only embraced by the Westphalian model because the conceptualization of what constitutes an international system is so narrowly defined. Existing conceptualizations fail to expose important differences between the modern international system and its seemingly similar predecessors. A theoretical framework that can reveal how international systems have evolved across the entire spatial and temporal sweep of human history needs to be much more elaborate than anything that currently exists.

When one confronts the existing concepts of international systems with the task of providing a world historical narrative, it becomes apparent just how seriously underdeveloped they are. Setting up an enriched theoretical framework of the international system pays significant dividends. Although there are other theoretical frameworks available to examine world history, we argue that the framework unfolded in this book generates a version and a vision of world history that are more coherent and comprehensive than any of the rival world historical narratives that have emerged in recent years. We aim to prove that Westphalia-based IR theory is not only incapable of understanding premodern international systems, but also that its lack of historical perspective makes it unable to answer, or in many cases even address, the most important questions about the modern international system. And we argue that the historical narrowness of most IR thinking goes a long way towards explaining why IR debates have had so little impact on debates in the other social sciences and history. Our view is that IR has failed to occupy a proper role in the macro-debates of the social sciences and history, and indeed that most of the interest in world history that does exist in IR is the result of its successful colonization by the world systems school deriving from the work of Wallerstein. Our hope is to show how this disastrous underachievement might begin to be rectified. Our historical account thus propels us to challenge the most fundamental theoretical assumptions about international systems that are found in the contemporary study of IR.

The book is built on three basic premises. The first is that none of the existing conceptualizations of the international system in IR can describe and analyse how international systems have emerged and evolved through the course of world history. The second is that the level of theoretical understanding in IR has been held back by a failure to examine international systems from a world historical perspective. The third premiss is that the international system constitutes the most effective unit for developing world history as well as for helping social scientists to advance a macro-analysis of social reality.

If these premises hold water, then it is surprising that so few links have been forged between world historians and IR theorists. Until recently, mainstream IR theorists have shown virtually no interest in examining international relations from a world historical perspective, nor have world historians shown much inclination to use an international systems framework to analyse world history. So although our theoretical framework and our world historical account of international systems are designed to be of interest to the general reader, we also wish, more specifically, to address and encourage a closer collaboration between IR theorists and world historians.

One of the great strengths of world histories is that they identify when critical transformation points have occurred in the past. Our framework shows that there have been three significant turning points in the world history of international systems. These are associated with a conjunction of step-level changes in some of the key components that make up our theoretical framework (all the components will be reviewed briefly at the end of this introduction). The first transformation point occurred more than 40,000 years ago when hunter-gatherer bands first began to engage in a form of exchange that resulted in the long-distance movement of goods and ideas (Bar-Yosef 1998). These goods and ideas were transferred from one group to another over hundreds and sometimes thousands of miles. Large numbers of hunter-gatherer bands were in indirect contact with each other and we associate these long lines of indirect contact with the first formation of pre-international systems. Because these hunter-gatherer bands were responsible for global colonization, these systems eventually encompassed virtually every corner of the habitable world and their last vestiges can still be dimly discerned today.

A second turning point can be traced back to 5,500 years ago when the very first state-like units began to emerge and interact. The mutual interactions between sets of these units formed the basis of the first fully-fledged international systems. Over time, the major units embraced by these systems became increasingly diversified and they included agrarian empires, nomadic empires, chiefdoms, city-states, and city leagues. For the next 5,000 years, this diversity persisted and represented a key defining feature of the ancient and classical historical era. During this era, pre-international systems and international systems coexisted, but international systems expanded at the expense of pre-international ones. Nevertheless, even by the end of this epoch, pre-international systems still occupied large sections of the globe, and for the majority of this period they also continued to expand into increasingly inaccessible and previously uninhabited regions. When the international systems expanded, they sometimes came into contact with each other and, over time, these separate systems coalesced. But an important feature of this epoch was the way that the economic and cultural sectors of international systems expanded further than the political sectors, so that international systems frequently established economic and cultural links without making political or military contact. Despite evidence of systems coalescing, a large number of discrete international systems persisted throughout this epoch.

The third turning point identified by our framework took place as recently as 500 years ago and it is most closely associated with the emergence of a new kind of political actor, the modern sovereign state. These actors formed initially in Europe, but by the end of the twentieth century, this mode of political organization had extended across the entire globe. The units in pre-international systems

were effectively eliminated, and so too was the diversity of actors that had flourished during the previous epoch. The various international systems that had
emerged and survived all around the globe over the previous 5,000 years coalesced
remarkably swiftly to form a single international system that extended over the
lands and seas of the planet. This extraordinarily rapid process was largely completed more than 150 years ago, giving birth to the fully global international
system, which in turn gave birth to the self-conscious study of international relations. But history has not stopped. There are debates about whether the Westphalian state is giving way to a postmodern state, and about whether military-political
relations are yielding pride of place to political-economic ones. These debates
open the door to questions about whether the modern era is now drawing to a
close.

On the basis of this short synopsis we can now say a little more about our three
basic premises. First, we need to justify our claim that existing frameworks are
unable to accommodate a world history of international systems. The importance
of the international system in IR thinking cannot be doubted. It represents one of
the central concepts in the discipline; indeed it is so central that the term is often
left undefined. Generally the international system is taken to be a shorthand way
of referring to the nexus of actors and interactions that constitute the subject
matter of international relations. It is this conception of the international system
that promotes the view that IR constitutes an independent discipline.

At first sight, it seems self-evident that the international system represents an
ideal vehicle for developing a world historical perspective. After all, in contemporary IR the international system constitutes a framework that makes it
possible to understand how international relations cohere across time and space.
Certainly it is taken for granted that the existing international system stretches
across the contemporary globe and that its origins can be traced back for several
centuries. So IR has habitually worked with the idea that the current international
system has extended across space and persisted over time.

But a significant factor has worked against examining the international system
from a world historical perspective. It is the deep-seated assumption in IR that the
Westphalian system epitomizes the international system. The assumption necessarily gives a strong Eurocentric bias to the discipline. Europe, it is argued, gave
birth to the modern sovereign state and so the international system defined in
terms of sovereign states must be viewed as an exclusively European product. Any
attempt to apply the concept to a previous era is deemed to be anachronistic. As
mentioned above, a softer line accepts that it is not inappropriate to apply the
term to earlier periods of history, and the Sumerian and Greek city-state systems
are sometimes cited as examples of international systems. But even from this
perspective, international systems only appear as relatively isolated episodes
within the context of a much broader world history.

The image of the international system as an interstate system is now so deeply ingrained that the two concepts are treated as synonymous. A whole network of terminology has grown up to reinforce this usage. So multinational companies, for example, are identified as transnational rather than international actors. At the same time, the background assumption is that these transnational actors operate within the existing international (meaning interstate) system. We have become so inured to the terminology that it is disorienting for us to think of international systems except in interstate terms. So, although the international system has sometimes been identified in terms of all the transactions that take place across state boundaries, this conception still privileges states as the defining unit of the system.

If the idea of international systems is to be extended to world history with any chance of success, it is essential to break free from this association. We need, for example, to be able to identify empires as international systems. Conventionally, when we follow the history of the Roman Empire, what we observe is a city-state expanding into an established international system to form the Roman Empire—a large and complex form of state. From our perspective, however, the Roman Empire constitutes a phase in the longer story of a Mediterranean–Middle Eastern international system: a phase in which the system's political structure takes a hierarchical rather than an anarchical form. At a very minimum, this change of labels matters in metaphorical terms. Just as it made a difference during the Cold War whether one thought of the Soviet Union as a state or as an empire (and thus as a kind of submerged international system), so it makes a difference whether analysts have to think of the Roman Empire as a state or as an international system in hierarchical form.

But we want to go beyond metaphorical analysis. Viewing the Roman Empire and the Soviet Union as types of international system forces us to reassess what we mean by an international system and how an international system should be conceptualized. The focus on sovereign states is too limiting. The established conceptualization only permits an understanding of the Westphalian system, and even for that purpose it is flawed. The underdeveloped nature of the concept becomes more apparent when one looks more closely at either the origins of the Westphalian system or the question of whether the contemporary international system is undergoing a transformation. In both cases, the existing theoretical framework proves inadequate and there has been a search for new vocabulary and new analytical tools (Ruggie 1993).

But little progress has been made so far. There have even been attempts to understand the contemporary international system by comparing it to the medieval era. But the literature on neomedievalism sharply divides between those who associate the term with an emerging cosmopolitanism and others who link it to a coming anarchy. There can be no clearer indication that IR lacks the tools to think clearly about either the past or the future than these references to neomedievalism. The only obvious feature that binds the medieval and contemporary worlds together is that neither can be accommodated within the Westphalian model. From our perspective, a more sophisticated framework is needed to see the similarities and differences between the three phases in the world history of international systems. Our world historical account suggests that although there is room for comparison, the future is going to look massively different from the historical epoch within which medieval Europe was located.

Our second premiss is that the development of theory in IR has been held back by its confinement to the Westphalian straitjacket. An IR-based world historical perspective challenges a range of theoretical assumptions that have become well established in IR. It therefore follows that the level of theoretical understanding in IR has been retarded by a failure to study international systems from a world historical perspective. For example, we dispute the widely held assumption, expressed with greatest clarity by the neorealists, that the shift from hierarchy to anarchy represents the most fundamental or deep structural political change that can be identified in world history. Our world history reveals a much more interesting picture. We can see, in the first instance, that anarchy and an absence of hierarchy persisted during the era of pre-international systems and again during the current 500-year epoch of the global international system. On the other hand, there were frequent and recurrent moves from anarchy to hierarchy in all of the international systems that formed during the 5,000-year period after international systems first came into existence. Our account of world history shows that it is change in the structure of the dominant units, not the move from hierarchy to anarchy, that represents the most fundamental, era-defining type of transformation in international systems. It can even be hypothesized within our framework that it is the nature of the dominant units that determines the propensity for, and (in)stability of, anarchic or hierarchic international system structures. The pre-international epoch was defined by interaction among hunter-gather bands, whereas the first international epoch was characterized by a whole host of structurally differentiated state-like units. Then, with the emergence of the modern sovereign state, all prior forms of units were effectively eliminated, marking the start of a second international epoch. It follows that we are also disputing the neorealist claim that anarchic systems are characterized by 'like units' that possess a common structure. Again, a comparison of the three epochs reveals the problem with the 'like unit' thesis. Although it holds for the first and third epochs, its universality is undermined by the intervening epoch that lasted for 5,000 years.

A further illustration of the problematic character of contemporary IR theory relates to the importance attached to polarity in IR theory in general and neorealism in particular. From a world historical perspective, the prolonged debate between advocates of the balance of power as opposed to hegemonic stability theory fails to take on board that it is a debate that only has relevance for the last 500 years of world history. The debate would have to be cast in very different terms if the previous two epochs were taken into account. As the details of our world history unfold, therefore, it becomes increasingly apparent just how many central IR assumptions are built on an understanding of the last 500 years and how many of them prove to be unfounded when a world historical perspective is adopted.

Our third premiss is that the international system constitutes the most effective unit for developing world history as well as for helping social scientists to advance a macro-analysis of social reality. World history, after falling out of fashion for some considerable time, has now undergone a significant revival, generating a renewed interest in the provision of overarching frameworks that can be used to trace the history of human beings across time and space. There is a desire to escape from the confinement imposed by histories written from within a specific time period or from a particular national or even continental perspective. Breaking loose from the confines imposed by these familiar and more parochial accounts of the past is not easy; and, as a consequence, world historians are engaged in a major debate about the kind of frameworks that can most usefully be employed to promote a world historical perspective. So far, IR has played little or no part in this debate. But if our assessment is correct, then the concept of the international system should be promoted as a framework for studying world history.

Sanderson (1995) claims that there are two leading approaches to world history. The first, now most closely associated with William McNeill (1991), but initially popularized earlier in the twentieth century by Spengler and Toynbee, uses the idea of a civilization as the central unit of analysis. Within the discipline of history, this is the dominant approach (Manning 1996: 777). The other, linked primarily to Immanuel Wallerstein (1974), focuses on world systems, and is rooted in historical sociology. Although they generate clear transformation points neither of these frameworks is as 'thick' as our conception of the international system. We accept that civilizations represent important units in world history. But there has been no attempt to identify the key processes and structures that define a civilization. Even more important, although McNeill recognizes the world historical importance of the mounted nomads who lived beyond the boundaries of the civilizations, he fails to embrace them systematically within his framework. Recently, McNeill (1998) has acknowledged the weaknesses in the civilizational framework, and has argued that a better framework is provided by what we call interaction capacity. What we show, however, is that although interaction capacity does play a crucial role in world history, its theoretical significance only becomes really apparent when examined in conjunction with the elements of process and structure.

The impact of Wallerstein's theory of world systems on world history and across the social sciences is indicated by the enormous literature it has inspired. He certainly does identify the basic economic and political structures and processes that define his world systems. Indeed, we would accept that he has developed a very powerful theoretical model. But we do not accept his argument that the military-political sector of a world system can be regarded as epiphenomenal and therefore ignored. From our perspective, the costs of eliminating this sector are very high. Another crucial problem with Wallerstein's framework is that he ignores the significance of interaction capacity. Moreover, his analysis only covers certain sections of the globe, leaving other sections as large 'black holes' (Adas 1998: 86). Finally, although Wallerstein does make reference to earlier periods, he is overwhelmingly concerned with the type of system he designates as a 'world economy' that emerged after AD 1500. It seems to us that both of the leading approaches in world history have produced theoretical frameworks that are relatively thin in comparison to the one that we formulate below.

Given how extensively Wallerstein's model has been adopted by analysts looking at the premodern world, despite being designed specifically to examine the post-1500 era, the preoccupation of IR theorists with a Westphalian model of the international system is probably insufficient to explain why world historians and others have failed to draw on these models. The truth is that attempts in IR to theorize about the international system have failed to resonate with world historians. Beyond the confines of IR, the international system is not widely regarded as an inherently useful or illuminating concept. For most people, the idea of the international system is opaque, conveying little meaning. Although theorists in IR have come up with a series of ill-assorted metaphors, from billiard balls and cobwebs to octopuses and egg boxes, designed to illuminate the nature of the contemporary global system, these metaphors have signally failed to penetrate beyond the boundaries of the discipline. The international system remains a shadowy, unfamiliar concept which has neither become part of popular parlance nor entered the general vocabulary of other social sciences.

Because there is a growing interest across the social sciences in fostering macro-approaches to analysis, this general lack of interest in international systems remains surprising. Anthropologists, sociologists, and geographers, as well as archaeologists, are acknowledging that they have devoted too much time in the past to observing what goes on within social units, and too little time to investigating the relations between these units. There has been a search for frameworks that will allow them to get a handle on macro-analysis. The framework that has been most extensively resorted to is Wallerstein's world systems. Almost all the attention has been centred on his conception of a world economy, and despite his injunction that no world economies existed before AD 1500, the framework has been extended all the way back to the fourth millennium BC. Ironically, therefore, Wallerstein's attempt to historicize the concept of a world system has been circumvented by his acolytes. They have taken the idea of a world economy out of its historical context and, by dehistoricizing it, transformed it into an ahistorical concept.

There is one area of literature, however, where reference to international systems has been made. As well as developing a wider spatial perspective on social systems, sociologists have also become increasingly interested in extending the temporal reach of their analysis and there has been an upsurge of interest in historical sociology. Here, contact has been made with international relations. Skocpol (1979), Tilly (1985), and Mann (1986) all draw on the idea that the anarchic character of the relations between states helps to account for the persistence of war. Although extremely illuminating in many ways, from the perspective of the international system, the work of these historical sociologists simply reinforces the long-established realist view in IR that the essential features of international politics are enduring and unchanging. None of them, not even Mann, who adopts a very long world historical perspective, makes any move to historicize the idea of the international system.

It is unreasonable to expect historical sociologists to carry out a task that falls squarely in the court of IR theory. To make progress, we believe that IR theorists have to join hands with all of those attempting to understand the macro, systems side of the human social world, whether they be historians, sociologists, political geographers, economists, or archaeologists. Theory and history may sometimes make strange bedfellows, but as the world systems school has demonstrated, the fruits of their union can be powerful and compelling in a way that neither of them can be when taken alone. From our perspective, the problem with IR theory is that it has treated the international system as standing outside history, and has then used history to reinforce this ahistorical assumption. Neorealists are particularly guilty of this fault. There is little point in turning to history with a framework that is incapable of exposing evidence of change. What we attempt to do in this book is to develop a theoretical framework that makes it possible to identify faultlines in history when the fundamental features of international systems have been transformed.

In *The Logic of Anarchy*, to which this book can be viewed as a sequel, we argue that despite the persistent criticism that has been levelled at neorealism, we nevertheless saw this approach as a useful 'foundation on which to construct a more solid and wider ranging Structural Realism' (Buzan et al. 1993). We employ a similar strategy in this book. We have deliberately favoured methodological pluralism over methodological monism. Many elements of both structure and realism are still prominent, but there is much else besides. The range and diversity of our borrowing also forbids calling the result a theory, for it contains no single line of cause and effect. Our position is that phenomena as massive and complex as international systems cannot be understood by any single method. The first task for international systems theorists *must* therefore be to show how existing theories stand in relation to each other. To say that they are simply different, or opposed, or mutually exclusive is not adequate. The job is to differentiate them in such a way as to expose their complementarities, to make clear how static and dynamic elements of systems can coexist, and to show how a division of labour can be constructed amongst them. We hope we have made a substantial start in this direction by deploying the matrix of levels and sectors of analysis as a way of organizing existing theories. We do not pretend to have produced a grand theory. But what follows might count as a grand theoretical framework within which a meta-theory might one day be constructed. And it does generate some of the meta-theoretical questions that such a theory will need to answer, and some of the meta-theoretical concepts it may find useful.

The first of the five parts that make up this book lays down the conceptual foundations on which the subsequent four parts rest. Part I provides, first, a genealogy of the international system, showing how the concept entered the language of IR theory and why we prefer the term to more long-established ones such as *states-systems* and newer ones such as *world systems*. We then go on to show that several mainstream approaches to the international system, although too narrowly focused on their own to provide the basis for a world history of international systems, can nevertheless be incorporated into a wider framework. Although world historians have not so far been tempted to use the international system as a concept around which to construct a world history, their interpretations can also be drawn upon to underpin our framework.

Having surveyed the field for useful ideas that we can draw upon, we then set out the tools that we intend to use to construct our account of how international systems have emerged and developed during the course of world history. There are three types of tools that come into play. First, we argue that international systems need to be sectorally differentiated. IR theory has tended to assume that international systems are first and foremost political systems. We argue that it is essential to separate out the military-political, economic, social, and environmental sectors of international systems. Focusing exclusively on the international military-political system makes it impossible to provide a comprehensive account of how international systems have evolved. For example, it is important to recognize that for most of world history, international economic systems have been more extensive than international political systems. This approach makes it possible to think of classical Afro-Eurasia as a weak international economic system linking together a number of separate international military-political systems. This divergence between economic and military-political systems has profound theoretical and practical implications which simply cannot be opened up for inspection if international systems are treated in undifferentiated terms.

The second set of tools highlights the fact that there are different analytical levels on which international systems can be investigated. This idea is already firmly embedded in the literature. We distinguish five levels of analysis: system, subsystem, unit, subunit, and individual.

The third set of tools are three sources of explanation that can help us to understand how systems are maintained and transformed: *interaction capacity*, *process*, and *structure*. Interaction capacity focuses on the system-wide capability of units to maintain contact with each other by moving goods, people, and information around the system. It is about the speed, range, and carrying capacity of physical systems (e.g. caravans, ships, railways, aircraft) and social systems (norms, rules, and institutions) for transportation and communication. Process is about the types of interaction that actually take place (e.g. fighting, political recognition, trade, identity formation, transplantation of flora and fauna) and the recurrent patterns of behaviour that form as a consequence (e.g. war, diplomacy, money, religion, plague). Structure concerns the principles by which the units in a system are arranged, and the effects of those arrangements on the behaviour of the units (e.g. anarchy, market, international society).

Interaction capacity and process are quite straightforward, but the very idea of structure remains controversial. Our methodological pluralism will probably add to the controversy about the place of structure in IR theory. We extend the challenge to Waltz's conception of structure that we first opened up in *The Logic of Anarchy*, using world history to show just how hugely mistaken Waltz's closure of the second tier (structural and functional differentiation of units) actually is. And because sectoral differentiation is such a crucial feature of our framework, we extend the idea of structure beyond the military-political sector to embrace the economic and socio-cultural sectors. International economic systems are structured either by the market or by some form of authoritative allocation mechanism—thereby closely mirroring the structures that regulate international military-political systems. Socio-cultural structures are more difficult to specify in any international system. But drawing on the work of the English school and the constructivists, who have focused on the idea of an international society, it seems clear that international units within an empire or an anarchic arena can be constrained by a common ideology or set of beliefs about appropriate norms and rules of behaviour.

The three sets of tools identified here are presented in Chapter 4 and their implications for an overarching conceptualization of an international system are then spelled out in Chapter 5. The next three main sections of the book (Parts II–IV) apply our conceptual framework to the historical record to provide a preliminary sketch of how international systems emerged and evolved. The notion of a sketch is appropriate because what is offered does not take the form of a regular or detailed narrative. What we are doing is putting some empirical flesh on the skeletal framework that is advanced in Part I.

After providing an outline of how international systems have emerged and evolved, we try, in Part V, to sum up and look forward. Chapter 16 applies our framework to the question of whether another systemic transformation is currently under way. What is the evidence that fundamental changes are taking place, analogous with those that have marked previous changes of era, and that would draw the modern, European-defined, era of the international system to a close? Chapter 17 explores the questions posed for IR theory by confronting it with the much wider empirical test that arises from a world historical perspective on international systems. Chapter 18 looks at the challenges that an IR theory approach poses to world historians. It compares the periodization of history that emerges when we examine the past from the perspective of IR theory with the periodizations associated with other social science and historical perspectives. Finally, Chapter 19 examines the implications of our analysis for future research.

# Part I

# INTERNATIONAL SYSTEMS, WORLD HISTORY, AND INTERNATIONAL RELATIONS THEORY

# Chapter 1

# SYSTEMS, HISTORY, THEORY, AND THE STUDY OF INTERNATIONAL RELATIONS

One central aim of this book is to provide a new way of thinking about international systems. Although there has been extensive analysis of the international system in mainstream IR, the concept remains deeply contested. Indeed, it is possible to argue that the most important methodological and theoretical debates that took place in IR during the second half of the twentieth century were all centred on attempts to identify the most appropriate way to conceptualize and then analyse the international system (as we show in Chapter 2).

These debates do tell us a good deal about why it is so difficult to conceptualize the international system. But they do not tell us how to develop an account of international systems from a world historical perspective. Mainstream conceptualizations of international systems in IR remain 'thin' and unidimensional, unable to assist in the task of telling the full story that we think needs to be told. Although parsimony in theorizing is a virtue, we argue that without a 'thicker' form of theorizing, a complex phenomenon like international systems simply cannot be adequately understood.

In the first section of this chapter we spell out some prevailing characteristics of the discipline that have prevented IR scholars from developing a 'thick' conception of the international system. Then in section 2 we examine the historiography of the discipline to see why these factors have been promoted and suggest that some of the inadequacies in the concept of the international system employed in mainstream IR can be attributed, at least in part, to the Americanization of IR that went on during the course of the twentieth century. The English school has developed along different lines, which can potentially give rise to a richer and more historicized conception of the international system. Finally, we show how world historical approaches transcend the history/theory divide that has had the effect of holding back the task of theorizing in IR.

# 1. THE UNDERDEVELOPED CONCEPTION OF THE INTERNATIONAL SYSTEM

Despite more than a century of intensive discussion about the nature of the international system, it is difficult to deny how underdeveloped the concept continues to be. Even the more sophisticated accounts of the international system fail to address some of the most elementary questions. Waltz (1979: 91), for example, talks about the international political system in terms of independent units co-acting, but he does not specify how much interaction, or what type, is necessary for a system to exist. Will *any* interaction suffice, or must we identify a boundary (or perhaps boundaries) defined by levels, types, and frequencies of interaction? On one side of this boundary will be international systems, and on the other will be sets of lightly interacting parts not yet defined as international systems. Neo-realism suggests (without specifically addressing the question) that an international system does not come into being until quite high levels of (strategic) interaction exist. On this basis Waltz's position is contradictory, because an international system does not necessarily, or even probably, form from the first point at which units begin to co-act.

This line of thinking points towards some interesting questions. Exactly what are the criteria for specifying that an international system exists? Is it useful or necessary to conceive of different types of international system—strategic, economic, cultural—in order to register the significance of different types of interaction? How far back in time can we apply the idea of international system? What does the history of the international system look like, and are there patterns in its development? When can we say that a fully global international system came into being? Existing research does not suggest obvious or uncontroversial answers to any of these questions, and before proceeding to suggest some possibilities it is worth considering why this is so. Why is it that such extremely basic questions about what is arguably the core concept in the discipline remain not only unaddressed, but almost unasked in IR? At least five complementary lines of explanation suggest themselves: presentism, ahistoricism, Eurocentrism, anarchophilia, and state-centrism.

## PRESENTISM

The discipline of IR has been mainly focused on contemporary history and current policy issues. The fast-moving nature of the subject, and the pressing demand for expertise on current events, encourage a forward- rather than a backward-looking perspective. Consequently rather few specialists within the discipline have had either a broad historical knowledge or an interest in acquiring it.

Occasionally, authors will raid further back and further afield, but these forays are usually guided more by the search for particular parallels with the modern

European experience than by any interest in capturing the character of the international system in history overall (Holsti 1967: 2; Watson 1992; Wight 1977). Following Burke (1993: p. xi), we refer here to this perspective as presentism, or
chronocentrism (Powelson 1994), which suggests that the dictum about using the
past to understand the present is reversed. As a consequence, the few historical
times and places that resemble the international anarchy of modern Europe get a
disproportionate amount of attention, most notably classical Greece, Renaissance
Italy, the 'warring states' period in China during several hundred years of the first
millennium BC, and, to a lesser extent, 'warring state' periods in South Asia.
Because these attempts to break away from presentism impose the present on
the past, they reinforce the problem of ahistoricism in the analysis of the international system.

## AHISTORICISM

Ahistoricism does not imply that the past is of no concern to social scientists, but
rather that they should be searching for general laws that apply to the past as well
as the present. Such a goal is dictated by the desire to emulate the invariant laws
of natural science that hold across time and space. Social scientists of a positivist
predisposition, anxious to emulate the natural sciences, also seek to identify laws
that are immune to historical variation.

In most areas of social science there has been a persistent debate about the
relative merits of ahistoricism and historicism. In anthropology and archaeology,
there has been a profound disagreement between formalists who subscribe to an
ahistorical position and substantivists who subscribe to a historicist position. The
former insist that concepts like trade and profit are universal and can be applied
in any time and place. The latter insist that these concepts are meaningless when
applied to tribal societies where it is not possible to identify a distinct economic
system. In such a setting, they insist, the practices that define the existence of an
economic system have no concrete reality. Identifying the exchange of goods in
such a setting as trade misunderstands the nature of the transaction.

Debates of this kind have rarely taken place in IR where until recently it was
widely accepted that the 'texture' of international politics did not change over
time, because 'patterns recur, and events repeat themselves endlessly' (Waltz
1979: 66). Twentieth-century realists have assumed that the balance of power provides the basis for a transhistorical theory that accounts just as well for behaviour
in the Greek city-states as it did for relations between the Soviet Union and the
United States. In the last quarter of the twentieth century the ahistoricism of
realism has come under increasing criticism. The easy assumption that we can
compare the conflict between Athens and Sparta with the conflict between the
United States and the Soviet Union rests, it is argued, on a 'gigantic optical illusion' (Rosenberg 1994: 90). The comparison requires the analyst to distort beyond

recognition the underlying social structures that form the Greek city-states. Similar criticisms have been levelled at attempts to apply realist thinking to the feudal era (see Hall and Kratochwil 1993 on Fischer 1992). As we will discuss in Chapter 2, this literature is now beginning to have an impact on the attempts to theorize the international system.

## EUROCENTRISM

Eurocentrism has bedevilled every aspect of the social sciences, and it is hardly surprising that it has had an impact on IR. At first sight, it might appear that there is nothing untoward about the familiar Eurocentric account of how the contemporary international system emerged. It seems to be almost self-evidently true that Europeans created the first global international system by bringing all parts of humankind into regular economic and strategic contact with each other. They occupied whole continents and stamped upon them a system of territorial boundaries, trading economies, and colonial administrations. The few places that they did not reduce to colonial status (Japan, Siam, Persia, Turkey, China) were forced to adapt to European models in order to preserve themselves. But as with ahistoricism, this story can only be told in this way by ignoring or distorting great swaths of the past. In particular, as writers like Hodgson (1993) have demonstrated, Eurocentric accounts invariably ignore the Afro-Eurasian system that existed long before the Europeans began to extend across the globe.

Rather than tracing the origins of Europe, we argue that it is this much wider history that constitutes the real antecedent of the contemporary global international system. Indeed, one can only explore the origins and significance of the idea of international system, and fully understand what is happening to it now, by comprehending its non-European dimension. Such comprehension requires more than merely selecting the handful of times and locations from the ancient and classical era during which anarchic structures similar to modern Europe's briefly held sway. It means addressing the whole sweep of ancient and classical history in terms of international system, and asking just what kind of system(s), if any, existed before the Europeans subordinated everything to their own anarchic model. Only by following this course can one bring the historical record to bear on the question of what are the necessary and sufficient conditions for an international system to come into being.

Eurocentrism is closely related to the idea of Orientalism. According to Said (1995; Sardar et al. 1993), the conception of European culture and identity gained in strength from the eighteenth century onwards by being contrasted with the Orient. Europe was seen to be outward looking, dynamic, and progressive whereas the Orient was depicted as inward looking, stagnant, and decadent. Marx, for example, contrasted the dynamism of capitalism with the static Asiatic mode of production. By the same token, the vibrant European system of states was not seen to have any counterpart in the Orient. Said insists that Occidental students of the Orient promoted an image of the East that helped the Europeans to see themselves as inherently superior to the rest of the world. The Orientalist thesis has probably been exaggerated (MacKenzie 1995), but there is no doubt that IR has been studied from a very Eurocentric perspective with a concomitant failure to come to terms with how non-European 'others' understood international relations or organized their world.

## ANARCHOPHILIA

The fourth reason why basic questions about the core concept in the discipline remain not only unaddressed but almost unasked is anarchophilia, which is very much a consequence of ahistoric and Eurocentric perceptions. This normative assumption is strongest in neorealism. Classical realists have often expressed more mixed feelings about the virtues of anarchy, and liberals have tended to see it as the main cause of war and disorder.

Adam Watson (1992, 1997) has opened an attack on anarchophilia, arguing that much of the international history of the last 5,000 years has not been anarchic, but has ranged across a spectrum with anarchy at one end, empire at the other, and hegemony, suzerainty, and dominion in between. Moreover, he argues that both anarchy and empire are extreme conditions, the natural instabilities of which tend to push the norm into the middle ranges of the spectrum. It is not easy to break free from the grip of anarchophilia because we are preconditioned to think of the international system in anarchic terms. Other disciplines are not so constrained. Historians like Gallagher and Robinson (1953), for example, find it appropriate to depict the links between Britain and Latin America in the first part of the nineteenth century in terms of an informal empire. As a consequence, it might be easier to tell the story of the British Empire, or the Soviet empire, for that matter, if they are identified as regional international systems rather than as states in the international system. Watson's framework raises the possibility that even the most abstract and successful theoretical development in the discipline has been profoundly, and probably unwittingly, shaped by an undue reliance on the peculiarities of the European and contemporary world experience.

## STATE-CENTRISM

Although almost inseparable from anarchophilia, state-centrism (or politicophilia) is a distinct reason for the underdeveloped conceptualization of the international system. There has, of course, been extensive attention paid to the economic, social, and environmental dimensions of international relations within the discipline. But attempts to conceptualize the international system have focused overwhelmingly on the military-political dimension. Perhaps even more important, politics has been linked almost indissolubly with the state. This is perhaps not that surprising after the Second World War, an era when the idea of the political system became little more than a synonym for the state (Easton 1953). A previous generation of pluralists in both Britain and the United States had endeavoured to dispense with the idea of the state when analysing politics (Little 1991, 1996). At the beginning of the twentieth century, pluralists began to argue that links between financial centres around the world were now closer than cities within the state had been in the past (Angell, 1912: p. viii). The state was characterized as a 'metaphysical spook' by the pluralists and during the inter-war era there were tentative attempts to analyse international relations from a non-state pluralist perspective (Fox 1975; Wilde 1991). It seemed possible in the 1960s and 1970s that the pluralist perspective would be resurrected and that a multi-centric and multi-layered image of the international system might be developed (Burton 1968; Keohane and Nye 1973). But the putative pluralists very rapidly drew back and refocused their attention on the state (Keohane and Nye 1977; Keohane 1984). Although Rosenau (1990) advocated the need to combine the pluralist and realist images of the international system, others have failed to follow this route and the most sophisticated attempts to conceptualize the international system have been restricted to the state-centric perspective.

### THE ALTERNATIVE

Within mainstream IR the concept of international system has almost invariably been depicted in one-dimensional terms. The resulting assessment is necessarily partial and there is generally no acknowledgement that a more comprehensive approach to the task of conceptualizing such a complex phenomenon is required. The underdeveloped concept of the international system has acted as a Procrustean straitjacket on the discipline. We hope to transcend the weaknesses discussed in this section by developing a very open-ended approach to international system which does not prejudge the nature of the dominant units in the system, privilege one sector of activity over another (for example, politics over economics), or give precedence to one mode of explanation over another (for example, structure over process). To achieve these objectives we need to draw extensively on both history and theory. But first, it is worth exploring briefly how this one-dimensional conception of the international system has come to prevail in IR.

## 2. THE HISTORIOGRAPHY OF INTERNATIONAL RELATIONS

During the last decade of the twentieth century, in the new post-Cold War era, IR underwent a large number of re-evaluations by scholars who were disturbed by the discipline's failure to forecast this ostensibly significant event. The putative weaknesses in the contemporary study of IR were frequently attributed to the dominance of realism in the era after the Second World War.

Can the failure to develop an adequate conceptualization of the international system also be laid at the same door? A plausible case can certainly be made that realism exemplifies all of the features identified in the previous section. Realists are preoccupied with applying their 'timeless' understanding of international politics to the exigencies of the contemporary international system. The focus on the competition between states as an inherent feature of the anarchic international system is the hallmark of realism. So ahistoricism does seem to be linked to state-centrism and presentism in realism. But realists are also drawn to anarchophilia and Eurocentrism: statesmen in the eighteenth and nineteenth centuries are viewed as having perfected statecraft and thereby stabilized the anarchic structure of the European international system. All five features discussed above have unequivocally been attributed to the work of the classical realists who dominated IR after the Second World War; and they are also present in the work of the neorealists who came to the fore in the 1980s.

Realism, it is often argued, was introduced into American IR by Europeans, like Hans J. Morgenthau, who came to the United States to escape the dangers that beset Europe in the 1930s. These key intellectual figures moved the basic tenets of realism to the centre of the academic stage in the United States (Guzzini 1998). Realist thinking made perfect sense during the ensuing Cold War; or certainly more sense than the approach of the inter-war idealists who had put their faith in international law and international organizations being able to override the long-standing imperatives of power politics. Problems with the state-centricism of realism, and its preoccupation with power and conflict, were brought to the surface briefly in the 1970s. But when relations between the Soviet Union and the United States deteriorated once more at the end of the 1970s, after the failure of détente, neorealists were able to move back to centre stage, where they stayed until the end of the Cold War. The neorealists distilled the essence of realist thought and then laced it with a large dose of scientific positivism. The scientific veneer, critics argued, blinded many to the deep-seated flaws of realism, and it also helped to deepen and widen the influence of the disabling factors discussed in the previous section. It was left to those writing on the margins to precipitate a post-positivist revolution in the 1980s. But they have still failed, as we move into the twenty-first century, to loosen completely the realist's grip on the IR tiller and turn the discipline decisively in an anti-realist direction.

If IR has unfolded in this way, it is unsurprising to find that the international system is such an undernourished concept. For over fifty years, its growth seems to have been stunted by a realism imported into the United States from Europe. But just how accurate is this assessment of how IR evolved? Recent attempts to reassess how IR has developed as a discipline suggest that the established historiography needs to be refigured. When this is done, it has significant consequences for how we account for the underdeveloped conception of the international system. The reassessment starts by undermining the familiar story that tells how the study of IR was largely a British and American response to the horrors of the First World War and that the desire to establish IR as an independent discipline was, until relatively recently, a long-standing, but quintessentially Anglo-American concern. The idea that Anglo-American IR was born in the ashes of the First World War can now be seen to be a romantic but erroneous myth. The roots of IR in both Britain and the United States are much deeper and rather less entwined than the myth suggests. Once the roots have been disentangled and traced back to their separate origins in Britain and the United States, moreover, our assessment of the role of the international system in the discipline's historiography becomes clearer although rather more complex than the conventional view allows.

## SYSTEMS AND THEORY IN AMERICAN IR

What is most fascinating about the revisionist historiography of IR in the United States is the recognition that the crucial debates that went on in the discipline throughout the second half of the twentieth century find their origins in the previous century. Schmidt (1998) demonstrates that the early foundations of IR in the United States were laid down long before the First World War by political scientists in the process of developing a theory of the state. The state, they argued, requires sovereignty, independence, and equality and, it inevitably follows, states operate in an anarchic arena containing similarly constituted entities. Domestic and international politics were depicted as opposite sides of the same coin. Although primarily concerned with establishing the scope and domain of Political Science, a space was thereby opened for the analysis of international relations. In the United States, Schmidt insists, IR was from the start regarded as an essential sub-field of Political Science.

By the end of the nineteenth century a very active debate existed within Political Science about the nature of the state and, because of the theoretical link between internal and external politics, about the nature of international relations. The debate persisted throughout the twentieth century. Advocates of a juristic theory of the state, derived from the position adopted by the English jurist John Austin, insisted that sovereignty meant that states operate within a Hobbesian state of nature that is 'atomistic', 'non-civic', and 'individualistic' (Willoughby, cited in Schmidt 1998: 90). The idea of international anarchy as a Hobbesian state of nature was deeply entrenched in American Political Science by the end of the nineteenth century. But the juristic theory of the state that generated this image was fiercely opposed by pragmatists like John Dewey, and pluralists like Harold Laski, amongst others. According to Laski, the juristic doctrine of state sovereignty was a dangerous fiction because a range of units had a corporate personality and it was a myth to assume that the state had an inherent right to subordinate these other corporate entities. Critics of the juristic theory also point-ed to the emergence in the nineteenth century of public international unions, like the Universal Postal Union, that revealed how states were becoming increasingly interdependent. Developments of this kind encouraged the view that it was much more appropriate to think of the anarchic international system as a 'society of nations' rather than a 'state of nature'. What happened during the inter-war years was not that the discipline slipped into a utopian phase, but rather that the image of the international system as a Hobbesian state of nature came under increasing attack. The image was seen to be anachronistic, resting on an outdated Austinian conception of sovereignty that had failed to take account of the changing nature of the international system.

After the Second World War and the onset of the Cold War, according to this revisionist historiography, the long-standing Hobbesian view of the international system was reasserted. European writers like Morgenthau were co-opted in sup-port of this position but in the process, their ideas were profoundly distorted. Schmidt (1998: 224) observes that Morgenthau 'thoroughly rejected' the image of the international system as a Hobbesian 'state of nature'. While this assessment oversimplifies Morgenthau's position, as we show in Chapter 2, it is certainly the case that the image of realism, depicted in Hobbesian terms, obscures more than it discloses.

The recognition that American IR represents a long-standing sub-field in Polit-ical Science has some important consequences. One is that it helps to account for the high level of uncertainty that exists about the status of IR as an academic discipline in the United States. In a major survey conducted in the middle of the twentieth century (Manning 1954), Harold Sprout, an important figure in the development of the subject, raised doubts about its 'inherent pedagogic virtue'. Twenty years later, William Fox (1970: 29) could still identify a sense of 'inferiority' amongst IR scholars when their discipline was compared with other social sci-ences. By the end of the century, references were still being made, inside and outside the discipline to the 'feebleness' and 'triviality' of theorizing in IR (Ryan 1998; Walker 1988). On the face of it, such concerns are surprising. After all, during the second half of the twentieth century the subject substantially came into its own. It had developed a wide range of well-regarded textbooks, and formed its own professional associations. Journals devoted to this area of knowledge steadily expanded in numbers. Nevertheless, as we enter a new century, with the study of international relations being taught and researched in a growing number of coun-tries across the globe, the American discipline of IR still seems to lack the status accorded to Economics, Anthropology, Sociology, and Political Science.

The sub-field status of IR also accounts for the anomalous role played by the idea of international system in American IR. The term came into increasing prom-inence after the Second World War when the idea of 'system' was seen in Political Science to play an important role in defining the disciplinary boundaries of all the social sciences. David Easton, for example, insisted that it was essential to be able to locate Political Science on the 'general map of social science' and that 'the idea of a political *system* proves to be an appropriate and indeed unavoidable starting point' (1953: 96). Other social sciences such as Economics, Sociology, and Anthropology were demarcated in similar fashion. It is interesting to note that although Easton acknowledged that the political system was a subsystem of the social system, he did not suggest that the social system was itself a subsystem of a more expansive international system. Such an admission was not compatible with the long-established idea of IR as a sub-field of Political Science. It is this institutional link rather than any link with realism that has ensured that anarchophilia and state-centrism have remained key features of American IR.

System thinking, however, was not only associated with the establishment of disciplinary boundaries, it was also closely linked to the 'behavioural' or 'positivist' turn which sought to ensure that the methodological rigour and technique of the natural sciences prevailed in the social ones. The attraction to general system theory was part of that process. David Easton's work on the political system epitomized this 'scientific' orientation. Easton wanted to use the idea of system to identify the recurrent relationships that open up a route to the formulation of theory about how the 'real world' political system behaves. The emphasis on systems thinking in American IR during the second half of the twentieth century is also associated with this desire to develop the discipline along scientific lines. The theorists most closely associated with the goal of turning IR into a science, such as Kaplan (1957), Singer (1961), and Waltz (1979), all focused on the idea of the international system and all identified the existence of systems by reference to recurrent patterns of behaviour. The desire to establish IR as a scientific discipline undoubtedly encouraged an ahistorical approach to analysis.

The promotion of a theoretical and scientific understanding of international relations was also associated with an attempt to break free from History. The behaviouralists believed that historians present the past as a unique series of events. It follows that their narrative accounts of the past cannot usefully be employed to develop a theoretical or scientific understanding of international relations (McClelland 1958; Morgenthau 1970: 67). Such theorists do not doubt the need to examine historical evidence, but insist that such an examination cannot be performed through a lens provided by the historian. Instead, specialists in IR must re-examine raw historical evidence using the tools of social science. This dichotomy reflects the view that whereas social scientists develop theoretical explanations through a constant distillation of the available facts, historians rely on the persistent accumulation of facts to account for the occurrence of unique events (Hexter 1971). This method has sometimes been demeaned by the suggestion that history is no more than the study of one damned thing after another. Historians, it is argued, eschew theory and are simply interested in identifying and then describing a particular chain of events. After the Second World War, the prevalence of this view throughout the social sciences led Meehan (1968: 109) to identify the emergence of a 'generation of social scientists with little knowledge and even less interest in history'. In IR, McClelland (1958), a widely acknowledged IR theorist, advocated a break from what he saw as the 'dead hand' of the historian that was holding back the development of the discipline. Towards the end of the twentieth century, although the importance of historical understanding was starting to be more widely appreciated throughout the social sciences, Richardson (1988: 316) could still observe 'the artificial separation between the disciplines of international history and international relations'. Ahistoricism and presentism have persisted as defining features of American IR.

There is little doubt that the status of American IR as an independent discipline was fostered by the onset of the Cold War and the emergence of the United States as a superpower. Hoffmann (1977) argues that it was at this juncture that IR emerged as an 'American Social Science'. An informal division of labour began to be fostered with Political Science examining what went on within the state and IR exploring what went on without (Easton 1981). This division reinforced the inside/outside image of the state that pragmatism and pluralism had begun to question during the first half of the century. Their ideas were completely lost sight of in American Political Science and it was nearly a quarter of a century before American IR began to point to the very complex transnational links forming among domestic actors operating within different states. These links established a much deeper conception of the international system, one that extended down into the hierarchical political structure of the state. They also crossed the boundaries between states and questioned the idea that the international system was essentially political in character. If the underlying premiss of general systems theory is accepted, that everything is linked to everything else, then it is not difficult to arrive at the point where the international system can be seen, in principle, to embrace everything that is going on in the world. The idea starts to encapsulate the breadth and depth of all human activity, pushing IR to become the study of humankind as a whole.

The changing metaphors used to depict the international system during this period neatly capture this transformation. For twenty years after the end of the Second World War, IR theorists were quite happy to think of the constitution of the international system in terms of states as billiard balls bouncing off each other (Wolfers 1962: 19). This metaphor is closely associated with the realist approach. But by the mid-1960s, a very different image of the international system was being advanced, depicting international relations in terms of cobwebs being constantly spun across the globe on many different levels (Burton 1968, 1972). This metaphor supported a pluralist approach. For the last three decades of the twentieth century there was a persistent debate between realists who insisted that the state continued to represent the dominant actor in an international system conceptualized in essentially political terms, and pluralists who argued that growing

necessary to go beyond the understanding of the international actors. Singer believes that the social scientist can identify systemic patterns of which the international actors may be unaware. By the same token, Waltz insists that a balance of power emerges as an unintended consequence of state action and such a pattern will form in an anarchic arena whether or not states are aware of the idea. We examine this position in more detail in Chapter 2. But it is worth noting here that Bull, in particular, was sensitive to the pitfalls of pushing a historicist line of argument too far. He suggested that 'we are not sufficiently flexible in our idea of what a "system" is. Morton Kaplan regards an international system as a "system of action". You can take any area and look for the pattern of the relations between the states in that area. It will form some sort of "system". There is no need to posit even any consciousness of system amongst the states involved' (Dunne 1998: 125). What is most interesting about this assessment is that the English school was aware of the divergent American position and, as we will see in the next chapter, endeavoured to take it into account.

The English school avoids Eurocentrism, ahistoricism, presentism, and, in the more recent work of Watson (1992) discussed above, anarchophilia and state-centrism. It is unsurprising, therefore, that we draw heavily on their ideas in our framework. But although the English school help to show the way, there has been a failure to pull their eclectic ideas together in a systematic fashion. Moreover, although their systemic approach produces a thicker conception of the international system than anything found in mainstream American IR, it is still not nearly thick enough to reveal how the international system has evolved across world history. The work of world historians throws an indirect light on the history of international systems, but since they have not used the concept their accounts of it are at best partial and inferred.

# 3. WORLD HISTORY

The idea that historians simply string together unique events into a storyline underestimates the complexity of how narratives work. It also fails to accommodate the diversity of approaches that can be observed among historians. They vary, first, in terms of the length of time that they focus on, and on this basis can be divided into 'lumpers' and 'splitters' (Hexter 1979). The 'splitters' are interested in developing ever more detailed pictures of increasingly narrow slices of time, and the 'lumpers' want to provide pictures of ever wider chunks of time. At the extreme end of this spectrum lie the world historians who wish to create a picture of the entire world from the beginning of time to the present day. As we will discuss in Chapter 3, some historians are deeply sceptical of such an approach. But McNeill (1986: 71) notes approvingly that 'World history was once taken for granted as the only sensible basis for understanding the past'. Rashid al-din Tabib, a court historian in Tabriz, for example, produced a world history at the start of the fourteenth century that embraced all of Eurasia (Rice 1976).

World historians generally presuppose that they do not proceed differently from any other type of historian. But perhaps the best-known approach to 'lumping', the French *annales* school, most closely associated with the work of Braudel, have argued more self-consciously that history is not simply concerned with surface *events* that are subject to rapid change over time, but must also take account of *processes* that must be observed over longer periods of time, and of *structures* that only become apparent over the *longue durée*. Similar ideas are implicit in the work of McNeill, Toynbee, and others who have told world history as the story of civilizations. The French school's ideas have had a very extensive impact. Certainly it is no longer controversial to argue that the divide between history and social science looks 'increasingly quaint, contrived and unnecessary' (Abrams 1982: 1).

But we can also find among this wave of world historians a self-conscious attempt to distance themselves from the work of those social scientists who have tried to break down the barriers separating Social Science and History. Fernandez-Armesto (1996: 7), who has provided an account of the last thousand years, insists that his book is a work of creative art that examines the activities of knights and peasants, but not feudalism; merchants and financiers, but not capitalism. Feudalism and capitalism, of course, are theoretical concepts and provide grist to the Social Science mill. It might appear that the gap between History and Social Science is as wide as ever.

We shall survey the work of world historians in Chapter 3 because some of it has foreshadowed or directly influenced our framework. But before concluding this chapter, we need to draw attention to the work of the sociologist Immanuel Wallerstein, who has anticipated some of the moves that we wish to make. In the 1970s, Wallerstein began to stress that the great weakness of the social sciences was the fact that they all operated on the basis of closed systems. He was opposed to disciplinary boundaries separating Political Science, Economics, and Sociology, to the boundary that divided History and Social Science, and to the impermeable boundary that shut political, economic, and social systems off from a wider world. He stressed the importance of using the idea of a 'world system' as the basic unit of analysis in the social sciences to break down these boundaries. What we find so striking is that although IR should have been well placed to make Wallerstein's points for him, the discipline signally failed to do so. Indeed, Wallerstein did not even mention IR. More disturbing for IR, Wallerstein's influence quickly became pervasive. In less than two decades, theorists across the social sciences, including IR, all became thoroughly familiar with his ideas and the many criticisms levelled against them. Just as important, the concepts associated with world systems are now regularly drawn upon within these disciplines. There is nothing like the same familiarity with any IR theorists of the international system. This concept quite simply has failed to resonate beyond what turn out to be the very circumscribed boundaries drawn around the study of international relations. It is difficult to avoid the conclusion that despite strenuous efforts, the discipline has not managed to establish a secure position for itself within the pantheon of the social sciences. Rather than integrating the other social sciences, it stands in some danger of being outflanked, or even reabsorbed, by them.

## 4. WHY PREFER THE LABEL 'INTERNATIONAL SYSTEMS'?

The term 'international' was first coined by Jeremy Bentham at the end of the eighteenth century to distinguish between domestic and international law. Before Bentham, international law was referred to in English as 'the law of nations'. He considered this expression to be inappropriate because it failed to capture the fact that law of this kind regulated relations *between*, not within, nations, though it took for granted that nations and states were synonymous (Suganami 1978). Bentham's term has proved resilient. But it now no longer refers only to relations between states, but covers any relationship that extends across state boundaries, be it an 'international' football match, the 'international' migration of individuals, or the 'international problem' of drug abuse. Given the potential for anachronism, it may seem perverse of us to wish to retain the term 'international system' but there are a variety of reasons for doing so. In some ways the term 'interstate', or the older 'states-system' would be a more accurate description for much of what is actually done in IR. Or why not use the more embracing 'world system'? There are several reasons why we prefer to stick with 'international system'.

First, the main rivals to 'international' are 'world' and 'global', both of which focus on geographical scale rather than on the nature of the relations involved. Although the international system has now become global in extent, this is a relatively recent development. We want to problematize the question of when the international system became global in scale.

Second, we wish to embrace the ambiguity now inherent in the term international. It has both political and sociological overtones. It can therefore embrace both interstate and transnational relations. Because we want to leave open the question of what units are appropriate for analysing international systems, this ambiguity can be turned to our advantage. The English school's 'states-system' is too explicitly state-centric for our needs.

Third, the term 'world system' is now closely associated with Wallerstein and his followers (see Chapter 3) and we do not wish to be confused with that school.

Fourth, one of the aims of this book is to reassert the autonomy of IR as a distinct field of study. We see the idea of international system as crucial to that project. There is the long-standing and complex debate about the status of IR as a branch of knowledge. From one perspective, international relations consists of no more than what Wight called the 'untidy fringe' of domestic politics. Up to a point there is nothing more at stake here than the self-esteem of specialists in IR who wish to accord themselves the status of operating within a fully-fledged branch of knowledge. But if the study of international relations is hived off to various established disciplines, with political scientists absorbing the political sector, and economists taking charge of the economic sector, our understanding of international relations will become very fragmented. Under these circumstances, international relations would, all too often, be accorded peripheral status within other disciplines and the subject would lose not only coherence, but also priority. Thus the idea of international system is necessary to consolidate the study of international relations as an independent field. Doing this requires deeper foundations on which to build an understanding of the international system than currently exist, and one of our purposes is to lay down those foundations.

A fifth reason, anticipating the discussion in Chapter 3, is because the idea of international system enables us to make the cross-disciplinary links between the work of world historians and the social science theories of IR. Without those links we cannot construct the foundations for a discipline. More on this in section 3 above and Chapter 3 below.

## 5. CONCLUSIONS

Our view is that international relations represents a subject of such immense size and complexity that it is best approached from a systemic or general perspective rather than an event-driven or particularist one. A systemic perspective presupposes that from the myriad events constituting international relations it is possible to abstract patterns and regularities that reveal the existence of international systems. To understand international relations, therefore, we need to start by looking at systems as a whole, rather than by opening with an examination of their component parts. This is why we start our enquiry in the next four chapters with a set of generalizing theories, and then introduce these to the historical narrative in Parts II to V.

The failure of history and theory to join forces has led to an impoverished understanding of international relations. We see the idea of the international system as providing the best possible location where history and theory can meet. By establishing a more extensive framework for the international system we hope to facilitate the task of pulling the work of theorists and historians together. And by enhancing our theoretical and historical understanding of the international system we hope to extend our overall understanding of international relations. We thus view this book as a marriage between the *longue durée* and a systems approach to IR. Our purpose is to change fundamentally the way in which the subject of IR is defined and understood, not only by its own practitioners, but also by those interested in the macro-side of the social sciences, and by world historians.

# Chapter 2

# COMPETING CONCEPTIONS OF THE INTERNATIONAL SYSTEM

---

Although the idea of an international system is now widely taken for granted in IR, critics argue that the introduction of systems terminology into the study of international relations has simply provided a source of confusion and obscurantism. The critics' view is that 'system' means no more than an interrelationship among component parts. Since the meaning of a system cannot be extended beyond this limit, then it should be discarded, being both 'irrefutable and useless' (Weltman 1973: 100). In this view, defining marriage as a system because husbands and wives interrelate adds nothing to our understanding of marriage. By the same token, identifying the relations between states in terms of a system is similarly unhelpful. According to these critics, the term has come into common currency simply because it provides the putative social sciences with a spurious sense of scientific rigour. But this criticism fails to acknowledge that theoretical debates in IR have conceptualized the international system in a number of different ways, most of which, as we demonstrate, invalidate Weltman's claim that a system means no more than an interrelationship among its parts.

Although this line of criticism can be dismissed, the problem remains that IR theorists have failed to generate any consensus about what is meant by a system. Despite the quite impressive evolution of systems thinking in IR over the past fifty years, IR theorists are still working from radically different perspectives. Not only have the competing approaches to the task of conceptualizing the international system been left unresolved, but all too often the range of thinking implicit in different approaches has not been fully mapped. One consequence is that the degree of difference amongst the competing systemic approaches to international relations has not been properly appreciated. Another is that there is a less sophisticated understanding of systemic thinking within IR than there should be.

Part of the problem is that the most methodologically self-conscious systems thinkers in IR have also tended to be theoretical and methodological monists, viewing the system from a one-dimensional perspective. Waltz, for example, has famously developed his theory of the international system in purely political terms. In contrast to these theoretical monists, we are working from the methodological assumption that theoretical pluralism is essential in order to establish an effective and comprehensive understanding of international systems. Some form of synthesis has to be accomplished. As we will see, there are systems thinkers in

IR who have adopted a position of theoretical and methodological pluralism, but because they have generally been among the most methodologically unself-conscious thinkers in the discipline, the implications of their approach have not been highlighted, nor have the shortcomings of their approach been explicitly explored.

Because the idea of the international system has been so central in the discipline, the literature surrounding the concept is vast. But most of it falls into three dominant schools. The *behavioural* school began by arguing that the study of international relations had been held back by its failure to develop a systematic approach to the collection and analysis of data about activity in the international system. *Neorealists* responded that behaviouralists had failed to appreciate the essential characteriztics of a systemic theory. Finally, *constructivists* provided a postpositivist challenge to neorealists, whom they accused of drawing an erroneous distinction between the structure of the system and the structure of its component units, failing to appreciate that they are mutually constituted. We will survey these schools mainly in terms of representative leading thinkers: Singer for behaviouralism, Waltz for neorealism, and Wendt for constructivism. We conclude the chapter by looking at the work of theorists who use a theoretically pluralist approach to the international system that is more in tune with our own orientation, particularly Morgenthau, Bull, and some of those in international political economy.

# 1.  SINGER AND THE BEHAVIOURAL CONCEPTION OF THE INTERNATIONAL SYSTEM

Singer starts from the premiss that every aspect of reality can be characterized in terms of interacting units that form a system. As a consequence, it is always possible to explore reality either from the perspective of the system or from the perspective of the units. Problems inevitably arise if one perspective is adopted to the exclusion of the other. So the familiar cry that an analyst cannot see the wood (the system) for the trees (the component parts) suggests that problems arise when analysts get so bogged down in the details of the parts that they cannot focus on more general patterns that are staring them in the face. But this difficulty needs to be set against the equally debilitating problem, at the other end of the spectrum, where analysts can see the wood but not the trees. Here, the totality of a system is in focus but at the expense of the details. We will discuss the way systems theory encourages us to shift levels of analysis in more detail in Chapter 4.

Singer is acutely conscious that developing a social systemic perspective, mapping the social 'wood', if you like, can be extraordinarily difficult because the task requires very special methodological tools. Without the systematic application of such tools it is perfectly possible to live in a social system, without having the least idea about its overall shape and composition. Developing a social systemic perspective, moreover, is particularly problematic because it requires the social scientists to operate at a level of abstraction that does not come naturally. As social foresters we are all much more familiar with individual trees than with the systemic wood.

The unwillingness to develop a systemic perspective was particularly apparent to behaviouralists in the 1960s when Singer observed a strong resistance expressed forcefully, for example, by Bull (1969), to any attempt to introduce the kind of methodological tools necessary to generate such a perspective. Yet he was convinced that it was only by operating from this perspective that our understanding of international relations could progress. Singer was to play a key role in applying the methodological tools that made it possible to provide such a perspective. He emphasized the need to move away from the prevailing preoccupation with relations between individual states—the unit level of analysis—and towards the formation of an aggregate picture of these relations—the system level of analysis. Once this picture has been formed, then systemic patterns appear that are invisible from a unit-level perspective. By analogy, flying at an appropriate height, the shape of a forest, which may be completely unknown to its inhabitants, becomes immediately apparent. But very distinctive methodological tools are required to generate this same image when operating, as pre-flight cartographers had to, on the ground. Like these pre-flight cartographers, social scientist also lack an aerial perspective, and similarly rely on special methodological tools to achieve it.

Singer sought to generate a systemic perspective on international relations by means of statistical analysis. His method made it possible to produce images of the international system that did not exist before. In one of the most intriguing pieces of research, Singer and Small (1966) wanted to demonstrate that within the international system it was possible to observe a diplomatic hierarchy. In a system made up of sovereign equal states, it is possible to argue that no such hierarchy has ever existed. Singer and Small attempt to demonstrate that this is not the case. They presuppose that the grade (there were traditionally four) and size of all the diplomatic missions established in a capital city measured the status that the other members of the system accorded to that state. By ranking the aggregated statuses and sizes of all the diplomatic missions established in each capital city, Singer and Small were able to demonstrate that the international system could be characterized in terms of a diplomatic hierarchy.

The data revealed significant differences in the aggregate status achieved by the members of the system. The result provides a purely systemic picture, telling us nothing about the status relations between individual members of the system. Nevertheless, Singer insists that the systemic picture is useful in its own right. It reveals, for example, how the systemic position of individual states in the diplomatic hierarchy can change over time; and there is no doubt that the results challenge conventional images of the international system. The aggregated data show that whereas the United States ranked 17, below Switzerland and Tuscany in 1817, it had risen to 6 by 1840 and 3 by 1849. To the extent that the data provide an index of integration into the international system, the United States was clearly much more tightly integrated and more significant than conventional views about its nineteenth-century policy of isolation suggest.

Singer, of course, is not alone in the attempt to develop a systemic perspective on international relations and many analysts have followed in his wake. But his methodological orientation certainly clarified the idea that the international system possesses properties which transcend the specific bilateral relations that form within the system. These properties are usually hidden from ordinary view, as the example of the diplomatic hierarchy illustrates. Through the systematic collection and processing of data, an increasingly complex picture of the international system has been established—embracing all its members, not just the limited number of great powers in Europe. The data that have been collected, certainly for the period since 1815, allow us to chart, *inter alia*, the changing levels of conflict in the system, the shifts in the distribution of power, the rise and fall in the number of alliances that have been formed, and the volume of territory that has changed hands over time. More significant, from the systemic perspective, is that because the data extend across time, we can investigate such questions as whether changes in the level of conflict in the system correlate with shifts in the polarization of power, or the rate of alliance formation (Singer et al. 1972).

Such correlations are based on systemic variables. As a consequence, a correlation between alliance formation and levels of conflict does not necessarily indicate that the states forming alliances were the same states that were involved in conflict. Such an inference commits the 'ecological fallacy': conflating properties of the system with properties of the constituent units of the system (Robinson 1950). Singer avoided this fallacy, and recognized that the systemic perspective is fabricated by the analyst. Although this systemic level of analysis produces 'a more comprehensive and total picture' of international relations than can be supplied at the unit level, in order to explain the systemic patterns it is necessary to drop down to the unit level of analysis 'where it is possible to make a more thorough investigation of the processes by which foreign policies are made' (Singer 1961: 91–2). While it is possible to chart the changing patterns in the variables used to operationalize the international system, the story or history behind these patterns is told most effectively at the level of the component units.

But Waltz reached a diametrically opposite conclusion, denying Singer the status of being a systems thinker.

## 2. WALTZ AND THE NEOREALIST CONCEPTION OF THE INTERNATIONAL SYSTEM

Distinguishing a systemic but essentially descriptive level of analysis from a descriptive but also potentially explanatory unit level of analysis oversimplifies Singer's position. But it helps to draw an unambiguous line between the theoretical positions held by Singer and Waltz, and their conceptions of the international system. From Waltz's perspective, Singer's view of the system is deeply flawed. His error springs from an entirely inappropriate methodology which requires the analyst to develop explanations of systemic patterns of behaviour at the unit level of analysis. Singer presupposes that the international system is, in Kaplan's (1957) terms, 'subsystem dominant' where Waltz presupposes that the international system is 'system-dominant'. In other words, for Singer, the behaviour of states is not dictated by the structure of the international system whereas for Waltz, it is. In Waltz's view this mistake is not idiosyncratic to Singer, but has been made by virtually every analyst who has endeavoured to develop a 'systemic' approach to international relations.

Although Waltz's formulation of the international system pulls us away from Weltman's assumption that a system is no more than a set of interacting parts, Waltz acknowledges that the systems examined by natural scientists are 'subsystem dominant'. As a consequence, natural scientists can generally use a 'reductionist' methodology. But Waltz insists that social systems are very different from natural systems and require a different methodology to understand them. He sees social systems as possessing a structure that constrains the behaviour of the constituent units. In developing this argument, Waltz is tapping into a long-standing debate within the social sciences conducted between holists and methodological individualists. Holists presuppose that there are distinct structural explanations that account for the behaviour of units. Waltz accepts the holist position, and argues that there is a level of analysis problem in IR because analysts like Singer develop a 'systemic' viewpoint that then requires explanations formulated at the unit level. They have no alternative but to adopt this strategy, argues Waltz, because of their failure to develop a conception of structure that excludes features of the units whose behaviour needs to be explained.

Waltz relies heavily on an analogy drawn from the work of economists to develop his argument that the international system possesses an independent structure that constrains the behaviour of states. States, he suggests, can be compared to firms operating in a situation of perfect competition. Entrepreneurs can, of course, price their wares at any level they wish, but if their goal is to optimize their position, then they have no alternative but to set the price at the level dictated by the market. In the economic world, the market represents a structure operating independently of the units and the transactions that take place between the entrepreneurs. Similarly, people in hierarchical organizations will find that their behaviour is constrained by the hierarchical structure within which they operate. An unintended consequence of their behaviour is to reproduce the hierarchical structure that is constraining their behaviour.

Identifying what constitutes the political structure of an international system is not easy. Waltz is quite clear that nothing can be inferred about the structure by looking at the nature or number of the component states. In his view we cannot say that the structure is enlarged when new states enter the system, as Kegley and Wittkopf (1987: 150) do; nor can we say that the system has a homogeneous structure, as Aron (1966) does, on the grounds that all the members are, for example, democracies. Waltz is equally clear that the interactions between states tells us nothing about the structure of the system. So changes in the level of conflict or the number of alliances formed leaves Waltz's structure of the international system unchanged.

From Waltz's perspective, Singer's methodology does not provide an increasingly detailed picture of the international system. Indeed, as we shall see, the very idea that an international system can become increasingly complex rests on a theoretical confusion as far as Waltz is concerned. Far from shedding any light on the nature of the international system, Singer's methodology at best simply tells us more about what is happening in it. But this amassing of empirical detail does no more than obscure the need for a prior conceptualization of the international system which must, according to Waltz's theory, precede any empirical investigation. Waltz's theory is diametrically opposed to Singer's. For Waltz, the international system is a theoretical concept and, as a consequence, we cannot learn more about the nature of the system by empirical means. By the same token, his conception of the system cannot be invalidated by empirical evidence, although Waltz acknowledges that an empirical investigation could lead to the conclusion that his theory is not helpful for understanding international relations.

Waltz argues that there are only two possible ways that political systems can be structured: one structure is characterized by hierarchy and the other by anarchy. In a hierarchy, the units perform different functions, which means that they are structurally dependent upon each other. The mode of organization amongst the units reflects subordinate–superordinate relationships, with the overall distribution of power giving the resulting hierarchy a distinctive shape. In an anarchy, by contrast, the units relate to each other as independent agents, and so must be functionally autonomous in order to avoid structural dependency. The division of labour associated with functional differentiation is a defining feature of hierarchies, whereas anarchic systems are characterized by the absence of a division of labour. Although power is present in both hierarchies and anarchies, it operates in a very different way. In hierarchies it reinforces the subordinate–superordinate relations. In anarchies it helps to reproduce the independence of the units, and when (as usually) power is unevenly distributed, it becomes possible to identify 'poles' of power, and thus the degree of polarity in the system. Waltz theorizes that the units in an anarchic system will be profoundly affected by the degree of polarity, and he distinguishes between unipolar, bipolar, and multipolar systems.

The assumptions drawn upon to distinguish hierarchical and anarchical systems are theoretically derived and Waltz readily acknowledges that when the theory is applied to the real world, it is to be expected that there will be evidence of hierarchy in anarchical systems and anarchy in hierarchical systems. But the structure of a stable anarchical system will tend to overwhelm any systemic effects generated by the 'flecks' of hierarchy that might be observed. And the same line of argument can be extended to hierarchical systems. Although much more can be said about Waltz's conception of the international system (Buzan et al. 1993) it is already clear that his theoretical assumptions are very different from Singer's. But as with Singer, the majority of the history of what happens within the system is most effectively told at the unit level of analysis. Waltz's framework is designed to explain why the international system has persisted through time. He is interested in system maintenance rather than system transformation. Waltz acknowledges that the international system can change, as when the international distribution of power changed with the collapse of the Soviet Union, but he argues that the source of such changes lies within the structures of the states, and therefore beyond the purview of the systemic perspective.

## 3. WENDT AND THE CONSTRUCTIVIST CONCEPTION OF THE INTERNATIONAL SYSTEM

Given that Waltz's chief criticism of Singer is that he lacks a theoretical conception of the international system, it is ironic that Wendt's (1992) main criticism of Waltz is that his conception of the international system is under-theorized. Wendt sees Waltz's inability to produce a fully theorized conception of the international system as a product of his methodological assumptions, particularly his insistence that an unequivocal distinction must be drawn between the structure of the system and the structure of its constituent units. Waltz's methodology treats the structure of the system as an environment which serves to constrain and contain the activities of the units in the system. When isolated, states have no need to be concerned about their autonomy. But the moment that states start to co-act, Waltz (1979: esp. 91) argues, the anarchic, power-oriented structure springs ready made into existence, compelling states to adopt a competitive relationship with each other in order to ensure that their autonomy is preserved. From Wendt's perspective, the anarchic structure only has this effect because of the self-regarding identity of the units, their interest in survival, and their reliance on self-help: characteristics that Waltz simply ascribes to the unit level. In Wendt's view, these characteristics are imported into neorealism as theoretical assumptions that, from Waltz's perspective, are not amenable to challenge on empirical grounds because they are assumed to be structural consequences of life in anarchic political conditions.

Wendt does not wish to challenge these theoretical assumptions on empirical grounds; he is more concerned with their theoretical and methodological status. For Wendt, the anarchic organization of the system does very little work in Waltz's theory other than explaining how states are reproduced as self-regarding units, interested in survival, and reliant on self-help mechanisms. But while Wendt is happy to acknowledge that states with these characteristics can be reproduced by the anarchic structure of an international system, he denies that they are reproduced in the way postulated by Waltz. To make this claim, he has to demonstrate that Waltz operates on the basis of an under-theorized conception of anarchy.

Wendt traces the root of the problem back to a fallacy in Waltz's method-ological position which means that, in neorealism, the structure of the inter-national system must exclude any reference to the structure of the component units. Wendt's methodology, by contrast, presupposes that in the case of social systems, the structure of the system and the structure of the component units are one and the same thing, because the system and the units are mutually consti-tuted. As a consequence, it is not possible to talk about the structure of the inter-national system without simultaneously talking about the identity and interests of the component units. What Waltz fails to recognize is that the way that the units conceive of the international system is constrained by their collective or intersubjective view of themselves; and it is this intersubjectivity which provides the mechanism that structures their actions. When states all recognize that they are operating in a system of self-regarding, survival-oriented, self-help units, they are constrained by this collective or intersubjective understanding to enter into a competitive relationship. This intersubjective understanding about the interest and identity of states constitutes an integral feature of the system's anarchic structure.

From Wendt's perspective, this intersubjectivive understanding does not emerge spontaneously. It can only develop on the basis of interaction. He insists that there would have to be a 'history of interaction' before actors would acquire their self-regarding identity, their interest in survival, and their reliance on self-help. Wendt further insists that the 'history of interaction' could give rise to a very different outcome, with states forming a less competitive, more rule-governed view of themselves, and because the structure of both the units and the system are mutually constituted, the international system would then also be defined by a more rule-governed structure of anarchy.

Such a possibility cannot be entertained by Waltz because his methodology presupposes that the anarchic structure of the system exists independently of any rules that might form inside the system. But for Wendt, Waltz has been deluded by his methodology, which prevents him from recognizing that, in practice, he smuggles a very Eurocentric, Westphalian conception of the state into his structural conception of anarchy. Unaware of his own bias, he fails to recognize that by changing the identity and interests of the component states, the conception of anarchy can also change. 'Anarchy', in Wendt's telling phrase, 'is what states make of it', and from this perspective Waltz's methodological posture results in an under-theorized view of anarchy. It locks him into a particular intersubjective view of it, while simultaneously making it impossible for him to identify the role played by intersubjectivity in the way anarchy structures the international system. The methodology also prevents him from appreciating the potential for rules to be introduced into the conception of anarchy.

In developing this argument, Wendt does not deny that Waltz allows for the existence of rules in the international system. On the contrary, Waltz readily acknowledges that rules associated with sovereignty have emerged as states have interacted. Recognition is an important rule that now underpins the autonomy of states in the international system. This rule has been generated by the processes of competition and socialization which are themselves depicted by Waltz as products of the anarchic structure of the system. But Waltz's methodology makes it impossible for him to acknowledge that the structure of the international system is affected by the emergence of rules associated with sovereignty.

By contrast, Wendt's methodology leads him inexorably towards the English school's view that the rules underpinning sovereignty form an essential element in the complex web of rules that help to constitute the structure of the international system. He observes that sovereignty is an institution dependent upon the implementation of rules that, like all rules, exist 'only in virtue of certain intersubjective understandings and expectations' (1992: 412). Because state and system are mutually constituted, these 'intersubjective understandings and expectations' inevitably shape the interests and identity of the state and, simultaneously, the structure of the international system. As a consequence, for Wendt, rules are not shaped by the structure of the anarchic system, as Waltz suggests; they are an integral part of that structure. And so as international rules change, so too does the anarchic structure of the international system. A story could be constructed around the changing structure of norms that help to constitute the international system, but, in practice, the constructivists have as yet failed to provide an overarching history of the international system.

## 4. THEORETICAL PLURALISM AND THE CONCEPTION OF THE INTERNATIONAL SYSTEM

The three analysts examined so far, along with their respective schools of thought, all operate from a position of methodological and theoretical monism. But when attention is turned to less methodologically self-conscious analysts within the classical tradition, it quickly becomes apparent that, perhaps unwittingly, they frequently adopt a position of methodological pluralism that permits them to conflate different theoretical positions. An examination of the perspectives adopted by Hans J. Morgenthau (1973), often depicted as the progenitor of classical realist thought, and Hedley Bull (1977), one of the central figures of the English school, reveals that neither sees any difficulty in drawing on theoretical perspectives that are considered starkly incompatible by the theoretical monists. For example, both Morgenthau and Bull pull together the apparently opposing theoretical positions that Waltz and Wendt seem so keen to keep apart.

Writing in the immediate aftermath of the Second World War, Morgenthau's methodological posture is overwhelmingly systemic in orientation, with international politics being characterized in terms of a 'complex system' (Morgenthau 1973: 168). He draws attention to two particular features of this complexity, first, the 'mechanical interplay of opposing forces' (p. 174), which he associates with the operation of the balance of power, and second, the existence of an intersubjective 'silent compact' (p. 219) that permits the emergence of an international society and smothers the effects of the balance of power. Bull also highlights these two features. So both the classical realists and the English school assume that there is no difficulty about yoking together the different methodologies advanced by neorealists and constructivists.

Morgenthau starts from the premiss that if a state increases its power capabilities in order to pursue an imperialist policy at the expense of a rival, then the policy will simply call forth a 'proportionate increase in the power of the other' (Morgenthau 1973: 174). The resulting balance of power not only maintains the precarious stability of the system, but also maintains the autonomy of both states. Bull uses this logic to define international systems as any situation 'where states are in regular contact with one another and where in addition there is interaction between them, sufficient to make the behaviour of each a necessary element in the calculation of the other' (Bull 1977: 10). Such systemic pressures are seen by members of the English school to 'act mechanistically in the sense that they act outside of the will of the community concerned' (Watson 1992: 311). Neither Morgenthau nor Bull manages to articulate the methodological implications of his position with anything like the clarity of Waltz; nevertheless, the underlying logic of system structure shaping the behaviour of units is exactly the same.

Morgenthau, however, goes on to argue that although the mechanistic process associated with the balance of power may appear to be an enduring feature of the international system, it has periodically been overlaid by a second feature which ameliorates the risk that the balance of power will precipitate self-destructive conflict. There have, he argues, been periods when the imperial drive for power has been constrained by certain 'moral limitations' that have been accepted by all the units in the system as the result of arriving at 'a silent compact' (1973: p. 219). On the basis of this compact it is possible to agree on an 'ultimate standard' of behaviour reflecting a body of rules that all the members of the system are morally obliged to follow. As Morgenthau puts it, during these distinctive periods, every ruler 'expected and was justified in expecting everybody else to share this standard', with the result that the mechanistic international system took on the form of a 'competitive society' (p. 220). Bull similarly acknowledges the existence of international societies where states are 'conscious of certain common interests and common values' on the one hand and, on the other, consider themselves to be 'bound by a common set of rules in their relations with one another, and share in the working of common institutions' (Bull 1977: 13). So like Morgenthau, members of the English school also depict the international society in terms of a 'superstructure, consciously put in place to modify the mechanical workings of the system' (Watson 1992: 311). This line of argument strikes a chord with the position advanced by Wendt, though again it was not articulated with his degree of methodological clarity.

The framework adopted by Morgenthau very clearly privileges the mechanical international system over the constructed international society. Although Morgenthau saw Europe during the nineteenth century as constituting an international society, he was clear that in the aftermath of the Second World War, with the emergence of the Soviet Union and the United States as dominant and antagonistic units, a 'new' but essentially mechanistic balance of power had returned to regulate international politics (1973: 340). At first sight, it might seem that Morgenthau had anticipated Waltz's neorealist and Wendt's constructivist positions and then applied them to different historical periods. But in fact, Morgenthau's position, although never made entirely clear, is more complex. The 'silent compact' permitting the emergence of a 'competitive society' is always undergirded by the mechanistic balance of power. States are consequently encouraged to maintain a rule-governed international society because they recognize that if they fail to do so, the mechanistic balance of power will once again reassert itself. Because of the privileged position occupied by the mechanistic international system in Morgenthau's systemic framework, it is possible to envisage an international system in the absence of an international society, but the reverse is not considered possible. Both Bull and Morgenthau thus reflect Waltz's theoretical position to characterize international systems, and Wendt's theoretical position to characterize international societies—a methodological marriage that would satisfy neither Waltz nor Wendt.

The position is further complicated in the context of the English school because Bull goes on to include a third element within his systemic perspective—a world society made up of individuals rather than states. Such a world society presupposes the existence of 'a world common good' defined in terms of 'the common ends or values of the universal society of all mankind' (Bull 1977: 84). The English school do not see world society as some kind of utopian dream. They believe that such societies have emerged at various times in different parts of the globe. And even more significantly, they argue that international societies have always been underpinned by a world society, although they do not pretend to understand the nature of the relationship between world and international societies.

The English school's systemic perspective is more subtle and complicated than Morgenthau's, and its view of the relationship amongst international system, international society, and world society needs to be clarified. Bull (1977: 22) offers the methodological injunction that the analyst must not 'reify' any of these elements because they form part of a larger and more complex reality. So although attention may be focused on any one of the elements at a time, it must never be forgotten that the element has been extracted from the broader reality. Bull insists that 'it is always erroneous to interpret events as if international society were the sole or dominant element' (1977: 55). When the features associated with the international society are highlighted, this must never be done at the expense of recognizing the continuing significance of the anarchic features associated with the international system and the transnational forces at work within the world society. All three elements exist coterminously, though in varying strengths. They can be separated only for methodological convenience (Cutler 1991).

But despite the obvious importance attached to the methodological injunction, Bull makes no attempt to clarify where the three elements fit into the conception of a broader reality. As a consequence, it is impossible to say whether there are other dimensions of reality that need to be brought into focus in order to achieve a comprehensive picture of the international system. Anticipating our discussion in Chapter 4, we can suggest that when Bull and Morgenthau distinguish between an international system and an international society, they are both operating at a systemic level of analysis, but they are operating in different sectors. International system draws attention to a military-political sector, whereas international society draws attention to a socio-political perspective. But having identified two sectors, the possibility of other sectors needs to be investigated. At the very least, attention needs to be drawn to an economic sector. In an international society, the dominant units are states, but in a world society they are individuals. So although world society can be located in the same sector as an international society, it draws attention to a very different level of analysis. Questions must therefore be asked as to how many levels of analysis and how many sectors need to be brought into the picture.

Despite these methodological shortcomings, the English school has succeeded in developing a much richer historical account of the international system than any of its competitors within the field of IR. By drawing a clear ontological distinction between international systems and societies, they are able to make the claim that over the last 500 years, during which the Europeans extended their power across the globe, the international system extended ahead of the international society. In other words, they suggest that European expansion in the military-political sector went ahead faster than the expansion that took place in the socio-political sector (Bull and Watson 1984). We will offer our assessment of this claim in the historical sections of the book, but can suggest at this juncture that failure to embrace the economic sector represents an obvious weakness in this account.

We are not suggesting that IR has ignored economics. For over thirty years, Susan Strange advocated the importance of international political economy (IPE) and insisted that the discipline must take economics into account. And without doubt, international economics now frequently occupies centre stage. Much discussion within IPE has focused on the rules that regulate international economics. Realists have insisted that power plays a crucial role in the nature of economic transactions, with the strength of rules governing free trade, for example, being primarily related to the presence or absence in the system of a hegemonic state subscribing to liberal principles (Krasner 1976). Economics is thereby subordinated to the political structure of the international system. Pluralists, by contrast, argue that the emergence and survival of economic regimes is more likely to be shaped by the level of information flowing around the international system rather than power (Keohane 1984). It has also been stressed that the nature of the international system is now changing as firms jostle with states in a way that simply cannot be accommodated by the neorealist theory of international politics. Although straining towards a new and more pluralistic theory to account for the part played by economics in the international system, pluralists have so far failed to emerge with a coherent alternative to the more established monistic theories.

# 5. CONCLUSIONS

It might appear self-evident that the international system is simply too complex to adopt a position of methodological and theoretical monism. But the issue is less clear-cut than this assessment suggests. It has long been supposed that our understanding of the world will only progress if an academic division of labour is employed. Although critics argue to the contrary, academic divisions of labour can be viewed as not arbitrary, but corresponding to divisions observable in the real world. That is why it is so important that the content of a discipline is defined by reference to a concrete system. For most social sciences, the individual represents the referent unit of analysis in the system. Realists have tried to promote the state as the core referent unit in IR, but this position has become increasingly contested. As Krasner (1976: 317) noted many years ago: 'students of international relations have multinationalized, transnationalized, bureaucratized, and transgovernmentalized the state until it has virtually ceased to exist as an analytic construct.' And this is partly where the problem lies. Each of these moves changes the content of the concrete international system in terms of the types of unit and types of interaction that compose it. The problem is not simply the complexity of the international system, but the fact that there is so little agreement amongst theorists about what constitutes it.

And there are other difficulties. The disposition in IR to adopt a posture of theoretical and methodological monism has meant that analysts have privileged political transactions and the anarchic political structure of the system. This has encouraged, largely unwittingly, a tendency to read the present structure of the international system into the past. The result is either that there are periods of time across the globe when it becomes impossible to examine the past from an international perspective, or that the analysis suffers from being anachronistic, Eurocentric, and/or ahistorical. In addition, as we will see in the next chapter, there are world historians who have adopted a systemic perspective that generates an image of the past which is very different from anything found in conventional IR. The only way to cope with these problems is to adopt a pluralistic perspective and put the broadest possible construction onto the international system. In that way it becomes possible to present a narrative that shows how the international system has changed over time. Moreover, only by adopting a theoretically and methodologically pluralistic perspective can we hope to accommodate some of the ideas developed by world historians. In the terms discussed above, we have to try to extend the pluralist approach of traditional realists and proponents of the English school, while hanging onto the more self-conscious theoretical rigour of Waltz and Wendt.

# Chapter 3

# SYSTEMIC THINKING IN WORLD HISTORY

The premiss that the contemporary international system can only be fully understood from a world historical perspective has not had much formal recognition in IR, even though the significance of world history is being acknowledged across a wide range of disciplines (Moore 1993; 1997). Although world historians offer a more encompassing narrative of the past than any found in conventional IR, we hope that the pluralistic toolkit presented in the next chapter will allow us to offer a perspective on the past different from anything found in either IR or world history.

Any discussion of world history is complicated by a distinction between *scientific* world history and *philosophical* world history (McNeill 1986; Callinicos 1995; Graham 1997). In the first section of this chapter we focus on these two conceptions of world history. In the second, we examine the perspectives developed on world history in IR, historical sociology, geopolitics, mainstream world history, and economic history. It is not possible to capture the full sense of systemic thinking in world history by looking at single representative authors as we did in Chapter 2. This chapter therefore focuses more on main schools of thought, though where we can do so through the work of one individual that is our preferred path. Since much of the work discussed here lies on or outside the boundaries of what is taught in mainstream IR, the chapter also serves as an introduction to authors who may be unfamiliar to IR readers.

## 1. SCIENTIFIC AND PHILOSOPHICAL WORLD HISTORY

### PHILOSOPHICAL WORLD HISTORY

The link between philosophy and history hinges on the idea that it is possible to ascribe some hidden meaning or purpose to history. Once this meaning or purpose has been divined, then the past, present, and future can be seen as conforming to some kind of structure or shape. Deeply rooted in the modern world, for example, is the belief that history reveals how human beings have advanced or progressed through time. It is widely assumed that by the exercise of human reason, this progress will extend into the future, with war, for example, eventually becoming a thing of the past. Such ideas are closely associated with philosophers such as Kant and Hegel who both stressed the importance of combining philosophical and historical reasoning.

Divining the meaning of history involves drawing on normative concepts like progress that can only be understood using philosophical tools of analysis. Although philosophers such as Aristotle and Hegel arrive at very different conclusions about the nature of progress (Graham 1997), the range of patterns associated with world history is in fact limited to four main options:

1. a trajectory of upward progress,
2. a trajectory of downward decline,
3. a cycle of civilizations endlessly rising and falling,
4. a spiral (linking the linear and cyclical patterns—Gruner 1985: 15).

McNeill suggests that Toynbee found this fourth option during the course of producing his multi-volume *Study of History*. Initially he operated on the basis of a cyclical model, with civilizations simply rising and falling. But in the later volumes, the cycles of civilization 'served, like wheels of some great chariot, to carry humanity onwards, ever onwards towards some divinely appointed and unknowable but plainly desirable end' (McNeill 1986: 137). McNeill (1986: 175) found Toynbee's work inspirational, but most scientific historians came to regard it as metaphysical nonsense. Karl Popper (1966, 1957) attacked Marx's approach to world history as dangerous, and linked his ideas to totalitarianism. Callinicos (1995) argues that all the philosophical world historians subscribe to an unacceptable teleology that sees history moving towards some predetermined end. For this reason Callinicos (1995: 45) opposes Kant's belief that world history reveals 'a hidden plan of nature' which is helping to realize a 'perfect political constitution as the only state within which all the natural capacities of mankind can be developed completely'. In the middle years of the twentieth century philosophical world history became extremely unfashionable, although the mood changed as the end of the millennium approached. Francis Fukuyama (1992, 1998) in *The End of History and the Last Man* provided a recent defence of a progressive view of the past and simultaneously helped to regenerate an interest in philosophical world history.

## SCIENTIFIC WORLD HISTORY

Throughout most of the twentieth century, there has been a desire to escape from what has been seen as a nationalist bias to history. With the onset of the First World War, the novelist and futurologist H. G. Wells decided that the only way to make sense of the tragic events that were engulfing the globe was to view them from a very long world historical perspective. An analysis of the immediate events that had led up to the world war did not, Wells argued, provide an adequate explanation of how and why Japanese warships came to be patrolling the Mediterranean when less than a hundred years previously Japan had been an isolated and feudal state. Wells (1925) set about writing a scientific 'outline' of world history that traced the crucial developments that have occurred across the globe back to the start of life on earth. As he wrote, he became ever more conscious of the extraordinary extent to which European historians had 'minimized' the role of non-Europeans in the 'drama of mankind' (p. 2). For Wells, events in Europe provided no more than a brief episode in a much larger story. Study groups and classes were established in Britain at this time in an attempt to encourage people to break free from the accounts of the past written during the 'long period of nationalist and particularist histories through which we have passed' (Cole 1923: 3). Yet at the end of the twentieth century, it was still being argued that the prevailing world-view lacked historical depth and remained highly Eurocentric (Blaut 1993; Hodgson 1993). During the course of the twentieth century, as Wells predicted, new synoptic accounts of world history came forward to take the place of his outline (Davies 1968; Roberts 1993). But McNeill (1986: 129) has argued that all too often these accounts tended to be the work of 'brilliant amateurs', like Wells, or textbooks that do no more than provide a catalogue of past events.

As the twentieth century came to a close, it became clear that during the last quarter of the century the fortunes of world historians had undergone a dramatic transformation (Burke 1993; Callinicos 1995; Moore 1997). Although postmodernists insisted that the time had come to discard what Lyotard (1984) called 'meta-narratives', there was a growing call throughout the social sciences for a restoration and reconstruction of a 'grand narrative' of human history (Sherratt 1995; Chase-Dunn and Hall 1997). It has been argued that the transformation was heralded by McNeill's *The Rise of the West*. While acknowledging the importance of the work of world systems theorists, Burke (1993: p. x) insists that this book had the effect of remaking the study of world history by unhooking the perspective from its 'Procrustean bed of metaphysics' that Burke associates, in particular, with Spengler and Toynbee.

Moore (1997: 945) has pushed the argument further, suggesting that world history is now the only credible paradigm that can satisfy 'an obvious and urgent need to understand the world we live in'. World history is being treated here as a vast time/space canvas. The methodology of world historians takes the whole canvas into consideration, and there is a growing number of attempts to understand the world we live in from a world historical perspective. These attempts have ranged from discussions of energy (Smil 1994) to circuses (Croft-Cooke and Cotes 1976). There is potentially an infinite number of topics that can be viewed from a world historical perspective, and this conclusion leads Moore to suggest that world history represents the 'set of all sets' because it is the only perspective in which 'all events, structures, and processes must ultimately be capable of being viewed' (1997: 949; 1993).

Depicted in these terms, world history generates a methodological injunction that every discipline must work from a world historical perspective: the tendency to study any subject exclusively in terms of a particular period of time or a particular geographical space must be eschewed. In line with this methodological injunction, Croft-Cooke and Cotes (1976), for example, associate circuses with the link that empires have had with the wider world and they compare the role played by circuses in the Roman and British Empires. The comparative method used in this instance is considered absolutely central for the study of world history. Archaeologists and anthropologists have led the way in developing this world historical approach (Moore 1997: 945). In both disciplines, comparisons are now regularly being made across time and space. The process of state formation, for example, has been compared in Mesopotamia and Mesoamerica at two points which are widely separated in both time and space. The increasing tendency for comparisons to be made in very different places and at very different points in time means that much conventional thinking has been questioned, with established disciplinary boundaries and familiar forms of periodization, in particular, being profoundly destabilized.

## 2.  DIVERGENT APPROACHES TO WORLD HISTORY

### INTERNATIONAL RELATIONS AND WORLD HISTORY

We claim to be providing, for the first time, a framework embracing a *continuous* narrative of international systems across a period of over 5,000 years. But it would be an exaggeration to suggest that the study of international relations lacks any kind of world historical perspective. Textbooks providing accounts of international history since 1945 (Calvocoressi 1996), or sometimes for the twentieth century or a bit longer (Barraclough 1967; Keylor 1984), are quite common. More than thirty years ago Holsti (1967) produced a major textbook that opened with a discussion of international politics in the Chou dynasty, 1122–221 BC, the Greek city-states, 800 BC–322 BC and Renaissance Italy. But as suggested in Chapter 1, understanding the origins and significance of the idea of the international system requires more than merely selecting the handful of times and locations from the ancient and classical era during which anarchic structures putatively similar to modern Europe's briefly held sway. It means addressing the whole sweep of ancient and classical history in terms of international systems, and asking just what kind of system(s), if any, existed before the Europeans subordinated everything to their own anarchic model. Only by following this course can one bring the historical record to bear on the question of what are the necessary and sufficient conditions for an international system to come into being.

We are not, of course, the first IR theorists to point to the problem of trying to develop a general theory of international systems on the basis of the European model. Perhaps surprisingly, Gilpin, an archetypal realist, has made just this point. He argues that throughout history international systems have been structured in three very different ways. First he identifies an imperial or hegemonic structure of control where a single state dominates the system. Second, there is a bipolar structure of control, with the system controlled by two powerful states. Finally, he identifies a balance of power structure where three or more states mutually regulate each other's activities. Gilpin (1981: 110–11) says that before the emergence of the European state system, the world history of international systems was characterized by a succession or cycle of great empires that 'unified and ordered' their respective international systems. It was only with the emergence of the European international system that the idea of international systems controlled by the balance of power came to the fore. Gibbon, Montesquieu, Heeren, Ranke, and more recently, Toynbee and Dehio have all made the same point (Gilpin 1981: 111). Gilpin argues that the cycle of empires in the ancient world was kept in motion as the result of the activities of barbarians that lay outside these international systems.

Gilpin accepts that the cycle of empires represents an oversimplified model, because he acknowledges the importance of city-states and feudalism, although he makes no attempt to fit these features into his theoretical framework. He argues that the cycle of empires was broken by the emergence of three interrelated developments—nation states, sustained economic growth, and a world market economy. The combination of these developments meant that the cycle of empires gave way to an international system controlled by the balance of power and a succession of political and economic hegemonies. Hegemonic powers are willing to supply public goods that benefit all members of the system. The power of hegemons, like the power of empires, has always waned, but in contrast to the cycle of empires, there are always contenders within the system willing to resort to war in order to challenge the reigning hegemon. In developing this thesis, Gilpin draws heavily on the work of theorists like Modelski (1987), who has suggested that the modern international system can be described in terms of hundred-year-long cycles, each of which began and ended with a cataclysmic war. Attempts of this kind to identify a pattern to the history of the modern international system have tended to eclipse work such as Singer and Small (1972) and Rosecrance (1963) that operated on a much narrower time-frame.

Gilpin and Modelski are not the only theorists who have endeavoured to provide a model that accounts for developments over the past 500 years. Kennedy (1989), for example, argues that the rise and fall of great powers is most effectively accounted for by the tendency of great powers to extend their strategic reach beyond the limits imposed by their economic resources. By contrast, Dehio (1963) suggested that what has prevented successive hegemons from establishing imperial international systems is the fact that the European international system was always an open system. As a consequence, there were always states waiting in the wings that could be used as a counterweight to any potential imperial state. Dehio was writing in the wake of the Second World War and he argued that now that the United States had been incorporated within the international system, there were no more external powers to draw upon and the balancing principle that had operated for the previous 400 years could no longer function. Toynbee (1954) developed a similar line of argument and both concluded that the international system would give way to a world state. But it became apparent after the Second World War that the United Nations was not going to provide an incipient world government and IR theorists became increasingly interested in the idea of an international system based on a bipolar structure. Although Kaplan (1957) tried to open up space for thinking about different kinds of international system, his hypothetical systems looked to the future rather than the past.

In recent years there has been a growing recognition that the neorealist preoccupation with anarchy has constrained theoretical thought. In an early move, Ruggie (1983) argued that Waltz's framework was so rigid that it was unable to identify feudalism as a distinctive form of international system. By focusing on the medieval period, Ruggie revealed a crucial weakness in the neorealist framework. More important, by drawing upon Waltz's own tools, he was able to extend the neorealist framework in a way that made it possible to accommodate feudalism as a particular kind of international system. Ferguson and Mansbach (1996) have also suggested that greater sensitivity to historical data quickly demonstrates the weaknesses of neorealism. They examine in considerable depth a series of fascinating case studies of political systems drawn from both the New World and the Old over the past five millennia. They adopt an essentially political and ahistorical perspective which effectively dissolves the state, revealing the complexity of the pluralist political arena, but without providing a way of moving beyond the complexity. Although a new generation of scholars are beginning to acknowledge the importance of developing theory from a more historicized and world historical perspective (Kaufman 1997; Reus-Smit 1997; Hall 1997), from our point of view, the most interesting body of historically aware IR writers are the members of the English school, one of whom, as we have already noted, provides an escape route from anarchophilia. More on them in Chapters 4 and 5.

## HISTORICAL SOCIOLOGY AND WORLD HISTORY

The origins of historical sociology have been traced back to the eighteenth century when the first attempts were made to compare societies and understand why some were more successful than others (D. Smith 1991). The first wave of contemporary historical sociology extends to the start of the twentieth century and embraces social thinkers as diverse as John Stuart Mill, Marx, and Weber, who despite their differences continue to have an enormous influence on the study of society (Hall 1985). All were interested in redrawing the parameters of society in a way that would permit a greater fulfilment of human aspirations and in understanding how Europe had managed to surge ahead of other centres of civilization. Marx and Weber provided competing foundations for the study of sociology throughout the twentieth century, although sociologists often lost sight of the historical dimension of their work. At the heart of Marx's philosophy of history is the assumption that world history can be described in terms of an evolving set of societies that are each held together by a distinctive economic mode of production. Weber also has a philosophy of history that distinguishes between agrarian and industrial societies. The latter is seen to be an accidental product of the civilization that evolved in Latin Christendom (Hall 1985). During the last thirty years of this century there was a resurgence of interest in historical sociology by advocates of both Marx and Weber. But in addition to acknowledging the need to take account of history, there was also a recognition that historical sociology had been held back by the tendency to treat society as a closed system. As we have seen, Wallerstein formulated one radical solution to this problem, but most historical sociologists were unwilling to put all their societal eggs in an exclusively economic basket. What they have endeavoured to do instead is to provide an international setting for a theory of the state and society.

Although contemporary historical sociologists have addressed a wide range of issues, they have all tended to draw on a common and essentially militaristic conception of international relations. The general argument (Tilly 1985, 1990; Hall 1985) is that the modern state emerged in an international context that embraced a wide variety of social units—including city-states, nation states, and empires—many of which coexisted for much of the last thousand years, and that in the long haul it was the superior warfighting qualities of the state that eliminated the other forms.

While sharing some of this view, Mann (1986, 1993) has endeavoured to locate the development of the state on an even broader historical canvas. He explores the role played by power throughout history in the process whereby people and space have been integrated. He traces the process back to 5,000 BC when, with the emergence of agriculture, volatile 'social networks' were rigidified into 'social cages'. Thereafter, he argues, two different social configurations can be identified—empires and multi-power-actor civilizations. Mann identifies four different sources of power (ideological, economic, political, and military). But despite acknowledging the existence of international norms, when addressing the role played by the international setting, he too tends to focus on the role of military power. Skocpol (1979) is similarly transfixed by the impact of war in her attempt to develop a theory of revolutions in the context of the European states-system.

Historical sociologists working in a Marxist tradition have also endeavoured to locate their unit of analysis in an international and world historical setting. Anderson (1974a and 1974b) argues that any attempt to understand the emergence of modern capitalism has no alternative but to follow the history of Western Europe back to antiquity along a unique historical pathway. In antiquity he demonstrates that the prevailing mode of production, based on slavery, resulted in economic stagnation. Economic expansion could only take place through conquest. Anderson shows how successive empires in antiquity each managed to overcome structural problems in the preceding empire which limited its capacity for expansion. But like the historical sociologists working within a Weberian tradition, Anderson also defines the international in essentially militaristic terms.

In recent years, there has emerged from within IR what appears to be a 'second wave' (Hobson 1999) in historical sociology. At the heart of this new movement lies a deep-seated dissatisfaction with neorealism and the absence of a historicized conception of the state. This literature is starting to challenge conventional views in both IR and historical sociology about how the modern state emerged. Spruyt (1994a, 1994b) argues that three different political forms emerged from feudalism: city-states and city leagues as well as sovereign states. It was the sovereign state, however, that persisted, proving most successful at reducing transportation and information costs as well as being able to produce the most credible commitments in the international system. In a similar vein, Thomson (1994) undermines the idea that international violence has always been monopolized by states. On the contrary, she suggests not only that in the heteronomous medieval period, violence was 'democratised, marketised, and internationalised' (Thomson 1994: 4), but that these characteristics were only brought to an end during the nineteenth century. Second wave theorists neverthe less argue that the neorealist view of the state is still flawed. Hobson argues that states cannot be treated as an ontological given, as neorealists do. In the nineteenth century, he argues, most states lacked the strength to impose their will on domestic forces and had no alternative but to tax trade in order to raise revenue. As states have become stronger during the twentieth century vis-à-vis their domestic constituencies, they have been able to rely on income tax rather than trade as a source of income. This line of argument challenges neorealist thinking on international political economy which has focused on the capacity of hegemonic states to impose their will on other states in the international system. The spread of free trade in the era after the Second World War is, as a consequence, not attributed to the hegemonic position of the United States, but to the widespread ability of states in the developed world to raise revenue by income tax.

Second wave theorists are not only working within this Weberian tradition of thought. There is also an important Marxist approach to historical sociology starting to be developed in IR. Within this Marxist tradition, the medieval period has been reassessed, for example, with Ruggie's (1983) approach being criticized for failing to recognize that the nature of the constitutive units in the feudal international system was determined by the property relations that existed within them (Teschke 1998). And in the same vein, Rosenberg (1994) has historicized familiar realist concepts such as anarchy and the balance of power. He argues that these are not timeless political features of the international system but character-istics that have taken divergent forms in different historical eras as determined by the prevailing mode of economic production.

## GEOPOLITICS AND WORLD HISTORY

At the beginning of the twentieth century it was very apparent to some geo-political analysts that the globe was rapidly becoming a closed and increasingly interdependent system. From this perspective, a seismic shift was taking place in world history that was bringing about a transformation in the geographical con-figuration of the globe. But because the two world wars convinced many analysts that the fundamental features of international politics had remained unchanged, the full impact of these ideas is only apparent as we move into a new century. The geopolitical perspective generated an assessment of world history that was radic-ally different from the one that came to prevail in the study of IR. Although our assessment of world history is different again, we acknowledge that elements of geopolitical thinking foreshadow aspects of what in Chapter 4 we call 'interaction capacity'.

Geopolitical thinking has been traced back to the ancient Greeks. Often con-sidered to be synonymous with power politics, modern geopolitics focuses on the great powers and presupposes that they are driven to expand in an attempt to secure natural resources and safe borders. The roots of modern geopolitics have been traced back to German theorists, such as Karl Ritter, writing at the beginning of the nineteenth century, who developed the theory of continents as 'natural wholes', and Friederich Ratzel, writing in the middle of the century, who argued that world history would come to be dominated by continental-sized states (Sen 1975). Later, the American Alfred Thayer Mahan drew a distinction between land- and sea-based powers. But it was the English geographer Halford J. Mackinder (1904, 1919) who gave 'mature expression to geopolitical concepts' (Sen 1975: 190). Building on the work of earlier theorists, Mackinder established a framework that was to underpin much of the twentieth-century geopolitical literature with sub-sequent theorists either supporting or contesting his basic thesis. Twentieth-century strategic planners in countries across the globe have unquestionably been influenced by Mackinder's framework, though they tend to ignore its world historical implications.

At the heart of his framework is the recognition that political relationships throughout history have been profoundly affected by the impact of geography on human mobility. Power, Mackinder presupposes, is ultimately delimited by mobil-ity. Geographical factors can facilitate or impede movement, and thus determine the capacity of political entities to interact. Because of developments in technol-ogy, the effects of geographical factors on mobility change over time, and this allows Mackinder to use his basic idea about the relationship between power and mobility to paint a very distinctive picture of world history.

Mackinder argued that the world was divided into three major regions. There is the Eurasian heartland, which consisted primarily of open steppeland and was depicted as wholly continental. Surrounding this pivot was the inner crescent where the bulk of the world's population resided. Beyond was the outer crescent which embraced the rest of the world which could only be linked to what Mackinder called the world island when oceanic transport developed.

From Mackinder's perspective, the landmass of Eurasia provided the starting point for world history, and prior to AD 1500, during what he calls the pre-Columbian period, this huge 'world island' constituted 'a closed political system' (Mackinder 1904: 428). The oceans acted as a barrier to the Americas and Australasia, while Southern and Central Africa were effectively cut off by the Sahara desert. Within this closed system, the population was very unevenly spread and divergent patterns of mobility developed at the core and the periphery of the system. Although there were rivers running through the heartland, they are depicted as 'practically useless for the purpose of human communication with the outer world' (1904: 429). The Volga, the Oxus, and the Jaxartes—three of the world's great rivers—run into salt lakes, while the other major rivers in the region flow into the frozen ocean to the north. This huge and sparsely populated area was historically dominated by horse- and camel-riding nomads who could aggregate into large, mobile military forces which posed a persistent and serious threat to the much more heavily populated regions of the inner crescent. Mackinder (1904: 430–1) argues not only that 'all the settled margins of the Old World sooner or later felt the expansive force of mobile power originating in the steppe' but also that the nomads were able periodically to divide India and China from the Mediterranean world. In the inner crescent, Mackinder (1904: 431) identifies four main areas of large, settled population: China, India, the Middle East, and Europe. This distinction between sedentary and mobile communities is not new. It can be traced back to at least the fourteenth-century historian Ibn-Khaldun's work *Muqaddimah*, or Introduction to History (Sen 1975: 174–5).

Mackinder then contrasts the land-bound horse and camel, the main sources of continental mobility, with the mobility permitted by sailing boats plying the oceanic rivers and coastlines that were accessible to the people living on the margins of the world island. Sea-borne vessels could establish links across enormous distances, but so long as Eurasia remained a world island, sea power did not help the civilizations of the inner crescent to prevail against the land mobility of the heartland. This situation was transformed in 1492 when transoceanic navigation transformed the world island from a closed to an open system. For the next four centuries, the Europeans moved off the world island and expanded into other parts of the inner crescent, as well as occupying the outer crescent 'against almost negligible resistance' (1904: 422). This sea-borne revolution endowed the

Europeans with the 'widest possible mobility of power' and had the effect of neutralizing the ability of the nomads to exercise pressure from the continental heartland (p. 432). The revolution shifted the balance of power decisively in the direction of the outer crescent of sea-based states (including Britain and Japan) which now effectively encircled the continental heartland but which were inaccessible to it (p. 433). Mackinder was here echoing the views of Mahan (Sen 1975: 189–90).

By 1900, however, the effects of the maritime revolution had been effectively played out, because with nowhere left for the further 'pegging out of a claim of ownership' (Mackinder 1904: 421), expansion was no longer possible. Mackinder associated this moment with the end of the Columbian epoch. He argued that world history was now moving into a post-Columbian age, because in the absence of any new territory to occupy, it was necessary to come to terms, once again, with operating inside a 'closed political system' although this time one of 'world-wide scope' (p. 422). From Mackinder's perspective, a closed political system operates in a radically different way from an open one. In an open system, the impact of major social change can be 'dissipated' into 'unknown space', whereas in a closed system, any change must necessarily reverberate, or 're-echo' as Mackinder puts it, all round the system (p. 422).

Mackinder also focused on the emergence of transcontinental railways, which he foresaw rapidly covering the heartland. Such a development could lead to the establishment of 'a vast economic world . . . . inaccessible to oceanic commerce' (p. 434) which could tip the balance of power once more in favour of the heartland, or more specifically, Russia. Russia could then extend its power across Eurasia, and build a fleet which would allow it to capture the outer crescent and establish a world empire. The image of an expansionist Russia initially dominating Eurasia and then the world exerted a powerful influence throughout the twentieth century. German geopoliticians such as Haushofer argued after the First World War for an alliance between Germany and Russia as a mechanism whereby Germany could dominate the heartland. Spykman, on the other hand, disputed the power of the heartland and favoured an alliance embracing the United States, the Soviet Union, and Britain as a mechanism for maintaining global peace (Sen 1975). After the Second World War, geopolitics was dismissed by Morgenthau (1973: 158) as 'pseudoscience' because of its geographic determinism, although its policy implications persisted (Taylor 1985).

The world historical implications of the heartland thesis were never really addressed by IR. The most interesting attempt to develop its world historical implications was by a historian with a geographic bent (Fox 1971, 1991). He argues that throughout much of history it is possible to distinguish between sea-based commercial communities and land-based administrative states. With the opening up of the Atlantic in the seventeenth century he sees this distinction becoming increasingly important and he uses it to reassess the familiar story which describes the rise of the 'nation state'. He argues that in conjunction with the developing state system there was 'a widespread and complex network of water-borne communication systems connecting islands and the fringes of continental masses' which permitted a global commercial community to emerge (Fox 1991: 1). There are some IR echoes of this in Rosecrance's (1986) idea of the trading state. Conventional approaches to IR have largely failed to assess these ideas systematically, though the current fashions for geopolitics and geo-economics (Luttwak 1990; Rusi 1997) suggest a propitious atmosphere for their revival.

## CIVILIZATIONS AND WORLD HISTORY

Civilizations represent the most frequently used unit of analysis in twentieth-century accounts of world history. At the beginning of the twentieth century, Max Weber explored how agrarian societies were transformed into divergent civilizations by the emergence of world religions. He compared Confucian China, Islam, Latin Christendom, and Hindu India in an attempt to account for the rise of capitalism in the West. Spengler and Toynbee similarly drew on the idea of civilization, as more recently did McNeill (1963) in what Hodgson (1993: 92) described as 'the first genuine world history ever written'. But our reason for focusing on McNeill is that, like Mackinder, he presents a view of the world which contrasts sharply with the one found in conventional IR texts.

McNeill is primarily concerned with the development of four world civilizations: Greece, India, China, and the Middle East. Like Mackinder, McNeill accepts that the world civilizations were separated by the territory of the steppe nomads, and he too establishes a sharp contrast, though in terms of culture rather than mobility. McNeill sees not a heartland pivot, but 'barbarian zones'. Although he also depicts the barbarians as posing a persistent threat, it is the civilizations who are clearly privileged in his account, with the 'barbarian zones' merely serving to insulate one civilization from another. In McNeill's account, before 500 BC the civilizations were unconnected and developed autonomously. Thereafter contact between the civilizations increased, but McNeill insists that their autonomy, and an overall equilibrium amongst them, was maintained for two millennia from 500 BC to AD 1500. He accounts for this by cultural diffusion: any development which might have enabled one of the civilizations to forge ahead was borrowed and adopted by the other civilizations.

From McNeill's perspective it is because of the barbarian insulation that the four civilizations coexisted rather than co-acted. He accepts that there was some interaction, but identifies this in terms of four major 'disturbances' or 'shocks' which temporarily upset the equilibrium between the civilizations between 500 BC and AD 1500, and represent major 'benchmarks' in the course of world history (McNeill 1979: 129). The spread of Islam from the Middle East and the capitalist expansion of the West are both seen to have major and long-term consequences for other civilizations. Far from identifying the re-emergence of the heartland to political significance at the end of the nineteenth century, McNeill argues that the various civilizations steadily expanded into and ultimately eliminated the significance of the 'barbarian zones'.

Twenty-five years after writing *The Rise of the West*, McNeill re-evaluated his view of world history. He acknowledged that, when writing the book, he had been unconsciously influenced by the 'imperial mood' which prevailed in the United States after the Second World War (1991, p. xvi). There was a widespread feeling that the twentieth century was the American century and that the advantages of the US political system and way of life were being diffused across the globe. He also recognized retrospectively that his text tends to look at history 'from the point of view of the winners' (1991; p. xvii). At the start of the 1990s, when there was extensive discussion about the inevitable demise of the United States as a great power (Kennedy 1989), McNeill felt obliged to revise his initial assessment. He argued that he had failed to take sufficient account of the 'communication nets' which link people together and that as he has taken this factor into account, his focus of attention has shifted from the idea of 'civilization' to the idea of 'world system' (1993: p. xii) and that much more attention needs to be given to the existence of transcivilizational links (1998).

He argues that, in the first instance, civilizations were autonomous, but that between 1700 and 500 BC, a cosmopolitan world system came into existence on the basis of the ever widening boundaries of a succession of great empires. McNeill argues that the tax- and tribute-collecting bureaucracies that sustained these empires 'worked in symbiosis with caravan and shipping networks that antedated the political empires and whose zones of activities always extended beyond even the most far-flung political frontiers' (1991: p. xxiv). McNeill observes how this emerging 'world system' suffered a setback in the third century BC as the result of diseases spreading along the trade routes. Later, he observes, with the rise of Islam, the world system became characterized by cultural heterogeneity, except at the two extremes, in Japan and China and Western Europe, where cultural homogeneity prevailed. And far from there being a rough balance of power amongst the four civilizations, he now felt able to trace how the centre of power within the world system moved around from the Middle East to China and then to Western Europe.

Although McNeill accepts that there were considerable strengths to his original world history, he now acknowledges that it failed to provide a sustained narrative of the fluctuations in the growth of the world system. He also accepts that such a narrative would have to start at the very beginning of the history of civilization. The existence of a world system that 'transcended political and cultural boundaries' is, he believes, beyond doubt. He accepts that it is not easy to see how to develop a narrative which takes account of both the history of diverse civilizations and the community expressed in terms of a world system, but he believes that this should provide the future agenda for world historians. Interestingly, Toynbee came to a similar conclusion. According to von Laue (1989: 229), Toynbee (1958) recognized that what was needed was not 'the internal dynamics of isolated or self-propelled cultural entities but the dynamics of their world-wide interaction'. A similar argument was also made by Hodgson (1993), who thought that because Islamic civilization crossed conventional regional boundaries, linking Africa, Europe, India, South-East Asia, and China, it was necessary to develop an inter-regional approach to the 'Afro-Eurasian complex'. In recent years, advocates of a civilizational perspective have started to insist that we must not only examine the links that pull civilizations together into a broader system, but also examine the friction points where civilizations meet (Huntington 1996; Fernandez-Armesto 1996).

## ECONOMICS AND WORLD HISTORY

Over the past thirty years it has been acknowledged with increasing regularity that the study of economics needs to be investigated from a world historical perspective. When one follows this methodological injunction, familiar facts often have to be reassessed, and the dominance of a Eurocentric perspective appears to have distorted our understanding of many aspects of economic history. It is generally assumed, for example, that Europe was primarily responsible for the African slave trade, whereas a world historical perspective suggests that the Islamic slave trade began earlier and lasted longer; and, albeit controversially, it has even been argued to have involved, in total, many more African slaves than taken by the Europeans (Bairoch 1993: 146–8). It is similarly taken for granted that Europeans must have been endowed with some special abilities that allowed them to industrialize before other parts of the world. It is uncontroversial for economic historians to ask, as a consequence, why the industrial revolution first occurred in Europe. The world historical perspective suggests that this is the wrong question to ask, and draws attention to the fact that in the eighteenth century 'the great industrial centres of the world were China and India' (Fernandez-Armesto 1996: 358). World historians endeavour to explain why the industrial revolution did not occur somewhere other than Europe. Two very different types of world historical frameworks have been developed to address this issue. One draws on the idea of world systems, whereas the other adopts a more comparative perspective.

The central ideas associated with world systems were formulated initially by Immanuel Wallerstein (1974) in the early 1970s and they have come to provide the basis for a highly distinctive picture of world history that has influenced every branch of the social sciences. The theory was initially designed to undermine the model of economic development which prevailed in the 1960s. According to this model, all states in the developing world were expected to go through a series of economic stages before becoming fully developed. Wallerstein argued that the model failed to acknowledge that these states had for a very long period of time been part of a worldwide economic system that first emerged at the beginning of the sixteenth century. Far from being autonomous units with the capacity to become fully modernized states, political units beyond Europe became locked into a world system which actively prevented them from becoming modernized. From Wallerstein's perspective, AD 1500 represents a crucial point of transformation, separating ancient and modern history. World systems theory, therefore, drew on the ideas of dependency theorists (Amin; Frank) who had already talked about the development of underdevelopment, and the French *annales* school of history (Braudel), which presupposed that the potential for change is restricted by the existence of deep-seated and expansive structures.

Wallerstein started from the premiss that human beings cannot survive on their own and that they rely on a division of labour which establishes a system of interdependence. The division of labour defines the boundaries of the system within which the basic needs of individuals can be met. If the individuals within an economic system start to rely on external parties for the satisfaction of their survival needs, then the division of labour extends, and with it the boundary of the system. On the basis of this conception of an economic system, Wallerstein identifies two historical watersheds, one in 10,000 BC and the other in AD 1500, and he suggests that critical systemic transformations occurred at those two points. Before 10,000 BC, a division of labour never extended beyond the bounds of a common culture, establishing what Wallerstein refers to as mini-systems. Such systems have a very distinctive mode of production based on hunting, gathering, and rudimentary agriculture. Survival depends on reciprocity, with a division of labour linking small extended families. In other words, social, political, and economic relations are all built on the basis of kinship. Although these mini-systems survived long after 10,000 BC, Wallerstein is clear that they have not persisted to the present day, having been absorbed into more substantial 'world systems'.

The form of world system that dominated across the globe for many millennia is identified by Wallerstein as a world empire. Although these empires took many different political forms over the millennia, they all shared the same mode of production, with the vast majority of the population working the land and producing a surplus that was then exchanged for goods produced by a smaller group of artisans and, crucially, to provide tribute that supported a distinct military-bureaucratic ruling class. This mode of production underpinned vast centralized political structures such as the Roman or Inca world empires, as well as the highly decentralized political structures that characterize the kind of feudal society found in Europe. Although Wallerstein acknowledges that these world empires sometimes interacted, the interaction was insufficient to generate a more extensive system because the interaction was not essential for the survival of any of the empires.

Wallerstein does accept, however, that when world empires collapsed a politically divided but economically interdependent system was forged. Relations within such a system were not governed by the principle of redistribution, as in the world empires, but, at least potentially, by the market. The existence of a market provides the basis for a capitalist mode of production and a new kind of world system that Wallerstein defines as a world economy. In practice, such systems were too unstable for a market to develop and they invariably gave way to the formation of a new world empire. For over 11 millennia Wallerstein sees world empires as the dominant unit in world history. After AD 1500, a second historical watershed is crossed and a new era emerges with the establishment of a stable world economy in Europe in the wake of feudalism. This world economy was stable, according to Wallerstein, because of the political structure which embraced strong states at the centre of the system and weak states at the periphery, with surplus produced at the periphery being extracted and accumulated at the centre. In contrast to earlier world economies, where eventually a dominant actor was able to reunify the system into a world empire, in this capitalist world economy the states at the centre of the system were all sufficiently strong that they could withstand the efforts of any single state to reforge an empire. The system was further stabilized by the emergence of what Wallerstein calls semi-peripheral states. These were states like the former Soviet Union, which lacked the necessary ingredients to form a state at the centre of the world economy, but possessed sufficient power to withstand being pushed into the periphery.

Wallerstein's framework has had an enormous impact across the social sciences from geography (Taylor 1985) to political science (Hollist and Rosenau 1981). But it has also come in for extensive criticism from two very different directions. On the one hand, it is argued that Wallerstein's attempt to locate the emergence of a stable world economy based on a capitalist mode of production represents a highly Eurocentric perspective. Abu-Lughod (1991), for example, pushes the origin of this world system back to AD 1250 when the system extended across Eurasia. She argues that the rise of the West can only be understood in conjunction with the simultaneous demise of the East. In an even more dramatic move, Frank and Gills (1993) push the origins of the contemporary world system back to 3000 BC. Frank (1995: 189) argues that the problem with Wallerstein is that he conflates 'systems' and 'modes of production' and thereby fails to identify the essential continuity that the focus on systems encourages. Following this logic, archaeologists and anthropologists see Wallerstein's fundamental error as assuming that the exchange of luxury goods does not create a division of labour. They argue that such goods played a crucial role in maintaining the hierarchical structure of the political units that overtook the egalitarian hunter-gatherer bands a very long way back in human history. It follows that the kind of world system that Wallerstein argues did not exist before AD 1500 has been traced back to at least the fourth millennium BC (Algaze 1993).

Wallerstein has also been attacked by analysts who have seriously engaged with the idea of modes of production. Mandel (1978) argues that although it is appropriate to describe the modern world system as capitalist because the trading links around the world were established by capitalists, these links have joined together societies that operate on the basis of very different modes of production. Extending this idea, Wolf (1982) argues that the nature of the world system only changed at the end of the eighteenth century when the new breed of capitalists who had gained control over the means of production within their own state began to extend this control over the means of production beyond their own borders. He associates this development with the formation of a self-regulating market in the international arena, precipitating what Polanyi (1957) called 'the great transformation'—300 years after the point identified by Wallerstein.

It has also been argued that Wallerstein's preoccupation with trade reflects an unacknowledged liberal bias (Brenner 1977). And political economists on the left of the political spectrum (Lewis and Malone 1996) are displaying increasing interest in reassessing Lenin's classic study of imperialism on the grounds that his analysis continues to provide profound insights into both world historical and contemporary developments. It foreshadows, in particular, the welter of contemporary literature on globalization. At the heart of Lenin's thesis was the argument that capitalism, initially based on competition amongst commodity producers, was giving way to a process of monopolization or concentration of both capital and production to counteract the falling rate of profits. This development had been accompanied by a process which had resulted in the entire globe being divided up amongst colonial powers that had pursued policies of monopolistic control over the territory that they had acquired.

Wallerstein has, nevertheless, had a major impact on the social sciences in part because of his world historical perspective. But there is an alternative economic approach to world history, exemplified by the work of E. L. Jones (1987), and also in a different sense by Jared Diamond (1997), that works from a comparative perspective. Both Jones and Diamond want to explain why Europe suddenly surged out of historical obscurity, achieved a whole range of astounding technological, economic, social, and political transformations, and in a feat unparalleled by any other civilization, imposed its power and its culture on the entire planet. To answer this question, Jones and Diamond both undertake careful comparisons of the circumstances, characteristics, and development of human civilizations. Jones focuses mainly on the four great civilizations of Eurasia, whereas Diamond ranges much more widely over the whole of humankind. In ways with some resonance in geopolitics, both authors put a lot of emphasis on how geographic factors advantaged some civilizations and disadvantaged others. Diamond focuses on how the east–west axis of geography and climate favoured all of the civilizations in Eurasia while the north–south axis disadvantaged those in the Americas and Africa. Jones argues how Europe's decentralized and diverse maritime geography favoured the development of bulk trade, and how its peripheral position insulated it from the attacks by steppe barbarians that so gravely affected the development of civilizations in the other population centres of Eurasia. Both authors agree that amongst the civilizations in Eurasia, Europe was favoured by circumstances in a variety of important ways.

Jones goes on to make more detailed comparisons among Europe, the Middle East, India, and China. He looks at the environment, and finds Europe less exposed to the depredations of weather and disease. He looks at population, and finds that Europe's long-standing habit of restraining reproduction gave it some economic advantages over the others, stimulating a sustained economic growth that long pre-dated, and established some of the foundations for, industrialization. He looks at geography, and notes Europe's enormous good fortune in having easiest access to the lightly defended resources of the Americas. He looks at government, and finds two advantages: first that Europe's decentralized economic geography made it easier for it to avoid becoming a single empire; and second that Europe's insulation from the steppe barbarians saved it from the imposition of extractive, economically crippling barbarian empires of the kind imposed on China (Mongol, Manchu), India (Mughal), and the Middle East (Seljuk, Mongol, Ottoman). He looks at trade, and notes how the development of bulk trade in Europe had widespread ramifications for society and politics, in contrast to the more superficial luxury trade that dominated elsewhere. He looks at markets, and notes how, in contrast to the other civilizations, Europe developed markets in land and labour, as well as in commodities. And he looks at technology, and finds in Europe a more consistent and sustained development and adoption of technology, compared with the flashes of brilliance elsewhere that were disrupted by periods of rejection and suppression.

The comparativists reject the idea that there was something intrinsically superior about European (or sometimes more narrowly British) civilization that enabled it to achieve industrialization and world domination. They assume that development is shaped by material circumstances, and that these have been unevenly distributed amongst the human stock. Jones (1988: 31) argues that 'History is to be thought of as repeated, tentative efforts of *intensive growth* to bubble up through the stately rising dough of *extensive growth*'. He sees Sung China (tenth to thirteenth century AD) and the Abbasid Caliphate in ninth-century Baghdad as examples where intensive growth emerged but was not sustained. In other words, industrialization was an option for other cultures as well, some of which might have obtained it before Europe, but for various reasons did not follow their option through. The miracle that Jones refers to in his title refers to just how many circumstances had to fall into place in order to explain why Europe, and not some other civilization, made the breakthrough to industrialization and world power.

# 3. CONCLUSIONS

Most of the literature examined in this chapter does not make explicit references to the international system. The main exception, to a degree, is the work of the historical sociologists who, according to Mann (1995: 555), went on a 'raiding party' and returned with a certain amount of 'loot' taken from the realists. But this analysis is made with a degree of hindsight, the link with realism being made after the historical sociologists had independently concluded that 'war makes the state and the state makes war' (Tilly 1985). Moreover, by focusing on the militaristic side of international relations, the work of these historical sociologists reflects a familiar, albeit a somewhat impoverished, view of the international system (Hobden 1998). Mann goes on to argue that analysts in IR, for their part, engaged in a similar raid on the work of historical sociologists, returning with some of the essential elements of the world systems literature. But whereas the ideas of Wallerstein have been revamped and used to considerable effect in disciplines like archaeology and anthropology (Chase-Dunn and Hall 1997) which were looking for ways to extend their spatial framework, these ideas have not had the same impact on mainstream IR theory.

When we turn to the work of geopoliticians like Mackinder, civilizational historians, like Hodgson and McNeill, and comparativists like Jones and Diamond, then we observe frameworks very different from anything found in IR. All rely on a framework which extends across Eurasia and embraces all the world historical civilizations as well as the mobile nomads that separated these civilizations. This is a framework that enables them to provide accounts of what happened across Eurasia over several millennia. The established conception of the international system found in international relations cannot begin to compete with this framework. It could be argued that this is because the framework does not constitute what IR theorists, particularly neorealists, would consider to be a system. But as we have argued, the theoretically monist approaches that have dominated IR thinking are incapable of generating an adequate conceptualization of international systems. The impoverished view of system in most IR thinking prevents IR from taking on the many valuable perspectives available in world historical accounts. These ideas must be incorporated in any attempt to develop an evolutionary and comparative conception of international systems that transcends the particular experience of modern Europe and the world it created.

*Chapter 4*

# THE THEORETICAL TOOLKIT OF THIS BOOK

---

This chapter sets out the basic concepts that underpin our approach in the rest of the book: levels of analysis, sectors of analysis, and sources of explanation. Most of these ideas are familiar to anyone engaged in the IR literature. We use these concepts to link together IR theory and world history and by doing so open the way to providing an overarching narrative or story of international systems.

## 1. LEVELS OF ANALYSIS

Whether implicitly or explicitly, the idea of levels of analysis is deeply rooted in the way we think about reality. It is possible to clarify the idea by contrasting two very different approaches to thinking about reality. Allport (1954: 43), working from a methodological individualist perspective, suggests that individuals see themselves as the central point of a series of expanding concentric circles, which starts with the family, moves out to the neighbourhood, then to the city, the state, and finally the human race. Each concentric circle draws in more and more individuals until eventually the entire global population is encompassed. All these circles, however, are operating on the same level of analysis, one that focuses on the individual. But it is also possible to reconceptualize the expanding set of concentric circles as a diminishing spiral made up of a diminishing number of increasingly abstract units that operate on different levels of analysis. At the base of the spiral is the global population of individuals. These individuals are members of a smaller number of families which can be analysed on a higher or more abstract level of analysis. Families can then be aggregated to form an even smaller number of neighbourhoods, which, in turn, form a smaller number of cities and then an even smaller number of states. At the bottom of the spiral, therefore, is the collectivity of individuals and at the top of this spiral is the collectivity of states. But states can, in their turn, also aggregate to form an even smaller number of international units, higher up the spiral. Idealists like to think of the United Nations forming a single unit at the top of this international spiral. Reality can be analysed on many different levels, because each level generates its own distinctive outcomes and sources of explanation. Identifying different levels of analysis represents an important methodological procedure for anyone interested in how reality is structured and organized. It is not unique to the study of international relations, and can be found in most of the natural and social sciences. In physics, for example, one can focus on the level of composite matter that forms us and the universe in which we live, or on the atomic level of atoms and molecules, or on the subatomic level of quarks and other exotic particles

For more than three decades, the debate about levels of analysis has been central to much of IR theory (Buzan 1994; Onuf 1995). There is not a universal acceptance of thinking about reality in this way, but theorists who favour a holistic, top-down, or systems approach to analysis have been particularly attracted by levels and especially by the interplay between systems and the units that compose them. In Allport's typology, the human race constitutes the total system and the individual represents the basic unit. But many other levels can be conceived of in terms of abstracted units and systems. Each level can be represented as a unit within a larger system, or as a system embracing the units at a lower level. So, the city can either be seen as a unit in the system of the state, or as a system made up of neighbourhood units. The choice of starting point reflects the interests of the analyst, and determines whether a given level is defined as a unit or a system. There is nothing intrinsic to levels themselves that suggests any particular pattern or priority of relations amongst them. Levels are simply ontological referents for where explanations and outcomes are located. They are not sources of explanation in themselves.

In the study of international relations, the five most frequently used levels of analysis are:

1. *international systems*, meaning the largest conglomerates of interacting or interdependent units that have no system level above them. Currently this encompasses the whole planet, but in earlier times there were several more or less disconnected international systems existing simultaneously;
2. *international subsystems*, meaning groups of units within an international system that can be distinguished from the whole system by the particular nature or intensity of their interactions/interdependence with each other. Subsystems may be either territorially coherent, in which case they are regional (ASEAN, the OAU), or not (OECD, OPEC), in which case they are not regions but simply subsystems;
3. *units*, meaning entities composed of various sub-groups, organizations, communities, and many individuals, sufficiently cohesive to have actor quality (i.e. be capable of conscious decision-making), and sufficiently independent to be differentiated from others and to have standing at the higher levels (e.g. states, nations, transnational firms);
4. *subunits*, meaning organized groups of individuals within units that are able (or try) to affect the behaviour of the unit (e.g. bureaucracies, lobbies);
5. *individuals*, the bottom line of most analysis in the social sciences.

Of course this set of labels, and the ranking it implies, reflects the analytical priority that we want to give to international systems. Someone pursuing foreign policy analysis might want to make the state, a bureaucracy, or even individual leaders the main system under analysis.

Levels provide a framework that one can use both to describe the phenomena that one observes, and also to theorize about causes and effects. The tension between description and explanation in the use of levels goes right back to the introduction of the idea into IR by Waltz (1959) and Singer (1961), already sketched in Chapter 2. Both concentrated their attention on two levels: the state as their unit of analysis and the international system as the highest level (i.e. not contained, and impinged upon, by some yet larger system). But even though Waltz was primarily interested in the international system from an explanatory perspective, it is important to understand that levels are not a theory in themselves. They enable one to locate the sources of explanation and the outcomes of which theories are composed. Theories may suggest causal explanations from one level to another: e.g. top down from system structure to unit behaviour (market to firms, anarchy to states), or bottom up from human nature to the behaviour of human collectivities, whether they be firms, states, or nations. Neorealism locates its source of explanation (structure) at the system level and its main outcomes (self-help, balance of power) at the unit level. Bureaucratic politics locates its source of explanation (process) at the subunit level, and its outcome (non-rational behaviour) at the unit level (Allison 1971). Waltz (1959) famously suggests that the three different types of explanation used to account for the recurrence of war between states each occupy a different level. Some writers explain war by human nature (individual level), others by the nature of the state (unit level), and others by the anarchic structure of the international system (system level). Analysts who explain war by human nature and by the nature of the state are identified by Waltz (1979) as reductionist in their mode of explanation, whereas those who locate the explanation in the international system are identified as system theorists. Waltz, however, confused himself (and others), by appearing to conflate his preferred level of analysis (system) and his source of explanation (structure) (Buzan et al. 1993: 28; Buzan 1994). If we are successfully to understand what international systems are, and how they work, it is essential to keep these distinctions clear.

Levels also, up to a point, enable one to locate many of the actors, forums and other elements involved in 'international' relations. Some organizations (the UN), structures (the global market), and processes (international law) operate at the system level, others (NATO, the EU, NAFTA, ASEAN) are clearly subsystemic. But it is not always possible to locate actors clearly within a given level. A lobby group such as the national farmers' union may well sit clearly at the subunit level, but transnational organizations such as Greenpeace or Amnesty International cross levels. They may act partly on the subunit level and partly on the subsystem and system ones. The same might be said for transnational firms and mafias.

   Although levels of analysis are widely used in IR they remain controversial on at least two grounds:

1.  their effect on what units become the main focus of analysis, and
2.  questions about the validity of the system level.

The first problem stems from the difficulty just described of fitting some types of unit, especially transnational ones, into the scheme. Because the levels of analysis debate in IR have been closely associated with neorealism it has tended to reflect that theory's state-centrism, picturing subunits as being within states, and subsystems and systems as made up of states. On this basis the levels of analysis scheme has been criticized for reinforcing the state-centrism and inside/outside assumptions typical of IR (Walker 1993; Onuf 1995). Much of IR theory, especially realism, is based on an inside/outside view of political reality, in which 'inside' is the hierarchic domestic realm of states, susceptible to progress, and 'outside' is the anarchic international realm of unchanging power politics. This distinction turns out to be very useful when it comes to tracing the historical evolution of international systems. The criticism of it is that levels are not just an innocent, abstract typology: the scheme presents a specific ontology that privileges the state, and obscures and discriminates against those transnational units that do not fit clearly into the scheme. Part of the dispute between realists and pluralists hinges on this issue, with the realists wanting to elevate the state to the status of prime unit, and the pluralists insisting that many types of actors (especially international governmental organizations (IGOs), transnational firms, and lobby groups) have independent status in the system. We accept the warning about the dangers of state-centrism, but think we can solve much of this difficulty by adding sectors to our toolkit, which opens up more room for diverse types of unit, on which see below.

   The question about the validity of the system level is embedded in the debate between reductionists and system theorists. While system theorists generally accept the validity of reductionist approaches (however critical they might be about their utility), the reverse is not always true. As noted in Chapter 2, some advocates of a reductionist explanation do not accept the validity of an international systems analysis (Weltman 1973). The system level has been seen by some to be a metaphysical, even a mystical, entity which, critics claim, has been an endless source of confusion not only in international relations, but in all areas of the social sciences where it has been suggested that human behaviour can be explained by reference to a system. In our view, this question replicates Waltz's confusion between level and source of explanation. This controversy is not about levels, but about structural explanations, which we discuss below.

   In this book we are committed to a system level of analysis for both descriptive and explanatory purposes. In line with Singer's view, we want to use the system level to provide an overarching picture of international relations, ensuring that we avoid the problem of not being able to see the wood for the trees. In line with Waltz's view, we want to retain the system level as an important location on which sources of explanation can be found. But we have a much more expansive conception of systemic explanation than Waltz, and wish to break free of the political constraints that he endeavoured to impose on what is meant by a systemic mode of explanation. At the same time, we will also make use of what in Waltz's view are 'reductionist' modes of analysis, looking at the nature of the dominant units in the system, and how their internal qualities affect the international system. Our systemic or top-down approach should be seen as a starting rather than a stopping point, and we wish to keep an open mind about what types of unit can compose international systems.

## 2. SECTORS OF ANALYSIS

Although it is acknowledged, in principle, that 'Knowledge is a unity' (Reynolds 1994: 1), it is accepted, in practice, that a division of labour is needed to study the world around us. The division of social and other sciences into disciplines is premissed on the need for such a division of labour. But these divisions also reflect a widely held belief that reality can be meaningfully segmented into different ontological sectors. As Braudel (1985: 17) notes, historians 'simplify matters by dividing history into sectors (and call them political, economic, social and cultural history)'. In IR, sectoral analysis refers to the practice of approaching the international system in terms of the types of activities, units, interactions, and structures within it. The use of terms such as 'the international economic system', or 'the international political system', or 'world society' indicates thinking in terms of sectoral divisions of the subject. Realists from Morgenthau to Waltz talk firmly in terms of *political* theory, assuming that dividing the subject into sectors is a necessary condition for effective theory-building. Michael Mann (1986: ch. 1) thinks about power in terms of sector-like distinctions amongst ideology, economic, military, and political power. Despite this widespread *de facto* acceptance, sectors have received much less discussion in the IR theory literature than have levels of analysis (Buzan et al. 1993: 30–3; Buzan et al. 1998). As a consequence, the practice of thinking in terms of sectors generally takes for granted that economy, society, history, and politics can and should be discussed separately without really thinking too hard about the consequences of doing so.

One way of understanding sectors and distinguishing them from levels of analysis is to see them as views of the whole system through an analytical lens which selects one particular type of relationship and highlights the types of unit, interaction, and structure most closely associated with it. The metaphor of a lens is a useful way of understanding what sectors represent and how they can and cannot be used (Manning 1962: 2). In the physical world, one can look at an object using many different types of 'lens', ranging from the naked eye and telescopes, through infrared sensors and radars, to X-ray machines and electron microscopes. In each case the lens is either sensitive to different types, or wavelengths, of energy (e.g. infrared and X-ray), or else sensitive to the same type of energy in a different way (e.g. microscope and telescope). Even though the observed object remains the same (ignoring Heisenberg), different lenses highlight different aspects of its reality. The naked eye sees mostly exterior shape and colour. The infrared sees the pattern of heat. The X-ray sees the pattern of physical density. The electron microscope sees molecular structure. The function of sectors is the same as that of these physical lenses: each one gives a view of the whole that emphasizes some things, and de-emphasizes, or even hides completely, others.

In analyses of the social world, there are at least five commonly used sectors:

- The *military sector* is about relationships of forceful coercion, and the ability of actors to fight wars with each other. It usually focuses on the two-level interplay of the armed offensive and defensive capabilities of actors in the international system, and their perceptions of each other's intentions.
- The *political sector* is about relationships of authority, governing status and recognition, and concerns the organizational stability of systems of government and the ideologies that give them legitimacy. Do actors accept other units as equals, or are relations hierarchical, with superior and inferior status acknowledged by both sides? Or do actors deny each other recognition, in effect treating each other as unoccupied territory available for seizure? The political sector can be interpreted in a more realist, state-centric, sense as being about government, or in a looser, more liberal, sense as being about governance, including norms, rules, and institutions above the level of the state. Some might wish to differentiate a *legal sector* from the political one.
- The *economic sector* is about relationships of trade, production, and finance, and how actors gain access to the resources, finance, and markets necessary to sustain acceptable levels of welfare and political power. For most of history, economic interactions have been about trade. Only in very recent times have they also come to be about the far-flung organization of production and finance.
- The *societal* or *socio-cultural sector* is about social and cultural relationships. It concerns collective identity, and the sustainability, within acceptable conditions for evolution, of traditional patterns of language, culture, and religious and national identity and custom. Interactions in this sector are about the transmission of ideas between peoples and civilizations. They may involve ideas about technology, or about political and religious organization.
- The *environmental sector* is about the relationship between human activity and the planetary biosphere as the essential support system on which all other

human enterprises depend. The most traditional environmental interaction is disease transmission, but since the European voyages of discovery one must add the intercontinental movement of plants, animals, and peoples, and local and global pollution.

From the analysts' perspective, sectors might be understood as follows. The military strategist looks at human systems in terms that highlight the offensive and defensive capability of actors, and justify restrictive assumptions such as the motivation of behaviour by opportunistic calculations of coercive advantage. The political realist looks at the same systems in terms that highlight sovereignty and power, and justify restrictive assumptions such as the motivation of behaviour by the desire to maximize power. The economist looks at them in terms that highlight wealth and development, and justify restrictive assumptions such as the motivation of behaviour by the desire to maximize utility. The sociologist will also see power and states, but in addition will see patterns of identity such as clan, class, and nation, and the desire to maintain cultural independence. International lawyers see states and to a lesser extent other legal persons such as firms and individuals, but focus on the customs, rules, and contracts that should constrain their behaviour. The environmentalist looks at the system in terms of the ecological underpinnings of civilization, and the need to achieve sustainable development. Each is looking at the whole, but seeing only one dimension of its reality.

The analytical method of sectors thus starts with disaggregation, but from our theoretically pluralist perspective must end with reassembly. The disaggregation is performed only to achieve simplification and clarity. To achieve understanding, it is necessary to reassemble the parts and see how they relate to each other. But just as academic disciplines are often accused of stunting understanding by dividing the world up in such a rigid way that they lose sight of what is going on in the whole, so the use of sectors has to be approached with some flexibility. In principle, one can justify the strict sectoral distinctions just listed. The separation of the military and political sectors might be thought controversial, but good justifications for it can be found in several quarters. Morgenthau took the view that politics was essentially about psychological control, a process that ended when control was attempted by direct coercion (Gellman 1988: 252). Clausewitz, who famously stated that war is a continuation of politics by other means, was not thereby stopped from arguing that military means have their own logic (Clausewitz 1976). Mann argues that political power does not necessitate a monopoly of force (Mann 1986: 10–11). But what holds in principle may not work so well in practice. Most IR theories involve some blending of sectors, in effect looking through two or more lenses simultaneously. To the extent that sectors are an analytical device, analysts can choose to combine sectors in order to select a particular type of view. Realism combines the military and political sectors, the English school combines the political and societal sectors, and international political economy (IPE), as its name implies, combines the political and economic sectors. Liberal economics famously tries to confine itself to a single sector, while sociology increasingly combines the societal and political sectors.

The use of sectors/lenses, whether singly or in combination, has the advantage of highlighting, and therefore making easier to see, certain qualities of whatever is being observed. It is a way of unpacking the complexity of the whole, and is therefore a very appealing device when one is faced with such a vast and many-faceted whole as an international system. Sectors serve to disaggregate a whole for purposes of analysis by selecting distinctive patterns of interaction. But the things identified by sectors generally do not have the quality of independent existence. Relations of coercion seldom exist apart from relations of exchange, authority, identity, or environment. Sectors identify distinctive patterns, but except in very particular circumstances they usually remain inseparable parts of complex wholes. The purpose of selecting them is simply to reduce complexity in order to facilitate analysis. The use of sectors confines the scope of enquiry to more manageable proportions by reducing the number of variables in play.

As with levels, there is scope for choice about which sectors to use. In principle, sectoral divisions are as clear as the divisions between different academic disciplines. But in practice how can one actually differentiate between the international political and economic systems? In thinking about any given historical event, it is difficult enough to disentangle the economic, political, societal, and military threads that make up the whole. Is the state an economic actor or a political one? Should one count the arms industry and its trade more as an economic phenomenon (production, trade, finance) or as a political (state power) or a military (arms racing) one? Because each sector is a partial view of the whole, what is seen through a sectoral lens necessarily overlaps and interweaves with the content of other sectors. Sectors are generally not separated by clear boundaries like those between levels of analysis. Indeed, when thinking in terms of sectors, the whole spatial metaphor of separation, boundaries, and the like is inappropriate. This is because, as with lenses, the distinction between sectoral boundaries is to be found as much, or more, in the equipment of the observer as in the nature of the thing observed. Sectors bring a selected type of activity into clearer view, but they do not establish grounds for thinking that in reality these activities are autonomous, and organized independently from what goes on in other sectors.

There are two dangers in the use of sectors. First is that the observer will begin to confuse the partial reality of the sector, with the total reality of the whole. Sectoral blindness is an occupational hazard of an academia divided into deeply institutionalized disciplines. The need to counteract this danger is one of the strongest reasons for establishing IR as a theoretically pluralist field of study in its own right, and for not seeing it merely as part of several other disciplines. If the study of the international economy is to be considered only a matter for economists, and the study of the balance of power only a matter for political scientists, then the possibilities for assembling a comprehensive view of international systems diminish sharply, and the danger that these sectors will be treated as real distinct entities rises in proportion. Academics are, in general, not good at communicating across disciplines, and consequently the division of the subject in this way effectively prevents any comprehensive understanding of international systems.

The second danger is that the lens metaphor makes it easy to lose sight of the difference between the natural world and the social world. The metaphor encourages us to think that the social world, like the natural world, is directly available for inspection by the analyst. But this is not the case. Unlike the natural world, the social world has already been interpreted by the actors under investigation, and can at any time be reinterpreted by them. These interpretations matter to what happens in social systems, and they provide a link between the subject of enquiry and the analyst that is not present in the natural world. Economic actors, for example, may not think, and may not be encouraged to think, that they are playing a vital role in propping up, or undermining, the established political order. Nevertheless, the activities of social actors operating in one sector may in practice be playing important roles in another sector. Whether these connections are perceived or not makes a difference to how the whole system operates, and analysts need to be aware of this factor. Awareness of just how much the self-understanding of people matters to social systems is what underlies Marxist projects to increase the self-awareness of the proletariat, and nationalist ones to increase the self-awareness of cultural-linguistic groups.

Patterns of understanding about sectors are part of the construction of the system itself, and this makes it difficult, or perhaps impossible, to separate scientific analysis from political action. Liberal ideology, for example, cultivates the idea that economic theory and practice can and should be delinked from politics. Analysts wanting to understand the nature of social reality must be careful not to accept uncritically the prevailing conceptions of sectoralization. Otherwise, as Morgenthau has noted, they become implicated in the system and play a role in the reproduction of the system they are analysing (Morgenthau 1971). Both accepting and questioning the conventional wisdom about the nature and relationship of sectors are political as well as scientific acts. Questioning may, by raising political consciousness, get social actors to recognize the consequences of their actions in other sectors, and in doing so change the construction and operation of the system.

The use of sectors goes a long way towards solving the disputes about units of analysis noted in the discussion about levels. Different types of interaction, and thus different units, become more—or less—prominent depending on which sectoral lens one is using to view the international system. Through the political and military lenses states will shine strong and dominant. Through the economic and societal lenses they will be less prominent, and other units such as firms and nations will come more clearly into focus. Much of the argument about units thus reflects confusion about sectors. Realists mostly want to confine themselves to the political sector, and in that view states *are* dominant, at least in the modern international system. Analysts in more pluralist traditions (such as IPE) or more sociological ones (such as world system theory) operate in several sectors at once, and thus see a more complex mix of units. Using a single sector preserves clarity at the expense of oversimplification. Using too many sectors risks complicating the picture to the point where theorizing becomes impossible. Given the large scale on which we are operating in this book, we will for most purposes merge the military and political sectors and treat them as a single lens.

## 3. SOURCES OF EXPLANATION

Sources of explanation refer to variables that explain behaviour. In the study of international relations, three sources of explanation encompass most of the debate: *interaction capacity*, *process*, and *structure*. They are the key to theory on any given level of analysis and in any sector. In principle, therefore, sources of explanation can be located anywhere on the matrix of levels and sectors illustrated in Fig. 4.1.

Adding sectors to levels enables one to specify the nature of theories more precisely than can be done with levels alone. Neorealism, for example, locates a structural explanation (anarchy/hierarchy, polarity) on the system level in the military and political sectors. World system theory locates a structural explanation (capitalism) on the system level in the economic and political sectors. Most of foreign policy analysis, for example bureaucratic politics, locates a process

| Levels/Sectors | military | political | economic | societal | environmental |
|---|---|---|---|---|---|
| system | | | | | |
| subsystem | | | | | |
| unit | | | | | |
| subunit | | | | | |
| individual | | | | | |

*Figure 4.1 Levels and sectors in the international system*

explanation at the unit level in the political sector. Integration theories are mostly found at the subsystem level in the economic and political sectors, and often focus on process explanations. Globalization theories also mostly operate at the system level, using process and interaction capacity explanations across most sectors. As noted above, the many theories of war can be found at several different levels (system, unit, individual), and scattered across most of the sectors. In practice, some of the boxes in Fig. 4.1 are much more heavily used than others. IR theory is still strongly skewed to the system and unit levels, and to the military and political sectors, though the economic one is catching up. In principle, however, all of the boxes are available. For those who are conditioned to thinking that structure is only a system-level property, it helps to remember that the analyst can choose how to specify levels. She or he may set the system level on a planetary scale, or may choose to identify a given state as the relevant system for purposes of analysis. Keeping this in mind makes it easier to see how structure, process, and interaction capacity can be applied at all levels.

Of course the specific meanings and qualities of these sources of explanation change as one shifts to different boxes. Within boxes they may change again as one looks at different periods of history. Because of the influence of Waltz, most people in IR have a pretty good sense of what *structure* means when located in the system level, confined to the military and political sectors, and placed in the context of the modern international system. But shift from the military-political to the economic sector, and one's definition of structure has to change. The general ideas of anarchy-hierarchy and polarity carry across quite well between the economic and political sectors (as they should do given the microeconomic source of Waltz's theory), but the nature of the structure shifts from politics to economics. If one shifts to the individual level, structure and process move into the psychological domain, and take on quite different qualities from those found at higher levels.

It is not our task here to set out the entire panoply of IR theory. Since this book is about international systems, we are going to focus mainly on structure, process, and interaction capacity at the system and unit, and up to a point, subsystem, levels. In order to unfold how such systems develop we need to range quite widely across the sectors. Part of our purpose is to show how systems defined in military-political terms are normally embedded in economic and societal systems that are often wider in extent and earlier in formation. Understanding international systems requires that one be able to see and appreciate their sectoral layers. Process, interaction capacity, and structure are all essential ways of understanding how systems develop, operate, and change, and these three concepts, along with units, play a major role in how we organize many of the chapters that follow.

## PROCESS

Process is probably the most easily understood and least controversial of the three sources of explanation, and it will feature prominently in the chapters to come. Systems are identified by the patterns of interaction that take place amongst their constituent units. Every pattern provides evidence of a process that is a product of the dynamics of the interactions among the units in the system and the use made of the existing interaction capacity by these units. Processes, therefore, tell us about the patterns of action and reaction that can be observed among the units that make up a system. Examples of the processes that can be observed in the international system extend across fighting, political recognition, trade, and identity formation to the transplantation of flora and fauna from one continent to another (Keohane and Nye 1987: 745). Process is distinct from structure, which is about how units are arranged in a system, and which is therefore more static and positional. Process as a source of explanation applies to all levels of analysis. By definition, processes are distinct from sector to sector, and definitions for the relevant differentiations were given on pp. 73-4. There is process within the international system (interactions amongst units), and also within the units that make up that system (every unit can be seen as a system in its own right). Process dynamics can be found within all types of collective organizations, and within individual human beings.

Perhaps the most interesting aspect of process for IR is the durable or recurrent patterns that occur in relations among units, which we label *process formations* (Buzan et al. 1993, 48-50). These are durable or recurrent patterns in interactions among units. Process formations include war, arms racing, balance of power, the security dilemma, security complexes, alliance, diplomacy, regimes, international organizations, trade competition, recession, liberal and mercantilist orders, and other patterns in international economic relations. Process formations often embody action–reaction theories of unit behaviour, and so are conditioned by structure, both at the system level (whether anarchic or hierarchic), and at the unit level (for example whether units are ideologically compatible or incompatible). Since international structure is often anarchic, many process formations such as the security dilemma, trade wars, and arms racing reflect system structure forces acting on units where there is no central government or authority, and where units are driven by imperatives of self-help and insecurity. Other process formations reflect the attempts of units to overcome the negative effects of anarchy by institutionalizing arrangements that enable them to seek joint gains, whether of political stability and peace, or of trade, resource management, and welfare.

## INTERACTION CAPACITY

Interaction capacity is probably the least well known of the sources of explanation. It refers to the amount of transportation, communication, and organizational capability within the unit or system: how much in the way of goods and information can be moved over what distances at what speeds and at what costs? It is about the technological capabilities (e.g. caravans, ships, railways, aircraft), and the shared norms, rules, and institutions, on which the type and intensity of interaction between units in a system, or within units, depends. Interaction capacity is about capabilities that are spread throughout any given system or unit (for simplicity's sake we will just talk about systems). It refers to the carrying capacity of a social system, its physical potential for enabling the units within it to exchange information, goods, or blows. If process defines what units *actually* do when they interact, interaction capacity defines what they *can* do.

Interaction capacity shapes not only how big a system can be, but also what its units will look like, and in what sector(s) the dominant forms of interaction will take place. Interaction in the societal sector requires only transfers of information, and can thus take place even when the level of interaction capacity is low. Economic interaction almost always involves the transport of goods, and therefore requires higher levels, though long-distance trade in high-value, low-volume goods can occur with quite modest capabilities. Military-political interaction typically involves the movement of armies from one unit to another and therefore requires quite high levels. Interaction capacity is thus a precondition for process and structure, defining the potential of a system to support them.

Interaction capacity is implicit in definitions of systems, all of which stress that units must be interacting in order for a system to exist (Bull 1977: 10; Reynolds 1994: 195; Waltz 1979: 95). Interaction is fundamental to any conceptualization of a system. But other than pointing out that this interaction must be sustained and in some way influential, the literature is generally silent about the nature of interaction. It can be inferred from some realist writings that the ability to wage war is the key to the interaction that defines international systems (Bull 1977: 10; Waltz 1979). From this perspective, a set of states that cannot pose each other a military threat fail to constitute an international system. It is the ability of states to create and communicate mutually credible military threats which generates a systemic relationship. This view both stems from, and feeds, the strong Eurocentric tendency in IR theory.

Preoccupation with military-political interaction has encouraged IR theorists to disregard non-military interactions because they are not seen as defining features of the international system. IR theorists invariably assume that units must be able to interact. But they have failed to show how, as capacities for transportation and communication contract and expand the capacity for interaction, so the nature of the international system itself must undergo fundamental change. When one looks more closely, it quickly becomes apparent that the capacity for interaction can change within a system over time, may vary from system to system, and will almost certainly vary within a system at any given point in time. As new technologies of transportation and communication spread, they change the quality and quantity of the interactions among and within units in the system as a whole. The failure to open up the concept of interaction capacity has meant that understanding of international systems is seriously stunted. As we have argued elsewhere (Buzan et al. 1993: ch. 4), even the operation of structural logic depends on the level of interaction capacity. If interaction capacity is low, then structure will have little or no effect. Higher levels of interaction capacity allow structural forces powerfully into play. By highlighting interaction capacity, and locating the concept at the centre of our analysis, we hope to create new space for theorizing about international systems. Interaction capacity captures both the physical and the social aspects of capabilities that are system- or unit-wide. These capabilities both play a role in defining the dominant units, and act as a distinct source of shoving and shaping forces playing alongside those generated by structure.

Physical interaction capacity is not differentiated by sector. The potential for transportation and communication is a fundamental property of social systems that cuts across all sectors. The availability (or not) of long-range, high-speed electronic communications capability, for example, has just as big an impact on military and political relations as it does on economic and societal ones. The form of physical interaction capacity is thus the same regardless of whether one is looking through political, economic, societal, or military lenses, and the main question to ask of any international system is whether its interaction capacity is high or low. Its consequences, of course, do vary from sector to sector. Low physical interaction capacity will prevent war between states located far away from each other, but it may not prevent either the transfer of low-volume, high-value goods over long distances, or the movement of ideas about everything from agricultural practices and technologies to astronomy and religion.

Three factors mediate interaction capacity:

- whether geographical factors make movement easy or difficult;
- what physical technologies are available for transportation and communication; and
- what social technologies are available for transportation and communication.

In a low-technology environment, interaction capacity is strongly shaped by geography. High mountains, vast swamps, and open oceans can simply block contact between human communities on either side of them. Open steppelands make movement easy once horses or camels are available, as do navigable rivers once even quite primitive boats become available. With the development of larger and sturdier ships, and knowledge about navigation, seas can become highways rather than barriers. Social organization also matters. The existence of domesticated horses may, in principle, allow a given speed and range of contact. But this can be greatly increased if society organizes a pony express system, in which there are regular stations placed along the route at which fresh horses and riders are based. Using such systems, the Persians and the Mongols were able to move information thousands of kilometres across their vast empires at speeds of nearly 300 km (186 miles) per day (Singer et al. 1954: 495–8). Diamond (1997) argues that the relative ease of east–west geographical communication in Eurasia gave its human occupants a great advantage in the development of civilization as compared with the more difficult north–south axis of communication in the Americas and Africa. People moving along an east–west axis can stay within the climate zone to which their lifestyle is adapted, but those moving along a north–south axis have to cross climate zones that may well be inhospitable to both their agriculture and their immune systems.

As physical technologies improve, geography becomes decreasingly important, and the large-scale movement of goods, information, people, and armies between any two points in the system becomes first possible, and then commonplace. Communication and transportation technologies are in an important sense system-wide in their deployment, as well as in their effects. Things like shipping capacity, telecommunications, and global forum organizations are more system- than state-based. Once developed to the point of cost-effectiveness, physical technologies tend to spread quickly throughout the system, just as steamships and telegraphs did in the nineteenth century, and civil aviation and computer networks have done since the Second World War. Although command of these technologies is unquestionably an element of unit power, their availability quickly transforms conditions of interaction for all units, and therefore transforms the system itself. As technologies in these areas spread, they change the quality and character of the system as a whole. This is both a characteristic, and an effect that is qualitatively different from the way in which the particular attributes of particular states affect their interactions with other individual states.

Interaction capacity is as central to the growth of units as it is to systems. Although humans are spatially organized into territorial units, the distance at which individuals can interact has a major impact both on the structure of these units and also on the structure and interactions among these units in the international system. Developments in interaction capacity were crucial to the early evolution of states and empires in Egypt and Mesopotamia. They also condition profoundly interaction within and between regional international systems, and underlie the long prologue to the quite recent development of a truly global international system.

Social technologies of transportation and communication include language (esp. the development of lingua francas and writing), shared ideas (religion, diplomacy, economics), money and bills of exchange, and more concrete systems of rules and institutions. One way to see them is as elements of process that become sedimented and embedded within the system to the point where, like physical technologies, they become part of the foundational conditions that determine how the system operates. Social technologies may develop unintentionally, as when modes of writing or lingua francas come into use through myriad incremental decisions. They may also, and more frequently, be intentionally constructed. Empires often cultivated social technologies as a matter of policy: lingua francas, legal systems, uniform systems of weights and measures, suppression of piracy, provision of roads, ports, and postal systems. As we shall see, international anarchies throughout history often developed norms and rules for diplomatic interaction, and in the modern world anarchy these have been supplemented by permanent institutions. The sharing of norms and values is a precondition for establishing organizations, but once established such organizations greatly facilitate, and even promote, interactions that shared norms and values make possible and desired. A system in which permanent diplomatic institutions exist, such as the United Nations, or the European Union, has a higher interaction capacity than one in which no such institutions have been created. Such institutions mean that diplomatic contact is easier, faster, and more frequent. If a crisis arises, familiar channels of communication will already exist, rather than having to be created from scratch. When the United States and the Soviet Union discovered during the Cuba missiles crisis that they could not easily communicate with each other in an emergency, they took steps to improve their interaction capacity by establishing the 'hot line'. The existence of such social technologies of communication raises the political interaction capacity of the international system by providing not only pre-set pathways for diplomacy, but also agreed rules and practices, and obligations to participate. In an international system that possesses such institutions, more political interaction is possible than in one that does not.

During the last two centuries, interaction capacity has grown enormously. Huge volumes of information can now be transferred almost instantaneously from one part of the planet to any other, and huge volumes of goods likewise flow across the planet. Myriad organizational networks exist to facilitate and sustain these movements. For individual states this development poses both threats and opportunities. Invasions or attacks can come swiftly from thousands of miles away. Economic and financial developments on other continents can have major local effects. Societies, cultures, and environments are all under intense pressure from global flows of language, style, information, goods, pollutants, diseases, money, propaganda, entertainment, and people. These threats are accompanied by opportunities. Military and economic assistance can arrive quickly if needed. Global sources of finance, information, and markets are available to assist economic development. It is becoming impossible for states to isolate themselves from these flows. Even major attempts by semi-continental states such as China and the former Soviet Union, and to a lesser extent India, have failed spectacularly. Isolation means relative poverty, backwardness, and eventually, weakness.

But engagement means loss of control over much of social, economic, and political life, and the massive penetration of state and society by outside forces that frequently have disruptive effects.

## STRUCTURE

There is a substantial debate about what is meant by structure in social science. In IR it embodies holistic explanations derived from the understanding that systems are more than the sum of their parts. Structure suggests that the behaviour of units is shoved and shaped not only by their internal processes and their interactions with other units, but also by the way in which their environment is constructed. Structure focuses on the principles by which units are arranged into a system, how units are differentiated from each other, and how they stand in relation to each other in terms of relative capabilities (Waltz 1979: ch. 5). Although the structures of military-political systems, economic systems, and socio-cultural systems are different (e.g. anarchy, market, international, and world society), they all share these general characteristics.

As suggested above, sectors are important to how structure is understood. Most IR theory, especially neorealism, has been concerned with political structure. Some other traditions (*dependencia*, world system theory) have contemplated economic structure, usually in terms of capitalism, but little attempt has been made to integrate these lines of thinking. Even in IPE, no real effort has been made to explore the apparent contradiction between hegemonic stability theory, with its explicit focus on a unipolar distribution of power, and balance of power theory, which suggests that such unipolarity should not be able to occur. The probable explanation for this anomaly is an inability or unwillingness to confront questions of structure that cut across sectors. The realist tradition firmly confines itself to the political sector, and IPE has so far not developed an explicit theoretical framework. Within IR, almost no explicit attempt has been made to think about structure in the societal or environmental sectors.

Our position in this book is that one cannot reach a full, or even an adequate, understanding of international systems, and especially not of their history, without considering structure in the economic and societal sectors as well as the military-political one. We admit defeat in trying to conceptualize environmental structure in IR terms. No doubt there is a physical structure to the planetary environment, and it could be argued that by the late twentieth century human activity was having an impact on this structure. But this falls outside the social realm that is our subject here, and we will not attempt to deal with it other than in terms of its consequences for international systems.

We use Waltz as our starting point, and try to build out from his basic ideas. At the centre of Waltz's analysis is the proposition that the most important source of explanation in the field of IR is the political structure of the international system, because it is this structure that explains how the system has survived over time. He has a great deal to say about the structure of international military-political systems, but is unconcerned about the structure of international economic and socio-cultural systems. Thus while we can start with Waltz, we certainly do not want to stop with him. Waltz's (1979: chs. 5-6) understanding of political structure suggests that international systems *always* have structure. For Waltz, 'a system is composed of a structure and of interacting parts', where 'structure is defined by the arrangement of its parts' (1979: 79–80). He divides political structure into three tiers: the organizing principle (anarchy or hierarchy, respectively the absence or presence of central government), the functional differentiation of units (are units like or unlike in terms of what they are structured to do?), and the distribution of capabilities (how many great powers are there in the system?). Waltz's case is that structure shapes and shoves the behaviour of units, but he does not argue that it is always or even usually the determining cause of behaviour. In many places he notes that there are other causes in play, and that these can override the effects of structure (1979: 48–9, 78, 87, 123; 1986: 328, 343). He also implies, though he does not develop the point, that structure may exist without having effects: 'A systems approach is required only if the structure of the system and its interacting units mutually affect each other. A systems approach [*sic*] is successful only if structural effects are clearly defined and displayed' (Waltz 1979: 58).

Waltz's formulation suggests that the effects of structure range along a spectrum from 0 to 100 per cent. It requires one to ask what it is that determines how much effect structure has. There are three possible answers to this question.

- First is that there is something within the manifestation of structure itself that determines whether its effect is strong or weak. Since structure either exists or does not, it is not easy to imagine what this 'something' might be.
- The second possibility is that some other variable impinges on structure in such a way as to vary its potency. Here the prime candidate is process, which in turn rests on interaction capacity (Buzan et al. 1993: ch. 4), and the argument is that structural effects vary directly according to the frequency and intensity of interaction. When interaction is high (e.g. frequent wars or regular trade amongst the units) structural effects should be strong; when it is low (e.g. infrequent and low-level conflict, sporadic and small-scale trade) structural effects should be weak.
- The third possibility is that structural effects exist, but are defeated by stronger rival effects from sources of explanation on other levels of analysis and/or in other sectors. For example, powerful unit-level developments such as a revolution within one or more states, or the spread of ideological homogeneity as in theories about 'democratic peace', might override structural effects from the system level. Or the effects of economic interaction might, as liberal free trade

supporters argue, cross sectoral boundaries and override the effects of political structure.

Waltz sees only political structure, and that is a key weakness of his theory for our purposes. Confinement to the political sector cripplingly restricts what can be thought of as an international system. It excludes systems that are defined by economic and/or socio-cultural interactions. This cuts off the economic and societal aspects of international systems from the political one, and this amputation has two dire effects. First, it forecloses much of the story of how international systems develop, with the consequence that IR theory gets boxed into Eurocentrism and ahistoricism. Second, it blocks enquiry into the cross-sectoral linkages that often seem to determine how strongly, and in what ways, the effects of political structure actually manifest themselves.

In the chapters that follow we use *political structure* more or less in Waltz's sense, though with the modifications discussed here. In doing so we consciously accept the blending of military and political sectors implicit in the idea of power politics. *Economic structure*, we understand in conventional deep structure terms as being about the difference between market and command economies, and in polarity terms as being about the spectrum from perfect competition (i.e. many small players) through oligopoly to monopoly. Here we stick with the liberals, taking a single sector view. There is no conventional understanding in IR of what should count as *societal structure*, so to fill this gap we need to innovate. In order to stay as much on familiar and relatively orthodox ground as possible, we use the English school ideas of international society and world society (discussed in Chapter 2, and elaborated below in Chapter 5) to stand for structure in the societal sector. Although we will refer to this as societal structure, we are fully aware that it is more complicated than that. International society is a blend of the political and societal sectors as defined above (p. 73), while world society is more strictly about socio-cultural matters. As well as having the advantage of being familiar, these English school concepts allow us to introduce the constructivist element of international structure that is so conspicuously missing from neorealist debates on system structure. The English school and constructivists share important areas of common ground (Rengger 1999).

On this basis we can now disagree quite strongly with Waltz's point that 'A systems approach is required only if the structure of the system and its interacting units mutually affect each other. A systems approach [*sic*] is successful only if structural effects are clearly defined and displayed' (Waltz 1979: 58). A lack of structural effects might well still require an analysis of structure at the system level, but it will probably take the form of an enquiry into how effects from other levels or other sectors have cancelled out, distorted, or overridden the expected effects from the system's political structure.

As well as departing from Waltz's limitation of structure to the political, we must also depart from his closure of the second tier of structure, the functional differentiation of units (are units like or unlike in terms of what they are structured to do?). This is a complicated issue which we have explored at length elsewhere (Buzan et al. 1993; Buzan and Little 1996). In our view, differentiation of units is one of the keys both to marrying IR theory and world history, and to understanding structural change in international systems. For this purpose, we take two steps away from Waltz's position. First, we reject his idea that units in anarchic international systems cannot be functionally differentiated. We think that units can sometimes be functionally differentiated even within the political sector (i.e. state systems vs. feudal systems—Ruggie 1983), and that they are by definition differentiated across sectors (i.e. states vs. firms). Second, we add the notion of *structural* differentiation to *functional* as a necessary tool for thinking about how the nature of units relates to system structure.

At this point we need to make definitions clear.

### Structural differentiation
The issue of whether units have similar or different institutional arrangements.

### Functional differentiation
If units are functionally differentiated, they each take on different, specialized, elements of the function of government. If they are not differentiated each unit performs the same tasks as all the others.

Unfortunately, the terms functional and structural differentiation overlap unhelpfully with those used by some anthropologists, sociologists, and political scientists in structural-functional theory. In their usage structure and function are linked, the argument being that for every socio-political function there is a matching structure. This linkage provided a way of comparing apparently unlike societies and polities. In the debates about neorealism these terms are used in a much more specific way, and with no necessary implication that they are linked.

In neorealism, function is about the tasks of government that political units perform. In other words it is about sovereignty (understood as the claim to self-government), and how it is distributed amongst the units in an international system. Sovereign states claim all the tasks of government. In Waltz's view, sovereign units in anarchic systems are thus functionally undifferentiated because they all claim all the powers of self-government (1979: 95–7). In this scheme, units are functionally differentiated when some of them claim less than all of these tasks (i.e. protectorates, vassals, or dominions). Waltz sees a determining link between anarchy and functionally 'like' units, whereas we see only a strong, and not a determining, pressure (Buzan et al. 1993: 37–47). In hierarchies, units by definition claim only some powers of government. We seek to stay within the neorealist understanding of functional differentiation. We reject the common misusage that equates it with the roles that states play in the international system: great power, middle power, neutral, and suchlike. A recent example of this error is Schroeder (1994), who uses the putative role played by a 'balancer' state to attack Waltz's claim that the international system is functionally undifferentiated. It is quite clear that Waltz does not associate functional differentiation with the performance of such roles in the international system. For Waltz, functional differentiation is related to the erosion of sovereignty as a defining feature of the units of an international system. It only emerges when sovereignty is not coterminous with the boundaries of the major political units which constitute the system. As Wæver (1994: 45) usefully reminds us, Ruggie's formulation of structural differentiation is clearer on this point than Waltz's. Ruggie (1983: 142) defines it as: 'the principles on the basis of which the constituent units are separated from one another. If anarchy tells us that the political system is a segmental realm, differentiation tells us on what basis the segmentation is determined.'

In neorealism, structural differentiation is about the way in which units are internally constructed. Where functional differentiation concerns claims to powers of government, structural differentiation is about how units are politically organized. Nomadic tribes, classical empires, and modern national states, for example, have all been autonomous, functionally undifferentiated, mainstream actors in international systems (at times all together), yet have radically different internal political structures. Structural differentiation is extremely important to the way in which historians define the major eras of human history. The most obvious example of this is the widespread consensus on the importance of 1500 as a defining date in the emergence of the modern era. What defines it is the rise of the modern state as a type of unit that was structurally differentiated from those that prevailed before. The state was not new in functional terms, for many other types of unit elsewhere in the world had claimed the right of self-government. It was, however, a functional change in a European context, where the preceding medieval order was characterized by extensive functional differentiation amongst units (Ruggie 1983; Buzan and Little 1996). What was new about it was that it had a different internal organization from earlier types of political unit. A structural change in the units caused a (second-tier) structural change in the international system.

# 4. CONCLUSIONS

In the chapters that follow we will use these three sets of ideas about levels, sectors, and sources of explanation to organize a chronological account of how international systems began and evolved. Since our focus is on international systems, and not international relations as a whole, we will not attempt to employ systematically the whole seventy five-box matrix that combining these three sets of variables generates. Before we can fine tune the analysis, we need to return to the idea of international system, and establish some firm foundations for the concept.

# Chapter 5

# ESTABLISHING CRITERIA FOR INTERNATIONAL SYSTEMS

This last introductory chapter focuses on the criteria for identifying international systems. We look first at the basic questions necessary to define an international system: how much interaction and of what type? What scale? What pattern? Section 2 goes on to look at second order questions: what are the constituent units? Are international systems mechanical or socially constructed phenomena? How do agents and structure relate? The third section sketches out how we will apply our toolkit to the empirical chapters that follow.

## 1. FIRST ORDER PROBLEMS OF DEFINITION

Given the amount of interest in international systems showed by IR theorists (though not outside the discipline), it is surprising that IR has generated no universally accepted, orthodox definition of what constitutes an international system. More surprisingly, there has been no great debate about the necessary and sufficient conditions for an international system to exist. To the extent that they think about the question at all, most people within IR accept some form of very basic general systems definition such as 'a set of interacting parts (or units)'. A little more thought generates a definition close to those cited in Chapter 1 for states-systems, for example Tilly (1990: 162): 'States form a system to the extent that they interact with each other regularly, and to the degree that their interaction affects the behaviour of each state.' Here the raw notion of interaction is supplemented by the idea that it must have some impact on the behaviour of the units. This supplement is formalized by neorealists, following Waltz, in the idea that political systems must have a structure, by which they mean that there must be organizing principles in the way the units in the system are arranged, and that it is these principles that affect the behaviour of the units (see Chs. 2 and 4). This formulation opens up the possibility of specifying cause–effect relations.

One can get away with such vague definitions only if the existence of an international system is taken for granted. Since most of IR concentrates on modern history, the existence of an international system can be taken for granted. But if one wants to investigate a wider historical range, then the existence of international systems cannot be assumed, and it becomes necessary to ask the more precise questions that enable one to identify where and when such systems exist and where and when they do not. Some might object that to push a modern idea such as 'international system' back into the past is to commit anachronism. We think not. If international systems are considered an important phenomenon, then there is an obligation to be able to tell the story of how they began and how they evolved. The fact that consciousness of international systems emerged only in the last few centuries does not mean that the phenomenon itself is not much older. And if one specifies the criteria for an international system more precisely than is currently done, then the danger of anachronism largely disappears. There are several first order issues that one needs to consider in thinking about whether international systems do or do not exist: how much interaction? What type of interaction? On what scale? In what pattern?

## INTERACTION

Interaction is fundamental to any conception of system. Without interaction, the parts or units are disconnected and free-standing. In our toolkit we differentiated between *interaction capacity* (what kinds of interaction *can* happen in the system), and *process* (what kinds of interaction *do* happen). But this still leaves the questions of 'how much' and 'what type' of interaction are necessary to constitute an international system, and these are difficult to separate. One can say with considerable confidence that a global international system now exists because both military-political and economic relations are conspicuously global in reach and organization. The balance of power, the process of diplomacy, the organization of trade, production, and finance, and networks of transportation and communication, all operate on a global scale. But it is not so clear by what date one could say that the process of globalization that led us to this point became sufficiently intense to supersede the sub-global international systems that dominated the planet's history for several thousand years.

   The historical record suggests that four types of interaction are significant for any broadly conceived understanding of international systems: military, political, economic, and societal (see definitions in Ch. 4). One could add environmental interaction as a fifth, but perhaps only at the cost of reading too much of the present into the past. Environmental interaction does not seem historically necessary to international systems in the way that is true of the other four. In order to determine whether an international system exists, one has to decide whether all four of these types count as interaction for this purpose, or whether only some of them do. What happens when some are present but not others? In addition, one has to fix criteria for both the necessary frequency and intensity of whatever interactions are seen as significant. One-off interactions, even if important, probably do not suffice to create a system. Thus, the battle of Talas (near Tashkent) in AD 751 between T'ang China and the Arab armies of newly mobilized Islam had major consequences for the cultural and political disposition of Central Asia in succeeding centuries. But it was virtually the only military contact between the East Asian and Middle Eastern international systems, and thus did not bind them together into a sustained strategic system. Similarly, one has to ask whether sustained economic interaction, unaccompanied by military-political relations, by itself constitutes an international system. Han China and Imperial Rome conducted a regular and quite substantial trade in luxury goods for several hundred years from the first century BC. The two empires knew of each other, but had no military or political contact, and very little cultural contact. Did this trade link suffice to make them part of the same international system? The crude definitions of international system currently deployed do not enable one to answer such questions.

Since the idea of system is an analytical concept, analysts have the right to set the criteria for it with greater or lesser degrees of stringency. They can, as most realists implicitly do, assume that international systems are only about high and regular levels of military-political interaction. This was a satisfactory position for many in IR until quite recently. But the rise of IPE has raised the profile of economic interactions, and the rise of constructivism, and concerns about nationalism, have raised the profile of intersubjective understandings and shared identities in debates about international relations. Narrow military-political conceptions of international relations no longer seem adequate for understanding the contemporary international system, just as they are not adequate for understanding world history.

Choices about what constitutes an international system have consequences for the way in which we understand and interpret the historical record. If the criteria for defining international systems are set in demanding and restrictive ways, then we will see fewer such systems, and they will come into being later. If the criteria are less restrictive, we will see more international systems and find them earlier. An example of a very open definition is provided by Frank (1990: 179 ff.), whose discussion of 'world systems' runs parallel in many respects to that of international systems. He argues that the essential signifier for the existence of a world system is whether it affects local history. In other words, a system exists if local events have unfolded differently from what would have been the case if the locality concerned had been proceeding in isolation. This is about as undemanding a definition as one could construct for an international system. It would include all four types of interaction, would give space to important one-off interactions like the battle of Talas, and would not require high or sustained levels of interaction. Unfortunately, Frank's definition is circular. It defines causes in terms of their effects, and is consequently useless for theorizing, though useful in opening up a sense of what the problem is.

In thinking about how to define international systems, it is worth restating the significance of interaction capacity (as defined in Ch. 4) for the four different types of interaction. As a rule, military interaction requires high levels of inter-action capacity. Fighting wars means moving large numbers of people, and their supplies and equipment, from wherever they are based to wherever they need to fight. In premodern times, the limitations of military logistics acted as a restraint on the ability of states to interact with each other. When armies had to march, and could only be moved short distances by sea, the difficulties of large-scale military movement limited both the size of ancient and classical empires, and their ability to interact with each other. Only when sturdy ocean-going sailing ships were deployed did military interaction on a global scale become possible, and it was only during the nineteenth century and into the twentieth century that indus-trialization (steamships, railways, automobiles, aircraft) began to make possible a global military logistics capable of rapid and massive movement to any part of the planet. One important exception to the limits of pre-industrial military logistics was the barbarians. Being nomadic, they could and did move as whole peoples, and their lifestyle equipped them for easy transportation of their herds and households. The general rule is that military interaction requires high interaction capacity. This can be achieved over local- and regional-scale distances with quite primitive technology, but to achieve it over interregional and global distances generally requires more technologically advanced forms of long-range mass transportation.

For most of history, political interaction has been closely linked to military, and therefore the same logic applies. Questions of political recognition and relative status generally do not arise, or do so only marginally, unless states come within military range of each other. There are some exceptions to this: Japan sent embassies to China in the first century AD even though the Chinese had never attacked or threatened it, and there were Chinese (Buddhist) embassies to India for much of the first millennium BC even though there was no military contact between South and East Asia. But as a rule, political relations are governed by the same logistical considerations as military interaction, which is one of the key reasons for lumping them together.

Economic interaction presents a quite different picture. Trade is of course also dependent on the logistics of transportation. Mass trade in bulk goods has very similar logistical characteristics to the movement of military forces, and therefore obeys the same rules in relation to interaction capacity. During the ancient and classical era, trade in bulk goods (grain, timber, stone) took place over the short and medium-range distances within the larger empires such as Rome, China, and the many empires that occupied the Middle East. But bulk trade over more than regional distances did not occur until modern times. Not all trade, however, requires the movement of bulk goods. Since very early times high-value, low-volume luxury goods (spices, silk, and other fine cloth, gems, ceramics, slaves) and highly valued metals (gold, silver, copper, tin) have been transported over long distances. The 'Silk Roads' and sea routes that connected Han China with Imperial

Rome before the first century BC carried such goods. The logistical demands of this type of trade were relatively modest: it could be done with caravans and coastal shipping. Consequently, even during the low interaction capacity of the ancient and classical era, substantial long-distance trade was possible between far-flung regions that had no military or political contact. Because significant trade can occur even with low interaction capacity, the economic component of international systems can form on a larger scale, and much earlier than is possible for military and political interactions. Gills and Frank (1992: 623) refer to this as 'the economy-polity contradiction', that 'the economic inter-linkage and integration of the world economy are always more intensive and extensive than its political ones, which tend to be more fragmented and territorially bounded'.

Socio-cultural interaction is a different story again. The transmission of ideas can be achieved by single individuals, and in principle can occur over long distances even in environments with very low interaction capacity. The transmission of Buddhism from South Asia to China, Korea, and Japan was basically achieved by individuals who walked or rode across the two regions, and the same was true for the spread of Christianity and Islam. Ideas can and do spread on the backs of military and economic interaction. Although they are not, in principle, dependent on them, in practice trade routes have been the principal transmission belts for many cultural ideas. This process can be slow—McNeill (1963: 218) notes that it took over 2,500 years for the ox-drawn plough to spread from the Middle East to China—though some ideas such as writing and horse-riding seem to have spread more quickly. It thus seems reasonable to question whether or not the transmission of ideas should count as interaction for purposes of identifying international systems. Cultural interaction does not require states. Its effects may be substantial, but tend to operate over much longer time-spans than military or economic interaction. Because cultural interaction has such low interaction capacity requirements (except for transmission across oceans), it can provide evidence for the existence of large-scale systems from a very early stage. Whether one wants to consider this as evidence for international systems is more questionable, though it clearly suggests the existence of large-scale social systems.

In sum, then, what we see is that interaction in different sectors (military, political, economic, socio-cultural) has strikingly different logistical requirements. Military and political interaction has the highest requirements, cultural interaction the lowest, with economic interaction in the middle for luxury trade, and towards the high end for bulk trade. The capability for transportation and communication is basically a function of the relationship between distance and geography, and transportation technology. This means that interaction requiring high levels of capacity can only take place over shortish distances or easy geography if the level of technology is low. Less demanding types of interaction can occur over longer distances even if the level of technology is low.

The logic that results from interaction capacity is fundamental to the shaping of both political units and international systems. Because states and empires are fundamentally military-political constructs, they require relatively high levels of interaction capacity within the territory they claim to control. Really successful empires may come close to absorbing a whole regional system, in the process becoming 'world empires' like the Aztec, Chinese, Inca, Persian, and Roman. If interaction capacity is low, as it has been for most of history, then this will limit both the size of states and empires, and the size of international systems defined in military-political terms. Since economic interaction, at least for low-volume, high-value goods, has lower interaction capacity requirements, it is reasonable to expect that both states and empires will normally be engaged in trading networks for such goods that extended well beyond the edges of their military-political control. This is the logistical explanation for 'the economy-polity contradiction'. Trade in bulk goods will tend to keep step with the boundaries of military-political interaction, but luxury trade can easily outpace them. Cultural interaction is virtually unrestrained by interaction capacity except when it meets ocean barriers. In all cases, the scale of a system is defined by the range across which interaction occurs.

In terms of how one defines international systems, this analysis suggests four options. The first, broadest possibility (in line with Frank's view) is to say that an international system exists whenever any kind of interaction has significant historical effects. The problem with this view is that one is faced with the prospect of a whole spectrum of international system types ranging from very tight and intense to very loose and sparse. An international system defined by the slow transmission of religion or technology is not really the same type of thing as one defined by regular warfare amongst its units. A loose definition thus undermines the possibility for both comparative studies and system theory. The second possibility is to eliminate cultural interactions as too diffuse, too slow, and insufficiently 'international' to count. This would give considerably tighter criteria for identifying international systems, but would still leave a substantial gap between military-political systems, and those defined by long-distance trade. The third possibility is to eliminate economic interactions, leaving only military-political ones to define the system. This is what many realists do, and it has the merit of being very tight and coherent, and producing comparable systems. Its cost is that by eliminating the economic sector, it removes an extremely important component of international relations from the picture, narrowing the whole conception of the subject in an unacceptable way.

The fourth option is to abandon the unqualified use of the term 'international system', disaggregate the idea into sectors, and refer separately to international military-political systems, international economic systems, and international socio-cultural systems. We have no hesitation in choosing this fourth option. It has the cost of being a bit verbose, but it has the merits of allowing all of the sectors to stay in play, and of providing clear foundations both for more precise system theories and for comparative work. Based on the hierarchy of logistical requirements it builds in a nesting assumption that, other things being equal, socio-cultural systems will coexist with economic ones, and both of these will coexist alongside military-political systems. It would be strange, though not impossible, to find war without trade.

On this basis we can differentiate and label three general types of system:

1. *full international systems*: these normally contain the full range of nested sectors, though in principle one might envisage (as in some simple-minded science fiction space war scenarios) military-political interaction without economic or socio-cultural exchange;
2. *economic international systems*: these lack military-political interaction, but would normally embody both economic and socio-cultural exchange;
3. *pre-international systems*: these comprise mainly socio-cultural interactions, though they may also contain elements of non-commercial trade. They are the main type of large-scale system found amongst non-urban, pre-civilizational peoples.

These three types can be seen both as a hierarchy from more comprehensive (1) to less (2 and 3), and as a possible (but not inevitable) development sequence (from 3 through 2, to 1).

If we settle the question of what type of interaction in this way, the problem of how much interaction still remains. This is an empirical question to which at this stage it is probably impossible (given limitations on data), and perhaps unwise (given the range of historical conditions), to try to give a definitive universal answer. But our general guidelines for thinking of interaction of any type as sufficient to form a system are as follows:

- It must be sustained, in the sense of recurring on a regular basis over a substantial period of time. One does not want to preclude the possibility of short-lived systems, but longevity is important in order for structural pressure to take effect.
- It must be substantial, in the sense that it penetrates the units involved more than superficially. This might mean either or both of penetrating widely into society and/or penetrating the ruling elite. It is important to avoid defining the degree of interaction in terms of its effects. Doing so confuses cause with effect and voids the possibility of theory.

## PATTERN

What patterns of interaction qualify as a system? When thinking in systems theory terms, one tends to assume that the pattern of interaction is two-dimensional: each actor in the system interacts directly with all of the others. This multiordinate model is suggested by modern European history, by other familiar anarchic international systems such as that amongst the classical Greek city-states, and by the hierarchical models of imperial systems. But it is not the only model in play.

For much of history, limits on interaction capacity meant that in many places international systems were linear, or one-dimensional, in construction. That is to say, interaction occurred in chain-like formations, with each unit interacting with its neighbours, but not with those further afield. Thus A and B interact, B and C interact, and C and D interact, but A does not interact directly with C or D, and B and D do not interact directly. Everything is, in a sense, connected, but much more weakly than in the case of a two-dimensional system, in which each actor interacts with all the others (see Fig. 5.1).

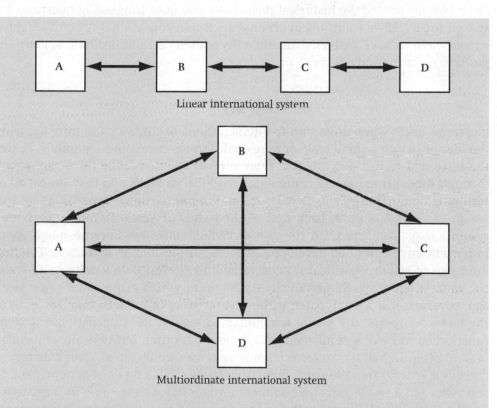

Linear international system

Multiordinate international system

*Note:* It is widely accepted in traditional IR that international systems are multiordinate and only emerge when the behaviour of each component unit forms a necessary element in the calculation of the others (Bull 1977: 10). With linear international systems, units only interact with their immediate neighbours. See Map 5.1 for an example of a linear international system in the Mediterranean of the fourth century BC.

*Figure 5.1 Linear and multiordinate international systems*

In the economic sector, the classical example of linear structure is the Silk Roads, which connected China, India, the Middle East, and Europe. Goods travelled from one end of this system to the other, but only very occasionally did individuals do so. Similar constructions can be found in the military-political sector. During the first millennium BC (before the great expansion of Rome) Carthage, Rome, the Greek city-states, and the Persian Empire formed a linear strategic system (see Map 5.1). Massive increases in interaction capacity have obliterated linear systems from the modern international system. But they do meet the basic criteria for being a system (a set of interacting units), and they are an important part of the historical story. They also pose interesting questions for system theory. If we count linear arrangements as international systems we must expect them to have weaker structural effects than do multiordinate systems, or perhaps no structural effects at all.

## SCALE

If systems begin when units start to interact, then nothing stops us from applying the idea either on a small scale or to several systems coexisting separately. In fact the historical record suggests that international systems range from very small, through subcontinental and continental, to global in scale, and that almost all of history is dominated by sub-global systems. Pre-international systems, as we will see in Chapter 6, stretch back tens of thousands of years. Primitive economic systems may have preceded the rise of civilizations, but became much more important once cities had developed as nodes for production and trade. The first examples of military-political systems came into existence on a quite small scale, the earliest being the Sumerian city-state system which arose some 5,500 years ago, covering only a small patch within the territory of modern Iraq. For most of the last 6,000 years, the planet has contained several full international systems functioning more or less independently from each other, but typically embedded in, and often linked by, larger economic systems (see Fig. 5. 2). Over this period there is a general trend towards increasing size for both types of system. Around 500 years ago a single global economic international system came into existence for the first time, followed within a few centuries by a full global international system. These global systems absorbed their older, smaller predecessors. The character of this history explains why we choose to stick with the label 'international systems' rather than opting for geographically determinist labels such as 'world system'.

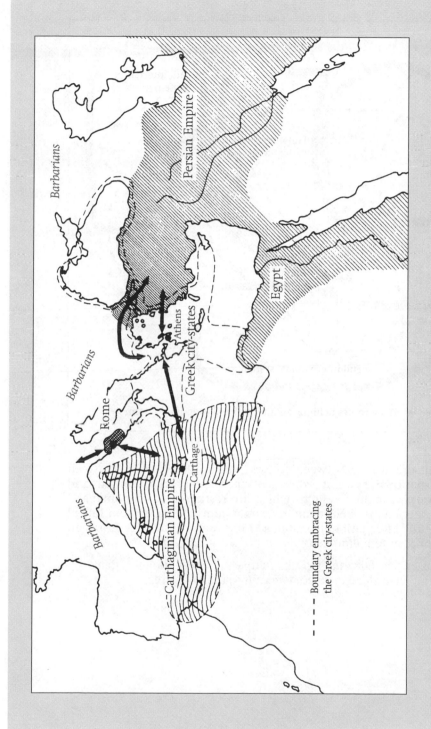

- - - -  Boundary embracing
the Greek city-states

*Note:* Contact with immediate neighbours was much more intense than with more distant powers in the Mediterranean world of the fourth century BC, suggesting a linear rather than a multiordinate system. See also Fig. 5.1.

*Map 5.1 The linear international system in the Mediterranean, fourth century BC*

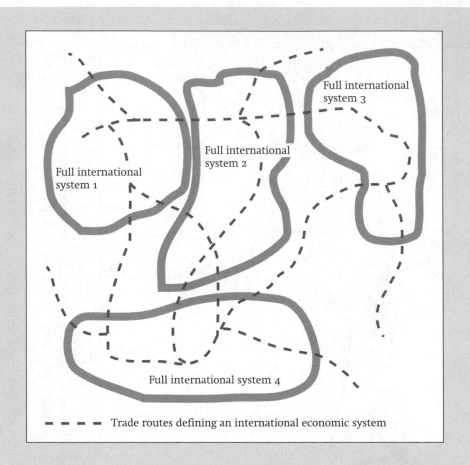

Full international system 3

Full international system 2

Full international system 1

Full international system 4

- - - - Trade routes defining an international economic system

*Note:* By distinguishing between sectors, we can differentiate between full international systems where all sectors are represented and international economic systems which are restricted to economic and societal transactions. A Eurasian economic international system linked several full international systems long before a full Eurasian international system emerged.

*Figure 5.2  The Eurasian model: multiple full international systems embedded in an economic international system*

## 2.  SECOND ORDER PROBLEMS OF DEFINITION

Solving these first order questions enables us to get much more precise handles on the basic idea of international system than are on offer in the existing literature. But in order to understand the full character of international systems we have also to tackle three second order questions: what types of units can constitute international systems? Are international systems a mechanical phenomenon or a socially constructed one? And what is the relationship between an international system's units and its structure?

### WHAT UNITS?

As suggested in Chapter 4, there is controversy within IR over the question of what units should be allowed to define international systems. This controversy arises primarily because of realism's strong commitment to the political sector, and its consequent privileging of the state. Given the long dominance of realism (and neorealism) in IR, and given the obvious importance of the state in almost any perspective on the modern international system, state-centrism has tended to squeeze out or marginalize other units. Our more open, multi-sectoral framework allows, and our longer historical view requires, a more pragmatic approach to units. That said, we do retain the idea from neorealism that in understanding international systems it is very useful to focus on the dominant unit, i.e. the unit whose arrangements and activities do most to define the system. Recall that in Chapter 4 we defined units in international systems as: 'entities composed of various sub-groups, organizations, communities and many individuals, sufficiently cohesive to have actor quality (i.e. to be capable of conscious decision-making), and sufficiently independent to be differentiated from others and to have standing at the higher levels (e.g. states, nations, transnational firms)'. This definition quite easily admits units other than the state, but the specification that units must be capable of self-directed behaviour, and that they must possess fairly high levels of cohesion rules out diffuse entities such as civilizations. Using this understanding, the Roman Catholic Church, NATO, and Hizbollah can be seen as units, but Christian, Western, or Islamic civilization cannot.

Using this definition of units, and combining it with the understandings about interaction discussed above, we take an empirical view of what units define any particular system. In pre-international systems, as set out in Chapter 6, the main units are pre-civilizational ones such as bands, tribes, clans, and perhaps chiefdoms. Such units display no or low levels of specialization and division of labour and cannot easily be analysed or differentiated by sector. They display behaviour in all the sectors—fighting, governing, trading, and identity formation and maintenance—but these activities are closely blended together. It is far from clear, for example, that the exchange of goods amongst such units can be understood in terms of modern economic logic with its emphasis on monetary value, profit, and individual motivation (Polanyi 1971).

Economic international systems, as will become clear in Part III, typically involve a range of units including tribes, empires, city-states, clans, and early forms of firm. Compared to pre-civilizational ones, many of these units had sophisticated forms of internal specialization (priests, kings, soldiers, scribes, slaves, artisans, etc.) and therefore a much more elaborate division of labour. But as a rule they lacked much differentiation into sectorally specialized types of international unit. One finds tribes, city-states, and empires playing the key roles in both the military-political and economic sectors. Cities normally grew and flourished as nodal points on trade routes. Empires were typically attempts to control a trading system and its revenues. Barbarian tribes played mixed roles, sometimes as raiders and wreckers, and sometimes as intermediaries, in the long-distance trading systems that connected different centres of civilization. That said, individual merchants were also important players in economic systems, as were communities of merchants organized as 'trade diasporas' (Curtin 1984).

Full international systems can also involve different types of unit. Such systems may be homogeneous, as Waltz's structural logic of military-political relations says they should be. They might be composed entirely of city-states, as in ancient Sumeria and classical Greece, or entirely of national states, as in the modern world system. Such homogeneous systems will tend to bind together closely the military-political and economic sectors, with the main political unit also being the main economic one. Mercantilist approaches to political economy in eighteenth-century Europe illustrate such a fusion of the political and the economic. But contra Waltz, full international systems can also be composed of unlike units. Much of the history of ancient and classical international systems can only be told in these terms, with strong military and economic interplay amongst empires, city-states, and barbarian tribes.

In our view more is lost than gained by ignoring the *de facto* diversity of units in order to hang on to the conceptual neatness of a system defined in terms of a single type of unit. In some times and places such neatness may actually reflect the empirical world. But when it does not, sectoral blindness is the danger, and the difficulties of diversity have to be faced rather than avoided. Embracing diversity of units also means abandoning the conventional (though little considered) assumption in much of IR that the dominant units must be territorial. States of course are the archetypal territorial unit, which is why this assumption is so strong in IR. Empires, city-states, and some tribes can also be conceptualized in territorial terms. But many bands and tribes are nomadic, as, in a different way, are many types of economic actor. In international systems both ancient and modern, non-territorial actors often play alongside territorial ones, sometimes amongst the dominant units.

In sum, we will take a pragmatic, empirical approach to determining what units compose and structure international systems in any given time and place. In practice, much of the story can be told in terms of five basic units (hunter-gatherer bands, tribes (including clans and chiefdoms), city-states, empires, and modern states) operating in our three types of international system. The five types of unit, can, like the three types of system they inhabit, in part be seen as stages in a process of development. The pre-civilizational units of pre-international systems, for example, were largely defined by the social ties of kinship. But kinship ties were inadequate for the larger and more complex units that followed on from the founding of cities, and were in many respects overlaid (though certainly not eliminated, even now) by cultural ties that constructed identity in terms of shared ideas such as religion and nation. Carneiro defines this process as 'the most important single step ever taken in the process of political development' (1978: 207). But while they are in one sense stages of development, these units also have to be seen as coexisting within full international systems, as most of them do even today, albeit with some no longer as dominant units. These basic five can, and often do, stretch across all the main sectors of activity. But in economic and full international systems there is also space for sectorally specialized units, most obviously varieties of economic actor ranging from merchants, guilds, and trade diasporas, through banks and some chartered companies, to TNCs.

## MECHANICALLY VERSUS SOCIALLY CONSTRUCTED SYSTEMS

In the discussion of our toolkit in Chapter 4 we differentiated structure by sector into military-political, economic, and societal (or socio-cultural). In doing so we noted that by using the English school concepts of international and world society to stand for societal structure, we could introduce a constructivist element into thinking about the structure of international systems. That remark hinges on the view that most realist and economic views of system and structure are essentially mechanical, and it is worth explaining this distinction in more depth.

A mechanistic or materialist view derives easily both from general systems theory and from analogies between the social and physical worlds, and is particularly strong in the American tradition of IR thinking about international systems. In this view, international systems are similar to physical ones. Just as the planets orbit around the sun, or millions of computers function together as the internet, so units (usually states) interact with each other like billiard balls on the table of world politics. Mechanical systems obey laws, and understanding these laws enables one to understand the system. Such knowledge usually leads to predictive capabilities: about the orbits of the planets; about the power balancing behaviour of states; or about the movement of markets. It may or may not provide the capability to manipulate the system: we can redesign the internet, but we cannot (yet) alter the orbits of the planets, and according to the harder sorts of realist and economists we cannot change the power-driven essentials of human political life, or the market-driven ones of economic life. Mechanical systems are about units interacting in ways that are structurally determined by some set of physical governing laws. In this view it makes no difference whether the units are lifeless (like planets) or sentient (like humans and their collective organizations). The behaviour of both types of unit will still be subject to objective mechanical laws deriving from material conditions, and the analyst's main job is to discover what these laws are. It is in these terms that liberal economists think about the law of supply and demand, Marxists depict the law of the declining rate of profit, and IR realists consider the law that maintains the international balance of power.

An alternative view thinks that sentience makes a difference, and on this basis separates social from physical systems. When units are sentient, how they perceive each other is a major determinant of how they interact. If the units share a common identity (a religion or a language), or even just a common set of rules or norms (about how to determine relative status, and how to conduct diplomacy), then these intersubjective understandings not only condition their behaviour, but also define the boundaries of a social system. This way of thinking has traditionally been stronger in European rather than American approaches to IR, though the current upsurge of social constructivism in IR may rectify this imbalance. It goes back at least as far as Grotius (Cutler 1991), and its classical roots are in the notion that international law constitutes a community of those participating in the international legal order (Mosler 1980: p. xv). Within IR, this approach, already identified in Chapters 2 and 3, has so far been mainly embodied in the concept of *international society* put forward and developed by writers of the English school (Dunne 1998; Wæver 1998), with the key founding figures being Wight (1966a, 1977), Bull (1977, 1984a), Gong (1984), Watson (1987, 1990, 1992), and Vincent (1974, 1986). There are of course elements of constructivism in realism and economic theory, but as a rule theorists in these traditions do not start out, as the English school does, from a constructivist position.

Bull and Watson's (1984: 1) classic definition of international society is: 'a group of states (or, more generally, a group of independent political communities) which not merely form a system, in the sense that the behaviour of each is a necessary factor in the calculations of the others, but also have established by dialogue and consent common rules and institutions for the conduct of their relations, and recognise their common interest in maintaining these arrangements'. This definition captures both the mechanical side of systems (units interacting), and the socially constructed one (the establishment and maintenance of rules and institutions). But as Little (1994, 1995) points out, the English school's position is more sophisticated than this definition implies. It is in fact based on a tripartite methodological distinction amongst international system, international society, and world society, sometimes codified as *Hobbes*, *Grotius*, and *Kant* (Cutler 1991). Broadly speaking, these terms are understood as follows: international system (Hobbes) is about power politics amongst states; international society (Grotius) is about the institutionalization of shared identity amongst states; while world society (Kant) takes individuals, non-state organizations, and ultimately the global population as a whole as the focus of global societal identities and arrangements. In the English school perspective all three of these elements coexist, the question being how strong they are in relation to each other.

We broadly accept the English school framework as a way of understanding international systems. We think that a purely mechanical conception is insufficient, and that the socially constructed elements provide valuable criteria both for benchmarking the development of international systems and for comparing them. That said, there is no escaping the fact that the English school's framework remains underdeveloped (Wæver 1992). It is all very well to say that the Hobbesian, Grotian, and Kantian elements always coexist, but not much work has been done on how they relate to each other, and no consensus exists.

Buzan (1993, 1996) argues that there is an important boundary between weak precursors of international society (i.e. where Hobbesian logic is still dominant), and a fully functioning modern international society (i.e. when Hobbesian logic begins to be significantly moderated by Grotian). Risking the charge of Eurocentrism he says that this boundary occurs at the point when the units not only recognize each other as being the same type of entity, but also are prepared to accord each other legally equal status on that basis. Mutual recognition and legal equality signify not only a turning point in the development of rules and institutions, but also acceptance of a shared identity. This act denies the possibility of suzerain, dominion, and imperial relations (though not hegemonic ones), and establishes the basis for international law and diplomacy. As Wight (1977: 135) puts it: 'It would be impossible to have a society of sovereign states unless each state while claiming sovereignty for itself, recognised that every other state had the right to claim and enjoy its own sovereignty as well.' Wight's claim for '*every* other state' is too strong. International society, like the international system, is largely defined by the great powers. It was quite possible for an international society to exist amongst the (European) great powers that sometimes extinguished states within its compass (Poland), and frequently did not recognize the rights of states outside it in Asia and Africa.

Once this boundary is understood, it becomes possible to think about the logic of potential degrees and developments of modern international society that fill the space between this bottom line, and the point at which the units within the society become effectively federated, so ceasing to be an international system. This space is large in terms of the spectrum of possible developments that it contains. The European Union (EU), for example, represents a very fully developed international society, with many shared norms, rules, and institutions co-ordinating, constraining, and facilitating the relationships amongst its members. Since nearly all existing states accord each other diplomatic recognition, there is a minimal international society embracing virtually the whole of the contemporary international system. Many of its members, however, are not much engaged beyond the minimal requirement, meaning that the degree of international society is quite unevenly distributed in the system.

There is confusion in the English school about how international society and world society relate. The more historical side of the school, represented by Wight (1977) and Watson (1987), think of world society (in the form of shared culture) as a *prerequisite* for international society. As Wight (1977: 33) puts it: 'We must assume that a states-system [i.e. an international society] will not come into being without a degree of cultural unity among its members.' Much of the historical record from classical Greece to early modern Europe supports this view, suggesting that a common culture is a necessary condition for an international society. A more or less opposite view is taken by Bull (1977: 151–3; 1984*a*: 11–18), as well as by more critical writers such as Linklater (1981: 23–37, 34–5). Here the argument is that the development of individual rights in international law could undermine state sovereignty. In other words, regardless of whether a measure of common culture is required as a foundation for international society, any serious attempt to develop a world society (by advancing human rights law for example) risks undermining the states that are the foundation of international society.

Buzan (1993) argues that both of these views are mistaken. Against the historicists, it is possible to find cases where elements of international society developed in areas not sharing a common culture. The messy multicultural history of the Middle East with its many waxings and wanings of empires, for example, suggests that significant elements of international society can form in a subsystem that does not share a common culture (Mann 1986: chs. 3–6, 8; Watson 1992: chs. 2–4, 6, 12; Cohen 1995*a*, 1995*b*). This points to the possibility of a more functional view, in which the development of international society can be seen as a rational long-term response to the existence of an increasingly dense and interactive international system. Against those who see the development of international society and world society as necessarily conflictual, it can be argued to the contrary that they cannot develop without each other. As contemporary developments in the West generally and Europe in particular show with great clarity, the development of an increasingly dense network of shared norms, rules, and institutions amongst states cannot continue without a parallel development of shared norms and identities among the peoples, particularly when the states are liberal democracies. More advanced forms of international society require matching developments of 'world' culture amongst the masses. Conversely, a world society cannot emerge unless it is supported by a stable political framework, and a state-based international society remains the only plausible candidate for this. At the time of writing, Wæver (1998) is probably the fullest and most sophisticated attempt to theorize international society.

In tracing the story of international systems we will make use of both mechanical and social constructivist views of the phenomenon. One problem is that these two approaches have tended to develop separately within IR, and not much thought has been devoted to how they relate to each other. As we showed in Chapter 2, Morgenthau was aware of the distinction, but the issue is more complex than he allows. For example, although at first glance Waltzian neorealism might seem to be purely mechanical and materialist in conception, its strong dependence on sovereignty and high levels of interaction suggest that the theory in fact depends on constructivist elements. Sovereignty only works if it is recognized by other units, and as noted above, this is the benchmark condition for a modern international society. Ruggie (1998: introd.) has noted the anomaly of Waltz's dependence on the constructivist process of 'socialization' in order to produce the 'like' (i.e. sovereign) units on which his theory depends. It is beyond the scope of this book to resolve the question of whether mechanical international systems can exist apart from socially constructed ones. What is clear is that both understandings are relevant to the development of international systems.

## STRUCTURATION

What disturbs many historians and some social scientists about the mechanical perspective on social systems in general and international systems in particular is the way that human beings get treated as cogs in a machine over which they have no control. The historian E. P. Thompson (1978: 267), for example, wrote a fierce denunciation of what he saw as a dehumanized view of the world where 'systems and subsystems, elements and structures are drilled up and down the pages pretending to be people'. But as Archer (1988) has stressed, the problem with endowing human beings with unfettered powers of agency and free will is that human beings are invariably aware that they are, in fact, constrained by structural forces. At the heart of the constructivist programme is the desire to make provision for both structures and human agents. As we saw in Chapter 2, Wendt moves in this direction by arguing that structures and agents are mutually constituted. What this implies is that practices habitually carried out by agents to maintain and define their own interests and identity simultaneously reproduce the social structures that make up the larger system of which they form a part. So, as argued in the previous section, when states engage in mutual recognition, they not only determine their own identity, but also the societal structure of the system of which they form a part. Subsequent actions that are premissed on mutual recognition, such as diplomatic codes of practice, simultaneously reproduce the component states and the international system of which they form a part.

The mutual constitution of agent and structure was originally identified by Giddens (1979: 93) as structuration and this concept indicates that far from being a cog in a machine, social agents are knowledgeable and skilful players who constantly monitor their own behaviour and the behaviour of others in order to

ensure their own survival. In doing so, whether intentionally or not, they reproduce the structure of the system within which they operate. The idea of structuration provides a way of conceptualizing the relationship between mechanical and
socially constructed systems. Because there is always a possibility that states will
pursue competitive rather than co-operative strategies in an anarchic system, the
assumption is often made that knowledge of this possibility will push all the
actors to pursue competitive strategies. Arms races and markets draw on this
logic. But we know that states can build up co-operative rule-governed relations
and that these relations will persist so long as none of the parties defects. In game
theoretic terms, this suggests that there is a dominant strategy that mechanistically pushes all parties to compete. But if states move into a position where they are
all co-operating, then they can form an unstable equilibrium that will persist so
long as no state breaks rank. The very knowledge that defection from co-operation
will lead to the reassertion of competitive strategy can help to maintain the
unstable equilibrium. Structuration is operating in both instances but the logic is
different. We are seeing the competitive logic as mechanical and the co-operative
logic as social.

Structuration raises another issue. Because constructivists argue that the units
and the structure of a system are mutually constituted, it seems to follow that any
theory of system structure must also contain a theory of the units. We have argued
elsewhere that this is true of neorealism, showing how Waltz's structural theory
of the international system contains a theory of the state. The central proposition
in Waltz's theory of the state is that under anarchic systemic conditions, states
will become 'like units'—i.e. functionally and structurally similar. The strong cir-
cularity of structuration logic is illustrated by the fact that Waltz's theory of system structure, at least in his view, requires that units be 'like' as a condition for
the existence of anarchy (Buzan et al. 1993: 37–47, 116–19). But as we will show in
subsequent chapters, there is an obvious problem with this formulation. Although
it is true that we now live in a world where the component units all take a
remarkably similar form, this has not always been the case in the past. What we
observe is that unlike units rather than like units are often the norm. We will
return to this issue in Part V.

## 3. USING THE TOOLKIT: THEORY MEETS HISTORY

In the chapters that follow we tell the story of how international systems, and
eventually a single global international system, developed. For purposes of simplicity and coherence, we tell this story as a chronological account constructed in
terms of our toolkit ideas. Most of the historical chapters in the book are organized around four headings (units, interaction capacity, process, structure), and

within those headings the discussion is divided into four sectors (military-political, economic, societal, environmental). Our approach to analysing international systems can be summed up in terms of the following questions that need to be asked about any international system:

- What is the scale of the system?
- Is its pattern linear or multiordinate?
- What kind of units dominate the system?
- Is its interaction capacity high or low?
- What types of process define the system?
- What types of structure does the system possess?
- How do units and structures interact with each other?

More specifically, we will be asking:

- How far back can we identify international systems and their precursors?
- How does interaction capacity increase, and what role does it play in the process of expanding and merging systems?
- What are the dominant units in international systems at their various stages of development, and are changes in units a principal key to understanding the major transformations in the story of international systems?
- If international systems are understood in terms of sectoral layers (societal, economic, military-political), how do the processes of interaction in different sectors interact with each other?
- How important is structural change in charting the evolution of international systems, and how do structures in different sectors relate to each other?

These questions form the theory framework that 'meets history' for the next eleven chapters.

There is a definite analytical pattern to the story which can be broadly summarized as follows:

- Precursors of international systems can be found in the extensive patterns of socio-cultural, and to a lesser extent economic, interaction that were typical of tribal peoples before the rise of cities and civilizations.
- What we will treat as fully-fledged international systems—those having substantial economic and military-political interaction—began with the rise of city-states, and grew up within these precursor systems. This created a sectorally layered arrangement in which fully-fledged international systems were typically embedded in geographically much more extensive systems of socio-cultural and economic interaction.
- Much of human history since the rise of civilization can be told in terms of multiple international systems structured in this layered arrangement. But while it was true that human interaction remained sectorally layered, it was

also true that the geographical size of socio-cultural, economic, and military-political systems all tended to expand. Socio-cultural and economic interaction tended nearly always to be wider in extent than military-political systems, but the general expansion meant that over time, more and more of the human population were absorbed into military-political international systems as well.

- The result of this process was the progressive merging of what had been distinct systems. By the sixteenth century AD the mergers had produced a single global economic system, and by the nineteenth century the military-political sector had caught up, producing for the first time a geographically coterminous set of systems in all three sectors that we know as the contemporary global international system.

- Although geographic disjuncture between the sectors no longer exists, it might be argued that interaction in the economic sector still races ahead of developments in the military-political one. This creates a disjuncture of relative development, with the economy much more advanced in its global organization than either the apparatuses of governance or the patterns of human identity.

Because we are dealing with such a vast time-span the level of generalization will inevitably be high, even by the standards of world history. To compensate, we will insert short boxed stories into Parts II–IV. These will provide more detailed accounts of the past that we hope will help to illustrate the more general points.

# Part II
# SYSTEMS IN PRE-INTERNATIONAL WORLD HISTORY

## INTRODUCTION TO PART II

The two chapters in this part sketch what we have labelled pre-international systems. These can be traced back for at least 40,000 years and they persisted outside the temporal and spatial boundaries of the international systems that first began to emerge in the fourth millennium BC. The task of drawing this sketch involves breaking new ground in the field of IR because both historians and theorists of international systems have generally given short shrift to areas of the world that lie outside the spatial and temporal limits of international systems. Indeed, to the extent that any consideration at all is given to the time before states, it tends to be in terms of abstract formulations about 'the state of nature' drawn from early political theorists such as Hobbes and Rousseau. Whatever their merits may be for constructing political theory, or for thinking about human nature, these formulations are demonstrably, and for the most part radically, wrong as descriptions of the actual precursors to states. There has never been a pre-social Hobbesian world of human beings in which life was just nasty, brutish, and short. We know that human beings have always lived in society, because they evolved from primates which are now all recognized to be innately social beings (Rodseth et al. 1991; Knauft 1991). In our view, it is essential to ground historical and theoretical approaches to international systems in a plausible account of what actually happened. There is enough empirical evidence to sketch such an account, and it turns out to be much more revealing than anything that fictive 'state of nature' stories have to offer. This pre-international world provides a vital backdrop for our discussion in Parts III and IV of how international systems were formed and developed.

Human communities have operated within international systems for 5,000 years: from the perspective of world history a relatively brief space of time. For most of history, human beings have operated in small hunter-gatherer bands (HGBs) which represent the most enduring kind of social unit yet developed. If we include the long period during which human beings evolved into their present form, then it is possible to trace this kind of unit back for several million years. But even if we restrict the time-scale to the span of fully modern human beings, then it is still possible to measure the history of hunter-gatherer bands operating within what we have labelled pre-international systems over a period of at least 40,000 years. Amazingly, despite the enormous impact of states on world history over the past 5,000 years, pre-international systems have managed—-just—to survive into the twenty-first century (Hemming 1998).

IR theorists have paid little attention to this dimension of human history because they largely take for granted that only with the emergence of states did social units begin to form coherent systems amongst themselves. They are not alone in making this assumption. It has been widely assumed throughout the social sciences that hunter-gatherer bands can be treated as autonomous, self-sufficient units which have roamed randomly across the landscape. But there is now a growing recognition that these units were, in fact, linked together into very much wider systems, sometimes extending across entire continents. Given this assessment, IR theorists need to acknowledge the existence of these pre-international systems that formed long before international systems ever emerged and survived long after international systems became part of the global scene.

In this part of the book, we draw on our theoretical toolkit to identify the essential characteristics of these long-standing pre-international systems, and then to explore the complex process of transition that eventually led from them to the establishment of the first international systems. In Parts III and IV, we go on to describe how these international systems extended across the globe, slowly but surely overtaking the established pre-international systems, eventually to coalesce and constitute a worldwide international system.

The main elements of the pre-international systems that were to transform into international systems can be summarized as follows:

- Pre-international world history is dominated by mobile, egalitarian, hunter-gatherer bands.
- A complex array of social mechanisms including speech, marriage, and gift-giving enabled these hunter-gatherers to extend their interaction far beyond the boundary that circumscribed the members of their immediate band, thereby leading to the formation of pre-international systems.
- Two new types of units—sedentary tribes and chiefdoms—began to emerge in the transitional era that preceded the formation of international systems.
- With the emergence of sedentary tribes and chiefdoms there was increasing linguistic division that had the effect of impeding social interaction capacity.
- Competition and ethnic divisions also began to consolidate amongst sedentary units, further impeding interaction capacity and promoting widespread conflict.
- War and alliances became endemic processes in the transitional pre-international systems.

As we tell the story of the pre-international systems, the reader needs to keep two important warnings in mind. First is that the labels placed on the three units identified in this section—bands, tribes, and chiefdoms—mask an enormous amount of variation. Each of these units comes in many different forms and the variation is so great that some theorists in the fields of anthropology and archaeology, where the labels are most extensively used, consider that they should be abandoned altogether. In their view these units should be located on a series of multidimensional continua which identify the scale, complexity, integration, and boundedness of the units. Reducing the complexity displayed on these various continua to three distinct kinds of unit represents a considerable oversimplification. But without the simplification it becomes impossible to tell the story of the pre-international world in a coherent fashion. Simplification is one of the costs incurred when trying to tell a comprehensible story, although an attempt is made to accommodate some of the complexity displayed by the units in the pre-international systems.

The second warning arises in part as a consequence of the initial simplification. Once the complexity of the units identified in the pre-international world is masked by our three labels of convenience, then it becomes remarkably easy to tell the story of this world in evolutionary terms, suggesting that there is a trajectory through which all units progress, with mobile egalitarian bands turning into sedentary egalitarian tribes which in turn get transformed into hierarchical chiefdoms, with the city-state lying at the end of this long trajectory. If the story is told in this way, then it starts to appear almost inevitable that, given enough time, all units will move along this line of trajectory. There are a variety of problems with this view. First, the image of a trajectory is an illusion created by the labelling process. If all the details of the units are spelled out then it becomes apparent that states have emerged from many different trajectories. Second, it is not inevitable that units will 'evolve' from one stage to another. For example, although the Aborigines in Australia did develop more complex systems over time, it is far from clear that given more time, before the Europeans arrived to affect the process irrevocably, they would have developed states. After all, some of the Aborigines were well aware of agriculture through their contact with farming communities in New Guinea, but apparently they did not see any advantages in turning themselves into farmers. Third, there is a tendency for the evolutionary model to take the units out of the context of the wider systems within which they all operated. By locating units within a more extensive system it becomes possible to tell a much more interesting story about how systems made up of hunter-gatherer bands were eventually to transform into a worldwide international system made up of sovereign states.

Chapter 6 describes the essential features of the systems made up of hunter-gatherer bands and shows how these systems helped the bands to colonize much of the globe. Chapter 7 goes on to describe the essential features of sedentary tribes and chiefdoms and how pre-international systems were affected by the emergence of these new kinds of unit. These new units coexisted and interacted within systems formed by the long-established HGBs. With the emergence of tribes and chiefdoms pre-international systems became increasingly differentiated, but only in a limited number of organizational hot spots across the globe. As we will see in Chapter 8, in a few of these hot spots, fully-fledged states came into existence and through their interactions brought international systems into existence. These international systems were initially nested in the much more extensive pre-international systems. In several areas of the world, such as Australia and North America, the pre-international systems remained largely untouched for several millennia by the international systems developing elsewhere.

## Chapter 6

# THE ORIGINS OF PRE-INTERNATIONAL SYSTEMS

This chapter constructs a model of the pre-international systems that have persisted across the course of world history. Knowledge of the early instances of these systems is scant, and so the details offered here are generally either hypothetical or draw upon more recent examples of these systems. From a methodological perspective, both of these procedures are potentially hazardous. Nevertheless, they offer the best way forward, because the alternative is to turn one's back on a fascinating and significant area of study. There are obvious problems with applying our toolkit to HGBs because they are so very different from the units that constitute full international systems. One benefit of these problems is that confronting them forces us to consider some of the hidden assumptions in the standard analytical tools of IR. Unlike the states that populate the modern international system, HGBs are neither hierarchical nor is their internal structure functionally differentiated. From a Waltzian perspective, HGBs can appear to be microcosms of the international system (i.e. anarchic and functionally undifferentiated). But this is not the case, because as we will show, the HGBs are not autonomous units, and relations within them operate on the basis of authority rather than power. This has important consequences for how one understands both process and structure in pre-international systems.

## 1. THEORETICAL INTEREST IN THE PRE-INTERNATIONAL

The very idea of pre-international world history represents very unfamiliar terrain in the study of IR. From a conventional IR perspective, it is considered unproblematic to start the study of international relations with the formation of states. As a consequence, questions about what existed before this point have not been raised. Waltz (1979) presupposes that when states first form they initially lack the power to have any impact on their neighbours. It is only when the power of states rises to the point where they can begin to impinge upon each other—to co-act in Waltz's terminology—that international systems come into existence. It follows that it is simply not necessary for IR theorists to push back into what archaeologists refer to as 'deep time'—the prehistorical and pre-international era before written records were produced.

By contrast, world system theorists say that their conception of a system enables them to identify an historical era that preceded the emergence of the state. Wallerstein (1991) argues that prior to 10,000 BC human beings all operated within self-sufficient cultural units such as bands or tribes that he identifies as mini-systems. He accepts that goods may have been exchanged between these mini-systems, but he insists that these goods were not essential to their survival, and so the exchange did not generate or constitute a systemic link which would require us to view each mini-system as a unit in a larger system. He also accepts that these mini-systems persisted into much later eras, although, because of the insidious character of the modern world system, they have now all been absorbed. Because of their interest in world systems, however, this school of thought has paid scant attention to these mini-systems.

## 2. UNITS

The basic units in pre-international systems are mobile, egalitarian hunter-gatherer bands, consisting of between fifteen and seventy-five people, and composed of a few closely knit families. These units could not be more different from the hierarchical, functionally differentiated, sedentary, political units that constitute international systems as described most explicitly by Waltz (1979). HGBs do not, of course, lack leaders. But their position rests purely on authority and the acceptance of the band. The status of leaders is achieved rather than ascribed. In contrast to hierarchical institutions, where leaders can enforce their decisions, leaders in egalitarian groups are obeyed because it is believed that they can give good reasons for the decisions that they make. In egalitarian groups, if leaders make mistakes or are seen to be unlucky, then they will either be replaced, or the dissatisfied can walk away and form a new band. As we will see in the next chapter, there are a variety of reasons why it becomes impossible to sustain egalitarian structures as groups increase in size. But because HGBs are so small, it would be counter-productive to establish an institutionalized division of labour in HGBs. If the band is to survive, then every adult must be self-sufficient; with such small numbers, functional differentiation would render a band extremely vulnerable. By contrast, in an international system, a division of labour or functional differentiation within the state is essential for its survival.

In a more detailed discussion than we can offer here, it would be necessary to develop the point that hunter-gatherers were much more varied than the picture being drawn in this chapter. Some bands contained more people, and were less mobile and more hierarchical than will be suggested here (Price and Brown 1985). Our intention in this chapter is not to provide a comprehensive picture of these units, but rather to move beyond the idea that hunter-gatherer bands can be treated as 'spatially discrete, isolated units' (Madden 1983: 191; Terrell et al. 1997).

We argue that the survival and resilience of these bands can only be understood in the context of their presence within much broader systems that sometimes encompassed 'entire continents' and generated 'continental-wide' patterns of exchange (Baugh and Ericson 1994: 4).

Although mobile, HGBs never lacked a sense of territoriality. The bands moved regularly from one campsite to another, but they did so around an 'estate' with which they were very familiar. Indeed, it was their very familiarity with the territory, and its resources and potential dangers, that helped to ensure the band's survival. Australian Aborigines, for example, identify very strongly with the landscape of their territory which they regard as sacred. From the perspective of their belief systems, they had been given custodianship over a clearly defined area of territory by their ancestors. It was their responsibility to preserve the landscape that their ancestors had created. These mobile HGBs were therefore fully aware when they were moving off their territory and encroaching onto the territory of others. But as the boxed story on the ochre expeditions illustrates, it is probable that HGBs saw themselves more as custodians than as owners of the territory they occupied. Their intrinsic mobility, even if normally confined to an estate, is one of the things that sharply differentiates HGBs from the more territorially rooted units that later came to dominate international systems.

*Ochre expeditions*

The Aborigines in Australia made very extensive expeditions for certain highly prized commodities such as the yellow and red ochre pigments which were used for cave paintings as well as body decoration. Small parties of Aborigines travelled all the way from western Queensland to the red ochre mine in the Flinders Ranges in South Australia to obtain the sacred iridescent ochre mined there (Flood 1995: 271–3). Because of the importance of ochre in funeral ceremonies, historical evidence suggests that the expeditions were allowed by the local bands to take away as much of the soft pigment-bearing rock as they could carry (McCarthy 1939–40a: 86–8).

Willingness to share resources can be seen as essential for the long-term survival of HGBs. Even in the most favourable environments, HGBs confronted inevitable 'risks arising from environmental unpredictability' (Braun and Plog 1982: 505). To contend with environmental unpredictability, HGBs formulated effective long-term 'risk-minimizing' strategies (Gould 1980: 87). Risk minimization was often achieved by risk-sharing, so that if the survival of a band was in jeopardy, the members could move onto a neighbour's territory without threatening the neighbour's survival. An ethos of sharing prevailed, so that an excess of any commodity was given away to kith or kin, thereby undermining an ethos of saving or storing as a buffer against future uncertainty.

For this strategy to work, the density of the population has to be well below the maximum that the territory can support. Evidence drawn from contemporary HGBs certainly substantiates this thesis. The maximum number of people in an HGB rarely exceeds 30 to 40 per cent of the actual carrying capacity of its territory (Service 1979: 26). This figure ensures that the population of a band can rise and still leave spare capacity for an emergency confronted by the HGB or its neighbours. There are also substantial buffer zones between the territory occupied by the bands, with the consequence that there are no clear-cut boundaries separating them (Moore 1981). Berndt (1976: 142) also suggests that because bands sometimes go out of existence, there have always been areas that are temporarily unoccupied. These empty zones provide an additional buffer against environmental unpredictability.

The size of the territory occupied by a band varies enormously, depending upon the level of resources available. When the Europeans first arrived in Australia, for example, the density of the Aboriginal population in the most fertile areas varied from 2.5 to 5 people per square km (0.4 square miles). This is a very high level of density for HGBs and is equivalent to the population density in farming communities throughout history. Generally, the population density for HGBs is much lower. In the desert regions in Australia, for example, the density of population did not exceed 1 person per 80–100 square km (30.8 square miles) (UNDESA 1973: 11). The figures in Table 6.1 are drawn from a computer simulation devised by Wobst (1976) that illustrates how the distance separating neighbouring bands consisting of twenty-five people is determined by the density of population that the land can support. (For reasons to be discussed in section 3, the figures presuppose that the band's territory takes an hexagonal shape.)

The distance between neighbouring bands is an important consideration for HGBs because they literally cannot survive as isolated units. To be autonomous, a population must be capable of reproducing itself. Although there is no consensus about what constitutes the minimum size for a self-sustaining population, an HGB of 25 people is certainly not viable. Wobst (1974) suggests that the minimum size for a stable breeding group or mating network is 475 individuals. If the bands were

*Table 6.1  Variation in the distance between neighbouring bands*

| Population density (persons/km²) | Area (km²) | Distance between neighbouring bands (km) |
|---|---|---|
| 0.05 | 500 | 24.0 |
| 0.01 | 2,500 | 53.7 |
| 0.005 | 5,000 | 75.9 |

*Source:* Figures taken from Wobst 1976: 51–2.

made up of 25 people, then a stable breeding unit would require 19 bands. So in the harshest environments, where the population falls to one person per 200 square km (77 square miles), the breeding unit would be covering an area of 95,000 square km (36,670 square miles), with the most distant bands being 304 km (189 miles) apart (Wobst 1976). There are much more conservative assessments (Jaffe 1992: 76) about the size of viable breeding groups, and as the number increases, so too does the distance over which HGBs need to maintain contact. The key point is that the territorial space occupied by a self-sustaining breeding group will steadily increase as the carrying capacity of the territory declines. The hunter-gatherer band therefore constitutes an extraordinarily flexible unit, with the capacity to expand or contract its territory depending upon the carrying capacity of the area occupied. But to survive under these varying conditions, it follows that the interaction capacity of the hunter-gatherer bands must also be able to concertina in and out, because, as we have seen, bands living in very harsh conditions will have to sustain reproductive relationships over much more extensive distances than bands living in very fertile conditions. To understand how this is achieved, it is necessary to look more closely at interaction capacity and the processes which help to sustain it.

## 3. INTERACTION CAPACITY

The long-term survival of an HGB requires it to maintain contact with other bands, some of which may be located a considerable distance away. Interaction capacity in pre-international systems is therefore an issue. There is evidence that HGBs produced seacraft, probably some form of raft, from a very early date, but they had no physical transportation technologies for land: no wheels, no pack or riding animals. On land, perforce, all direct contact depended upon the capacity of individuals to walk from one place to another. But in the most sparsely populated regions, a band will be several walking days distant from neighbouring bands. This suggests that the interaction capacity of pre-international systems must have diminished steadily as the population density of these systems decreased. But if this was the case, then it would follow that as regions become progressively less favourable to human habitation, so the bands living there would become ever more isolated and vulnerable. A risk-minimizing strategy that depended upon the co-operation of neighbouring bands would be impossible to sustain if the risks confronted by bands were negatively correlated with their capacity to maintain contact with neighbours. Yet the historical record indicates that bands survived very successfully in extraordinarily harsh environments, which suggests that interaction capacity was not an insuperable problem.

For interaction capacity to be maintained under these circumstances, there have to be compensatory mechanisms at work, and these cannot have been physical technologies for transportation and communication. Perhaps the most obvious compensation was the intrinsic mobility of HGBs. The concept of inter-action capacity presupposes a system of territorially rooted units whose problem is bridging the distances between them. But if the units themselves move lock, stock, and barrel, as HGBs did, then even if this movement is slow, interaction capacity is a less compelling variable than it is in systems of fixed units.

The other compensation is that HGBs developed two social technologies to facilitate the contact necessary to their survival and reproduction: language and proximity. There is a close correlation between language diversity and the risk to survival posed by the environment. Research has demonstrated that language diversity decreases as risks posed by the environment increase (Nettle 1996, 1998; Blanton et al. 1993: 48). A common language represents an important mechanism for overcoming physical impediments to communication. By analogy, two prisoners separated by a dividing wall but who share a common language and culture may well find it easier to communicate than two prisoners in the same cell who lack a common language and culture. Certainly Terry Waite and John Anderson who occupied adjacent cells when they were held hostage in Lebanon found ways of communicating to each other through the wall that separated them. A common language and culture enormously facilitates communication for bands that can only come into contact on an irregular basis.

A second social mechanism to enhance interaction capacity is to maximize the number of proximate neighbours possessed by each band. Studies of HGBs show that the mean number of neighbours with which bands maintain direct contact 'consistently approaches six' (Moore 1981: 198). It follows that the best model to describe the territorial configuration of HGBs is an hexagonal lattice (see Fig. 6.1). Moore (1981) and Peterson (1976) suggest that the hexagonal landscape of HGBs emerges because it generates the most efficient information network and this is essential for the HGBs' risk-minimizing strategy.

For this strategy to work, HGBs have to ensure that channels of communica-tion are constantly kept open with bands further afield who may be needed at some time in the future to provide either mates or assistance when their own local environment fails them. Not only will it be necessary to maintain good relations with neighbouring bands, but information needs to be passed con-stantly along the channels of communication so that a band will know who to turn to when a need arises. Proximity and common language provide the min-imum conditions for interaction capacity. But for the risk-minimizing strategy to work, there has to be a general willingness to share. This willingness has to be fostered by a set of social processes that maintain the channels of communica-tion and simultaneously allow bands to monitor conditions in distant areas (Rautman 1993) and facilitate the task of identifying mating partners. Maintain-ing social technologies for interaction capacity requires active social processes. Once in place, these processes make possible a 'release from proximity' which

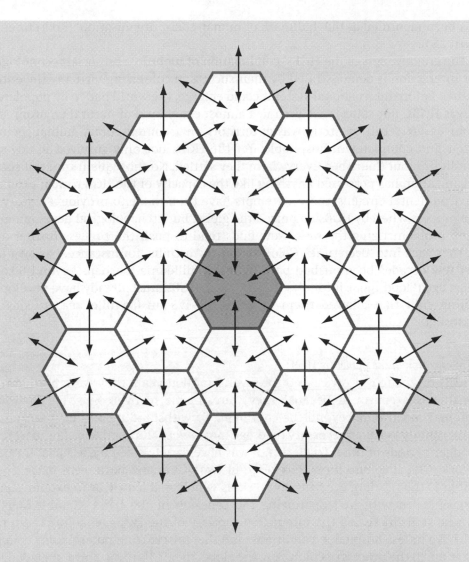

*Note:* In this figure, each hexagon represents a hunter-gatherer band (HGB). Each HGB contains too few people to form a self-sufficient breeding unit. Computer simulations suggest that an HGB made up of twenty-five people will need to be in regular contact with eighteen other HGBs to form a viable unit. In the diagram, only the shaded HGB in the centre achieves this total. The remaining HGBs will need to be in contact with other bands further afield.

*Source:* Peterson 1976.

*Figure 6.1  The hexagonal lattice model of HGB systems*

has been identified as the 'hallmark of human social organisation' (Rodseth et al. 1991: 240).

The effectiveness of the HGBs' combination of mobility and social technologies for interaction is demonstrated by their success in colonizing virtually the entire planet. Before international systems could emerge, the world had to be populated. It was HGBs, not states, that occupied almost every kind of natural environment from desert scrub to Arctic waste: territory that contemporary human beings often find completely inhospitable. Yet the HGBs not only survived in adverse conditions, but flourished everywhere they settled. No subsequent mode of social organization has possessed anything like the capacity of the HGB to adapt to new environmental circumstances. Attempts have been made to provide a history of the process whereby HGBs colonized the globe, but archaeological developments keep problematizing the task. New finds tend to push the process further and further back into 'deep time'. Colonization of Australia, for instance, has over the last few decades been pushed back by many millennia, perhaps beyond 60,000 years ago (Flood 1996). It follows that, by then, HGBs must already have developed sailing craft that allowed them to make the 128-km (80-mile) sea crossing to Australia.

*Colonization of the planet by HGBs*

HGBs originated in Africa and for several million years they were bottled up within this continent because they were unable to overcome the environmental constraints beyond the continent. To withstand increasingly seasonal environments it was necessary to forage more widely for food and stay apart for longer periods of time. To do this, it was necessary to stretch the social framework. Global colonization took place in two waves and both were made possible as the result of evolving social skills which enabled HGBs to extend their social reach without jeopardizing the cohesion of the band (Gamble 1995). These skills increased the interaction capacity of the HGBs, enabling them to survive in less hospitable conditions, and thereby creating potential for colonization. In the process of colonizing the globe, the HGBs invariably left evidence of their stone tool-making culture, and so it is possible to trace the extent of the colonization.

What the evidence reveals about the first phase is that while HGBs occupied large stretches of Eurasia, they were unable to colonize arid regions deficient in water supplies, or the Eurasian plains, covered in snow during the winter, or oceanic islands which could only be reached by sea, or dense forests where communication was difficult. As a consequence, large sections of Afro-Eurasia were left unoccupied, and the Americas, the Pacific islands, and Australasia were never colonized at all. The early humans who engaged in the first wave of colonization lacked the necessary skills to bring these regions within their reach. The routes they took and the areas they colonized were profoundly affected by the repertoire of social skills that had evolved in Africa. As they moved into less hospitable territory, they needed to maintain contact over increasing distances. As Gamble puts it, 'If the social networks could not cope with such stretching then colonisation did not occur' (1995: 142).

During this long first stage of global colonization, evolution continued, giving rise to new forms of the human species. But although there is some regional variation in the composition of the kit of stone tools that were carried out of Africa, the archaeological remains identify a remarkably standardized technology which persisted with relatively minor changes for a million years. At the end of this period, however, there is evidence of very major behavioural changes. Humans began to engage in distinctive cultural practices such as burying their dead and looking after the sick and the old. New social skills created the potential for establishing an even wider and more complex 'web of relations' than had previously existed, leading to very rapid advances in social organization and interaction capacity. An unintended consequence of the enhanced interaction capacity was to bring about a second phase of global colonization. From around 60,000 years ago the empty areas of the globe that had resisted HGBs for hundreds of thousands of years were rapidly filled up. From Gamble's perspective, the ability of these HGBs to complete the process of global colonization indicates unequivocally that the members of these bands were fully modern human beings. Even more important from an IR perspective is that while the HGBs made up of modern humans did not create any kind of global system, they did generate networks of interaction that were eventually to cross entire continents (see Map 6.1).

## 4. PROCESS

In Chapter 4 we argue that systemic processes can be distinguished by sector. But this formulation supposes that the units in the system have hierarchical and functionally differentiated domestic structures. The absence of both these features in HGBs means that it is impossible to identify separate sectoral processes with any clarity. Because there is no clear differentiation between political, economic, social, and environmental processes within the HGBs, these processes cannot be neatly distinguished at the systemic level either. HGBs generate processes that permit their 'release from proximity' by ensuring that relationships mingling political, economic, and social elements between distant bands are regularly reproduced. It is perhaps easiest to think of these relationships as basically socio-cultural, with admixtures of elements from other sectors. There are three main processes in the pre-international systems formed by HGBs: marriage, exchange of goods, and gatherings. It is also likely that some fighting took place.

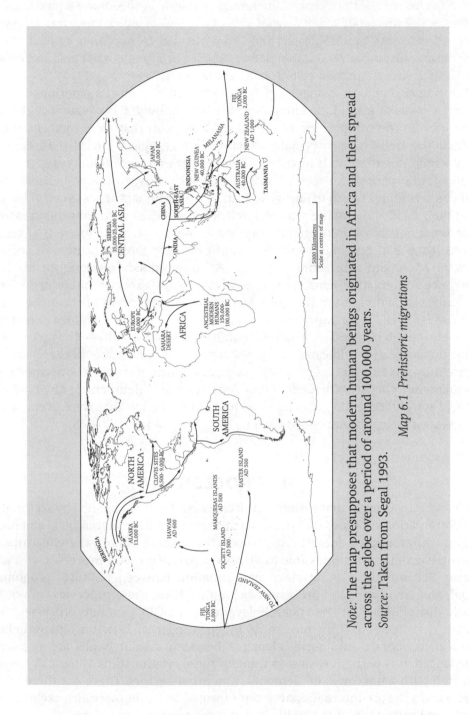

*Note:* The map presupposes that modern human beings originated in Africa and then spread across the globe over a period of around 100,000 years.
*Source:* Taken from Segal 1993.

*Map 6.1 Prehistoric migrations*

What is significant about marriage, as opposed to the mating that takes place amongst non-human primates, is that it establishes a permanent link between two spatially separated families. A non-human primate may join another group in the hope of mating, but it will not maintain links with its former group. By contrast, marriage in HGBs establishes a consanguineal alliance between two families (Rodseth et al. 1991). Marriage therefore has political and economic as well as social significance because it serves to tie families from different bands together. Complex rules governing kinship relationships developed amongst HGBs and although these rules could take many different forms, according to Service (1979: 37) they all represent 'different forms of exogamy'. Exogamy is the custom whereby an individual is required to marry a partner from another band or tribe. Because HGBs are exogamous, the rules of marriage determine whether the man or the woman leaves their own band and land to join another. Either way, the partner who moves maintains the link with their blood relatives. In times of emergency, an endangered band can draw on this link and expect assistance.

The nature of kinship systems has important consequences for the scale and intensity of interaction established amongst the bands. If the rules require marriage between first cousins, then the effect will bind two bands very closely together. But there are also rules that promote ties with a broader range of bands. In Australia, for example, Western Desert Aborigines prefer second cross-cousin marriages. This means that a man is expected to marry a woman who is related to him as his mother's mother's brother's daughter's daughter. Because the population is widely dispersed in the Western Desert, the cumulative effect of this complex kinship system is to produce a shortage of potential marriage partners near where any individual male normally lives and forages. It is necessary to look further afield, and often the partner located will live hundreds of miles away. As a consequence, because these Aborigines are polygynous, multiple long-distance marriages can be arranged in several different directions, so that throughout the Western Desert there are 'widely ramified and interconnected kin-sharing networks' (Gould 1980: 85).

The strategy of risk-sharing depends upon having a range of reliable allies in a variety of different locations. Marriage represents an important process that has the effect of stretching social organization, sometimes over very substantial distances. But when mates are exchanged between non-proximate bands, the constraint of low physical interaction capacity means that contact will not occur frequently. There will thus always be a danger that the marriage 'alliances' established between bands will either wither or weaken over time. To maintain the social network, lines of communication have to be reinforced by additional institutionalized processes that take place on a more regular basis. A strategy of sharing within and between bands has the effect of strengthening links and ensuring that social networks are constantly being reproduced. HGBs regularly engage in the institutionalized exchange of goods, not only because of their utilitarian value but also because of the intrinsic importance attached to maintaining alliances and reproducing established lines of communication. The strategy of 'prestations'—obligatory gift-giving—helps to keep social networks open (Leach 1983: 536).

Wallerstein's conception of HGBs as autonomous 'mini-systems' presupposes that 'prestations' fail to generate systemic ties between bands. But his argument rests on the assumption that the items exchanged are luxuries that can be forgone without any loss. This fails to appreciate the real significance of gift-giving. The exchange of goods represents simultaneously a social, economic, and a political process. Goods may well be exchanged in the first instance because of their economic utility. In South-East Australia, stone axes were traded as far as 800 km (500 miles) (Flood 1995: 269). Pituri, which contains nicotine and is a psychotropic plant, was also widely traded amongst the Aborigines and played an important role in the process of barter. The narrow leaves of the pituri grown in Queensland and Western Australia were packed tightly in bags and traded for up to 1,000 km (620 miles) from its source. The evidence also shows that because such goods had an intrinsic or utilitarian value, most would be retained by the recipient. As a consequence, the amount of any these goods that gets passed 'down the line' to another recipient diminishes, and the availability of such goods declines as the distance from their source increases (Ammerman et al. 1978; Helms 1988). As the good becomes more scarce, so the value attached to it increases and, unsurprisingly, as the value of a good changes, so too, as the story of the Kimberley point illustrates, does the use to which the good is put.

*The Kimberley point*
The 'point' is a flake of stone that can be produced from a type of rock found in the Kimberley district in north-western Australia. These points are valued because they retain their cutting edge. In the Kimberley region the points provide the tips of the spears used for hunting kangaroos. But as they are also traded into other regions, they become increasingly scarce, raising their value and simultaneously precipitating a change in the use made of them. In the Central Desert, the points were held to be endowed with evil magic and it was believed that any injury caused by them would prove fatal. Further afield, in the Western Desert, over 1,000 km (620 miles) away, the Kimberley points were used exclusively in a sacred ceremony to circumcise young novices. Gould (1980: 143) argues that 'purely profane objects' became 'increasingly sacred when transported further into a situation where they were scarce and where the social context was different'.

This finding is readily explainable by conventional economic thought which supposes that as goods become more scarce, the value attached to them will rise.

But it is not difficult to demonstrate that the exchange of goods served the additional political purpose of consolidating alliances. Archaeologists have shown that the stone flakes used to make adzes in certain areas in the Western Desert of Australia were imported from much further afield despite the fact that the local stone produced a higher-quality blade (Gould 1980: 153). This finding cannot be explained in conventional economic terms and helps to substantiate the argument that the process of exchanging goods had an additional social and political value for HGBs.

It is not difficult to demonstrate the enormous scale over which ideas and goods moved between HGBs. Archaeologists have carefully monitored the distance that humans have carried the stone used to produce their tools. Although the evidence is still very fragmentary, it would seem that a major change began to take place from as far back as 200,000 years ago, when humans were no longer content to use the stone that most readily came to hand. Stones began to be carried several kilometres from their source (Roebroeks et al. 1988). From around 40,000 years ago there seems to have been a step-level increase in the distance that stones were moved. Stone tools are identified at increasing distances from their original source. In the era between 40,000 and 20,000 years ago, for instance, a distinctive chocolate-coloured, high-quality flint was transported from the quarry sites in the Holy Cross Mountains of Poland over distances of up to 400 km (250 miles) (Gamble 1986: 337). As the technology associated with the stone tools became more sophisticated, so the demand for more exotic stones increased and the stones were moved over ever greater distances. One of the most remarkable recent discoveries reveals that as far back as 20,000 years ago, obsidian, the black volcanic glass that played an essential role in making Stone Age tools, was moved over 350 km (217 miles) by sea along the islands that form the Bismarck archipelago (Flood 1996). There is also evidence of rare or technologically sophisticated goods, from a very early stage, being moved over very great distances. Amber from the Baltic has been found among the palaeolithic remains in Moravia, Austria, and France, while shells from the Red Sea have been found in Switzerland (Morgan 1965: 9).

The same phenomenon can be observed in many places. In North America, shark and alligator teeth from Florida have been discovered in Ohio and Illinois (Fagan 1991). In Australia, pearl shells from the north-west coast were moved 1,600 km (990 miles) to the Great Australian Bight. Similarly, the baler shells from Cape York were shaped into oval ornaments and exchanged as far as the coast of South Australia (Flood 1995: 269; McCarthy 1939–40a: 92–8), and boomerangs were similarly traded over very long distances. McCarthy (1939–40a: 98–104) talks of 'trunk trade routes' that criss-crossed the continent carrying not only commodities but also cultural practices, such as ceremonial dances. He accepts that these trunk routes were not always marked by well-defined paths, but they represent, nevertheless, metaphorical highways along which goods were traded. These trunk routes reveal that far from being isolated groups, the Aborigines were part of a 'complex social and economic network' (Flood 1995: 273) that extended across the Australian continent (see Map. 6.2).

And as McCarthy indicates, the network was not restricted to the long-distance movements of goods and artefacts. Common styles provide another indicator of the existence of extensive networks.

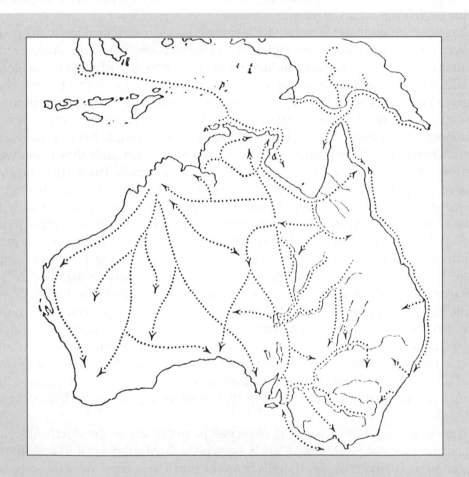

*Note:* The Aborigines exchanged goods with neighbours that then got passed 'down the line', establishing what McCarthy (1938–9) describes as 'trunk routes' that extended across Australia. The Aborigines also traded with their island neighbours.

*Source:* Taken from Numelin 1967.

*Map 6.2 Exchange networks across Australia*

Between 23,000 and 21,000 years ago, when climatic conditions in north-west Europe deteriorated very substantially, stone 'Venus' figurines made their appearance throughout this region. These figurines, identical in style, are found all the way across Europe from Poland to the Pyrenees. These visual symbols made it easier to cement social alliances (Gamble 1982; 1986: 210–11).

Although bands must generally have interacted on a bilateral basis, there is also evidence that they could aggregate into larger groups on special occasions. It has even been argued that these aggregations represent a universal process amongst hunter-gatherers (Hayden 1993: 163; but see Hofman 1994). Such gatherings provided opportunities for group rituals, mate-finding, information-sharing, and gift-giving (Hofman, 1994: 345). But the process of aggregation could only occur in locations where there was a superabundance of food, and a macroband—an aggregation of HGBs—could only stay together for so long as the food lasted. As the boxed story on feeding macrobands illustrates, a variety of very different sources of food have been used to feed macrobands. The most important sacred sites for Australian Aborigines were all located where there was an important seasonal source of food, thereby allowing full-scale ceremonial festivals to take place. Many of these festivals occurred irregularly, because they could only take place when the source of food was in particularly plentiful supply (Strehlow 1970).

*Feeding the macrobands*

Every year, a species of small brown moth (*Agrotus infusa*) flies in vast numbers to the uplands of the Great Dividing Range in Australia where they spend the summer in a dormant state. The moths, clustered several feet in depth, can be found in crevices in these Alpine regions and, because of their dormant condition, they are easily gathered. The bodies of the moths contain a high fat content and can feed large numbers of people. Archaeological and historical evidence has shown that the Aborigines in the region joined together in large campsites where they collected and roasted the moths (Flood 1995). In the same way, in southern Queensland, the Aborigines joined and feasted together on the edible Bunya pine (Gould 1980).

At the opposite end of the spectrum from these macroband festivals is conflict amongst HGBs. Knowledge of the early history of these bands is extremely limited, but evidence from contemporary HGBs suggests the possibility. Keeley (1996: 29) observes evidence of raiding amongst some Australian HGBs. He argues that because of the small numbers of people killed we are predisposed to refer to the outcome as murder rather than war. But when we hold population constant, although the validity of doing so can be questioned, then some surprising statistics emerge. The homicide rate amongst the Kung San (or Bushmen) of the Kalahari desert, for example, was four times higher than that of the United States during the period 1920 to 1955. Critics of this position (Ferguson and Whitehead 1992) insist that it is contact with 'civilization' that produces these figures. Numelin (1967: 44) also thinks that conflict was generally avoided, even when macrobands formed, because of the ceremonial and religious nature of these encounters. Messengers sent to invite neighbouring bands to these ceremonies were held in high esteem and were permitted to pass safely from one estate to another (Numelin 1967: 83). Numelin insists, therefore, that the essential elements of modern diplomacy can be observed amongst prehistoric people.

# 5. STRUCTURE

There are obvious problems about applying concepts of structure derived from modern international systems to pre-international ones. As we showed in the previous section, economic, political, and social processes are difficult to distinguish in relations between HGBs. This is a problem because our toolkit establishes definitions of structure that are sector dependent. It is unclear what form the structures of pre-international systems can take, or even whether, from an international systems perspective, these systems should be considered unstructured. Concepts such as anarchy, hierarchy, markets, command economy, and international society simply cannot be applied meaningfully to systems composed of HGBs. We can, however, do two things under this heading. First, we can look at the patterns of interaction to see whether these pre-international systems are linear or multiordinate. And second, we can explore the possibility that if system structure means anything during this era, it can perhaps best be thought of in socio-cultural terms as an early species of world society.

Thinking about the patterns of interaction in pre-international systems draws one back to the idea from section 3 that HGBs arranged themselves in a network of contacts taking the shape of a hexagonal lattice. One can imagine this as a large number of bands linked together like pieces in a vast jigsaw puzzle. If we start the historical clock ticking at 100,000 years ago the jigsaw is still very incomplete. But over time, new pieces get added until eventually all habitable sectors of the globe are occupied. Recall that neighbours are needed to supply both mates, and assistance when a band confronts environmental stress. It is unclear how many neighbours are needed to cope with environmental stress, but accepting the calculations of Wobst (1976), a hexagonal lattice must contain a minimum of 19 bands to form a viable breeding group. Each individual band is thus at the centre of a kind of subsystem composed of 19 bands. Because the membership of each group of 19 overlaps heavily, it becomes easy to see how goods and ideas get passed down the line over long distances. It is also easy to see that in this arrangement, bands on the edge of the system suffer locational disadvantages that encourage them to splinter and occupy new terrain. Lacking neighbouring bands beyond the edge of the system, they have to find all their 18 partners in the interior. This will generate competition for partners with other interior bands which can most easily be relieved by the occupation of new territory. This model might also help to account for Wobst's (1976: 56) observation that linear environments, such as seacoasts, were not exploited by HGBs until 'quite late in the course of human evolution'.

In principle, if each band retained contact with all of its immediate neighbours, there would be a kind of very weak world system in this. Such a system would be much more linear than multiordinate in its interactions, though it does not fit either model all that well. It has linear character because each unit interacts mainly with those next to it, and not much if at all with those further away in the lattice. The alliances of any given HGB were all local in character. They certainly helped to extend the interaction capacity of individual bands, but they did not reflect the existence of direct contacts across continents. The goods and ideas which traversed continents did so on a relay basis, with each item only being carried a short distance by any individual; the goods were moved 'down the line' by people who never themselves travelled far from their own home base (Curtin 1984: 17; Hodder 1978: 157). In principle it would be possible for a relay system to have weak connecting bonds linking all of its units. In practice, however, there was no global scale pre-international system even in this weak sense. As shown in the previous section there were some whose exchange processes reached near continental scale but relay processes were not strong enough to make a continental system.

These pre-international systems were certainly not political systems nor economic systems nor international societies. They had no structure in these senses, and neither Waltz nor Wallerstein nor Morgenthau would acknowledge them as being international systems at all. Yet it might be worth exploring the idea that pre-international systems were structured as a type of world society. We have already noted that substantial networks of HGBs shared language, marriage customs, and festivals. A social structure emerged spontaneously among them as a result of their mutual recognition that if they wished to survive then they needed to maintain close relations with neighbouring bands. This basic self-interest was reinforced by a set of common beliefs. HGBs operated within what Strehlow (1970) calls a 'totemic landscape'. All HGBs seem to have adhered to a view of the world which not only explained their origins, but also linked them very closely both to each other, and to their environment. The people of the sub-Arctic in North America, for example, all claim to have been descended from an animal or a legendary ancestor linked to an animal. Each family had a particular animal as its totem. The word is drawn from *ototeman* which roughly translates from Algonkian, one of the major languages of this region, as 'he is my relative' (Farb 1969: 63). The term 'totem' has been applied to the world-view of HGBs throughout the world. Totems are not restricted to animals. They embrace plants, or any aspect of nature that is conceived to be 'in a mystical social relationship with the members of a group'

(Service 1979: 44). Comaroff (1992) argues that it is a historically specific form of the universal process of classification, allowing the members of a band, as well as the interlinked bands themselves, to be portrayed as both similar and yet different. Totemism enables bands to define themselves as either 'independent or interdependent units within a common humanity'(Comaroff 1992: 51).

*Totemism and the Penobscot*

The classification system associated with totemism takes the form of dualities or opposites and this mode of classification has important social and political consequences. The bands of the Penobscot, who occupy territory near the Maine coast in North America, for example, subscribe to a creation myth which simultaneously joins and divides the various bands. A giant frog, they believe, swallowed all the world's water, causing a universal drought. The water was then released when the frog was killed by a mythical hero. Those people who rushed to drink the water, however, were turned into either salt-water creatures, such as whales, perch, and lobsters, or freshwater creatures such as frogs and eels. Relatives who survived then adopted the creature of their transformed kin as a totem, and it was believed, moreover, that they possessed the essential characteristics of the creature adopted as their totem. Myths and totems, therefore, have to be seen as a totality, because they demonstrate that despite the diversity of the bands, there is always an underlying unity (Farb 1969: 63–4).

The 'dreaming' *Zeitgeist* of the Australian Aborigines illustrates very clearly the high level of interconnection that can form among HGBs. Spiritual ancestors of the Aborigines are seen to have created the landscape when they travelled along 'dreaming tracks'. The tracks extend over hundreds of miles (Strehlow 1970: 94) and link members of different HGBs. The tracks form 'channels of communication' along which humans as well as mythical ancestors travel (Berndt 1976: 140). And along the 'dreaming tracks' are 'dreaming sites' where sacred ceremonies take place to ensure that the 'dreaming' continues. Songs play a very important role in these ceremonies and initiated members of the HGBs must ensure that the songs are performed. Strehlow (1970: 132) argues that the 'perpetual well-being of the universe and the whole welfare of the material world' are seen to depend on these ceremonies. The songs sung on the sites link individuals who live along the dreaming tracks and form what Chatwin (1987) graphically called 'songlines'. Because the dreaming tracks criss-cross and intersect at many points, they establish 'a network of spiritual bonds' (Ross et al. 1987: 102) which tie the bands of a region together. As Morphy (1990: 316) notes, each HGB is essentially outward looking because its identity is established in part 'through its position in a cosmic network of connections'.

The integration engendered by totemism was reinforced by the belief that the plants and animals that were totemically linked to the HGBs would only flourish if each totemic group carried out the ceremonies that ensured the continuity and well-being of the living thing associated with a totem. It follows that the economic well-being of any particular band depended on the survival of all the bands, because only if the totemic rites were performed by every band would the full repertoire of plants and animals be preserved (Strehlow 1970: 102–3; Service 1979: 44–5). HGBs, therefore, operated in a totemic landscape that not only defined relationships within and between the bands, but also indissolubly linked the bands and their natural environment.

This view of HGBs suggests that while their pre-international systems may have been unstructured in a mechanical sense, they were not without socially constructed identity structures. These early 'world societies' were embedded in a structuration process precipitated by a mutual recognition amongst HGBs of their interdependence.

# 6. CONCLUSIONS

The pre-international systems of HGBs were quite unlike the international systems that came into being with the dawn of civilization. The characteristics of HGBs as the dominant unit—their small scale, their mobility, their lack of internal structure or differentiation, their quite high degree of interdependence and consequent inability to exist as self-contained entities—sharply differentiate them from the dominant units of historical times. Nevertheless HGBs laid the foundations for their successors in several crucial ways. Their primary colonization peopled the planet. Mobile units continued to be influential in international systems until a few hundred years ago. HGB relay networks for exchanging goods over long distances set out the basis for later trading systems, and the basic mechanism of relay trade lasted well into the ancient and classical era. And their world societies paved the way for the distinct civilizational areas that are still a strong feature of human organization. It was the particular character of HGBs as the dominant unit that shaped pre-international systems, and it was changes in the nature of this dominant unit that marked the transition from pre-international to international systems.

*Chapter 7*

# THE TRANSITION FROM PRE-INTERNATIONAL TO INTERNATIONAL SYSTEMS

---

The transition from pre-international to international systems began and ended at different points in time in different parts of the world, and the whole process covers a period much longer than the time that international systems have been in existence. Although it is impossible to put even a rough date on the start of this era, it began in most parts of the world at some point between 20,000 and 10,000 BC. Its end point is the well-documented formation of city-states and empires, which in Eurasia began in the Near East during the fourth millennium BC, and in the New World, in Mesoamerica, during the second millennium BC. During this very long period of time, two fundamental transformations occurred in the long-standing pre-international systems: first, the emergence of sedentary societies; and second, the development of hierarchy within some of these units. Larger and more self-contained units came into being, in the process laying the foundations for cities, states, and war. These transformations were as dramatic and significant as anything that has happened in the subsequent international systems. Without them, international systems could never have emerged.

The formation of larger, sedentary units which were internally more hierarchically structured utterly transformed the pre-international systems of small, mobile, egalitarian HGBs. During the transition, hunter-gatherers gave up their mobile way of life and settled down, living in close proximity to each other in small villages, a process known as *nucleation*. On the face of it, there seem to be so many obvious advantages to living together in one location that this development might not seem to require explanation. But there are serious costs attached to this development. Apart from the fact that their overall health declined, settled hunter-gatherers began to experience a much greater degree of physical insecurity than before because of the risk of being attacked. Nucleation was a defensive move to reduce this insecurity, and villages became the dominant units within the evolving pre-international systems. These villages were politically autonomous, but from an economic and social perspective they were never completely self-sufficient. They remained part of the extensive pre-international systems that continued to embrace the remaining mobile hunter-gatherer bands. To help clarify the distinction between mobile HGBs and settled communities we shall refer to the latter as *tribes*.

In settled communities social differentiation between individuals increased, leading to the evolution of more hierarchic domestic structures, and the eventual emergence of a chief who possessed distinct political power. Since, on the face of it, the emergence of hierarchy produced substantial benefits for a very limited number of people, and costs for a very large group of people, it is more difficult to account for than the emergence of sedentary tribes. One plausible explanation is a security-driven, neorealist-type process of structuration, with the emergence of hierarchy being an unintended consequence of the struggle to survive in the evolving anarchic system that the sedentary communities both found themselves in, and were instrumental in reproducing. We label these new hierarchical units *chiefdoms*. With their formation, the pre-international systems began to take on the contours of a full international system. But chiefdoms were generally unstable, and their regular collapse meant that hierarchical units constantly reverted back to egalitarianism. It was only with the emergence of city-states that hierarchy solidified, beginning the story of the first full international systems that is the subject of Part III.

In digesting this story, readers should recall the cautions sketched out in the Introduction to Part II. There is much that is simply not known about this huge period of time. New findings will undoubtedly necessitate changes in the story. The account given here does, however, have considerable advantages over the more familiar story that the emergence of sedentary hierarchical units originated in population growth. In this view, there was a slow but discernible increase in population during the hunter-gatherer era. As a consequence, HGBs began to develop agriculture in those areas where population growth created pressure on resources. With the development of agriculture, the HGBs turned themselves into farmers and further increases in population resulting from the availability of food meant that it was eventually impossible for these farmers either to revert back to being hunter-gatherers or to move off into virgin territory. The egalitarian tribes of farmers ultimately found themselves completely immobilized. The door on their iron cage swung closed and the farmers found that their leaders, who in the past had operated on the basis of authority rather than power, were now in a position to coerce their followers. Before the development of agriculture, it had been possible for groups to fission, thereby preventing the emergence of coercive leadership. Any leader who endeavoured to develop a coercive stance would simply find that their followers melted away. But this option was no longer possible and the route to hierarchy was opened up, leading eventually to the formation of the state.

This account may seem plausible and it has certainly seduced some historical sociologists (Mann 1986). But it is flawed by lack of evidence either that agriculture developed as the result of population pressure, or that agriculture accounts for the formation of sedentary units (Runnels and van Andel 1988). What the evidence seems to suggest is that in certain favoured areas where resources were both reliable and plentiful, it was possible for HGBs to adopt a much more settled way of life. It is argued that as the result of climatic changes in the post-glacial or Holocene period around 10,000 BC some hunter-gatherers found themselves in such favourable locations that it was not necessary for them to move around their 'estate'. They could acquire all the food they needed from one location. In the coastal regions of South-East Asia, for example, where seafood and wild rice were readily available, archaeologists have concluded that humans began to settle, building houses and establishing cemeteries, before the process of domesticating plants and animals had started (Higham 1989). The Fertile Crescent defined by the Tigris and Euphrates rivers was another area where food was readily accessible. Animals were plentiful for hunting, and there was an abundance of wild cereals on the mountain ridges. Maisels (1990: 68–9) estimates that a family group could move up the slope of the ridge as the season progressed and in three weeks collect more wild wheat than they could consume in a year. Under these circumstances, there was a decreasing incentive for hunter-gatherer bands to move around, and a virtue to establishing a base where surplus food could be stored. From 8000 BC not only were the bands in these favoured areas across Afro-Eurasia adopting a sedentary pattern of life, but they were also starting to live in small villages or hamlets. For all its virtues, the practice of storing food in fixed sites created security problems that were never experienced by mobile HGBs, which specifically eschewed this practice. Stored food is a source of wealth that becomes a target for raiders, a pattern that was to become a major feature of relations in the international systems of the ancient and classical world.

Supporting this interpretation of what led to settlement is the fact that contemporary HGBs still vary from being highly mobile to being completely sedentary. By the same token, in areas where bands rely on the meat from big game animals, there is a greater need for leadership to organize the kill, thereby generating a degree of hierarchy within the band. Variations that can be observed amongst contemporary HGBs reflect a degree of complexity (Price and Brown 1985) that tends to undermine the evolutionary, population growth theory about how sedentary, hierarchical units emerged. The fact is that egalitarian farming tribes continue to exist today, sometimes living alongside sedentary hunter-gatherer tribes who also live in villages. These tribes have not been pushed to develop hierarchies as a consequence of their loss of mobility. And as we shall show in Part III, the nomadic tribes that formed in Central Asia and Arabia around 1000 BC were mobile, but also hierarchical in structure. These nomads by linking mobility with hierarchy were to have a huge impact on world history, often proving more than a match militarily for the sedentary empires that existed on the periphery of the nomadic terrain. The nomadic case demonstrates very clearly that there is no necessary link between egalitarianism and the potential for fission. Settlement and hierarchy, therefore, need to be treated as independent dimensions and their relationship must be treated as more complex than the familiar evolutionary story suggests.

As before we will use the central concepts drawn from our toolkit to organize this chapter, looking first at the defining characteristics of the sedentary tribes and hierarchical chiefdoms that joined the mobile HGBs as the dominant units of pre-international systems. In section 2 we examine changes in interaction capacity that occurred with the emergence of these new units. Section 3 surveys processes in pre-international systems that helped to form and reproduce tribes and chiefdoms, and section 4 explores the structural implications associated with the introduction of these new units.

# 1. UNITS

We argued in Chapter 6 that it is only possible to develop a meaningful picture of the HGB by seeing this unit as an integral feature of a larger system. The same line of argument will now be extended to tribes and chiefdoms, locating them within a wider pre-international system. The differences between tribal and chiefdom villages can only be fully explained by treating the village as a unit in a larger system. There has been a tendency to ignore the systemic links that form between villages (Liu 1996: 238) as well as the broader systemic processes and structures that develop between tribes and chiefdoms on the regional and macro-regional levels (Blanton et al. 1993). The basic differences between tribes and chiefdoms will be spelled out in this section and then the systemic context within which tribes and chiefdoms operated will be examined in more detail in the following two sections.

## SEDENTARY TRIBES

Sedentary tribes operate from a village base, and tribal villages have persisted down to the present day. According to McNeill (1997: 274) such villages provide an essential 'nexus for sustaining continuity of human life across the generations', though this assessment fails to acknowledge that for the vast bulk of history, the same could be said for mobile HGBs. As discussed above, the formation of villages represented a radical transformation from the system of mobile HGBs. Humans adopted a sedentary way of life, which seemed to arise in areas where food supplies were stable and abundant, and security concerns meant that they chose to live close together. From 8000 BC, the inhabitants of these favoured areas across the globe started to live in small villages or hamlets without the benefit of either domesticated animals or plants. As we see in the next section, the formation of villages is the product of a fundamental systemic process which also determines the size of the villages. When villages first started to form in the Near East they contained about 50 people. By the middle of the seventh millennium BC this had increased to around 100 and by the end of that millennium the size had grown further to about 300 (Maisels 1990: 128–9). The enlargement of the villages was in part a consequence of the gradually increasing size of the population in the region. But the increase in size would not have been possible without a concomitant growth in the availability of food within the immediate vicinity of the village. What happened during this period was that the village communities began to experiment with new techniques which over a very long period of time moved them from being hunter-gatherers to fully-fledged farmers. The innovations occurred at different times and in different places, but eventually they extended across the region. This brought about a revolution because, as regions were occupied by more people than could be sustained by hunter-gathering techniques, humans found themselves ultimately dependent on agriculture for survival. This outcome was an unintended consequence of the many innovations that occurred during the millennia after 8,000 BC. But it was also not an inevitable development, because there are today villages in New Guinea made up of around 100 hunter-gatherers living alongside similar sized farming villages (Roscoe 1996).

Two factors constrained the size of tribal villages. The first was the amount of food available. When a village reached its optimum size, the population divided and a new village was 'budded off' from the first village (Maisels 1990: 130). Second, it has been hypothesized that there is an optimum size for any social unit organized on an egalitarian basis. If the size of the group extends beyond this limit, then it is no longer possible to maintain the cohesion and internal order of the group on the basis of face-to-face, egalitarian relationships. Game theory demonstrates why egalitarian behaviour is the best strategy for individuals operating in small groups. Because everyone knows each other in such groups, individuals who attempt to cheat and maximize their returns at the expense of others will quickly find that nobody in the group will interact with them. As the size of the group increases, a point is reached when it is no longer possible for all members to engage in face-to-face contact, and at that juncture individuals can start to cheat more effectively because social sanctioning becomes less efficient (Kantner 1996: 45–6). Estimates of the largest coherent social unit that can be organized on a face-to-face, egalitarian basis vary between 300 (Forge 1972) and 500 (Kosse 1994).

Forge (1972) refers to these egalitarian units as ritual groups because they have a complex internal structure which forms the basis for the organization of the group's rituals. When villages 'bud off', the new group takes exactly the same form as the original village and Forge compares the process to the splitting of a cell, with the structure of the new cell replicating the structure of its parent. Chagnon's analysis of the fissioning that takes place within the villages inhabited by the Yanomamo Amazonian Indians who live on the border of Brazil and Venezuela illustrates this process very effectively (1977: 70–2).

Although villages persisted for several millennia as the most significant form of autonomous political unit, over the last three millennia they have been steadily engulfed by larger-scale political units.

*The demise of small-scale political units*

Throughout most of world history, humans have been organized in terms of small, distinct, although not autonomous units. Up to 8000 BC these largely took the form of mobile HGBs. During the next 7,500 years, the total human population expanded from around 5 million to around 100 million people, an increasing proportion of whom were living in villages. When communities become sedentary, the population starts to rise. One explanation for this is the reduced transportation demands on women, who in mobile HGBs had to carry small children, and who could not therefore support a second child until the first one could walk. Sedentary life permitted closer child spacing. But this rise is small, with a ceiling of about 1 per cent on the annual growth of population occurring even in very favourable circumstances. Maisels (1990: 121–3) estimates that at the start of the neolithic period the rate of increase was as low as 0.01 per cent.

It has been estimated that around 1000 BC there were 600,000 separate units mainly consisting of about 100 people (Carneiro 1978: 213–14). At that time, only a tiny fraction of the total number of units took the form of large-scale autonomous political organizations. By AD 500, despite a steady rise in population to nearly 200 million, the number of political organizations had dropped, according to Carneiro, to about 200,000 units, a very much more substantial percentage of which consisted of large-scale organizations such as city-states or empires. This tendency for large-scale organizations to engulf smaller political units has continued ever since with the result that today, when the population has risen to around 6,000 million, the vast majority of the global population is housed within just under 200 autonomous political units.

## CHIEFDOMS

As set out above, hierarchy provides the crucial structural difference between tribes and chiefdoms. In contrast to the egalitarian tribal villages we have just discussed, chiefdom villages were hierarchically structured and they also formed part of a broader hierarchy of villages which collectively constituted the chiefdom. Hierarchy is now such an embedded, almost defining, feature of political organization that it is surprising to learn how extraordinarily difficult it was to put this structure into place. Chiefdoms were generally unstable political systems and early attempts at consolidating political hierarchy often failed (Earle 1991: 4; Flannery 1999). As Brun (1995: 13) observes chiefdoms were characteristically fragile; they formed in one place, only to collapse and reappear elsewhere.

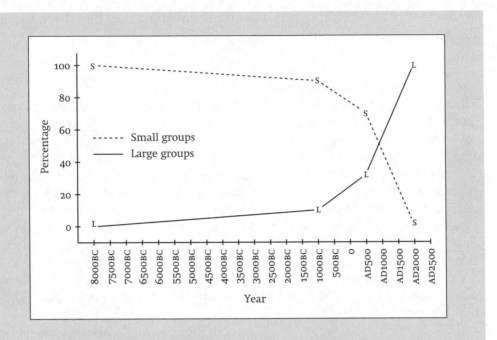

*Note:* The figure extrapolates from calculations made initially by Carneiro (1978: 213–14). Although the estimates are very crude, they suggest that, for most of world history, most human beings have lived in small rather than large groups.

*Source:* Taken from Kosse 1994.

*Figure 7.1 The demise of small-scale units*

Nevertheless, chiefdoms play a crucial role in our story because we accept the argument that the emergence of states is best explained as the unintended outcome of competition within and amongst chiefdoms (Savage 1997; Liu 1996).

Informal leadership exists in the tribal setting, but, as we will see in section 3, hierarchy is a very difficult structure to impose and a complex systemic process is required to reproduce it. Once established, however, it can become increasingly complex, and a distinction needs to be drawn between simple chiefdoms which consist of one level of hierarchy embracing several thousand people, and complex chiefdoms which consist of tens of thousands of people and two levels of hierarchy (Earle 1991: 1). Each village, therefore, has a chief, who is related to the chief on the next tier of the hierarchy, although only the chief at the top of the hierarchy has the authority to engage in diplomatic relations with other chiefdoms. This distinctive function means that with the formation of chiefdoms, functional differentiation was introduced as a defining feature of domestic political organization.

> *Hierarchy and the expansion in numbers of villages*
> Typologies of settlement systems often presuppose that as the number of settlements increases, so the potential for hierarchy increases. Nissen's typology (see Figure 7.2) demonstrates, for example, that although the number of settlements may be constrained by geographical factors, as the number increases, so it becomes apparent that centrally located settlements will have a natural advantage over their neighbours. As a result, there is a correlation between central location and position in an emerging hierarchy. The complexity of the hierarchy is also seen to be directly related to the number of settlements in the system. The problem with this explanation of hierarchy is that it fails to account for the non-emergence of hierarchies when settlements are egalitarian in structure. As we will see in more detail in sections 3 and 4, a more complex explanation is required for the emergence of hierarchy.

## 2. INTERACTION CAPACITY

Despite the emergence of new units, the transition period did not see any changes in physical technologies from those available to HGBs. But there were some dramatic, and mostly negative, changes in social interaction capacity resulting from a substantial increase in the number of languages spoken amongst sedentary tribes. Amongst HGBs there is low linguistic diversity and so individuals can communicate with each other over very large distances. Inuit populations from Greenland to Siberia only spoke between five and ten dialects from one of two language families, Eskimo and Aleut; and all Australian Aboriginal languages south of the northern coastal region belong to one language family (Nichols 1992).

The contrast with sedentary tribes could not, at first sight, be more marked. Amongst the sedentary farming tribes in Papua New Guinea, for example, Robb (1993: 752) observes that the maximum number of people speaking exactly the same language is about 500. It is unsurprising, therefore, that nearly one thousand of the modern world's remaining 5,000 languages are spoken here (Diamond 1997: 225). But a closer investigation of the evidence prompts a degree of caution. A survey of the native languages spoken in North America reveals that as one moves from the horticultural subtropical regions in the south, through the cultivated temperate regions, and then into the Arctic and Boreal regions occupied by hunter-gatherers, the size of territory within which a common language is spoken steadily increases (Robb 1993: 752). This finding can be generalized. Linguistic

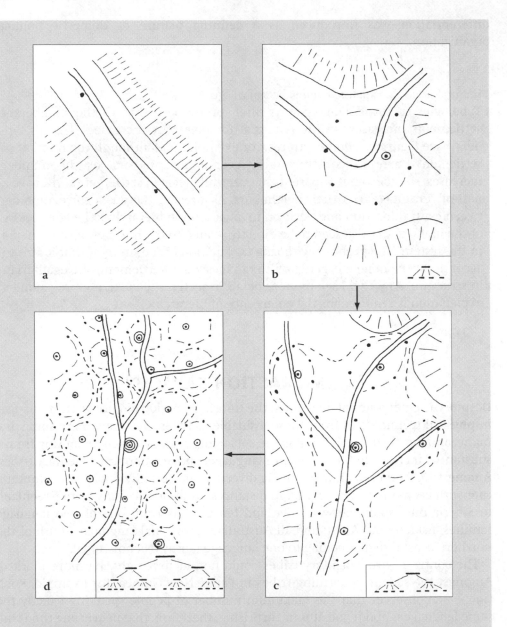

*Note:* The figure illustrates four systems that display increasing hierarchy: (a) isolated settlements in a narrow valley; (b) a one-tiered settlement system; (c) a two-tiered settlement system; (d) a four-tiered settlement system.

*Source:* Taken from Nissen 1988.

*Figure 7.2 Hierarchy of settlements*

diversity at the global level is inversely correlated with latitude and seasonality (Nichols 1990; Nettle 1998). It would seem that as uncertainty about food supplies increases, so individuals become involved in ever larger social networks in order to mitigate the risk. Farming, therefore, reduces but does not eliminate insecurity. Food supplies based on farming become more precarious as climatic conditions become harsher and more uncertain. As a result, the introduction of farming does not dispense with the pattern of social networks we associated with HGBs. Social networks can concertina in and out depending upon the level of risk and uncertainty confronted by a community (Nettle 1996).

As already noted, the adoption of a sedentary way of life led to the storing of food (O'Shea 1981) which in turn reduced the effects of environmental uncertainty. As a consequence, communities that had access to plentiful food supplies that could be easily stored, such as grain, no longer needed to participate in extensive social networks. But as discussed in Chapter 6, it is not only uncertainty that determines the size of a social network: small social groups need to participate in a viable breeding population. It might be thought that the boundaries of a language must embrace such a group. Yet it is not difficult to find recent examples of tribes that exchange brides despite speaking different languages. This phenomenon suggests that additional factors are needed to explain why villages establish linguistic markers that serve as a barrier to communication with adjacent tribes. These will be explored in the next section.

The emergence of hierarchical chiefdoms is also associated with very significant developments in interaction capacity. Again, attention has to be focused on language. Two important factors emerge. First, we find that as chiefdoms began to overtake sedentary tribes, so the size of language areas begin to increase again. But, second, and just as significant, there emerged elite languages which were distinct from the indigenous language spoken in any given area. This development meant that while language acted as a barrier, reducing the interaction capacity of the general population within a polity, the existence of a distinct elite language simultaneously facilitated social interaction capacity at the chiefdom level while helping to reinforce hierarchy within these political units (Robb 1993).

*The production and extinction of languages in Europe*
John Robb (1993) has provided a hypothetical history of language distribution in Europe from the end of the palaeolithic period, when HGBs prevailed, through to the onset of the historical era at the end of the Iron Age in the first millennium BC, by which time much of Europe was covered by agricultural villages and chiefdoms prevailed in many areas. What the story reveals is that initially there was very low linguistic diversity in Europe, but that languages proliferated very rapidly during the neolithic era. Mallory (1989) estimates that between 4500 and 2500 BC the number of languages spoken in Europe increased from between 20 and 40 to 400. Then, as population density increased

and large-scale political units began to overtake small-scale political units, an increasing number of languages became extinct and we returned to a situation of low linguistic diversity in Europe. We have assumed that this reflects a general process in world history.

What we see during this transition period is thus a weakening of the social networks that characterized relations amongst HGBs. The emergence of larger and more self-reliant units prefigures elements of international systems, and the

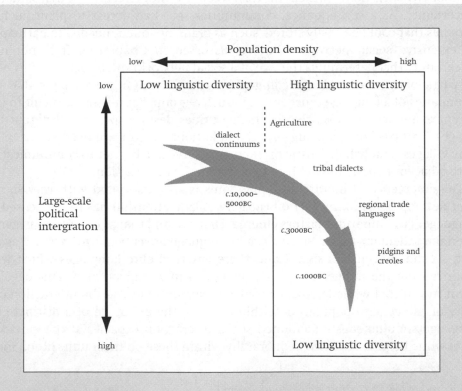

*Note:* This figure provides a theoretical model of how linguistic diversity changed over time in Europe. Initially, when population density and political integration were low, so too was linguistic diversity. As population density increased, so too did linguistic diversity. But with an increase in political integration, linguistic diversity contracted.

*Source:* Taken from Robb 1993.

*Figure 7.3 Linguistic diversity*

development of elite languages points towards the lingua francas and diplomatic practices of later times.

# 3. PROCESS

We have argued that it is very difficult to apply the idea of sectors to the internal and external activities of HGBs because of the way in which their 'military', 'political', 'economic', and 'social' behaviour blended together into a sectorally undifferentiated whole. Up to a point the same argument could be extended to sedentary tribes and chiefdoms, and it remains important not to lose sight of the social whole. But we accept O'Shea's (1981: 167) position that it is useful to draw sectoral distinctions in order to make sense of these transitional systems. As societies become larger and more complex, sectors take on more autonomy.

## SEDENTARY TRIBES

When HGBs became sedentary tribes they unintentionally generated a greater level of political insecurity without completely eliminating their economic insecurity. As a consequence, the social processes that linked HGBs now started to perform important economic and political functions.

### Military-political processes

One of the most paradoxical features that distinguishes the systems of sedentary tribes that have survived into the modern world is the persistent recurrence of war amongst communities that are tightly bound together by social and economic ties. Chagnon (1977: 162) for example, describes the Amazonian Yanomamo as the 'fierce people' not because war is occurring all the time, but, as in Hobbes's formulation, because 'warre' is an ever-present possibility, and 'even the least warlike villages suddenly find themselves embroiled in an active war'. Intervillage warfare amongst South American tribes takes the form of surprise raids with the purpose of killing as many of the enemy as possible together with a secondary aim of looting. Seizing land or gaining access to natural resources is not the objective of tribal warfare (Redmond 1994: 45). The war parties can range from 5 to 50 men and they can raid villages as much as ten days' walking distance away, so that the inhabitants of the warring villages will often speak different languages. Indeed, Meschner and Meschner (1998) report that villages on islands in the north Pacific carried out raids on other villages as far as 700 km (435 miles) from each other. Tribal villages, therefore, are always defensive units and in the case of tribal villages in South America, they are never closer than half an hour in walking distance (Redmond 1994: 46–8). Archaeological evidence reveals that as villages move closer to each other, they become progressively more heavily defended. Archaeologists who have examined the Tripolye cultural grouping in the Balkans, around 5000 BC, for example, show that, as the density of population increased in the area, settlements which were originally spaced at intervals averaging 23 to 24 km (14–15 miles) apart, moved progressively closer together, to within 3 to 4 km (2 miles) apart from each other. In the process, the settlements acquired defensive architecture such as palisades, ditches, and earthen banks (Mallory 1989: 196 and 242). As distances between villages shrink, so also do the interaction capacity requirements for warfare.

The evidence seems to suggest that once tribal villages come into existence, they find themselves locked into military competition with each other. It is not surprising to find anthropologists arguing, in a phrase that echoes the familiar assessment of the origins of the European state, that 'war makes states and states make war' (Tilly 1990: 28, 191). Harrison (1993: 18) insists that it is not so much 'groups that make war, but . . . war that makes groups'. In a classic restatement of the security dilemma, Roscoe (1996: 662) argues that violence may not be an inevitable contingency in human affairs, but 'the *perception* that violence is a *potential* contingency may be, and may therefore prompt measures to enhance physical safety against violence'. From this perspective, there may be less concern about violence amongst HGBs, not because they are inherently more peaceful, but because if population density is very low and the bands are constantly on the move in search of food, potential warring bands would find it difficult to come into contact. HGBs who feel threatened can move to a less densely populated area. But as areas become more densely populated and settled, the potential for dispersal diminishes. Roscoe (1996: 655) argues that at this juncture a different logic comes into place: a military logic of mutual defence. According to this logic, the level of security can be raised not by dispersal, but by increasing the number and proximity of people living together.

Yet for two reasons the need for security from external threats does not give rise to ever larger villages. First, the size of villages is constrained by available resources, though this can be offset as horticulture becomes more effective. More intractable is the constraint on nucleation for security purposes created by the size limitation of egalitarian organization. The potential for internal conflict rises geometrically with village size (Roscoe 1996: 655). The constant tendency for tribal villages to fission suggests that the new units must be secure units.

Egalitarianism also has a profound affect on the process of war, creating an asymmetrical relationship between offence and defence. Tribal villages are more defensive than offensive units. Members of a village have a vested interest in collaborating to defend themselves, but this does not extend to operating offensively. In the absence of a hierarchy, there is no one to organize offensive operations. Indeed, it is considered an arduous task to persuade villagers to join a war party and villages sometimes seek the help of a successful warrior from another village to lead a war party (Redmond 1994: 45). On the other hand, there are always incipient leaders within tribal villages, and raiding is one way that these individuals can gain prestige. But this feature of war is not necessarily a warlord route to hierarchy. Tribes are often suspicious of war-band leaders, and keep them from other leadership roles. In addition, tribal villages contain various factions that operate quite independently when establishing war parties (Roscoe 1996: 654). The very existence of competing internal factions deters the emergence of hierarchy and encourages the tendency for villages to fission whenever the possibility of hierarchy emerges (Spencer 1991). Nucleation thus provides a partial solution to the security dilemma which arises once human beings begin to adopt a sedentary way of life, but it does so at the expense of consolidating the conditions that precipitate the initial sources of insecurity.

Numelin (1967) reveals, however, that insecurity is not completely endemic. The potential for conflict is mitigated by a capacity for diplomacy. Heralds were given effective diplomatic immunity when they entered an enemy village. Heralds often had kinsfolk in the enemy village, thereby helping to bolster their immunity. The heralds or ambassadors frequently carried a 'message stick' which Numelin (1967: 96) equates to the 'diploma' presented by diplomats to a foreign monarch in Renaissance Europe to confirm their status. Numelin (1950) has also suggested that whereas war leaders of tribes were generally temporary appointments, peace leaders frequently held more permanent positions. The process of peace-making between two warring tribes was invariably accompanied by extensive ceremony.

### Economic processes

Since insecurity is a product of adopting a sedentary way of life it follows that there must be some advantages to encourage this development. These lie in the economic arena. Unlike HGBs, which rely on their mobility, low density, and the reciprocal support of neighbours, the adoption of a sedentary way of life generates the very different strategy of storage to reduce vulnerability, and this strategy stimulates more explicit economic processes of trade. Settled communities abandon the mobile HGBs' practice of coming together to consume surplus subsistence commodities at a particular point in time. Wild grain, fish, nuts, and many fruits, for example, can be stored. Goods that are capable of being stored can also be exchanged. Sedentary groups thus have incentives to trade with others who produce goods different from their own, embarking on the road towards a process of complementary exchange. Trade amongst settled human communities usually follows the natural division of labour created by the products of different climate zones. Along the Pacific coast of South America, for example, trade developed between highland farmers and coastal fishermen.

### Complementary exchange in North America

Throughout North America widespread exchange was, from a very early stage in the human history of the continent, always the norm. Environmental diversity had the effect of generating interdependence amongst people operating over vast distances. Interdependence developed after they started trading staple foodstuffs as well as luxury goods. These goods were passed along a complex network of trails, some of them marked by carvings on rocks (petroglyphs) and shrines. The obsidian trade was a vital element in these trading networks. But down these trails, linking a multitude of small bands and larger tribes, there also passed a wide range of goods. According to Fagan (1991: 191), along the Pacific coast, for example, there was trade in 'acorns, salt, fish, shell artefacts, clothing, baskets, even dogs'. The trails ran from Vancouver Island, onto the mainland, and then all the way down the coast to southern California. As part of this trading network, the nomadic bands of the Diegueño peoples in southern California moved into the interior each year to collect acorns which were then passed along the trails. In later times, beads made of clam shells or *olivella* were used as a simple form of 'money'. The Pacific region was also linked with the south-west. One well-established trail brought Pacific sea shells from near Los Angeles across the desert, linking up with the Gila River and then distributing the shells to the villages along the various tributaries (Fagan 1991: 191, 217, 279).

There is also a second form of exchange, 'redundant exchange' (O'Shea 1981: 173), which occurs in situations of broad and undifferentiated environments. Here individuals in villages can deal with localized shortages by drawing on foods that have been stored. But such a strategy cannot help in the case of large-scale disturbances such as drought and the timing of frosts and by the same token, nor can help be sought from immediate neighbours. Redundant exchange systems, therefore, will tend to be more extensive than complementary systems and there will be a greater emphasis on non-food commodities. So while, in the case of a complementary process, foodstuffs will be a regular part of the exchange network, in the case of a redundant process, foodstuffs are only moved in times of local shortage. But because the exchange links must be maintained, trade channels will be kept open by the exchange of prestige goods. The acquisition of these prestige goods thus forms a very important form of indirect storage. This form of storage 'encompasses all those processes which transform foodstuffs into a more stable, alternative form, from which food value may later be recovered' (O'Shea 1981: 169). As a consequence, when trading partners experience a shortage of a subsistence commodity, then they will have to part with some of their durable prestige goods in return for the deficient non-durable subsistence commodity. As we will see in the discussion of chiefdoms, this process lays the basis for the growth of hierarchy.

### Societal processes

Given the persistence of war in tribal settings, it follows that exchange is a potentially dangerous activity. Peaceful relations must be secured in terms of the exchange process itself. This is one of the reasons why it is difficult to draw a clear-cut distinction between political, economic, and social processes. The economic ratio, or terms of trade, becomes a diplomatic move unrelated to the laws of supply and demand. The result is that the rate of exchange can be seen to take on the functions of a peace treaty and it has been observed that when these trading encounters take place there is a tendency to over-reciprocate. Intertribal relations under these circumstances are characterized by generalized reciprocity, with trade taking place under the cover of gift-giving. The kula provides a useful illustration of the important role played by social ceremonies in sustaining both economic, social, and political relations (Persson 1983). Processes like the kula are extremely important in tribal situations because tribes are not highly centralized and hierarchical institutions like the state. As a consequence, social relations are very fluid both within and between the tribes.

*The kula*

The kula ceremony takes place around an archipelago of islands in the western Pacific (see Map 7.1). The ceremony involves the exchange of two types of valuable ornament: long necklaces made of red shell which travel clockwise around the islands, and arm bracelets made of white shell which move in an anticlockwise direction. Every other year, all the members of a tribe who participate in the kula gather together and travel clockwise in their canoes to an adjacent island. All members of the expedition have a lifelong partner from whom they will receive a number of bracelets in the course of the kula, although the kula also involves other less permanent partners. On a return expedition, the partner will receive some necklaces in exchange. A central objective of the kula is to facilitate trade. It is a peace-making ceremony conducted with a potential enemy while at the same time, the tribes can barter over more utilitarian goods without friction as a 'side issue' (Fortune 1932: 208–9). More recent analyses of the kula have suggested that it is a much more complex process than was originally recognized (Leach and Leach 1983; Persson 1983). The bartering, for example, is 'predicated on the temporary presence of a society' instantiated by the kula (Hodges 1988: 99; Hart 1986). The kula promotes cross-cutting cleavages which promote stability within and between the tribes (Uberoi 1962). Because the kula operates on a principle of generalized reciprocity, with reciprocation always being delayed to the future, there is considerable scope for sharp-practice or *wabuwabu*. Indeed, tribes outside the kula dislike the process for this very reason (Chowning 1983). For example, an individual with a very famous bracelet may receive a number of very valuable necklaces from various partners, each believing that he will receive the valuable bracelet in return. On the return expedition, only one of the partners will receive the bracelet. The animosity of the disappointed partners is not directed

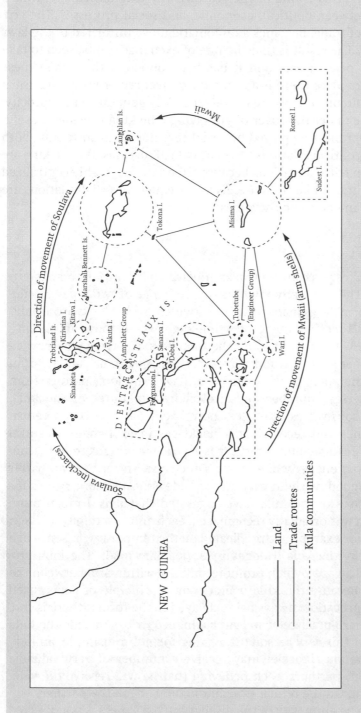

*Note:* The map identifies the archipelago of islands in the western Pacific that participate in the kula ceremony. Long necklaces made of red shell travel clockwise around the islands, and arm bracelets made of white shell move in an anticlockwise direction. The dotted circles represent the kula communities. The dotted squares represent the districts indirectly affected by the kula.

*Source:* Taken from Hodder 1978.

*Map 7.1 Islands participating in the kula*

at the individual who practised the *wabuwabu*; instead, it is turned against the member of their own tribe whose prestige has risen with the acquisition of the bracelet. A comparison can be made with the complex of rivalries which often exist within and between cricket or football teams operating in the same league, where the rivalries within the teams are offset by the rivalries between the teams. Both sets of rivalries have to be contained if the overall process is to persist. The kula ensures that trade can take place peacefully, and also that conflict within and between tribes is contained.

## CHIEFDOMS

The economic and social processes associated with tribal villages are closely linked to the integrated processes of HGBs because these processes are designed to deal with the vulnerability of individuals in a potentially hostile environment. It is the emergence of war that distinguishes these two types of units and we have linked this development to the sedentary nature of the tribal villages. The systemic processes generated by chiefdoms, however, move us even further from those of HGBs because not only is war a persistent feature of the system, but, like economic exchange, it is also concerned with the promotion and consolidation of hierarchy.

### Military-political process
Amongst tribal villages, war was an ever present phenomenon, but because of the egalitarian nature of the units it was not a source of major political change. Because of the larger size and resources of chiefdoms, war is a more significant process in pre-international systems made up of chiefdoms. By themselves, chiefs could raise a war party made up of hundreds of men, but with the help of allies they were sometimes in a position to extend the war party to many thousands of men (Redmond 1994: 46). In contrast to tribal raids, which aimed to settle scores, or bolster the prestige of the members of the war party within their own villages, the aim of chiefdoms which went to war was to extend the land and power of the chief. The political environment of chiefdoms was thus very different from that of tribal villages. Whereas all tribal villages were potential targets of attack, with the emergence of chiefdoms, villages formed a hierarchy, and it was the village at the top of the hierarchy, the paramount village, that was most vulnerable to attack. In contrast to villages lower down the hierarchy which were often left undefended, the dominant village was very heavily defended. One of the features of the paramount village in a chiefdom is that it will sometimes absorb the local population and begin to look much more like a town than a village. By the same token, handicraft industries that are initially decentralized throughout the village system become concentrated at the centre of the chiefdom.

Because chiefdoms rarely if ever form in isolation, the potential for expanding control by means of military force is both limited and unstable. Although warfare is a prevalent feature of these pre-international systems, Earle (1991: 6) argues that chiefdoms often effectively block each other, making it difficult for any one of them to expand spatially by absorbing neighbouring areas in the vicinity. But, if anything, chiefdoms intensify the competition for power and status both within and amongst themselves. Internal factions in the paramount village compete for power at the centre, and there are also factions vying for power in the subordinate villages. This factionalism within chiefdoms explains their instability, and makes it difficult for a paramount chief to consolidate his power or use it effectively to expand. It is generally agreed, therefore, that military force alone cannot adequately account for the emergence of chiefdoms or explain the dynamics of the resulting system. It is necessary to turn instead to the economic and social processes at work within pre-international systems of chiefdoms.

### Economic processes

The emergence and consolidation of hierarchy can be most effectively accounted for in terms of the economic processes of pre-international systems. It seems probable that the exchange of scarce and unevenly distributed agricultural commodities commenced long before the development of agriculture 'had become capable of furnishing a major portion of the food supply' (Runnels and van Andel 1988: 98). In tribal villages, these 'cash crops' were traded for the prestige durables (things like stone axes, shell jewellery, and precious stones such as lapis lazuli and carnelian) which provided a form of indirect food storage. But with agricultural innovations, these prestige goods could accumulate differentially and at that juncture, these items became more clearly identified as a source of wealth as well as a form of insurance against environmental disaster. Moreover, once animals were domesticated, in addition to providing a very effective buffer against crop failure (O'Shea 1981: 169), they also became an important independent source of wealth, as the boxed story on New Guinea illustrates.

*Agriculture and the emergence of social stratification in New Guinea*
Farming communities have been traced back for 9,000 years in the western highlands of New Guinea. Cultivation for several thousand years focused on the taro, a tuber which flourishes in moist conditions. Under dry conditions, a good crop yields between 4 and 5 tonnes per hectare (1.5–2 tons per acre), but in the swamplands, which began to be drained over 2,000 years ago, production was increased to almost 13 tonnes per hectare (5 tons per acre). This increase encouraged the domestication of pigs which became a valuable object of exchange as well as a major source of protein. About 250 years ago, however, the sweet potato was introduced to New Guinea. Not only does the sweet potato generate much higher yields than the taro but its food content is much superior

for both pigs and people. Pigs became an even more important object of exchange. Feil has observed that as production increased, 'social credit was established by sending pigs outwards along lengthy expanding exchange chains'. Pigs became 'the "essential coin" for proliferating transactions' and politics and competition increased as the range of transactions grew (Feil 1987: 29). Pigs, therefore, became a crucial source of wealth and power.

The intensification of agriculture can be seen as the unintended consequence of attempts, initially, to provide a buffer against environmental risk and uncertainty, but later, of attempts to generate wealth. Trade was the essential process needed to achieve these related but ultimately very different ends. The intensification of agriculture was also, in its turn, the source of two further unintended consequences which then created the potential for the formation of chiefdoms. First, agriculture enabled the size of villages to increase. In New Guinea, egalitarian tribal villages grew in size during the nineteenth century to 1,500 people (Roscoe 1996). And in terms of world history, agriculture made the establishment of towns, and ultimately cities, possible. But a second and very important unintended consequence of the intensification of agriculture was the promotion of status distinctions and social rank within and between villages. There appears to be a feedback loop linking the intensification of agriculture, the acquisition of wealth, and the emergence of hierarchy. What the boxed story of stratification in New Guinea demonstrates is that agriculture is not sufficient to generate wealth or hierarchy—these attributes only emerge when there is an expansion in the production of cash crops and animals which are capable of being stored and traded.

When an individual has accumulated wealth, it becomes possible to use the wealth to establish allies, thereby overcoming factionalism and beginning the process of stratification and centralization which can ultimately end in the formation of the state. To consolidate his position, an incipient chief will act to monopolize the source of his wealth by regulating the flow of goods into and out of the village. He establishes himself as a middleman, regulating the economic links with the outside world. This development does not account for the hierarchical relations that a paramount village establishes with its neighbours, but paramount villages will generally be located close to a strategic resource. Raijgir, a paramount village in the north-east of India during the second millennium BC, for example, is very close to the largest deposits of iron ore in India (Allchin 1995: 82). Higham (1989: 234) also argues, in the context of South-East Asia, that the emergence of chiefdoms can be related to access to a circumscribed resource. The access might be to 'salt, copper, tin or good land; control over a strategic position such as a mountain pass or a river crossing; or a monopoly, through the fortunes of geography, over access to prestige exotic goods such as glass beads, iron or agate jewellery'. But whatever the resource, the critical factor is that it generate wealth through the process of trade. Sometimes, a resource can be sufficiently important and widespread that it can sustain several chiefdoms.

*Salt and the rise and fall of chiefdoms in Austria*
Salt played a significant role in the establishment of chiefdoms in Austria during the first millennium BC. Between 1000 BC and 500 BC deep mining shafts were dug in Hallstatt and the salt was exported over extensive distances. It is assumed that during this era, tribal leaders used their control over the resource to consolidate their position and establish themselves as chiefdoms. Local cemeteries, contemporary with the mines, contain very rich jewellery and metalwork which had been traded over a distance of 500 km (300 miles) and buried with the local chief. These chiefs collapsed soon after 500 BC, at the same time that the inland salt mines in Europe were replaced by solar evaporated salt from Europe's north-west coastline. The change in the direction of the salt trade has been attributed to large-scale population movements and the disruption of long-established trading routes (Alexander 1993: 653–7).

*Societal process*
Because the sense of hierarchy is still relatively tenuous, and attached more to individuals than to institutions, chiefdoms are extraordinarily fragile units. Many of their societal processes are consequently aimed at establishing and maintaining hierarchy. Factions remain a feature of chiefdom villages so that the potential for villages to fission persists and there is also a potential for villages to switch allegiance to a new village or another chiefdom. Because the strength of a chiefdom, like the strength of a tribal village, is very largely determined by the number of people it embraces, chiefs are very anxious to prevent any fissiparious tendencies. Factions pose a constant threat to the power of the leader and the coherence of the unit. By the same token, chiefs are always willing to absorb new people and villages in an effort to maintain or enhance the strength of the chiefdom. It is unsurprising, therefore, that chiefs relied on a wide range of strategies in an effort to maintain and foster societal cohesion. They were constantly aware that their support could always be threatened by an aspiring chief who could usurp the power of the dominant chief by cultivating ties with dissident factions within the various villages which constitute the chiefdom (Spencer 1991).

As we have seen, chiefs relied heavily on economic and political processes to preserve their position. On the political front, where the paramount village was heavily defended, the remaining villages in the chiefdom were left undefended. This strategy not only emphasized the status of the paramount chief, but it also pushed the undefended villagers to the centre for protection in the event of an attack. On the economic front, the paramount chief endeavoured to monopolize the storage of subsistence resources—another reason to protect the centre (Wesson 1999). This strategy not only enabled the paramount chief to take charge of the redistribution of these resources but it also gave him control over the resources for feasting which was a crucial social institution used to garner support. The system of centralized storage also ensured that a paramount chief had to act as middleman in trade relations with the outside world.

Social contact with the outside world was absolutely crucial to maintaining the power of paramount chiefs. It was this factor which elevated them above their peers. In the first instance, it gave them a monopoly access to prestige goods which, by definition, were only obtainable from the outside world. Their control over prestige goods served two important ends. First, these prestige goods could get passed down through the local hierarchy, in return for tribute, thereby consolidating power relations at every level. But as prestige goods were circulated locally, the goods lost their value as a source of status, thereby undermining their second role, which was to differentiate paramount leaders on the basis of access to prestige goods that only they possessed. To relieve pressure from internal factions these prestige goods would eventually enter general circulation, creating a constant need for new and exclusive prestige goods. This persistent demand accounts for the changing motifs on prestige artefacts as well as for the introduction of new items into the exchange circuits, such as copper daggers and amber beads in the case of European chiefdoms. Given the nature of this process, it is unsurprising to find that new exotic products, like the fine pottery associated with the bell beakers, or the elaborately designed copper daggers, would be exchanged or emulated across the expanding trade networks, thereby generating a degree of cultural commonality across the extensive areas covered by these trading networks. Paramount chiefs were linked together by their demand for and access to prestige goods that reflected the existence of an international style. The importance attached to these prestige goods simultaneously linked paramount chiefs to each other, and dissociated them from their followers.

This need for chiefs to try to distance themselves from their followers is a universal feature of chiefdoms. Chiefs endeavoured to promote a sense of awe in their followers by possession of exotic goods to which no one else had access. In this way, the transfer of exotic goods became delinked from the task of maintaining links between widely dispersed bands, and shifted towards helping to consolidate the power of an emerging elite. In traditional societies members of an elite are expected to be 'especially familiar with esoteric resources' and the distance travelled by a good plays an important part in rendering the good exotic (Helms 1988: 263). It was not only the possession of goods brought from distant and 'mysterious worlds' which was significant. Chiefs would be expected to have knowledge of the goods and their places of origin. Renfrew argues that it is 'in the nature of things that only those who travel may return as bearers of exotic knowledge as well as exotic goods' (Renfrew 1993: 9). With the emergence of chiefdoms, exotic goods were not always passed down the line, but may have been procured directly by elites as a mechanism for validating their authority and status. There is a growing recognition that this control of distance can play an important role in the establishment and consolidation of hierarchy. In systems made up of tribal villages, as with HGBs, the amounts of any exotic product decline with distance from its source. But as studies of amber—an important prestige good—illustrate, with the development of hierarchy, such prestige goods start to be found in considerable amounts at significant distances from their source (Beck and Shennan 1991).

Paramount chiefs also endeavoured to awe their followers by associating themselves with exotic knowledge and supernatural forces. As a consequence, chiefdoms are not only associated with hierarchical settlement patterns, but also with elaborate monuments such as chambered tombs and massive ceremonial centres, such as the henges which exist across the length and breadth of Britain and Ireland. With the establishment of an ever wider network of contacts between paramount chiefs, not only did commonalties in culture develop, but prototypes of monuments developed in one region were then copied in another, and built in a larger size and more complex form (Bradley 1993). Competitive activities of this kind are a product of the hierarchical world of chiefdoms, where chiefs constantly had to strive to assert their superiority against aspiring chiefs within the chiefdom and other paramount chiefs on the outside. Survival depended not only on political and economic processes but also upon the capacity to monopolize societal links with the outside world, a process which simultaneously helped to internationalize the system while deepening internal hierarchies.

## 4. STRUCTURE

The shift from HGBs to tribes and chiefdoms begins to unravel some of the difficulties encountered in the previous chapter in applying structural concepts to HGBs. As units become larger, more settled, and more complex, elements of sectoral differentiation begin to emerge out of the more or less undifferentiated social organization and interaction of HGBs. Settlement and food storage beget both war and trade as distinct activities. Trade stimulates social differentiation into a recognizably political hierarchy, which in turn stimulates trade in durable prestige goods in order to reproduce itself. Larger units with stored food become more self-contained in terms of both reproductive and food requirements, and one can begin to see entities that are much more state-like in character than HGBs, albeit not yet stable in construction. Although these developments stimulated an increase in the range and volume and diversity of trade, it would still be a gross distortion to talk about market structures for even the most developed pre-international systems. Although some aspects of trade were becoming more distinct there was still heavy linkage between exchange and social relations with-in and between these units. Central storage of food, and the monopoly position of the paramount chiefs could perhaps be interpreted as a precursor of command economies, but again one still runs serious risks of anachronism.

Somewhat clearer, and therefore worth discussion, is the apparent move towards fulfilling the conditions for structure in the neorealist, military-political sense. Tribal villages systems, and even more so systems of chiefdoms, display many of the necessary qualities for neorealist structure. The units become more distinct and autonomous, and relations amongst them might be thought of as anarchic. They engage in warfare with each other, and consequently live in per-manent insecurity and fear of attack, requiring increasingly elaborate defensive measures. Can it therefore be argued that these late pre-international systems are structured in the neorealist sense? Probably not. What we see instead is that these pre-international systems raise questions for neorealist assumptions both about how international systems begin, and about the nature of the units necessary to form politically structured international systems.

In Waltz's formulation, units emerge in isolation and only become constrained by structural forces when the units begin to co-act. But the story unfolded here shows that this is not how pre-international systems develop. HGBs, tribal vil-lages, and chiefdoms have always been dependent, although for different reasons, on participation in a wider social system for their survival. There has never been a time when units developed and operated in isolation from each other. If we never-theless accept Waltz's argument that once units begin to co-act they must be constrained by structural forces, it follows that units must always have been con-strained by the anarchic structure of the systems within which they operated. Three questions arise: (1) what type of interaction qualifies as 'beginning to co-act'; (2) are these systems anarchic; and (3) does the nature of the structural constraints change according to the nature of the dominant unit?

On the first question, since neorealism seems to presuppose military-political interactions, HGB systems probably do not qualify because they have too little that could be identified as war or politics. Tribal systems begin to qualify, and chief-dom systems definitely seem to fit. The answer to the second question seems to fall similarly. HGB systems are not anarchically structured in the neorealist sense because the units are not self-contained. The members of the unit are outwardly oriented and this outward orientation is essential to their survival. Tribal villages retain some of the outward orientation of HGBs, but being settled also take on some appearance of anarchic structure. Chiefdoms become more self-contained and territorial, and it does not seem an exaggeration to think of chiefdom systems as anarchic.

On the third question, it would seem that the structural constraints do vary according to the nature of the dominant unit. Our analysis in this chapter suggests that in pre-international systems of tribal villages and chiefdoms there is a more complicated and interesting story to tell about structure than the oversimplified one offered by Waltz. With the emergence of sedentary tribes the effects of military-political structure become much stronger. Sedentary units are much more vulnerable to attack than mobile units, and this sense of vulnerability represents a structural constraint which precipitates nucleation. With the formation of villages, the basic elements of an anarchic political structure are put into play. But Waltz's conception of a political structure does not yet function, because although the units are positioned in an anarchic fashion, there is still very little by way of a power structure in place. Tribal units are too decentralized to generate much in the way of unit power characteristics. Their egalitarian domestic structure means that they are not organized to make concerted attacks on each other. While villages are in danger of being attacked, it is from factions in other villages rather than by the village as a whole. It is thus by no means obvious that larger villages are necessarily more powerful attackers, although they may be more capable of defending themselves. For this reason, egalitarian tribal villages are defensive rather than offensive organizations. They are not self-sufficient units, and like HGBs they are constrained to establish economic and social links with other tribal villages in order to ensure their survival.

An examination of chiefdoms also reveals that Waltz's conception of structural constraints is still not in place. A chiefdom is made up of loosely linked villages and it is difficult to say whether the village or the chiefdom is the fundamental unit (a problem that will recur when we come to think about empires in Part III). If we take the chiefdom as the basic unit, then it can be argued that the units in the system are 'like units', with clear signs of structural and functional differentiation within the unit, because the paramount village is defended whereas the others are not, and the paramount chief exercises power/authority over the chiefs who rule the subordinate villages. However, these units are very fragile and the location of power is constantly shifting as villages (especially those on the periphery of the chiefdom) and individuals shift their allegiances. Thus although chiefdoms might at first seem to fit within the neorealist model, their fragility as units means that they do not meet its requirements. Chiefdoms are largely the creation of individual leaders whose status is achieved rather than ascribed. In other words, they lack institutions stable enough to give them much permanence or robustness as units in international systems. Because of this, structural pressures cannot work as neorealists envisage because the unit is as likely to disintegrate as to adapt. Because the units are ephemeral, structural forces cannot work in the way that they do amongst more institutionally developed, and so more robust, units.

One other point that might be made is about societal structure. In Chapter 6 we argued that HGB systems displayed something analogous to 'world society' in their shared systems of belief and identity. By creating more autonomous and self-reliant units, and increasing the barriers of language, the shift from HGBs to tribal villages eroded this world society. One might, however, see some of the developments in chiefdom systems as precursors either of a world society at the level of elites, or perhaps of an international society in which ruling elites shared elements of culture, language, and an exclusive right of mutual contact that has some resemblance to diplomacy.

# Conclusion to Part II

We hope that these two chapters have provided an answer to those readers who might at the start have been sceptical about the utility of trying to push the concept of international systems, and its associated theoretical baggage, back into prehistory. Sceptics might have wondered both about the methodological validity of pushing modern concepts so far out of their formative historical context, and about the substantive purpose of adding the vast swath of prehistory, with all its baggage of archaeological and anthropological debate, onto the already crowded subject matter of IR.

It is clear that many of the concepts from our toolkit do not fit well with the empirical referents of prehistory. But there are two big rewards to be reaped from attempting to apply IR concepts to prehistory. First is that the attempt enables us to tell a plausible story about the precursors to international systems. As the development unfolds from HGBs to tribes to chiefdoms we find more and more elements that either fit with, or are reasonable functional analogues for, the concepts in our toolkit. There is a clear unfolding towards more state-like entities and more international system-like behaviours. We can elaborate in some detail the conditions out of which international systems developed, and as the fit with our toolkit thickens, we can also draw a pretty firm boundary between pre- and full international systems. The methodology thus does produce useful results, and the story it reveals is clearly necessary to understanding how international systems formed. They did not just spring into existence *de novo* when units began to co-act.

The second reward is that grappling with the material of prehistory in terms of IR concepts exposes many fundamental assumptions within IR theory that otherwise remain obscured from view. When one uses IR theory on modern international systems it is all too easy to lose sight of the fact that the theories are mostly rooted in modern history, and that this link carries with it a whole raft of built-in assumptions. Looking at prehistory forces one to ask both what types of interactions and what type of units are necessary to form international systems. Prehistory reveals the enormous difference made by whether the units in the system are mobile or territorially fixed. It shows the difficulty of thinking in IR terms about units that are not hierarchically structured internally, and whose activities consequently lack sectoral differentiation. It also shows how IR theory assumes units that are robust and durable in the sense that they possess institutions capable of reproducing both themselves and the unit. Without such institutions, as shown by the discussion of chiefdoms, the units are too ephemeral to respond to structural pressures.

Prehistory also throws into sharp relief just how much IR theory, in particular neorealism and neoliberalism, builds on the assumption that political units can be thought of as having an inside and an outside. This assumption also prevails in most of the historical sociology literature that assumes the state can be treated as a 'power container' or an 'iron cage'. But the inside/outside distinction has little meaning in the context of HGBs because each band forms an intrinsic part of a much broader and highly interdependent totemic landscape. The same is less true of tribal villages, because despite complex links with neighbouring villages, an incipient security dilemma encourages individuals to look to their own village for protection. Nevertheless, institutions such as the kula demonstrate that villages are not autonomous political units that can be unambiguously con-figured as having an inside and an outside. And the same can be said of villages operating within chiefdoms, although the inside/outside dimension does start to become more firmly outlined in the case of paramount villages. But the inside/outside configuration is much less firmly etched in the case of peripheral villages.

Because IR theory assumes that units are territorially fixed, that they are hier-archically structured (and functionally and structurally differentiated in their internal organization), that they have robust and durable institutions, that they have an inside and an outside, and that they engage in sectorally differentiated activities such as diplomacy, war, and trade, it is unsurprising that IR has had such difficulty dealing with the many weak states that entered the international sys-tem with decolonization. But for the fact that they are being held in place by strong patterns of international recognition and support, many of them (think of Afghanistan, Tadjikistan, Somalia, Liberia, Sierra Leone, Congo, and others) could almost be understood as chiefdoms.

That said, readers should remember the warning given in the introduction to this part of the book that we have oversimplified the story of prehistory by bund-ling it neatly into the three packages of HGBs, tribal villages, and chiefdoms. It is important to avoid reading into this an overly determined story of evolution lead-ing from one to the other and eventually to states and international systems. The reality is that HGBs and tribal villages continued to exist in many parts of the world right up to modern times. Only in some places did the transition from HGBs to settled tribal villages take place, and only in some of those places did chiefdoms develop. Very special circumstances had to be in play before HGBs became tribal villages and before tribal villages became chiefdoms. Over the whole of the planet there are huge variations in how this story unfolded, and these variations matter for the story we will tell in Part III about the international systems of the ancient and classical world. Different kinds of chiefdoms gave rise to different kinds of state. In Mesopotamia, for example, the first city-states were a product of intense competition among very hierarchical chiefdoms, with populations concentrating in emerging cities. In such city-state systems, like those in Sumeria, Greece, and Mesoamerica, urbanization was very high (up to 80 per cent) and power was root-ed in the cities. In China, Egypt, and the Andes the precursors to the early states were much less hierarchical chiefdoms, and the result was territorial states in which urbanization was relatively low, and cities were smaller. In these kingdoms cities were administrative and ceremonial creations of the state, rather than being self-made centres of power in their own right (Trigger 1993: 1–26).

# Part III

# THE RISE AND INTERLINKAGE OF MULTIPLE INTERNATIONAL SYSTEMS IN THE ANCIENT AND CLASSICAL WORLD

## INTRODUCTION TO PART III

The chapters in this section carry the story across the divide from pre-international to full international systems. We will be looking at the establishment, consolidation, and evolution of the first generation of real international systems: 'real' in the sense of sharing enough features with modern international systems to establish them as members of the same general class of phenomena. One way of understanding this transformation is in terms of Walker's (1993) 'inside/outside' distinction introduced in Chapter 4. In the pre-international world described in Part II, it was not really possible to differentiate between the domestic and the international. Units were mostly too small, too inter-dependent, and not sufficiently hierarchical in their internal organization to generate 'inside' and 'outside' political realms, though chiefdoms clearly began to do so. But with the formation of city-states and empires, units became large and internally complex enough to consolidate an inside/outside political construction. The point at which such an inside/outside construction takes hold is the point at which true international systems come into being.

As also shown in Part II, the first international systems did not simply materialize into being where nothing had been before. They evolved in places where the productivity and trade of the pre-international systems were most fully developed, and where populations had reached sufficient mass and concentration to enable new types of unit, the city-state and the empire, to come into being. In other words, the first international systems were nested in pre-international systems. Once established, this first type of international system had a very long run, occupying nearly five millennia between the rise of civilization in Sumeria, and the creation of a world economic system by European national states during the sixteenth century AD. During that period, several versions of this type of system arose at different locations and different times, and it was normal for there to be a number of them in existence simultaneously in different locations around the planet.

We cannot tell this immense story in any detail. During these five millennia dozens of peoples, cultures, religions, and empires came and went; hundreds of cities were founded, some to flourish and others to die; and thousands of battles were won and lost. Happily, our toolkit allows us to simplify this epic. It reveals that underlying all the complexities is a manageable set of themes that captures the development and consolidation of international systems across the entire ancient and classical era. For although this era occupies the bulk of recorded human history, in terms of international systems, most of it can be seen as repeated variations of a basic pattern. Setting out that pattern, and characterizing the distinctive first-generation international systems that evolved within it, is the purpose of the next four chapters.

Its main elements can be summarized as follows:

- The crystallization of two new types of unit out of the more developed and populous parts of pre-international systems: city-states and sedentary empires; and two new types of units in the undeveloped and more sparsely populated desert and steppe regions of Afro-Eurasia: nomadic tribes and empires.
- The persistence of sedentary tribes and hunter-gatherer bands in pre-international systems and the growth of contacts between international systems and pre-international systems.
- Increases in interaction capacity in international systems arising from a package of technological developments, most notably the wheel, roads, sailing ships, and the domestication and breeding of animals suitable for pulling, packing, and riding.
- Increases in interaction capacity in international systems arising from a package of social developments, most notably, multilingualism and lingua francas, writing, 'universal' religions, money and credit systems, trade diasporas, and rudimentary forms of diplomacy.
- Intensification of trade in international systems with knock-on consequences for many pre-international systems as a result of higher populations, more diversified production and demand, and improved interaction capacity.
- The steady expansion of international systems into the territory occupied by pre-international systems (see Map 8.1).

Not all of the elements distinguishing international from pre-international systems needed to be present in every case. For example, the Incas did without writing, none of the civilizations in the Americas developed the wheel, and the wheel largely disappeared from the Middle East at the time of the Roman Empire when the camel took over from other means of transport and roads went out of use (Bulliet 1990).

Locating the nomadic tribes and empires within international systems rather than pre-international systems may seem, at first sight, perverse. Certainly the Eurasian civilizations all regarded the nomads as barbarians who pursued an alien and uncivilized way of life. The nomads were seen to descend like locusts on civilized communities, all too often laying them to waste—an alien force that periodically and unpredictably invaded developed sectors of the globe where international systems had become established. But such an account fails to note that the steppe nomads only emerged at a relatively late date in world history. Their survival depended on access to wheeled vehicles, the domestication of vital animals like horses and camels, and continuous interaction with sedentary communities which provided them with a wide range of essential goods. The nomads could, of course, be depicted as a final stage in the development of pre-international systems. The social structures of their tribes and empires were very much akin to those of the sedentary tribes and chiefdoms discussed in Part II, putting them on the borderline of the inside/outside construction. But because they only emerged spontaneously in Eurasia at a relatively late point in world history, at least two millennia after the first formation of international systems, we think it makes more analytical sense to view them as a feature of the evolving international systems. Their economic reliance on communities operating within established international systems ties them relatively unambiguously into these systems, and their military challenge to the settled agrarian civilizations gives them a major role in the inside/outside construction of most ancient and classical international systems.

All of these early international systems were locked into a similar framework that limited their ability either to expand or to develop beyond a certain point. Thus despite the length of time involved, and the number and variety of international systems that developed, there is a certain static quality about this whole gigantic era. As Hodgson (1993: 127) puts it, agrarian civilizations were profoundly conservative in the sense that: 'the prime object of all institutions was the preservation of what had been attained rather than the development of anything new.' In saying this we certainly do not subscribe to 'Orientalist' fallacies about decadence and stagnation in non-Western civilizations. As we shall see, there was a great deal of development during this era, some of it highly significant. In particular, there was a general tendency for both economic and full international systems to expand, with the result that over this era such systems steadily absorbed and replaced pre-international systems over most of the planet. Nevertheless, all of the international systems during this era were constrained by technological limits on interaction capacity.

The fundamental revolutions in transportation and communication that were vital to bringing the first international systems into being—the horse (and later camel), the wheeled cart, and the sailing ship—also put a ceiling on its development. All of these components underwent sustained processes of incremental improvement during this era. But until the development of ocean-going ships during the fifteenth century AD, there were no really fundamental transformations in the speed, range, or carrying capacity of the transportation technologies available to human civilization. For nearly 5,000 years the limits of human ability to exchange goods, information, or blows across a distance was set by the speed, range, and carrying capacity of horses, camels, and wooden sailing ships. Some incremental developments made a substantial difference: lighter wheels, stronger horses, stirrups, knowledge of wind patterns. Social technologies also could and did improve what could be done with mechanical ones, as in the organization of 'pony express' relay systems to carry information quickly across vast empires. But neither incremental improvements in the mechanical technologies nor support from social ones could overcome the basic logistical constraints that defined and confined both the first generation of international systems and the units that comprised them. The quite striking similarity of pattern uniting international systems across the ancient and classical era thus stems from two constants:

1.  the limits of a particular set of transportation and communication technologies; and
2.  the dominance of the same set of military-political-economic units (city-states, empires, and barbarian tribes).

The four chapters in this section cover the rise and development of first-generation international systems during the ancient and classical era. Chapter 8 examines the new units that generated the first full international systems. Chapters 9, 10, and 11 then look, in turn, at the interaction capacity, processes, and structures of these international systems. Together these chapters show the development, expansion, and growing inter-linkage of the international systems that took place during this long era, and the parallel contraction of pre-international systems as they were steadily overrun. Although the story of medieval Europe falls within the time period covered by these four chapters (c.3500 BC to AD 1500) we defer examination of it to Part IV, where it serves as the background to the rise of the modern state in Europe.

*Chapter 8*

# THE NEW UNITS: CITY-STATES, EMPIRES, AND BARBARIANS AS THE MAIN ACTORS OF THE ANCIENT AND CLASSICAL WORLD

This chapter examines the main units of the ancient and classical international systems. They are located at the core and the periphery of the world's civilizations which steadily extended across the globe during the five millennia being examined in Part III (see Map 8.1). The rise of new types of unit, larger and more complex than the hunter-gatherer bands, tribes, and chiefdoms that dominated pre-international systems, is one of the two principal factors differentiating the ancient and classical era from what came before. These units were capable of generating an inside/outside structure in a way that pre-international units were not. Section 1 looks at the linked stories of city-states and empires, the units at the core of the ancient and classical world. Section 2 examines the linked stories of nomadic tribes and nomadic empires which subsequently formed on the periphery of the newly emerged international systems in Afro-Eurasia. As we will show in the later chapters, the existence of these highly mobile units not only posed a common threat to the sedentary states in Eurasia, but also helped to link these systems together in a way that did not happen in the Americas, where nomadic tribes and nomadic empires failed to form.

## 1. CITY-STATES AND EMPIRES

One of the main keys to the emergence of international systems was the development of new types of unit that were more specifically military-political in nature than the hunter-gatherer tribes and neolithic villages and towns that preceded them. Tribes were perfectly capable of dealing with the organizational problems associated with the onset of agriculture. But in one of the great steps in human social development, kinship ties were eventually superseded by the process of urbanization. With this development, the decentralized mode of socio-political organization based on kinship which had dominated most of human history gave way to a more centralized form that we can recognize as being a type of state. As

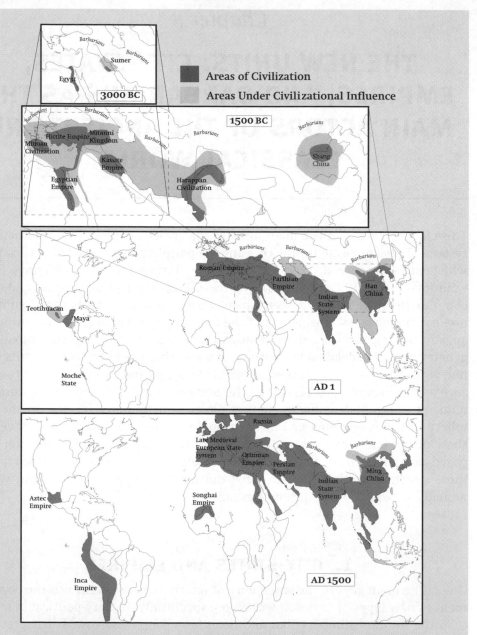

*Note:* The maps provide four time-shots showing the spread of civilization across the globe over a 5,000-year period. Initially, there are pockets of civilization formed within a global arena of pre-international systems. But civilizations and their associated international systems steadily extended at the expense of the pre-international systems.

*Map 8.1  The spread of civilization:* 3000 BC, 1500 BC, AD 1, AD 1500

McNeill (1991: 30–1) notes, 'Kinship, the oldest basis of human society, came to be supplemented and then supplanted by a new principle of social cohesion: mere propinquity.' With the emergence of city-states, increasingly large numbers of people came to live in close proximity. These individuals identified with their city as well as with their immediate kinship group. Kinship remained a powerful principle at many levels of society, not least in the hereditary practices of most ruling elites, and the importance of blood ties to the merchants who organized long-distance trade, but it no longer set limits to the overall scale and complexity of socio-political organization.

Urbanization gave rise to cities, which in turn gave rise to city-states and empires. These city states and empires were larger, more concentrated, and more differentiated than any type of unit that preceded them. Their internal structures (especially the existence of distinct instruments of government), their behaviour (especially their pursuit of security and power), and their ways of relating both to each other and to tribal peoples (especially their use of war and diplomacy) clearly identify them as early types of state. Tilly (1990: 1–2) defines states as 'coercion-wielding organisations that are distinct from households and kinship groups and exercise clear priority in some respects over all other organisations within substantial territories'. States generally seek political autonomy (i.e. the right of self-government) and are usually both able and willing to go to war in pursuit or defence of that goal. The emergence of city-states and empires as the first types of state correlate closely with the first international systems. As we will show later (Chapter 12), the development of new types of state, with different internal and external characteristics, is equally closely associated with major transformations in the nature of international systems.

The story of Sumeria tells how the first city-states developed, and how they generated the first empires.

---

*Sumeria*

The rise of the first full international system in Sumeria contains many of the elements that marked the emergence of subsequent international systems as far afield as China and Mesoamerica. Sumeria was located in southern Mesopotamia between the Tigris and Euphrates and embraced the southern region of Sumer with its own distinctive language and Akkad to the north, a Semitic-speaking area (Roaf 1990: 82). Political power shifted from the south to the north during the fourth and third millennia BC, and by 1800 BC Sumerian had become a dead language. But the term Sumerian is now used to describe the entire region and the civilization associated with it (Crawford 1991: 11–20)(see Map 8.2).

Farming began in this region around 4000 BC, but it was difficult because although the soil is fertile, rainfall is sparse. Initially the farmers operated on the banks of the rivers, but with the development of irrigation schemes, cultivation extended further afield, thereby allowing an expansion in population. But with the expansion of the population, the farming communities became dependent on the maintenance of ever more complex irrigation and supply systems. If the annual flood waters failed to arrive, or washed away the dykes, production was disrupted, and food supplies then depended on storage of previous surpluses. By 3000 BC, when the first written documentation becomes available, it is clear that elaborate irrigation networks and storage schemes had been long established. Ever more elaborate social structures and divisions of labour developed in tandem with the expanding population and the ever more complex task of maintaining food supply.

Centralized management of food production was not the only distinctive feature of the Sumerians. From an early stage in their history they established religious centres which provided a focal point for pilgrimages. The Sumerians attached much more importance to their gods than was usual at that time. A possible explanation is the Sumerian dependence on irrigation and their extreme vulnerability to the vagaries of natural forces like floods and droughts which were seen to be controlled by the gods (Roberts 1993: 42–3). But Sumerian mythology established a much more direct link with the gods. According to this mythology, humankind was created in order to serve the needs of the gods, and failure to satisfy these needs led to dire punishments: people were effectively slaves to the gods (Maisels 1993). They produced food for the gods and built increasingly lavish temples for them. Priests tended the temples and craftsmen built and embellished them. Cultural developments of this kind were only possible when agricultural surpluses could be produced more or less reliably.

The communities which developed in Sumeria increasingly diverged from other neolithic villages. In place of small fields, worked by the farmer, the Sumerians' irrigated land was divided into large areas which were owned by the gods and administered by the priests. The farmers lived in concentrated settlements, focused on the temple which provided the earthly household of the city's god. Territory was no longer regulated by kinship but by centralized institutions located in the city. Crone (1980: 60) has argued that at this stage it becomes appropriate to identify the emergence of a fully-fledged city-state. Although the priests were responsible for managing many aspects of the city-state and in particular the irrigation system, there was also a separate political structure which was initially very egalitarian. Political decision-making took place in an assembly which consisted of all the adult males in the city (Roberts 1993: 45).

The emergent city-states established by the Sumerians remained highly unstable and insecure institutions. Natural disasters posed a constant threat to food supply. But as the wealth that flowed from agricultural surpluses and trade started to accumulate in the city-states, they also became vulnerable to raids from nomadic pastoralists to the south and west while mountain tribesmen to the north and east came to see them as sources of rich pickings (Roaf 1990: 108, 117). There was also growing conflict between neighbouring cities, which were often located quite close to each other. For example, Umma was only 30 km (18 miles) from Girshu, a town within the city-state of Lagash. The written records indicate that there was continual fighting over the land that separated them (Roaf 1990: 82). By 3000 BC, there were around thirty major cities in Sumeria and intercity warfare throughout Sumeria was common (Maisels 1993). From this point it does not seem unreasonable to see the Sumerian city-states as a fully-fledged international system, albeit on a small scale. In response to the urgencies of warfare both with local tribes and neighbouring cities, individual Sumerians claiming to represent the city's god usurped the power of the assemblies, established themselves as kings, and took on the responsibility for ensuring the survival of the city-states. This internal struggle between democratic and autocratic forces was to be a recurrent feature in the subsequent history of city-states.

As the Sumerian city-states vied with each other, the two primary mechanisms for enhancing security were to establish city walls against raiders and to engage in pacts designed to undermine the autonomy of neighbouring city-states. The city-states, in other words, initiated processes of empire-building and diplomacy from a very early stage. The first empires established in Sumeria were unstable. The first really successful empire which managed to unite all the city-states was established by Sargon of Akkad in 2334–2193 BC (Roaf 1990: 96). Sargon broke away from the city-state of Kish and established a new and purely administrative capital, not a city-state, at Argade. This was an important step in moving towards a new territorial form of control (Crawford 1991: 25; Hammond 1972: 50). But while Sargon's empire did implant the big political idea in the region, for the next 600 years power fluctuated in Mesopotamia between peripheral tribes, city-states, and fledgling empires. McNeill (1963; 1991: 51–8) has argued that, during this period, perpetual insecurity and instability created constant pressure for greater political centralization. With the establishment of the Babylonian Empire by Hammurabi, c.1700 BC, the essential elements for imperial stability were finally in place, and it was possible to sustain centralized and secular authority over very extensive areas of territory for long periods of time.

McNeill (1963, 1991) identifies four key features in the making of stable empires. First was the availability of a non-parochial ideology which could help to consolidate the empire as a coherent entity. The initial attempts by the Sumerians to establish a stable empire ultimately failed because each city-state was ruled by a separate god. It was therefore difficult for any one city-state to exercise legitimate authority over the internal affairs of the others. But Sumerian mythology did acknowledge the existence of one god who stood above the others and had the right to arbitrate between them. This god's city could thus legitimately exercise hegemonic authority over the other Sumerian city-states (Watson 1992: 24–9). The Babylonians drew on this mythology, but for their own purposes. The Babylonians claimed that their god Marduk had overthrown the other gods and established a kingship over them. This ensured that the Babylonian emperor's right to extend his control over the city-states of Sumeria and further afield was underpinned by stable ideological foundations. As a fully-fledged emperor, Hammurabi had the right to regulate the domestic activities of the political communities within his control. This was important, because it enabled him to regulate water-rights over the whole of the Tigris–Euphrates watershed.

The early attempts at empire also lacked the necessary administrative and military structures to maintain stability over a wide area. The second key feature which was in place by the time of Hammurabi was an effective bureaucracy and a professional army. Royal judges, tax collectors, and garrison commanders were strategically located across the empire. The evidence indicates that Hammurabi kept a very close watch on the activity of these officials. Intimately related to an effective administrative structure, and the third key feature of empire, were advances in administrative techniques. To maintain control over administrators who were widely dispersed, it was necessary to have extensive recourse to written communication. Writing was also necessary to maintain a record of the terms and conditions of agreements reached within the empire. The origins of writing are found in the records kept on goods supplied to the temple storehouses in the Sumerian city-states and it seems likely that the evolution of writing was closely related to the administrative needs of the empire. The final development was the creation of a merchant class which facilitated the distribution of goods both inside and outside the empire.

The civilization stemming from Sumeria generated a long succession of empires all sharing the same cultural roots. The last flourishings of this civilization were the Assyrian and Babylonian empires during the first half of the first millennium BC. After the Persian conquest in 539 BC, that culture, with its distinctive cuneiform script, began to wither and by the second century AD was completely submerged by Persian, Greek, and other cultures (Yoffee and Cowgill 1991: 44–68; Crawford 1991: 173).

## City-states

The Sumerian city-states were eventually overtaken by the emergence of empires. In the course of world history this has been a common fate for city-states, and yet they have managed to survive as significant actors on the world scene, a handful persisting even to the present day. Unlike bands and tribes, city-states were not

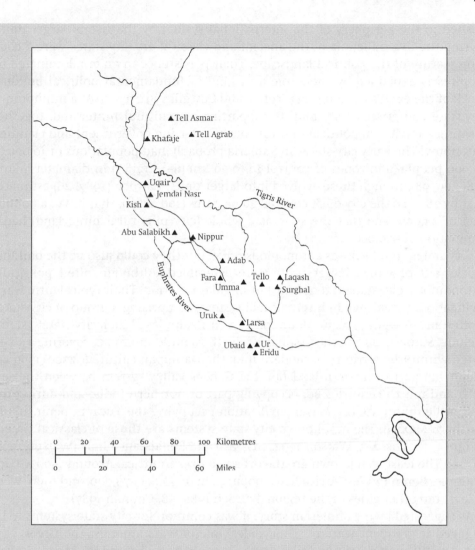

*Note:* From around 3500 BC settlements on the Sumerian plain developed into city-states that were fiercely competitive but formed a common civilization because of their shared cultural beliefs.

*Source:* Taken from Crawford 1991.

*Map 8.2  The cities of the Sumerian plain*

pushed to the periphery of the international system by the rise of larger units. During the five millennia of the ancient and classical era city-states were a common feature of the political landscape. Their persistence in an era dominated by empires is explained by their role as a kind of fundamental political building block of the era (Fagan 1993: 233; Yoffee and Cowgill 1991: 33–7). At a minimum, a city-state comprised a city and its supporting agricultural hinterland, together forming a territorial political unit capable of asserting government and claiming autonomy. The early city-states in Sumeria probably had populations of 10,000 to 20,000 people, and zones of control 10 to 30 km (6–18 miles) in diameter (Mann 1986: 89–98), though these evolved into larger units. Bairoch (1987: 26) estimates that by 2800 BC the city of Ur covered 40 hectares (100 acres), that it had a population of 24,000, and that the state as a whole (city plus rural hinterland) had a population of 500,000.

City-states could exist as autonomous units, but they could also be the building blocks out of which larger units were assembled. Although often politically autonomous, city-states did not exist in singular isolation. Their typical form was a civilizational area, and an international system, comprising a group of city-states (Yoffee and Cowgill 1991: 36; Mann 1986: ch. 3). Examples of such city-state systems include: Sumeria during the first half of the third millennium BC, covering a small patch within the territory of modern Iraq; the Harappan culture (c.2500–1500 BC) occupying part of modern Pakistan; the Ganges valley system between the seventh and fourth centuries BC, occupying part of northern India; and during the first millennium AD, the Mayan civilization occupying the Yucatan peninsula in southern Mexico. The best-known city-state systems are those of classical Greece (Wight 1977: chs. 2–3; Watson 1992: chs. 5–6) and Renaissance Italy (Watson 1992: ch. 14). The least well known are the urban centres in Africa. Around 1500 AD, for example, Benin in West Africa had a population of 60,000–70,000, and there were at least ten other cities in the region (Bairoch 1988: 58; Connah 1987).

As suggested by the Sumerian story, it was common for city-state systems to be engaged in frequent warfare. Thucydides' tale of wars amongst the Greek city-states is still an IR classic, and similar stories could be told of the Mayan and Italian city-state systems. This habit sharpened their combat skills against outsiders, and city-state systems could sometimes successfully take on empires, as indicated by the famous defence of Greece against invading Persians starting in 490 BC (Trigger 1993: 11–12). But just as often internecine warfare debilitated them, leading either to collapse (one explanation for the disappearance of the Maya) or take-over (the eventual fate of Greece and Italy). City-states could also be prolific colonizers and spreaders of urban civilization. During the first millennium BC, the classical Greek and Phoenician city-states seeded dozens of reproductions of themselves all around the coasts of the Mediterranean and Black Seas. The Phoenician colony of Carthage became an imperial centre in its own right, and Greek cities such as Syracuse, in Sicily, rivalled the biggest of the city-states in Greece. The Greek cities on the Black Sea became a major frontier zone between urban and nomadic peoples, and projected cultural and economic influence right into the heart of Eurasia (Ascherson 1996). A not dissimilar process took place during late medieval Europe, when 'Latin' culture expanded into central and north-east Europe, implanting new towns and cities as it did so (Bartlett 1994).

City-state systems could provide a platform for empire-building, and a common mechanism for this was when a powerful city-state expanded itself into an empire by taking control of other city-states. Athens, Babylon, Carthage, Delhi, Nineveh, Rome, Tenochtitlan, and Ur are merely the better-known city-states that accomplished this trick. When empires disintegrated, which all of them did eventually, some after a few years, others after many centuries, they generally collapsed back to the city-state level, which meant that when imperial control collapsed it did not normally endanger civilization. Power simply fragmented back down to city-states and small kingdoms (Fagan 1993: 178). Only when the cities themselves died, and social organization reverted to village level, was civilization threatened, as happened to the city-state systems of the Maya and the Harappan civilization (Yoffee and Cowgill 1991: 69–101, 273). This was a rare event; indeed, Bairoch (1988: 34–5) argues that the 'stability of urban networks' represents a 'constant' in the history of cities. Collapses were usually caused by one or more of three factors: environmental changes undermining food production; tribal depredations; and/or the breakdown of trade.

Less common was the construction of city-state leagues which emerged at various times in the ancient and classical world. Bairoch (1988: 29–30), for example, notes similarities between the way the Phoenician city-states of Byblos, Acre, Aradus, Beirut, Ugarit, Sidon, and Tyre related and the various links formed between medieval European cities in Italy, Germany, and the Netherlands. There were also leagues established amongst some of the weaker city-states in Greece. The Aechaean League, made up of city-states on the Gulf of Corinth, for example, had an annually elected general who was responsible for the league's foreign policy (Hammond 1972). But the most significant and long-lasting league was the Hanseatic League, which was a force by the twelfth century AD, eventually linking 70 to 80 major but non-sovereign towns and 100 or so smaller towns covering northern and eastern Europe (Braudel 1985: 101–6). Although the league lacked any formal governmental apparatus, apart from a general assembly which met annually at first and then with increasing irregularity, the league could wage war, implement blockades, and deal, as Scammell (1981: 54) notes, 'on more than equal terms, with sovereign states'. For a time such leagues became a feature of the political landscape in late medieval Europe but they could not compete against the emergent modern states (Spruyt 1994a, 1994b).

There has been much dispute about why city-states emerged, but no general theory has gained acceptance (Mann 1986: ch. 2). It is now generally agreed that city-states were the product of a very long historical development and were not the result of any single cause. It is not disputed that systems of city-states emerged independently in several different places but at very different times. Also not in dispute is that the formation of city-states is closely associated with the formation of civilizations, with whole groups of such states sharing elements of a common high culture (language, religion, script, etc.), and developing stratified class structures (priests, kings, merchants, craftsmen, soldiers, etc.) based on ever more complex divisions of labour (Fagan 1993: 167–8; Mann 1986: ch. 3). Quite common, for example, was the development of skills in astronomy (often associated with the temples). Observation of the stars led to an ability to measure time, and therefore to begin locating oneself accurately in the cycle of seasons. Such knowledge was hugely important in societies dependent on knowing when best to plant crops. McNeill (1979: p. v) argues that civilizations are 'unusually massive societies, weaving the lives of millions of persons into a large yet coherent life style across hundreds or even thousands of miles and for periods of time that are very long when measured by the space of an individual human life'. Roberts (1993: 32) argues that civilizations are distinguished from pre-civilizational cultures in terms of greater scale and complexity. The Sumerian city-states are regarded as the onset of civilization. Their shared religion provided an overarching framework, so even though there was competition between the cities, their inhabitants distinguished themselves sharply from the barbarian peoples surrounding them. In the ancient and classical world, peoples drew the boundaries between civilized and barbarian more sharply than those between city-states within a civilizational area. This pattern is consistent whether one is looking at ancient Sumer or at classical Greece, China, or Rome, or indeed at modern Europe.

The fortunes of city-states waxed and waned during the ancient and classical era. Sometimes they flourished as city-state systems, as in early Sumeria, classical Greece, the Maya civilization, and medieval Europe. In other periods they lost independence to imperial power. City-states were effective generators of wealth and power, a trait that remained conspicuous in medieval Europe in the run-up to the formation of national states (Chirot 1985; Braudel 1985).

### Empires

Doyle (1986: 19) defines empires as 'relationships of political control imposed by some political societies over the effective sovereignty of other political societies'. Not everyone is happy with this definition (Wæver 1996: 222–6), and it is important not to underestimate the legitimacy often carried by empires, and to see them as more than just coercive impositions. During the ancient and classical era, agrarian empires were the dominant form, typically comprising a core city extending varying degrees of administrative and military control over its neighbours. In some cases (Egypt, China, Incas) empires arose without stemming from a dominant city-state, and with lower levels of urbanization. In such cases, empires generated cities rather than the other way around, and monuments and administrative centres might be established separately from cities. Some analysts see these as a distinct type of political form (Trigger 1993: 8; Maisels 1990). In their expansionary phases, empires often seeded new cities, as most notably by the Greeks during the Hellenistic expansion into the Middle East, one of whose many fruits was Alexandria (Walbank 1993: 43). Agrarian empires, whether city-state-based or not, had their cores in areas of dense population and high agricultural production, and often had a major transportation route, usually a navigable river (Euphrates/ Tigris, Nile, Indus, Ganges, Hwang Ho), as their spine. One main incentive for building empires was the desire to control and tax trade routes. The rise of cities stimulated trade by creating centres of wealth, production, and demand. The Sumerians, for example, had to import stone, wood, and metal, and could trade in food, textiles, and luxury goods. Imperial control was usually good for trade in that it provided protection and stimulated demand for, and production of, goods. In turn, the tax revenues from trade (and also the loot from successful conquests) funded the monumental display and the military might of the empire. These empires were extractive, but offered important services in return: security of trade routes and food supply; protection against barbarian raiders; provision of public goods (roads, temples, coinage, property rights, promotion of lingua francas, standards for weights, measures, and values); and military demand for goods and services (Watson 1992: 37).

While the agrarian empire was much the most common form, it was not the only one. Tribal empires sometimes arose amongst the nomadic barbarians who were in regular contact with agrarian civilization. More on these below. There were also trading empires, such as that of Carthage, in which military and administrative control were less intense than in agrarian ones. Although Carthage stationed troops abroad on the territory of trading partners, and may have exercised extraterritorial jurisdiction over its own citizens who lived within the boundaries of a foreign port, these mechanisms were designed to foster trade rather than to exercise power (Whittaker 1978). Nevertheless, Carthage did regard the western Mediterranean as its sphere of influence and was anxious to cut the area off from the expanding influence of the Greek city-states (Warmington 1964: 61). The fact that Carthage exercised hegemonic influence over the region means that trading empires must be distinguished from city-state leagues, discussed above, which embraced a range of autonomous city-states.

The empires of the ancient and classical era were in some ways remarkably flexible units. They had neither fixed geographical limits nor a uniform degree of internal political control. They can be seen in terms of concentric circles of control, ranging from complete absorption at the core, through varying degrees of control over foreign, military, and domestic policy in the middle zones, to mere hegemony at the outer margins (Watson 1992; Buzan and Little 1996). They did not have uniform sovereignty within a firm boundary, but rather faded away through zones of diminishing control. They comprised a spectrum of units ranging from totally subordinate, through semi-independent, to independent but under heavy influence. In this sense, although empires can be seen as units within international systems (albeit loose ones, containing a measure of functional differentiation within themselves), they can also be seen as a kind of hierarchical international system in their own right (see Figs. 8.1 and 8.2). Wight (1977: 23–4), for example, characterizes them as 'suzerain state-systems' in which the principle is not balance of power but divide and rule. More on this later. Tambiah (1976: 113), uses an astronomical metaphor to capture this idea, talking of the political structures found in India and then extended to South-East Asia as 'galactic polities' on the analogy of 'a central planet surrounded by differentiated satellites, which are more or less "autonomous" entities held in orbit and within the sphere of influence of the centre'. The rise of great military captains—Alexander the Great, Chandragupta Maurya, Charlemagne, Genghis Khan, Hammurabi, Julian, Sargon, Timur—often made empires, while weak rulers, or fragmenting rules of royal succession, often dismantled them. Random events such as plagues or barbarian assaults could weaken or destroy empires. So too could structural problems, such as reaching the limits of expansion, and so losing the input of new resources of land (Ottomans) or slaves (Rome) which had previously been used to buy off internal problems or to sustain the economy. Secessionism was a constant problem, borders were always in question, and the balance between central and local power was continuously in flux.

But there was a learning process, and as history unfolded, the techniques of imperial control improved enabling larger and more durable constructions to be built (see Map 8.3). In such a turbulent environment military power and skilful, energetic, and ruthless leadership were the keys to successful empire. But even possession of these did not guarantee more than short-term success. Creating a broader and more deeply rooted ruling elite better able to survive variations in the talent of leaders was one key. Another was the attraction of the imperial idea itself. This took root especially strongly in China and the Middle East, so that even during periods of fragmentation, the warring states were often motivated by the desire to re-establish a wider imperial domain. Over the five millennia of this era, there is a pattern of progressive development from Sumeria through Rome to the Ottoman, Chinese, and other empires that overlapped with the rise of Europe, in which the techniques of imperial construction and control discussed above (ideology, bureaucracy and administrative technique, professional army, merchant class) became more effective. With the development of bureaucracies and professional armies, ruling elites acquired a broader social base, which enabled empires to become larger and/or better integrated. Rome even extended citizenship to its peoples, and in Western Europe, nostalgia for Rome lasted for more than a thousand years after its fall (Bozeman 1960). Some historians (e.g. McNeill 1963, 355; Mann 1986: ch. 9) rate internal developments in classical Greece and Rome, such as civil law and citizenship, as perhaps sufficient to distinguish

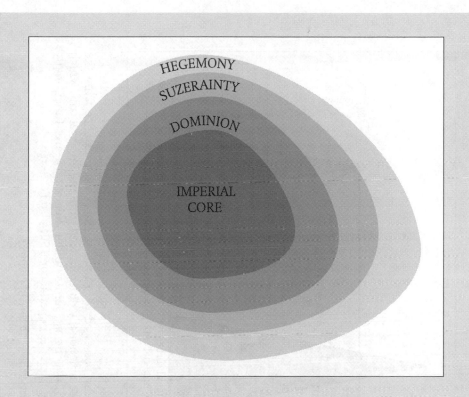

*Note:* Drawing on Watson (1992: 14-16), this figure indicates that the power and influence of an empire over other units wanes as the distance from the imperial core increases. It distinguishes between hegemony, where units are nominally independent but in practice their foreign policy is severely constrained by the power exercised from the imperial core; suzerainty, where units acknowledge that the imperial core can legitimately regulate their foreign policy; and dominion, where aspects of domestic policy are also controlled by the imperial core. See also Fig. 8.2.

*Figure 8.1 Watson's model of functional differentiation within empires*

between ancient and classical eras. But there are dangers of Eurocentrism in this move, which appears to privilege the precursors to modern Europe. From the perspective of international systems, this evolution had little effect, and so we prefer to see the empires of the ancient and classical world as a single type of unit evolving more effective means of control.

Despite this learning process, all empires were still subject to patterns of rise

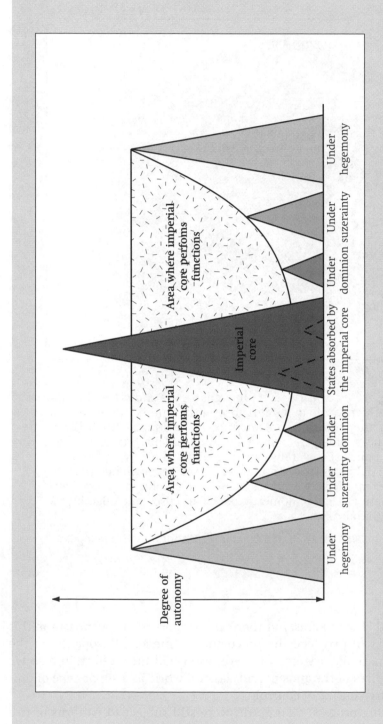

*Note:* The figure indicates that the degree of autonomy possessed by a unit increases with distance from the imperial core. Units under dominion and suzerainty are functionally differentiated from the imperial core which is responsible for some of their key functions. By contrast, units under hegemony are functionally undifferentiated because they claim to be independent from the imperial core. See also Fig. 8.1.

*Figure 8.2 The 'international' structure of empires*

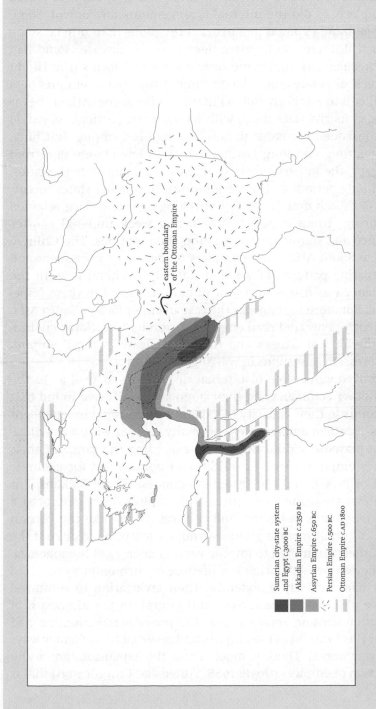

eastern boundary
of the Ottoman Empire

Sumerian city-state system
and Egypt c.3000 BC

Akkadian Empire c.2350 BC

Assyrian Empire c.650 BC

Persian Empire c.500 BC

Ottoman Empire c.AD 1800

*Note:* The map shows how the empires of the Middle East have become progressively more extensive. But, in addition to the restrictions imposed by interaction capacity, the emergence of other effective political units elsewhere has always placed limits on imperial expansion. The Persians, for example, were unable to defeat the Greek city-states in the fifth century BC, although their descendants were able to hold the Roman Empire at bay.

*Map 8.3 Ever bigger empires in the Middle East*

and fall. The rhythms and reasons of the waxing and waning of empires varied greatly from place to place, as did the internal arrangements for control. Some civilizational areas were more exposed to barbarian invasions than others, some suffered environmental disasters, some were devastated by disease, some had unstable succession mechanisms, and some developed social forms (the Hindu caste system, the Greek city-state, the Islamic umma) that made empires less necessary or more difficult to establish and maintain. Unlike Rome, Athens never successfully transcended its city-state form, with its intimate, participatory style of politics, and was consequently unable to build a long-lived empire. In China, empires tended to be strong and long lasting, and to follow closely one from another, and as in Egypt, the imperial form itself was dominant over the cities. Only occasionally did long periods of fragmentation into 'warring states' occur, and as Ferguson and Mansbach note (1996: 193–222) kingdoms and clans retained some power even during strong imperial phases, and weak imperial centres retained some influence and status during 'warring state' periods. The Chinese pattern was reversed in South Asia, where empires tended to be infrequent and short lived, and fluctuating patterns of warring states the general rule. In the Middle East, the tendency was firmly in favour of empires, some of them (especially Egypt) long lived. But more so than was the case in either East or South Asia, this civilization frequently generated rival empires within its area. Some civilizations, most notably the ancient Greeks and the Maya, firmly resisted empire, finding their main expression as systems of warring city-states.

All empires have proved vulnerable to internal dislocation, as well as to the corrosive activities of other actors beyond their boundaries. All have found that ultimately there are limits to their capacity to expand by absorbing independent political communities. Agrarian empires were normally centred within a civilizational area, and often played a significant role in extending the range of their civilization. Sometimes empires crossed civilizational boundaries: for example Alexander's conquest of Persia, and the Ottoman conquest of the Balkans. But even within civilizational areas the more successful empires often embraced a wide variety of language groups, religions, and cultures. Some, like the Persian Empire, incorporated culturally diverse groups without attempting to disrupt the indigenous cultures. Others attempted to impose varying degrees of homogenization on the peoples they absorbed. During the lifetime of such empires, it could easily look as if they had successfully extended their civilization to colonized regions at the expense of indigenous socio-cultural groups. In the aftermath of empire, however, it often became apparent that the pre-imperial situation had simply been frozen for the duration of the empire, and reverted to its former ways once the imperial power waned. There is much about the expansion, and more especially the contraction of empires (Doyle 1986; Yoffee and Cowgill 1991) that is not well understood.

# 2.  NOMADIC TRIBES AND THEIR EMPIRES

Although attempts have been made to accommodate units as different as city-states and agrarian empires within established theories in IR, little, if any, effort has been made to take account of nomadic tribes. The lack of interest is perhaps unsurprising because these units have had no major role in world history for the past 500 years. But during the previous two millennia, nomadic tribes and empires played a crucial part in international relations. Nomadic tribes were responsible for establishing the Mongol Empire in the thirteenth century AD, the largest land empire yet to appear on the world stage, as well as being intimately associated with the rise of Islam, one of the world's great civilizations. Both of these developments had transformational consequences for world politics and so a failure to bring the nomads into focus necessarily results in a partial and distorted assessment of the past. Settled tribal peoples had always existed on the periphery of civilization, and had been a continuous source of military threat. Nomadic tribes emerged some two millennia after cities and empires came into existence. They presented a new kind of threat to agrarian civilizations which greatly increased when the tribes consolidated to form an empire. Nomadic empires were very different from sedentary empires and they constitute distinctive international actors with a unique role to play in the evolution of international systems. By examining the relationship and essential characteristics of nomadic tribes and empires and their respective international roles it also becomes less paradoxical than it might otherwise seem that nomadic tribes could be involved in the creation of both a world empire and a world civilization.

## NOMADIC TRIBES

The emergence of nomadic tribes is inextricably linked to the spread of agriculture and the domestication of animals. As we saw in Part II, these developments can be traced back for many millennia. Pastoralists, who tended flocks of goats, sheep, and cattle, were a familiar feature of the ancient Afro-Eurasian world and are often identified as nomads, although they invariably led a semi-sedentary life. By contrast, the nomadic tribes that Khazanov (1984: 7) identifies as 'real nomads' and Cole (1975) refers to as the 'nomads of the nomads' are tribes that have given up all the trappings of sedentary life and this kind of unit only came into existence relatively late in the history of the ancient world—around the start of the first millennium BC. The explanation for this long gestation period before the development of true nomadism is not difficult to identify. Although animals were domesticated and herded relatively early in the history of agriculture, the 'real nomads' were capable of riding either horses or camels as well as using them for pack and draught purposes (Levine 1999). The full domestication of horses and camels required a repertoire of skills and technological developments associated with riding which did not take place for several millennia after the process of domesticating these animals started. Horses needed to go through a long process of selective breeding before they were strong enough to carry a rider. When eventually the necessary skills and animals were acquired, the resulting mobility enabled semi-sedentary tribes to adopt a completely nomadic way of life. The true nomads occupied territory which had previously resisted penetration by tribes engaged in pastoralism and agriculture. They moved deep into the steppes and deserts of Eurasia, Africa, and Arabia, where it was always difficult and often impossible for the agents of city-states and empires to make contact with them.

For millennia before this juncture, pastoralists and agriculturalists had lived side by side in a mutually dependent relationship (Schwartz 1995: 253). After the formation of states, the movement of the pastoralists and their herds of animals over their long-established traditional routes often required them to cross the frontiers of city-states and agrarian empires, and this was an accepted feature of the ancient world in Africa and the Near East. As a consequence, pastoral tribes retained some political independence from city-states and agrarian empires, although they were locked into the economies of these centralized political units, supplying them with meat, milk products, skins, and wool in return for manufactured and agricultural products (Maisels 1990: 186–90). Barth (1964: 70) observes that the pastoral herders were one of several 'specialised occupational groups within a single economic system'. But the balance of power generally lay with the sedentary units, and the degree of political independence displayed by the pastoralists was necessarily correlated with the power possessed by the city-states and empires.

By the end of the third millennium BC, however, written texts describe the pastoralists as 'dangerous and disruptive' (Schwartz 1995: 253). Indeed, the kings of Ur embarked on a massive military project, building a wall from the Tigris to the Euphrates designed to keep the Amorites, pastoralists who lived to the west of Sumaria, at bay (Postgate 1992: 43). When the empire established by Sargon began to collapse, it came under pressure from the Amorites to the west and the Guti, mountain tribesmen from the east. But it was all too easy for empire-builders to blame the pastoralists for the persistent tendency of the early empires to give way to the forces of decentralization (Schwartz 1995: 253). The military threat posed by the pastoral tribes tends obscure the constant tendency of pastoralists to move into the city-states and adopt a sedentary way of life (Crawford 1991: 10). In fact, most of the texts describe the intercourse with the pastoral tribesmen as peaceful (Postgate 1992: 43) and it is now widely accepted that the military raids precipitated by the pastoralists occurred when economic relations with the city-states broke down (Schwartz 1995: 251–4). It is also acknowledged that the pastoralists provided a 'crucial channel of communication' (Crawford 1991: 11) along which goods and ideas could flow, linking settled populations that were otherwise separated by very considerable distances. The Sumerian cities were separated from the cities in the north of Mesopotamia by tracts of desert. As the agrarian empires came into existence, with the emergence of merchants and messengers, the significance of this role steadily diminished.

Once the fully-fledged nomadic tribes moved into territory that lay beyond the control of the city-states and empires, the nature of their relationship with these units began to diverge from the one that had operated in the past with the semi-sedentary pastoralists. On the Arabian peninsula, this development is associated with the 'bedouinization' of the Arabs (Khazanov 1984: 99). Sedentary Arabs have always remained deeply ambivalent about the Bedouin Arabs; depicting them as primitive and yet at the same time marvelling at the skills that allow them to survive in the desert (Cole 1975: 53). The ambivalence is widespread and deep-rooted, with nomadic people almost universally being identified as 'barbarians', drawing on the terminology devised by the ancient Greeks. Yet it is important to recall that when visiting the Greek colonies on the Black Sea in the fifth century BC—'the hem of Greece sewn onto the fields of the barbarians' as Cicero put it, (Adshead 1988: 32)—and seeing at first hand the Scythians, the nomadic tribes that surrounded these colonies, Herodotus acknowledged that while they lived a way of life that was very different from the urbanized Greeks, it was their mobility that had enabled them to defeat the Persians. He associated the mobility of the Scythians with a military strategy that he believed the Greeks should emulate in order to ensure that they too could escape domination by what he regarded as the Persian barbarians (Ascherson 1996; Hall 1989; Hartzog, 1988).

Nomadic tribes formed independently, although at roughly the same time, in Eurasia, Arabia, and Africa, around 1000 BC. By that time, the horse had not only been exported from its original home, possibly in the Ukraine, across Eurasia, but the techniques and technology necessary for riding these animals were also beginning to be mastered and diffused very rapidly around the continent (Azzaroli 1985; Clutton-Brock 1992). The same was true for the camel in Africa and Arabia (Bulliet 1990; Khazanov 1984). On the other hand, the absence of horses, camels, or their equivalents in other parts of the world made it inevitable that there were no nomads beyond the boundaries of Afro-Eurasia, although, as we shall see in Part IV, some of the native American peoples rapidly turned themselves into nomads when the Europeans imported horses onto this continent after AD 1500 (Vajnsh-tejn 1978). The ease with which the North American tribes turned themselves into mounted nomads makes it less surprising that nomadism spread so rapidly around Afro-Eurasia.

## NOMADIC EMPIRES

Most pastoralists have remained semi-sedentary throughout history, resisting the opportunity to become true nomads, and they have, as a consequence, generally operated under the suzerain power of empires and city-states. By contrast, fully nomadic tribes experienced complete autonomy; and having escaped the power of empires and city-states, they had the potential to play an independent inter-national role. The ability to realize this potential depended upon a suite of factors which distinguish one region from another and, as a result, it is necessary at the very least to contrast the desert nomads of Arabia and Africa with the steppe nomads of Eurasia (Crone 1980). At the heart of the difference was the capacity of the steppe nomads to form stable empires.

The nomadic tribes in Arabia throughout most of their history have resisted attempts at centralization. Constant intertribal feuding prevented both the forma-tion of larger political units and the development of any economic co-operation (Halliday 1974: 39). The desert nomads engaged in persistent raiding of each other and the sedentary population on their periphery, as well as collecting tolls from the merchants who passed down the trade routes that crossed Arabia. But this was the extent of their contact with the outside world. Because there was little social stratification within the tribes, nomadic leaders also lacked real political power and they had to work through consensus (Crone 1980: 23). Although 'desert empires' built upon oasis settlements did emerge occasionally, they were always ephemeral and invariably succumbed to the constant feuds that went on within and between tribes. Nevertheless, the Bedouin tribes evolved a common poetic language and an orally transmitted culture which transcended local tribal dialects (Lewis 1966: 30–1). As Crone (1980: 25) notes, 'their mobility had given them a common identity such as other peoples acquire only through their state struc-tures'. What the prophet Muhammad did, in the seventh century AD, was to create a state structure in Arabia and then harness the common Bedouin sense of iden-tity to a divine mission to spread the word of Allah. Although the factors under-lying the emergence of Islam are still heavily contested (Ibrahim 1990; Crone 1987) there is no doubt that Muhammad succeeded in overcoming tribal divisions and drawing on the common identity of the desert nomads to produce an 'expansion-ist dynamic with military backing' (Halliday 1974: 42). The resulting empire was, however, from the start, centred on the major cities that lay in the agricultural regions to the north. It was a sedentary empire and the Bedouin tribes soon broke their ties of allegiance with the imperial centre and reverted back to their decentralized and feuding way of life.

The feuding which characterized the desert nomads was also a common feature of the nomadic tribes living on the steppes of Central Asia. But unlike the desert nomads whose movement was restricted to the Arabian peninsula, the steppe nomads operated on a vast arena spanning 11,000 km (7,000 miles), with the trade routes providing a fragile 'continental bridge' from Japan to Europe (Hayashi 1975: 9) being established soon after the nomads moved onto the steppes. Because of their mobility, for over 2,000 years steppe nomads like the Scythians in the eighth and seventh centuries BC and the Huns of the fourth and fifth centuries AD were able to change their location by travelling thousands of miles across the Eurasian continent. This extraordinary capacity for movement created an arena which is radically different from the conventional image of an international system and deserves more investigation than it has received so far in IR. These long-distance movements were never the norm (indeed, the most widespread pastoral tribes in Eurasia were all semi-sedentary (Khazanov 1984: 121)) and they were far from being the only feature distinguishing desert and steppe nomads. The steppe nomads were ethnically divided and conflict between the tribes was much more ferocious than anything experienced on the Arabian peninsula (Crone 1980). There was also much more evidence of hierarchy both within and between the steppe tribes (Barfield 1989). It was the combination of these factors that opened the way to the development of nomadic empires.

Nomadic empires, like sedentary ones, expanded and collapsed with predictable regularity. But unlike sedentary empires, the nomads left no urban infrastructure. They disappeared without trace, leaving only the nomadic tribes that had joined forces under the leadership of a dominant tribe. In contrast to political units that were often involuntarily brought together within a sedentary empire, nomadic tribes could not be coerced into a tribal confederation, because their mobility always left them with an avenue of escape from imperial control. The periodic movement of tribes in Eurasia could have been caused by nomads exercising this option. But by the same token, semi-sedentary nomads were much more vulnerable to pressure from what Kwanten (1979) describes as the 'imperial nomads'. Because nomadic empires were not built on coercive foundations they were very decentralized in structure. Tribes retained control of their own affairs and were only required to accept that the imperial ruler was responsible for the conduct of international relations. Nomadic empires came into existence, therefore, almost solely for the purposes of playing an international role (Phillips 1965; Kwanten 1979; Barfield 1989).

By confederating, the nomads managed to transform themselves from being isolated raiders capable of being a nuisance to their sedentary neighbours into a political and military unit which could pose a serious threat to the largest agrarian empires. During most of the first millennium BC, for example, the Chinese never saw the tribes on their borders as constituting anything more than a minor irritant. But by 300 BC, these tribes had acquired horses and used their equestrian skills to develop very effective cavalry tactics. During the next century, the Hsiung Nu tribes, from the Gobi desert, confederated into a powerful nomadic empire which controlled all the territory north of the Great Wall stretching at one point in the empire's history from Korea to the Altai Mountains. For several hundred years the Hsiung Nu's nomadic empire provided a formidable rival to the sedentary Chinese Han Empire. As happened to other agrarian imperial states, the Chinese found that they had no alternative but to abandon their chariots and adopt the cavalry strategy perfected by the nomads (Phillips 1965: 91).

But the steppe nomads were not usually interested in posing a threat to the survival of the sedentary empires. Their aim was to stabilize trading relations. Desert and steppe nomads shared this aim. In Arabia, for example, the Bedouins prized their horses as much as, if not more than, their camels. But to survive, the horses required grain which had to be imported from the sedentary societies. In the steppe regions, there was also a demand for luxury goods to maintain the status distinctions which were an essential feature of the nomadic tribes on the steppe. The graves of tribal leaders reveal that there was a substantial appetite for luxury goods. For example, the leaders of successive nomadic tribes which occupied the Crimea—the Scythians, Sarmatians, and the Goths—were all interested in conspicuous wealth. The craftsmen living in the Greek colonies on the edge of the Black Sea produced some of their very finest works of art in the style required by these nomadic elites (Ascherson 1996: 222–3). When this trading relationship broke down, the nomads almost invariably resorted to force in order to re-establish the link. When Alexander the Great attempted in 329 BC to close the frontier of his expanding empire and shut out the nomads who lived beyond the River Jaxari, thereby changing the established Persian practice of maintaining a 'swinging door' (Holt 1988: 57) on the frontier, conflict was precipitated immediately. Order was only restored when the policy was reversed and Alexander, to the horror of his troops, married the daughter of a tribal chief.

The Hsiung Nu and the Scythians at opposite ends of the Eurasian steppes coexisted with very substantial agrarian empires for several hundred years. They are the first recorded nomadic empires. The Scythians had travelled west much earlier in the millennium under pressure from other tribes. This was a cyclical feature of the steppes. In the early second century BC, the Hsiung Nu began a policy of expansion which again had consequences right across the steppes. The Yueh Chi, their immediate neighbours, were forced off their land, and attempts to settle further west were thwarted by the Wu Sun tribes, allies of the Hsiung Nu. The Yueh Chi eventually settled in Bactria, destroying in the process the cities built in this region by Greek colonists (Phillips 1965: 110–12). The tribes, however, adopted a sedentary way of life; they united, and then extended their control over neighbouring areas to form the Kushan Empire which was as extensive as the Parthian Empire and played a crucial role in the transport of silk from China to the Roman Empire (Boulnois 1966).

Nomadic empires continued to form, and for brief periods the Turks even succeeded in uniting the entire steppe region, first in the sixth century AD and then again at the end of the seventh century. But by the time the second Turkic Empire collapsed, the tribes in the areas bordering the agrarian empires were adopting a more sedentary way of life. The same pattern followed the collapse of the Mongol Empire. Significantly, the Mongols ruled their empire from a city, Qaraqorum, the first nomadic city established on the steppes, and then, after the conquest of China, from Peking. Sedentarization was always to prove the ultimate threat to nomads.

# 3. CONCLUSIONS

With the emergence of these new units, international systems began to form at certain nodal points in the established pre-international systems. The role of these pre-international systems in the emergence of the initial international systems has never been explored. Although it is recognized that all non-agricultural products had to be imported into Sumeria, for example, the obscure sources of some of these products do not seem to occasion surprise. Lapis lazuli, and very probably tin, was imported into Sumeria from Afghanistan, over a distance of 2,400 km (1500 miles) across deserts and mountains (Herrmann 1968). And carnelian stones arrived from the Harappan civilization. Yet no thought has been given to how these extraordinary links were established. It is simply asserted that this evidence 'makes an impression of a dimly emerging international trading system already creating important patterns of interdependence' (Roberts 1993: 45). The more obvious answer is that these new units were embedded in, and responsive to, the long-established 'trading' networks of pre-international systems.

Given the emergence of the new types of units discussed in this chapter, what was the character of the first generation of international systems that they generated and how did these systems relate to the established pre-international systems? We can examine this development in terms of interaction capacity, processes, and structures.

# Chapter 9

# INTERACTION CAPACITY IN ANCIENT AND CLASSICAL INTERNATIONAL SYSTEMS

As noted in the introduction to this group of chapters, developments in interaction capacity define much of both what differentiates the ancient and classical era from pre-international systems, and what set limits on the size and type of both the units and the international systems characteristic of the era. In line with our toolkit we divide this story into physical and social technologies. The basic story here is of the development, and also the limits, of physical and social techniques that allowed the movement of more goods, people, and information over wider distances, more easily, and at lower cost, than had been possible in earlier times.

The story of the Silk Road provides a good illustration of the complex social and physical factors that can affect the evolution of interaction capacity.

*The Silk Road (see Map 9.1)*

Two thousand years before the Europeans began taking advantage of developments in interaction capacity to connect all corners of the globe, the major civilizations across Eurasia were all starting to be linked together in such a way that goods and ideas were able to circulate amongst them. During the nineteenth century, this feature was romantically associated with the existence of a 'silk road' stretching across the land mass of Eurasia, although, in practice, there was no road but rather a network of routes across land and sea that carried much more than just silk. But the reference to silk is important because for millennia it was only produced in China. So the presence of silk in other parts of Eurasia helps to confirm the existence of active trading routes and it is estimated that silk constituted 90 per cent of the trade between China and the Roman Empire (Hudson 1931: 93). There is, however, a range of other goods, such as pepper and cinnamon, that also help to identify the emergence of extensive Eurasian trading routes from a very early stage in world history (Miller 1969).

The existence of silk in Greece and elsewhere in the Western world has been traced back to the fifth century BC, long before the West had any knowledge of its source (Hayashi 1975: 9). The most likely way that the silk could have travelled to the West was along the Scythian route established by the steppe nomads around the sixth century BC. The route extended from the Scythian nomadic tribes on the Black Sea to the nomadic tribes on the Pacific along a route which has been speculatively plotted by Hudson (1931: 37; Rolle 1989: 13–14) on the basis of an account given by Herodotus. The Scythians set out from the Black Sea with caravans of horse-drawn wagons to engage in substantial trade with the other nomadic tribes across Eurasia. Trade was facilitated by the existence of the common language and culture which extended across the Eurasian steppe (Rice 1957: 39). It is presumed that the Scythians were particularly interested in the gold that was mined in the Altai Mountains in Mongolia. Rice (1957: 24) suggests that the Altai Mountains were a point of 'two way contact' with the tribes in the area having links with both Greece and China. Hudson argues, however, that with the collapse of the Scythian nomadic empire in the third century BC, the Scythian trade route also effectively came to an end.

But by this time, Persia was extending its influence to the east, while at the same time, China was extending its influence to the West. By the end of the second century BC, the Chinese had sent an embassy to Persia along with gifts of silk. Interest in silk quickly spread westwards and, within a century, significant trading routes had been established linking the Roman and Han empires together and to the subcontinent of India. Separating these two empires were the Parthian and Kushan (and later the Sassanian and Gupta) Empires that provided the political stability that Boulnois (1966) argues was vital to the persistence of this trade. Hudson (1931: 71) argues, however, that the piracy associated with political instability could be rendered insignificant if the commercial expeditions were sufficiently large and strong. But even more important was the existence of sea routes. Towards the end of the Roman Empire, an all-sea route from Egypt to Tongking had been established, but it never became commercially significant, whereas the routes to Burma and Bengal did become important and had the consequence of substantially reducing the price of silk to the point where it became very widely available in the Roman Empire (Hudson 1931: 77). But market forces never operated in the Romans' favour because the Persians were able to dictate the price of the silk that came by both land and sea (Hudson 1931: 112).

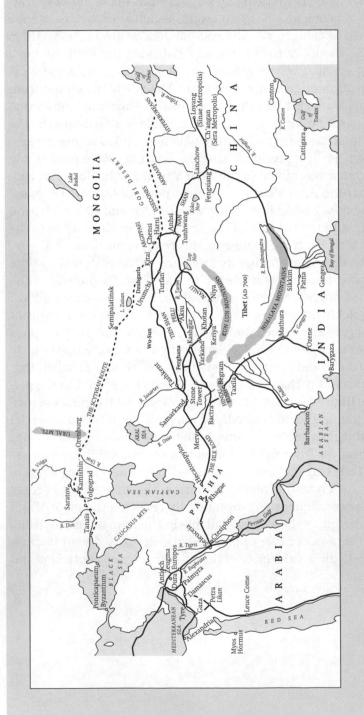

*Note:* The first link between China and the West, as described by Herodotus, was established by nomadic tribes that exchanged goods along the Scythian route in the sixth century BC. Trade across Eurasia became much more regular when the Silk Roads opened up between the Han and Roman Empires. These land routes were soon supplemented by sea routes (see Map 10.1).

*Source:* Taken from Miller 1969.

*Map 9.1 The Silk Road*

# 1. PHYSICAL TECHNOLOGIES OF TRANSPORTATION AND COMMUNICATION

With physical technologies, the basic pattern is a series of breakthroughs in transportation and communication by land and by water, followed by a very long period of incremental but not transformational improvements. As Bentley (1993: 20–1) notes, the breakthroughs accelerated cross-cultural exchanges amongst many branches of humankind. On land, the story in Eurasia hinges on the invention of wheels, the domestication of animals suitable for pulling, packing, and riding, and the development of roads, 'pony express' systems. On water, it hinges on the development of proper ships (as opposed to rafts), sails, knowledge of navigation techniques, and harbours. One has to understand the importance of geography in this era given the relative weakness of transportation technology. Geography could both pose huge barriers (seas, mountains, deserts, harsh climate zones), and offer huge assets (navigable rivers, inland seas, predictable trade winds, and, for nomadic peoples, open steppelands). One estimate of transportation cost ratios for ancient and classical era is: 1 by sea, 4.9 by river, and 28 by land (Meijer and van Nijf 1992: 133). In the Americas the ratio is even more dramatic, with transport by water being 40 times more efficient than transport by land (Hassig 1985: 133). These numbers give immediate insight into the importance of water-borne transport in shaping the empires and international systems of the ancient and classical era. Because of the high relative cost of ground transportation, distance overland was a major barrier for all but high-value, low-weight and low-volume goods. One calculation has it that 'in classical antiquity, every 100 miles of land transport roughly doubled the price of heavy or bulky goods' (Singer et al. 1956: 493). Such calculations shaped both the economic and military-political potentialities of the era, though the potential for overland trade in high-value, low-volume goods should not be underestimated. There is ample evidence of substantial overland trade from a very early stage. The archives of Assyrian merchants record caravans of donkeys travelling over 1,100 km (700 miles) from Assur to Cappadocia carrying tin and textiles and then returning with silver and gold (Larsen 1976: 89; Silver 1985: 61). The fact that the donkeys fed on grass meant that the fuel for transport was free.

As we saw in Part II, physical interaction capacity in pre-international systems was essentially defined by the speed and carrying capacity of human movement on foot. There were established trails for long-distance trade in materials for tool-making such as flint and obsidian (Singer et al. 1954: 704), and for some luxury goods. Neolithic peoples used floats, log rafts, and crude boats (e.g. dugout canoes) for river transportation (Singer et al. 1954: 730–40), and some of these were good enough to take human beings across the substantial sea gap separating Australia from Indonesia perhaps as long as 30,000 years ago (Diamond 1997: 41). But even very crude improvements in land transportation such as sledges do not seem to have materialized until as late as 5000 BC (Singer et al. 1954: 707).

On land, the first revolution in transportation seems to have begun during the fourth millennium BC. Its major element was the application of animal power to transportation, which greatly raised the limits of both speed and carrying capacity. The use of domesticated pack animals pre-dates 3000 BC, and donkey caravans connected Mesopotamia and Asia Minor as early as 2000 BC (Bentley 1993: 20–1). Wheeled carts existed possibly from 3500 BC, and definitely after 3000 BC. These carts had heavy solid wheels, and were initially pulled by oxen and onagers. Only after 2000 BC had the breeding of horses produced large enough variants of this key species to be put into harness, enabling wheeled vehicles to achieve higher speeds and longer ranges. This combination was crucial in enabling the develop-ment of nomadic lifestyles on the Eurasian steppe. Lighter spoked wheels developed c.2000 BC in Persia/Mesopotamia, reaching China by 1300 BC (Singer et al. 1954: 203–11, 705–6, 720–6). This marriage opened the way for what became an important war machine of the second millennium BC: the horse-drawn chariot.

The use of horses for riding developed from early in the first millennium BC. This required not only the development of riding skills, but also the breeding of still larger horses capable of carrying a human, a process that culminated in the heavy horses necessary for carrying the armoured cavalry that developed during the first millennium AD. Stirrups, probably developed in Asia, did not reach Europe until around the fifth century AD, after the fall of Rome, and the harnesses used by Rome were also notably inefficient in their design (Singer et al. 1956: 495, 515, 555). Stirrups gave mounted riders much more freedom to use a variety of weapons, thus greatly increasing the power of cavalry, both light and heavy. Camels were also domesticated, playing a major role in opening up transportation routes across desert areas in Central Asia, Arabia, and Africa. Camels played a crucial role in the Silk Roads across Central Asia and the Incense Route across Arabia. They reached Egypt around the middle of the first millennium BC and were essential to opening up the cross-Sahara caravan routes that developed thereafter (Curtin 1984: 15–37; Bulliet 1990).

Along with the application of animal, and particularly horse, power to transportation went the development of roads. By roads we mean not just paved highways, but also maintained tracks, which might include fords, bridges, way-stations, and guard houses. Given the high relative cost of land transport, ancient and classical road systems were primarily built for the strategic communications and military movements of empires, and only secondarily for trade. City-state systems, such as that in classical Greece, did not develop roads other than for local and ceremonial purposes. Water transport, by river or sea, was favoured for trade (Forbes 1955: 146).

The technology for paved roads can be found as early as the third millennium BC in Egypt (in relation to pyramid-building) and in the second millennium BC towns of the Hittite Empire. But early roads were largely short and ceremonial, and were not used for long-distance exchanges (Singer et al. 1956: 494–5). They could, nevertheless, be impressive achievements. The Mayan network of causeways linking civic and ceremonial centres to satellite centres could be 3 to 20 m across and up to 99 km (60 miles) long, but they performed a largely symbolic function (Earle 1991: 13). There is evidence of an extensive road network in China with five grades of roads during the Chou dynasty, early in the first millennium BC (Singer et al. 1954: 713–14). A major regional road system was established by the Assyrians during the seventh century BC and inherited by the Persian Empire. This was more in the nature of a maintained and guarded track, only partly paved, with over 100 permanent stations along the way. The use of stone bridges also seems to date from this time. The Persian road stretched 2,500 km (1,600 miles) from the Aegean coast to their capital at Susa, and its use, as also in the later Roman road system, was primarily for strategic communication and military movement (mostly marching armies), rather than for commerce. Messengers could move along this road at five times the speed of general travellers—or invading armies (Singer et al. 1954: 713; 1956: 495–8; Meijer and van Nijf 1992: 141–2). The Roman road system began to be extended in 312 BC, reaching its fullest extent by AD 200, constituting some 90,000 km (56,000 miles) of paved roads, and 300,000 km (186,000 miles) of roads of all classes. There were several grades of roads, ranging from fully paved, through gravel, to maintained footpaths. Communication could move at 75 km (46 miles) per day. The Roman system fell into disrepair in Europe after the fall of Rome, but was kept up in the East by the Byzantines and the Arabs. Even in Europe, Roman routes continued in use for communication and light trade (foot and horse traffic) (Singer et al. 1956: 500–27; Forbes 1955: 146). The Incas in South America followed a similar strategy and built 5,230 km (3,250 miles) of road running from north to south across 35 degrees of latitude. These roads enabled the Incas to maintain the coherence of the empire, despite the absence of any draught animals. There were posthouses every five miles along the roads, some of them fortified, and relays of runners could transport messages 240 km (150 miles) a day (Lanning 1974a: 85).

As noted in Chapter 8, many of the early city-state systems and empires were built around navigable rivers. This was true of most of the Mesopotamian empires, Egypt, the Harappan civilization, and China. Given the substantial cost advantage of river transport compared with overland, the presence or absence of navigable rivers significantly shaped the possibilities of empire. Egypt was particularly blessed in having a prevailing wind blowing in the opposite direction from the river current, so providing easy water transport in both directions. This, in conjunction with the surrounding deserts, gave Egypt its basic shape. Likewise, Roman penetration into Europe was substantially shaped by access to rivers (Rhone, Rhine, Danube). Many cultures in the ancient and classical world built canals to extend the irrigation provided by rivers. The Sumerian cities, for example, were criss-crossed with canals, used primarily to supply the population with water, but also as a means of communication, linking the city with the outside world. The cities had harbours within the city walls where trading activities were carried out (Stone 1995: 239). A few cultures, most notably China, also built canals to extend the river transportation network. The Grand Canal built AD 584–618 linked the two major river systems around which Chinese civilization was centred, enabling food to be transported from south to north.

### Interaction capacity in Mesoamerica

With no wagons or draught animals in Mesoamerica, goods were carried in cane containers on the backs of people called *tlamemes* along roads built and maintained by the state. The main roads were wide, but often rough, and they could also be steep and turn sharp corners, because they were designed for foot traffic and to minimize the distance travelled. It was possible for the *tlamemes* to carry 23 kg (50 lb) over a distance of five leagues (about 29 km/18 miles). The transport system, therefore, generated an overall picture in Mesoamerica of small cities sustained by small hinterlands. In Eurasia, cities tended to be larger and spaced further apart.

The huge cities developed in the Valley of Mexico represent an obvious exception to this generalization. Tenochtitlan, the capital city of the Aztec Empire, for example, contained over 200,000 inhabitants when the Spaniards arrived at the start of the sixteenth century. Before the rise of the Aztec Empire, the Valley of Mexico had been dominated by five city-states. The size of these cities is explained by their access to water transportation. Built on an island in Lake Texcoco, Tenochtitlan was joined to the mainland by three causeways and six canals that ran through the city, providing docking facilities for the 20,000 canoes used to provide transport throughout the Valley of Mexico lakes (Fagan 1993: 239). Although the canoes travelled at the same speed as the *tlamemes*, they could propel one tonne per person—an efficiency ratio of 40 to 1 over the *tlamemes* (Hassig 1985: 133). The effect of this mode of transport was to draw towns surrounding the lakes into much closer commercial interaction than would otherwise have been the case. Nevertheless, the *tlamemes* were an essential part of the transport system; and their role was particularly important in the case of long-distance trade. Mesoamerica was organized at the local level into small districts with their own capital city which was responsible for ensuring that there were *tlamemes* available for portering goods across the district. Each district, therefore, formed part of an interlocking transport system. Merchants would hire the *tlamemes* to porter goods from one district to another. Despite hostile relations between some districts, the transport system was relatively immune from these political tensions, except in times of war. Local authorities were responsible for the main roads along which the long-distance trade travelled. But in the Aztec Empire there were also messengers stationed along the route at 2-league intervals (just over 8 km/5 miles). Messages were carried in relays, allegedly at 4 to 5 leagues per hour. This meant, in theory, that messages could cover 400 km (250 miles) a day. These messengers undoubtedly played an important role in the security of the empire where there was a constant danger of internal revolt. Messages could be carried in written form. This development was not unique to the Aztecs. Four separate writing systems evolved in Mesoamerica, linked to the Maya, Zapotec, Mixtec, and Aztec regions (Marcus 1992). These systems have been traced back to the time of pre-state societies, between 700 and 400 BC, and are associated with attempts by chiefdoms to maintain control of genealogy and history. Although less sophisticated than the Maya script, the Aztec writing system was still an effective means of information storage and communication. Two days after Cortés landed in Vera Cruz, for example, Montezuma received a written account of the arrival of the Spaniards, with descriptions of their ships, their horses, and their weapons (Gaur 1992).

The development of transportation by sea was altogether more demanding than that by river. It required larger and sturdier ships, better sailing gear, and, if one wanted to do more than follow the coastline, knowledge of navigation techniques and patterns of wind, tide, and current. There is evidence for the use of sails on Egyptian boats as early as 2400 BC, and by the eighteenth century BC wooden ships up to 55 m (180 feet) in length, with crews of 120, and capable of carrying 1,000 tonnes of cargo were plying the Mediterranean (Singer et al. 1954: 733–5). The use of stronger keeled hulls dates from at least 1000 BC, and by that time there was a trans-Mediterranean sea trade stretching from the Levant to Spain. By 500 BC, Carthaginians were trading by sea as far as the British Isles and the West African coast. They may have circumnavigated Africa, and there is evidence that such coastal trade goes back much earlier. The Sumerians, for example, during the third millennium, traded with various regions along the coastline of the Persian Gulf (Hourani 1995: 6). During the Hellenistic period (late fourth to early second centuries BC), both the Seleucid and Ptolemaic Empires traded with India by sea using coastal navigation via the Red Sea or Persian Gulf, then along the coast of the Arabian Sea. The Greek explorer Pytheas circumnavigated Britain c.320 BC, and Polybius explored the Atlantic coast of Morocco (Walbank 1993: 204–6). Early navigation was coastal and cautious, with primitive navigation techniques creating a well-founded fear of open water (Singer et al. 1956: 568–9; Neuberger 1930: 499–500).

Some of the classical cities of antiquity, notably Athens and Rome, became dependent on trade by sea to import the building materials and foodstuffs necessary to maintain both their populations and their navies. Despite the general restriction of cross-Mediterranean navigation to the summer months, Rome imported perhaps 200,000 tonnes of wheat annually from Egypt, Africa, Sicily, and the Black Sea (Meijer and van Nijf 1992: 98–118). This bulk trade encouraged the development of harbours, lighthouses, and port facilities (warehouses etc.), a major feature of first-millennium BC maritime development, especially by Athens, Carthage, Alexandria, and Rome. Once the working of the trade winds across the Arabian Sea was understood around the first century BC, sea trade opened up between Rome (via Egypt) and South Asia (Meijer and van Nijf 1992: 128–9). By the time the Arabs had established their vast Islamic empire, ships were strong enough, and navigational knowledge good enough, to allow voyages from the Middle East to China, the round trip taking 1.5 years (Curtin 1984: 103–8). The Chinese seem to have developed ocean-going junks some time around AD 1000. The lateen sail (for sailing into the wind), the compass (from China, reaching Europe c.AD 1250), and the stern-post rudder all date from Byzantine times (Singer et al. 1956: 584; van Creveld 1991: 51–6) and were to become part of the revolution in global shipping that took place in the fifteenth century (see Chapter 13).

The rowed galley that dominated Mediterranean sea power from the time of the Greek–Persian wars up to the encounters between European and Ottoman fleets in the sixteenth century AD, was already well developed by the seventh century BC, and probably dates from several hundred years earlier, when a marked differentiation between fast rowed warships and slower, more capacious, sail-powered merchantmen began to develop. During Roman times, wooden vessels reached the size, though not the strength of construction, of mid-nineteenth-century galleons (Singer et al. 1954: 735–43; 1956: 563–7, 572–3; Meijer and van Nijf 1992: 152–8). But although important militarily, rowed vessels had limited range, and their large crews made their carrying capacity small, and their need for provisions large.

Putting all of this together, one way of understanding the physical side of interaction capacity during the ancient and classical era is to see it as quite constrained on land, but increasingly liberated by sea. This is of course an oversimplification. The nomadic barbarians could and did move powerful military forces as well as goods across large distances, and briefly established empires spanning much of Eurasia on several occasions. The wheel, the horse, the camel, and roads facilitated huge improvements in the speed and carrying capacity (though not the range) of overland transport when compared with the foot traffic of prehistory. Rivers, and in China also canals, went some way towards compensating for the difficulties of land transportation, which is why they played such a prominent role as the spines of empires. But the ability to compensate for the difficulties of overland transportation by using navigable rivers was restricted to relatively few geographical areas, and goes a long way towards explaining why this era featured multiple international systems, loosely connected to each other in Afro-Eurasia, and largely unconnected in the Americas. There seems little doubt that there were geographical and environmental factors that meant that interaction capacity was easier to develop in Eurasia than the Americas. Although the llama was used as a pack animal in South America, it could not compare with the horses and camels which made transcontinental links possible in Eurasia (Diamond 1997). Just as important were the open steppes which made it possible for the nomads to establish direct transcontinental links in the first millennium BC. The nomads acquainted the West with Oriental goods, although it was eventually the empires and city-states that consolidated the sea trading routes stretching from one end of Eurasia to the other.

Once the ocean-going sailing ship was invented, however, a major key was in hand to unlock the long-distance transportation of both people and bulk goods. In principle, as the Chinese and the Europeans were to prove during the fifteenth century AD, such vessels could open up intercontinental economic and military contact, and create a global international system. But in practice, that development took some four millennia to reach fruition. Many innovations in ship design and construction, and much accumulation of knowledge about navigation, especially in the open sea, had to occur before maritime transport had the capacity to generate and sustain a global international system. Along the way, this development generated both maritime empires like those of the Greeks, Carthaginians, and Romans, and trading systems, which ranged far beyond the boundaries of any single empire or civilization. Seen from this perspective, it was clearly no accident that sea power and commercial shipping were crucial elements in Europe's eventual creation of a global international system. This was neither a chance event nor some development exclusive to Europe. It represented the culmination of a long development that had been a major factor in shaping the whole political economy of the ancient and classical world, and whose sustained flowering in Europe led quickly to the destruction of that world.

## 2. SOCIAL TECHNOLOGIES OF TRANSPORTATION AND COMMUNICATION

As noted in Chapter 4, the social side of interaction capacity can be seen as 'elements of process that become sedimented and embedded within the system'. This section thus needs to be understood in conjunction with the chapter on process that follows. As discussed in Part II, social technology played a vital role in the creation of pre-international systems. Social mechanisms like marriage and exogamy ensured that individual bands, tribes, or clans operated within systems that extended over vast distances. What the social technology of prehistory was not able to do was to create the infrastructures necessary to support systematic and large-scale movements of goods and information, or to create wider realms of authority.

The larger and more sophisticated units of the ancient and classical world were able to do all of these things, and over time learned how to extend many of them beyond the sphere of individual city-states or empires so that they became as essential as shipping to facilitating the development and expansion of international systems. Sometimes these social technologies were developed intentionally, as when imperial powers promoted a particular language, currency, script, or religion. At other times, they arose spontaneously, such as when the operation of trader networks spread religions (Buddhism, Islam), languages (Aramaic, Arabic, Malay), and written scripts. Sometimes a long-dead empire would pass on its social technologies to successor states or systems. The Sumerian civilization of city-states left an important cultural legacy for the empires that followed in its wake, although perhaps the best known example of this is Rome's legacy to medieval Europe of Latin, Christianity, and law, all of which survived much better than the physical technology of Roman roads.

Many types of social technologies went into the making of units in the ancient and classical world, and were particularly important to the construction and maintenance of large empires. In a world still highly fragmented by language, geography, religion, and culture, creating common standards was an important part of the imperial process. Uniform systems of weights and measures, standardized currencies and accounting systems, postal services, an infrastructure of roads and ports, and widely imposed systems of law and law enforcement (especially against piracy) all facilitated trade. In doing so they supported imperial prosperity, and sometimes thereby imperial legitimacy. Athens, for example, imposed a single currency and standardized weights and measures on the other city-states within its empire (Meijer and van Nijf 1992: 33–51). Higher religions were also a feature of the imperial process. These enabled much wider patterns of shared identity to develop, which could be useful in bolstering imperial legitimacy as well as in generally greasing the wheels of social interaction in otherwise diverse societies.

But more important for our purposes are those social technologies that grew beyond the boundaries of individual units, or were left behind when larger units disintegrated into systems of smaller ones, so supporting international systems and not just units. Of these, six stand out as important to the development of international systems in the ancient and classical era: multilingualism and common languages, scripts, higher religions, money, diplomacy, and trade diasporas and credit systems.

## MULTILINGUALISM AND LINGUA FRANCAS

As we showed in Part II, when communities became sedentary and their population increased beyond the minimum size required for a viable breeding group, languages increasingly began to diverge and ethnicity became an ever more important feature of an individual's sense of identity. The languages of adjacent groups could become mutually incomprehensible, perhaps as a mechanism to heighten the social differentiation between the groups (Renfrew 1987: 113). The proliferation of languages therefore has the effect of putting a social brake on interaction capacity. This development is most evident today in New Guinea, where over 1,000 mutually unintelligible languages are spoken within an area the size of Texas. Many of these languages seem to have no common roots with each other or with other languages in the world (Diamond 1997: 231–2). The extraordinary diversity of languages is in part a function of the fact that these communities have been undisturbed by outside forces for many millennia and in part a result of the fact that, prior to European colonization, there was no political unification of any kind linking them. This is an unusual phenomenon. It contrasts sharply with Africa, where, because of recent migration, there are relatively few languages with distinct linguistic roots.

Linguistic diversity is not a problem if there is no need for interaction, but as indicated in Part II, there is a range of reasons why communities will want to interact. If communities only need to interact with their immediate neighbours, which was often the case in the neolithic systems that formed before the emergence of city-states and empires, then bilingualism or multilingualism provided an adequate social mechanism for overcoming the language impediment to interaction. But with the emergence of civilization and the development of merchants who travelled along trading routes that crossed many linguistic frontiers, and the growth of merchant or commercial cities where traders came from many quarters to buy and sell their wares, multilingualism became an unsatisfactory solution to the problem. By the same token, once the world of city-states began to be overtaken by the multi-ethnic empires which proliferated in the ancient and classical worlds, the task of administering and trading within these new units was also necessarily complicated by the existence of divergent and competing languages. In both these cases, the linguistic obstacle to interaction was overcome by the development of a lingua franca or common language which either replaced or supplemented the indigenous languages. The processes whereby one language overtakes another are various, often complex, and not fully understood (Renfrew 1987; Mallory 1989). The most obvious sources of lingua francas are imperialism and trade. Although indigenous languages survived, Latin served as the common language across the Roman Empire, just as Babylonian and later Aramaic had served as lingua francas in the Near East (Bozeman 1960: 29). But trade can also serve as the basis for a lingua franca. The Hittites, for example, who occupied the dominant trading city of Kanes, provided the lingua franca across central Anatolia in the second millennium BC (Mallory 1989: 28) But lingua francas are not the preserve of civilized communities. As argued in Part II, common languages are spoken over vast distances in areas where the population is mobile. Turkic, for example, provided a lingua franca for the nomadic tribes who lived on the Asian steppes (Kwanten 1979).

## SCRIPTS

The development of writing has had huge consequences for interaction capacity because it transforms the way that individuals can communicate across time and space. Of course, it was always possible for information to be preserved over time or passed from one place to another by oral means. But inevitably there are severe limitations on the complexity and volume of information that can be conveyed orally. Even the most simple information can be forgotten or distorted in the process of transmission. Scripts, moreover, are not the only way that information can be stored. Cave paintings, for example, can be seen as a way of storing information although we will never be able to retrieve with any certainty the meaning that is locked in them. Nevertheless, the range of mechanisms that can be used for storing information is obviously enormous. Some of these mechanisms have been regarded as precursors of scripts. Counting devices, in particular, are of crucial importance from this perspective. It is argued that scripts have never evolved in societies that had not already developed elaborate counting systems. The earliest known writing script was developed in Mesopotamia where, from the ninth millennium BC, the development of farming was accompanied by the emergence of clay tokens which were used to keep records of the number of animals in a herd and the volume of a product such as oil, wool, or grain that was being stored (Harris 1986).

What this development suggests is that when societies become more complex and start to produce surpluses, verbal communication, which is a perfectly satisfactory mechanism for transferring information in less highly organized settings, becomes increasingly inadequate. Trade and administration beyond a certain level of complexity require some form of writing because their transient character requires records that can be established with a reasonable degree of speed and a high degree of accuracy. Gaur (1992; Dickinson 1994: 193–7) argues that when societies in Egypt, Mesopotamia, and the Aegean reached the point in their trading and administrative relations where it was necessary to rely on systematic writing, they either developed their own form of writing or borrowed it from elsewhere. He suggests, as a consequence, that most codified forms of writing using phonetic elements have developed in capitalistically oriented societies. Such scripts appear to have developed first in the Fertile Crescent between 4000 and 3000 BC (Crawford 1991: 151–6). To support his claim that scripts are associated with capitalistically oriented societies, Gaur (1992) points to the fact that many of the early documents relate to property.

But this generalization needs to be treated with some caution. Not all scripts are phonetically based and the assumption that other types of scripts, such as those developed in the Far East around 2000 BC (although recent discoveries suggest that another millennium needs to be added to this date), and in Central America around 1000 BC, are less advanced is now seen to be yet another example of Eurocentrism. In such societies the development of writing may have had nothing to do with trade or property. Many early documents in such societies related to dynastic history, and it has been suggested that scripts were developed in order to allow ruling dynasties to use the past as a resource to legitimize their rule. This is true for both China and Central America (Marcus 1992). Attention has also been drawn to the importance of sacred scripts in the evolution of religion. Such scripts can be seen to guarantee once and for all the words of God, as spoken by his prophets (Burkert 1996: 178). But whatever the reasons for inventing scripts, the fact remains that the development has enormous consequences for interaction capacity. Scripts free societies from the impermanence of speech and it becomes possible to transfer information across space and time without the intervention of an interlocutor.

The invention of scripts represented the first real revolution in information storage. Although all human societies store information at some level or other, scripts are distinctive because they provide a mechanism for reproducing and storing the spoken word. One can think of scripts as frozen speech. The emergence of the written word played a crucial role in the formation of centralized and hierarchically structured states and, as we will see in subsequent sections, organized religions and international diplomacy. But the advantages of adopting writing were not always seen as compelling. Nomadic societies throughout history failed to adopt scripts despite living alongside societies that used them. Such societies could maintain contact over vast distances, with oral communication providing the basis for the interaction required at their relatively low level of organization. Written scripts, therefore, are not needed to maintain the cohesion of societies that interact across expansive tracts of territory. They only become necessary when a higher level of organization develops. Scripts do not create the basis for communication to be sustained over very large distances, but they do permit a much greater density of interaction across these distances. Only with the formation of their vast empires, for example, did nomadic chiefs find it necessary to take advantage of writing.

## RELIGIONS

The evolution of universal religions also had an impact on the development of interaction capacity. Burkert (1996: 6) argues that religion manifests itself through interaction and communication, with the divine representing a 'social tool' that shapes the way that communication takes place. From this perspective religion can have a profound effect on regular transactions within and between societies because it becomes possible to draw on a culturally defined supernatural dimension to reinforce the import of a message communicated through more conventional channels. It has been argued since the time of Herodotus that religious belief is a defining feature of all human beings, but it is necessary, at the very least, to draw a broad distinction between universal and folk religions. In practice, even this distinction is too restrictive and these two modes of religion need to be seen as the ends of a spectrum with national religions sitting between them (Schneider 1970: 74). In very general terms, folk religions can constrain interaction capacity whereas universal religions can facilitate communication within and between societies and provide an added depth to interaction capacity. But because universal religions compete, they too can act as a barrier rather than a bridge to communication.

A folk religion is tied to a particular group such as a band or a tribe whereas a universal religion is detached from any specific group and appeals, in principle, to individuals across the known world. But classifying any religion is problematic. Islam, like Judaism, for example, has been classified as, ultimately, a national religion. Hinduism, by contrast, is associated with a particular caste, and has been classified as a national folk religion, with Buddhism being identified as 'the export form of Hinduism' (Schneider 1970: 75–7). It has been estimated on the basis of anthropological evidence that during the course of world history there have been more than 100,000 religions in existence. In the contemporary world, however, it is possible to restrict the major religious traditions to Hindu-Buddhist, Chinese, Judao-Christian, and Islamic (Fallding 1974: 1). All these traditions have developed over three millennia and each came to form the dominant faith over an extensive geographical zone during the ancient and classical period (see Maps 9.2 and 9.3). At that time, of course, there were major religions in the Americas but these were regional rather than universal in form and they also failed to survive during the period of European expansion. The contemporary significance of these four dominant traditions will be examined in Part IV. But in this section we still need to look more closely at the link between religion and interaction capacity.

The four dominant religious traditions all formed on the margins of Asia during the course of the first millennium BC (Fallding 1974). Karl Jaspers (1953) refers to the period 800–200 BC as the 'axial age' when ethical and reflective thought flourished in India, China, the Middle East, and Greece. Bentley (1993: 24–5) argues that during this period, thinkers as different as Confucius, the Buddha, the Hebrew prophets, Socrates, and Plato all displayed a profound interest in political and social stability, ethics and personal morality, and standards that would rationalize human relationships. He argues, however, that we are never likely to possess the necessary documentary evidence to verify Jaspers' (1953) claim that this efflorescence in thought was at least in part the result of the threat that the steppe nomads posed to all the sedentary communities that lay on the fringe of the steppe, although we do know that the Greeks found the Scythian success against the Persians to be very unsettling (Ascherson 1996). But, more important in terms of this section, it is possible to view the efflorescence as part of a much broader development whereby folk religions gave way to universal religions with the density and breadth of interaction capacity increasing as a consequence.

In preliterate agricultural societies, religion suffuses every aspect of life, from

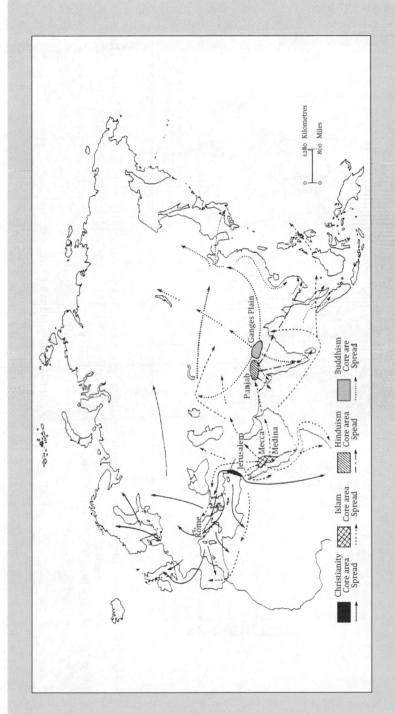

*Note:* The map indicates how the four major world religions have dispersed across Eurasia over the last two millennia. It does not reveal the important divisions within these religions (see Map 9.3).

*Source:* Taken from Park 1994.

*Map 9.2 The origin and dispersion of four major world religions*

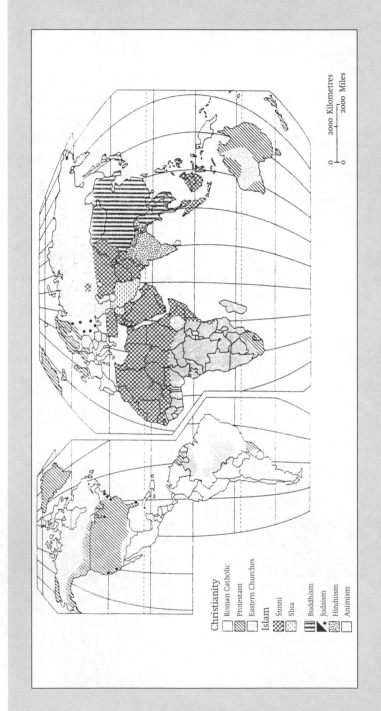

Christianity
☐ Roman Catholic
▨ Protestant
▨ Eastern Churches

Islam
▨ Sunni
▨ Shia

▤ Buddhism
◣ Judaism
▨ Hinduism
☐ Animism

0 ———— 2000 Kilometres
0 ———— 2000 Miles

*Note:* There have been innumerable religions established across the globe during the course of world history. The map illustrates the contemporary distribution of the major world religions and demonstrates that only a very few religions have been successfully exported (see Map 9.2).

*Source:* Taken from Park 1994.

*Map 9.3  The world distribution of major religions*

the family to the workplace. Such religions play a crucial role in binding people together into tight *Gemeinschaft* communities and separating them from other communities. Exclusion from the religiously defined group is extremely hazardous. (O'Dea and O'Dea Aviad 1983; Schneider 1970). One of the features of the early city-based societies that distinguishes them from the preceding agricultural societies was the emergence of organizations whose main function was religious. Religious organizations were an important aspect of the increasing division of labour and specificity of function that accompanied the growth of urbanization. This development is also associated with the consolidation of hierarchy. But from a very early stage, the interaction between neighbouring city-states was fostered by a religious component. In Mesopotamia, for example, it was acknowledged that every city-state had its own distinctive god, who participated in a pantheon of gods, but that they vied with each other as did the city-states. The dominant city-state at any point in time claimed that its god took precedence over the others (Watson 1992). With the development of empires, such ideas helped to stabilize internal as well as external relations. That Egypt, for example, saw itself as the centre of the world helped to consolidate relations with trading partners beyond the limits of the empire by incorporating and subordinating their gods within the pantheon of Egyptian gods (Morenz 1973: 232–57). This development, although subversive of folk religions, gives way to national rather than universal religions.

The emergence of universal religions can be associated with another distinctive development in interaction capacity. As empires expanded and consolidated, established patterns of folk religions were often disrupted. Christianity took root in Palestine, for example, at the time that Rome had absorbed this area into the empire. In the face of this expansion, the boundaries defining traditional groups and values were destroyed and there was a need for a more expansive world-view and a new kind of community. Christianity provided a more cosmopolitan way of viewing reality which embraced what the stoics referred to as 'the sympathy of the whole' (O'Dea and O'Dea Aviad 1983: 44). Like other universal religions, Christianity was founded by a charismatic figure who was at odds with the established norms and institutions of society and who advocated a new spirit of unity and coherence. The survival of this new religion, however, ultimately depended upon what Weber (1947: 363–92) calls the 'routinisation of charisma'. The new religion required an organizational structure which enabled it to extend far beyond the borders of Palestine and even the frontiers of Rome—a development encouraged by the Romans (Blockley 1992: 15). In similar fashion, Buddhism, which originated in India, was to become the dominant religion in Ceylon, Burma, Thailand, and Tibet and, much later, Islam was to move out of Arabia and become the principal religion in North Africa, Central Asia, and parts of South-East Asia. Each of these religious communities can be viewed, in our terms, as potential 'world societies' constituted by shared values, rules, and practices. The common world-views associated with these different religions helped sometimes to create and sustain vibrant societies and communities even when political structures were weak and unstable. The capacity of religions to help bind world societies together has also persistently been undermined by the acute schisms that beset these universal religions such as the divide between Sunni vs. Shia in Islam and between Catholics and Protestants in Christianity. Nevertheless, there is no doubt that universal religions have had a profound effect on the capacity of individuals and communities to bind themselves together.

But the importance of folk religions for interaction capacity must not be underestimated. The local religious leagues or Amphictyonies that formed in ancient Greece provide one of the earliest examples of interstate organizations. The members of the Delphic Amphictyony were bound by oaths to refrain from the destruction of any of its members. They were also forbidden to interrupt the water supplies to any member during peace or war and any city that failed to comply with this injunction risked being razed to the ground (Adcock and Mosley 1974: 186, 229–30). By the same token, it was known that the gods offered safe and honest dealing, so that the temples of the ancient Near East and the Graeco-Roman worlds served not only as places of worship but as centres of intercity and international commerce (Silver 1985: 7)—a custom that notably annoyed one Jesus of Nazareth.

### Entry of Buddhism into China

One of the intriguing features of Buddhism as a universal religion is that having initially spread across India over a period of nearly three centuries, becoming consolidated as one of the major religions on the subcontinent by the end of the third century BC, then successfully moving further afield through Asia, over the next millennium the religion failed to penetrate any other parts of the world and it was eventually to be largely overtaken in India by Hinduism and Islam (see Maps 9.2 and 9.3). The ability of Buddhists to win converts is a complex story that we do not need to go into here, but the dispersal of Buddhism is generally agreed to be closely associated with the evolving pattern of Indian trade. Indeed, Buddhism represents an important social institution that fostered trade by enhancing the interaction capacity on which trade depended. From the start, the class of Indian merchants that emerged in the second half of the first millennium BC found Buddhist teachings much more amenable than the exclusionary beliefs adhered to by the Brahman priests. The merchants began to give financial support to the Buddhists whose monks depended on the charity of the laity. At the same time, the Buddhists aimed to win converts and monks followed the merchants down the trade routes that were being established across Asia. Monasteries were built along these routes and they were to provide places of hospitality and sanctuary for the merchants. As the merchants established trade diasporas, therefore, they simultaneously created

Buddhist communities. By this process, Buddhism was to reach China. The beliefs were alien to the indigenous population, but by a process of syncretism, the Buddhists did eventually win converts. Between the third and ninth centuries AD, thousands of Indians travelled to China and similar numbers of Chinese went to India to learn Sanskrit, copy religious texts, and visit holy shrines. In the long haul, the Buddhists failed to maintain their influence in China, although important elements of this cultural link persist to the present (Bentley 1993: 42–53, 69–84; Boulnois 1966: 92–106; Simkin 1968: 61–73). Why the Buddhists failed to penetrate the West will be discussed in a later box.

## DIPLOMACY

It is unwise to draw any absolute distinction between religious and secular activities in the ancient world because as the Amphictyonies illustrate, religious organizations and activities could have important secular consequences. Nevertheless, it is still worthwhile attempting to distinguish the role played by diplomacy in the development of interaction capacity in the ancient and classical worlds (Mosley 1973: 1). In the absence of any diplomatic relations, only two options exist: ignore each other, or go to war. It has been argued that such conditions prevailed during the early history of the Greek city-states. Greece is seen then to have consisted of a multiplicity of inward-looking communities that coexisted without co-acting (Adcock and Mosley 1974: 10). But although one may be able to identify situations in the ancient and classical world in which neighbouring political units had no diplomatic relations, in practice, such cases are rare. The norm was for most neighbouring political units to have at least intermittent contact with each other, regulated by some kind of diplomatic relations. Diplomacy, however, is not restricted to anarchic international systems, although it is most necessary in such sharply fragmented systems, and it is no surprise that it found its highest development in such systems. Diplomacy can also be found in more hierarchical systems, where imperial cores exercised different degrees of control over their vassals.

The institutional character of diplomacy varies from one international system to another, but in all cases, the emergence of diplomacy demonstrates a willingness of political units to work within a framework of rules—or, in the terms of the English school, to establish elements of an international society. Undoubtedly, the evolution of diplomacy has had important consequences for interaction capacity because the mechanisms associated with diplomacy enormously facilitate the ability of political units to communicate with each other. There are many examples of such practice in the ancient and classical world, ranging from Mesopotamia, through Greece and the Chinese 'warring state' period, to Renaissance Italy (Ferguson and Mansbach 1996; Watson 1992). Cohen (1995a; see also Watson 1992: 30–1) provides evidence that there was a highly developed and extensive diplomatic system in the Middle East during the period 1460–1220 BC including permanent ambassadors, and well-established protocols and procedures. It conducted trade as well as alliance relations, and was based on a hierarchy of kingships in a multicultural environment. In the case of the Greek city-states, the system of *proxenia* represented a surrogate form of permanent diplomatic representation. A city was represented in other cities by one or more citizens of those cities. Such representatives were called *proxenoi*, and the function of each *proxenos* was to find ways of harmonizing the interests of the two cities (Adcock and Mosley 1974: 160–3; Watson 1992: 88–9). Walbank (1993: 141–58) notes many instances of mediation and arbitration during the Hellenistic period, as well as joint attempts to reduce piracy and feuding. And when the Portuguese penetrated Asia, they found a well-developed system of diplomacy including exchanges of envoys, credentials, and embassies, and awareness of 'the necessary privileges and immunities' (Alexandrowicz 1973: 106–7).

The origins of diplomacy seem to be closely tied to religious belief. In Sumeria, for example, the kings of the city-states were considered to be the underlings of gods who occupied a cosmic universe. As a consequence, the territorial dispute between the city-states of Lagash and Umma was depicted as a clash between the divine owners of these two city-states. The powerful king of Kish resolved the dispute by establishing a boundary line between the two city-states revealed to him by his divine overlord (Bozeman 1960: 22). Common religious beliefs seem to have facilitated the development of diplomatic practices. But as empires expanded, inevitably they came to confront societies with incompatible, even inimical, belief systems. As a consequence, it is unsurprising to find that in the early days of the Roman Empire, for example, there was a tendency to define relations beyond its frontiers in terms of war. Diplomacy was regarded at best as an adjunct to war. By the fourth century AD, when further expansion was no longer possible, the Romans had no alternative but to resort to a secular-based form of diplomacy to stabilize their frontiers. But these diplomatic relations could take very different forms. The links established with the Persians who had successfully resisted Roman attacks were very different from the diplomatic links made with the nomadic and sedentary tribes from the East that were endeavouring to enter the Roman Empire. The tribes were willing to accept the traditional posture of Rome that the empire acknowledged no equal and they were willing to accept that only a hegemonic relationship could be formed between the empire and the tribes. But the Romans insisted nevertheless that these relations were based on formal albeit unequal and time-limited treaties and they further assumed that these relationships were of a temporary character. By contrast, the Romans and the Persians came to accept the existence and authenticity of each other. Although their treaties were also time-limited, they were established on 'equal terms', and the Romans accepted that Persia would persist after a treaty terminated and that a state of war did not automatically take its place. Embassies of equal status were exchanged between the two parties and it was acknowledged that both Persia and Rome had their own legitimate interests, as well as sharing some common interests (Blockley 1992). A similar divergence in the pattern of diplomatic relations that China formed with neighbouring states and the tribal communities that lay on its borders can also be observed (Barfield 1989; Boulnois 1966).

Although diplomacy was surprisingly sophisticated in the ancient and classical world, it was for the most part conducted on an ad hoc basis (Blockley 1992: 167). Only at the very end of this era did the Italian city-states develop a more elaborate process of representation, with states permitting ambassadors from other states to reside permanently on their territory. This process formation, along with sovereignty and the establishment of precisely defined territorial boundaries separating one state from another (Kratochwil 1986), was transferred to the rest of Europe during the Renaissance, and became a core feature in the rise of Europe and the creation of a global international society. Aspects of this distinctively different system of diplomacy were foreshadowed in the earlier period, as with the Greek system of *proxenia*, although such developments were generally facilitated by the absence of any significant language differences (Mosley 1973: 95). Nevertheless, the nature of diplomacy that developed in Europe and extended across the globe possessed unique features that were to have profound consequences for interaction capacity.

## MONEY AND BILLS OF EXCHANGE

The origin of money in the form of coins in the ancient world is contested. Polanyi (1977: 119–20) argues that there was a complete absence of coins in the great civilizations of Babylon and Egypt and that the first evidence of coins in Asia Minor is as late as the seventh century BC. By contrast, Silver (1985: 123) argues that money, 'in the generic sense of a common medium of exchange', was a familiar feature of the ancient Near East. If one accepts that the key function of money is to provide a universal, portable means of exchange, then there is little doubt that money was used from a very early date. By the second half of the third millennium silver was used in Mesopotamia to pay rents as well as for the purchase of dates, oil, and barley. Silver argues that there is evidence of coins much earlier than suggested by Polanyi, although generally the origin of coins is traced to Greece by the seventh century BC (Hammond 1972: 166). Coins not only operated as a very convenient means of exchange; they also had important symbolic functions in expressing the power of empires and kings (whose faces often appeared on them). Metal coins had an intrinsic value based on the scarcity of the elements used in making them (usually copper, silver, gold). Since these metals were valued by most cultures, they provided a means of exchange not only within, but also between, units in the system. Money made trade enormously more fluid by replacing barter (trading one good for another) with a single unit of exchange that could be traded for any good. The existence of money thus hugely increased interaction capacity in the economic sector.

But even metal money was not without its problems. The value of the metals varied from place to place, and metal coinage was vulnerable to debasement (reducing the percentage of precious metal in the coins), resulting in inflation and loss of faith in the value of the coinage as a stable medium of exchange. Inflation was even more of a problem with paper money, first invented in China in the eleventh century AD. Paper money was easier to transport than metal coins, and in principle its value was supported by the state's guarantee to redeem notes for their value in metal. But this system was vulnerable to the still familiar abuse of excessive printing (not to mention forgery), and subsequent inflation, a problem that the Chinese never mastered before they abandoned paper money during the Ming dynasty (1368–1644).

Because trade in this era was generally conducted by merchants who moved with their goods, it was possible for foreign trade to take place without an international currency. The traders sold their goods for local currency which they used locally to buy goods which accompanied them on the return journey. It was also possible to exchange currencies. This was a complicated procedure because there were so many separate political entities, from city-states to empires, each having its own coinage with different weights and different contents of precious metal. The task was undertaken by a money changer (who can be thought of as an early species of banker), and the transaction required a good deal of knowledge (not least about which currencies were being debased) to determine an appropriate rate of exchange. But money changing, then as now, was also a lucrative source of profit, and money changers could be found throughout the ancient world.

Once money was in operation, then credit became another way of increasing the fluidity of economic transactions, both by expanding the supply of capital, and by increasing its mobility. Because of the danger of robbers, never mind the burden of carrying heavy metal coins, traders have always preferred not to take currency with them. As far back as 2000 BC in Babylonia, there is evidence of traders relying on written assurances that they would be paid in the future and in a place other than the one where their goods were actually sold. Shipping loans, in which repayment was contingent on the success of the voyage, also go back a long way. T'ang China (AD 618–906) developed the so-called 'flying cash system', whereby merchants could pay money at the capital in exchange for a certificate from the government which, when presented at any provincial treasury entitled the bearer to draw an equivalent sum (Elvin 1973). Such an assurance illustrates the essence of what later came to be called a *bill of exchange*, defined by Pounds (1994: 410) as a contract in which 'money received in one place was repaid at a later date, in a distant place and in a different currency'. In Europe, bills of exchange developed in Genoa during the twelfth century, and reached Europe more generally during the fourteenth century, but sophisticated versions of them were already operating in the Middle East and in Mughal India several centuries before then. From the twelfth century onwards, the mercantile market slowly but surely came to be bolstered by and entangled with an international money market which depended upon the development of a closely integrated network of international banks. But before that development, despite the early signs of an incipient money market, the bulk of foreign trade relied upon local currency (Pounds 1994: 410–22; Cipolla 1981: 197; Curtin 1984: 115–16, 196; Morgan 1965; Abu-Lughod 1989: 93–4, 216–24).

## TRADE DIASPORAS

Trade diasporas reflect the almost universal historical rule that the development of economic networks precedes and outpaces the development of political structures (Fagan 1993). Norms and rules for cross-cultural trading developed from very early times, but trade diasporas mark a major institutional development to make this process easier and more efficient. Trade diasporas comprise groups of merchants, usually linked by race, religion, or kinship, and forming a long-distance trading network connecting different polities and often different cultures. They are linked to credit systems by the need to establish the levels of trust necessary to operate economic transactions over long distances in the absence of quick or reliable means of communication. Curtin (1984) argues that trade diasporas were a recurrent feature of the ancient and classical world from its earliest times. They stemmed from the increased specialization, including merchant classes, that developed with the rise of cities. Trade diasporas were an institution helping to overcome the cultural barriers to long-distance trade, easing the creation of networks of trust, credit, and security. They were a kind of symbiotic solution to the tension in the trading process between the state, with its desire to control, contain, and tax (but also obtain goods from outside its area of control), and the merchants, with their need for freedom to travel safely over long distances without excessive hindrance or danger. From a very early phase states and empires established ports where traders could come and go, and enjoy a degree of autonomy from the direct political control of local rulers. When the Phoenicians were extending their trading activities across the Mediterranean during the first millennium BC, for example, they were incorporated into the Assyrian Empire. But their main coastal cities, such as Byblos, Tyre, and Arwad, were given a special role within the empire, operating under treaties which left them free to establish and implement their own economic strategies. The Phoenicians were able to maintain contact with their Mediterranean colonies as well as their major trading partners, such as Egypt (Larsen 1979). In the same way, during the early medieval period, the coastal trading cities in East Africa, such as Mogadishu and Kilwa, which provided a focal point for trade embracing the Middle East, India, and China, were also established as ports of trade unfettered from the control of local rulers (Chaudhuri

1990). In some ways one can see trade diasporas as a precursor to the liberal trade doctrines that emerged in nineteenth-century Europe. Laissez-faire was intended to institutionalize this detachment of the trading process by locating trade firmly within the sphere of civil society as opposed to the sphere regulated by the state (Rosenberg 1994). It is not surprising that, as liberal doctrines took hold, trade diasporas declined as the expanding West imposed a cosmopolitan culture on the whole world.

Trade diasporas were also a solution to the discrimination against commercial activity that marked many ancient and classical cultures. Ancient and classical civilizations often accorded a low status to merchant activity and so were content to leave it to outside peoples. This was true of ancient Egypt, and also of classical Greece and Rome, who left trade in the hands of peoples such as the Phoenicians (Meijer and van Nijf 1992: 3–51; Trigger 1993: 71). Confucian China and Japan held merchants in contempt, as in many ways did Catholic Europe. This attitude created opportunities for peoples not afflicted by it, or, like the Jews, excluded from mainstream society for other reasons. Merchants created a common culture of outsiders, and trade diasporas were often built around specific peoples (Phoenicians, Jews, Armenians, Chinese, Gujaratis) or religions. Islam was unusual in the ancient and classical world for giving merchants high social status (Curtin 1984: 116; Bentley 1993: 89–100; Anderson 1974b: 496–520). Hodgson (1993: 97–125, 176–94) argues that the commercial orientation of the Islamic world reflected both its position straddling the ancient Eurasian trade routes, and its offsetting of agrarian elites (who normally dominated ancient and classical societies) by nomadic and merchant ones. Islam became a successful merchant religion based on mobile trading and investment. Buddhism also found favour as a merchant religion, and was transported from South to East Asia by merchants, as was Islam to Africa and the Indian Ocean (Bentley 1993: 42–53, 117–31). Jews were uniquely placed to work across the Christian–Islamic boundary, being based on both sides and having their own networks (McNeill 1963: 509). The fact that Jews were persecuted by both sides (more by Christians, especially in Spain, than in the Islamic world) points to the danger of combining alien status and wealth, which was a weakness of trade diasporas.

It is perhaps worth speculating about how much of the political diplomacy in this era grew out of the practices of the trading networks and merchants' enclaves that had for a long time established the need and the means for societies and states to deal with outsiders.

# 3. CONCLUSIONS

It was argued in Part II that social technologies played a much greater role than physical technologies in the development of interaction capacity. We have seen in this chapter that interaction capacity was transformed during the ancient and classical world as the result of developments in physical technology. But some of the most crucial developments, such as the domestication of the horse and the camel, and the ability to take advantage of trade winds, only had an effect in Eurasia, allowing relay, if not direct contact, to take place from one end of the landmass to the other. These developments had no impact on interaction capacity in the Americas, and this fact sharply differentiates the development of Eurasia from that of the Americas. Relay links across the length and breadth of the Americas only developed after the arrival of the Europeans. Social technologies, however, had a dramatic impact on interaction capacity in both Eurasia and the Americas. But again there were crucial differences. Religion had a powerful integrating effect on both landmasses, but it was only in Eurasia that folk religions gave way to universal religions. In pre-international systems, social technologies were designed to ensure that individuals could remain integrated across vast tracts of territory, despite relatively low levels of contact. In the ancient and classical world, by contrast, social technologies substantially increased the depth of interaction capacity, permitting a much greater density of process. This density becomes apparent in the scale on which process formations developed, a subject to be examined in more detail in the next chapter.

# Chapter 10

# PROCESS IN ANCIENT AND CLASSICAL INTERNATIONAL SYSTEMS

Process is about how units interact with each other, and particularly about how that interaction settles into the durable patterns we call *process formations*. In international systems most process is a variant or combination of a few basic types:

- fighting/threatening;
- alliance-making;
- trading;
- negotiating over recognition and status;
- inflicting changes on the natural environment.

Process can be either conflictual or co-operative, or various mixtures. As we saw in Part II, pre-international systems displayed their own versions of process, some of which foreshadowed later developments, and therefore the shift to economic and full international systems was not about the initiation of process *per se*. The key to understanding the change lies in the transformation of units and interaction capacity. As we showed in Chapter 8, the units that defined the ancient and classical world were not only much larger and more elaborate than those of pre-international systems, but they also commanded a far greater range and scale of resources. Their populations were much bigger, and were hierarchically differentiated into specialized class and professional structures. This made them capable of more complex and sectorally differentiated relations with their neighbours. By the time the Roman and Han Empires were at their height, the global population stood at some 170 million people, more than twelve times the number (*c.*14 million) at the beginning of civilization, and more than forty times the 4–5 million hunter-gatherers who constituted humankind before the agricultural revolution. Thus what was new about process in this era was not the mere fact of it, but its scale, richness, and diversity, and the emergence of types of process formation still familiar in contemporary international relations. The basic story in this chapter is the development and evolution of practically the whole set of behaviours and patterns that we now think of as constituting international relations, from arms racing and war, through diplomacy, trade, and balance of payments problems, to imperialism and clash of civilizations. Looking at this by sectors gives a clearer impression.

# 1. MILITARY-POLITICAL PROCESS

Here we focus on military interactions, starting with the neorealists' claim that their theorizing on conflictual processes applies across time to like units in anarchic structures, whether these units are empires, city-states, or national states. Waltz (1979) makes much of the fact that processes observed in the Greek city-state system can also be observed in the contemporary international system. He highlights, in particular, features like war and imperialism. Any reader of Thucydides' account of the Peloponnesian War will recognize not only these features, but also the more general operation of the security dilemma which lies at the heart of neorealist understandings of the nature of international relations in anarchically structured systems. The security dilemma arises because of the inability of states to distinguish reliably between the offensive and defensive intentions of other powers in the system. Because of the ambiguity of military strength, states recognize that there is no policy available in the international system which will enable them to enhance their security. On the one hand, if a state enters into an agreement with a potential adversary to engage in a reduction of weapons in an effort to enhance their mutual security, neither state can ever be completely sure that the other state has complied with the agreement. So if either state does observe the agreement, then it will experience a diminished sense of security, because it will then be less prepared in the event of an attack from the adversary. On the other hand, if the state attempts to increase its security by expanding the number of weapons it possesses, then it will observe its adversary adopting a reciprocal policy. It will then be confronted with a more highly armed enemy and will experience a decreased sense of security. So, whether the state increases or decreases its level of arms, it will experience a loss of security: hence the dilemma.

The history of ancient and classical international relations gives a lot of support to this view. As Singer et al. (1956: 695) note, between 700 BC and AD 1500, the states in the Mediterranean and Europe 'were essentially fighting states; their prosperity depended upon their ability to subdue their neighbours, to defend their civilization against barbarian invaders, and to protect their trade. When they ceased to be able to do these things, they collapsed.' This remark could be applied to any of the civilizations of the ancient and classical world, and sets the scene for the operation of the neorealist logic of socialization and competition, in which the imperative of survival pushes units to emulate, or find counters to, successful power-generating practices developed by those with whom they interact. Not surprisingly, given these conditions, one of the process formations that developed during this era was the arms dynamic (Buzan and Herring 1998), including arms racing. On land, innovations such as iron weapons (as opposed to copper or bronze ones), formation fighting (developed by the Greeks, and improved by the Romans), chariots, the compound bow, techniques of fortification, siege machinery, and cavalry spread quickly, even though different types of unit used them in different ways according to their preferred style of warfare. Because of the constraints of interaction capacity military dynamics had relatively limited range. No military-political process extended across the whole of Eurasia, though the Mongols came quite close. As a rule, military dynamics were largely confined to subcontinental areas: Roman power could stretch as far as Britain and Persia, but it could not reach India or China.

Technology was a military variable in this era in a way that was true only in embryo during prehistory. That said, the rhythm and impact of ancient and classical military technology was in some ways quite different from current norms. Since the onset of the industrial revolution, technological innovation in the military sphere has been rapid and continuous. Some types of weapon become obsolete and disappear (battleships, Zeppelins), and new types of weapons are continuously being introduced (nuclear weapons, radar, missiles). In the ancient and classical world, this pattern did exist, but it operated far more slowly. Technological breakthroughs were infrequent, and separated by long periods of incremental development. Prevailing technologies might rule for hundreds of years, a situation that put the emphasis of military power on numbers, warrior skills, training, and leadership. Roman legionnaires, for example, were not radically different in their equipment from the soldiers of Assyria a millennium before. Military forces tended to reflect the type of political economy from which they sprang, with nomadic peoples developing fast-moving light cavalry, and agrarian civilizations cultivating the arts of infantry and fortification. Occasionally, technology might be crucial, as when iron-wielding Hyksos defeated copper-armed Egyptians c.1600 BC, or when the nomads first developed cavalry. But in general military technology diffused fairly quickly, and it was innovations in tactics, such as the Greek wedge and the Roman legion, that gave one side an advantage over another. Brilliant generals such as Alexander, Genghis Khan, and Chandragupta Maurya could cut a large swath across the map, and efficient military machines such as those of Assyria, Sparta, Athens, Macedonia, Rome, the Ottomans, and the Mongols could create and hold large empires.

Thus although not as technologically driven as the modern world, the ancient and classical world none the less possessed all of the requisites for a realist international relations of power politics. Its units cultivated military power, engaged in military competitions and wars with each other, and suffered the difficulties of the security dilemma. Because of the far greater resources and the more specialized skills possessed by city-states and empires, the arms dynamic was perhaps most spectacularly visible at sea.

*The naval arms dynamic in the Mediterranean*

The development of warships on the Mediterranean reveals a number of major advances which inevitably triggered off naval arms races between seafaring states. Initially, ships were used to transport soldiers. But from about 1500 BC specialized warships began to be built. The development of the trireme in the seventh century BC represented a major step forward. It had 170 rowers sitting on three levels. The enormous cost of the boat held back its development, but in 480 BC, the Greek city-states under the leadership of Athens were able to sail 200 triremes, requiring 34,000 rowers, against the Persian navy at the battle of Salamis. Despite its later defeat in the Peloponnesian Wars, Athens still managed to double the size of its navy, so that by 330 BC it possessed 400 triremes. Yet within a decade, the Athenian navy had been rendered obsolete because new super galleys had been developed, dwarfing the trireme, and involving a cost which was beyond the reach of any of the Greek city-states.

The size of galleys began to increase dramatically at this point, until, a century later, a galley was built to be propelled by 4,000 rowers. It was a catamaran, with three levels of oarsmen, eight men to an oar on the top layer, seven on the second layer, and five on the bottom layer. On each section of the catamaran, there were 2,000 men, with 50 rows of men, 40 men to a row. This boat was referred to as a 40, and it never went to sea, but boats with 20 and 30 to a row did. The size of the boats steadily increased during this 100-year period. Two factors account for this extraordinary arms race. First, with the collapse of Alexander the Great's empire, three smaller empires came into existence. Two of these, the Antigonid Empire in Macedonia and the Ptolemaic Empire in Egypt, were naval powers and it was these empires which possessed the resources to drive the arms race. But there was also a good strategic reason for wishing to increase the size of these galleys. Larger galleys could carry towers on which archers and javelineers could be mounted. In addition, they could carry torsion catapults for firing large stones. These super galleys, in turn, however, were also rendered obsolete when the Romans eventually came to control the Mediterranean (Casson 1994).

# 2. ECONOMIC PROCESS

The main economic process in the ancient and classical world was trade. As we set out in the discussion of interaction capacity above, trade generated some quite sophisticated process formations, most notably trade diasporas and bills of exchange. But during this era, finance did not really take on a life of its own at the system level. Monetary phenomena such as inflation were certainly present: Silver (1985: 130), for example, identifies periods of steep inflation in both Babylonia and

Egypt. But they tended to occur within units rather than between them, albeit sometimes being exacerbated by trade deficits. Thus the main story we have to tell here is about the expanding volume, sophistication, and range of trade, and particularly the making of an economic international system embracing the whole of Eurasia and North Africa.

In the early part of this period trade networks were relatively localized. They went mostly overland or by river, and only tentatively by coastal sea routes. Most of the newly forming areas of civilization were not in any kind of conscious contact with each other. As the various cores of civilization grew more populous, more productive, and more sophisticated, their demand for goods increased, as did their ability to provide other goods in return, and the range and complexity of their trading activities expanded. Egypt, Mesopotamia, and the Harappan civilization in the Indus valley established trade links during the third millennium BC. By the second millennium BC a trading network was flourishing right across western Asia, Europe, and North Africa. Fagan (1993: 194–5) reveals the scale and sophistication of this early trade with an account of a shipwreck dating from the fourteenth century BC off southern Turkey. It contained an amazing array of goods from as far apart as the Baltic and Africa, including more than 5 tonnes of copper ingots (enough metal to equip a small army), a ton of resin, numerous blue glass ingots, hardwood, amber, tortoise shells, elephant tusks, pottery, olives, and ostrich eggs.

This development was being matched in East Asia, around the hub of Chinese civilization, and more slowly in North and South America around the hubs of the Mesoamerican and Andean civilizations. A big breakthrough occurred during the first millennium BC when the eastern, southern, and western Eurasian trading systems linked up to form a single Eurasian trading system moving goods between all of its four great centres of civilization (China, India, the Middle East, and the Mediterranean) (see Map 10.1). The steppe nomads played a crucial role in opening up trans-Eurasia trade, anticipating the later development of the Silk Roads by filtering Chinese tribute goods westward (Bentley 1993: 29–42). Chinese silk had reached as far west as Armenia by 750 BC (Curtin 1984: 185), and shortly thereafter the Persian Empire had expanded sufficiently to create firm trading contact between Central Asia and the Mediterranean. Chinese ships were trading as far as Malaya by 350 BC, and during the Han dynasty (202 BC to AD 220) Chinese trade reached overland into Central Asia and India and overseas to India, meeting with the Middle Eastern trading system at both points. From the first century BC, the land route was accompanied by an extensive sea trade between the Red Sea and the Gulf, and South Asia, and between China and the Indian Ocean. Around 120 BC, Ptolemaic Egypt pioneered coastal and then, once the seasonal wind patterns were mastered, open-ocean sea routes to India, making Alexandria a key entrepôt for the eastern trade with the Mediterranean. At about the same time, Chinese ships reached the Bay of Bengal, meeting up with Indian traffic to South-East Asia. By the second century AD, these developments had evolved into a regular sea route

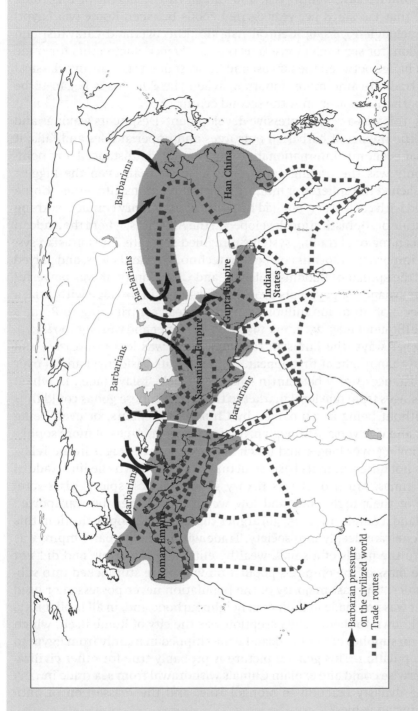

*Note:* In the fourth century AD extensive land and sea trading routes had opened up among the Eurasian empires. Trading routes embraced the steppe and desert nomads and extended far into the pre-international systems.

*Map 10.1 Trade, empire, and barbarians in fourth-century AD Eurasia*

connecting the Middle East, South Asia, and China. At the height of this trade records suggest that 120 ships per year carried goods between Rome (via Egypt) and India (Barraclough 1978: 70). Central Asia (for the overland caravans) and South India/Ceylon (for sea trade) were thus the two key contact points for trade and cultural exchange between the far east and far west of Eurasia during classical times. The sea trade became more important when the Silk Roads began to be threatened by barbarian power after the second century AD.

In some ways, this was a very impressive development. Despite its waxings and wanings under the impact of barbarian outsurges and imperial rises and falls, it created a kind of economic international system that far outdistanced any political one. Not only was the trading system much larger than even the biggest empire, it outreached the spheres of military-political relations altogether. China and Rome traded with each other, but had no political or military contact. Nothing comparable in scale or sophistication developed in the Americas, where the Andean and Mesoamerican regional trading systems remained separate. The Eurasian system acted as an important transmission belt for technologies and ideas, and played a major role in the spread of Buddhism, Islam, and Christianity. It was powerful enough to create balance of payments problems for Rome in its trade with Asia: a net drain of specie of up to 100 million sesterces a year contributing to Rome's imperial decline (Braudel 1985: 25; Frank 1990: 205–6; Meijer and van Nijf 1992: 129).

And yet in other ways, the Eurasian trading system was less impressive and more superficial than might at first appear. For a start, its basic mechanism over the very long distances was what Curtin (1984: 17) labels 'relay trade', in which goods move by stages from one local market to the next. Chinese goods could thus reach Rome without being accompanied by Chinese merchants, or even being aimed at Rome, and vice versa. Although involving larger volumes of more sophisticated goods moving over longer and much better organized stages in the relay, this system was not different in its basic structure from the down-the-line trade of pre-civilization times. Much of it was luxury goods (fabrics, spices, glassware) which because of their high value and low weight could even be transported profitably overland. Pounds (1994: 25, 30) argues that for all its sophistication, this trade did not penetrate deeply into society. Trade within the Roman Empire was largely geared to the needs of a small, wealthy elite, and the army, and did not much affect the mass of the empire's population who were still locked into subsistence economies: 'the vast majority of the population never possessed or used any artefact that was not made in their own neighbourhood and, in all probability, by a craftsman known to them.' The exception was the city of Rome itself, which was dependent on supplies of grain, oil, and wine shipped in mainly from Egypt to feed its huge population. This general picture is probably true for other civilizations. How otherwise could one explain China's withdrawal from sea trade in 1433 as part of Ming dynasty reaction to Mongol rule, and the reassertion of anti-mercantile Confucian values?

These contrasting evaluations lie at the heart of the debates about Wallerstein's distinction between world empires and world economies. The existence of a Eurasian trading system embracing several of his 'world empires' would seem to bring his whole scheme into question. Even isolated civilizations, such as the Aztec Empire, were located in broader trading systems that reached out far into pre-international tribal areas. Yet the question remains about how significant these wider networks were for what remained in many respects largely autonomous 'world empires'. There are two ways of answering this question. The first is to stress that even though the trade between the empires that formed in the ancient and classical world may not have been large, it would be a mistake to under-estimate the significance of luxury goods. The demand for silk and spices was persistent and the flow of goods around Eurasia did reflect the existence of a continuous process which provides the necessary hallmark of a Eurasian international system. Second, as we will see in the next two sections, the existence of the Eurasian-wide international economic system provided the basis for two other types of process.

## 3. SOCIETAL PROCESS

If neorealist theory can readily account for the conflictual features of international systems, then the English school comes into its own in accounting for the co-operative dimension of interstate relations. Neorealism's logic of socialization and competition can be used to account for the emergence of diplomacy (Buzan 1993), but is not yet generally used in that way. As discussed above, diplomacy was an important process in the ancient and classical world, and one found in most areas of civilization. Yet although diplomacy in one form or another is a more or less universal feature of the ancient and classical world, it did not link the world together on anything like the scale of trade. As a rule, diplomacy operated at about the same range as war. Because of the physical limits on interaction capacity, this meant in practice that diplomatic relations were confined to sets of neighbours within regions. Japan could send embassies to China, Carthage could make treaties (and war) with Rome, and the shifting configuration of empires in Egypt, Mesopotamia, and Anatolia were in regular diplomatic contact. But China and Rome even at their height had no diplomatic contact, and China had only sporadic, short-lived periods of political contact with the Middle East and South Asia.

But this assessment fails to draw attention to the extraordinary processes whereby universal religions and their related cultures have expanded far beyond their places of origin. The most striking cases are Christianity, Buddhism, and Islam. Bentley (1993) identifies two major eras when cross-cultural encounters became particularly intense. The first occurred with the emergence of Buddhism and then later Christianity. Buddhism was founded at a time of great change in India during the sixth century BC. By the middle of the third century BC, King Asoka began to promote Buddhism and sent missions to Burma, Ceylon, and Bactria. But it was the merchants who were most influential in encouraging the spread of Buddhism, establishing the religion in merchant diasporas that formed along the silk routes. In subsequent centuries, Indian merchants formed diaspora communities in the coastal regions of South-East Asia and invited both Hindu and Buddhist authorities from India to join them. Over time, Indian culture came to have a very profound effect on the region.

Although the origins of Christian thought can be traced back through Jewish history and, more controversially, to Hellenistic thought (Nash 1984), its expansion was initially and most closely associated with the impact and expansion of the Roman Empire. Christianity extended west into Europe, but only after the Roman Empire had brought the region under its control. After the conversion of Constantine, the Romans encouraged the Christians to move beyond the borders of the empire and convert both the inhabitants of other empires, like Persia, and the members of the illiterate tribes that were bearing down on Rome.

After the establishment of Islam, Bentley (1993) argues that the volume of Eurasian international trade far outstripped the amount that circulated when the silk routes were first established. During this period, the tempo of cross-cultural contacts increased dramatically. Christianity extended into northern Europe. Buddhism came to flourish in China as well as South East and Central Asia. At the same time, Islam extended into North Africa and across Asia. In the first instance, Islam was a state-sponsored religion. Populations were not coerced, but conversion occurred as the result of economic, social, and political pressures. But after the initial imperial phase, Islam was spread by trade diasporas. Local populations voluntarily adopted Islam in sub-Saharan Africa, South India, South-East Asia, and East Africa.

Cross-cultural contacts were a constant feature of ancient and classical times with populations periodically engaging in very substantial cultural changes as the result of these contacts. But it would be a mistake to exaggerate the extent of the changes or to assume that there must have been increasing cultural convergence taking place as a consequence of this process. Alien cultures frequently met with resistance, but even when they did not, attention must be drawn to the importance of syncretism which reflects the idea of co-optation. For Buddhism to be accepted in China, for example, it had to undergo some radical changes in order to accommodate deeply rooted Chinese beliefs. Chinese Buddhism therefore developed along lines which were quite distinct from those found in India. Moreover, although these cultural conversions laid down potential foundations for world societies that transcended the boundaries defined by political, diplomatic, and military relations of that time, in fact, they failed to generate any persistent patterns of interaction that would build upon these foundations.

This is not to say that there were no interactions between these communities that were bound together by powerful cultural links, but they were episodic and involved only a handful of people. Pilgrimages, for example (which might be thought of as the ancient and classical version of tourism), were inspired by the universal religions and could draw people over very long distances. Christian pilgrims went from north-west Europe to Jerusalem. Islamic pilgrims ventured from West Africa and South-East Asia to Mecca, and Buddhist ones made the difficult journey from North-East Asia to India. But except, perhaps, for a handful of missionaries, this interaction did not match the scale of the trading system that helped to precipitate the cultural transformations in the first place.

As the boxed story of Persia's role in the silk route helps to show, although the Eurasian trading system promoted some remarkable cross-cultural encounters and transformations, it could also act as a barrier to cultural contact. The position of Persia on the silk route, for example, may partially explain why Chinese pilgrims failed to set their sights on Europe or the Middle East, and why Europeans felt no compulsion to visit the Buddhist sites in India.

*Persia and the Silk Road*

The close correlation between the movement of Indian traders and the spread of Buddhism raises the as yet unanswered historical question of why Buddhism failed to spread to the West (Boulnois 1966: 101). There are no obvious or uncontroversial reasons why Buddhism should not have penetrated the Roman Empire as well as the Han Empire. But it is worth noting that although the Indian traders were able to establish trading routes all the way to China, they failed to make similar contacts with the Roman Empire. To reach the Roman Empire by land, they had to cross the Parthian Empire, and this they failed to do. It is not that the Parthians were uninterested in trade. Quite the contrary. The main trade routes from China crossed the Parthian Empire and the tax on trade was a crucial source of revenue for the Parthians. Persians traders were known to be less interested in marketing their own goods than in 'an active transit trade' from East to West and West to East (Wiesehofer 1996: 194). By regulating trade in this way, as Colledge (1967: 80) notes, the Parthians 'held their two greatest customers firmly apart, to avoid any embarrassing comparison of prices'. The Han records indicate that the Chinese were well aware that the Parthians aimed to prevent the Romans from establishing direct contact with the Chinese. Despite attempts from both sides, no 'direct intercourse' between the Romans and the Chinese ever took place (Hudson 1931: 83). Attempts by the Romans to circumvent the Parthian and subsequent Sassanid Empires by establishing a northern trade route met with limited success. The Parthian and Sassanid Empires were also very effective at controlling the sea routes via both the Persian Gulf and the Red Sea (Wiesehofer 1996: 194–7).

Persia's role in the silk routes is undoubtedly insufficient to explain why Buddhism failed to establish a base in the West. But it illustrates, nevertheless, how trade does not automatically lead to cross-cultural encounters.

# 4. ENVIRONMENTAL PROCESS

In general, the human impact on the environment during the ancient and classical era was too small and too localized to have any international system dimension. In some places the human impact was large (clearing of forests, exhaustion or salination of farmland), and sometimes the environmental consequences caused particular civilizations to decline or disappear. There are two exceptions to this localism: first, the movement of flora and fauna, still relatively minor during this era, and second, and of major impact, the movement of plagues across long distances.

The movement of plants, animals, and peoples from their place of origin to other continents only became major when oceanic navigation got under way during the fifteenth and sixteenth centuries AD. Before that, there was some exchange of food crops among Africa, Asia, and the Middle East starting around 200 BC (Jones 1987: 154, 163), and a long-standing trade of horses into China, India, and the Middle East.

But the big environmental process during this era was disease. The onset of civilization, and particularly the rise of densely populated cities and the herding of domesticated animals, gave rise to a variety of epidemic diseases (McNeill 1976; Diamond 1997). The concentration of disease in urban populations eventually gave them immunological advantages over non-urban peoples, and this was a significant factor in allowing civilization to expand at the expense of hunter-gatherer populations. But different centres of civilization hosted different diseases, and with the opening of regular trade contact during the first millennium BC, plagues began to travel down the trade routes from areas where the population had acquired some immunity to areas where it had not. After 500 BC, this opening of contact between civilizations began to transmit plagues between different pools of disease on a recurrent, if episodic, basis. Although generally not an intentional process (except where besiegers catapulted diseased corpses into walled cities) the transmission of plagues is a key feature on the historical landscape of the ancient and classical world. From the second century AD, for example, it gravely weakened the Chinese and Roman Empires as waves of disease spread across Eurasia causing huge population die-offs (McNeill 1976: 112–40). It can be argued that the complex disease environment of South Asia explains both the relative weakness of empires there, and the evolution of the caste system (McNeill 1976: 90–4). McNeill (1976: 184) also argues that the establishment of bubonic plague in the rodent population of the Eurasian steppe during the Mongol Empire played a role in the decline of barbarian power that accompanied the end of this era.

# 5. CONCLUSIONS

The processes of international systems in the ancient and classical world are strikingly similar to those of the contemporary international system. War, diplomacy, the arms dynamic, trade, balance of payments problems, religious proselytization and pilgrimage, and disease transmission are all present, and this should assuage the doubts of those worried about the potential for anachronism in pushing a modern concept such as 'international system' back into premodern times. That said, it is clear that many of these processes are either relatively weak compared with their modern versions (such as trade), or else relatively short ranged (such as war). The full international systems defined by process in the ancient and classical world tended to be confined to subcontinental scale regions. The economic systems were larger, but relatively thin and fragile.

# Chapter 11

# STRUCTURE IN ANCIENT AND CLASSICAL INTERNATIONAL SYSTEMS

In Part II we suggested that the effects of structure on pre-international systems were often very weak or non-existent and that it is not possible to establish a sectoral analysis of structures in a pre-international system. In our analysis of the ancient and classical world we have not only demonstrated that units are much more autonomous and functionally differentiated but that they operate within a system where interaction capacity has become much wider and deeper in scope and where sectorally differentiated process formations become a persistent feature of the system. It is unsurprising to find, therefore, that sectorally differentiated structures also come into play and, as a consequence, help to account for systemic behaviour.

## 1. MILITARY-POLITICAL STRUCTURE

As defined in our toolkit, military-political structure is generated by the Hobbesian, power politics, side of international relations, and results in what we have labelled 'full international systems'. Since the historical record of the ancient and classical world contains vast amounts of war and coercion (not to mention the security dilemma and arms dynamic processes discussed above), we should expect to find political structure in the Waltzian sense. Recall that military interaction is the most demanding in terms of physical interaction capacity, and that physical interaction capacity in the ancient and classical world was generally low except over relatively short distances. It follows, therefore, that we should expect full international systems in this era to be fairly limited in extent. This is indeed the case.

Although there was a general tendency for full international systems to expand during this era, with a few exceptions they never developed much beyond what would today be thought of as a regional scale. From a global perspective, what developed during this era was a set of local, regional, and occasionally inter-regional, full international systems that for the most part were completely disconnected from each other strategically. As systems of city-states, and then empires, grew up in the core areas of civilization they formed local international systems. These generally grew into regional-scale systems as the civilizational cores themselves expanded. In quite a few cases, these regional systems remained completely self-contained in military-political, if not always in economic and cultural, terms. The Andean and Mesoamerican civilizations, for example, remained completely cut off both from each other and from the rest of the world in all respects. Egypt enjoyed more than a thousand years of military-political isolation after the onset of civilization in the Nile valley. China's isolation was less intense. It did develop some economic and cultural ties with the rest of Eurasia, and, on a few occasions, short-lived military-political contact. Sassanid Persia and T'ang China aimed at making common cause against the Arabs in the seventh century AD, but the Arab defeat of China at the battle of Talas in AD 751 caused China to withdraw from Central Asia. In the early fifteenth century AD, the voyages of Cheng-ho briefly took Chinese military and political power around most of the northern coast of the Indian Ocean (Jones 1987: 203–5), but these exceptions only underline the general absence of sustained strategic contact between China and the other civilized military powers of Eurasia.

Because of its geographically central location, and accessibility by both land and sea, Middle Eastern civilization had the widest array of military-political relations. As early as the middle of the first millennium BC, the Persian Empire had made contact with Greece in the west, the kingdoms of South Asia in the east, and Egypt in the south. Alexander the Great's battles took him as far east as present-day Pakistan, and the successor Diadochi Empires formed an international system stretching from the eastern Mediterranean to the Gulf. Watson (1992: 69–76) argues that this system stretched from Carthage in the west to India in the east. The rise of Rome absorbed most of this into a single empire, but there was repeated war for nearly a thousand years between Rome and Parthia, and their respective successors the Byzantine and Sassanid Persian Empires. The rise of Arab-Islamic power during the seventh century AD overwhelmed the Sassanids, pushed back the Byzantines, and for a time created a military-political system that stretched from the Atlantic to the borders of China.

It might be objected that this account leaves out the nomadic barbarians, and in doing so neglects major military powers that in some ways spanned Eurasia, connecting together the otherwise mostly separated international systems centred around the cores of civilization. But while it is true that barbarian military power was both great and highly mobile, the very nature of its mobility gave it a special character that for the most part made its significance more local than inter-regional. As we saw in Chapter 8, the nomads were capable of establishing settled empires that coexisted with sedentary empires. But unlike the sedentary agricultural empires, when the nomadic empires collapsed, the nomadic barbarians were capable of very extensive overland movement. And when they moved, they moved lock, stock, and barrel. This meant that when nomadic tribesmen turned up at the gates of civilization, as they did regularly all across Eurasia throughout this era, this did not represent power projection from a distant base in the sense that Britain was able to project power into the Far East during the nineteenth century, or the USA into Europe, Asia, and the Middle East during the twentieth. The barbarians were for the most part not power projected over a distance from a fixed base, but a genuinely mobile power that could and did move from one territorial base to another. In order to understand the barbarians one has to suspend the usually unquestioned assumption in IR that military-political units are territorially rooted. It is thus appropriate to see the barbarians more as part of the local and regional systems into which they intruded than as some kind of strategic link that created a full international system across Eurasia from an early stage. The only exception to this was close to the end of the era, when the last great barbarian outsurge (the short-lived Mongol Empire during the thirteenth century AD) took imperial form itself, creating a single military system that stretched from China to the borders of India, Europe, and Egypt. In this context, Rossabi (1992) notes the thirteenth-century Christian and Mongol attempts to enlist each other in a two-front crusade against Islam. This suggests at least the conceptual existence of a Eurasian strategic international system, though nothing emerged in practice.

So far this is pretty straightforward. The ancient and classical world contains a number of easily identified full international systems in which war, alliance, the arms dynamic, and power politics operate vigorously. The basic conditions for a Waltzian type of international system are all in place. Neorealism posits anarchic systems as the natural form of international relations. Once individual units begin to co-act strategically, the imperative of survival and the pressures of self-help should ensure both that units converge (a survival of the fittest logic), and that balance of power logic amongst them preserves the anarchic structure. But the history of the ancient and classical era throws up two problems: first, the normal form of its strategic international systems was, in Waltzian terms, hierarchic, with anarchy being the exception, and second, even anarchic systems did not go very far towards creating 'like' units. We have therefore to ask, as in Chapter 4, why the predicted effects do not occur. Does some other variable undercut the potency of structure, or create strong effects in opposing directions?

In strategic terms, there were four significant types of unit in ancient and classical international systems: city-states, empires, nomadic and settled tribes. As we saw in Chapter 8, these units were extremely dissimilar in terms of their internal structures, most notably so in the case of the nomadic tribes. They could be functionally alike, in the sense that all of them could, and sometimes did, claim political autonomy. But they could also be functionally differentiated, as most commonly when city-states, other empires, or sedentary tribes acknowledged the suzerainty of an imperial core, without surrendering all of their political autonomy to it. This is captured by the part of Watson's (1990: 102–6; 1992: chs. 1, 12) spectrum that covers suzerainty and dominion. A suzerain system retains elements of anarchy in that separate political units still exist, but these units formally accept lower status in relation to the suzerain power, and cede some elements of control to it. In a dominion system, the control of the dominant power extends into areas of domestic governance of the other units, but these still retain a notional identity as independent actors. From Waltz's perspective, of course, these are both types of hierarchy. Many of the claims for anarchic systems composed of like units during this era are dubious. The most frequently cited is the Greek city-state system with its many internal wars. But one has only to mention the famous Persian invasions, not to mention the Greek expedition to assist Egypt against Persia, to undo this claim. Although the Greek city-states certainly did fight amongst themselves, they also fought regularly with a major empire, and were part of a strategic system that included units other than city-states.

This structural and functional differentiation of units remained in force as the norm of this era for more than four millennia. Although nomadic tribes were more or less eliminated as a significant military player during the last century of this era, they remained a potent force for almost its entire span. Although they could challenge sedentary empires by a process of confederation, provided they maintained their mobile way of life, there was no way that these nomadic and sedentary empires could be regarded as like units. The position of sedentary tribes in this equation is more complex. As indicated in Part II, sedentary tribes could give way or transform into chiefdoms and it is widely accepted that this process was accelerated when sedentary tribes came into contact with sedentary empires. The Roman Empire, for example, engaged in extensive trade across its frontier, in particular, importing slaves. The wealth associated with this trade had the effect of promoting chiefdoms beyond the border. But this transformation was quite unrelated to the creation of like units as described by Waltz.

City-states and empires also persisted as unlike units well into modern times. The explanation for this failure of the theory does not seem to lie either in the logic of Waltzian structure or in the effect of interaction capacity. Although logistical constraints do explain the limited size of full international systems during this era, it would be difficult to argue that they cut down the shoving and shaping forces of socialization and competition within those systems. Wars in the ancient and classical world were often about survival: Rome eventually obliterated Carthage, and it was not uncommon for losers in the wars amongst the Greek city-states to have all the male population killed and the women and children sold into slavery. The Huns and the Mongols laid waste to large areas of agrarian civilization, sometimes destroying both cities and agricultural systems. If it is fear of such outcomes that generates like units, then this should have worked in the ancient and classical world, at least within its various international systems.

The most plausible lines of explanation for its not working seem to lie in the nature of the units themselves. We do not have the space to address this question in detail, but a number of possibilities suggest themselves. One is that the imperial form was both legitimate and unstable. Because empires were widely accepted, and provided useful services (trade, security, peace), other units might quite readily bandwagon with a rising empire, accepting a vassal status, rather than always resisting it in favour of independence. But because empires were often unstable, and subject to periods of weak leadership or excessive extraction, they regularly fell to pieces, releasing a host of smaller units and thus keeping city-states on the map. It could also be that none of the main political forms was so inherently superior to any of the others as to make the logic of socialization and competition converge on a single form (as it did after AD 1500 around the modern state—Tilly 1990). Note, for example, how the Greek city-states were able to stand off the Persian Empire, and much later how Venice and Genoa were able to hold their own against the Byzantine Empire. The barbarians certainly had no reason to think that agrarian empires were militarily superior, and neither form established any general advantage over the other until right at the end of the era, when guns, and perhaps plague, undermined the warrior skills of the barbarians. And given the fundamental differences in political economy between these two types of unit it is impossible to see how they could converge short of one replacing the other.

Some of these points make contact with the question about anarchy and hierarchy. The undeniable fact is that hierarchy was the dominant structural form during the ancient and classical era, and anarchy the exception. Most of the full international systems during this era spent most of their time under some form of imperial sway. Multi-actor systems of independent units certainly did occur, but they were not stable, usually, as in China, the Mediterranean, and the Middle East, giving way to overarching empires. Perhaps only in South Asia was empire more the exception and anarchy more the rule, but even there empires were a recurrent feature. Numerous cases in this era offer reasons to question the neorealist argument that anarchy is self-sustaining: in South Asia, East Asia, the Middle East, and the Mediterranean, anarchic systems regularly and repeatedly collapsed into empires or suzerain systems. Indeed, if one focused only on East Asia and the Middle East (rather than on medieval and modern Europe, as most IR theory does), the obvious theoretical question to ask would be: why do hierarchic systems persist?

As Watson's scheme suggests, hierarchy under these conditions could be quite tight, as when major empires like Rome and China held direct control over most of their known worlds. Or it could be quite loose, as when weak imperial cores held fairly notional suzerainty over an array of vassals. This predominance of hierarchy creates some awkward but interesting questions about the definition of international systems. It is partly a matter of common sense, but also partly an expression of what in Chapter 1 we called 'Eurocentrism', that the very idea of 'international system' is closely tied to the existence of multiple, independent political units, or, in neorealist terms, anarchies. The inside/outside logic of 'international' or 'domestic' is powerful and pervasive, and thus the idea that a hierarchically structured system might also be an 'international' one seems at first a contradiction in terms: hierarchy must mean that politics become domestic. But the imperial systems of the ancient and classical world, just like the current political development of European Union, challenge this excessively rigid assumption.

In trying to grasp this, it is important to keep in mind that a full international system has to be more or less self-contained, meaning that it has some kind of frontier at which regular *strategic* (but not necessarily economic or societal) inter-action ceases or fades away. This frontier can of course expand or contract, but it must be there. Within such a frontier there may of course be an anarchic inter-national system. But it is also possible, and in the ancient and classical world not uncommon, that the area comes more or less to be filled by a single empire, either totally, as in the case of the Chinese and the Andean systems at the peaks of imperial power, or nearly so, as in the case of Rome. When that happens, we argue that there are still two good reasons for thinking of it as an international system.

One reason is structural, and rests on the fact that empires usually contain a variety of other units. Some of these, as we saw in the discussion of Watson's scheme above, retain degrees of political autonomy as dominions or vassals. Empires are by definition about one group of people controlling another (Doyle 1986: 19) and this usually means that distinctive subunits continue to exist within them. The second reason is temporal, and rests on the fact that empires, even where they establish foundations of legitimacy, are unstable. There is thus a quite compelling case for understanding 'international system' not only as referring to a state of affairs existing at a given point in time, but as a historical phenomenon, residing durably across long periods of time. At different times in its history, such a system might be structured as either anarchy or hierarchy. If centralizing phases of empire are seen as temporary, then there is less difficulty in thinking about such phases in terms of 'international systems'. The assumption is that no struc-tural phase is permanent: anarchies are vulnerable to centralization, and empires are vulnerable to fragmentation.

## 2. ECONOMIC STRUCTURE

Understanding the structure of economic international systems during the ancient and classical era is not so easy as explaining interaction capacity and process. The relevant units are not too problematic. For the most part, political units, whether tribes, city-states, or empires, are also the main economic actors. Merchants, as discussed above, had some autonomy, but did not generate organ-ized units equivalent to the modern firm. In principle economic structure is either command or market, but one cannot infer from the dominance of political units that economic structure was therefore necessarily command. Political hier-archy can support either command or market economies, and it can be argued that political hierarchy of some sort is a necessary condition for stable markets (Buzan et al. 1993: part III). In the ancient and classical world, there is evidence for both market and command structures. Most empires, as one would expect, ran their internal trade largely on command lines. Most of what might be called tribute trade also seems to fit the command model. This was where vassal kingdoms or tribes paid tribute to imperial suzerains, or, depending on the balance of power, imperial suzerains paid appeasement bribes to supposed vassals in return for not being attacked by them (as was often the case in Chinese and Byzantine relations with neighbouring barbarians).

But there was also room for markets, as the boxed story shows.

*The Assyrian silver trade*

Traders must possess some understanding of the geography and pricing system of the market. For example, Assyrian traders residing in the area between Mesopotamia and Anatolia came to recognize that it was worth opening up trading routes between these two areas because of the way resources were distributed, with some goods being scarce in one area and plentiful in another. To facilitate the process of redistributing goods, the Assyrians opened up a trading colony in Kanesh, in the centre of Anatolia, and traded goods between Mesopotamia and Anatolia via Assur, at the heart of the Assyrian state. The principle underlying the process was very straightforward. Silver was scarce in Assur, and the silver-to-tin price ratio was 1 : 15. By contrast, in Anatolia, where silver was relatively plentiful, the price ratio was about 1 : 7. It follows, other things being equal, that by moving 15 units of tin from Assur to Kanesh, it was possible to acquire just over 2 units of silver. These units of silver could then be used to purchase more than 30 units of tin after the trader returned to Assur from Kanesh (Yoffee 1991). On this basis, it was possible for traders to amass substantial profits, and a significant Assyrian state came into existence on the basis of this foreign trade.

But market structures in the ancient world were extremely fragile, as the Assyrian case also demonstrates. The Assyrian trade flourished during an era when there was local autonomy in both Mesopotamia and Anatolia. But by the early eighteenth century BC the situation had undergone a substantial change. Mesopotamia had come within the centralized control of the Babylonians, under Hammurabi, while Anatolia was starting to be dominated by the Hittites. The Assyrian traders had been able to take advantage of the absence of centralized political control in these areas. Indeed, profits depended upon the traders having relatively unrestricted access to the resources in both regions. When restraints were imposed by strong governments aiming to control production and exchange, Assyria's foreign trade collapsed, and with it, the Assyrian political system. From being one of the most powerful actors in the region, Assyria underwent a total demise, demonstrating just how dependent the state had been on the trading system of which it formed the central part (Yoffee 1991).

But while all this tells us something about economic structure in the ancient and classical world, it says more about such structure within units than it does between them. Market forces were clearly at work in impelling the movement of various goods across the vast distances of Eurasia. Indeed, no polity existed on anything like the scale necessary to impose command over that trade. And yet it seems risky to characterize the structure of the Eurasian, or any other, trading system of this era as a market. International trading systems were very thin and superficial in relation to the largely command economies embedded in them. In Eurasia, the linear shape and many-staged relay process put huge impediments in the way of any powerful operation of market forces. Such forces may at times have been locally powerful, as in the case of Assyria, or in the waxing and waning of the cities along the Silk Roads. But although the economic international system of the ancient and classical world was impressive in its scale and process, and arguably the most important achievement of the whole era in terms of interaction capacity, its structural effects on the system level were probably small. Trade was certainly moved by comparative advantage, and market forces did generate some specialization. But it would be hard to find any great pressures for efficiency, and market dynamics certainly had little impact in countering the technological and social conservatism of the ancient and classical political economy.

## 3. SOCIETAL STRUCTURE

Within our framework, structure in this sector is about the existence (or not) of socially constructed communities, particularly those defined by the English school categories of *international society* and *world society*. Aside from whether or not these phenomena existed, we need to know about the ranges over which they extended, and the intensity with which they were held.

Martin Wight (1977) was probably the first to try to examine the ancient and classical world in terms of international society. He certainly thought he found it there, albeit in more complicated form than that of modern Europe. Wight posited two types of international society (he used the term 'states system'): international states-systems, such as that in Greece, which were based, like modern Europe, on mutual recognition by sovereign units; and suzerain states-systems, by which he meant imperial cores and their relationships with their surrounding vassals, such as the Persian Empire. The idea of suzerain states-systems implies that Wight would not have had any objection to the idea of hierarchical international systems discussed above. He also identified two configurations: primary systems (with states as units) and secondary ones (with primary systems as units). Secondary systems covered cases like the relationship between classical Greece and the Persian Empire, where two culturally distinct international societies formed a meta-international society, and like the diplomatic relationships amongst the various empires in the Middle East during the later second millennium BC (i.e. a meta-society of suzerain states-systems). Wight saw four institutions in these international societies: messengers/ambassadors, conferences and congresses, a diplomatic language, and trade (1977: 29–33). He posited that low number systems such as that formed by Rome and Parthia would not generate strong rules (1977: 25).

Watson is also interested in this era, and the Greek–Persian case (1992: 40–68), but he has problems seeing that the societal institutions of ancient and classical international systems were well enough developed to count as fully-fledged international societies. He tries to deal with this by positing some kind of boundary between pre- and full international societies hinging on recognition of shared values amongst the units (1987: 147–53). His concern is reflected by others. Wight (1966a: 120–30) argues that the Greeks had some cultural community but no sense of legal community amongst states, and that the Romans knew only imperial relations, not a system of equals. Mosler (1980: 1) points out that there was no conception of a universal community of rules or laws in classical times.

As suggested by the discussion of societal process above, societal structures in the ancient and classical world were by today's standards regional in scale. World societies ('world' here meaning an identity capable of overarching many other levels of social identity, not necessarily global) certainly developed on a regional scale, and sometimes, as most spectacularly with Islam, encompassed several geographical regions (the Middle East, North Africa, south-west and south-east Europe, South Asia, Central Asia, parts of South-East Asia). The world societies of the ancient and classical era are most easily understood as civilizations (on which see McNeill 1963; Braudel 1985: 65–9), and although things like common scripts may have been significant, the main identity core of these civilizations was almost always a common religion. As was shown in the story of Sumeria in Chapter 8 common, or at least related, religions were a feature of international systems from the very beginning of civilization. One of the few really major social innovations during (as opposed to at the beginning of) this era was the whole series of 'universal' religions and ethical systems that began to appear in the middle of the first millennium BC (Buddhism, Confucianism), and ended with Islam a thousand years later. These religions were capable of transcending the intense, parochial localism of ancient and classical times, and creating wide communities that bridged many languages and cultures. They remain perhaps the most active and significant legacy from classical civilization to our own time. But although some of these (Christianity, Islam) stretched tendrils right across Eurasia, there was nothing like a world society even in Eurasia during this period. And the bigger

religions all experienced fissions serious enough to redivide the larger communities that they created (Sunni vs. Shia, Catholic vs. Orthodox vs. Nestorian,
etc.).

International societies were an even more limited development, being both
smaller in scale, and weaker in the level of common identity that they embodied.
Even at their best developed, as in classical Greece, they were in many ways not
much more than basic expressions of their relevant world society (in this case,
distinguishing members of Greek civilization from a 'barbarian' rest-of-world).
And while the Greeks did make at least some separation between rights and
power (by recognizing each other's independence), it could be argued that in
suzerain systems (or the Athenian Empire) the niceties of diplomacy and recognition were little more than reflections of raw power relations. One area that does
merit more attention than we can give it here is the role played by the legitimacy
of empire as a political form. If this was a norm of ancient and classical international society then it explains a lot about the dominance of hierarchy over
anarchy, and opens up an interesting perspective on imperial international systems. We are used to thinking of modern international society as reaffirming the
value of anarchic political structure. But the ancient and classical experience, and
Wight's idea of suzerain states-systems, suggest that international society can also
be organized around norms that differentiate units and place them in hierarchical
relations with each other, without at the same time simply creating domestic
rather than international politics. There is a link here between the international
politics of the ancient and classical world and post-Westphalian developments
such as the EU, which reinsert hierarchy into the international without crossing
the boundary into the domestic (Deudney 1995).

During this era, the trading systems were altogether more impressive than both
the societal and military-political ones both in terms of their range, and in the
sophistication and permanence of their institutions. While diplomacy had
advanced little beyond the idea that it was a useful practice not to kill, or take as
hostage, messengers, traders had built durable institutions and succeeded in carving out a significant sphere of freedom from political control. There is nevertheless a view that, seen in a very general societal perspective, the development of
civilization across Afro-Eurasia can be understood as a single process rather than
four distinct evolutions. Hodgson (1993: ch. 1), for example, sees the linkages
amongst the four centres of civilization in Eurasia as at least as important as what
separates them, and traces these linkages back into prehistory. This perspective
rests on the general similarity of both the processes of development across Eurasia
and the general pattern of civilization expanding at the expense of barbarians and
hunter-gatherers. Hodgson's point is to deny European exceptionalism by making
it part of this general development. But while these similarities are undeniable, it
is less clear whether they represent some kind of societal linkage, and therefore a
system, or merely parallel development in response to similar sets of conditions. A

case can be made for a deep, slow, and systematic process of diffusion of physical and social technologies in Eurasia, though interaction of this glacial sort is well outside the boundaries of our definition of international system. Although they remained distinctive, the Eurasian civilizations did influence each other by the exchange of technologies, arts, religions, and to a lesser extent, ideas about social organization. The argument for mere parallel development is supported by the many similarities between civilizations in the Americas and Eurasia, where the case for systematic contact of any sort is almost impossible to sustain.

# 4. CONCLUSIONS

Structure is the most difficult of our toolkit concepts to apply to the ancient and classical era. It is not quite so difficult as in the case of pre-international systems, but it lacks the clarity that we find in the modern era. This difference is sufficiently striking that it could almost serve as the basis for differentiating pre-international, ancient and classical, and modern types of international system. Where modern concepts of international structure seem clearly to apply to the ancient and classical world, as in the military-political sector, the expected theoretical outcomes do not occur. In the economic and societal sectors, the intensity of process is generally not high enough to generate much in the way of significant structural effects.

# Conclusion to Part III

Given all of the above, what can we say about the international systems of the ancient and classical world? We are quite satisfied that it is appropriate to think of this era in terms of international systems. It demonstrates both a general inside/outside structuration and a set of behaviours and processes that are clearly 'international' in form and content. The whole era can be framed and made sense of in terms of concepts familiar from contemporary IR. That said, it is also clear that this first generation of international systems differs from the modern international system in some significant ways. The general character of ancient and classical international systems can be summarized as follows.

1. During this era there are several distinct full international systems operating at the same time, and over the course of the era all of these systems tended to expand, sometimes merging with others in the process. There was no global international system by any definition.

2. There are also two different types of international system operating throughout this era: larger, but rather tenuous, economic systems defined principally by patterns of trade, and smaller, but more intense, full international systems, defined principally by patterns of war, diplomacy, and security dilemma. In Eurasia, the economic system expanded until it embraced all of the full international systems.

3. Technological constraints set a level of physical interaction capacity that goes a long way towards explaining the geographical limits of full international systems, and the tenuous quality of economic ones throughout this era.

4. Full international systems were clearly structured in the neorealist sense, yet diverged markedly from neorealist expectations of structural effect. There can be no doubt that the security dilemma operated powerfully and permanently in such systems, and that unrestrained power politics was very much the order of the day. But in the ancient and classical world this resulted neither in 'like units' nor in an anarchic structure permanently sustained by balance of power behaviour. What we see is the durable existence of unlike units (unlike always in terms of structural differentiation, and sometimes—within loose empires—in terms of functional differentiation), and the predominance of hierarchically over anarchically structured international systems. The most plausible explanations for this dramatic overriding of neorealist logic seem to be found on the unit level, in the character of empires and the perceived legitimacy of imperial rule.

5. Economic systems show some signs of market structure, but their linear arrangement and relay type of interaction, as well as constraints of interaction capacity generally, made them too tenuous to generate much in the way of structural effects.

For all its apparent conservatism, the ancient and classical world nevertheless fits into a picture of overall human progress. Although technological innovation was slow after the initial burst, the range and depth of civilization expanded quite steadily. Trading networks grew, and the political skills of humankind, among which one might count the development of universal religions, developed impressively. The human population expanded, and the long-standing threat from the barbarians was eventually contained and defeated. The ancient and classical world provided the foundation on which the European development was built. If the rise of Europe had not intervened, it is easy to imagine that the process of slow expansion from several cores of civilization might have continued. Trade and contact might have increased as the different zones of civilization overlapped more with each other, eventually resulting in a global system. This system would have been quite different from that which the Europeans eventually created. But once Europe had overwhelmed the two weakest of the old civilizations in the Americas, wiped out more than 90 per cent of their population with imported diseases, and added two re-peopled continents to its power base, its world historical momentum was unstoppable (Jones 1987: 4). Europeans went on to create the West and two centuries of global control.

Thus a global international system was created, but one that was exceptionally lopsided in the sense of being dominated by a single centre of civilization and a single regional international system. This was the second generation of international systems, and it is to that story that we now turn.

# Part IV

# THE ESTABLISHMENT AND EVOLUTION OF A GLOBAL INTERNATIONAL SYSTEM

## INTRODUCTION

There is a fairly wide consensus amongst world historians and historical sociologists that the middle of the second millennium AD marks a major transformation in the structure and character of world history. International Relations theorists do not give the matter much explicit thought, but implicitly nearly all of their theorizing is based on the world after AD 1500, and especially after 1648. Because of this assumption they generally take as given that there is only one international system, that it has become global in extent, and that it is a full system, with military-political and economic interaction occupying the same geographical space. Given that this section covers the historical home base of most IR theory, it comes as no surprise that there is a better fit between theory and history here than in Parts II and III. That is not to say that there are no problems at all. Making the theoretical divisions explicit, as our chapter structure forces us to do, reveals just how murky some of the everyday concepts in IR actually are, and how ill-defined the boundaries between them are. For example, the discourse of IR theory talks easily about process and structure, but actually distinguishing these two is not so clear-cut as one might expect. We try to spotlight some of these difficulties in Part V.

With something as vast and epochal as a change in world order, one would not expect an instant conversion from one condition to another, but a process taking place over some decades or centuries. This is indeed the case. The most obvious and rapid transformation came in terms of the scale of the European international system. The late fifteenth-century European openings of the sea routes around Africa and across the Atlantic were quickly followed by voyages across the Pacific. By the last decades of the sixteenth century a basic global system of navigation was firmly in place. In line with the ancient and classical pattern of economic systems being larger than military-political ones, this breakthrough in interaction capacity quickly generated a global-scale trading system that not only linked Europe, Africa, and Asia directly, but brought the resources of the Americas into the Eurasian system for the first time. The global spread of full international systems followed more slowly. The Americas were very quickly brought into the European military-political system (and with disease transmission, and the import and export of biota, also the environmental one). This merger resulted in the rapid obliteration of the indigenous civilizations and empires in the Andean highlands and Mesoamerica, as well as the pre-international systems in North America. But the making of a full global international system lagged considerably behind the making of a global trading one. India came under European sway during the eighteenth century, but not until the middle of the nineteenth century could the Western powers bring sufficient military power to bear in East Asia to force open Japan and China. The interior of Africa was the last to fall to European guns a couple of decades later, even though it had been penetrated by the Eurasian economy for a very long time before 1500. Thus not until the middle of the nineteenth century was there a single, full, global international system. Since the system then became geographically closed, the story thereafter is about its intensification rather than about its further expansion.

From this summary it is apparent that Europe is absolutely central to this phase of our story. On the face of it, that is puzzling. During all of the ancient and classical era, most of Europe was either a pre-international backwater or a colonial periphery. Only its southern countries were main players during the classical age. But around 1500, a new unit, the modern state, begins to come into focus along the western fringes of Europe, and begins its march to world domination. When Europe finally emerged from the feudal era with its largely localized history of unstable petty kingdoms and warring barons (mitigated to some extent by the extensive links maintained by the Western Christian Church) and began its rise to economic and military power, the newly formed modern states found themselves in a world still shaped by ancient and powerful civilizations. Connecting the Eurasian civilizations was a well-developed pattern of trade which Europe was once again able to tap into, and which the West quite quickly came to dominate. The classical era provided many of the key ingredients, economic, cultural, and technological, that went into the making of the European miracle, and were then overwhelmed by it.

The case that a major transformation in international relations got under way at this time is compelling, and the purpose of these four chapters is to examine the nature of the changes involved, and how they have unfolded up to the present day.

# Chapter 12

# UNITS IN THE MODERN INTERNATIONAL SYSTEM

## 1. INTRODUCTION

The rise of a new type of dominant unit in Europe around AD 1500 is one of the main foundations on which the differentiation of the modern from the ancient and classical era rests. There is widespread agreement that a unit transformation took place at this time, and there has been growing interest amongst IR theorists, in recent years, in the nature of feudalism and the complex shift from feudalism to the Westphalian system of sovereign states that took place in Europe at the end of the Middle Ages (Ruggie 1983; Fischer 1992; Hall and Kratochwil 1993; Watson 1992: ch. 13; Spruyt 1994*b*: ch. 3; Ruggie 1998: ch. 5; Teschke 1998). How and why this transformation took place is still far from being fully understood. Traditionally, non-Marxist historians argued that the modern European state emerged from a 'feudal anarchy' into which Europe had degenerated in the wake of the Carolingian Empire's collapse. That empire had extended across the territory that was occupied a millennium later by the original six members of the European Union, and it had returned a degree of order to Europe after the destruction of the western end of the Roman Empire. But with its collapse, warring barons are depicted as precipitating an era of 'feudal anarchy' before a new order was once again restored with the rise of modern states.

But there is now an important reassessment taking place. It is acknowledged that the demise of the Roman Empire left 'successor states', and Reynolds (1997: 132) goes further to suggest that 'a good deal of Western Europe was governed throughout the Middle Ages by polities that can reasonably be called states'. But these feudal or medieval states were very different from the states that eventually precipitated the global expansion of Europe. They were weak states and often very small, especially those that formed on the periphery of the Carolingian Empire and, later, in Western Europe following the collapse of that empire. Attempts are being made to categorize the changes that occurred in European state structures during the Middle Ages. Teschke (1998: 349) distinguishes three phases: feudal empires (650–950), feudal anarchy (950–1150), and a feudal states-system (1150–1450). Increasing attention is being paid to the fact that, initially, modern states were not the only dominant units to emerge from feudalism. As we noted in Part III, in northern Europe, the city league known as the Hanse became the dominant unit in this region, while in southern Europe, the Italian city-states flourished (Spruyt 1994a, 1994b). Empires also survived into the modern era, although they increasingly came to resemble modern states (Tilly 1990), and in Central Europe the Holy Roman Empire retained many medieval features of political organization until it was replaced by the new German state in the nineteenth century.

The medieval world looked radically different from the contemporary world of sovereign states that will be discussed in this chapter. It was constituted by a patchwork of overlapping and sometimes competing authorities. The Roman Church and the Holy Roman Empire, for example, both claimed authority over the same constituency of Christian believers. But in practice, neither possessed sovereign authority. During the era of feudal anarchy a highly decentralized mode of political organization developed based on personal ties of obligation. So it was not only the Roman Church and Empire that claimed to exercise authority in Europe; there were also, among a host of political actors, kings, barons, city bur-ghers, trade guilds, and bishops (see Fig. 12.1). In an attempt to distinguish the resulting structure from hierarchy and anarchy, feudalism has sometimes been labelled as heteronomy. IR theorists increasingly acknowledge that their existing concepts simply cannot begin to capture the complexity of medieval political organization. We lack the space to enter into a detailed discussion of this period. And to do so, moreover, would divert us from our main intention in this chapter which is to discuss the units which have come to play a crucial role in the global international system. From our perspective, the medieval period is interesting theoretically as a challenge to IR concepts of political structure, and historically as the precursor to what became the world-spanning Westphalian international sys-tem. We do not, however, see it as a world historical era in its own right (more on this in Chapter 18).

Initially, it was mainly in the West, particularly in England, France, and Spain, that the modern state took root. It was some time before it became apparent that the diverse unit types that persisted across Europe would be unable to compete successfully with the modern states that eventually swept to one side every kind of unit that had existed in the ancient and classical international systems as well as in the pre-international systems. Because they are different from any of the units that had dominated previous international and pre-international sys-tems, attention will be focused here on the modern states that began to crystal-lize out of late medieval Western Europe. It was ultimately the modern state rather than the empire, city-state, or city league that was to represent the wave of the future.

The modern state did, in fact, share many of the features that characterized earlier forms of state, but they were also distinctive in a number of crucial ways. Although the picture in much of Europe remained very mixed until as late as the nineteenth century, the modern states increasingly cultivated precise, hard boundaries rather than fuzzy frontiers, and within those boundaries they claimed

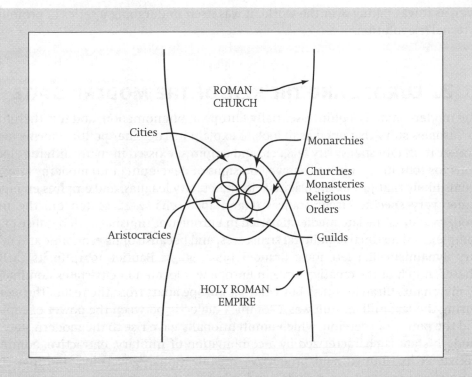

*Note*: The figure illustrates very schematically the complex and overlapping sovereignties that operated in the feudal era in Europe. The major challenge was between the Roman Church and the Holy Roman Empire. But within this contested arena there were also a host of additional rights and duties formed between individuals and feudal institutions.

*Figure 12.1 The feudal system: multiple overlapping sovereignties*

absolute sovereignty. The modern state tightened up the inside/outside construction of world politics. Within three or four hundred years of its arrival on the scene as a distinctive player it had obliterated and replaced, colonized, or subordinated nearly all of the other political units on the planet. The few older units of the previously dominant types that retained their independence (Japan, China, Ethiopia, Ottoman Empire, Thailand) were forced to adapt furiously to take on state-like forms (Gong 1984; Tilly 1990). The ancient and classical arrangement where empires, city-states, and barbarian tribes had coexisted as the dominant units for many millennia was rapidly replaced by a system in which only one type of unit, the modern state, was dominant. And this new unit did not stand still.

Even as it was taking over the world, it was itself undergoing a series of profound internal (r)evolutions.

## 2. EUROPE AND THE RISE OF THE MODERN STATE

The modern state is a quintessentially European phenomenon, and it is therefore to Europe's story that one has to look to explain it. The older political forms most similar to it, city-states, city leagues, and empires, existed in many different locations for four millennia and showed no signs of developing into modern states. It seems likely that just as the original city-states, city leagues, and empires emerged under very specific circumstances (Mann 1986: chs. 2–4), so too did the first modern states. The late medieval period in Europe was unusual both because of its complex and distinctive political structures, and because of its economic and military dynamism (Bartlett 1994; Braudel 1985: 45–57; Bautier 1971). In its earlier phases, much of the creative force in Europe was located in city-states dominated by merchants (Braudel 1985). But what set Europe apart from the rest of the world during the last millennium was a complex dialectic between the power of capital and the power of coercion, which unintentionally gave rise to the modern state. A modern state is characterized by a combination of military, extractive, administrative, redistributive, and productive organizations, 'governing multiple contiguous regions and their cities', and mixing capital and coercion both in its formative process and in its empire-building style. The key synthesis in such states is that the holders of capital provide financial resources for the state, while the holders of coercion allow capital a significant role in government. This combination proved to be more efficient in mobilizing the human potential of populations, making for high effectiveness in both war and economics (Tilly 1990; 2–3, 21, 31, 91–5, 137–51; Spruyt 1994a, and 1994b; Braudel 1985: 277–97), and is the key to why this new unit so quickly achieved global dominance.

At the end of the Middle Ages, however, Europe was still very fragmented politically and the international political system was characterized by a high degree of structural and functional differentiation. The Norsemen, for example, had by AD 1100 established the first Atlantic maritime empire that linked Scandinavia to Iceland, Greenland, and North America. In the twelfth century, Scandinavian merchants were trading across northern Europe, into Russia, Byzantium, and beyond, as well as westwards across the Atlantic (Scammell 1981; Crosby 1986). The maritime supremacy of the Norse, however, was destroyed and surpassed by the cities that belonged to the Hanseatic League. To the south, a small number of Italian city-states dominated the trade in the Mediterranean and acted as intermediaries between Europe and Asia (Scammell 1981). In other parts of Europe, effective power rested with manorial barons whose rule often embraced no more than a handful of villages. But there were also areas, like Flanders and Normandy, that were effectively governed from the centre by powerful rulers (Reynolds 1997).

It was by no means obvious at this stage that the inchoate but distinctive modern states that were emerging in Britain and France would eventually constitute the dominant unit that would shape the political, economic, and social sectors of the emerging European international system. But over time it became apparent that these modern states possessed a combination of advantages that none of the other types of unit could match. In the first place, the modern states generated a more effective economic environment than either the city-states or the city leagues could produce. As a consequence, they emerged as the dominant economic units in both the European and eventually the global international economic systems. At the same time, the modern states were able to draw on this economic success to become the most powerful political actors in the system because they were to prove more effective than the agrarian empires at fighting wars. Under the pressures of socialization and competition, the agrarian empires at one extreme, and the city leagues at the other, began to emulate the modern states, with the result that the systemic characteristics of structural and functional differentiation were reduced and eventually eliminated. Over the long haul, the European and then the global international systems came to be constituted by 'like units' that were all modern states.

The complex array of competing political units and the low level of systemic political links across medieval Europe has often obscured the fact that by the end of the Middle Ages Europe formed a coherent international economic system (Jones 1988: 168). At that juncture, cities were still the dominant economic units in the system. At the heart of the European international economic system lay a band of cities, forming an urban corridor stretching from north-west Italy to southern England, cutting across an essentially agrarian Europe. At the northern end of this corridor, merchants engaged in a high-volume bulk trade, in goods with low profit margins such as timber, grain, and herring. The towns were small in size and wealth and Spruyt (1994b) postulates that as a consequence they needed to pool their resources by forming the Hanseatic League to provide protection and promote a favourable economic climate for themselves. By contrast, at the southern end of the corridor, the Italian city-states, while also engaging in bulk trade, became extremely wealthy by trading in luxury goods on which there was a very high profit margin. Throughout the later Middle Ages, Venice and Genoa vied for control over this trade, and by the fifteenth century, the Levant was the exclusive preserve of the Venetians (Scammell 1981: 86). The Italian city-states were much larger and wealthier than their northern counterparts and they did not experience the need to combine forces by establishing a league.

When the European economy started to expand, towards the end of the eleventh century, the towns and cities that already formed the urban corridor began to flourish. New towns were established and the corridor widened. In the ancient and classical worlds, capital tended to be drawn into cities from the surrounding regions, so that they could become wealthier even in the absence of economic growth. Expanding wealth was often only the product of a concentration of capital. But in the medieval period, as the European economy grew, cities in the urban corridor became wealthier *not* at the expense of neighbouring cities. Across the system, wealth accumulated but without any concentration of capital. This environment encouraged the cities to maintain their independence, or at most to form loose associations such as the Hanseatic League. It was not conducive to the promotion of political hierarchy or the establishment of clear-cut territorial boundaries. But just beyond this corridor of cities, there lay a number of medieval kingdoms, in particular, Britain, France, Spain, and later Prussia, that were beginning to develop into modern states. These states contained towns that just fell within the penumbra of the accumulating capital that was being generated within the urban corridor. The volume of trade and the profit margins were lower in these towns than in the towns at the centre of the urban corridor. Spruyt (1994b: 64) suggests that the merchants in these towns responded positively to the moves being made to consolidate the state as a hierarchic and clearly demarcated unit, recognizing that these developments would help to improve their economic position. An unintended consequence of this development was that these modern states eventually became more effective economic units than either the city leagues or the city-states.

The emerging hierarchy and the consolidation of the borders that demarcated these new modern states proved beneficial to merchants in a number of different ways. First, the national units were able to lower the transaction costs experienced by merchants, by standardizing measures and centralizing the minting of coins. Taxes were also standardized, which meant that merchants confronted a much more stable and predictable environment than that experienced by merchants in city-states and city leagues. Second, in modern states, free riding became difficult or impossible. The defence of the realm, for example, was provided as a public good and it was not possible for merchants or cities to renege on contributions to military campaigns and rely on the efforts of others as happened in the Hanseatic League and the Italian city-states. In the same way, it was much easier for the modern state to engage in agreements that bound all their subjects than it was for the Hanseatic League to bind its members. Spruyt (1994b: 177) concludes that because city-states were more like modern states than the city leagues, they managed to survive for much longer by turning themselves into mini-modern states. But because they lacked a clear internal hierarchy and precise boundaries, they remained much less effective economic units.

National states proved to be not only to be the most effective economic units in the European international economic system, but also more effective warfighting machines. Tilly (1990) argues that modern states emerged as the dominant unit in the global arena primarily because they proved to be more successful than any of their competitors when it came to waging war. A first intimation of this development came in 1494 when the French overran the Italian city-states. But the modern states were not only able to defeat city-states, they also outperformed the agrarian empires. So the success of the modern states is not attributed by Tilly to sheer size but to the fact that they were so much more effective than the other units at resource mobilization. Tilly distinguishes in the first instance between capital and coercive intensive resource mobilization. In empires, rulers rely on the coercive power of the state to requisition or extract from its population the resources needed to fight a war. By contrast, city-states illustrate a capital-intensive mode of resource mobilization, where the imposition of taxes on commerce relatively painlessly provided the revenue needed to finance war. What Tilly sees as distinctive about the modern state was its ability to combine capital and coercive modes of resource mobilization. Kingdoms operating within the penumbra of the urban corridor were able to enhance the economic position of the towns and cities that had formed within their territorial boundaries and then extract revenue from trade as well as land. States that followed this trajectory produced the first modern states and the story of England is a good example.

*The making of England*

At the end of the first millennium AD, England was a country with a number of significant towns tied into the international trading network. Although these cities were still on the periphery of this network, they were an important source of wealth, and the Danes, who lacked any significant urbanization, found it well worth their while to force the British into their tribute-taking empire. This relationship was overthrown by the Norman invasion of Britain in 1066. The Normans began to colonize Britain, distributing land in fiefs to their soldiers who then became agents to the crown. A century later, Henry II laid claim to much of Britain and a large section of France. His ambition was under constant challenge from rivals within the family and from local barons whose support was required to wage the wars required to consolidate these claims. To secure the support of the barons, the Norman rulers had to make concessions to them. A great council was established which curbed the power of the king, especially because its approval was required for any new taxation.

With the passage of time, English kings found that there was a second powerful group which needed to be accommodated. Wool, produced on the land of the barons, was initially exported, but this wool was increasingly processed in England. As a result, a new merchant class began to grow up in England. Their co-operation and capital was also required if kings were to consolidate their power at home and abroad. The merchants, like the landlords, were given a voice in a lower chamber, consolidating the role of Parliament in the process of government. In contrast to agrarian empires, where landowners had the most influential voice, and to city-states where merchants held sway, in the emerging modern states, there was an uneasy alliance between these two groups. It was the growing commercialization, proletarianization, and economic expansion which provided the foundations on which the modern state was built. Not only did it enable kings to prosecute wars abroad, but it also enabled them to eliminate the feudal armies of the landlords. The modern state emerged as the result of a complex process of brokerage between rulers and power groupings within the state.

The modern state thus emerged on the periphery of a dynamic area of economic growth. Competing power groups—landlords and merchants—both benefited from their interaction with this area of wealth. These two groups proved willing to finance the growth and war-making capacity of the state in return for an increasing say in the activities of the state. After 1500, when new technology (cannons, much larger warships) made wars increasingly expensive to fight, this development gave emerging modern states like England an increasing advantage over other forms of state because they could finance these wars more effectively. This advantage increased with time. As the modern state became more commercialized and urbanized, it also became more monetized as individuals increasingly came to work for wages. With this development, it became possible to introduce income tax and the state came to reply on surveillance rather than coercion to maintain its revenues. The modern state became increasingly responsible for managing the economy, and, by the end of the Middle Ages, was already moving towards being the central economic actor in the international system. This position facilitated the task of turning the modern state into the foremost fighting machine.

Tilly's account sees the modern state emerging as a specific form of compromise where coercion and capital come into a kind of balance. First in Europe, and later in the wider world, this synthesis proved more effective than either city-state forms, where capital remained dominant, or empires, where coercion ruled. The rich city-states could not match the scale and military strength of the modern states, and the empires, while having no problems with scale, could not match their wealth and technological innovation. At an early stage the Hanseatic League gave way to the emergent states of northern Europe, and the previously autonomous city-state system in Italy increasingly fell under the sway of France and Spain. The Netherlands survived only by taking on state-like qualities during its long war of independence against Spain. And the city-states of Germany survived only because they constituted a convenient buffer in the balance of power game played amongst Austria, France, Prussia, and England.

# 3.  THE EVOLUTION OF THE MODERN STATE

Although largely keeping their exterior form (hard boundaries, strong sovereignty), the leading modern states evolved rapidly inside, growing in power as
they did so, and quickly rising to become the dominant type of unit in the global
international system that was being made by Europeans. The internal development of this new unit involved a progressive shift of political centrality from
leaders to people. Starting out from absolutism, with sovereignty located in the
monarch, the leading states shifted to a national form, locating sovereignty in the
people, and making them citizens rather than subjects. Nationalism evolved to
mass democracy, albeit not before flirting with various forms of totalitarian mass
society (communism, fascism).

We have already noted that none of the dominant units in the ancient and
classical world led the evolution into modern states. Instead, the new unit arose in
a relative backwater of classical times, where the collapse of the Western Roman
Empire gave rise to the unique configuration known as medievalist. But as we
argued in Part III, the classical empires were not politically stagnant. They constantly attempted to achieve higher levels of internal integration, and although
their general form remained the same, they did learn how to improve the range
and stability of imperial government. Rome, remember, eventually extended citizenship to most of its subject peoples. But this integration was mostly associated
with mechanisms of territorial control and was about guaranteeing the cohesion
of the ruling elite.

National states, by contrast, have become much more concerned about linking
rulers to people, and state to society and territory. Compare, for example, the
absolute monarchies of Europe and Asia, or the despotic empires of ancient and
classical times, with contemporary democratic national states. In their domestic
politics the early absolutist states in some ways resembled classical empires. In
absolute monarchies, the state was little more than the personal property of the
ruler. It provided a measure of order and security for those within it, though it
may also have been a major source of insecurity for them. The people were subjects rather than citizens. There was little in the way of socio-political integration
except that provided by the hierarchies of the feudal social order and the coercive
and extractive powers of the ruler. People and territory were added to or sub-
tracted from any given state quite casually. Boundaries changed according to the
fortunes of war, the balance of power, and the manipulations of dynastic marriage
and succession. Both absolutist states and classical empires learned the trick of
creating an administrative bureaucracy to manage the (e)state, collect taxes,
maintain standing armed forces, and suchlike. As it developed, this bureaucracy
both extended the powers of government and created a state establishment considerably broader than the ruling family. Among other things, it provided a buffer
against weak rulers, the appearance of which often led to the break-up of both

ancient empires and medieval kingdoms. In absolutist states, security concerns focused very much on the interests of the ruling family. The main difference was in the harder boundaries and more exclusive claim to sovereignty of the absolutist state compared with the classical empires.

But this comparison was quite short lived. From the eighteenth century onwards, the increasing pressure of capitalism and industrialism extended the compact between capital and coercion that lay at the heart of the modern state. As a result, the development of the national state took place within the shell of territorial sovereignty provided by the absolutist one. This process occurred first in the leading north-west European states, and spread from there to a few others in the Americas and Asia. A substantial majority of contemporary states have not completed it, and some have barely begun. At least three major developments took place which differentiated modern states both from their absolutist pre-decessors and even more so from classical empires. First was the rise of an independent commercial class. This was a trick almost never mastered by ancient and classical empires beyond a fairly basic level, as with the main Phoenician coastal cities, such as Byblos, Tyre, and Arwad, that were given a special role within the Assyrian Empire, leaving them free to establish and implement their own economic strategies (Larsen 1979). In the same way, during the early medieval period, the coastal trading cities in East Africa, such as Mogadishu and Kilwa, which provided a focal point for trade embracing the Middle East, India, and China, were also established as ports of trade unfettered from the control of local rulers (Chaudhuri 1991). But more frequently, the demands of the commercial class were stoutly resisted (the anti-mercantile moves in fifteenth-century China). Creating legal, political, and social space for commercial actors not only increased the resource base of the state, but also created a more complex class structure, and a more pluralist distribution of power and interest within the state, separate from the traditional dynastic ruling establishment (Tilly 1990).

Second was the invention of nationalism as an ideology of the state. By national-ism we mean the political ideology that locates the right of self-government in a people who share a common culture. Nationalism can come in *ethno* form, where the cultural group is seen as pre-existing, organic, *Gemeinschaft* in nature (Russian, German, Japanese, for example), or 'civic' where shared identity is more a matter of contractual, *Gesellschaft* type agreement amongst those who participate in a given political system (most obviously in New World countries such as the USA, Australia, Brazil, but also in some ways France). In practice this distinction between ethno and civic nationalism is often hard to sustain. Ostensibly ethno states have often played a big role in creating a sense of common language and culture amongst their peoples, and ostensibly civic ones often try to create com-mon language and culture, so moving towards ethno form. Despite its powerful myths of ancient roots, nationalism as a political force is a development of the late eighteenth and nineteenth centuries in Europe. Its timing is closely associated with the rise of industrialization, and it can be seen as a successful answer to the growing threat identified by Marx that the class conflicts generated by industrialism would overthrow the state (Gellner 1983). In effect, nationalism provided a strong overarching bond of identity to set against and ameliorate class divisions.

Nationalism helped to transform the people from subjects into citizens. The spread of political inclusion meant that the relationship between state and people was increasingly mediated by law, and that sovereignty became diffused throughout society rather than concentrated in the ruling elite. It welded government and society together into a mutually supportive framework, and it strengthened the bond between a state and a particular expanse of territory. As Mayall (1990) argues, the rise of nationalism changed not only what states were internally, but also many aspects of how they related to each other. Nationalism overrode more extensive, cosmopolitan forms of shared identity such as religion (Piscatori 1986). It generated a whole set of conflict issues within and between states to do with minorities. It threatened multicultural states with dismemberment, whether by secession or irredentist demands, and it drove some modern states to seek to bring into their rule all the components of 'their' nation. It created a new set of problems for stateless minorities, most notably Jews, who had previously been persecuted on grounds of religion. In many ways nationalism called into question the existing territorial order of the European states-system. But it did so without calling into question the principles of either hard territoriality or hard sovereignty on which the modern state rested. Indeed, it reinforced the 'inside/outside' construction of politics. In principle, though somewhat less in practice, nationalism offered the possibility of creating both strongly self-legitimizing states (the ideal nation-state fusion), and principles by which such states could recognize each other's political and territorial legitimacy (Herz 1968: 82, 89). In the ideal nationalist world, nations would all have their own state, and like individuals would all treat each other as legal equals. This ideal was realized in a few places, but mostly fell victim to power politics, to the political difficulty of giving states to small nations, and to the extreme messiness of the national map compared with the territorial one. Yet despite its responsibility for generating conflicts in Europe, nationalism was also part of the process of industrialization that enormously strengthened the European states against the still formidable imperial remnants of the ancient and classical world.

The third development was the introduction of democracy in the leading modern states. This institutionalized the transfer of sovereignty from ruler to people implicit in nationalism, and made the state actually as well as notionally representative of its whole citizenry. But democracy was not the only possible evolution from nationalism. One way or another, mass society was on the cards, not only in the sense of mass participation in politics, but also in the senses of mass literacy, mass education, mass identity, and the possibility of mass mobilization. Mass society was implicit in both nationalism and industrialism, and fascist and communist forms of mass society both emerged strongly during the twentieth century as possible alternatives to mass democracy. Much of the history of the twentieth century, and especially its three world wars (First, Second, and Cold), can be read as the struggle amongst these alternatives to capture the future of industrial society. In the event, the liberal reading of nationalism proved to be the most effective in generating both wealth and power. Like nationalism, democracy also not only changed the state internally, but also impacted on the nature of relations between states. Most obvious has been the spread of the 'democratic peace', in which good empirical grounds exist for thinking that democratic states very rarely if ever go to war with each other (Doyle 1983a, 1983b; Chan 1993; Russett 1993). But equally important to non-democratic states has been the agenda of human rights now embedded in the strongest states in the system, and projected by them throughout it. At least initially, democratization seemed to take place within the hard territorial and sovereign legacy of the absolutist state. Whether this remains so is a question we will take up in Part V.

The modern state is a concept whose content has thus undergone a remarkable expansion (see Fig. 12.2). The most advanced states have steadily fused govern-

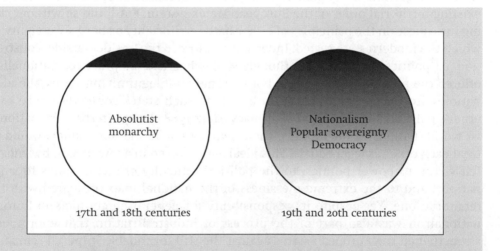

*Note:* The figure illustrates very schematically how the process of governing within modern states has been transformed over the past four centuries. Initially, a small elite was responsible for the government of the state. But over the past two centuries, with the growth of nationalism and democracy in the modern state, most of society is now involved, to some degree, in governing the state.

*Figure 12.2 The evolution of government in the modern state*

ment and society, in the process becoming much deeper, more complex, and more firmly established constructs than either their predecessors or contemporary 'weak' states.

*Weak and strong states*
Weak states are those with low levels of socio-political cohesion. Because they have failed to integrate society and government, they typically have authoritarian governments and violent domestic politics. Strong states have high levels of socio-political cohesion, are usually democratic, and tend to have peaceful domestic politics. The weak–strong state spectrum contrasts with (and often does not correlate with) the more traditional spectrum of weak and strong powers. Iceland, for example, is a strong state but a weak power. Nigeria is a weak state, but a substantial regional power. (See Buzan 1991: 96–107.)

They have expanded not only to incorporate, but also to represent, an ever widening circle of interests and participants. Their functions and capabilities have expanded along with their constituency until the state has become involved in all sectors of activity, and responsive to all sectors of society. Nationalism and democracy have transformed the way in which states relate to each other, creating new grounds for both co-operation and conflict.

In domestic perspective, the advanced modern state appears to have grown much more solid and deeply rooted. Compared with its ancestors, it is an altogether more developed entity, much better integrated with society, much more complex and internally coherent, much more powerful (in terms of its ability to penetrate society and extract resources from it, and to project its influence and activity outside its boundaries), and much more firmly legitimized. Along with this development, and stemming from it, is a much more comprehensive security agenda. States have now to worry not just about their military strength and the security of their ruling families, but also about the competitiveness of their economies, the reproduction of their cultures, the welfare, health, and education of their citizens, the stability of their ecology, and their command of knowledge and technology. On this basis, it is difficult to explain why there is so much questioning of the viability and relevance of the state as the defining unit of the international system. If the leading states have become so much more powerful and inclusive, why should they not still be at the centre of world politics? More on this below.

## 4. THE SPREAD OF THE MODERN STATE AND THE DEMISE OF OLDER UNIT TYPES

In AD 1500, it was still not clear what kind of actor would constitute the dominant unit in the global international system. Hunter-gatherer bands and sedentary tribes had for long been unequivocally marginalized in Eurasia during the ancient and classical era. But they remained the only significant actors in lands that other types of unit shunned (the far north) and where the Eurasians had not yet been able to reach (Australasia, Oceania, and much of the Americas). The nomadic tribes that had cut such a swath through ancient and classical history were still around, but on the brink of extinction as a major player in international relations. On the one hand, the steppe nomads were increasingly adopting a sedentary way of life (Kwanten 1979), while on the other, the advent of firearms from the four-teenth century AD onward spelled the permanent doom of the long-standing nomadic military superiority based on light cavalry. Equipped with guns, peasant infantry could stand off nomadic raiders, and so push the area of state control into the steppe. The Russian expansion across Siberia beginning in the sixteenth cen-tury and the assertion of durable Chinese control over the eastern reaches of Central Asia during the Manchu expansion of the eighteenth century, marked the final extinction of classical nomadic control in the steppe. Only in a few areas (Afghanistan, Kurdistan) did barbarian culture remain strong enough to resist total absorption by other units, though even in these places it was no longer strong enough to count more than locally in the balance of power. The collapse of nomadic power is almost as important in defining the end of the ancient and classical era as is the rise of the modern state in Europe.

In the core areas of civilization, empires, city-states, city-state leagues, and (in Europe) emerging modern states coexisted and competed with each other. It took a couple of centuries before it became clear that neither tribal federations, city-states, nor empires would be able to compete effectively with the modern state. Tribal federations were mostly absorbed into expanding empires (Chinese, Russian, Ottoman, British, French, and United States). Individual city-states were mostly absorbed into contiguous modern states or empires. Federations of city-states, such as the Netherlands, as well as empires, such as the Austro-Hungarian, Ottoman, and Russian, began to adopt some of the structural features, most not-ably hard boundaries, that would allow them to exist in a world dominated by modern states.

As the leading modern states gained speed in the processes of internal devel-opment described in the previous section, power in the international system shifted decisively although possibly only temporarily away (Jones et al. 1993) from the long-established areas of civilization in China, India, the Middle East, Meso-America, and the Andean highlands, and came to rest firmly in Europe. The hand-ful of leading modern states in Western Europe began to build vast overseas empires (see Maps 12.1–12.4): first Spain and Portugal in the sixteenth century, then the Netherlands in the seventeenth century, and then Britain and France from the seventeenth century onward. Some of the classical-type land-based empires also expanded during the sixteenth, seventeenth, and eighteenth centuries, most notably the Chinese and Ottoman. So also did the Russian, which was a hybrid between the forms of modern state and classical empire. Even quite minor European powers such as Denmark were able to take substantial overseas territories. European latecomers to the process of making modern states, such as the Germans and the Italians, who did not cohere into modern states until well into the nineteenth century, were left with the dregs of overseas empire. They did not do as well as the United States, a European offshoot, which carved out both a continental and an overseas empire. Neither did they do as well as Japan, which was the only non-European society able during the nineteenth century to construct a modern state successful enough to itself enter the empire-building game in Asia in its own right. In 1500, Europeans controlled 7 per cent of the world's land area. By 1800 they controlled 35 per cent. By 1914 they had substantially re-peopled three continents (North and South America and Australia), and controlled 84 per cent of the world's land (Headrick 1988: 3, cited in Tilly 1990: 183). The British, however, possessed the lion's share of this overseas territory—their empire extended over 30 million square km (12 million square miles), which was three times the size of the French Empire (Smith 1981).

*Four centuries of European expansion*
During the sixteenth century, Russia began its eastward march, occupying the Urals and penetrating into western Siberia. Spain destroyed the empires of the Aztecs and the Incas, built up its own empire in Mexico, Central America, the Caribbean, and Peru (Rosenberg 1994), and introduced the diseases that within a century had killed off more than 90 per cent of the native population in the Americas. By 1564 Spain had also taken the Philippines. Portugal established forts and trading posts along the western and eastern coasts of Africa, at the mouth of the Persian Gulf, in India and Indonesia, and set about establishing naval and commercial control of the Indian Ocean. It created a chain that linked to trading contacts in China and Japan, and began the transfer of the Asian trade with Europe from land routes to sea ones. Portugal also began the slave trade to South America where it was establishing a colony in Brazil. In this century, the Europeans successfully devastated the pre-Iron Age civilizations of the Americas, and had a major impact on tribal peoples in the Americas, Siberia, and increasingly Africa. But they had not yet called into question the power of the leading classical empires. Right on Europe's doorstep, the Ottoman Empire was taking Egypt, much of the Middle East, and Hungary, and laying siege to Vienna. It was in alliance with France against the Hapsburgs, while at

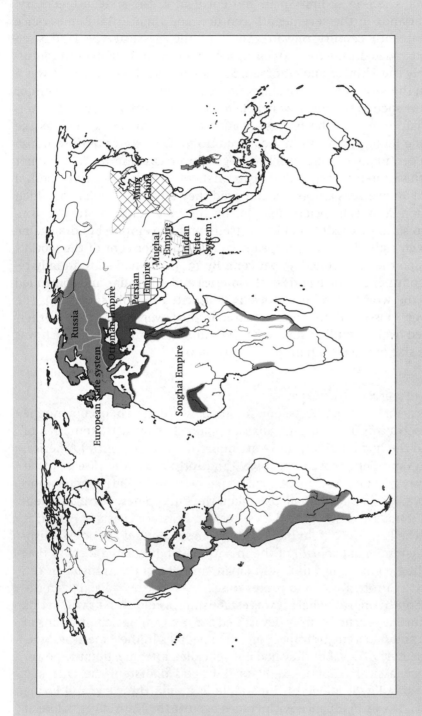

*Note:* Maps 12.1–12.4 illustrate the major political changes that took place across the globe over a period of four centuries.

*Map 12.1  Imperial expansion in the sixteenth century*

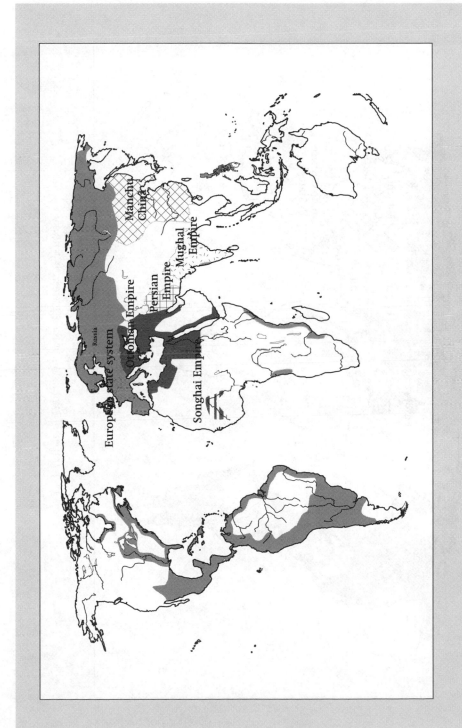

Russia

Manchu
China

Mughal
Empire

Persian
Empire

Ottoman Empire

European state system

Songhai Empire

*Map 12.2  Imperial expansion in the seventeenth century*

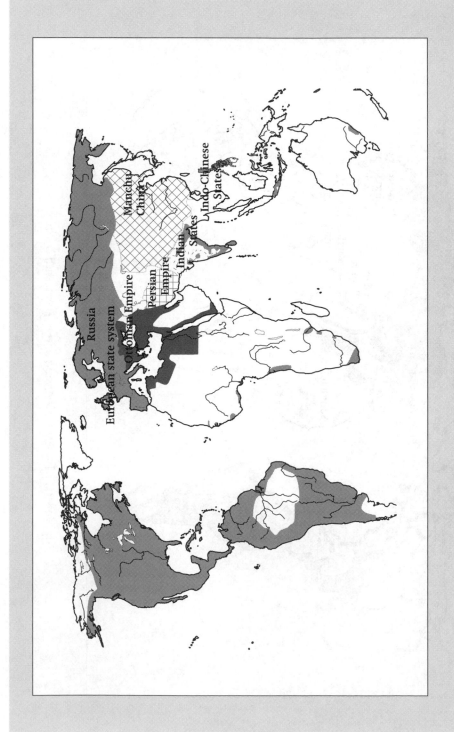

*Map 12.3 Imperial expansion in the eighteenth century*

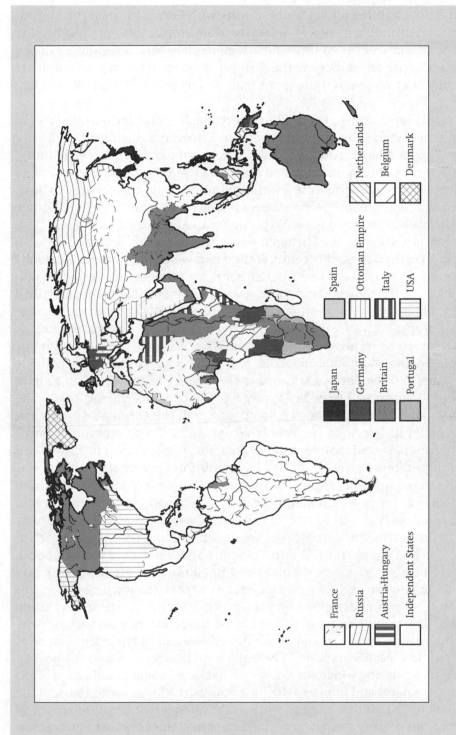

Map 12.4 Imperial powers in 1914

the same time fighting a long series of wars with Persia. In India the Mughal Empire was expanding its power, while the Ming Empire in China was beating off tribal attacks from the north and attempted Japanese invasions of Korea. With their superior sea power, the Europeans were beginning to dominate Asian trade, but they were little more than players in what was still an Asian game.

During the seventeenth century, Russia occupied central and eastern Siberia, reaching the Pacific coast in 1637. Europeans discovered Australia but did not settle it. France, Britain, and the Netherlands began a competitive penetration and settlement of North America, and also challenged the existing Spanish and Portuguese hold on Central and South America, and on the trade with Asia. Britain and France began their rival penetrations into India. The Dutch established themselves on the coasts in West and South Africa, took Formosa in 1619, and began to challenge the Portuguese in Indonesia, and for the trade with China and Japan. During this century, the main weight of European colonial expansion and settlement was in the Americas. European penetration into Africa and Asia was mostly about trade, involving the establishment of fortified coastal trading stations rather than attempts to seize or control large territories. The European advance was beginning to challenge the classical empires of Asia, but had by no means overthrown them. The success of the trade routes by sea replaced the traditional overland routes through Central Asia and the Middle East, and thereby undermined the prosperity of the Ottoman Empire (and Venice) which had previously served as the conduits for this trade. The Mughal Empire was still strong in South Asia, and the Ottoman Empire was able to mount its last offensive against Vienna (1683). China ousted the Dutch from Taiwan (1662) and took control of Korea (1627), while Japan instituted and successfully enforced its policy of closure against foreign contact.

During the eighteenth century the main expansions were Russia's extension of its hold over the northern part of Central Asia, across the Bering strait into Alaska, and down the west coast of North America; and Spain's extension of its control northwards through Mexico and up the Pacific coast, and in South America, from Peru northward into Colombia and Venezuela. In both South Asia and North America, Britain succeeded in eliminating French power, and consolidating its own exclusive control. At the end of the century, however, this British success was undermined by the (French assisted) American revolution (1776–83). This revolution founded the United States as a new sovereign member of international society, and began its career as an independent centre of power and 'European' expansion. The eighteenth century was also the peak of the slave trade, during which the Europeans extracted some 10 million Africans to work the estates and mines of the Americas (Barraclough 1978: 166) and the Arabs took over 4 million more to work in the Middle East (Segal 1993: 54). By the end of this century the power of the European states and their empires was beginning to register seriously against some of the Asian empires, and competition amongst the Europeans was more significant than that between the Europeans and the local powers. India was largely under British sway, and the Ottoman Empire was being pushed into retreat by the advances of Russia and Austria. China, however, remained vigorous, reasserting its control in Central Asia, conquering Tibet (1751), invading Burma (1765), and establishing suzerainty over Nepal (1792). China followed Japan's policy of closure by restricting European trade access to the single port of Canton (1757).

During the nineteenth century, the balance tipped decisively in favour of the modern state, with only vestiges of the classical empires managing to hang on. In Europe itself Germany and Italy finally took on modern state forms, though in Eastern Europe the Austro-Hungarian and Russian Empires still managed to retain older forms, albeit influenced by the modern state. European expansion abroad was combined with mass migrations of Europeans. The United States occupied the western two-thirds of its present territory, pushed Mexico southwards, purchased Alaska from Russia, and extended colonial control across the Pacific to the Philippines, and into Central America and the Caribbean. Russia occupied Central Asia and the Vladivostok region. In South America, a set of new states established their independence from Spain and Portugal in the early part of the century. During this century the Europeans penetrated and then colonized nearly all of Africa, eroded and penetrated the Ottoman Empire and Persia, extended colonial control over most of South-East Asia, and, along with the United States, forced China (1842) and Japan (1853–6) to abandon their policies of closure, and open themselves to Western trade, culture, and political influence.

By the beginning of the twentieth century, the modern state was unquestionably the dominant unit in the international system, and yet the system was not itself fully composed of modern states. The European powers, joined by their offshoot in the USA, and their successful mimic in Japan, had nearly all acquired empires. In one sense, the international system was thus a mixture of modern states and colonies, plus the scattered remnants of older forms: a few classical empires and tribal societies. But this picture is too simple. The Russian and Austro-Hungarian Empires were still similar in form to classical empires even though they had acquired the harder boundaries of the modern state. Some European overseas empires, most notably the British, made a pretty firm distinction between the core modern state and the colonies, dominions, and protectorates that made up the empire. But others, most notably the French, treated at least some of their colonies as integral parts of the metropolitan polity, and even the British crossed this line in Ireland (Smith 1981). As a consequence, right up to the middle of the twentieth century the modern state was still not the dominant unit in the global international system. Empires with modern states at their core were the dominant unit. These empires shared some qualities with their classical predecessors in that they often contained layered sovereignty (ranging from outright colonies to dominions and protectorates). But many of them were far-flung overseas empires, which broke the classical mould (even the famous maritime empires of classical times, such as those of Athens and Carthage tended to concentrate around their core city-state). And the hard territoriality of the modern state was also reflected in the Europeans' practice of precise territorial demarcations of their colonies. The ideology of many of the classical empires was also universal in form and they aspired to control their known world, whereas the European empires acknowledged that they were members of an international system largely constituted by modern state empires.

Although the modern state had, by the nineteenth century, clearly created a revolution by becoming the new dominant unit of the international system, a global system of modern states did not emerge clearly until the process of decolonization was complete (see Fig. 12.3). The European empires can thus be seen as the nursery, or mechanism, by which the political form of the modern state was transposed onto the rest of the world.

The timing and the method of this transposition varied from place to place, but its outcome was always the same. Whatever had been there before, what remained was a set of modern states, some well made and some badly, but all copies of the new political form that had arisen in Europe. Unlike ancient and classical empires, which tended to disintegrate into pre-existing units, modern state empires from the French and British to the Russian have tended to disintegrate into the administrative units created by the empire.

The first round of this process took place in the Americas, where European immigrants had largely displaced, subordinated, and to a considerable extent exterminated the native population. In the late eighteenth and early nineteenth centuries, these European populations revolted against the colonialism of Britain and Spain, setting up the United States and the Latin American countries as independent states. A few countries escaped direct colonization by Europeans, but these had to adapt to European political norms and forms in order to retain their independence. For Japan, Thailand, Turkey, Ethiopia, Persia, and China it was the threat of colonization that acted as the transforming spur, a story excellently told by Gong (1984). Another round of the empire-to-modern state process occurred in Europe before and after the First World War, when the Austro-Hungarian and Ottoman Empires dissolved, and the Russian Empire retreated eastward. A band of new modern states stretching from Finland to Turkey came into being. The Middle Eastern parts of the Ottoman Empire came under British and French rule, in the process getting divided up into the entities that were later to become today's states. A few states in the Middle East—Egypt (1922), Iraq (1932)—and some of the settler colonies—Australia (1901), South Africa (1910), Canada (1931), New Zealand

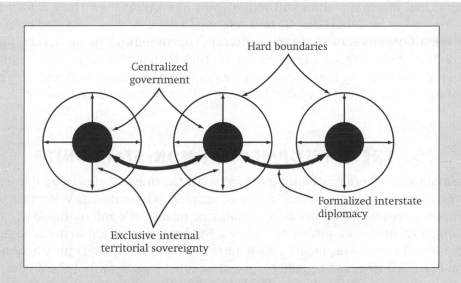

*Note:* The Treaties of Westphalia signed in 1648 are often taken to symbolize a new kind of international system made up of units that recognized the legitimacy of each other's boundaries and internal sovereignty.

*Figure 12.3  The basic form of the Westphalian international system of states*

(1941)—also achieved independence. But the main event began after the Second World War. Between 1947, when Britain withdrew from South Asia, and the 1960s, most of the European, American, and Japanese colonies in Asia and Africa either took or were given independence, becoming part of the ever widening community of modern states. The last big round in this process took place in 1992, when the Soviet Union imploded, releasing fifteen new modern states into the system.

With that event, and barring a few small and scattered colonial remnants (most resisting decolonization), the modern state had become virtually universal as the political form within which human life was organized. In 1914 there were 44 states, in 1930, 64, in 1945, despite the huge turbulence of the war, still 64, in 1960, 107, in 1978, 148, and by the start of the new millennium, more than 190. As noted in section 3 of this chapter, many of these states were not well made, and only a few of them were close to the leading edge in terms of shifting sovereignty from the rulers to the people. Some, most notably China, Indonesia, Pakistan, and

Russia, had internal politics still reminiscent of empires even though formally constructed as modern states. No unit referred to itself as an empire, and even the few remaining city-states (Singapore, Kuwait, Luxembourg) took on the trappings of modern states. Within a space of five centuries, ancient and classical empires, nomadic empires, city-states, and even the empires of the early modern states had all disappeared, leaving a political landscape of unprecedented uniformity.

## 5. THE DEVELOPMENT OF NON-STATE UNITS

The main story about units during this period is the one told above about the rise of the modern state to replace a mix of empires, city-states, city leagues, and nomadic tribes and empires as the dominant unit of the international system. Accompanying this is a subordinate story about how the modern state encouraged and allowed types of secondary unit to form and operate under its jurisdiction. In good part, this story can be read as a more detailed look at part of the process by which sovereignty shifted from rulers to people as the modern state developed out of the absolutist one. As more civic and legal space opened up within and between states, the governments of the leading modern states found it to their advantage to create, or make room for, other types of organization to operate with a degree of independence defined by the state, and to undertake tasks that the state either could not do, or did not want to do. This is essentially the story of corporations, understood as autonomous, self-reproducing, collective entities licensed by the state (or sometimes by the Church) to create a synthesis of private interest and the fulfilment of various social purposes (Davis 1971). The history of corporations as a distinctive form or organization can be traced back into medieval times, having roots in ecclesiastical bodies such as monasteries and religious orders, and secular ones such as chartered towns, guilds, and universities. There are also links with the very large family-based medieval merchant-banking companies, such as the Peruzzi Company of Florence that was established in the thirteenth century (Hunt 1994).

For the purpose of understanding the modern international system, two types are prominent. First, and also earliest, are the chartered companies that laid the foundations for the modern firm, and its offshoot the transnational corporation, with their primarily economic functions. Second, and focused almost wholly in the twentieth century, are international non-governmental organizations (INGOs). These are neither economic nor (for the most part) governmental, but a wide spectrum of political and social organizations whose interests range from sports to human rights. Neither of these types defines a new class of dominant unit, for they both remain subordinate to the state.

It may be asked whether intergovernmental organizations (IGOs) should be counted amongst these secondary units. Some authors unquestioningly treat IGOs as actors (Russett and Starr 1996: 64 ff.). We think not. While their appearance late in the nineteenth century is an important landmark in the way in which the international system develops during this period, most IGOs do not have sufficient autonomous actor quality to count as units. Units have to be seen as independently acting subsystems within a larger system. IGOs are standing bodies set up by groups of states to serve particular collective interests. An IGO like the UN can only be characterized as an independent actor in the weakest sense. It is barely more than the sum of its parts, and exists much more to serve its members than to become an independent actor. It is important primarily as an institutionalized forum and network which facilitates communication between states. The UN Secretary General has a little bit of autonomy to speak on behalf of the world, but not much. The question about the actor quality of such IGOs comes into clearer perspective if they are seen as a kind of permanent conference. Conferences do not generally have actor quality. Some IGOs such as the IMF and the WTO may be moving towards more robust forms of actor quality, but even they are still essentially slaves to their state members. Amongst the IGOs, only the EU has clearly crossed the divide and begun to acquire status (albeit still ambiguous) as a unit with actor quality in its own right in the international system. For these reasons it is more appropriate to treat IGOs as part of the social technology of interaction capacity, and so we will take up their story in Chapter 13.

## FIRMS

The roots of the modern firm can be found in the processes and practices of ancient and classical times, such as groups of merchants funding sea voyages, or forming trade diasporas, or organizing bills of exchange. The commercial revolution of the fourteenth century in Europe saw the spread of more sophisticated economic partnerships, with better bookkeeping, formalized shares, and the beginnings of durable institutional forms. Family firms created trading and banking networks, branch offices, and suchlike. Italian banking houses, such as the Medici, Bardi, Acciauoli and Peruzzi, had branch offices in London, Paris, and Bruges, and were part of a network of perhaps 150 Italian banks operating multinationally (Dunning 1993: 97–8).

From the sixteenth century onwards, the newly ascendant modern state increasingly imposed itself not only on the highly distributed autonomies of medieval Europe (religious orders, guilds, cities, feudal lords, and suchlike), but also on an expanding domain of overseas territories and peoples. Initially, the new Leviathan lacked the capacity to undertake the expansion of trade, and the colonization of remote territories, that it desired as a means of increasing the national wealth and welfare. It was this lack of state capacity that, from the sixteenth to the eighteenth centuries, gave rise to the chartered companies which became one of the main instruments of European overseas expansion. These companies were an amalgam of economic and military-political rights. Their purposes ranged from opening up new trade to developing new production and colonization, and to carry out these missions they were often given the right to exercise military and political power within their designated zones of operation. But as state capacity in Europe grew, the new Leviathan steadily seized back the military and political powers that it had delegated to the chartered companies, thereby laying the foundation for the emergence of the more strictly economic modern firm (Davis 1971: ii, chs. 3–8; Thomson 1994: 59–67).

The Spanish and Portuguese were the first European states to venture out into the wider world, and they did so initially in the mercantilist, statist form of classical empires. The Iberians did not initially favour private firms. Their 'Casas'— the Spanish Casa de Contratación (1510); the Portuguese Casa da Mina and da Guinea, and Casa das Indias (c.1500)—were more in the form of state bureaucracies. They did not have independent shareholders, and their capital and their ships were provided by the state. As state institutions, they were interested in territorial acquisition, most notably in the Americas, where the ability of local peoples to oppose such expansionism was much weaker than it was in Asia. The Spanish and Portuguese thus set about appointing viceroys, and carving out territorial empires, much earlier than the northern European states. Unlike the Iberians the later-starting French used the form of chartered companies—such as Compagnie des Indes Orientales (1664), liquidated 1769 as bankrupt—but like them very much at the instigation of the state, and substantially under its control (Coornaert 1967: 229).

The northern Europeans, most notably the Dutch and English, relied on the *chartered company* (Curtin 1984: 152–7; Davis 1971: ii, chs. 3–6), which was a more or less private group recognized by government charter as being entitled to pursue specified activities that were thereby closed to other citizens of that state. Precursors of the chartered company can be found in a Genoese company formed in 1373 to capture Cyprus in order to establish a commercial monopoly over the Egyptian trade. More examples can be found during the sixteenth century as the European expansion got under way—the Company of Merchant Adventurers (1553), 200 London merchants with a monopoly to explore for north-eastern and north-western passages to Asia, which later (1555) becomes the Muscovy Company for trade with Russia; the Baltic Company (1579); and the Levant Company (1581). But the heyday of the chartered companies was in the seventeenth century, when earlier forms of regulated company based on shares in particular ventures were superseded by more sophisticated joint stock companies. Dozens of these were formed, not only in England and the Netherlands, but also in France, Prussia, Sweden, and Denmark. Among these were: the Dutch East India Company (1602), the British East India Company (1602), the Portuguese East India Company (1623), and Compagnia Geral do Comercia do Brasil (1649), and the Hudson's Bay Company (1670). Lloyd's of London was also founded at this time (1688), initially as a coffee shop where shipping insurance was bought and sold. Some of these companies were formidable quasi-state entities. The Dutch East India Company, for example, had an initial capital of 64 tonnes of gold, and commanded 100 ships, most of them armed (Braudel 1985: 220–35).

The chartered company did not take a single form, but came as a varied set of institutions. Chartered companies reflected a mixture of the transition from feudalism to capitalism, the mercantilist state interest in extracting wealth from abroad (more than controlling territory), and the inability of the still-forming modern states to handle overseas expansion in their own right. As Coornaert (1967: 225–6) notes: 'The overseas expansion of Europe ran on parallel lines to the development of modern states. . . . for all the countries of Europe, overseas expansion accompanied a movement for strengthening and reorganizing their internal administration and government.' From the beginning, the English and Dutch used semi-public organizations which left more of the initiative to private citizens. The chartered companies originated in the feudal practice of sovereigns granting fiefs to vassals in exchange for acceptance of obligations to the suzerain. The charters basically assigned monopoly trading rights to a group of merchants over a specified territory, or else rights to colonize a specific territory, for a fixed period. They often included quasi-state rights such as the power to make treaties with local rulers, collect taxes, mint currency, and create armed forces to defend themselves against both locals and European rivals. 'In the colonies both political organization, in so far as it existed, and above all economic development were in the hands of the chartered companies' (Coornaert 1967: 236). This practice of delegating core state functions to private actors operating outside the state was not out of line with other practices of the time, such as the use of mercenaries, or the licensing of 'privateers' to attack shipping in return for a share of the booty. The modern state's monopoly of legitimate violence within its territory was achieved much earlier than its monopoly of the legitimate exercise of violence by its citizens outside its territory (Howard 1976: chs. 2–3; Thomson 1994: 22–6).

During the seventeenth and eighteenth centuries, the chartered companies themselves evolved into substantial organizations. They started as congeries of commercial partnerships with a shared interest in excluding interlopers and securing the safety of their ships and fixed assets in parts of the world where no efficient or friendly state was to be found. Groups of merchants pooled their resources to finance voyages and hopefully divide the profits if the voyage was successful: a type of temporary partnership arrangement common in the ancient and classical world. These short-term partnerships gave way to the more novel, permanent, and sophisticated form of a joint stock company, where the company itself owned capital, and 'a permanent capital ultimately became the unifying basis for corporate action' (Coornaert 1967: 253). Once the capital became fixed in the company, rather than being held by the owners, the idea of tradable shares took root enabling companies to find new capital either by issuing new shares or raising loans. Such companies developed elected directorates ('boards' or 'courts') to enforce their rules, deal with disputes amongst their members, and negotiate with outsiders. They also developed procedures for annual accounting.

The Iberian/French and Anglo/Dutch models eventually evolved towards a single norm. The Iberian Casas steadily surrendered activity to economically more efficient private companies. The chartered companies of northern Europe were eventually unable to keep up with the demands of colonial expansion, territorial rule, and provision of security. They were increasingly hard put to defend their monopoly against free riders who benefited both from the falling costs of shipping and from the evasion of any contribution to the provision of security. There was also rising ideological unease about the dangers of moral impropriety, and corruption raised by individuals engaged in both political administration and commerce. Between 1788 and 1806 private trading rights were withdrawn from the civil and military officials of the East India Company. As a consequence of these pressures, the chartered companies were steadily brought back under government control by the increasingly capable and coherent modern state, which itself took over the provision of security abroad. 'When expansion gave place to conquest . . . the old chartered companies gave way to the empires of the future' (Coornaert 1967: 239). Most famously, the British East India Company, which had substantially taken over India, was subordinated to the crown by legislation in 1773 and 1784, and then abolished in 1858 after the Indian Mutiny.

Given the scale of their activities, it is not unreasonable to see the chartered companies in some senses as the ancestors of today's transnational corporations (TNCs). But the line of succession is not direct. Very few of the chartered companies (the Hudson's Bay Company being a rare exception) survived the takeback of powers by the state. The more exclusively economic limited companies that arose during the nineteenth century were nearly all new enterprises, institutionally distinct from their forebears, though owing something to the institutional developments pioneered by the chartered companies. Stavrianos (1990: 95–111) argues that what made Europe distinct from China in the race for world domination was not just the rise of states, but also the rise of limited companies. Some of the key ideas underpinning the development of this new type of actor were:

- *partnership*: in which several people own the firm jointly and are personally fully responsible for it (unlimited liability);
- *corporation*: in which the firm has a separate legal identity from its owners, becoming what Davis (1971: ii. 215) calls 'an immortal person' for the purpose of exercising legal rights and ownership of property;
- *limited liability*: in which the owners have only limited responsibility for the company's debts;
- *public listing*: in which the company's shares are available on the stock exchange

(as opposed to a private company, in which the shares are not available for public subscription).

The publicly listed limited company, in corporate form—in other words the modern firm—begins to appear in numbers after 1830, and expands rapidly from 1850 onward. In Britain, a key turning point was the Companies Act of 1862, which marked a general shift to limited liability, both reducing the cost of forming a company, and removing the necessity to get an Act of Parliament in order to form one. The rise of the modern firm is closely associated with the industrial revolution, the new firms providing both the vast amounts of capital, and the organizational form, necessary to develop both industrial production and the huge new infrastructure projects of railways and telecommunications. Its development thus occurred largely within the leading industrial states, and especially the more liberal ones such as Britain and the United States (Davis 1905: ii. 252–60). Although ostensibly private, many of these firms retained a variety of links to the state, not least through subsidies such as the British government gave to shipping companies for the carriage of mail. Right from the beginning of the modern firm, the state has treated this new entity as an element of its own power, and so taken an interest in its welfare. The modern firm increasingly became a player both within the far-flung empires of the modern states, and more significantly as a true transnational corporation, crossing the boundaries between sovereign states. The essential quality of a TNC is that its activities (extraction of resources, manufacturing, provision of services) can take place in more than one country, and that there is an organizational hierarchy crossing national borders. The forerunners of the modern TNC were visible in the early nineteenth century, with cross-border financing of economic enterprise. The modern TNC emerged from 1870 onwards as foreign direct investment (FDI) sought to reduce transport costs, find more efficient places for production, and get around the tariffs and import controls imposed by many newly industrializing states. The United Fruit Company dates from 1889, around which time Cadbury was investing in cocoa plantations in the Gold Coast and Trinidad. Many banks started to go transnational during the later nineteenth century. All of this took place in the context of the high water of Western imperialism, posing the technical problem of whether activities in colonies count as 'across national borders'. But, *de facto*, much FDI did go from one independent state to another, as in British investment in the USA, and the problem of colonial investment of course disappeared with decolonization. The post-1945 period saw an extraordinary growth in the number of multinational corporations from a handful to 37,000 by the early 1990s (Hirst and Thompson 1996: 53; UNCTAD 1993: 20–1). At first these were mostly American, but the Europeans and Japanese created their own TNCs during the 1970s and 1980s, and some of the NICs joined in during the 1980s and 1990s (Gilpin 1987: ch. 6).

## INTERNATIONAL NON-GOVERNMENTAL ORGANIZATIONS (INGOS)

The story of INGOs is mostly one of developments within the civil societies of the leading states eventually breaking out into the expanding civic and legal space that democratic states opened up between themselves during the late twentieth century. In recent years they have been increasingly associated with the idea of 'pluralising global governance' (Gordenker and Weiss 1996) and have variously been identified as 'international pressure groups' (Willetts 1982) and 'new social movements'. The INGO label has been institutionalized by the diplomatic community, in general, and IGOs, in particular (Willetts 1996: 2). A very tight link has now been established between INGOs and IGOs and in determining whether an INGO can be formally associated with an IGO, four essential criteria have emerged—the INGO must be non-profit-making, non-violent, eschew political action designed to damage the governments of the IGO's member states, and support the goals of the IGO (Willetts 1996: 3–5). Although the origins of INGOs can be traced back to the committees, societies, and associations that began to develop from the eighteenth century onwards in Europe and the United States, it was the growth of the middle classes and improvements in international communications in the nineteenth century that provided the crucial fillip to the formation of the first INGOs (Seary 1996).

As leading states created more open civil societies within themselves during the nineteenth and twentieth centuries, they generated large numbers of non-governmental organizations concerned with everything from religion, politics, class, and the professions, through sport, hobbies, and entertainment, to animal welfare, peace, and the environment. Some of these organizations linked up with similar ones in other countries, and others expanded their membership and organization abroad. In doing so they added huge numbers and variety to the category of non-economic corporations previously occupied largely by religious and essentially cosmopolitan institutions dating from the classical era, most notably the Roman Catholic Church. The growth of nationalism, therefore, was also accompanied by a growth in internationalism. By the UN's count (Yearbook of International Organizations 1994–5: 1739), INGOs increased from 176 in 1909 to 973 in 1956 and 4,928 by 1994 (though a looser definition gives a number of 26,157 for 1994). The idea of INGOs as a global extension of civil society sounds all very nice. But it is important to recognize that civil society has its dark side in organized crime (mafias, Hell's Angels), some kinds of sexual perversion (paedophile networks), terrorism (Aum Shinrykyo), extreme cults (fascists, racists), and suchlike. These phenomena also get extended into the international system via illicit INGOs that are usually, although not invariably, denied association with IGOs, and more recently via the internet. Some political INGOs, such as the South West African Peoples Organization and the Palestine Liberation Organization, manage to cross the divide from illicit to legal, both of these having eventually been given observer status in the UN's General Assembly.

Unlike with IGOs, and more in line with firms, there is not usually much question about the actor quality of INGOs, although the degree of centralization varies considerably from one INGO to another. Some are highly centralized. Amnesty International, for example, consists of an international tier that co-ordinates the activities of the 53 sections that operate on the national tier. Other INGOs are much more decentralized, with the International Planned Parenthood Federation, for example, simply consisting of 109 family planning associations. In principle, and mostly in practice, they represent private interests, and operate with a substantial degree of autonomy. The very first INGO was the World Alliance of YMCAs which was established in the middle of the nineteenth century (Seary 1996: 15). Ever since then, there have been organizations that have aimed to tie together groups of people with shared interests across national boundaries, whether they be academics (the International Studies Association, the International Peace Research Association), game players (chess, tennis), or simply fans of Star Trek or Elvis Presley. But many of these organizations are ephemeral and are certainly not associated with the United Nations.

INGOs endeavour to become associated with IGOs because they wish to act as pressure groups and play a part in world politics. At the Rio Environmental Conference held in 1992, there were representatives from 178 countries and 650 INGOs. And the INGOs were not simply there as observers. The knowledge-based INGOs, such as the International Union for the Conservation of Nature and Natural Resources (IUCN) and the International Council of Scientific Unions (ICSU), helped to shape some of the agenda items and, equally important, had an input into some of the conventions that were established at the conference (Morphet 1996; Buzan et al. 1998: ch. 4). In the same way, Amnesty International, soon after it was established in 1961, was given consultative status at the United Nations which enables it to attend relevant UN meetings, to submit documents, and to make statements. Amnesty devotes a considerable amount of its time, expertise, and resources to performing these tasks in order to promote observance of the Universal Declaration of Human Rights. It also endeavours to put pressure on a wide range of regional IGOs, from the Council of Europe to the League of Arab States (Cook 1996).

In a number of instances, the link between IGOs and INGOs is institutionalized and the hybrid organization consists of both governments and INGOs. The International Red Cross, for example, has government and non-government representatives. The organization is governed by a conference that meets every four years, with each state and each national society having a representative and an equal vote. There is, however, a functional division of labour, with governments funding the International Committee of the Red Cross which protects prisoners of war and acts as an intermediary in conflicts, and national societies funding the Red Cross

International Federation which assists refugees and provides disaster relief. The International Labour Organization is another important hybrid organization, because although its members are states, the representatives of the states come from the government, trade unions, and employer associations and they are free to cast their votes as they like.

INGOs are certainly not a contender, as is sometimes argued of TNCs, to take over the role of dominant unit in the international system. But they do now play an increasingly important role in world politics. Both TNCs and governments have backed down, on occasions, when confronted by concerted pressure from INGOs. But as many INGOs discovered to their chagrin in the aftermath of the Rio Environmental Conference, governments do not always deliver what they have promised in internationally agreed conventions. Nevertheless, the actor status of INGOs is not in doubt. And the growing transnational links being established by the myriad of INGOs that have formed during the twentieth century not only affect world politics, but also represent a development that becomes significant when we think about world society in Chapter 15.

# 6. CONCLUSIONS

The rise of the modern state as the dominant unit of the global international system shaped the character of international relations in a number of ways. Most obviously, it imposed its own strict standards of territoriality and sovereignty on the whole system. The world became much more territorially demarcated, and the right to govern was located much more exclusively within these territorial packages. The strong claim to sovereignty meant that this international system was prone to war, and firmly committed to balance of power and anti-hegemonic principles. But it also provided fertile ground for the development of international society, particularly diplomacy and international law. The linkage between anarchy and frequent war is not unique: the Greek city-state system was famously war-prone, and it is no accident that the main anarchic period in Chinese history (403–221 BC) is known as 'the warring states period'. During its absolutist phase, the war motives of the modern state had much in common with those prevailing during the ancient and classical era: territorial and imperial aggrandizement, booty, royal claims to inheritance rights, and the sport of kings. Nationalism added new reasons (*Lebensraum*, irredentism, social Darwinism) as did mass politics (human rights, open markets, the various ideological crusades of liberals, fascists, and communists).

There is now a question as to whether the spread of democracy amongst the leading states is not causing a sharp move away from war. This question ties into the development of international society, which amongst the leading states has generated a wide range of norms, rules, and institutions for the conduct of interstate and transnational relations, and which increasingly makes room for non-state organizations to acquire a degree of autonomy as international actors. There is nothing new about dominant actors projecting their own characteristics into the international system. As argued in Part III, it seems quite possible that the legitimacy of the imperial idea helps to explain why neorealist predictions are so frequently not met in ancient and classical international systems. But it would be a very significant departure indeed if democratic states were able to do so sufficiently to eliminate, or even seriously degrade, war as the primary process defining international systems, shaping their units, and determining their structure.

# Chapter 13

# INTERACTION CAPACITY IN THE MODERN INTERNATIONAL SYSTEM

## 1. INTRODUCTION

Alongside the change in dominant units, physical improvements in interaction capacity play a big role in differentiating the modern era from the ancient and classical one. They are essential to the expansion of the international system up to global scale, and therefore to the shift from a world of multiple international systems to a single, global international system. They do not, however, play any great role in the formation and early stages of the rise of the modern state itself. Not until the nineteenth century do new technologies for transportation and communication, different from those used by the ancient and classical world, become available. There is almost certainly a significant link between that development and the evolution of the modern state beyond absolutism described in the previous chapter. At the same time, and in some ways also related, there is a development of social technologies that begin to transform the way in which the international system operates, if not quite yet the way in which it is defined.

## 2. PHYSICAL TECHNOLOGIES

The story of the transformation in physical technologies comes in two quite distinct stages. The first stage is the culmination of a process, under way from possibly even before the beginning of the ancient and classical era, of developing seagoing sailing ships and improving navigation techniques. Certainly some of the most remarkable developments in maritime exploration were precipitated within pre-international systems, with Polynesian sailors, for example, gathering increasing expertise over two millennia, so that they were eventually able to occupy even the most distant islands in the Pacific a full millennium before the arrival of the Europeans (Irwin 1992). Equally enterprising, the Waqwaqs from Indonesia also succeeded in crossing the Indian Ocean around AD 400 to colonize previously uninhabited Madagascar (R. Hall 1996: 23–6). But more regular and durable contacts were established by the Persian, Indian, Arab, and Chinese navigators who opened up the Indian Ocean to traders who exchanged goods between

China, Indonesia, India, Arabia, and East Africa for over a thousand years before the Europeans came upon the scene (R. Hall 1996; Hourani 1995).

Although remarkable, these voyages were not truly transoceanic; the Indian Ocean often being viewed as the Asian counterpart to the Mediterraean Sea (Steensgaard 1987). These trading routes undoubtedly supplemented and reinforced links that had already been established overland, and helped to promote Eurasia as a single international economic system. But by the fifteenth century, skills in shipbuilding and navigational knowledge had reached a point both in China and in Europe where regular transoceanic voyages were within reach. At that point, the oceans ceased to be geographical barriers, and like the smaller seas before them opened up into highways. The voyages of Cheng-ho, in 1405–33, from China to Arabia provided early intimations of this development. But although his huge vessels had the potential to withstand the rigours of transoceanic voyages, in fact, he travelled along familiar, mostly coastal, sealanes that had been regularly used for many hundreds of years. Political developments, however, snuffed out the Chinese venture, leaving the field clear for the Europeans. Even so, it was another century before they accomplished true transoceanic voyages. Improvements in shipbuilding technology meant that the Europeans could have crossed the Pacific in 1421 rather than in 1521 when Magellan traversed the globe. But what was not understood at that time was where and when the winds blew over the major oceans, with the exception of the Indian Ocean. That knowledge was acquired during the course of the fifteenth century (Crosby 1986: ch. 5) and, once in place, transoceanic communication provided the first essential step towards the formation of the global economic system, and later of the full global international system.

By the early to middle decades of the nineteenth century a wholly new series of unprecedented transformations in interaction capacity was under way. These were part of the wider transformation of the industrial revolution, beginning in the eighteenth century, which Landes (1969: 41), oversimplifying somewhat, describes as the use of machines plus heat engines plus minerals, as opposed to the technologies of the ancient and classical era which relied on human skill, plus animal power, plus vegetable and animal materials. This technological revolution was not necessary to the making either of the modern state or of a global international system, both of which preceded it by more than two centuries. But once under way, its consequences for interaction capacity allowed both of these political developments to spread and deepen with a singular speed and intensity. The marriage of steam and steel enabled the maritime revolution to continue with ever larger and faster ships. This same marriage in the form of railways also swept away the age-old constraint on overland transport. Horses, wagons, and canals quickly gave way to the new iron roads, overturning forever the adverse cost ratios for transportation of 1 by sea, 4.9 by river, and 28 by land (Meijer and van Nijf 1992: 133) that had played such a big part in defining the international relations of the ancient and classical era. The spread of railways was augmented late in the nineteenth century by the marriage of internal combustion engines to wagons, starting another revolution in which motor vehicles transformed the importance of roads to overland transport. In the early twentieth century, that revolution took to the air, opening a whole new dimension of transportation. At the same time, yet another technical breakthrough enabled the separation of communication from transportation. First the telegraph, and a bit later radio, meant that communication no longer had to be considered as a form of light freight. Freed from material form, it took on light speed, enabling virtually instantaneous communication across the planet.

*The revolution in speed*

The impact of the nineteenth-century revolution become apparent not in the range of transportation and communication, which the sailing ship had already made global, but in its speed. Five hundred years ago transportation remained painfully slow as well as limited in scope. From Venice to Lyons took 12 days, to London 27 days, to Lisbon 46 days, to Constantinople 37 days, to Damascus 80 days (Barraclough 1978: 144). During the seventeenth century the *Mayflower* took 66 days to cross the Atlantic (Woodruff 1966: 237) and during the eighteenth century it took three years for a caravan to make the round trip from Moscow to Peking (Braudel 1985: 454). In 1776 it took 29 days for news of the Declaration of Independence to travel 800 km (500 miles) from Philadelphia to Charleston, and 44 days for it to reach Europe (Braudel 1985: 390; Woodruff 1966: 237). By 1812, before the impact of steam technology, range had improved a lot, but speed only a bit. The average journey time from Berlin to countries such as England, France, or Austria was 5–10 days; to Italy or Hungary, 10–15 days; to Moscow, Spain, the Balkans, Turkey, or North Africa, 15 to 30 days; to the east coast of North America, or the coast of West Africa, 30–60 days; to the Mississippi valley, Mexico, Peru, Argentina, or Cape Town, 60 to 90 days; to Chile, California, Johannesburg, Somalia, or Bombay, 90 to 120 days; to Bolivia, Central Africa, Bengal, Japan, or the coastal cities of Australia, 120 to 150 days. Nearly the whole planet was accessible to the European traveller, but it might take five months just for a one-way journey. A century later, the second revolution in interaction capacity had radically transformed these timetables. By 1912, a traveller from Berlin could reach most parts of Europe in 1 or 2 days, and within 5 days could be as far afield as Egypt or the Caucasus. The journey time to the Mississippi valley, Central Asia, or Siberia was 5 to 10 days; to California, Cape Town, India, or Japan, 10 to 20 days; to Uganda, Bolivia, Alaska, or Vietnam, 20 to 30 days. Only the remotest parts of Africa, South America, Tibet, and Australia required more than 40 days (Woytinsky 1927). In just a single century, and even before air transport had, so to speak, got off the ground, the technological revolution in transportation had shrunk most journey times to one-fifth of their former duration.

Put in other terms, this shrinkage of the world can be told as a story of the average speed of prevailing forms of technology for mass transportation. Up until the middle of the nineteenth century, neither ships nor horse-drawn coaches could average much over 16 km (10 miles) an hour. Once steam technology matured by the late nineteenth century, railways could average over 97 km (60 miles) an hour, and steamships over 48 km (30 miles). By the 1930s, propeller-driven aircraft managed average speeds of over 480 km (300 miles) an hour, and with the coming of jet passenger aircraft in the late 1950s, this was doubled to more than 970 km (600 miles) an hour. The supersonic Concorde can carry passengers at over 1,900 km (1200 miles) an hour, but has not become a form of mass transportation. Thus in under two centuries, the average speed of the prevailing technology for mass transportation increased more than 60 times from around 16 km (10 miles) per hour to over 970 km (600 miles) per hour. As a consequence, a journey halfway around the world that would have taken a year or more in the sixteenth century took five months in 1812, one month in 1912, and less than a day in our own time. The impact of this revolution on everything from war and trade, through diplomacy and tourism, to identity and migration has been enormous.

## THE FIRST REVOLUTION AT SEA

The first revolution at sea culminated with the development of sailing ship technology, a story we have already largely told in Part III. There is no single key to this story. Rather, it involves the coming together of many incremental developments in both ship design and construction, and knowledge of navigation techniques. Important elements in ship design and construction included the stern-post rudder (thirteenth century, giving better steering qualities), improved rigging and sails (fifteenth century, giving more manoeuvrability, and ability to sail against the wind), and robust hull construction (fifteenth century, able to withstand stormy weather). Important elements in navigation technique include maps, knowledge of trade wind patterns, and better instruments for determining one's position on the open ocean (the compass, which arrived from China during the thirteenth century, for determining direction; the quadrant and sextant, for estimating latitude; and in the eighteenth century, the chronometer, for determining longitude).

There is some evidence for development of robust, high-seas sailing junks in China by thirteenth century AD (McNeill 1982: 42–3). The voyages of Cheng-ho (1405–33), involving seven expeditions with as many as 60 ships and 25,000 men as a military, economic, and political reconnaissance by China into the Indian Ocean (Bentley 1993: 168–70; Curtin 1984: 124–7; Jones 1987: 203–5), suggest that the time was ripe elsewhere, as well as in Europe, for breakthroughs in ocean-going ships. The north European sailing ship underwent steady development during the fourteenth and fifteenth centuries. By 1300 it was able to penetrate the Mediterranean, and with the arrival of cannon was quickly able to outgun both Mediterranean galleys and Asian warships. During the fifteenth century King Henry ('the Navigator') of Portugal played an important role in improving ship design and construction, gathering knowledge about maps, and pushing exploration southward down the coast of Africa. In the fourteenth and fifteenth centuries, sailors worked out the wind patterns that enabled them to sail to the Canary, Madeira, and Azores Islands, thus making the first step towards crossing the Atlantic (Crosby 1986: ch. 4). Towards the end of the fifteenth century the European voyages of exploration began to open up systematic contact with the wider world, the key breakthroughs in this respect being Columbus's crossing of the Atlantic (1492), and Da Gama's voyage around Africa to India (1498). These voyages demonstrated that the world was round (conclusively proved by Magellan's circumnavigation 1519–22), and that European ships were sturdy enough to reach any part of it. By making it possible to carry goods and soldiers all around the planet, these ships opened a 200-year period of transition from land- to ocean-centred international relations.

## THE SECOND REVOLUTION AT SEA

The second revolution at sea greatly intensified the effects of the first by increasing both the speed and the carrying capacity of ships. Basically, the move is from wood-built, sail-powered vessels, which had more or less reached their technological limits, to iron, and then steel-built ships powered by engines, first steam piston engines, and later diesels and steam turbines. Iron and steel construction meant that ships could get much larger: wooden vessels could not exceed five or six thousand tonnes. Engines both freed ships from dependence on wind (though at the cost of dependence on a supply of coal or oil), and allowed average speeds to triple.

This maritime revolution of steam and steel rested on the wider base of rapid improvements in metallurgy, precision engineering, and mechanical design that were part of the industrial revolution. With improved knowledge and technique, the cost of metal fell sharply, and the quality rose. Iron was at first too brittle (and too expensive) to be used safely in ship construction, but by the 1830s, the quality of metal had improved so that iron-hulled vessels such as Brunel's *Great Britain* were becoming common. Steam engines made their first appearance as early as 1698, but were far too big and inefficient to be used for anything but pumping mines. Watt's design improvements dating from 1769 yielded a 400 per cent improvement in efficiency, which in turn unleashed a huge expansion in the use of steam power. Fuel efficiency increased by a factor of 12 between 1776 and 1850, and the resulting drop in cost multiplied the use of steam power by a factor of 100 in Britain between 1800 and 1850 (Landes 1969: 100–4), and made steam-powered freighters economic by the 1860s (Woodruff 1966: 238). Boiler pressure, a measure of engine efficiency, increased from c.0.35 kg per square cm (5 pounds per square inch (psi)) in the 1830s to 2 kg per square cm (30 psi) by the 1870s, then to 14 kg per square cm (200 psi) towards the end of the century, rising to 45 kg per square cm (650 psi) by the 1970s. During the nineteenth century, as steam engines got smaller, more powerful, and more fuel-efficient, they began to be installed in ships, initially driving paddle wheels, and later the more efficient screw propeller. At first, steam power was a supplement to sail (only 9.8 per cent of tonnage was steam by 1860), but by 1913 steam tonnage accounted for 97.7 per cent of shipping (Woodruff 1966: 256). As a result of these improvements, ocean freight rates dropped 80 per cent during the nineteenth century (Curtin 1984: 251–2), with a corresponding expansion of the volume of trade. These new ships were able to take advantage of two new canals, Suez (1869) and Panama (1914). By eliminating lengthy journeys around Africa and South America, these canals cut the length of many major shipping routes by between 25 and 60 per cent.

In the years before the First World War, some 2 million passengers per year crossed the North Atlantic by sea. A journey that took between five and seven weeks under sail, and two weeks in the early steamers, could by then be done on a scheduled liner in three to four days. The biggest of these liners, such as the *Titanic*, weighed nearly 50,000 tonnes, ten times the size of the largest wooden ships. By the 1980s bulk carriers (mostly oil tankers) as big as 500,000 tonnes were being built, and their huge capacities reduced shipping costs to a tiny fraction of the value of the goods being carried. Many trade goods had also become lighter, smaller, and more sophisticated (CDs, computers), making transportation costs a lower proportion of their total value. The container revolution that got rolling during the 1960s also massively reduced the costs of shipping freight (*Economist* 15 Nov. 1994: 89–90).

## THE REVOLUTION ON LAND

Because there were no land transportation technologies maturing to a point of breakthrough, the revolution on land was much slower arriving than the one by sea. There was no potential for transformational improvement in animal-powered vehicles, though Europe certainly had room to catch up with developments in road- and canal-building already familiar to some classical civilizations. Roads in Europe, for example, did not surpass Roman standards until the eighteenth century (van Creveld 1991: 114), and French and British engineers then subsequently developed cheap methods for constructing reliable all-weather roads suitable for wheeled vehicles (McNeill 1982: 163–4).The second half of that century saw much canal-building in Europe for both commercial and strategic transportation purposes, and by the mid-nineteenth century the USA also had a well-developed canal network in the north-east. And one should not forget the impact of the transfer of old technologies to peoples newly brought within the ambit of the global international system. Horses (and guns) transformed the life-style of the Plains Indians, and the colonial history of North America reveals the speed with which these new technologies spread amongst the indigenous popula-tion once they were introduced (see Maps 13.1 and 13.2). These developments certainly made a difference, but they did not overcome the long-standing barrier of the high cost of transport over land.

The land barrier was only broken in the nineteenth century by the same mar-riage of steam and steel that made the second revolution on the sea. Like ships, only more so because of their smaller size, trains required relatively compact and efficient steam engines. Stephenson's *Rocket* in 1814 was the first demonstration of a practical locomotive. Widespread railway-building began in Britain during

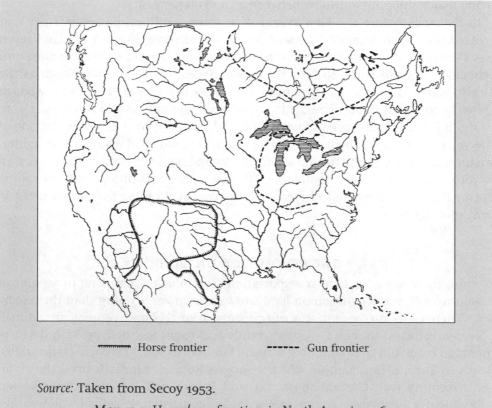

━━━━ Horse frontier       ------ Gun frontier

*Source:* Taken from Secoy 1953.

*Map 13.1  Horse/gun frontiers in North America: 1675*

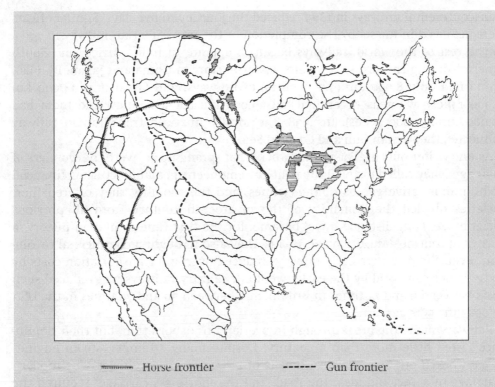

────────── Horse frontier    - - - - - - Gun frontier

*Note:* These two maps illustrate how horses entered the pre-international systems of North America from the south whereas guns entered from the north. Both were diffused very quickly through the systems and transformed the culture of the indigenous people.

*Source:* Taken from Secoy 1953.

*Map 13.2 Horse/gun frontiers in North America: 1790*

the 1820s and spread to France and Germany during the 1830s. By 1840 there were 7,700 km (4,800 miles) of railways worldwide, and coherent national networks were appearing in leading countries such as Britain, France, Germany, and the USA. By 1870 the world total had risen to over 209,000 km (130,000 miles), and by 1900 to nearly 800,000 km (half a million miles), over a third of which was in Europe. By the 1860s a dense network of railways covered the north-eastern USA from New England to the Mississippi river, and, less densely, also in the South, and the first link to the Pacific coast had been made. By the 1890s, there were half a dozen transcontinental railways. In 1850 it might take up to three weeks to cross the continental USA by a combination of train and stagecoach. The coming of the transcontinental railways in 1869 reduced the journey to five days. Similar effects were achieved in Russia by the completion of the trans-Siberian railway in 1903. In the rest of the world, railways began to operate in India, Africa, and South America during the 1850s, but were slower to start in China and Japan. By 1920, China had only 8,000 km (5,000 miles) of railways, and Japan only 14,000 km (8,500 miles), whereas Argentina had 36,000 km (22,500 miles) and India had 60,000 km (37,000 miles). In 1938, the locally financed trans-Iranian railway connected the Persian Gulf and Caspian Sea.

As one writer puts it: 'The rail networks that sprang up . . . were the wonders of their age. They called forth all the political, engineering, manufacturing, financial and administrative genius of their times, and the mobility they offered their societies divided the humanity of the nineteenth century from all previous societies. . . . Long-distance travel became, for the first time in human history, a matter of routine' (Mead 1995–6: 16–17). They also wrought a commercial revolution. Even the primitive early railways reduced overland transportation costs by 50 to 75 per cent, and by the early twentieth century railways had reduced such costs between 9 and 14 times in Britain, and between 30 and 70 times in the USA (Woodruff 1966: 225, 254).

Railways made the breakthrough in overland transportation, but their dominance lasted little more than a century. Despite many attempts, steam engines never worked out as a practical means of powering road vehicles. The modern marriage of a very old idea, the road, and the 'horseless carriage' required the development of the internal combustion engine. Such engines became available towards the end of the nineteenth century, triggering the age of the automobile and the road network that are familiar features of our own landscape. Automobiles did not become a form of mass transport until the 1930s, and even then only in the USA. They did not begin to challenge the railways as carriers of freight until the latter half of the twentieth century, by which time road networks had become a feature in nearly all countries, and a highly dense feature in the most advanced ones.

## THE REVOLUTION IN THE AIR

The revolution in the air also stemmed from the availability of reliable internal combustion engines, though unpowered balloons have a much longer history. The overall trajectory of this revolution is quite similar to that of the automobile, except that in the case of aircraft, the two world wars provided periods of intense technological and industrial development. The first manned and powered flight took place in 1903, not much more than a decade after the appearance of the first practical automobiles. Up to the First World War, both were mostly playthings of the rich, though lighter-than-air craft, in the form of the rigid-frame airships known as Zeppelins, were taken seriously because of their ability to go long distances without refuelling. Already by 1910, transatlantic flight using Zeppelins was under discussion in Germany (Hugill 1993: 257).

The First World War saw not only great improvements in the size, range, speed, and reliability of aircraft, but also the creation of a substantial manufacturing industry to produce them. The 1914–18 war established a link between military requirements for aircraft and civil possibilities for their use that was greatly to accelerate the employment of aircraft for mass transportation. The military requirement for fighter aircraft emphasized the development of speed, while that for bombers emphasized range, carrying capacity, and accurate navigation. The implications for the development of commercial airmail, freight, and passenger services were obvious, and at the end of the war there was an abundance of redundant military aircraft, trained pilots, and aircraft manufacturing capacity.

The first airmail services started immediately after the First World War, and during the 1920s, air passenger services developed that linked much of Europe and parts of North Africa. By the 1930s Britain, France, the Netherlands, and Germany had all developed imperial air services linking Europe to most of the Middle East, Africa, South and East Asia, and Australia, while the USA used flying boats to extend air services to South America, and by island-hopping across the Pacific, to New Zealand and the Philippines. Crossing the North Atlantic was a major technical hurdle, requiring not only long-range aircraft, but also ones that were capable of flying at night, and that were reliable in all weathers, for there was nowhere to land in an emergency. Zeppelins opened the Atlantic route in 1936–7, but aeroplanes were only just acquiring that capability when the Second World War intervened. Only American flying boats achieved an operational service on the eve of the war.

The Second World War also saw a major surge in flight technology, especially in the development of jet engines, and of the four-engined heavy bombers that pioneered the technology for long-haul mass air travel. During the war, airports were constructed in Newfoundland and in Ireland, which made it possible to fly the North Atlantic non-stop, and after the war, this capacity was used to open commercial air services. With the journey time cut from several days in even the fastest ship to just 15 hours by air, a great boom in transatlantic air passenger travel followed the Second World War. Air travel began to compete seriously with passenger ships, passing a million passengers a year in the mid-1950s, and surpassing the sea trade in numbers of people carried during the late 1950s. In the late 1950s, the arrival of jet airliners cut the time for the transatlantic crossing in half, to not much more than seven hours. This stimulated further growth in North Atlantic air travel, reaching 8 million passengers by 1970, and pushing 40 million by the early 1990s, by which time passenger traffic by sea had shrunk to negligible proportions (Davis 1964; Hugill 1993). Within the USA itself, distance also continued to shrink. In 1929, the fastest passenger journey across the USA could be done in 2 days by a combination of train (by night) and plane (by day) involving ten stops. By 1953 it could be done non-stop by air in just over 7 hours (Woytinsky and Woytinsky 1955: 529). On the basis of this fast maturing technology, the world total of airline passengers, domestic and international, rose from 9 million to 1,171 million between 1945 and 1993. Between 1983 and 1993 combined domestic and international flights in terms of tonne-kms performed rose from around 90 billion to around 230 billion (mail, freight, and passengers) (IATA 1993: 38).

The revolution in the air not only multiplied the speed of travel ten or twenty times, it also hugely increased the volume of passenger traffic, making possible the worldwide mass transportation system that came into being during the 1960s and 1970s. In the process, it substantially dissolved the long-standing and historically crucial distinction between transportation by land and by sea. By the 1970s, long -range 'jumbo' jets could fly almost anywhere non-stop, making it a matter of indifference whether what was passing underneath was land or water.

A more specialized aspect of the revolution in the air concerned the development of rockets. These had no impact at all on mass transportation, but they had two very specific and important impacts on the revolution in interaction capacity as a whole. The first was in their role as fast, long-range, impossible to stop, delivery systems for military payloads. This role developed rapidly during the Second World War, but came to full fruition during the Cold War with the marriage of rockets and nuclear warheads. By the late 1950s, intercontinental range rockets were available that could carry a large nuclear weapon between the USA and the Soviet Union in about 30 minutes, and deliver it within a radius of 5 km (3 miles). This very specific achievement of transportation technology changed the entire face of great power war and strategic thinking. From the 1960s onward, much the same capability was used to put satellites into orbit, and these quickly created both an intense, real-time surveillance of the planet, and a new, highly flexible, and earth-spanning communications network.

## THE COMMUNICATIONS REVOLUTION

Until some 300 years into this era, communication was simply a function of the various revolutions in transportation sketched above. It was also a function of printing presses and cheap paper, which made mass communication possible. Communication was in the form of letters and newspapers, and was thus a type of light freight. Being light, it could take advantage of the fastest ships and pony express services, but was still chained to the speed and range of land and sea transportation technology. Even so, it still had advantages over the movement of bulk goods. As Braudel notes (1985: 215), during the first half of the seventeenth century, 'news travelling overland always reached the Indian ocean more quickly than the Dutch or English ships sailing towards it. The Portuguese authorities were always forewarned via Venice and the Levant, of the Dutch expeditions on their way to attack them.' Not until the late eighteenth century did the real communication revolution occur, which involved the separation of information from paper for the purposes of transporting it. The breakthrough technology was the telegraph. Optical telegraphs capable of sending messages 400 km (250 miles) per day were available by the late eighteenth century, albeit mainly for military purposes. During the nineteenth century these were outpaced first by railways, and then from the 1830s by the electromagnetic telegraph (van Creveld 1991: 153–66).

The spread of the telegraph ran in parallel with that of railways and steamships. Indeed, telegraph lines were often built alongside the railways, and steamships laid the submarine cables that took the telegraph network across the seas and oceans. During the 1840s, telegraph networks spread through Europe and North America. In 1851 the first underwater cable was laid across the channel to connect Britain and France, and the first transatlantic cable opened in 1866. During the 1870s much of East Asia, including Australia, was linked by telegraph, though the trans-Pacific cable was not complete until 1902.

The impact of the telegraph on the speed of communications was dramatic, far outpacing even the impressive improvements in the speed of transportation. For example, communication times between Britain and India dropped from 5–8 months during the 1830s (sailing ship), to 35–40 days during the 1850s (rail and steamship), to same day during the 1870s (telegraph) (Curtin 1984: 251–2). That kind of speed was not achieved in the realm of transportation for another hundred years. By the late nineteenth century telephones were replacing the telegraph, still relying on wires, but replacing the cumbersome coding and decoding process with direct voice communication. At the same time radio (so-called 'wireless') technology was becoming available which made long-distance communication possible at the speed of light, and this also moved quickly from code to direct voice. The ability to broadcast using radio, and by the late 1930s also television, meant that communication became not only instantaneous, but also extremely flexible. Radio meant that communication networks could be extended to ships and aircraft and automobiles, and also that mass audiences could be contacted simultaneously with very low distribution costs.

These developments had major impacts on all kinds of human activities. They greatly accelerated the movement of information, and the range of people to whom it could be available. Governments could now know about political and military developments almost as they happened, and business people had much faster access to information about worldwide market movements and the factors that might affect prices. One consequence was to enable much more concentrated command structures to extend over long distances. With instant communication, ambassadors did not have to be given nearly so much independence of action, and firms could keep tighter control over distant subsidiaries or partners. The close parallel between the spread of high-speed communication technology and the rise of the TNC is not without significance. Another consequence was that news became part of public and political life, giving rise to the media as a fifth estate, and to a general sense that since information was available, there was a public right to be kept informed. The other side of this was of course propaganda (now sanitized as 'spin'), which sought to use the mass flow of information to shape society in various ways.

The fundamental breakthroughs in speed and flexibility that made the communications revolution were thus made by the telegraph, telephone, and radio. Since then, television, which became part of the mass media only after the Second World War, has added another layer to the revolution. And as from the 1980s, the rise of the internet promises to add yet another dimension to mass communication. Starting from military communication facilities during the 1960s, the internet became a network of networks during the 1980s, and took off into mass communications with the introduction of the world wide web format in 1993. The number of host computers on the internet has risen from 130,000 in 1989 to over 30 million in 1998, and conservatively estimating an average of five users per host, this suggests something like 150 million people were on-line by the late 1990s (Christensen 1998), with exponential growth in prospect. These developments greatly increase the social reach and impact of the communications revolution, though they extend what was done before rather than amounting to a new breakthrough in interaction capacity. They do not increase the range or the speed of communication, though they do add mightily to its volume, and in myriad ways to its content. These things make a substantial difference, and make possible everything from CNN to cyberwar, and global money markets to the world wide web. But in interaction capacity terms, they do not compare to the fundamental breakthroughs of the late nineteenth and early twentieth centuries that forever demolished the historic role of distance as a barrier to human communication.

## 3. SOCIAL TECHNOLOGIES

The mind-boggling transformations in the physical technologies of transportation and communication are a hard act to follow, and the story of social technologies is indeed more modest, though in its own way equally important. There are of course lots of carry-overs from ancient and classical times, often expanded in scale along with the global international system. Lingua francas continue to be important, though mostly on a regional basis until the rise of first French, and then more widely English, as world lingua francas. By the end of the twentieth century, English was looking well positioned to become a genuinely embedded world language, serving not just political, intellectual, professional, and business elites, but also a considerable chunk of the public at large. Alongside human languages, a different sort of lingua franca was evolving in the software of the increasingly ubiquitous computer networks.

Money became much more universal, though still divided into myriad national currencies. As a consequence, the density of interaction within the international economic system during this epoch increased spectacularly. Much of modern European history before the twentieth century can be read as a search for new supplies of gold and silver with which to create the monetary foundations for expanding trade. From 1493 to 1800, 85 per cent of the world's silver and over 70 per cent of its gold came from the Americas, and during the seventeenth and eighteenth centuries an average of roughly 15 tonnes per year of silver was shipped to the Philippines to finance the China trade (Barrett 1990: 224, 249). Shortages of specie stifled economic growth by restricting the money supply, whereas the discovery of new sources of gold and silver stimulated trade. But more profoundly, Europe's economic history can also increasingly be read as the continuous working out of how to increase the volume of credit that could be built on a given capital stock of specie. As the world economy grew ever larger, it tended to outrun the supply of specie, thus increasing the pressure to find stable forms of credit. Braudel (1985: 365–85) picks out the British invention of the national debt in 1688 (linking government borrowing to taxes) as a particular stroke of genius in this regard. This still ongoing financial experiment resulted in many crashes when credit got overextended and confidence collapsed, but this drove a learning process which helped to expand the money supply. Braudel (1985: 244–5) argues that credit was the key to power, noting that during the eighteenth century Dutch 'paper' (i.e. credit) exceeded the amount of specie in circulation by between 4 and 15 times, and that major financiers could raise more money than most governments. For a time during the nineteenth and twentieth centuries gold provided a universal standard of value. Strong currencies, most notably the British pound before the First World War and the US dollar after the Second World War, also acted in some ways as a kind of global money, and the development of sophisticated money markets made currency exchange easy.

Universal religions also continued to provide important social networks. Islam expanded the number and geographical range of its adherents despite the fall from power of its military and political heartlands. Christianity, by contrast, rode to world scale on the back of Western power. There was, however, a price to be paid for size in the increasing subdivision into rival doctrines and sects. Both Islam and Christianity fragmented to such a degree, and with such intensity, that it could be argued that they lost much of their use as social lubricants, becoming instead sources of division and conflict.

But the main event in the development of social interaction capacity during this era was the development of a much richer, deeper, better organized, more formal, and more extensive international society than anything that had ever existed before. The story of this international society cuts across several of our categories: it is partly about the new units already sketched in Chapter 12, partly about process formations, and partly about structure. We cannot avoid fragmenting the narrative somewhat, and we will draw the threads together later. Here it will suffice to set out a general sketch in the form of two key points.

First is that this new, global international society unfolded simultaneously along two paths: one more socio-political, to do with the rise of diplomacy, international law, and international organizations; the other more socio-economic, to do with the shift from mercantilist to liberal ways of understanding the international political economy.

The socio-political path is about the development and spread of the European system of formal interstate diplomacy, and its accompanying framework of international law. This path unfolds steadily from the fifteenth century onwards, expanding first from Italy to the rest of Europe, and then being carried by the European expansion to the rest of the world. As Tibi (1993: 11) notes, before their encounter with Europe: 'advanced non-European civilisations . . . were unfamiliar either with the sovereignty of nations or with sovereignty under international law.' With decolonization, as described in Chapter 12, the system of formally unequal relations between Europe and the rest of the world came to an end, and states and peoples treated each other more or less as legal and moral equals, albeit acknowledging differences in power. The European form of diplomacy and international law provided a universal framework for this type of political relationship, and also provided the basis for intergovernmental organizations (IGOs) to became a significant feature on the global political landscape.

IGOs have become a central social technology of interaction capacity in the modern international system. Their existence raises the political interaction capacity of the international system by providing not only pre-set pathways for diplomacy, but also agreed rules and practices, and obligations to participate. In an international system that possesses such institutions, more political interaction is possible than in one that does not. Indeed, as we will show in the next chapter, IGOs have become necessary for many of the poorer states in the system to sustain their diplomatic presence. The precursor to IGOs was international conferences amongst the powers, and particularly the series of such conferences in the nineteenth century that goes under the label 'the concert of Europe'. Such conferences remain an ongoing feature of diplomacy, and it is not uncommon for them to turn into standing organizations, as UNCTAD, UNEP, and the Islamic Conference have done.

The first permanent IGOs began to emerge during the 1860s and 1870s as a limited set of narrow functional organizations. Some, like the Universal Postal Union, the International Telecommunications Union, and the International Bureau of Weights and Measures, were aimed at setting common standards to facilitate desired forms of interaction, and at enhancing the interoperability of the new physical communication technologies. Others, like the Red Cross and various river management commissions, began to occupy environmental and humanitarian niches. The big breakthrough came after the First World War, when the League of Nations and its associated functional institutions such as the International Labour Organization and the Permanent Court of International Justice were established. These set the form for the present UN system, and established the idea that a permanent global forum was a desirable, and perhaps necessary, addition to bilateral diplomacy and periodic conferences. But the league's ambition to be a global collective security device was much too far in advance of what was politically possible, and the core of the inter-war IGO system was pushed into irrelevance during the 1930s. After the Second World War, the remnants of the league system were incorporated into the new UN system, demonstrating the consensus amongst most states that a global forum organization, and a set of specialized functional agencies, had become necessary for the management of the international system. Several further waves of IGOs were created during the 1950s, 1960s, and 1970s, some adding to the global UN system, others providing forum organizations at the regional level. From nothing in the eighteenth century, IGOs grew to 37 by 1909, reached a peak of 369 in 1986, and declined to 263 by 1994, a bit more than the number of states in the system (Yearbook of International Organizations 1994–5: 1739).

The socio-economic path is primarily about the shift from mercantilist to liberal ways of thinking about international economic relations, and the consequent changes in the rules, institutions, and attitudes that accompanied the spread of liberal understanding and the extension of market conditions to the global level. This development has been depicted as a nineteenth-century phenomenon (Rosenberg 1994). But the impact of socio-economic institutions on interaction capacity has very much deeper roots. In the Middle Ages, the Italian merchant banking companies played a crucial role in the expansion of commodity trading. The Peruzzi Company, for instance, was particularly concerned with moving grain, a high-volume, low-value commodity, into a number of different markets where both the demand and the price were extremely volatile. Such 'super-companies' needed large amounts of capital, a sophisticated organization, and an international network which, in the case of the Peruzzi family, extended from London to Constantinople (see Map 13.3).

The company acted as an intermediary, providing the ambitious rulers who controlled the basic commodities with a reliable source of cash and the expanding industrial cities with the supplies of basic foodstuffs necessary for survival. Without the merchant banks, it would have been difficult to establish this link (Hunt 1994). The effect of new institutional modes of organization on interaction capacity is even more clearly demonstrated through an examination of some of the effects of the mercantile companies established in the seventeenth century. Their new mode of operation began the process of creating a more transparent market which had the consequence of eliminating the less efficient intercontinental caravan routes.

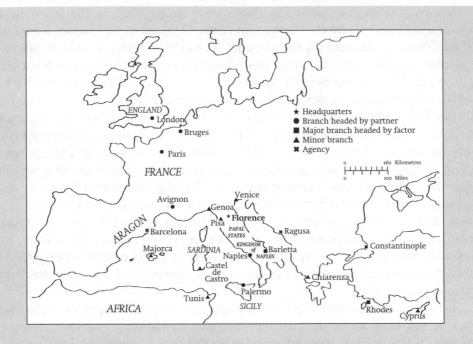

*Note:* The map shows that the Peruzzi Company had branches that were located across Europe and the Mediterranean. There were twenty-one partners in the 1330s who shared the profits and losses made by the company and an even larger number of factors or paid employees (Hunt 1994: ch. 3).

*Source:* Taken from Hunt 1994.

Map 13.3  *The Peruzzi Company network: 1335*

*Caravans, carracks, companies, and the pepper trade*

The caravans that travelled along the silk routes provided a vital link across Eurasia for over fifteen hundred years. Yet within a hundred years of the Europeans rounding the Cape of Good Hope and discovering a sea route to India and the East, the caravan routes became uneconomic and suffered a rapid demise. But the opening up of the sea route was not sufficient to put the caravans out of business.

The caravan trade initially survived the competition posed by the Portuguese carracks that first plied the sealanes linking Europe to Asia during the sixteenth century. But this, according to Steensgaard (1972; Lane 1966), was because the Portuguese and the caravan traders worked within a redistributive rather than a market framework. For example, the price of pepper, a vital commodity brought to Europe by land and sea in the sixteenth century, was never determined by transparent market forces. For the caravan traders, a crucial element of the price was determined by very substantial and highly unpredictable 'protection costs' related to custom duties, the risk of attack by robbers, and extortion by local officials. Although economists are prone to exclude such costs from market calculations, it is more appropriate to suggest that for the caravan traders, the market lacked transparency. Although it can be argued that the Portuguese had a monopoly on the sea-borne pepper trade, the monopoly rested not on their exclusive access to the source of pepper, but on their ability to use force to control the trading route along which the pepper was carried. There was, however, no attempt to factor the cost of this 'protection' into the price at which pepper was sold. Instead, the Portuguese sold their pepper at the same price as the pepper that had been brought along the caravan routes. The mercantile companies, by contrast, were profit-making organizations. As a consequence, the companies were not interested in assisting their home state in its conflicts with other states by acting, for example, as privateers. In this way, they minimized their protection costs. At the same time, they devised elaborate mechanisms, withholding pepper from the market when prices were low, for example, to stabilize prices. They were interested not in maximizing profits, but in establishing a long-range commercial policy that included price stability. The effect was to increase the transparency of the market and by this means they rendered themselves more efficient than the caravan traders.

It was the organizational structure of the mercantile companies, not the opening up of the oceans, that led to the demise of the intercontinental caravan trade between Asia and Europe.

Although we are still a long way off establishing a fully transparent global market, it has been a persistent goal for liberals from the eighteenth century onwards. Governments have taken up the goal with varying degrees of enthusiasm from the nineteenth century onwards. A convenient date for marking the development is the repeal of the Corn Laws in Britain in 1846, which lowered the cost of food by removing tariffs on imports, thereby exposing British agriculture (and the landowning class) to competition from abroad. According to mercantilist thinking, national economies were in a zero-sum relationship with each other: the gains of one must be the losses of another. This understanding acted as a barrier to economic interaction. Under mercantilism, everyone sought the advantages of being an exporter, because having a trade surplus meant that wealth was accumulating. But nobody wanted to import unless they absolutely had to, because to do so would drain the national wealth. The negative perception of imports meant that mercantilist states encouraged self-reliance in production, even where it was not efficient to do so. This kind of economic self-reliance also served strategic ends. It gave states maximum resistance to blockade, and maximum independence in mobilizing for war. Such features could be useful for self-defence, but they just as easily served military aggressors, and by associating control of territory with ownership of wealth they encouraged states to pursue military expansion (Buzan 1984).

Liberalism supported a quite different view of economic relations. It argued that societies should open themselves to imports not just out of necessity, but whenever foreign producers could outcompete domestic ones in terms of price and quality. There was a strong case for this both in terms of direct benefits to consumers (lower prices, higher quality, more choice), and in terms of its stimulative effects on domestic production (seek higher efficiency or go out of business). Against the mercantilist doctrine of self-reliance, liberal ideology promoted specialization and interdependence. It worked for the abandonment of autarkic national economies and the opening up of world markets, arguing that what was lost in protected national markets would be more than compensated for by the wider opportunities of a global market. In the liberal view, trade was not a zero-sum game (wins=losses), but a positive-sum one in which everyone could win. On the strategic side, liberals argued that free trade and economic interdependence would reduce the incentives for war, not least by delinking the acquisition of wealth from the control of territory.

After their adoption by Britain—then the most powerful state in the world—in the middle of the nineteenth century, liberal economic ideas spread steadily to other countries, albeit meeting much resistance, and enduring much backsliding in the process, and sometimes being imposed by force (as on China and Japan). As they did so, the social interaction capacity of the system increased. States became more open to trade, and many were prepared to stimulate trade by reducing tariffs, and by adopting most favoured nation agreements (MFN). Economic organization adapted to this increasing openness. As noted in Chapter 12, transnational companies and banks began to appear during the later decades of the nineteenth century. Gilpin (1987: 231–8) argues that such companies are both products and supporters of liberal economic systems: their extension of managerial control beyond state boundaries is consistent with economic liberalism, and becomes a bulwark of it.

At the same time, more and more countries followed Britain onto the gold standard, thus stabilizing exchange rates and facilitating trade. The First World War suspended the process of liberalization, and attempts to revive it after the war were weakened by the communist revolution in Russia, and fascist ones in Italy, Germany, Japan, and elsewhere. All of the totalitarian ideologies espoused neomercantilism, and rejected the openness and interdependence of liberalism. The liberal revival was also weakened by the financial crash of 1929, and the great depression that followed it. In some ways these events exposed the dangers of a liberal world economy, particularly its vulnerability to systemic financial instability. But in other ways, they confirmed liberal views about the linkages between free trade on the one hand, and prosperity and war on the other. Economic liberalism revived under American leadership after the Second World War, bringing with it new institutions (GATT (now WTO), IMF, IBRD), a renewed commitment to free trade, and, at least until the 1970s, a more cautious attitude towards financial liberalization. With the defeat of communism at the end of the Cold War, liberal economic ideology acquired hegemonic status, becoming effectively universal as a social technology for increasing interaction capacity.

Thus in both the socio-political and the socio-economic domains, international society developed in such a way as greatly to facilitate interaction in the international system.

The second key point about social interaction capacity takes the form of a question about causality and connectivity. It arises from the strikingly parallel occurrence during the nineteenth century of three things:

- economic liberalization;
- the industrial transformation of physical interaction capacity; and
- the internal evolution of the leading modern states into their mass national and then democratic forms.

It beggars belief to think that these concurrent developments are mere coincidences. Yet thinking of them as connected implies the existence of a very considerable transformation in the international system whose causal pathways are not at all clear. It would be nice to take the simple view that the physical developments in interaction capacity essentially drove the other developments. In this perspective, mass transportation and communication enabled both the shift from rulers to people within the leading modern states, and the emergence of global norms, rules, and institutions. But while this view undoubtedly has considerable force, it seems unlikely to represent the whole truth. The developments in physical interaction capacity were themselves pulled along by the fact of an already existing global economy, and the impetus towards democratization has clear political, social, and economic roots that pre-date the technological marvels of the nineteenth century.

We cannot solve this causal puzzle here, though we can note its significance for the story of international systems.

# 4. CONCLUSIONS

The revolutions in interaction capacity during the last 500 years, and especially the last 150 of those, have changed the nature of the international system in a number of profound ways. Most obvious has been the death of distance and geography as major determinants of international systems. First, the culmination of sailing ship technology transformed the oceans from barriers into highways, and then railways, roads, and aircraft did the same for continental spaces. Over a period of just over 400 years, the physical constraints on human interaction that had shaped international systems for nearly five millennia largely disappeared. One consequence of this was the making of a single global system. A second was the elimination of the significance of different levels of interaction capacity for different types of interaction. When interaction capacity was generally low, it made a difference that societal interactions, and some types of economic interactions, could still take place over long distances, whereas bulk trade and war could not. But when interaction capacity became high, the different requirements of military-political, economic, and societal interaction ceased to matter so much. All types could flow rapidly over the new global transportation and communication systems. This led to a third consequence, which was the merging of military-political and economic international systems into a single geographical space, ending the long differentiation between the two types.

Alongside this intense physical networking of the planet, a parallel social wiring was also being built up. This is somewhat harder to grasp than the physical dimension because it lacks many of the concrete manifestations such as railway networks, telegraph lines, and global systems of satellite communications. It does have some concrete symbols, most notably the TNCs, IGOs, INGOs, and international regimes that provide the organizational nexus for international and world society. But underlying these is a set of attitudes that is different from anything that existed in the ancient and classical world. There is, to start with, a much higher consciousness of being part of an international system. This is perhaps a natural development given the great spread and intensification of that system during modern times. The existence on a global scale of war and peace, and economic boom and bust, is hard not to notice. In addition to being aware of the fact that they are embedded in an international system, most of its units also value the pursuit of order and stability in that system (which is not to say that disagreements about how this should be done do not sometimes lead to conflict). For the most part, they are willing to initiate or accept norms and rules that make economic and political interaction within the system run more smoothly. Sometimes they are even willing to establish collective organizations either to serve as forums (the UN, many regional IGOs), or to pursue shared functional objectives (WHO, WTO, IAEA). This social wiring of the planet underpins everything from diplomacy and banking to trade and tourism. All of these activities depend on units being willing to accept rules about how various cross-border activities are to be conducted. The modern international system has become deeply infused with such rules, and just like the physical hardware of the railway lines, the shipping routes, the telephone systems, and the internet, the software of socially constructed norms and rules also removes obstacles to the flow of interaction.

The physical and social aspects of interaction capacity meet and merge on questions of standards and interoperability. Most countries will eventually adopt a standard gauge for their railway lines, a standard voltage and code system for their telegraph systems, a standard set of rules for their ships and aircraft, and suchlike. It makes a difference to interaction capacity whether countries agree to share standards, or prefer to mark their borders by difference. If two countries use a different width of railway track, then goods and people travelling between them have to stop and change trains. The existence of railways is a physical technology. But the existence of an international standard gauge is a social one, reflecting, among other things, a judgement that the risk of railways being used to assist military invasions is low.

Despite all this, there can be no doubt that the international system is marked by quite extreme uneven development in interaction capacity as in many other spheres of life. Both physically and socially, the global system was made by a small number of leading states. All of humankind is embraced by this system, and as the density and flexibility of electronic networks grows, that embrace grows tighter everywhere. Yet interaction capacity remains very uneven, as do the flows of interaction that rest on it. Any map of air, sea, or telephone traffic immediately reveals a centre–periphery pattern, with heavy concentrations amongst the most developed states, thinner traffic between centre and periphery, and thinnest between units in the periphery. Some parts of the periphery are even going backward, as in those African countries that have proved unable to maintain the road and railway systems they inherited from the Europeans. Much the same pattern would be revealed by a map of the socially constructed world, with the degree of acceptance of norms, rules, and institutions following a similar centre–periphery pattern (see Map 13.4).

So there are some awkward questions here about the relationship between units and interaction capacity. It is clear that the leading units both led the revolution in interaction capacity, and were its principal beneficiaries. Initially, and in different ways still, they were and are able to use their superior ability to project power to impose themselves and their interests onto others. The uneven distribution of interaction capacity gave them a longer reach, and this is still visible in the very small number of states that have the capability to operate militarily outside their own region. At the other end of the spectrum, there is room for serious questions about how, or if, weak states like many of those in Africa *can* achieve economic and political development while being embedded in a powerful and penetrative international system (Buzan 1998). Yet even so, the development of global networks for transportation and communication has extended the reach of all actors. Unless they are forbidden to do so by governments, or lack the cash, individuals can send letters or emails, or make phone calls, worldwide. Firms can

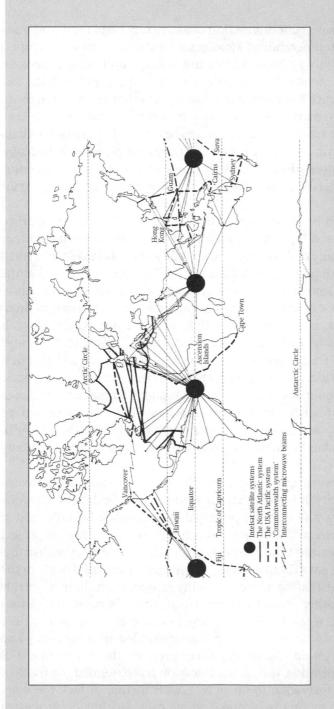

*Note:* The map identifies the main cable and satellite trunk routes for telecommunications that existed in 1970. Although the map reveals the existence of a global network of communications, with over 90% of all telephones located in the developed world at that time (Cherry 1971: 61), centre-periphery disparities were accentuated rather than diminished. Further developments in communications have meant that the capital cities of many developing countries are now in closer contact with London and New York than with their own rural communities (Brunn and Leinbach 1991).

*Source:* Taken from Cherry 1971.

*Map 13.4  The world's principal intercontinental trunk routes for telecommunications*

ship and receive goods worldwide. Terrorists can set up global networks and deliver violence in the location of their choice. Criminals can launder and then bank their proceeds anywhere in the world. And governments both rich and poor can conduct diplomacy in regional and global forums.

# Chapter 14

# PROCESS IN THE MODERN INTERNATIONAL SYSTEM

## 1. INTRODUCTION

Expansion of the international system to global scale was one main change for most types of process. Processes either became global, such as trade and war, or if they remained local had to function in a globalized context. The various revolutions in interaction capacity described in the previous chapter also meant that most types of international process became more intense, though there were some notable exceptions such as China's fifteenth-century failure to follow through its breakthrough in ocean-going shipping. Generally, the higher carrying capacity of the system meant that interaction increased not only in range, but also in volume, value, diversity, and speed. Trade multiplied relentlessly, wars became wider ranging and more destructive, diplomatic contact increased, and global flows of information began to create an ever more generalized awareness of events on the planet as a whole. One way of understanding this is to say that the units in the system became more interconnected, and in many ways more interdependent. Another way of looking at it is to say that the international system became stronger in relation to the units that composed it—even though the units themselves, as described in Chapter 12, were becoming stronger than they had been in the past. This means that structural forces generated by increasing interaction began to operate more powerfully, increasing the external pressures on both how units behave, and how they organize themselves internally. More on this below.

But while it is true to say that the international system became larger, more intense, more interdependent, and more strongly shaped by structural forces, it would be false to claim that this happened evenly. It should already be clear from the discussions of units and interaction capacity in Chapters 12 and 13 that the global international system unfolded in a highly uneven manner. The new units and the revolutions in interaction capacity all came out of Europe/the West, and they enabled one civilization to create a global system by expanding to dominate, occupy, or sometimes obliterate all the others. The very making of the global international system rested on major inequalities of development. Such inequalities were not new. The ancient and classical world was divided into zones in which development was certainly different, and arguably uneven: the agrarian zones of cities and high civilization; the barbarian zone of pastoral nomads and primitive agriculturalists who did not generate cities; and on the fringes the residual hunter-gatherers.

These older differentiations lasted well into the modern era, and in a few places are with us still, but increasingly they were overridden by a newer, more dynamic, and more intrusive pattern which is probably best labelled centre–periphery. The three zones of ancient and classical times reflected adaptations to particular physical environments and climates, and although they did intrude on each other, these features also insulated them from each other. Only very slowly, and with many reversals, did agrarian civilizations manage to extend their sway into the other two zones. The industrial civilization that developed in Europe during the eighteenth and nineteenth centuries was more aggressively expansionist than agrarian civilization—or perhaps just more successfully so because of its greater absolute and relative power. In its search for resources and markets it quickly spread its influence into all parts of the planet, inspiring, forcing, or seducing all other peoples to relate to its standards and modes of operation. Unlike agrarian and barbarian society, industrial society was not tied to particular types of land or climate. In principle it could locate in any geography, though in practice it seemed to require particular types of social and political conditions before it could take root. Industrial society spread quickly and effectively within the West, and to a limited extent elsewhere (most notably Japan). In some other places the attempt to transplant industrial society had only partial success, and has often, as in China, Russia, and India, run up against cultural obstacles. And in yet other places (most notably Africa and parts of Asia) industrialism has scarcely put down local roots at all. The result is a global hierarchy of development. There is an industrial core whose influence penetrates everywhere, a semi-periphery of partly industrialized societies, and a periphery of underdeveloped ones. This hierarchy is clearly reflected in most of the main patterns of process. Whether in air traffic flows, sea routes, communications, investment, or international institutions, the core dominates and the periphery is at the end of the line. Thus while everyone is caught up in the international system, there are huge inequalities in power, mobility, welfare, life expectancy, and so forth. Whether these inequalities are a necessary, and therefore more or less permanent, feature of industrialism, or whether they are simply a transitional condition that will disappear as more and more non-Western cultures discover how to adopt industrialism, is a matter of heated and long-standing debate. We cannot resolve that question here. But we can safely assert that uneven development has been a central feature of the modern international system, and that even on the most optimistic prognostication will certainly remain so for many decades, and probably for several centuries, to come.

## 2. MILITARY-POLITICAL PROCESS

In the realm of military-political process there was much that remained familiar from the ancient and classical world. The basic institutions of war, alliance, arms racing, security dilemma, and suchlike all carried over into the modern era. But within this general framework of continuity, there were three significant differences:

- expansion to global scale carried on the back of the revolutions in physical interaction capacity;
- a very marked acceleration in the pace and significance of technological innovation in weaponry; and
- the growth of fear of the war process itself as a rival to the long-standing fear of defeat by other actors in the system (although this occurred only at the centre of the system).

The expansion to global scale imposed a single, system-wide standard of military capability, removing forever the different standards that had marked the various international systems of the ancient and classical world. The first victims of this were the indigenous Stone Age civilizations of the Americas, whose level of development was roughly on a par with that of the early Egyptians and Sumerians. Any one of the late agrarian empires in Eurasia could, in principle, have overwhelmed the Incas and the Aztecs almost as easily as the Spaniards did. The Amerindian civilizations had no metal weapons, no horses, no guns, and little immunity to Eurasian diseases. Interaction capacity across the Americas was so weak that when the Spaniards arrived in the Inca Empire, its leaders did not know that the conquistadores had recently obliterated their Aztec neighbours, of whose existence they were unaware (Diamond 1997: ch. 3). Black Africa was similarly poorly equipped and one reason that it was so vulnerable to European and Arab penetration and exploitation was that its peoples had developed no coastal shipping of their own and had made no attempt to explore either the seas or the deserts that bordered them (Braudel 1985: 430–41). The last victims were China, Japan, and the many African peoples who gave way in the face of superior European military power during the nineteenth century, and whose defeat marked the making of a full global international system. The demise of barbarian military power after the great Mongol outsurge during the thirteenth century relieved the world of their threat of invasion, but for non-Europeans the threat of barbarian invasion by land was quickly replaced by the threat of equally catastrophic (and in some eyes equally barbaric) European invasions by sea (McNeill 1994: 128).

Europe's military and imperial apprenticeship occurred during the late Middle Ages, when Latin Christendom expanded into its surrounding periphery, sometimes overthrowing fellow Christians (England, Ireland, Byzantine Empire), sometimes colonizing or ethnically cleansing tribal peoples (the Baltic), and sometimes taking on the Islamic world (the Levant, Iberia). By the eleventh century, European naval power was sufficiently developed that its armies could be landed anywhere within their known maritime world (Bartlett 1994: 292–4). From the seventeenth century onward, Europeans were not only fighting amongst themselves, but also with local powers across all parts of the planet. During the eighteenth century the military rivalry between Britain and France took place in Europe, North America, the Middle East, and South Asia. The interconnected set of wars that hinged around the French and American revolutions can almost be seen as the first real world war, though East Asia was not much touched by it. The rise of Japan during the late nineteenth century, and its coming of age as a great power by allying with Britain in 1902, and defeating Russia in 1904–5, set the stage for what was undoubtedly a world war during 1914–18. Although the fighting was centred on Europe and the Middle East, Europe's imperial reach meant that troops were sent from all corners of the globe. The dismantling of the German empire after the war ensured that the peace settlement had worldwide ramifications. The Second World War was much more fully global, with all of the great powers—European, Asian, American—in play, and two main cores of conflict, one in Europe, and the other in the western Pacific. As wars became global, so did other aspects of military-political interaction. The Washington Naval Agreements of 1922, for example, represented one of the first attempts at global management of the military balance. The five great naval powers agreed to proportion their strength in capital ships on a ratio of 5 (USA), 5 (Britain), 3 (Japan), 1.67 (France), 1.67 (Italy).

Accompanying, and driving along, the expansion of scale in military-political interaction was a very marked acceleration in the pace and significance of technological innovation in weaponry. This is an often told tale (Buzan and Herring 1998) and does not need to be more than summarized here. Military technological innovation, as was shown in Part III, is an old story. Things like iron swords, chariots, metal body armour, and stirrups caused periodic military revolutions in the ancient and classical world. But in the modern era, three revolutions transformed military-political relations away from the ancient and classical model: the arrival of gunpowder in the fourteenth century, the making of ocean-going sailing ships in the fifteenth century, and the nineteenth-century industrial revolution(s).

The ocean-going sailing ship and gunpowder both represent developments firmly rooted in the last centuries of the ancient and classical era. In some ways they fit the general pattern of that era's occasional technological revolutions, but they also undid some of that era's defining features. As we have seen, the ocean-going sailing ship transformed military-political relations by hugely extending the range over which military power could be projected and so breaking down one of the main insulators that separated the international systems of the ancient and classical world from each other. Gunpowder had similarly revolutionary effects. By providing increased firepower, it both made fortification more difficult, and undermined the power of cavalry. It made life much harder for city-states and feudal lords, neither of whom could keep up with the rapidly rising costs of both offensive and defensive military technology, and it broke forever the military strength of the nomadic barbarians.

The nineteenth-century industrial revolution(s) were an altogether new and more fundamental departure. Rather than being just particular revolutions with particular effects, they constituted a revolution in the process of innovation itself. Put in the simplest terms, what happened was that military technological innovation became the rule rather than the exception. In the ancient and classical world, military technological revolutions were infrequent, and typically separated by long periods. The galleys with which the Greeks fought the Persians in classical times were not so different from those with which the Venetians fought the Ottomans 2,000 years later. And the ships and guns with which the British fought the French early in the nineteenth century were not fundamentally different from those used to fight the Thirty Years War nearly 300 years earlier.

But from the middle of the nineteenth century onwards, there was a tremendous acceleration in the pace of technological innovation. Between 1850 and 1870, wood-built, sail-powered warships disappeared to be replaced by steel-built, steam-powered ones, solid shot gave way to explosive shells, and smooth bore, muzzle-loading cannon to rifled, breech-loading ones. Thereafter, and right down to the present day, major technological innovations in military affairs followed close on each other's heels: machine guns, submarines, poison gas, aeroplanes, tanks, radio, aircraft carriers, nerve gas, radar, helicopters, long-range rockets, computers, nuclear weapons, surveillance satellites, precision guided munitions, pilotless aircraft. Once invented, each of these innovations underwent rapid improvement in performance capability. It became not uncommon for whole classes of weapon to disappear once improvement elsewhere made them disfunctional. Horse cavalry was more or less redundant by the time of the First World War, and heavy armoured battleships succumbed to submarines and aircraft carriers after a reign of less than a century. On current trends, manned aircraft and big surface ships may well disappear within a few more decades. And not only did innovation become the norm, but industrial production capacity allowed new weapons to be made in huge quantities.

This third revolution introduced many new elements into military political process. Most obviously it changed the nature of war by making the instruments of destruction far more diverse, numerous, and potent. War became faster moving, longer ranged, bigger in scale, more expensive, and more elaborate than ever before. Military interaction moved into several new dimensions (underwater, air, space), and technological quality and production capacity became important determinants of outcomes. Big wars required the total mobilization of society to support the military effort, and it was the mass national mobilizations for the First World War that provided the template for the totalitarian governments of the inter-war years. The frenzied pace of technological innovation meant that no two wars would be alike, and that military planners could no longer count on the accumulated wisdom of the past to give them much guidance for the future.

The third revolution also had a big impact on military-political relations short of war. Military rivalries and arms competitions were not new, but the acceleration of technological innovation added several new twists. Now one had not only to keep up with the size and training of rival forces, but also with the rapidly changing technological standard of their equipment. New weapons quite quickly became obsolete, meaning that armed forces had to run in order to stand still in maintaining the quality of their equipment. In serious arms races, a technological lead could be as decisive as a quantitative one, which meant that military rivalry and technological advance fed on each other. In such an environment, only a handful of great powers could muster the resources to keep their military production at the leading edge. Non-industrial countries, no matter how populous, could no longer aspire to great power standing. Lesser powers wishing to have modern armed forces had no choice but to buy leading edge weapons from those able to produce them, making the arms trade one of the more conspicuous aspects of centre–periphery relations.

Perhaps the most striking aspect of this revolution was the huge power gap that it opened up between the West and the rest of the world during the nineteenth and much of the twentieth century. For more than a century this gap gave the industrial powers an unbeatable advantage. It enabled them both to subdue the most resilient of the remaining classical empires (China, Japan, Ottoman), and to take over all the remaining areas occupied by barbarians and hunter-gatherers. As the famous lines by Hillaire Belloc note: 'Whatever happens we have got The Maxim gun and they have not.' The ability of the Maxim gun, and other early machine guns, to fire 600 rounds per minute meant that quite small European forces could and did defeat larger numbers of more primitively equipped Africans, Asians, and native Americans. But the revolution in firepower eventually turned against the European powers that had generated it, and in the twentieth century made intra-European wars so destructive that they undermined the foundations of Europe's world power.

The growing cost and destructiveness of both weapons and war underpinned the third significant difference in military political process during the modern era which was the rise of the defence dilemma. Perhaps the first glimmerings of this were the Hague Peace Conferences in 1899 and 1907 which considered various restraints on war and weapons. But the defence dilemma really got rolling as a result of the First World War, whose huge human and economic costs, apparently trivial causes, and monumental examples of military mismanagement created a widespread revulsion against war itself in many of the participating societies. The desperate propaganda slogan of 'the war to end war' that had been invented during the war by the Western powers to justify the carnage fed into this reaction, as did the fear of the social revolutions that the war had unleashed in Russia, Italy, and several other countries. There was a real fear, shared at all levels of society, that another such war would destroy European civilization. Continued development of weapons of mass destruction, particularly bombers and chemical weapons, reinforced this fear. In the event, the Second World War did not obliterate Europe to the extent anticipated, but the arrival of nuclear weapons in 1945 quickly confirmed the view that a new world war might well risk not just the demise of European civilization, but of the human species itself. Amongst the leading powers, the technologically driven intensification of war that unfolded during the twentieth century brought the whole process of war increasingly into question.

One reaction to this rising concern about the destructive impact of weapons and war was the development of disarmament and arms control as new types of mainstream military-political process. During the inter-war years there was much effort (though not much result) to find agreement on limiting the numbers and types of weapons that states could make, possess, and sell. Although success in this enterprise was limited, and broke down in the face of fascism, there was a clear move in the more liberal countries away from the traditional view that war was a normal and expected practice of states, and towards the view that the resort to war should be confined to exceptional circumstances. This pattern continued after the Second World War, with arms control and disarmament negotiations becoming a central feature in the management of the Cold War. Again, the specific results of these negotiations were seldom all that impressive, but the general drift towards the idea that war should be exceptional practice rather than normal continued to gain ground. The ending of the Cold War removed the one remaining ideological conflict that might have caused a great power hot war, and revealed more clearly the existence of an impressive security community embracing all of the West, as well as some Westernistic powers such as Japan, amongst whom war had ceased to be a possibility. Most of these countries were linked together in military co-operation arrangements which not only combined their strength, but also increased their military dependence on each other, and made collective action central to legitimizing any major use of force. Even outside the Western core, some regional arrangements to eliminate war within a group of states were beginning to appear, most notably in South-East Asia. The warrior culture, which since the beginning of history had played a big role in making war not only acceptable, but also desired, seemed to be fading away as a central feature of the most powerful and advanced societies in the international system.

## 3. ECONOMIC PROCESS

In some respects the transformation of economic processes was even more dramatic than that of military political ones. There was of course a similar expansion of scale with the making of a global system, and this came earlier for global economic relations than for military-political ones. But the intensity of economic relations increased relatively more than that of military-political ones. World trade not only underwent an enormous increase in volume, but also shifted from being primarily about luxury goods for small elites to being about bulk goods and items of mass production that directly affected the lives of a much larger proportion of the population, both as consumers and producers. The revolutions in interaction capacity meant that long-distance trade became direct. The relay trade system of classical Eurasia was replaced by a global maritime trading system in which buyers and sellers were generally in face-to-face contact with each other. European ships could now pick up Far Eastern products directly, so bypassing the multiple stages of the Silk Road routes. No longer could it be argued, as it was of the long-distance trade of ancient and classical times, that world trade was superficial and largely unconnected to society at large. Finance and investment grew up alongside trade as massive new dimensions of international economic relations.

The breakthrough to a global trading system had many late classical precursors, and was more the result of a host of incremental developments than some kind of bolt from the blue. These precursors started to show in the eleventh century, when transportation and trade revived in Europe and when China's period of industrial and commercial greatness expanded the whole maritime trading network linking East, South-East, and South Asia to the Middle East (McNeill 1982: 53–4). In the West, direct sea trade between Italy and the Netherlands was under way by 1277 (Braudel 1985: 98–101). Circa 1340, the Eurasian revival was dampened by the closure of the Mongol Silk Roads connecting East Asia and the Black Sea, which reimposed the Islamic barrier on European trade (Braudel 1985: 79). This closure stimulated the European search for maritime routes to East Asia. The Portuguese begin exploring down the African coast in 1416, reaching the Azores in 1430, the Cape of Good Hope in 1487, and India in 1498. Columbus reached the Americas in 1492, and thirty years later, Magellan's expedition crossed the Pacific. Initially, the world trade that these discoveries made possible was quite modest in scale (though rich in profit), resembling the luxury trade of ancient and classical times. From 1500 to 1634, for example, the entire Portuguese Asian spice trade was carried by around seven 1,000-tonnes ships per year (Curtin 1984: 142–4).

Coherent trade figures only begin during the eighteenth century, but various estimates have been compiled that enable one to link into the contemporary UN statistics in order to get a rough idea of how world trade has grown in relation to both population and the global GNP. Since 1750, the world's population has grown about 8 times, from around 770 million to around 6 billion. Bairoch (1981: 7; 1993: 95) suggests that the global GNP has increased by a multiple of 41, from $148 billion in 1750 to $400 billion in 1900, $1,224 billion in 1950, and $6,080 billion in 1990. Curtin (1984: 251–2) calculates the growth of world trade by a factor of 54.5 from $700 million in 1700 to $38,150 million in 1914, including a ninefold increase

1820–80. Rostow (1978: 669) calculates that world trade increased by a factor of 54.2 between 1750 and 1938. Over the same period, Woodruff (1966: 313) comes to a similar conclusion, giving an increase by a factor of 65.9 from $700 million in 1750 to $46,100 million in 1938. Woodruff's figures blend into those from the UN Statistical Yearbooks for 1964, 1982, and 1994 (1965: 464–5; 1983: 874–5; 1996: 672–3) which show a multiple of 174.6 for the years 1938 to 1995, rising from $47,900 million to $8,364,321 million. If we multiply together Woodruff's increase and that of the UNSYs, we get an aggregate increase in the value of world trade from 1750 to 1994 of 11,506 times. This rather astonishing figure suggests that during the last 250 years world trade has outperformed the growth in the human population by over 1,400 times and outperformed global GNP by 281 times. Up to 1997 the value of world trade was still increasing at around 6 per cent per year, double the rate of growth of the global economy as a whole (*Economist* 15 Nov. 1997: 89).

Even allowing for quite substantial inaccuracies in these estimates, and for temporary downturns like that of the late 1990s, it seems abundantly clear that world trade has expanded during this period with a ferocity that is only rather marginally explained by parallel expansions of population and GNP. Jones (1987: 165) notes that compared to even the early manifestations of this Western economic explosion of bulk trade, the economies of the ancient and classical world 'were thus watered and fertilised by only a tiny, circumscribed and often inessential trade sector'. It is not our task here to provide an explanation for this extraordinary transformation, although the correlation with the increases in both physical (transportation technologies) and social (liberal norms) interaction capacity sketched above is obvious. Doing so would also require reference to the effects of the industrial revolution and the sharp rise in the standard of living of a substantial part of the world's population, though interestingly it was not until 1957 that the value of manufactured goods within world trade exceeded that of primary products (Kennedy 1989: 415). The vast expansion of trade is a major process factor in its own right, but from the nineteenth century onwards it also generated frequent and intensive negotiations on the rules for international trade as a central part of economic process. This was especially true after 1945, when the desire to avoid any repeat of the 1930s disaster was very strong. What started as simple 'most favoured nation' agreements on trade had by the late twentieth century turned into a system of multilateral institutions. Regular rounds of GATT negotiations reduced tariffs and other barriers to trade, culminating in the creation of the WTO in 1995.

It is impossible to comprehend the development of trade without a simultaneous appreciation of the way that trade has been financed. The invention of money obviously lies at the heart of this process and the origins of money are very closely associated with the development of trade. As a consequence, it is possible to tell a large and crucial part of the story of money in terms of the persistent attempts to improve the financial arrangements for conducting trade without 'the cumbersome and inefficient mechanism of barter' (Kindleberger 1984: 17). As we have already seen, money is not a recent invention. Indeed, we can find evidence of 'money' being employed in pre-international systems. And so it would be a mistake, according to Kindleberger, to tell the story of money in terms of an evolution from barter, to economies based on money, through to the recent formation of credit-based economies. For a large chunk of world history barter, money, and credit have coexisted and certainly elements of all three can still be identified in the contemporary international economy. Vilar (1976: 8) suggests that economists who are convinced that credit and the world bank are completely new features of the international economy have simply failed to examine the historical record. But there are good reasons for thinking that a financial revolution did take place at the start of the epoch we are now examining, the effects of which are still being worked out today. Indeed, after an investigation of the origins of international capital markets which he traces back to the start of the sixteenth century, Neal (1990: 2) concludes that he was 'impressed with the modernity of their operations'. History reveals that the financial processes that have come into play since the start of the sixteenth century have facilitated the emergence and consolidation of modern states while, at the same time, in conjunction with increasing international trade, they have pulled national economies into an ever closer and more integrated network of relations. But because national currencies have persisted, increasing interdependence has meant that the need for financial mechanisms to allow international transactions to take place has become ever more significant. A consequence of these developments, in conjunction with rising interaction capacity, has been the emergence of international money markets which have been graphically and disturbingly described in terms of 'casino capitalism' and 'mad money' (Strange 1997, 1998). Even if the fears reflected in these expressions are exaggerated, it is now commonly assumed that the financial side of the global economy dominates the 'real' economy of production and trade: the financial tail wagging the production dog.

The importance of finance as a key aspect of economic process is certainly not new. Even the ancient and classical world possessed some advanced financial techniques such as the practice in the Roman Empire of sending payment orders from one bank to another. The Romans, however, failed to take the crucial step of creating credit through negotiable instruments and the initiation of such 'modern' financial management techniques is considered to be primarily a product of late medieval Europe (De Ligt 1993: 104). The first crucial steps were taken in some of the medieval fairs where international trade was conducted. The fairs in Champagne, for example, were initially involved with local trade but, during the twelfth century, the Flemish and then later the Italians came to exchange goods there and the resulting international trade began to provide the principal *raison d'être* for the fairs. Although there is evidence of fairs in the classical world, for example, the Roman Empire, although not the Chinese Empire, except on the frontiers with the steppe nomads (De Ligt 1993: 22), the medieval fairs in Europe were very different because they quickly began to play an important and independent role in European finance. This was primarily the result of the introduction of bills of exchange from the twelfth century onwards. Although they were initially intended simply to facilitate the transfer of money from one region to another, 'this seemingly simple invention quickly developed into the preferred form of commercial credit and speculation' (De Ligt 1993: 103). The bills of exchange represented a 'quasi-currency', a form of international paper money that crossed all the political and monetary frontiers of Europe and had the effect of making capital much more liquid and internationally mobile. As the bills of exchange became increasingly recognized as a form of paper money, the fairs became financial centres.

*Financing trade in the medieval fairs of Europe*
Medieval fairs took place at specific points in the year and, for the duration of the fair, foreigners were placed under the protection of the local seigneur. To accommodate the international merchants, new financial arrangements were introduced in order to minimize the number of financial transactions that had to take place and also to reduce the amount of bullion (gold or silver ingots) and specie (coins) that the international traders had to travel with. Settlement involved a form of clearing, with each merchant keeping a book in which transactions were recorded. At the end of the fair, there was a period set aside for settlement when an official of the fair would validate the claims made and liabilities incurred by a merchant as a result of the trading he had done. The claims would then be used to cancel the liabilities and the merchant would have either a surplus or a deficit at the end of the fair. Uncancelled balances could be paid in currency, bills of exchange brought to the fair, or new bills drawn to carry the claim or debt to the next fair. Over time, the role of the fair widened beyond trade to embrace purely financial transactions. Tax collectors began to come to fairs to make use of the bills of exchange to facilitate their financial transactions that occurred in different parts of the country and agents of royal borrowers attended to raise cash in return for pledges of taxes, valuable possessions, or concessions. The range of financial transactions at these fairs proliferated and embraced foreign exchange, real estate, banking, early forms of insurance, and lotteries. By the end of the thirteenth century, financial activities became more important than the exchange of goods in the Champagne fairs. Within a few decades, however, the influence of the Champagne fairs waned and they once again became the location for local markets. New fairs in Geneva and Lyons took their place. This was mainly the consequence of shifting trade routes, with sea routes becoming of increasing significance. But eventually, for more deep-seated reasons, all of the great international fairs

degenerated into local markets. In the first place, there was an obvious need for financial centres to operate on a continuous basis. And, second, with the growth of trade there was also a need for a location where international trading could take place on a continuous basis. The spread of new business techniques in the areas of goods storage and dispatch furthered this development. By the end of the fifteenth century a city such as Antwerp that had become a major trading and financial centre could be viewed as a 'permanent fair' (Kindleberger 1984: 36–9; De Ligt 1993: 14–25).

The impacts of the financial mechanisms developed in the Middle Ages were eventually to have revolutionary consequences in the sixteenth century, enabling the Europeans to trade on a global scale and giving rise in the process to the formation of international capital markets. With the opening up of the sea routes at the end of the fifteenth century, merchants found that they could not meet the costs of trading on this scale. Financial intermediaries were required who were capable of 'mobilising larger sums, waiting for longer periods, and dealing with greater numbers of clients spread over greater distances than ever before' (Neal 1990: 4). The financial intermediaries were responsible for providing capital, first, to construct the thousands of ocean-going vessels that were built in the sixteenth century, and second, to pay for the goods that were being carried on these vessels. Bills of exchange provided the main source of credit used to meet the increasing cost of financing trade. But the merchant bankers who acted as the financial intermediaries came to use these long-established bills of exchange to create their own financial market where the bills and other claims on the physical stock associated with international trade became negotiable and transferable.

The merchant bankers were interested in profit, but their financial innovations became inextricably linked with the activities of the rulers of the emerging modern states who were concerned not with profit but with the projection of power, both inside and outside of the state. The successful projection of power was expensive and financial innovations were required to meet the escalating costs incurred by the emerging modern states. A key innovation was initiated by the Hapsburg Empire in the first half of the sixteenth century when Charles V pledged taxes in Holland to service a new source of finance for the crown in the form of heritable annuities. Other modern states followed suit, endeavouring to cover their mounting debts, almost invariably incurred as the result of wars, by encouraging individuals to lend them money, for example, through the issue of Exchequer or Treasury Bills (Kindleberger 1984: ch. 9). Because these state annuities were transferable, they were suitable for resale, giving rise to financial intermediaries who were willing to buy and sell them, and thereby generating a capital market. These intermediaries dispersed throughout Europe and they were

able to 'operate across market boundaries, whether defined by geography, language, religion, or political authority' (Neal 1990: 4).

Two key financial innovations were in place by the end of the sixteenth century.

- capital, in the form of bills of exchange, could be moved from one country to another quickly and safely;
- the market in annuities had facilitated the process of long-term investment.

These two innovations joined forces with the creation of joint stock companies initiated by the Dutch East India Company at the beginning of the seventeenth century. The initial stockholders in the company each provided a share of the non-refundable capital on which they then received an annual dividend. Unsurprisingly, therefore, like bills of exchange, the shares entered the emerging international capital market where they were bought and sold. The East India Company followed the lead of the Dutch East India Company, and the accumulation of wealth in London during the seventeenth century encouraged the formation of other joint stock companies. By the end of the century, a hundred new companies had been formed (Kindleberger 1984: 196), and by 1681, if not earlier, the prices of shares sold on the London Stock Exchange were being published every week (Neal 1990: 21). In 1723, at the latest, shares in the chartered joint stock companies were being traded simultaneously in the London and Amsterdam stock exchanges (Neal 1990: 141). For the next seventy years neither country attempted to promote an independent monetary policy with the result that the two capital markets became increasingly integrated. As Neal (1990: 165) notes, 'two remark-ably modern capital markets were permitted to interact in an unfettered (and hence unmodern) fashion'. But with the French Revolution and the Napoleonic era, these international capital markets disintegrated and although a process of reintegration did slowly take place, two centuries were to pass before unfettered international capital markets were to be restored (Neal 1990: 229–30).

A crucial feature behind the reintegration of international capital markets was the promotion of foreign direct investment which became a notable feature of international economic process in the nineteenth century and a major one in the twentieth century. As always it is possible to find antecedents in the Middle Ages, as the Peruzzi family's super firm mentioned earlier illustrates. But not until the nineteenth century was there sustained interest in gaining access to foreign markets through direct investment rather than through trade. Foreign direct investment occurs according to Kindleberger (1984: 262) 'when the investor keeps control and makes decisions for foreign enterprise from abroad'. Initially, much of the investment was in developing the infrastructure of other counties. British firms, for example, played a major role in building the railways in India and parts of Latin America. But over time there was an increasing interest in setting up manufacturing plants abroad. Kindleberger argues that given the difficulties in communications that still persisted in the middle of the nineteenth century 'what is baffling is not why there was so little direct investment in manufacturing before 1850, but how there happened to be so much in finance' (Kindleberger 1984: 263). Nevertheless, the figures demonstrate that foreign direct investment increased steadily during the nineteenth century and spectacularly in the twentieth century. For example, British FDI during the nineteenth century rose from $500 million in 1825 to $12.1 billion in 1900 and $19.5 billion by 1915. Much of this was in the Americas, and it was not until the Second World War that the USA shifted from being a net debtor to Europe (Woodruff 1966: 120, 150). According to Dunning (1983: 87) the total estimated stock of accumulated FDI worldwide was $14.3 billion in 1914, $26.4 billion in 1938, $66.7 billion in 1960, $172.1 billion in 1971, and $392.8 billion in 1978. UNCTAD (1993: 14; 1996: 5) takes the figures up to $999 billion in 1987 and $2,730 billion in 1995, an increase of 191 times since 1914. During the mid-1980s the average annual outflow of FDI had reached $77 billion, rising to $318 billion by 1995 (UNCTAD 1996: 4).

These dramatic developments in economic process have occurred within an international monetary system that displays the same underlying features and problems that existed in the fifteenth and sixteenth centuries. Throughout this period a distinction has persisted between money that circulates within the boundaries of modern states and internationally valid currency which is exchanged among merchants, firms, and states. As one of the most perceptive students of money has observed, the distinction generates 'a problem of our times, as much as it was the problem of the past' (Vilar 1976: 15). National states have endeavoured to overcome this problem by linking the value of national currencies to the value of gold or silver. But gold and silver, of course, are commodities which have a market value. In the fifteenth century, for example, the price of gold rose throughout Europe, so that anyone possessing gold could buy an increasing volume of goods with the same amount of gold. During the course of the century, as a consequence, new sources of gold were sought and found in West Africa. Columbus's search for gold at the end of the century was to be even more successful, with the Americas proving to be a major source of gold and more especially silver (Vilar 1976: 64–5). The increasing volume of gold and silver did not allay the fears of many Europeans, because they were aware that gold and silver coins were constantly being drained out of Europe to pay for the goods being imported from the East (the Chinese preferred specie to bullion). The fear was understandable because the gold available at any point in time has always been very limited. It is estimated that the amount of gold available in Europe in 1500 was 8 cubic metres (10.5 cubic yards) (2 metres each way) and by 1905 the total volume of gold taken from the earth through world history only equalled 1,000 cubic metres (1,300 cubic yards) (10 metres each way). The quantity of gold has never equalled the total money circulation (Vilar 1976: 19). As we have seen, however, the financial revolution precipitated during the sixteenth century reduced the need for specie in conducting national and international financial transactions. This is not the place to tell the complex story, still far from fully understood, of how governments have endeavoured over the centuries to deal with the problems of maintaining a stable currency (see Vilar 1976), but it is worth noting that from the late sixteenth century onwards, European states began to establish central banks in an attempt to end the monetary disorder precipitated by private banks. The Bank of England, for example, was formed for this purpose in 1694 (Vilar 1976: 213), marking a further step in the direction of centralizing and institutionalizing the state. The British thereby laid the basis for what was to become the world monetary system based on the gold standard and bank notes. Paper money increased liquidity, but only at the cost of creating major problems of managing inflation and interest rates, a set of issues that often put national interests in tension with the stability of the international financial system. The cost of mismanaging this tension was graphically demonstrated by the great crash of 1929 (Gilpin 1987: 118–31).

Particularly in the twentieth century, financial affairs have grown to a dominant position in the global economy, outpacing even the enormous growth in trade. The expansion of credit has proved a great stimulus to production and trade, but only at the cost of massive erosion of national economic autonomy, and sustained concern about the potential instability of the whole international financial system. According to UNCTAD (1994: 128), the gross size of the international banking market rose from 12.4 per cent of world trade in 1964 to 215.6 per cent in 1991, and it is now frequently observed that the value of trading on the world's currency markets exceeds the value of trade by 40 times or more. The size of these financial flows makes it impossible to insulate national economies from the global money markets, and the financial crash in East Asia in 1997–8 was a painful reminder of the dark side of the huge expansion of global financial processes. After the Second World War, serious attempts were made to put in place international institutions that would prevent a repeat of the economic disaster of the inter-war years. The Bretton Woods system liberalized trade, while stabilizing exchange rates and putting firm controls on finance, a formula that allowed the development of the welfare state (Ruggie 1982). This system rested on the hegemony of the US economy and currency, and for a time proved a solution to the management problem. But this solution carried its own problems, and was undermined both by the relative weakening of the US economy, and by America's exploitation of its hegemonic position. By the 1970s US leadership was coming unravelled, exchange rates were floating, and the restraints on international finance were being hacked away (Gilpin 1987: 142–70). By the end of the twentieth century, economic processes were dominated by finance, and it remained unclear whether or not the self-regulation mechanisms of the global financial system were adequate to control the instabilities inherent in the ongoing attempt to devise new and more sophisticated forms of credit such as futures and derivatives.

These financial developments point to increasing interdependence within, and integration of, the global economy on a basis of processes other than trade. By the 1990s, global capital had become sufficiently powerful and necessary that wooing it was a main task of governments. The need for states at all levels of development to appear attractive to international capital in terms of acquiring investments and loans had repercussions that extended deep into domestic political and social life. The great intensification of economic processes, and the consequent rise in economic interdependence and integration amongst national economies, generated a whole new array of economic problems as an element of mainstream international relations. The increasingly integrated global economy delivered prosperity for unprecedented numbers, but it also delivered inequality and marginalization for many, and an increasingly complex and massive global management task. The pressures on states easily pushed them into competitive exporting of the burdens of adjustment through exchange rates, tariffs, and employment policy. If joint gains were one side of intensified economic interaction, then 'beggar-thy-neighbour' strategies were the other.

The character of contemporary economic interdependence suggests that the old rule that economic systems are always larger in scale than military-political ones has not disappeared with the achievement of global scale but simply changed form. Within the closed confines of a global system, the new rule seems to be that economic systems outpace military-political ones in their degree of intensity. More on this in Chapter 15.

Liberals view the economic processes associated with interdependence as having broadly benign and positive connotations. But there is a darker side to the coin. Interdependence is also associated with uneven development. Lenin (1996) conceptualized uneven development as an inherent feature of the final stage of capitalism. But, in fact, it is widely acknowledged that all market structures create uneven development as a natural part of their operation. In the global economy, market structures have had the effect of producing a centre–periphery pattern of uneven development on a planetary scale. At the centre are situated rich, well-organized, and powerful societies, while the periphery is made up of poor, chaotic, and weak societies. And, as Lenin indicated, this process formation spawns struggles both between centre and periphery, and within the centre for dominance.

We agree with Lenin that this centre periphery formation is radically different from the zonal arrangement of ancient and classical times. For the periphery, and for both better and worse, the global market puts the whole question of development on the system level as much as or more than on the local one. But we do not see this development in structural terms. It is a process formation, although, as a consequence, here lies the whole debate about the causes of and cures for underdevelopment, with some seeing the centre as responsible for underdeveloping the periphery (*dependencia* thesis), and others seeing the centre as the main hope for developing a periphery that has fallen behind in part because of its own local

The logic of these numbers is one explanation for the emergence of forum IGOs, both global, like the League of Nations and the UN, and regional, like the Organization of African Unity and the Arab League, sketched in Chapter 13. Such organizations allow the poorer members of the system to conduct their diplomacy at a small number of central locations. Indeed, regional IGOs, as well as the UN, have played crucial roles in holding the fragile subsystems of post-colonial states in place and giving their boundaries time to set. IGOs also play an increasingly important role in meeting the complex management problems generated by the huge expansion of the global political economy. These range from economic monitoring and assistance (IMF, IBRD), through the making, setting, and adjudication of rules of conduct (WTO, ICJ), and the allocation of scarce resources such as transmission wavelengths and satellite orbits (INTEL-SAT, ITU), to arms control monitoring and inspection (IAEA). Since the logic of the n(n–1) formula also applies to the problem of language translation, it explains both the enduring attraction of lingua francas, and the economic necessity for IGOs of restricting interpretation and translation services to a few key languages: six at the UN: English, French, Russian, Chinese, Spanish, and Arabic (the latter specially paid for by the Arab states).

At the individual (world society) level, international societal interaction is basically about cross-cultural contact. The structural question is about the impact of this contact on identity. It is undeniable that there has been a huge increase in the amount of contact amongst individuals worldwide. As in the other sectors, this increase has ridden on the back of improvements in interaction capacity. In the early centuries of this era, cross-cultural contact increased as (mainly) European explorers and traders encountered other peoples and cultures for the first time. European explorers quite quickly opened up the whole world to 'first contact', and they were followed by traders and settlers who deepened the contact and made it permanent. There was a strong element of unevenness in this process because the Europeans met all of the rest of the world, whereas most of the rest of the world met only the Europeans. And many of these contacts were disastrous for the non-Europeans. Some were obliterated by disease or military action, some were pushed aside by settlers or captured and sold as slaves, and many were politically and economically subjugated.

As the global international system unfolded and intensified, so the level and variety of cross-cultural contact increased. Initially, such contact was largely carried by people, but with the rise of the mass media it became more and more a matter of dominant cultures being transmitted directly. As transportation became more efficient, more and more people moved either under coercion or voluntarily from one continent to another. As they did so, both ethnic and cultural mixing became more common. Again this mixing was uneven. Most of the people moving around in the system were Europeans, whether as traders, settlers, soldiers, missionaries, or colonial administrators. With the transportation revolutions of the nineteenth century Europeans (and particularly British and Irish, who comprised nearly a third of the total) migrated abroad in huge numbers. Woodruff (1966: 61, 103, 106–8) estimates that between 1851 and 1960, the United States and Canada received more than 40 million immigrants from Europe, another 6.5 million went to South America, and 2.5 million to Australia and New Zealand. Nearly one million went to Africa, mostly to South Africa and Algeria. Russia sent 15 million settlers eastward into Siberia. The peak of the flow was just before the First World War, when 1.5 million Europeans a year emigrated abroad, more or less coinciding with the demographic peak of European population, which topped out at nearly 27 per cent of the world total (up from 20 per cent in 1750) (see Maps 14.1 and 14.2). Since Europeans were generally in dominant positions, this meant that Western culture was strongly transmitted worldwide. Elites in most parts of the world, and in many places also substantial parts of the wider population, were exposed to Western culture either through education, or during recent decades via the global media (press, radio, TV) which are also Western dominated.

*A civilisational perspective on European world domination*
Some writers (Hodgson 1993: 19–28) take the view that modernist universalism takes over from around 1800, bringing Europe into pre-eminence and ending the agrarian age. Hodgson (1993: 44–71, 207–24) argues that a revolution of 'technicalization' occurred in Europe from the sixteenth to eighteenth centuries, creating new and more complex economic and political institutions based on rationalism, and marking a shift of power from landed classes to commercial ones. By the beginning of the nineteenth century, Europe had not only caught up with the institutions of classical civilization, but surpassed them. Once this revolution was under way, it accelerated the speed of history in the Occident, and pre-empted similar developments elsewhere. Other civilizations could not repeat the European development both because they lacked its antecedents and because they were under severe and immediate pressure from its expanded presence and power. As the development gap opened up, especially during the eighteenth and even more so the nineteenth centuries, it created the power differentials that underpinned an increasingly easy European imperialism. From a Western perspective, the classical world seemed static and stagnant, but the reality was simply a difference in the pace of development, with Europe transforming itself on a scale of decades, compared with change measured at a pace of centuries in the classical world (Chase-Dunn 1994: 86–92). This disjuncture parallels that between the onset of cities and civilizations in the ancient and classical world, and the hunter-gatherer peoples that it left behind. Many elements in the European development came from the classical

world, but that world was unable either to adapt to, or emulate, the modernist revolution in Europe. By the late eighteenth century, many of the Asian polities were becoming weak compared to the European state. Despite the impressive size and products of its economy, China never developed an efficient tax base. In India, the success of the societal structure (caste system) resulted in shallow state roots and a recurrent inability to defend the area. The Islamic world failed to develop a stable state structure (Hall and Ikenberry 1989: 22–34).

The Islamic and Chinese civilizations, both of which saw themselves as dominant world cultures, suffered a 'sense of radical spiritual defeat' as Western power surged around them (Hodgson 1993: 224). In the case of Islam, the early period of European expansion corresponds to the height of Islamic power, 1503–1800, when three Islamic empires (Ottoman, Safavid, Timurid) held sway from the eastern Mediterranean to South Asia. Islam had undergone a tremendous period of expansion 1258–1503 taking in Anatolia, the Balkans, India, and swaths of South-East Asia and Africa. But in the eighteenth century, as Europe was reaching its peak, the Islamic world was in decline. Splits between Sunni and Shi'a Islam manifested in, and reinforced, enervating conflict between the Ottoman and Safavid (Persian) Empires, and the fundamentally land-based Islamic empires did little to resist European penetration by sea (Hodgson 1993: 194–204). Jones (1987: 161) argues that nearly all of the great Asian civilizations were burdened by extractive military despotisms (Ottoman, Mughal, Manchu) originating in invasions.

Unlike most classical agrarian civilizations, Islam was supportive of merchant culture and became a successful merchant religion based on mobile trading and investment. The Islamic world played a central role in the Eurasian trading system. One reason for this was that the Arab-Islamic system unusually favoured town and trade over country and agriculture, allowing a greater role for tribal and merchant elites, and not just agricultural ones. Despite this inclination, and despite its early development of sophisticated financial instruments such as bills of exchange, the Islamic world failed to develop property rights, a clear legal order, or independent guilds or merchant associations (Anderson 1974b: 496–520). Although the Ottoman Empire had quite vigorous internal production and trade, its finances were crude, and it did not keep up with developments in money, credit, and banking in Europe (Braudel 1985: 467–84). And one cost of the bias towards town and trade was a general failure to advance, or even maintain, the irrigation systems on which the earlier agricultural prosperity of the Middle East had rested (Anderson 1974b: 496–520; Diamond 1997: 409). The Islamic world's failure to construct political institutions stable enough to guarantee the fixed investments necessary for industrial investment became a liability once the European modernization based on such investments had begun. The contradiction between religion and politics in the Islamic world blocked its path to modernization because while it was socially cohesive it was politically incoherent, lacking both clear boundaries and well-rooted states (Hodgson 1993: 97–125, 176–94; Ferguson and Mansbach 1996: 301–23; Hall and Ikenberry 1989: 22–34).

Western culture picked up elements from the many other cultures it encountered, but these other cultures did not have that much contact with each other. The major exception to this rule was when the Western system moved other peoples to other continents: between 10 and 15 million Africans to the Americas (with another 4 million moved by Arabs to the Middle East) (Austen 1988: 29, 33; Segal 1993: 54; Lovejoy 1996: 497; Curtin 1969: 3, 268; Castles and Miller 1993: 48); and perhaps 3 million Indians to Africa and the Caribbean (Castles and Miller 1993: 49). Other peoples took advantage of the new transportation links to migrate: perhaps 20 million Chinese to South-East Asia, and several hundred thousand Chinese and Japanese to the Americas (Segal 1993: 16–18) (see Maps 14.2 and 14.3).

Not until decolonization did any kind of balance begin to appear in global societal interaction. After 1945, outward migration of settlers from the West faded away, and a counter-flow of peoples from the third world into Europe and North America began. Over 8 million people from Latin American and the Caribbean migrated to the USA between 1945 and 1980 (Segal 1993: 25), and during the 1990s, both Europe and the USA were receiving more than a million migrants per year (SOPEMI 1995: 195, 240). With the economic rise of Japan and the East Asian NICs during the 1970s and 1980s non-western peoples began to flow around the whole system, rather than just their own region, as traders, tourists, and students in substantial numbers.

In recent decades some of the forms of this interaction have changed. While physical interaction capacity continues to increase, political and societal barriers to population mobility have risen sharply. Migrations from the West to the rest of the world have largely ceased, and migrations from the rest of the world to the West, though they still take place, face ever higher barriers. Much migration is now between neighbouring states and is in response to local conflicts or ecological crises. In 1994 there were some 16 million refugees, more than two-thirds of them in Africa and the Middle East, sheltering in countries neighbouring their own (*World Refugee Survey*, 1995). Travel for business and tourism remains high, and access to global media continues to spread and deepen. The rise of the internet during the 1990s as a kind of global public service still reflects Western dominance in its content and centre–periphery structure. But in principle, and increasingly in practice, the internet offers the prospect of open access from anywhere to anywhere else, thus removing the unevenness that has for so long put the West at the centre of societal interaction.

One measure of the degree to which this expansion of societal process has

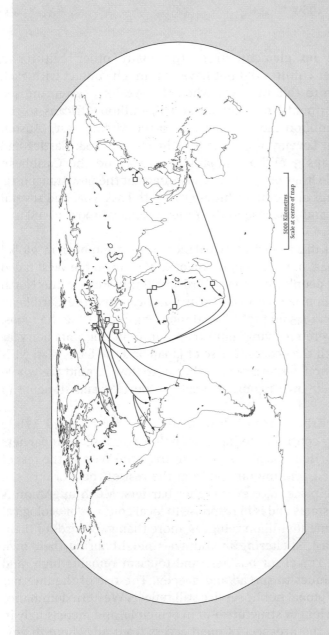

5000 Kilometres
Scale at centre of map

*Note:* The map identifies the main voluntary migrations over three centuries from 1500. Most of the migrants were from Western Europe. But there was also a significant movement of Chinese into Taiwan from the seventeenth century onwards. There were also several important shifts in population within Africa.

*Map 14.1 Global voluntary migrations: 1500–1814*

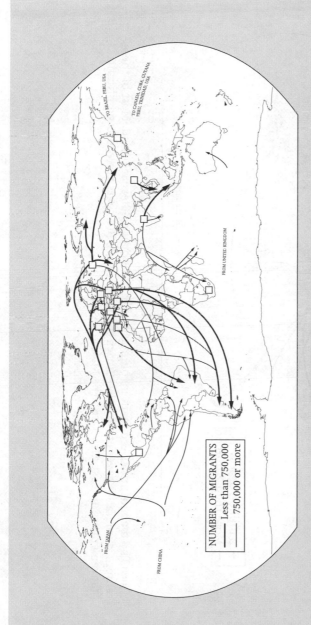

TO BRAZIL, PERU, USA

TO CANADA, CUBA, GUYANA
PERU, TRINIDAD, USA

FROM UNITED KINGDOM

FROM JAPAN

FROM CHINA

NUMBER OF MIGRANTS
Less than 750,000
750,000 or more

*Note:* The map identifies the main voluntary migrations in the nineteenth and early twentieth centuries. Most were from Western and Eastern Europe. But there were also significant migrations from Japan, China, and India, although two thirds of the four million Indians who migrated to Malaya returned to India.

*Map 14.2 Global Migrations: 1815 – 1914*

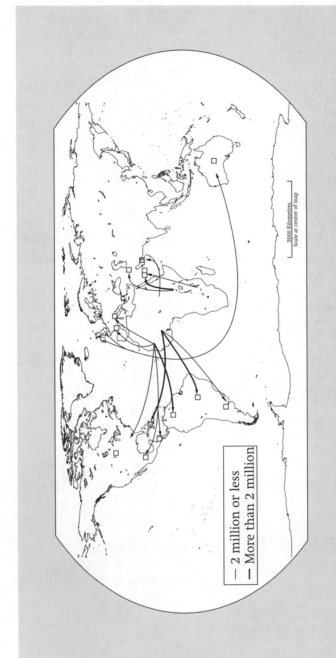

*Note:* The map identifies the main involuntary migrations over a 400-year period. Most of these enforced migrations were from West Africa to the Americas. But there were also significant movements from East Africa into the Middle East.

*Map 14.3  World involuntary migrations: 1500–1900*

pervaded the international system is that we now live in a world in which encounters with the truly foreign are becoming almost unknown for Westerners, and are increasingly rare even for the cultures in the periphery. Contrast this with the situation just 500 years ago, and for all of previous human history, when most of the world beyond one's immediate sphere was either totally or largely unknown, and contact with the truly foreign defined the work of explorers and traders. But as will be shown in the next chapter, this undeniably large expansion of societal interaction, and the unprecedented intermingling of cultures and civilizations, has so far had rather little structural effect.

## 5. ENVIRONMENTAL PROCESS

In the environmental sector, the story of process during the modern era is very much a mixture of old and new, but with the old getting, for the most part, less serious, and the new becoming dominant. Continuity with the past is represented primarily by the continued role of disease transmission along trade routes. There have been two new developments: first a massive mixing of previously separated flora and fauna; and second a rising impact of pollution on the ecosphere.

Disease transmission peaked with the major role played by Eurasian diseases such as measles, typhus, and smallpox, and African ones such as malaria and yellow fever, in the European conquest of the Americas. These diseases devastated the native peoples, both civilized and tribal, often spreading ahead of direct contact between the natives and the new arrivals. Because they lacked large herds of domesticated herd animals (a key source of disease pools in Eurasia) native Americans had little immunity to the diseases that came with conquistadores and colonists from Europe, and later with slaves from Africa. Some 95 per cent of a native American population of perhaps 100 million in 1500 was wiped out, mostly by disease, in the century and a half following the first contact with Europe (McNeill 1976: 185–216; Diamond 1997: 67–81, 195–214; Crosby 1986: ch. 9).

*Depopulation of the New World*
Our image of the pre-Columbian Amerindians that occupied North America is heavily influenced by textbook accounts of US history and the representations found in popular culture. The Amerindians are almost invariably depicted as living in relatively small unstratified tribal societies. Such an assessment was not far off the mark when the United States was founded. But it provides a highly inaccurate picture of large sectors of North America in the millennium before the arrival of the Europeans. In the south-east, for example, a wide range of different cultures that are now collectively known as the Mound Builders were operating at the level of the Sumerians just before the city-state system

described in Chapter 8 emerged. At Cahokia, one of the great ceremonial centres of this region, it is estimated that there was a settlement of an estimated 40,000 people organized on a steeply hierarchical class base. The first Europeans who traversed the region observed densely populated settlements set in extensively cultivated fields. By the time the Europeans started to settle the area, at the start of the eighteenth century, it was an empty wilderness. Only a few scattered tribes of Amerindians remained. The explanation for this catastrophe is almost certainly epidemic disease. As Crosby (1986: 213) observes, 'No other factor seems capable of having exterminated so many people over such a large part of North America.'

Disease transmission continues to be a problem during the modern era. A severe epidemic of pneumonia killed some 20 million people after the First World War, and the last decade of the twentieth century has heard a continuous drumbeat about the spread of AIDS, and the danger that more easily transmitted and more quickly fatal plagues such as the Ebola virus might spread out of Africa. But although the mechanisms of disease transmission are still in place, the twentieth century has seen great advances in medicine that have taken much of the sting out of diseases—at least for the developed world. Only if these defences suffer severe breakdown—such as the feared rise of bacteria immune to all available antibiotics—will disease transmission regain its former standing as the leading international environmental process.

  In the meantime, the opening up of a global international system, and particularly the development of a global economy, and widespread European migration and settlement, created new types of environmental interaction. As we have already described in the previous section, the making of a global international system involved an unprecedented cultural and genetic mixing amongst the races and nations of humankind. A very similar, but much more wide-ranging, process of transportation and mixing was also going on amongst the world's flora and fauna. This was particularly so in relation to food crops and animals, and animals used for transportation, but also applied to a great range of other plants and animals: tropical birds taken to Europe as pets, Asian and American trees and shrubs likewise transported for use in ornamental and botanical gardens. This process was not entirely new. Within the Eurasian-African trading system, some plants and animals had been moved from their native ranges during ancient and classical times (horses, yams, bananas, rice). But now it became worldwide, occurred on a much larger scale, and had a much greater impact on the local ecology and economy. From the Eurasian system to the Americas went horses, cattle, pigs, sheep, sugar cane, rice, wheat, barley, oats, tea, coffee, bananas, citrus fruits, peaches, and yams. From the Americas to Eurasia went maize, potatoes, tobacco, cacao, several varieties of bean, manioc, sweet potato, peanuts, pine-apples, tomatoes, and cotton (Woodruff 1966: 170; Barraclough 1978: 155).

The impact of these transfers was often dramatic. Horses transformed the life-style of the Plains Indians in the Americas, and new crops greatly increased the food supply in China, Europe, and Africa, as well as opening up new sectors of trade in the world economy. There were also very substantial changes to global ecology, with new arrivals sometimes displacing local species and often occupying huge tracts of land when taken up as food or industrial crops. In the longer run, the focus on a limited number of commercial crops and animals tended to reduce bio-diversity, building up to a possible assault on the structure of the biosphere. The processes of mass biota transfer initiated during the sixteenth century are ongoing. Species of mollusc and fish are carried from one continent to another in the ballast tanks of ships creating local environmental problems (e.g. in the Great Lakes). Intentional attempts at bio-engineering, as when foreign species are imported in order to try to improve production (the African bee into South America) or attack some local or imported pest (disease control against Australian rabbits), also involve continued mixing of the world's biota.

The second new form of environmental interaction has arisen only during the last few decades, but has the potential to make major impacts on the operation of the international system. Part of it is about the depletion of resources such as soil, fresh water, forests, and minerals, but the main thread concerns pollution arising from human activities and impacting on the composition and operation of the planetary ecosphere and climate systems. The cause is a combination of rising human population, spreading industrialization, and increasing per capita con-sumption of a wider range of products both agricultural and manufactured. The effect is to move what can broadly be referred to as 'the environment' from the background to the foreground of human affairs. For most of human history the environment has been either a background constant, or, if it did change, a force with its own logic of climate change or local catastrophe (flood, drought, volcano, meteorite, earthquake, tidal wave, ice age) about which humans could do little but pray, die, adapt, or move. It is noteworthy that the entire span of human civilization has taken place during an interglacial period, when the planetary climate has been both relatively benign and relatively stable.

But during the last few decades, realization has grown that human activity has now reached sufficient scale and intensity that our total activity as a species is capable of changing the composition of the atmosphere and thus, *inter alia*, of altering the planetary climate. There is of course a local dimension to this in which pollution spillovers such as smoke, acid rain, radioactive fallout, or fouled lakes, rivers, and seas become an issue in regional international relations. But the bigger concern is with impacts on the global environment as a whole. The two defining cases here have been the deterioration of the protective ozone layer first noticed during the 1980s, and the apparent (still contested, but increasingly accepted) trend towards global warming. The thinning of the ozone layer over the poles exposed the people and other living things below it to higher, and health threatening, levels of solar radiation. The cause of the thinning was clearly identifiable as a number of ozone-destroying industrial gases reaching the upper atmosphere, and this precipitated international action to reduce the emission of these gases. Global warming threatens at best some noticeable rises in sea level (say up to a metre) and some marked changes in climate (the currently fashionable el Niño effects). At worst it threatens huge rises in sea level (tens of metres), major transformations of climate, and a wholesale change in the nature of the planet as a venue for human habitation. The causes are less clear (given still quite large uncertainties about the natural operation of the global climate system), but at least in good part relate to emissions of gases such as $CO_2$ and methane. Since such gases are generated by very many mainstream industrial and agricultural processes, reducing them requires big, costly, and difficult changes in the global economy, and as yet there is no consensus about what action can or should be taken.

What is clear is that by the late twentieth century pollution of air and water by the scale of industrial and agricultural production was introducing a wholly new element of environmental process into international relations. Human activity was redefining the biosphere, the atmosphere and the climate. Such things had happened locally in earlier times, but human-generated environmental processes were now able to threaten the natural structures of the planet. Environmental issues thus also created a new agenda for international diplomacy, and a new focus for IGOs and INGOs. Like developments in the economic sector, the rise of global environmental problems confronted humankind with a new, durable, and system-wide management problem. Failure to respond to this management problem carried the threat of massive disruptions to the functioning and development of the international system.

# 6. CONCLUSIONS

It is clear that international process has undergone a phenomenal transformation during the last 500 years. Up to a point, this transformation can be explained by the twelvefold multiplication of the human population between 1500 and 2000, but this is obviously not the whole story. More people means more interaction almost by definition, but what we have witnessed here is a multiplication of a quite different order. Because of the industrial revolution, and everything associated with it, each individual is empowered to do more things: travel further and faster, consume more, produce more, transport more, know more, communicate more, love and hate more widely, destroy more. This empowerment has been distributed very unevenly. Hundreds of millions of people in poor countries still have little more individual impact than their forebears from ancient and classical, or even prehistoric, times. But hundreds of millions more have greatly increased opportunities, and a few have almost godlike powers to create and destroy on a planetary scale. Following this uneven pattern, much of the international process of the modern era fits into the centre–periphery model sketched out in the introduction to this chapter. Most economic and societal interaction fits the model closely, and so also does much of the process in the military-political sector. But some does not, most obviously the systemic aspects of the environmental sector. While the causes of environmental change might be related to the centre–periphery model, the consequences operate planet wide, distributing their effects with no reference to the social, political, military, and economic patterns of humankind.

Yet despite the transformations of scale and intensity, the basic framework of international process remains familiar. We are easily able to tell the story using the same headings as those for the ancient and classical era, and many of the main types of process from older times—trade, war, military competition, disease transmission, diplomacy, belief systems—remain prominent. But across the board there is huge expansion and intensification of these processes, and several new branches spring up within the main categories: arms control and disarmament, IGOs, international finance and investment, pollution, biological mixing. With the closure of the global international system during the nineteenth century, intensification and diversification replace expansion as the principal means along which process develops. And as the impact of the industrial revolution really begins to bite during the nineteenth and twentieth centuries, the overall pattern of interaction that defines the international system begins to change. War, which had always been central, remains so almost throughout this period, but towards the very end of it faces serious pressures both from the excesses of its means of destruction and from the impact of spreading democratization. From the late twentieth century onwards, it was not unreasonable to think that great power war—world war—might never occur again. At the same time, interaction in other sectors was growing both in absolute and relative importance. The expansion of economic process was unprecedented by any measure, and although less superficially impressive, so also was the expansion of societal processes. Much of environmental process was too new to evaluate properly. It clearly contained the potential to become a central feature in the operation of the international system, but whether it would do so or not remained hard to predict.

What all this added up to was a strong case for thinking about the balance of the processes that define the international system. All experienced terrific growth during these five centuries. But at the very least, the balance amongst them was changing, with non-military processes making relative gains. Under the general heading of 'globalization' it became fashionable to debate whether or not this amounted to a case for an unprecedented sectoral transformation in the nature of the international system. More on this in Part V.

# Chapter 15

# STRUCTURE IN THE MODERN INTERNATIONAL SYSTEM

## 1. INTRODUCTION

From the story told in the three preceding chapters—stronger units, uneven development, enormous increases in interaction capacity, huge intensification, and diversification of process—one might well anticipate that system structure also became stronger during this era. This is indeed the case. Although structure is different from interaction capacity and process, it nevertheless depends on them. If interaction capacity is low, or process thin, then structural effects will be small. But as both of these things surged forward during the last half of the second millennium AD, they expanded and energized system structures across the board.

It helps at this point to recall that international systems are composed of units interacting within a structure. In order to simplify the jumble of something as complicated as an international system we are following the neorealist practice of looking at systems in terms of their dominant units and the dominant type of interaction. One way of understanding what happened to the international system during the modern era is to observe the changes in the basic design of the system that took place. Not only did the system become global, but the lines of contact amongst the units within it became much more numerous and much fuller. In the ancient and classical era it was not uncommon for systems to be linear, and for much interaction to be indirect. One example of this is the Eurasian economic system connecting Rome and China, in which, for the most part, each major unit was in direct contact only with its neighbours, but goods moved in relay fashion down the line. Military-political relations could also take linear form, as in the early modern case of the Ottoman Empire fighting both the Europeans and the Persians, while the latter had hardly any direct contact with each other. As noted in Part I, systems with this arrangement are not structured in any Waltzian sense. During the modern era the international system became multiordinate, and all of these constraints were swept away. In principle, and mostly in practice, each of the units in the international system could relate directly to all of the others. Thus Portugal and Spain could trade directly with China by sending their ships to East Asia. Britain and Japan could make an alliance in order to co-ordinate their mutual rivalry with Russia. In forums such as the League of Nations or the UN, and their many specialized functional offshoots, diplomats from all of the recognized units in the system could gather to discuss the operation of the global system, and to make laws and treaties to standardize their behaviour, improve the interoperability of the units in the system, or confront common problems of system management.

In this way, the system itself became much stronger in relation to the units. Units now related directly (for better or worse) with all of the others in the system, and not just with their neighbours. Whether in terms of military security, trade, or recognition of political status, all units found themselves having to deal with a much wider, more varied, and in many ways more penetrative international system from which there was no escape. Many peoples and countries found themselves forced to participate by the arrival of superior European/Western power on their doorstep. Even when relations became considerably less directly coercive, as in the late twentieth century, it was still not possible for units to isolate themselves from the system without paying a very high price. Although units also became stronger during this period (and for many of the same reasons of improved interaction capacity and enriched process within their boundaries), there can be little doubt that overall there was a relative shift in favour of the system. Both the units and the system became absolutely stronger and more capable. But the system became relatively more pervasive, more penetrative, and more powerful. The local became steadily weaker, and the regional and global steadily stronger. As this happened, system structural effects became stronger, shoving and shaping the units, and shifting the balance of the forces determining their development from inside to outside.

## 2. MILITARY-POLITICAL STRUCTURE

The story of military-political structure during the modern era can largely be told in the familiar terms of neorealist theory. As in the ancient and classical world, there is intense military interaction, but with the difference of a rising technological content (and therefore rising cost and destructiveness, and increasing disparities of power), and a shift from regional to global range. But unlike in the ancient and classical era, the neorealist predictions are fulfilled: one type of unit does become universally dominant, and the system retains a stable anarchic structure with no sign of a deep structure shift to hierarchy. These two developments feed into each other, with the fierce independence of modern states working to support the maintenance of international anarchy, and the anarchic structural pressure of self-help pushing the units towards the 'look after yourself' imperative identified by Waltz (1979: 107).

The rise to dominance of the modern state, and the demise of other types of military political unit, was covered in Chapter 12. In structural terms it is about socialization and competition producing like units. Its essence is the emergence of a new type of unit that proves to be more effective both economically and militarily than other types. From a slow start in what until then had been one of the more obscure corners of the planet, the modern state makes a swift rise to world power. In Europe, the modern state steadily outcompetes city-states and empires, forcing both either to give up or change their form. Abroad, the new European states embark on an unprecedented expansion which at one time or another brings nearly the whole planet under their sway. In the Americas they quickly obliterate both the local empires and (also later in Australia) much of the native population, and set about a colonization process that eventually produces more than two dozen European-style states. In the civilized zone of Asia they either occupy the local empires, becoming a new ruling elite (as in India and most of South-East Asia), or break them up (the Ottoman Empire, and closer to home the Austro-Hungarian one), or subordinate and manipulate them without actually assuming direct rule (Persia and China). In Africa, and the pre-international system areas of Asia, they carve out colonies and impose boundaries and sovereignty on a diverse array of tribal peoples with greatly varied levels of political and economic development. The few places that escape direct take-overs (Japan, Turkey, China, Thailand, Persia) are forced to adapt to the European model in order to preserve their independence.

A few of the classical empires survive by taking on state-like appearances (China, Iran, Ethiopia) as does one of the modern empires that grows up on the periphery of Europe (Russia). All of the leading modern states in Europe, and most of the minor European powers as well, acquire overseas empires, in the process stamping both their languages and their political and economic practices onto the peoples under their rule. But all of them (even, up to a point, Russia) eventually surrender their empires, with the various waves of decolonization leaving behind a global political system structured in Europe's image (modern states), based on European ideas (sovereignty, nationalism), and operating according to European practices (diplomacy, international law). No more comprehensive demonstration of neorealist structural logic could be desired. The logic of anarchy works by socialization and competition (i.e. a mixture of coercion and copying) to produce a system of like units which in return reproduce the anarchic structure. And this structure continues to operate, in the process increasing the depth of 'likeness'. The history of the twentieth century can be read as a struggle about how the political economy of industrial society would be organized, with monarchy, fascism, and communism losing out to liberal democracy in a series of wars both hot and cold (Buzan 1995a; Hobsbawm 1994). In this way, by the end of the twentieth century, the main units in the system had become much more ideologically alike, all of them allowing market forces to play a central role in their political economies.

But note how neorealist logic depends both on a strong system and on units that embed its values. Remember that although the interaction requirements of neorealism were met in the international systems of the ancient and classical world, its predictions were not. In the modern era, the international system embraces its units much more intensely, and the modern state itself incorporates values that help to sustain international anarchy. The strict territoriality and fierce commitment to sovereignty of the modern state strongly underpins anarchy, as does the doctrine of nationalism as the centrepiece of political legitimacy. All of these made anti-hegemonism the natural doctrine of the European international system and its global successor. This is in sharp contrast to the unit effects in the ancient and classical world, where empire carried substantial legitimacy, and bandwagoning in pursuit of peace and order was as common as balancing to preserve independence.

So one of the defining features of the modern era is that international political structure grows strong, and its effects become pervasive. Under pressure from the system, units become structurally and functionally more alike. Those that fail to adapt disappear or are forcibly remade.

Neorealist theory puts a lot of emphasis on polarity (the number of great powers in the system) (Waltz 1979). But in a long historical perspective, polarity looks to be of fairly limited interest. Its prominence in the theory seems to have more to do with the temporary ascendance of bipolarity during the Cold War than with any long-term significance. Polarity does tell us some useful things about the dynamics of deterrence, alliance-making, and military competitions (Buzan 1987) and economic orders (hegemonic stability theory), but in the longer view it is the deep structures (anarchy-hierarchy; functional and structural differentiation of units) that carry the greater significance. In the ancient and classical world, anarchy-hierarchy is an important benchmark of system change (Watson 1992) and in the modern world the structural effect of anarchy is very prominent. Changes in the functional and structural differentiation of units seem to mark the biggest transformations of all. The medieval to modern change in Europe was defined by a shift from functionally and structurally differentiated units to functionally and structurally undifferentiated ones, and the general shift from the ancient and classical era to the modern one was defined by a shift from structurally differentiated to structurally undifferentiated units (i.e. barbarians, city-states, and empires to modern states) (Ruggie 1983; Buzan and Little 1996).

One other notable feature of the modern era has been the emergence of regional security complexes as a substructure of the global international system (Buzan and Wæver forthcoming: chs. 1–2). The formation of these regional complexes occurred as newly decolonized states, released from the overlay of external colonial powers, were forced to make their own (mostly conflictual) security relations with their neighbours. Following the logic that military and political threats travel more easily over short distances than over long ones, most newly independent states found their security concerns focused much more within their regions than outside. A variety of local rivalries (e.g. India–Pakistan, Arab–Israel, Iran–Iraq) provided the cores for these rivalries. Mouritzen (1980, 1995, 1997) argues that regional security structures will be a natural feature of any large, anarchic international system in which the units are territorially fixed rather than mobile. Wæver (1997) sees regional security complexes as a fourth tier of structure within the neorealist framework. They constitute durable features in the global international system, and often play a central role in mediating how outside powers get drawn into regional security politics. Polarity, and in some cases anarchy-hierarchy, are as structurally important within regional security complexes as they are in the international system as a whole (Buzan and Wæver forthcoming: ch. 1).

# 3. ECONOMIC STRUCTURE

The rise to prominence of a global market structure is one of the biggest differences between the modern international system and those of the ancient and classical era. In premodern times, as we saw in Chapter 11, economic interaction was too thin and too linear to generate significant structural effects. The economic international system in Eurasia was more impressive in size than in intensity. As we have seen, the making of a full global international system eventually merged the global economy into the same geographical space as the military-political one. At the same time, global economic interaction began the extraordinary rise in intensity that still continues today. The combined effect of the huge surge in interaction capacity, the overall shift from linear to multiordinate system structure, and the huge increase in trade and financial activity, rapidly empowered a global market which became an increasingly important and penetrative influence on all the actors in the system.

Like the military-political structure, this economic one also initially emanated from Europe. It can in one sense be seen as resulting from a steady expansion of the markets in Europe from local to national to global. The process of state-making in Europe involved the creation of a national market, which was partly a function of economic growth, partly of better transportation and communication, and partly of breaking down the numerous local tolls, tariffs, and inspections which worked to preserve local markets (Braudel 1985: ch. 4). It was also about providing the political-legal collective goods necessary to support a national market, such as a tolerably stable national currency, a central bank, a framework of laws about property, contracts, and finance, and an effective system of enforcement for these laws. This was the mercantilist project that was dominant in Europe until well into the nineteenth century. The most successful national economies generated pressures to extend these same processes beyond the boundaries of the state, either into empire (Hobson 1938), or into the international system at large (liberalism).

Almost certainly one of the first global markets to develop was that in gold and silver which underpinned the emergence of bills of exchange which played a crucial role in lubricating the newly formed world trading system. But the liberal project was interested in a much fuller elaboration of international trade, and this required extending to the international system the same processes that made the national market: i.e. removing tolls, tariffs, and inspections, and providing the necessary collective goods and institutions. In the absence of global government, the only way of creating and sustaining a global market was if states agreed to co-ordinate their economic policies, and create the necessary international rules, regimes, and organizations. As we saw in the previous three chapters, this was a project that got rolling during the nineteenth century, and was sometimes accomplished by agreement (mostly in the case of other Western states), and more often by coercion (especially in Africa and Asia). India was relatively easy to pene-trate because it already had a well-developed money economy, lacked domestic supplies of specie, and had a long-standing tradition of openness to trade dating back to before Roman times. China and Japan, with traditions of closure, offered more serious resistance (Braudel 1985: 489–503). The operation of this market empowered some states (particularly industrial ones), and overpowered others (especially those in the periphery, both before and after decolonization).

The effects of a global market structure are numerous and diverse and we can-not do more than sketch them briefly here. It is also the case that the global market structure is continuing its headlong intensification, and that many of its effects are yet to be either discovered or fully understood. The operation of the market creates pressure towards a single universal price for like goods (Gilpin 1987: 15–18). It overrides local economies both by challenging them with cheap imports, and by demanding from them particular types of product, and it overpowers older eco-nomic systems (barter, luxury trade, command economies). Because it ties together production, trade, and finance on a system-wide scale, a global market imposes the patterns of economic cycles on the whole system. These may be benign, as when all boom together, but they may be malign, as when the whole system crashes into recession or depression, as happened most strikingly during the 1930s. Another example is the debt crisis of the 1980s, which linked US monet-ary policy, oil politics, development policy in LDCs, and the behaviour of banks and financial markets (Gilpin 1987: ch. 8). The large literature on the many types of economic cycles reflects this system-wide connectivity of the global market, and tries to define and explain its effects. Cycles may vary in length from a few years to centuries or more, and since several different cycles are always in play the questions of how they relate to each other causally, or just how they interact with each other, have as yet no clear answers. (Braudel 1985: 70–88; Gilpin 1987: 100–11; Mager 1987; Goldstein 1988; Kleinknecht et al. 1992).

Whatever the struggles it might generate, there can be no doubt that a world market creates a system management problem that grows in size as the market becomes more extensive and more elaborate. Markets are not autonomous. They depend in various ways on political and societal structures, and yet they affect these structures in both positive and negative ways. At bottom lie the basic issues of providing stable currency, credit, rules, and security identified by Kindleberger (1981). But as the global economy grows ever more complex, more and more rules and arrangements need to be negotiated in order to facilitate interoperability and to keep it stable. As Gilpin (1987) argues at length, there are serious and permanent tensions between the territoriality and authority of state power on the one hand, and the non-territoriality of trade, money, and markets on the other. He sees an ongoing contradiction between the drive of global markets for efficiency, and both the welfare and power aspirations of states. Among other things, global markets create increasing pressure for harmonization of domestic policies as a consequence of international trade and financial regimes, and this undercuts the autonomy of the state (Gilpin 1987: 221–30). More obviously, there are the problems caused by intensifying trade competition and the increasing social and political adjustment costs it imposes on both winners and losers, and the ever-present danger that the financial system will become overextended and suffer a collapse of confidence (Buzan 1991: ch. 6; Buzan et al. 1998: ch. 5). Keeping a global market economy stable might be done by the right sort of hegemonic state, or it might be done (more problematically: Keohane 1984) by a coalition of leading states, or by international institutions. But it must be done somehow if the global market structure is to be preserved, and this management problem is one of the effects that results from an increasingly powerful economic structure.

Somewhat paradoxically, and partly in parallel with military-political regional substructures, economic regionalism can also be read as a structural effect of the global market. Because states fear both being weak actors in the world economy, and being victims of economic instability (whether caused by mismanagement or cyclical imperatives), they have incentives to create regional groupings. Such groupings can generate their own subsystems by reducing local tariffs and other barriers to trade and investment. But they can also serve to increase local bargaining power in the wider system, as in the case of Mercosur and the EU, or to act as bastions if the world economy crashes. The EU, and especially its moves towards monetary union, can be seen as in part a reaction against the instabilities and costs of the dollar hegemony (Gilpin 1987: 142–51; Helleiner 1994).

## 4. SOCIETAL STRUCTURE

As in the other sectors, the societal sector also experienced a great strengthening of structure consequent upon the huge increases in interaction. But the rise of structure was much more apparent in international society than in world society. During the nineteenth and twentieth centuries European international society and its 'standard of civilization' widened to encompass first the West, and then the global international system as a whole (Bull 1977; Bull and Watson 1984, Wight 1977; Zhang 1991; Gong 1984; Alexandrowicz 1967, 1973). This meant that the system of states became fully conscious of itself as a legal and political construct whose component parts nearly all accepted each other as being the same sort of unit as themselves. No such dramatic development took place at the world society level. Despite dramatic increases in the level of cross-cultural contact, and a sustained and powerful projection of Western culture worldwide, only the first glimmers of what might be the beginnings of a world society were visible by the end of the twentieth century.

The same forces that enlivened global neorealist and market structures also drove the creation for the first time of a global international society. European international society, with its highly formalized diplomacy, and mutual recognitions of sovereign equality, reached full flower in the much celebrated Treaty of Westphalia in 1648. During the centuries of European imperialism, the expansion of European power made this regional international society into a kind of global one, but only at the cost of excluding the colonized peoples from it. Because the Europeans, and later the West, controlled virtually the whole planet, their international society was *de facto* global. But European international society was not properly globalized until decolonization required the awarding of recognition as sovereign equals to the great bulk of the world's peoples (or rather, to the new states in which they were contained). Thus a fully-fledged global international society did not really take shape until after the Second World War. Its bottom line was the mutual recognition of its members as legal equals in the international community, with the exceptions that the 'big 5' retained a veto in the UN Security Council, and the recognized right to hold nuclear weapons under the NPT.

In the three decades since this international society became more or less complete it has made some advance in the scope of its shared identity. Within the 'like units' framework of sovereign, territorial states a vast amount of diversity is still possible: think of the internal political differences amongst the former Soviet Union, the USA, Saudi Arabia, Nigeria, and Japan. But in a few areas, most notably the regimes for nuclear non-proliferation and international trade, global international society has advanced beyond this baseline and adopted norms and rules that are accepted by the great majority of the states in the system. In this sense, even though it has only been up and running for a few decades, the global international society shows signs of being progressive, of extending the range of shared norms, rules, and institutions that define it. There can be little doubt that the massive pressure of economic globalization, and the pressing need to respond to the international management problems created by economic interdependence and integration, have been main drivers of this development.

But nevertheless it comes as no surprise that given the uneven genesis of this international society its development has also been uneven. The Cold War can be read in part as a competition for how global international society would develop, with the communist world offering an alternative to the Western model. For a time, in effect, international society had two cores competing for the allegiance of the periphery. But the main story of unevenness focuses on the difference between the West and the rest. Especially in the later twentieth century, the Western states began to develop a much more intense set of shared rules, norms, and institutions amongst themselves on a wider range of issues than they shared with the rest of the international system. The EU constituted a kind of core-within-a-core, with its member states creating such a thick web of common law and institutions, penetrating so deeply into their societies, that it was no longer altogether clear whether they should be seen as a set of highly 'like' units, or as some kind of *sui generis* confederal unit—in some senses an actor in its own right in international society. But the wider West too was bound together by an increasingly dense network of shared norms, rules, and institutions covering everything from democracy, through military co-operation, and trade and finance, to human rights and environmental standards. One of the most striking structural effects of this development was the rise during the 1990s of a consensus about the 'democratic peace', based on the strong empirical evidence that democracies very seldom go to war with each other. The existence of the democratic peace helped to consolidate the sense of the West as a security community, and thereby to create a sense of commonality and understanding amongst its constituent states and peoples. Amongst the Western states, the sense of what 'like unit' encompassed was now extended to a wide range of political, legal, economic, and societal characteristics.

The question is how this more highly developed core relates to the progressive tendency in global international society. There can be little doubt that a strong core of international society represents a comparative advantage for the states within it, and as such operates with the same 'socialization and competition' logic as neorealism to produce like units (Buzan 1993, 1996). The original creation of a global from a European international society can be read in this light, and there is every reason to think that this structural effect continues to operate. In other words, the core of international society creates pressures (both coercive and persuasive) on the periphery to follow the core's path towards a deeper and wider understanding of what 'like unit' means. One very powerful example of this structural effect at work is the recent conversion of most of the world to market economics consequent on the end of the Cold War. So strong is this effect that we even have states such as China, still claiming to be communist, clamouring for admission to the WTO and marketizing their economies as fast as they can. This process is not smooth, and not without conflict. Both in the Islamic world and in much of Asia there are strong reactions against Western values, particularly human rights and democracy. Many countries in the periphery resist, in varying degree, the attempt by the core to impose its own 'standard of civilization' on them (China, India, Brazil, Iran, Myanmar, etc.), and the line between international society and the hegemony of the capitalist core can sometimes be difficult to draw. Major elements of international society thus remain contested, and a durable centre–periphery process formation marks global international society. But there is also an expanding circle of Westernistic states such as Japan, South Korea, Taiwan, India, South Africa, Turkey, and Russia that already represent deep fusions between Western ideas and practices and indigenous cultures (Buzan and Segal 1998a, 1998b). To the extent that these hybrids add weight to the core, they also increase pressure on the periphery to conform.

The development of international society is a response both to the general problem of disorder in an anarchic system, and to the specific problems created by the increase in interaction capacity. In many ways, international society is supportive of state security. It provides the legitimization of external sovereignty and some legal protection against aggression. It also provides ways for states to deal with some of the threats and opportunities arising from increased interaction capacity. Participation in frameworks of rules and institutions gives states some power to shape their environment, and provides a greater element of stability and predictability than would otherwise be the case. But international society can also threaten states. It limits their freedom of action, seems to subordinate them to larger bodies, and may erode their distinctive identity. Many periphery states feel threatened by international societal norms coming from the centre that go against either their own political and cultural identity, or what they perceive as their foreign policy rights and interests. Less powerful and weaker states are more vulnerable to this type of threat, but as reactions against the process of European integration show, the intensification of international society can threaten even quite powerful strong states.

As the discussion of societal process above indicated, there was little in the way of a parallel development in world society. World society structures form the conspicuous exception to the general rush for globalization. Even allowing for the expansion in scale to global level, and the intense bombardment of Western culture, patterns of identity remained enduringly parochial. Much of the story simply carries over from the ancient and classical era, with 'universal' religions such as Christianity, Islam, and Buddhism continuing to expand. In the nineteenth and twentieth centuries, they were joined by universalist secular ideologies (liberalism, communism), but like their older religious counterparts, these also tended to fragment humankind as much as they united it, both by precipitating opposing camps and by themselves fragmenting into factions. But the nineteenth and twentieth centuries also saw the rise of powerful particularist ideologies (nationalism, fascism) which sought to focus identity in narrow and intense ways. It might even be argued that the interlinked universalization of nationalism and the modern state, and the struggle amongst fascism, communism, and liberalism, intensified the parochialism of identity in the international system. In the sphere of identity there is only globalization in the sense that the rivalries amongst these various identities move to a global scale. Identities themselves conspicuously failed to achieve, or in many cases to aspire to, globalization. In this sense, nearly all of the most obvious and powerful societal and political identities in play work against rather than towards the formation of a world society structure. Looked at in this light, world societal structure has been much less affected by uneven development than have military-political and economic structures. Parochial identities have remained strong despite (or some might argue because of) uneven development.

But despite the durable fragmentation of mainstream identities it was becoming possible to argue at least that some important foundations for a world society were being laid. Buzan and Segal (1998a) labelled this 'Westernistic civilisation', seeing it as a fusion of several basic Western ideas with a variety of other cultures, producing complex multicultural societies and individuals with multiple identities. One of the main foundations for a Westernistic world society was the widespread acceptance of a universal norm of human equality which arose from the process of decolonization. Acceptance of all humans as fundamentally equal in rights was a wholly new departure in human history. It was perhaps a necessary parallel to the award of sovereign equality to states, especially states perceived as modern states, that their peoples had also to be accepted as equal. The largely successful campaign against the slave trade, which preceded this by more than a century, was based on much the same idea. A second foundation was the rise and spread of INGOs sketched in Chapter 12. The proliferation of INGOs provided a basic organizational framework for the development of global civil society, and at least in principle, if still only a little bit in practice, allowed the development of grassroots global politics. This development was, however, still at a very preliminary stage by the end of the twentieth century. The roots of most INGOs were still very much planted in the leading liberal states, and so although leaning towards a world society, still very much reflected the centre–periphery substructure characteristic of most of the structures of the international system. As in domestic civil society, this development also had its dark side as well as its light one, with organized criminals, terrorists, and paedophiles featuring as much as worthy causes and supportive social networks.

In addition to these fundamental breakthroughs were some more superficial, but none the less significant, developments. Towards the end of the twentieth century some elements of a possible global identity became manifest in such things as the spread of English as a global lingua franca, the culture of global business, and the achievement of global icon status by some consumer products (jeans, coke, some computer software) and some features of the entertainment industry (sports, music, cinema). Huntington (1996: 57) dismisses this as 'Davos culture', seeing it as global, but confined only to a thin veneer of business and political elites. This comment is not without force, for there is no doubt that a strong case could be made for a kind of world society at the elite level. But it neglects the many elements of mass culture, and the shared symbols and metaphors that they provide, that have filtered down to a much wider segment of the world's people. Why do English football clubs, for example, have big fan clubs in Chinese cities? This does not as yet constitute a world society in any sense significant enough to produce structural effects. But it does represent a quite profound change from the prior run of human history in which the world's people shared no common language or common icons, had little sense of each other as members of the same species, shared no understanding that they occupied the same planet and were embedded in its all-embracing ecosystem, and had little or no information about each other's affairs.

The structure of identity politics at the individual level seems to have stronger local roots, and to be more resistant to large-scale redefinition, than either economic or military-political structure. Consequently, despite huge changes elsewhere, the twentieth century did not create a functioning world society in anything more than the limited 'Davos' sense. But in a whole variety of important ways it laid the foundations for such a development in succeeding generations.

# 5. CONCLUSIONS

When several structures are in play, the obvious question to ask is how they relate to each other. If they do relate to each other, then there is a deeper question about whether some metastructure exists that ties them all together. In the great bulk of the IR literature these questions are seldom asked, let alone answered. For the most part, debates about political structure (anarchy) and economic structure (markets) take place in isolation from each other. The field of international political economy (IPE) has tried to unite them, but although it has changed the agenda of IR, it has not been very fruitful in developing integrated theories. Its main attempt, hegemonic stability theory, has not achieved widespread acceptance. Our use of English school concepts to represent structure in the societal sector is in itself a radical departure, but even without that move, there has been little attempt to relate English school ideas to other IR theories. The task is much too big for us to try to make good these deficiencies here. But the long historical perspective does enable us to point out some ideas about possible linkages, and take note of where the various structural effects seem to act together or separately.

There is, for example, a debate as to whether and how the economic structure of the market and the political one of anarchy are connected. Some writers think that there is a strong connection, though they disagree on how to define it. On the face of it, anarchy would seem to be a necessary but not sufficient condition for an international market. Anarchies have existed without markets, but not markets without anarchies, so the political sector seems to have a prior claim (Buzan et al.

1993: part III). But political fragmentation alone is not enough to generate capital-ism, as witness India and the Islamic world (Hall and Ikenberry 1989: 27). Most of the analyses that ask why Europe and not China ended up making the global international system stress the anarchy-market structure of the former, and the empire-command economy of the latter. But it may well be the case that although anarchy is prior, once market structures are established they play an important role in supporting anarchy. If so this might help to explain the resilience of anarchy in the modern era versus its relative fragility in the ancient and classical one.

Another debate about the linkage between structures is that within the English school about the relationship between international society and world society (Buzan 1993, 1996). The English school starts from the idea that some sort of world society is a necessary underpinning for the development of international society, the illustrative cases being the shared culture of both classical Greece and modern Europe. But when looking to the future rather than to the past, the relationship is much less clear. Many English school writers see the two as competitive on the grounds that the cosmopolitan identities necessary for a serious world society would undermine the political foundation and rationale of the modern state. Conversely, the self-maintenance of the modern state with its particularistic iden-tity stands as a principal barrier to the development of world society. In this view, one of the key purposes of international society is to sustain a political framework (anarchy) that supports and sustains the pattern of cultural diversity that is one of humankind's great legacies from history. This view rests on a rather narrowly political view of English school ideas, in some ways similar to that of neorealism. But if one allows the economic sector to have more play in the thinking, then an alternative view becomes possible. In this view, international society is progres-sive, seeking to widen the range of shared rules, norms, and institutions. The development of world society becomes a necessary condition for this to occur. Unless there is convergence on the world society level, like that which has taken place amongst the Western states in general, and the members of the EU in par-ticular, it is not politically possible to extend the scope of international society beyond a rather limited range. One of the attractions of this English school debate is that it seems to offer a framework that potentially relates all three sectors of structure.

In terms of structural effects, it is striking that both neorealist and international society logics push towards like units, suggesting that there may be more com-mon ground between them than is generally acknowledged. Market structure relates to this effect in a contradictory fashion. In some ways market forces gener-ate follow-the-leader type adaptations that also work towards like units. The recent triumph of liberalism provides a good example. Yet in other ways, market structures push towards difference, whether in the logic of specialization or in uneven development and the centre–periphery process formation. Alongside this set of effects is another one that relates to the status of the dominant units in the system. Neorealist and international society logic work together to support the state and reaffirm it as the dominant unit. But world society and market logic can, and sometimes do, work against the state. The current debate about globalization is very much about this erosion of the state by forces and institutions rooted in the economic and societal sectors.

# Conclusion to Part IV

In summary, the modern international system displays six sharp distinctions that differentiate it from those of the ancient and classical world.

*   First, and most obviously, it achieved global scale and geographic closure. This meant that there was a single international system instead of multiple ones, and that economic and military-political systems merged into the same geographic space. The weaker, unstructured system forms of linear and relay systems gave way to a single, stronger, multiordinate form.
*   Second, a new type of dominant unit arose whose success was so great that it remade the whole world in its own image, imposing not only a pattern of hard boundaries, but also a global international society. As it did this, the modern state also underwent a series of internal developments that progressively raised the profile of civil society and gave birth to new forms of non-state organization, the firm and NGO. The evolution of the modern state led to the opening up of international civic-legal space into which firms and NGOs were able to move with increasing autonomy as TNCs and INGOs.
*   Third, interaction capacity increased out of all recognition. New physical technologies brought unheard of speeds and carrying capacities to old dimensions, and occupied new ones in air and space. New social technologies in the form of diplomacy, law, IGOs, and liberalism arose which both complemented and facilitated the physical technologies, and made possible a much stronger international society than ever seen before.
*   Fourth, most international processes underwent massive expansion, intensification, and diversification. In particular, warfare became far more destructive; international trade and finance grew hugely in relation to domestic economies (which also grew hugely); a system of formal global diplomacy became universal; cross-cultural contact increased to the point where the truly foreign has become almost extinct; and the worldwide environmental impacts of human activity rose sharply.
*   Fifth, system structures became vastly stronger than they were in the ancient and classical era, and so did their effects, shaping both the units and the system. In a mutually supportive loop, military-political structure worked powerfully to create like units, and modern states promoted the defining unit features of hard sovereignty and territoriality that sustained anarchic structure. The structure of international society reinforced this effect by intensifying the content of 'like units' and offering comparative advantages to those states that became part of an international community, though limits were set to this development by the much weaker development of world society. Global market structure fed into the making of both international and world society, but also created uneven development and the centre–periphery substructure.

- Sixth, the vigorous global operation of military-political and economic struc- tures, reinforced by the enduring parochialism of world society, generated significant regional substructures in the global system: security complexes, regional IGOs, and a variety of regional economic zones.

Perhaps the central question arising out of this analysis of the modern inter- national system is about how the units and the system relate to each other. It is very clear from the story both that the dominant units and the system as a whole have become much stronger than in the ancient and classical era, and that these two developments are closely linked. It is equally obvious that many of the units in the system are not strong. Many of these weak units are indeed better under- stood as products of the strong system than as self-generated entities. Certainly for these states, and possibly also for the strong states, the system has become a relatively more powerful force. Compared to ancient and classical times, more things are determined by global and regional forces than by local ones, whether it be the nature of the polity, the organization of the economy, the content of people's identity, or the functioning of the planetary environment. In principle we have the makings of a simple matrix comprising weak and strong units and weak and strong international systems. We will attempt in Part V to address this and other questions arising from the meeting of theory and history.

# Part V

# SPECULATIONS, ASSESSMENTS, REFLECTIONS

## INTRODUCTION TO PART V

This last group of chapters draws together the threads from the previous fifteen along four different lines. Chapter 16 stays in the mould of Parts II to IV, but looks forward rather than back. It applies our framework to the present and near future, addressing the question of whether we are undergoing another systemic transformation. Part of the argument for marrying IR theory and world history is to enable us to break out of the Westphalian theoretical cage, and think more clearly about the nature and process of system transformation, so putting our framework up against the future seems a fair test. What is the evidence that changes are taking place sufficiently fundamental that they would draw the modern, European-defined, era of the international system to a close, in the process creating a historical turning point analogous with those that have marked previous changes of era? What does it mean to say that the international system is getting stronger?

The final three chapters shift the focus from history back to the theory concerns of Part I. Chapter 17 explores the questions posed for IR theory by confronting it with the much wider empirical test that arises from a world historical perspective on international systems. How well has our framework stood up to the task of dealing with premodern history? What insights do we get from taking a long view that might help with the development of international system theory? Chapter 18 looks at what an IR theory approach offers to world historians and historical sociologists. It proceeds by comparing the periodization of history that emerges when we examine the past from the perspective of IR theory with the periodizations associated with other social science and historical perspectives. What does our framework contribute to debates about distinguishing really important from merely secondary turning points in understanding the pattern of world history? Can we offer new turning points, or deeper justifications for thinking some conventional ones more, or less, important than others? Finally, Chapter 19 looks forward by setting out some of the research questions for the future towards which this whole exercise seems to point.

*Chapter 16*

# OUTLOOK: A POSTMODERN INTERNATIONAL SYSTEM?

## 1. INTRODUCTION

In this chapter, we reflect on what our multi-tracked, long-view approach to studying the international system tells us about where it may be headed. In the still-turbulent wake of the ending of the Cold War there is a fairly widespread consensus that the international system has undergone a significant change. But there is much less agreement about how to define the main features of this change, and almost none about how to assess in what direction it might be taking us. Perhaps the most obvious change is that fear of world wars has moved into the background. But while some think this a permanent change, others see it as a temporary effect of the ending of the Cold War. Neorealists focus on the change in polarity, but cannot agree whether we are in a unipolar or multipolar system. Liberals focus on globalization, and the economic, and to some extent cultural, knitting together of an ever stronger international system. Some even talk of the 'end of history', by which they mean the solving (by liberal democracy) of basic questions about how best to organize human political economy. Marxists continue to see an impending crisis of capitalism, and some environmentalists continue to predict ecological catastrophes from a variety of sources (pollution, meteorites— though fears of resource depletion and Malthusian population crises have retreated somewhat). More old-fashioned types of realist, and some postmodernists, are increasingly concerned with identity questions as a source of conflict, whether locally, or in some grand 'clash of civilizations'. People of various persuasions think that we are heading for a 'two worlds' arrangement, with a rich and largely peaceful core surrounded by a poor and largely conflictual periphery.

All of this leads to the question of whether we are on the brink of another transformation of the international system. Or is talk of 'a new world order' overstating the significance of seemingly large-scale turbulences and transformations such as the end of the Cold War, simply because they are close to us in time? In other words, are the events currently swirling around us merely expressions of the continued unfolding of the modern era, or are they sufficiently transformational to support a case that we are indeed heading into a new world order, significantly different both from the ancient and classical era and the modern one? To answer this, we need once again to review the basic components of the international system in the light of current developments, though it will be clearer if we change the order to: scale, interaction capacity, process, units, structure.

## 2. SCALE

Transformation in the scale of international systems was one of the key changes defining the transition from the ancient and classical to the modern era. But since the habitable land areas of the planet are now fully incorporated into the international system, no further transformations of this kind seem possible in the near or even medium-term future. Projects for large-scale human habitation on or under the oceans would increase the density of the system, but not its size. Outer space offers two options for expanding the system: colonization and visitation. Colonization requires the human species to move into space on a fairly large scale (such as self-sustaining colonies on the moon or Mars, or in orbit), but unless there are some unanticipated breakthroughs in technology which lower the cost of escaping earth's gravity well, this does not look likely any time soon. Visitation requires the arrival of aliens, and although a surprising number of people think this has already occurred, the mainstream evidence (silence on the SETI—Search for Extra-terrestrial Intelligence—airwaves) suggests otherwise. Were such an event to occur, it would be a rather different story from the one we have told of an expanding human system, though there would be some analogues for it (hopefully not close analogues!) in the surprise meetings early in the sixteenth century between European civilization and the previously isolated civilizations in the Andean highlands and Mesoamerica.

But short of some very big surprises, at present the international system has reached geographical closure. It has only the option to grow more intense, and not the option to expand. This assessment is not new. As we noted in Chapter 3, writers as different as Mackinder, Lenin, and Toynbee all came to the same conclusion in the first half of the twentieth century.

## 3. INTERACTION CAPACITY

Increases in interaction capacity driven by profound developments in both physical and social technologies were another key element in the transformation from the ancient and classical era to the modern one. Without improvements in physical technologies neither the global system nor the huge expansion of process would have taken place. But from the perspective of the end of the twentieth century, physical technologies for interaction capacity seem to have reached a limit almost as absolute as that affecting the size of the international system.

Further transformational developments are hard to envisage except in relation to moving off planet, and there is little sign as yet of cost-effective mass transportation systems for doing this. Most of the classical technologies for transportation and communication have reached maturity. Whether one looks at ships, trains, planes, or automobiles only marginal improvements in size, speed, carrying capacity, or range seem possible. One can already cross the planet in a matter of hours, and transportation costs are so low that they no longer constitute a significant element in the price of most goods. It is hard to see how improvements in existing capabilities would make any fundamental difference to the operation of the international system.

Communications technology is in some ways similarly mature. It is possible to shift huge amounts of information around the planet almost instantaneously in several different forms. Because there is so little room for breakthroughs in the range or speed of communication, there does not seem to be any possibility for new conquests of time and distance of the kind that previously transformed international systems. Where room for change is still available is in the carrying capacity of information and communications systems (even though this already seems huge), and in the numbers of people having easy access to them. This might be seen as no more than incremental improvement of existing capabilities, and therefore not transformational. But it is still relevant to ask how much difference it will make when 3 billion people are on the internet rather than 30 million, and it is not yet clear whether we understand the impact of the current provision of mass communication. Existing networks have already had discernible effects on economic, social, and political life. In the economic sector instantaneous global information pushes the trading and financial systems towards perfect information, reducing the opportunities for arbitrage. In the societal sector the internet enables transnational interest groups and diasporas to remain in close and immediate contact, introducing new social and political organizational possibilities into the international system. And in the political sector, these networks have weakened state boundaries and governments' ability to control, in ways that are not yet fully understood. We are still a long way from any kind of coherent global grassroots politics, but the potential shape and character of such a development are already clear in the form of numerous transnational INGOs and internet groups. Whether these things are harbingers of a fundamental transformation, or superficial adornments of late modernity, is still impossible to judge. There may well be potential for international system transformation in the emergent quantity and low cost of mass communication systems. If so, it would be a change in physical interaction capacity quite unlike those that transformed earlier international systems. Judging by its impact in the economic sector, its most likely effect would take the form of a serious assault on the territorial organization of politics and culture (Ruggie 1993).

Social technologies are by nature less concrete and quantifiable than physical ones, but here too it is hard to think of revolutionary breakthroughs that might lie just over the horizon. The framework of diplomacy, international law, IGOs, regimes, and liberalism that mark the modern era already take in hand much of what is possible. It is easy to imagine more of the same as economic and environmental pressures create demand for higher levels of planetary management, and new forms of standardization and interoperability. But as the case of the EU illustrates very clearly, if even just this evolutionist line is pushed very much further, we begin to spill over into questions not of social interaction capacity, but about the nature of dominant units and the structure of the system. Is the EU now a unit in the international system? Is what goes on within it domestic or international politics, and is its internal structure therefore hierarchic or anarchic? The fact that it is not unreasonable to ask such questions, as well as the real difficulty in answering them clearly, shows just how close to structural transformation the great European experiment with post-Westphalian political economy has come, its many day-to-day problems notwithstanding. In addition, for the near future at least, there seems to be as much concern to place caps on some aspects of interaction capacity (such as restrictions on migrants, financial markets, criminal activity, disease control, and even trade) as to try opening them up further. Indeed, there are clear signs that some communities, concerned that globalization is undermining their cultural identity, are drawing on social technologies to restrict interaction capacity. There is a tendency for some Islamic communities, for example, to retreat behind a very strict interpretation of the Koran. This development has major consequences, particularly for women who are often required to withdraw from the public and male-controlled spheres of society. Language is also often used as a social technology to bind a community together and lower interaction capacity with other communities. Even in the United States there are 329 different languages in use, although only the 17 million Spanish speakers pose any real threat to the 'universalism' of English. Paradoxically, the growth of global communications facilitates these attempts to use social technology to promote identity formation—a phenomenon sometimes referred to as 'glocalization'. Thus social technologies may be used as effectively to block as to promote increases of interaction capacity.

It does not seem likely that changes in either physical or social technologies for interaction capacity will redefine the international system in the near future. One has, however, to keep an eye on the ever expanding carrying capacity of physical communications systems, the effects of which may at some point create qualitative rather than incremental change in the international system.

# 4. PROCESS

As argued in Chapter 14, all processes have undergone immense intensification during the modern era. Even though such intensification is unlikely to be driven by further breakthroughs in the range and speed of interaction capacity, it is easy to imagine incremental developments across the board that will make international processes ever more diverse, elaborate, universal, and quick. But probably the major transformations have already been made, and it is therefore not to further intensifications of process that we should look for the makings of a new world order.

Neither does there seem to be much scope for immediate changes in the dominant process formations. In particular, the centre–periphery formation looks durable for some time to come. It is firmly embedded not only in economic processes, but also in military-political ones and in international and world society, and there is little sign that the strong pattern of uneven development is about to disappear from the international system. This is perhaps best captured in the widely held view that uneven development is pulling the international system into 'two worlds' (Keohane and Nye 1977; Buzan 1991, 1998; Goldgeier and McFaul 1992; Singer and Wildavsky 1993; Rana 1993; Keohane 1995: 165–86). This view supposes that a partial transformation of the international system has taken place. Rather than being a single strategic-political space, with a single set of rules of the game, the international system has divided into two worlds. One world (call it the zone of peace) is defined by a postmodern security community of powerful advanced industrial democracies, and international relations within this world no longer operate according to old realist rules. In the zone of peace, states do not expect or prepare for war against each other, and since this zone contains most of the great powers this is a very significant development for the whole of the international system. Reflecting the character of postmodern states, economies and societies are highly open and interdependent, transnational players are numerous and strong, and international society is well developed.

The other world (call it the zone of conflict) is comprised of a mixture of modern and premodern states. In relations amongst (and within) these states classical realist rules still obtain, sovereignty remains sacred, and war is a usable and used instrument of policy. In this zone, international relations operate by the traditional rules of power politics that prevailed all over the world up to 1945. States expect and prepare for the possibility of serious tension with their neighbours. Some restraint is provided by deterrence (in a few places nuclear deterrence) but economic interdependence between neighbours is generally low, and populations can often be easily mobilized for war. Especially within premodern, but also within some modern states, political power is frequently contested by force. Even in the modernizing states of East Asia where economic interdependence between neighbours is growing, the states are still often fragile and highly protective of sovereignty, and use of force amongst some of them cannot be ruled out.

To divide the world in this way of course oversimplifies. Some places close to the core of the zone of peace behave like the zone of conflict (ex-Yugoslavia, Albania, Northern Ireland), and some ostensibly in the zone of conflict have managed to build substantial regional barriers against local wars (the Association of South-East Asian Nations (ASEAN), the Southern African Development Community (SADC), and possibly Mercosur in the Latin American southern cone). An alternative view is that these two worlds exist not as distinct and separate territorial spaces, but as interleaved modes of living. Thus parts of some cities in the West contain their own zones of conflict. Nevertheless the general distinction seems valid, even at the risk of creating an exaggerated sense of spatial separation, and the claim for two parallel modes of international relations seems plausible, even though there is significant overlap between them. There are fundamental qualitative differences in the way in which the states and societies of Europe, North America, and Japan relate both to each other and to their populations on the one hand, and the way in which states in the Middle East, South Asia, and many other places do so. These differences are rooted deeply in the form and character, and therefore also the history, of the states and societies within the two zones.

A central issue in the two worlds formulation is how the zone of peace and the zone of conflict relate to each other, for that they do relate in many and significant ways is beyond question. In the past, the relationship between different zones of political economy was often the mainspring of history. Before the rise of Europe, the relationship between the barbarian and civilized zones was crucial. Again, during the European expansion, the relationship between the modernizing European core and the premodern periphery was the defining feature of world history. As a rule, the nature and shape of zones in the international system changes over time, but the fact of them does not. At whatever point in history one looks at the international system, some strong pattern of uneven development and different forms of political economy will be present. The diffusion of goods, ideas, and people works continuously to erode uneven development, but never (yet) succeeds in doing so. Some cultures have great difficulty absorbing new goods and ideas without self-destructing. And the game is not static. The leading edge cultures are themselves continuously evolving (or in some cases declining), so opening up new space and new zones to maintain the pattern of unevenness.

In recent times, some attention has focused on the relationship between centre and periphery, and with the Cold War out of the way we can expect this to intensify. How the two zones will relate to each other is one of the great unanswered questions for the twenty-first century. Will the weaker, but perhaps more aggressive, zone of conflict begin to penetrate and impinge upon the zone of peace through threats of terrorism, long-range weapons of mass destruction, migration, disease, debt repudiation, and suchlike? Or will the unquestionably more powerful zone of peace seek to penetrate and influence the zone of conflict, using the levers of geo-economics, and occasionally more robust forms of intervention, to manipulate state-making in the zone of conflict? Or will the postmodern world try to insulate itself by constructing buffer zones in Mexico, Central Europe, Turkey, and North Africa, and trying to stay out of the more chaotic parts of the zone of conflict? Or will it try to engage with the whole, pushing towards a new world order in its own image? We can only guess at the answers to these questions, but what is clear is that complete, or even substantial, separation of the two zones is highly unlikely.

It also seems clear that the developments traced here open up the space for some powerful logics of regionalism (Buzan and Wæver forthcoming). During most of the modern era, the worldwide dominance of European/Western power overlaid most of the possibilities for indigenous regional dynamics to operate. But during the nineteenth and twentieth centuries decolonization opened the space for regional military-political dynamics, and the ending of the Cold War enabled these dynamics to operate much more free from high levels of superpower intrusion. In many parts of the world locally generated regional security dynamics dominate international relations. At the same time, the growing power of the global market has generated regional economic initiatives both as a way of building stronger positions within that market, and as fallback positions in case it falls into crisis.

Despite the prominence of regional subsystems, there can be no doubt that the actors (states, TNCs, INGOs) in the zone of peace are largely responsible for creating and maintaining the international system and international society within which the actors in the zone of conflict have to operate. Everything from norms, rules, and laws, through capital and information flows, to the structure of power is shaped by the zone of peace, and *strongly* shaped. The international system and society in which the zone of conflict is embedded is arguably the most powerful, comprehensive, and pervasive ever seen on the planet. So great is its impact that it is possible to ask whether (or to theorize that) the core in the zone of peace is in some ways responsible for the social, political, and economic weakness in the periphery. Does economic, cultural, political, and military pressure from the core actually destabilize the periphery and inhibit its development, or does it provide role models, resources, and capital that should help the periphery to overcome obstacles to development that are rooted in its own cultures and history? The answer to that question is hotly contested and far from empirically clear, but it is not unreasonable to ask it. Neither is it unreasonable to ask whether the power differential between core and periphery is so great that it is only a matter of time before the core assimilates much of the periphery. The vast modernization process under way in much of East Asia (notwithstanding the periodic crises to which all such capitalist developments have been subject), and possibly beginning in South Asia, will forever change the balance between wealth and poverty, and core and periphery, in the international system. If it succeeds, the core will no longer be rooted in just one civilization (the West), but will span several continents in a global network of power and prosperity.

There *are* two worlds whose political life is defined by differences in their level and type of political, social and economic development. But while these worlds may well be different, they are not wholly separate spatially. There is a strong, if lopsided, interaction and overlap between them, and whatever their differences, both worlds are firmly embedded in what might best be labelled the late modern international system.

If process formations look relatively stable, and the main breakthroughs in the quantitative side of process have already been made, can we write off process as a source of system transformation? No. What is now interesting about process is not so much its absolute measures (how much . . .), but its qualitative (what type . . .) and relative (which dominates . . .) ones. As hinted in the conclusions to Chapter 14, a case can be made that some quite fundamental transformations are under way in the relative importance of one sector as opposed to another. Two stories can be told about this.

The first feels like a very real story that is actually happening as you sit here reading this. It can be told simply as a product of two contemporary debates about liberalism: 'democratic peace' and 'globalization'. Democratic peace is about the apparent end of great power war in the international system. It is about the quality, political salience, and perhaps also the amount, of interaction within the military-political sector. Explanations for the apparent abandonment of war amongst a growing group of states vary from fear of nuclear weapons, through economic interdependence, to democratic peace, but for the purposes of this particular argument the causes matter less than the simple fact. If sustained, the cessation of great power war would dethrone military interaction from its millennia-long reign as the principal defining process of international systems. The shift from negative (conflict formation) to positive (security regime, security community) security interdependence not only changes the dominant type of interaction within the sector, but makes the sector as a whole a less urgent and less prominent feature in the day-to-day life of units.

Now place this debate alongside that on globalization, which is the heir to earlier debates about free trade (nineteenth and early twentieth century) and interdependence (1960s–1970s). Globalization is about the truly enormous, and ongoing, rise of economic interaction in the system, and the effects of that on other sectors. The globalization argument is that economic interaction is not only becoming more and more important in the day-to-day life of units, but also transforming the units themselves (more on this in the next section). The pursuit of economic liberal goals requires a big reduction in the state's control of the national economy, and a general opening of borders to economic transactions. It creates powerful roles for TNCs and some IGOs (WTO, IMF, IBRD), and because of the knock-on effects of trying to separate economic from political life, many argue that the state itself is being hollowed out.

If both of these stories are true, putting them together creates grounds for arguing that we may be entering a *sectoral transformation*: a shift from military-political to economic processes as the *dominant* (i.e. system-defining) form of interaction: 'Geopolitics' to 'Geo-economics' as Luttwak (1990) puts it. These are, of course, both liberal stories, and liberals have predicted the end of war before. Hardened realists dismiss them as temporary aberrations from the time-honoured norms of power politics. They point to the rise of Chinese military and economic power, or to the proliferation of weapons of mass destruction, or to the dangers from terrorists, to suggest that post-Cold War euphoria will soon give way to business as usual in world politics. And no clear image is to hand about what such an economics-dominant system would look like. Few believe that any kind of liberal utopia is around the corner, and IPE writers such as Cerny (1995, 1996), who have tried to think about it, find it easy to come to worrying conclusions. It is easy to make the case that even if interstate military security issues become much less salient for the core states and peoples, insecurity itself will not whither away. Other dimensions of security (intrastate military, economic, societal, environmental) will rise to take their place (Wæver et al. 1993; Buzan et al. 1998; Buzan and Wæver 1998). But at this juncture these two liberal stories both have much more empirical support than ever before. Great power war does seem to have disappeared from the system, and the agenda of international politics is dominated by issues of trade, finance, property rights, and the powers and functions of international economic institutions. It is possible to imagine that this transformation is temporary, that the system could once again fall back into great power military rivalry. But the pressures against great power war are very strong, and the penetrative effect of an expanding global economy continues to grow. Even if the system does fall back into the realist model, it will do so in such a highly constrained way as to suggest that we would still be in the process of a sectoral transformation, if not yet through to the other side. So these two liberal stories do not point to any immediate liberal utopia, but to a sectoral transformation, which, when it comes, would have profound effects on both units and structures. And since economic processes are not culturally neutral (note, for example, the strong projection of individualism in most pop music and much advertising) one might also expect that this revolution would affect patterns of identity. A sectoral transformation along these lines would be an unprecedented development in the history of international systems, almost sufficient by itself to justify talking about a new world order.

The second story is also about sectoral transformation, but it has the feeling of being a potential story: more likely to happen some way in the future than now, and perhaps never going to happen at all. This story is about the rise of environmental processes not only as a new key variable in human affairs, but as a candidate for being the dominant process. Mead (1995–6: 27), for example, argues that the key to current history is 'the shift from progress to sustainability as the task confronting contemporary society', and Kaplan (1994: 58) that environment is 'the national-security issue of the early twenty-first century'. If true, this would require subordinating economic and military interactions to environmental priorities or necessities. This view is of course contested, but many share a feeling that the environment could go badly wrong. In the ancient and classical era environmental interaction was largely confined to disease transmission, with human-caused pollution and ecological collapse being local events. In the modern era, the mass movement of plants, animals, microbes, and humans across the oceans was added. By the late twentieth century, driven by both a rising human population and increasing industrial activity, pollution and mass extinctions of species had become major new elements of environmental interaction. Human activity was threatening to make radical changes not only to the composition of the biosphere, but also to the composition of the atmosphere and consequently to both the planet's climate and its defences against solar radiation. There is no question that environmental processes have become and will remain more important than in the past. As we study the effects of our pollution we are laying the foundations for an ability to engineer the planetary climate against, for example, a natural return to ice age conditions. There is a possibility that if things turn very bad (major climate change, rampant disease transmission, or suchlike) environmental process could become the dominant concern of humankind, but there is no way of predicting how probable such a development may be. It is also easy to imagine that some environmental catastrophes, such as big rises in sea level, could reinstate military primacy as people resisted mass migrations, and fought over shrinking land areas. If the economic sector is becoming dominant, then that move very much depends on the environment remaining tolerably stable, and on military processes remaining in the background.

# 5. UNITS

The possibility that the international system might be entering into a sectoral transformation raises questions about the standing of the dominant unit. Judging by our account of the rise and evolution of international systems, the really big question in IR is about when and how a new type (or types) of dominant unit will arise, bringing with it (them) new forms of domestic and international political, economic, and social order. As the accounts in Parts III and IV show, since the beginning of civilization the dominant units have always been military-political ones, and mostly (the nomadic barbarians excepted) territorially rooted. Can that pattern be sustained if the military-political sector is losing dominance as the defining process of the system, and if globalization is pushing the state out of many aspects of the economy?

When one looks at the leading contemporary states, there are quite strong grounds for thinking that the series of (r)evolutions which characterized their development throughout the modern era (from absolutist to nationalist to democratic, not to mention from agrarian to industrial to post-industrial) is still under way. The much commented upon 'hollowing out' of the state might be seen as a fourth round representing yet another shift in the empowerment of civil society, and particularly economic actors (firms, banks), process formations (IGOs, regimes) and structures (markets), in relation to governments. Cerny (1995) labels this phase 'the competition state', though others see it more as a regression to nineteenth-century laissez-faire, before the state became so intrusive into economic and social life. But is this best understood as a fourth round of the modernist development, or as a transition to a different kind of dominant unit—the postmodern state? If one accepts the idea that a sectoral transformation from military dominant to economic dominant is under way, then it becomes easier to argue that we are looking not just at a change *in* the dominant unit, but a change *of* it. If true, this would be a quite different form of unit transformation than occurred between the ancient and classical and modern eras. Then the new unit did not evolve from the existing dominant ones, but emerged on the periphery to challenge the older unit types. It would have more in common with the unit transformation that occurred between the pre-international and ancient and classical worlds, when some chiefdoms evolved into city-states and agrarian empires.

There are two steps to the argument that we may be witnessing a change *of* rather than *in* the dominant unit. First is the erosion of hard boundaries and strong sovereignty as the declared (if not always fully practised) defining elements of national states and their relations, and their replacement by a negotiated arrangement of permeable boundaries, layered sovereignty, and common international and transnational 'spaces' (cyberspace, civic space, commercial space, legal space, civilizational space). For many purposes (trade and finance, communications and media, tourism, some aspects of law, human rights) boundaries have become not just permeable, but shot through with large holes. If hard boundaries and hard sovereignty are being politically abandoned in enough important ways, then perhaps we are no longer looking at modern states but at something else: the postmodern state (Cooper 1996). This development is most obvious within the subsystem of the EU, where the question of unit transformation arises in relation both to the EU itself as a new type of entity with actor quality, and to its effect on its member states. The EU does not seem likely to become simply another large federal state. Instead it is experimenting with a new form of both unit and subsystem structure, where the sharp inside/outside features of the modernist era are blurring into a mixture of the domestic and the international. States still exist, but they are embedded in a layered sovereignty, and for many purposes their boundaries are highly porous. The British and Irish governments took advantage of this development when they established a series of interlocking institutional arrangements embracing both countries as part of the 1998 peace agreement.

The second step is to see that this change is not just about the state, but also about upgrading the relative autonomy of the economic and civic units that had until recently gestated within the modern state. Are we seeing a combined move away from the dominance of military-political units, and (back) towards a situation in which there is variety of dominant units? If so this development is not the same as the ancient and classical system in which there were different types of dominant unit, all of them predominantly military-political in character. It would be a new and more complex development, albeit with some resemblance to medieval arrangements. The key would be that there are not only multiple types of units, but these types are functionally and in some ways sectorally differentiated. The postmodern state has both dissolved its borders for many types of interaction and begun to disperse its sovereignty to other levels. This is most obvious in the EU where layered governance is explicit, and the principle of subsidiarity is the guiding rule. But it is also apparent, though more weakly, in the international system at large, where a variety of regimes and institutions are providing elements of global governance in some specific areas of policy (think of the WTO, or the nuclear non-proliferation regime and its inspection arm, the IAEA). Non-state actors such as TNCs, banks, mafias, and INGOs (Amnesty International, the World Wildlife Fund, Greenpeace) are able to move with considerable autonomy in the transnational legal space created by open borders and layered governance. In a sense, part of the civic space that was opened up *within* the national state as it moved towards democracy is now being shifted into the system level, the space *between* states, especially democratic ones. In the process, the sharp inside/outside delineation of the Westphalian system is breaking down, not just in practice, but as declared policy. If this development continues, it points towards an international system that has no single, clearly dominant, multi-purpose, multi-sectoral type of unit, but instead has a variety of more sector-specialized units. Some of these, most obviously TNCs and mafias, do not require territorial bases, and in practice are quite mobile: the new barbarians of the postmodern international system? The idea of a coming world order that is much less rooted in territorial logics is reinforced by the spreading impact of mass communications discussed above.

Unsurprisingly there is no consensus about this interpretation. While it is clear that something interesting is going on, it is not clear that the departure from the modernist unit is yet so deep or so widespread as to count as a transformation of units. The modern state still retains its unique multi-sectoral role, and it still remains the primary source of political legitimacy. Its boundaries may have become more permeable, but as would-be migrants from poor countries can attest, boundaries remain hard for some purposes. And as the state abandons or downgrades some functions (economy, military), it picks up others (human rights, environmental protection). The main centres of supposedly postmodern evolution in North America, Europe, and Japan also remain remarkably parochial, culturally self-centred, and politically inward looking. And while some IGOs and INGOs might have achieved significant levels of relative autonomy, it is much less clear either that they have escaped the dominion of the state, or that they are themselves plausible candidates for status as new types of dominant unit.

There are many contending voices trying to capture current developments. Albert and Brock (1995) put forward the idea that 'debordering' is effectively dismantling the Westphalian system, making way for a non-territorial politics combining elements of neomedievalism and world society. Rosecrance (1996) also sees deterritorialization, and advocates surrender to economic forces in a mobile, meritocratic world. McRae tends to agree (1994: 21–3, 185–205) arguing that we are at the beginning of 'reestablishing markets, as opposed to state bureaucracy, as the main method of allocating resources', with the state shifting from being a provider of services (failed model) to being a regulator, and a new class of internationally mobile professionals emerging. Watson (1997) sees all this as good, making a sustained argument against the excesses of sovereignty and non-intervention in international society, and in favour of more acceptance of hegemonial authority. He sees the modernist European anarchic model as too prone to excess, and not possible in a world with micro-states and weak states. Many cosmopolitans, however, would be unhappy with his solution: the system managed by a hegemonic coalition of great powers, adopting a value base wider than just Western. McNeill (1994), like Watson, postulates a turn away from the extreme of the nation state towards more polyethnic political constructions reminiscent of classical empires. He sees migration and ethnic loyalty creating ghettos just as in the classical empires, and dismisses the nation state as a temporary throwback to the simpler patterns of barbarian, and classical Greek times. Buzan and Segal (1998a), building on the analogy with classical Greece and its Hellenistic successors, argue that we are entering a 'Westernistic' era of civilizational fusions. And yet it is also possible to argue that territorial boundaries have become more stable than ever before in the sense that movement of boundaries is much less common than it used to be until very recently (Jackson and Zacher 1997), and that for some purposes they remain hard.

All of this suggests that the question of unit transformation is firmly, and rightly, on the agenda of contemporary international systems analysis, but that the jury is still out. Not least of the problems involved is that there are no agreed criteria for distinguishing when changes *in* the dominant unit add up to a change *of* dominant unit.

## 6. STRUCTURE

The unfolding of the modern international system over the last 500 years has seen a great strengthening of structural forces as compared with earlier times. As with process, there is not much reason to expect imminent transformations in the main shapes of structure, though there might well be reasons to expect a shift in the relative importance of the various structures in play within the system.

In terms of military-political structure, opinions are rather mixed. Some (Waltz 1993; Mearsheimer 1990) expect neorealist logic to soldier on more or less unaffected. They expect the USA to become the target of balance of power behaviour, and the EU to break down into a balance of power subsystem. Huntington's (1993, 1996) 'clash of civilizations' thesis implausibly tries to extend this hard realist structural logic from the state level up to the civilizational (or in our terms 'world society') level. Some agree with Huntington that 'Euramerica' (Lind 1996), or the core West, is and should be a unit in the global power balance, whereas others see Europe and America as natural singularities, not a unit except when seriously threatened (Harries 1993). But what seemed at the end of the Cold War to be the exciting prospect of a shift in polarity turns out not to be all that significant after all, and to be increasingly difficult to capture in meaningful terms. Although it is pretty clear that the system is no longer bipolar in any general sense, it is far from clear what it has become. Seen through military-political lenses it might be unipolar (USA as last superpower), bipolar (USA and Russia, emphasizing nuclear weapons), or diffuse (many regional great powers: Russia, China, India, Iran, South Africa, etc.). If one adds in economic and political factors, the picture gets even more confused. This polarity puzzle seems to stem from the sectoral shift under way in process. Because polarity is distributed differently in different sectors, and because the military sector is declining in importance relative to the economic, it is much more difficult than it was during the Cold War to calculate polarity in aggregated terms.

Indeed, questions need to be asked about how the whole logic of neorealism functions in a strongly marketized global system without great power war. Such a system can remain anarchic and stable both because a strong international society provides a framework of rules and principles that legitimizes the functional and sectoral differentiation amongst the units, and because of the different quality of the survival imperative in the economic realm as compared to the military one. As Waltz (1979: 95) himself points out, firms die more naturally and frequently than do states. The neorealist logic of like units might well survive, but only in relation to classes of units (all postmodern states become like, all TNCs become like, all INGOs become like, etc.) and not in the way that a single type of unit must become dominant. This might be thought a more accurate reading of the social Darwinist metaphor of realism: not that 'survival of the fittest' logic generates a single dominant 'species', excluding all others, but that it results in the filling of myriad ecological niches by units best adapted to them (we are grateful to Eric Herring for this observation).

To the extent that conflict is replaced by mutual security (security regimes, security communities) the shoving and shaping forces of socialization and competition become less driven by military considerations, and more driven by economic and societal ones. The comparative advantage that enables some units to dominate others (or inspires some to emulate others) will shift away from military capability, and towards economic prowess, societal dynamism, and the diplomatic skills necessary to build, and to expand, strong subsystems of international society. Military skills will certainly not disappear in a postmodern international system. They will continue to be central in many relationships amongst states outside the core (e.g. India–Pakistan, Iran–Iraq), and will also play a selectively important role in relations between core and periphery where periphery states get designated as threats to international order (e.g. Iran, Iraq, Libya, North Korea, Serbia, possibly China). But they will matter less than they did before in building comparative advantage. Real comparative advantage will lie with those most able to sustain and expand zones of economic and political openness within which the threat and use of force between states is largely replaced by diplomacy. The Cold War itself, and its outcome, might be taken as an illustration. Whereas the West was able to construct an expanding zone of security community and economic openness, the communist world remained economically primitive, and not only failed to establish a security community amongst its members but quite frequently resorted to military-political confrontation (China–USSR, USSR–Yugoslavia) or invasion and war (China–Vietnam, Vietnam–Cambodia, USSR–Hungary, USSR–Czechoslovakia).

The intensification of the global market structure seems almost certain to continue, carrying with it an increasingly dense regulatory framework at all levels of governance. This is essentially a continuation, but it could be argued that the global market has, like the ocean-going sailing ship, been a development long in the making where a series of incremental improvements eventually culminates in a transformational breakthrough. That breakthrough occurred late in the twentieth century, when the global market reached sufficient strength that it could begin to change the political structure by unpacking the hard borders and centralized sovereignty of the modern state. This is the story we have told above under the labels 'sectoral transformation' and 'postmodern state'. But while there is little doubt that the global market structure is powerful while it operates, there is much argument about how stable it is.

The liberal triumphalist view is in fashion and, as Fukuyama's (1992, 1998) notion of 'the end of history' suggests, assumes that the triumph of the global market will endure. But there are still many visions of gloom in play, often with roots in Marxian thinking, painting pictures of a rampant and self-destructive capitalism impoverishing the Third World and hollowing out the advanced industrial states (Stavrianos 1990: 139–87; Wallerstein 1993). Chase-Dunn (1994: 102) sees the victory of neoliberalism as having 'occurred within a context of a capitalist crisis of immense proportions' caused by irrationality, inequality, ecological damage, fiscal crises, and racial antagonisms. Some (Judt 1994) interpret this as a crisis not just of capitalism, but of modernism *per se:* he sees Europe as 'about to enter an era of turmoil, a time of troubles' because of the disarray in its enlightenment ordering ideas. Others have a less apocalyptic view, but still one that questions the stability of the liberal order. Calleo (1996) sees capitalism heading for a time of troubles as the demise of the Soviet Union unleashes fiercer intra-capitalist competition. McRae (1994: 97–119, 209–24) sees the coming crisis in terms of demography, with a growing divide between a young, unstable, poor world and a rich, old, stable one, and in terms of declining US leadership, and withdrawal of American support from internationalism and liberalism. Horsman and Marshall (1995: 208, 212) worry that the state is being dismantled by liberal capitalism, taking with it citizenship, accountability, and the general framework of socio-political stability. They worry that 'the creation of risk has outpaced the creation of trust'. They hope for a more layered form of politics up and down from the state, but fear that the economic sector is outpacing the political framework, and that there is 'no global liberal consensus on how capitalism should operate'. Buzan et al. (1998: ch. 5) focus on the operating instabilities of the global market in terms of credit bubbles and reactions to the political and social effects of intense competition. But gloom about the fate of capitalism is of course perennial. Wood (1995) rejects the easy calling of yet another terminal crisis of capitalism, rightly noting that capitalism is 'the system that dies a thousand deaths'.

There are good reasons for thinking that this pattern will continue: capitalism endlessly in crisis, but also endlessly inventing new technologies, both physical and social, with which to keep itself in business. The crisis of capitalism is always in motion, and seems likely to remain so until some fundamental change, such as the final solving of the problem of production by technology, sweeps away the conditions on which it rests. Major crises over trade or money, such as that which hit much of East Asia during 1997–8, will doubtless remain a recurrent feature of the global market, but there is little sign that the market structure itself is under terminal threat, either from its own operation or from a reassertion of military primacy. Only the worst of the environmental scenarios could easily unseat the power of the global market.

Along with the intensification of the market comes an intensification of international society, again, more of the same, marked by a steady spread (both by voluntary acceptance and by imposition) of a wider range of rules, norms, and institutions, especially economic liberal ones. Again, there is no consensus on how to understand the current condition and prospects of international society. Both 'clash of civilization' and 'decline of the USA/West' views carry the implication that international society is not much more than a projection of Western power, and that as the West declines so inevitably will international society. Similar worries about the excessively Western character of international society can be found in the work of Watson (1997) and Cohen (1995b). These concerns have to be set against the fact that both of their underlying assumptions are disputed. Not everyone thinks that the West/USA is declining (Strange 1988; Nye 1990), and some argue that international society is not Western but Westernistic (Buzan and Segal 1998a). This latter view is based on the understanding that the originally Western ideas on which international society rests—the state, sovereignty, nationalism, and diplomacy—have now become effectively universal—as, almost, has acceptance of the market. If this is so, then the foundations of international society no longer depend on Western power. What one sees through this lens is neither a subtle form of Western imperialism nor a new kind of socio-political universalism. It is, in part, both. There is universalism in the general acceptance of sovereign equality and the framework of international law and diplomacy based on that. And there is Western imperialism both in the projection of some contested values (human rights, democracy), and in the fact that the Western core and its immediate circle of Westernistic associates have developed a much thicker version of international society amongst themselves than they share with the rest. International society may be unevenly developed, but it is not fragile.

Indeed, others (Clapham 1996: 15–16, 245; 1998) note that international society is now sufficiently powerful and embedded that it is actually responsible for creating many of the states in the system, not just in Africa and parts of the Middle East, but also in Eastern Europe (after the First World War). These states, and in some ways also several of the successor states to the Soviet Union, have been given 'juridical sovereignty' by international recognition, without having first established 'empirical sovereignty' in terms of effective government over their territories (Jackson 1990). Alan James (1992) argues that international society, in the form of the doctrine of legal equality amongst states, has significantly constrained the exercise of power in the contemporary international system. Hedley Bull (1984) goes even further, developing the view that the sovereign rights of states derive from the rules of international society and are limited by them.

Bull's is a very advanced view of international society, placing rights in the system rather than in the units. If correct, this view of a strengthening and universally rooted international society slots in nicely to the stories above about sectoral transformations and the possible emergence of a new type of postmodern dominant unit which shares international space with TNCs, INGOs, and some IGOs whose legal status gives them a quasi-autonomous status in the system. If this 'neomedieval' image of multiple types of units is where things are going, then the function of the strong international society will change. In Westphalian mode, international society has rested on reinforcing sovereign equality amongst states, excluding other units, and thus supporting a neorealist international system of like units. But as indicated in the discussion of units above, this Westphalian mode is already under question, and may be entering into a significant change. A postmodern international society might well still rest on the state as the ultimate source of political authority, albeit moderated by some international legal bodies with independent power to generate some types of international law (e.g. ICJ, European Court of Human Rights). In this way, international society would retain a strong Westphalian foundation based on like units with equal legal and diplomatic rights. But it would have to add to this an agreed set of principles of differentiation, which set out the rights and obligations of different types of unit—states, TNCs, INGOs, IGOs—and how they relate to each other. The rationale for these principles of differentiation would have to rest on the liberal logic of division of labour. Firms and states would have to accept the historical evidence that neither performs efficiently when it tries to do the other's job, and that their legal rights and obligations need to be clearly demarcated. There are already signs of developments in this direction in the framework of laws about incorporation, finance, property rights, and suchlike that define the relative autonomy of non-state units and how they relate to the postmodern state. Ultimately, however, states would be responsible for enforcing these laws, although IGOs, such as the UN and NATO, are also likely to be given increasing responsibility for enforcing international law by means of force where necessary. As a consequence, the norm of non-intervention will become increasingly less significant.

Perhaps the biggest space for transformation of structure in the international system lies in world society. This most laggardly of sectors is, in historical terms, much the most resistant to globalization, and its relative backwardness might be counted as one of the major impediments to the further expansion of global international society (Buzan 1993). Mosler (1980: 27) argues that 'Today's international society cannot find its identity as a community in an ideal concept of the world supported by all the members', and this view is supported by the often anti-Western outbreaks of parochialism such as 'Asian values', 'Islamic fundamentalism', and 'Hindu nationalism'. All of these are projections out of the ancient and classical era into what some perceive as a post-Western future, and they underpin the fashionable speculation about a 'clash of civilizations'. But as argued in Chapter 15, foundations have now been laid that might permit the emergence of a stronger world society—'Mondo culture' as Buzan and Segal (1998b) have called it. While not impossible, this looks like a slow-moving development, albeit one that, like further developments in social interaction capacity, would have implications for both dominant units and system structure.

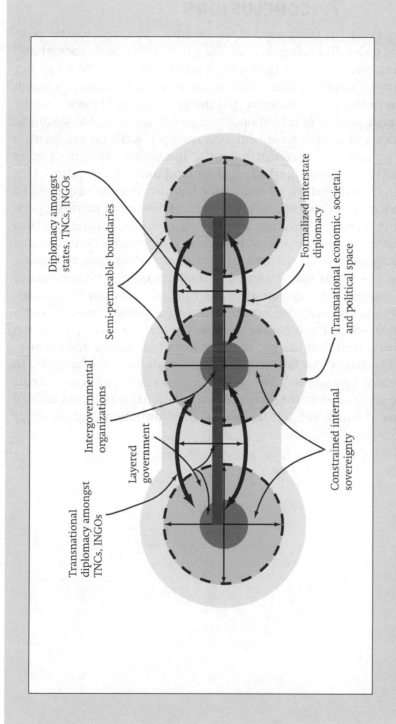

Diplomacy amongst
states, TNCs, INGOs

Semi-permeable boundaries

Formalized interstate
diplomacy

Transnational economic, societal,
and political space

Intergovernmental
organizations

Layered
government

Constrained internal
sovereignty

Transnational
diplomacy amongst
TNCs, INGOs

*Note:* The figure suggests that although some elements of the Westphalian system remain in place (see Fig. 12.3) other features have undergone a radical change. In particular, the boundaries of states are no longer impermeable, internal sovereignty is constrained, and transnational space has opened up.

*Figure 16.1 The basic form of the postmodern international system*

# 7. CONCLUSIONS

Does this add up to a case for thinking that we are now entering a fourth, post-modern, 'new world order' following on from the pre-international, ancient and classical, and modern ones reviewed in this book (see Figure 16.1)? Probably not yet, though it certainly provides evidence both to show that the question is worth asking, and perhaps to inspire the thought that the international system may be entering another major process of transition. The case for thinking that we might be witnessing a process of system transformation rests primarily on the sectoral shift in dominant process, and secondarily on the increasing capacity of mass communication, and their unfolding effects on dominant units and structure. This is something new in human history. Of course one has always to be suspicious of those making claims for the dawn of a new era. Such claims often privilege present events. They structure perceptions of both the past and the future, and they are nearly always aimed at steering present behaviour in directions desired by the proclaimer. Our analysis has the strength of resting on a long and systematic historical overview. But it has the weakness of tracking quite a wide range of variables, and this means that it cannot offer a definitive, universal formula for saying when such a transformation has occurred. If we are moving into a new era, then the changes that define it are not the same as the ones in scale, interaction capacity, and dominant unit that marked the shift from the ancient and classical to the modern world order. Those favouring a transformational view have also to confront the problem of 'two worlds'. Rather than being a single political-strategic space, with a single set of rules of the game, the international system has divided into two worlds, one of which exhibits features of transformation, and the other of which does not.

# Chapter 17

# WHAT WORLD HISTORY TELLS US ABOUT INTERNATIONAL RELATIONS THEORY

In this chapter we will sum up and review the lessons that a long view of world history seems to offer for IR theory. Marrying theory and history not only expands the empirical universe that IR theory has to address, but also puts its methodological pluralism into a larger systemic perspective. Over a global scale and a longer time one sees more easily not only what the different 'islands' of IR theory apply to, but how the islands relate to each other in a kind of archipelago. One also sees more clearly how Eurocentric much of IR theory actually is. Despite its pretence to be abstract and objective, the bulk of it is closely derived from the rather narrow historical experience defined by the period of European/Western domination. While most of the key concepts of IR theory fit quite comfortably into premodern times, some of the Westphalian assumptions and logics in the theories need to be reconsidered. We will organize this discussion using the same set of headings as in the empirical chapters: units, interaction capacity, process, and structure. But first we need to consider what history has to tell us about the core concept of this book: the international system itself.

## 1. INTERNATIONAL SYSTEM

Perhaps the most striking inadequacy in IR theory revealed by world history is its impoverished view of international systems. The standard model assumes that international systems are composed of a number of units amongst which contact is direct, and processes include diplomacy, war, and trade. Although interaction may be uneven, in principle any unit in the system can be ally, enemy, and/or trading partner with any of the others. This model can be called a full, multiordinate, international system. Its Eurocentric vision underpins most of IR theory, and makes sense for most of the modern era. But its unconscious linkage to that particular patch of history means not only that it is incapable of dealing with both past and future international systems, but also that IR theory is weaker than it should be because it is largely based on a narrow set of conditions. Without a fuller understanding of all the forms that international systems can take, and all the variables that shape them, one cannot theorize properly about either structure or process, and can hardly theorize at all about system transformations. Because an international system has obviously existed throughout the modern era, little or no thought has been given to what constitutes the necessary and sufficient conditions to say that an international system exists. Almost no thought has been given to when the first international systems might have come into being, and surprisingly little thought has been given to how the present system might transform into something else. Because these things have not been on the agenda of the discipline, there is little understanding of how international systems have evolved, and consequently there are real difficulties in trying to conceptualize where our current one might be going.

The first lesson of history for theory is that we need to look more closely at how international systems are composed, and to appreciate much more explicitly the diversity of the elements that make them up. History suggests that international systems can vary along six dimensions:

- the intensity of interaction;
- the geometrical arrangement of the units;
- the scale of the system relative to the geographical environment;
- the type of interaction;
- the time-span over which the system is observed; and
- the nature of the dominant unit or units.

## THE INTENSITY OF INTERACTION

The standard model of an international system assumes that the units are all in direct contact with each other. But as we have seen not only in pre-international systems, but also in those of the ancient and classical world, direct contact is not the only possibility. Particularly in economic and societal transactions, contact by relay is an alternative to direct contact. In both prehistoric and ancient and classical times significant amounts and values of goods, not to mention ideas, moved across long distances by being passed from one neighbour to another. This mechanism connected large numbers of units together, and some even think that it was powerful enough to create balance of payments problems for the Roman Empire in its trade with Asia. Relay contacts are clearly weaker than direct ones. They are usually slower moving and involve lower volumes. It also seems to be the case that relay processes only work for economic and social interactions, and not for political ones. If we accept relay interactions as constituting international systems—and we think that the historical evidence, especially for economic systems, is strong enough to justify doing so—then we clearly have to theorize such systems differently from those defined by direct interaction. Because they involve a lower order of contact, relay systems may well not generate significant structural effects. Indeed, one can think of relay systems as almost by definition politically unstructured, and perhaps unstructured in any sense.

## THE GEOMETRICAL ARRANGEMENT OF THE UNITS

The multiordinate or omnidirectional model of the international system pre-supposes a cluster of units all in direct contact with each other. As in most parts of the modern world, many units might have more than two neighbours, and also be in direct contact with units remote from their borders. An alternative to this is linear systems, where each unit is directly in contact only with two neighbours, one on either side (or with only one in the case of units at the end of the line, or possibly with three if the system has a branch line). Linear systems were surprisingly common in the ancient and classical world, the most dramatic being the economic system that connected Rome and China along the Silk Roads. In a pure linear system most of the interaction will by definition be relay rather than direct, and such systems will therefore have little or no structure. The systemic quality of linear economic systems is quite clear because the movement of goods crosses all the units in the system. But whether linear arrangements of military-political relations should count as systems is more open to question. If Carthage fights the Greeks, and the Greeks fight the Persians, but there are no strategic contacts between Carthage and Persia, or if the Hapsburgs fight the Ottomans and the Ottomans fight the Safavid Persians, but there are no contacts between the Hapsburgs and Persia, are these full inter-national systems?

## THE SCALE OF THE SYSTEM RELATIVE TO THE GEOGRAPHICAL ENVIRONMENT

The standard model generally assumes that the international system is global in scale. But as we have seen, for most of history this was not the case, and multiple international systems existed at the same time. When international systems are not global, a whole range of issues arises that do not exist when one system fills the whole available geographical space. Sub-global international systems have boundaries, or more likely frontier zones, where they fade away into the zones of pre-international systems. Such systems can and do expand into the terrain of pre-international systems. Sometimes they meet and merge, as the Mediterranean and Middle Eastern systems did when the Greeks and Persians began to war with each other. In other words, sub-global international systems are open in that they have an environment with which they interact, and from which they differentiate themselves. Because the modern international system is closed in this sense, IR theory has not considered these issues. And as we have seen, when international systems are sub-global, it becomes necessary to differentiate between military-political, or full, international systems (generally smaller), and economic ones (generally larger). Such sectoral and geographical differentiations disappear when a full global international system comes into being.

## THE TYPE OF INTERACTION

Awareness that economic international systems can and have functioned on a separate scale from military-political ones gives insights into international political economy that are lost if one's thoughts are confined only to the realm of full global systems. The fact that economic international systems historically have some ontological, as well as analytical, standing validates IPE's claim for the necessity of a multi-sectoral approach, and undermines the monistic approach of realists. Furthermore, the ability of international economic systems to exist substantially (though not wholly) apart from military-political ones, makes it less puzzling that the economic sector consistently leads the military-political one in degree of globalization once both systems occupy the same closed geographical space.

Sensitivity to sectoral factors is essential not only to defining the necessary and sufficient conditions for an international system to exist, but also to telling the story of how international systems have evolved up to the present day. A good case can be made that sectors are also essential to understanding how our present international system might evolve. In principle, as our distinction between full and economic systems shows, an international system can be defined by any type of interaction. Historically, military-political interaction has been dominant, but this does not always have to be the case. International systems are defined not only by dominant units, as neorealists hold, but also, and perhaps more so, by dominant forms of interaction. IR theorists need to think more about the relationship between dominant units and the dominant form of interaction. Sectors are essential to methodological pluralism, and as we have shown, system structure has to be considered in sectoral terms. Doing so allows things to run in parallel that otherwise might seem forced into an unhelpful relationship of apparent mutual exclusivity—such as *materialist and constructivist conceptions* of system structure.

## THE TIME-SPAN OVER WHICH THE SYSTEM IS OBSERVED

Because of its Eurocentric origins, much of IR theory is rooted in the assumption that international systems must be anarchic. Neorealism, with its rigid distinction between anarchy and hierarchy, includes this assumption as part of the definition of international systems. In the neorealist view, international systems cannot be hierarchies, and hierarchies cannot be international systems. In the short perspective of the modern era, this formulation serves reasonably well and does not raise obvious problems. But in the longer view it is hopelessly inadequate. When one looks at the more extensive history of international systems during the ancient and classical era it becomes clear that it is quite normal for such systems to cycle back and forth between anarchic and hierarchic structures. This phenomenon has already been observed by Adam Watson (1992). Typically, anarchies give way to universal empires, which then decay back into anarchies. In some places (China, Middle East) empire is more common than anarchy, and in others empires tend to be short lived (South Asia) or absent (Europe), with anarchy the dominant form.

It seems quite inadequate to say that international systems simply disappear during periods of empire and reappear when empires crumble. Doing so makes one unable to tell a coherent story about the system and its evolution. Given the anarchophilia of much IR theory, it is asking a lot that people should open their minds to the possibility that international systems can also be hierarchic. But that is what we propose. The shock can be eased by noting that in most empires the units do not disappear. The hierarchical structure of empire is present across the system, but it varies very considerably in its impact. Some units will be absorbed by the core, but others will retain degrees of independence as dominions or vassals or more or less independent actors on the fringe who simply acknowledge imperial hegemony (see Figs. 8.1 and 8.2).

While observing the pendulum swing between hierarchy and anarchy in the political sector, however, it is also necessary to keep a weather eye on transactions in other sectors. Market processes, for example, operate alongside imperial economic command and almost invariably stretch far beyond the political reach of an empire. The cultural influence of empires can also extend to areas that lie outside of the imperial political frontiers. Hierarchic international systems, as a result, generally contain the seeds of their own (re)fragmentation. They lack complete political domination within their own frontiers and, at the same time, when other sectors are brought into focus, they can be seen to be embedded in much more extensive systems.

The relevance of allowing hierarchy into the definition of international systems is not confined just to ancient and classical history. The real difficulty posed by the EU, and the uncertainty as to whether what goes on amongst its members is better thought of as international or domestic politics, underlines the contemporary relevance of hierarchy in analysing international relations.

Allowing that international systems can have hierarchic phases means that such systems do not generally, or at least easily, come to an end. There are two possibilities for the extinction of an international system. First, it could decay to the point where there was insufficient interaction to sustain a system (as might have happened to the Mayan and Harappan city-state systems). Or second, it could transform into a universal *state* (which is quite a different thing from a universal empire, or a political union like the current EU), in which all earlier units were dissolved into a single sovereignty. A universal state can be contemplated in theory (with opinions very divided as to whether it would be a good thing or a terrible disaster), but in practice the world does not seem to be headed in that direction. Perhaps surprisingly, traditional realists (Morgenthau 1973; Claude 1962) have strongly favoured such an outcome. But, if anything, what we see is a momentum towards an international system in which a variety of units exercise degrees of autonomy within an ever denser network of norms, rules, and institutions that define their rights and duties in relation to each other. This seems to be moving away from Westphalian-style anarchy as classically understood, but it is not moving towards a universal empire, and even less towards a universal state. Whatever it is becoming, it still seems to make excellent sense to think of it as an international system, even if it passes beyond what neorealists understand as anarchic structure.

## THE NATURE OF THE DOMINANT UNIT OR UNITS

Waltz's idea that a system is defined by its dominant units is a useful one. It is worth retaining not only because it simplifies the identification of international systems but also because it works for the whole span of history. For neorealists, the dominant units are states, and in the modern era that small number of states that count as great powers. Thus neorealists see dominant units as neither structurally nor functionally differentiated. During the ancient and classical era, great powers could be any or all of empires, city-states, or barbarian tribal federations, and thus they were structurally, if not functionally, differentiated. Given the apparent permanence of uneven development, international systems will normally contain structurally differentiated units, though as at present, some of these may not be counted in the ranks of the great powers. History so far gives exclusive primacy to military-political units as the key definers of international systems. But there is nothing determined about this. In principle, economic or societal units could dominate. This issue is historically contingent, and we should not close our minds to evolutions in which other sectors become dominant, carrying with them new types of dominant units to define international systems.

## 2. UNITS

Perhaps the main lesson of history for theory in this area is that changes at the unit level, and not in the structural variables identified by neorealists, define the biggest transformations of international systems. It turns out that the biggest type of transformation hypothesized by neorealists—from anarchy to hierarchy—is actually rather common, and not as they suggest of only theoretical interest. Indeed, it was almost the normal pattern throughout the ancient and classical era. The really big changes that define transformations of era are caused by changes in the nature of the dominant units whose actions largely define the international system. The transformation from pre-international systems to those of the ancient and classical era was caused by the rise of new types of dominant unit, first the city-state, and later empires and barbarian tribes. The transformation from the ancient and classical to the modern era was caused by the rise of the modern state as a new type of dominant unit. During the 5,000-year history of international systems it has been changes, or new developments, in the internal structure of units, more than functional differentiation between them, that provide the key to the biggest changes. Modern states, city-states, empires, and barbarian tribes were all more or less autonomous political entities and therefore hard to differentiate in functional terms. Functional differentiation did of course arise in the suzerain–vassal pattern of political relations that typified both ancient and classical empires, and the modern ones of the European imperial age. But this did not mark the biggest changes. Transformations of era arose only when changes of internal organization allowed a new type (or types) of unit to rise to power and project their distinctive internal dynamics out into the international system. Neorealists are thus right to focus on dominant units as the key definers of international systems, but wrong to focus on system structure as the only key to understanding system transformation. How one is to foresee such developments remains a problem. Who would have anticipated that the ramshackle kingdoms of late medieval Europe would swiftly evolve into the world-spanning empires of the nineteenth century and the global economy of the twentieth?

Neorealists are also wrong to close off the second tier of structure. Structural differentiation amongst the dominant units was almost the defining feature of ancient and classical international systems, and when they were in hierarchic mode, functional differention was also notable. But because their theory is Eurocentric, neorealists have difficulty thinking of hierarchical systems as international, and so they miss these points. Even in the modern era structural and functional differention of units was quite normal until the process of decolonization dismantled empires. Neorealists will point out that this applied only to the minor powers in the system, and not to the great powers. But some colonized countries (India, Egypt) were great powers in their day.

We thus cannot avoid the conclusion that constructivists (Wendt 1992; Ruggie 1998) are correct in arguing that structural theory is not independent of the character of the units in the system, and that structural forces do not wholly determine the nature of the units. In a competitive environment there is no doubt that structural pressures do work strongly in favour of like units. It might also be argued that the particular character of the national state, most notably, its obsession with hard boundaries and highly focused sovereignty, worked to reinforce the pressure for like units, at least amongst the great powers, during the modern era. Part of the problem for neorealists is the narrow cast of their theory, which is confined to the military-political sector, and which except for the loophole of socialization (Ruggie 1998: 16) is cast in material (power) rather than social (norms) terms. Our methodological pluralism allows us to bring in other structural effects, such as those of international society. These can reinforce the pressure for like units, as they did during decolonization. But they can also provide countervailing pressures. International society in the ancient Middle East seemed to encourage a hierarchy amongst kings, and it might be argued that late modern international society is encouraging the emergence of sectorally differentiated units (states, firms, INGOs). It is clear that there is more in play here than just material power and the dynamics of rivalry. Dominant units and structure are locked together in a mutually constitutive embrace. How the dominant units are internally structured makes a difference to what kind of influence they project into the system. Liberal powers will project different influences from mercantilist ones, and sovereignty-obsessed Westphalian states will reinforce anarchic structure in a way that suzerainty-seeking (and accepting) empires and city-states, or highly differentiated medieval units, might not. The character of the dominant units thus affects what kind of structural effects the system feeds back into them: whether anarchy is robust or fragile, whether global market forces are strong or weak, whether the norms of international society supports difference or homogenization of unit type.

While we are concerned about the excessive narrowness of the neorealist approach, we do not go along with those, such as Ferguson and Mansbach (1996: 10, 400–19), who argue against the state as a meaningful unit of analysis. They note that many other units are in play, that politics is much more complex than just interstate, and that the apparent 'like unit' construction of postcolonial world politics actually disguises the role of other units because some 'states' are dominated by families, some by clans or tribes, and some by religions. They seem to go too far in the other direction, celebrating the complexity of political life to the point where theory becomes impossible. There is of course no question that other units are in play, and that politics is complicated. One has to be impressed, for example, by the extraordinary longevity of kinship as an organizing principle in political and economic life. Before the rise of civilization and functional differentiation, kinship was *the* organizing principle for most of human life. During the ancient and classical era, and much of the modern one, it remained influential both in the dynastic policies of ruling elites, and in the trade diasporas of the merchant classes. Although professionalization, specialization, and meritocracy created a whole new universe of organizational structures, the old principle of kinship remained important in some central ways. This continues even today. One cannot fail to notice the central role of family in East Asian business life, or the dynastic tendencies in South Asian politics, or the importance of clan in much Middle Eastern and African political life. The Israeli army retaliates against the families of suicide bombers by blowing up their houses. A prestigious think-tank observes of Iraq that the principle on which Saddam Hussein has generally relied in his rule is that: 'a secure power base can only be founded on blood relationships' (*Strategic Survey* 1991–2: 97).

But there is another story to be told, and we think a more important one. While it is interesting to know that ancient principles of organization still play significant roles in modern life, the point is that such principles are no longer the *main* ones in operation, either in the system as a whole or in the dominant units. From our perspective, the really interesting story is the rise of ever more complex, sophisticated, and durable hierarchical units. One thread in this book has been a story about the evolution of units that started with the almost unstratified and undifferentiated hunter-gatherer bands of prehistory; moved up to hierarchical, but unstable chiefdoms; went from there to the more stable and more highly stratified form of city-states; thence moved to empires, which were at first unstable, but over the millennia learned arts of government that made them much more long lived; and ended up with what might count as the ultimate form of hierarchical unit, the Westphalian state. Historical sociologists such as Mann and Tilly have told this story compellingly in terms of 'the state makes war and war makes the state'. This is a story about social learning and innovation over very long time-spans. It is related to the neorealist story about socialization and competition, but it is not so directly evolutionist as that might imply. Sometimes, as in the case of the rise of Europe, key developments took place on the fringes of international systems. The modern state was much more a fresh start in a marginal area than a direct evolution from classical empires.

This story is one of ever more complicated and durable units, with ever more differentiated internal structures resting on ever more sophisticated principles of organization. Kinship remained in play throughout, but it was steadily joined by, and subordinated to, new principles such as bureaucracy, meritocracy, codified law, ideology, democracy, and markets which allowed the construction of ever more populous and powerful units. This story is that of the dominant units, which is also the story of the major transformations of international systems. It is a story that continues to unfold. As suggested in Chapter 16 we may be living in a noteworthy phase, during which the trend to ever greater degrees of hierarchy in the construction of dominant units begins to give way to sectoral differentiation, the layering of sovereignty, and the abandonment of war as the defining system process. While in one sense this would represent a major discontinuity with the pattern of the past, in another it represents a very significant continuity. What we see is the ongoing development and unfolding of ever more sophisticated principles of organization, and the social learning process that drives them. This development continues because it opens up new resources of power and wealth that far outstrip the expansion in the human population. It also seems to threaten not only the basic structure of the Westphalian state, but also the long-standing dominance of military-political units as the defining actors of international systems. The challenge for coming generations will be to find what kinds of social and political organizations are both possible and desirable within the strong structure of a global market economy.

## 3. INTERACTION CAPACITY

History shows that interaction capacity is central to understanding how international systems change and develop. It determines the scale of international systems, and the range, pace, and volume of the processes that take place within them. Before the quite recent advent of a full, global international system, the constraints posed by interaction capacity underpinned an important differentiation between larger, but thinner, economic international systems and smaller, but more intense, full ones. The colonial history of North America reveals the speed with which new technology spread amongst the indigenous population once it was introduced (see Maps 13.1 and 13.2). It becomes clear from very early on in our story of international systems that social technologies for interaction capacity are just as important as physical ones. Indeed, during the era of pre-international systems social technologies were totally dominant. With the rise of civilization a more balanced pattern developed with physical and social technologies both in play. Often the two are hard to disentangle. Pony express systems get the best out of horses (or runners) by organizing relay stations to ensure that communications are moving continuously at the highest available speed over long distances. Air traffic control systems allow more planes to fly in a given airspace than would otherwise be safe.

But although we think that we have demonstrated the importance of interaction capacity to understanding, and theorizing about, international systems, we have to admit that the concept posed some difficult problems of classification which we are not confident that we have fully solved. This is hardly an unusual problem in IR. Many people remain confused about, or in disagreement about, how to draw the boundaries between process and structure. Although these classifications are used frequently in IR literature, insufficient attention has been paid to the problem of differentiating them. Neorealist and neoliberal discussions do not usually make both structure and process explicit at the same time, and the boundary problem between them is therefore less visible than it should be. Linking these theories to an account of world history thus highlights problems that are already a feature of orthodox IR theory, but which are hidden by its excessive abstraction. It is not therefore so surprising that introducing a new category should compound the difficulty. In principle, we think the distinction between interaction capacity (what interaction *can* happen) and process (what *does* happen) is clear. In practice, physical technologies pose few problems, but allocating social technologies to their 'right' place often proved difficult. Most social technologies take the form of sedimented processes, and could therefore also be classified as process formations. This would be true of diplomacy, trade diasporas, higher religions, and the elaborate norms, rules, and institutions of international society, including most IGOs. But not all process formations are social interaction capacity: namely wars, the arms dynamic, trade 'wars', and suchlike. This double hatting has made our story a bit messier than we would like, and perhaps suggests the need for more thinking about how to differentiate the basic components of international systems.

## 4. PROCESS

The long view of history generates three observations about process. The first, picking up on the discussion immediately above, is to note the deep embeddedness of social processes in international systems. This stands out most clearly in pre-international systems, where social technologies for interaction capacity played a major role in facilitating interaction long before physical technologies came into play. Social technologies continued to play a major role in facilitating process right through the ancient and classical era, and on into the modern one down to the present day. The continuity and centrality of this role lends weight to the social constructivist view of international systems, and constrains the relevance of more mechanistic interpretations. As many a second-rate science fiction plot demonstrates, military interaction between units is conceivable without their sharing any mutually constructed social ground. But economic, societal, and political interactions are not. Diplomacy, proselytization, trade, credit, and currency exchange all require that the units share some common social understanding of themselves, their relationship, and their activity.

The second observation is the durability of a familiar set of process formations over very long stretches of history. Deep back into the ancient and classical era we find most of the main process formations also present in the contemporary international system: diplomacy, war, trade diasporas, trade wars, balance of payments problems, inflation, arms competitions, international societies, and so forth. One can even find uneven development as a standing feature of world economies (Braudel 1985: 26, 35–45), albeit with the different twists set out in the introduction to Chapter 14. Uneven development not only carries implications of durable centre–periphery process formations, but also ties into the central importance of structural differentiation of units as an enduring feature of international systems (see section 2 of this chapter). At the very least, all of this lays to rest fears that by pushing the modern idea of international systems back into the past we would construct a false and anachronistic image of earlier times. The idea of international systems is historically robust. It is valid both as a way of looking at history, and as a way of connecting theoretical analysis of the present to the data base of the past.

The third observation, and perhaps the main lesson of history for IR theory under this heading, is the central role of process in defining not only the scale of international systems, but also their intensity, and their character. None of this stands out clearly if all one is looking at is the last 500 years of the European/

Western era, when the system is in a sense borderless, and all sectors of process operate in the same geographical space. But both come into clear perspective in the longer view. Because premodern interaction capacity was relatively low, all types of process were constrained. Military-political interaction tended to be confined to subcontinental scale. Even great imperial powers such as Rome and China could not project military power much beyond their core area, and Alexander the Great could not convince his exhausted army to push on into India. Economic systems achieved greater extent only because the movement of low-volume, high-value luxury goods over long distances, unlike the movement of armies, did not require high levels of interaction capacity. The expansion, and occasional merger, of international systems during the ancient and classical era was thus closely determined by the range over which various types of interaction could be sustained. And the separation of economic from full international systems rested on the different interaction capacity requirements of trade and war. The story of ancient and classical international systems, and their transformation into the modern era, can thus be told in terms of the expanding range of process, first linking up economic systems and later military political ones. It can also be told in terms of the growing intensity of interaction as less intense relay processes gave way to more intense direct ones. More than 2,000 years ago this steady extension of range had already created a single economic system embracing all of Eurasia and North Africa. Fifteen hundred years ago, riding on the back of breakthroughs in transportation technology, it leapt the Atlantic, and shortly thereafter the Pacific, to create first a global economic system, and within 300 years a full global international system.

The gegraphical range of processes defined not only the scale of international systems but also their character. It is of more than passing interest that for thousands of years economic international systems were not coextensive with military-political ones. This is of course not to argue that economic systems were *totally* separate from military political ones, for it is abundantly clear that the waxing and waning of imperial power made a big difference to the sustainability of the Eurasian trading system. But it is to observe that economic processes have logistics and modes of organization sufficiently different from military-political ones to enable them to form distinctive international systems in their own right. If one looks at international history only for the last few centuries this independent quality of economic systems is largely lost to view because of the conjuncture of economic and military-political international systems on a global scale that emerged from the eighteenth century onward. Knowing that economic international systems are capable of semi-independent self-definition does more than simply justify the use of sectors as an analytical tool. It also tells us something quite profound about the full international system in which we live. It suggests that seeking to understand that system by using the tools of methodological monism, as both neorealists (viewing it through purely political lenses) and world-system theorists (putting economics in the driving seat) try to do, is at best a highly distorting exercise, and at worst a futile and counter-productive one. It is true that IPE has yet to develop much in the way of coherent theory, but one cannot fault its guiding impulse that in order to make sense of international relations one has to understand the interplay between markets and political authority, and that one can only do so using a methodologically pluralist approach.

Knowing that economic systems can in principle function semi-autonomously from military-political ones, and have in practice done so, opens up an interesting perspective on the current condition of the international system. As suggested in Chapter 16, one way of reading current developments seen through sectoral lenses is to suggest that we may be in the early stages of a sectoral shift in which economic processes are becoming more important to defining the international system and military-political ones less important. The key issue here is no longer, as in the ancient and classical era, the *range* over which different types of process can function. Now it is about the relative *intensity* of different types of process, and therefore the balance of influence and power in how they interplay with each other in constructing the international system. We have already noted that the economic international system reached global scale more than two centuries before a full global international system came into being. The explanation for the leading role of the economic sector in expanding the scale of international systems is that many economic processes, especially finance and the lighter end of trade, have lower interaction capacity requirements than most military-political processes. This explanation still has a lot of power even though the relationship between sectors has moved from relative range (no longer in play since the system is now geographically closed) to relative intensity. It is now a commonplace to observe the extraordinary dynamism of the global economy, and the relative underdevelopment of the global polity and global society. The very words give the game away. We talk easily of a global economy, but there is no sign of a world government, and even talk of a global polity, or global governance, is ringed with hesitations, as is talk of international or world society.

Thus another way of looking at this explanation is to say that economic processes are more responsive to the opportunities offered by any given level of interaction capacity. Since interaction capacity has been increasing by leaps and bounds since the spectacular breakthroughs in physical and social technologies during the nineteenth and twentieth centuries, it is hardly surprising that economic processes have outpaced military-political and societal ones. Knowing that economic systems once flourished separately from military-political ones in terms of geographical domain makes it easier to understand that they still have a semi-autonomous status even within the shared global domain, and that what differentiates them now is the relatively greater intensity of economic processes. That difference hinges on the greater ease with which economic process respond to increases in interaction capacity: think, for example, of the way in which global financial markets have seized the opportunity created by global mass communication. And since interaction capacity continues to grow, even if only by incremental improvements of existing technologies, it is not unreasonable to think that the economic sector will continue to outpace the military-political and societal ones in terms of its relative intensity and depth of development. If so, and given the constraints on war imposed by both democracy and weapons of mass destruction, this could easily lead to changes in the relative importance of economic as opposed to military-political structures in defining the character of the international system.

# 5. STRUCTURE

Our discussions about structure reveal not only major gaps in theorizing international systems, but also big questions for neorealists, and an expansive research agenda for methodological pluralists.

As the discussion in section 1 of this chapter argues, a long view of history shows that the whole concept of international systems is under-theorized. This weak conceptualization particularly affects the understanding of structure, which is the most abstract of the elements that compose social systems. Throughout our discussion it has become apparent that interaction capacity, process, and structure are linked, and these links can be summed up in the following propositions.

- Interaction capacity constrains what kinds of process *can* occur, but it does not determine what kinds of process *do* occur.
- Where interaction capacity is only sufficient to support relay processes we are unlikely to find much in the way of political process or structural effects, and might well classify such systems as unstructured across all sectors. This is likely to be true of systems with a linear geographical arrangement.
- The strength or weakness of process determines whether systems are structured or not, and whether structures have significant effects or not.

Thus low interaction capacity=weak process, but the strength of interaction does not necessarily increase as interaction capacity rises. Units can decide not to make full use of available opportunities for interaction. The relationship between process and structure is more direct, and it seems reasonable to hypothesize that strong process=strong structure. These formulations mean that there is a link between interaction capacity and structure, but that it is not a simple or straightforward one. Since structure depends on process, and process depends on interaction capacity, there is a sense in which structure, like process, is constrained, but not determined, by interaction capacity. Weak interaction capacity will definitely mean weak or no structure, especially if process is confined to relay modes, which seem capable of supporting extensive, if slow-moving, economic and social processes, but not political ones. Strong structure will require high levels of inter-action capacity, but high interaction capacity does not necessarily mean strong structure. In the pre-international systems of Australia and North America, low levels of interaction capacity were capable of supporting only relay processes, and these processes were too weak to generate structural effects. These systems must thus count as unstructured, as also must the Eurasian economic system of classical times, which also displayed only relay processes. Unstructured systems can still generate process formations (e.g. balance of payments problems, centre-periphery), but they will not generate structural effects (e.g. convergence of prices).

Perhaps the main point to be drawn from all of this is that structure is, like process, itself variable. It is not controversial to say that processes vary in strength: the destructiveness of war, the value and volume of trade, the extent of collective identity, and so forth. But it would be easy to infer from a Waltzian account that this is not true of structure, that structure either exists or does not. As we have shown, this is not valid. Structure depends on process, and other things being equal, structural effects will get stronger in proportion to the strength of the processes that generate them. This is most obviously true in the economic sector, where larger volumes of trade and finance, accounting for higher proportions of GNP, generate stronger market effects. But it is also true in the military-political sector, where, as in the story of the rise of the modern state, intensification of warfare strengthens the processes of socialization and competition that generate like units. If structural effects vary with process in this way, then it becomes hard to avoid the conclusion that such effects will become increasingly powerful in shaping the international system over the coming decades.

In addition to this general observation, our survey has revealed a number of specific questions about structural theory, but since these have been discussed fully earlier, there is no need to do more than summarize them here.

Chapter 11 argued that while the conditions for neorealist theory were met in the international systems of the ancient and classical era, its predictions about 'like units' and stable anarchic structures were largely unfulfilled. The reasons for this failure could be found in neither interaction capacity nor process, both of which were sufficient to support structural effects in the military-political sector. An argument was offered that explained the failure of neorealist expectations in terms of the character of the dominant units in those systems, reinforcing the arguments of those from Wendt (1992) to Braudel (1985: 26, 35–45) that also focus on the internal qualities of dominant units as one key to understanding how international systems operate. More generally, the long view of history challenges quite a number of the assumptions and assertions underpinning neorealism. As we argued in *The Logic of Anarchy*, the neorealist view that international systems have always been anarchic, and units always 'like', is simply wrong. There are many instances of international systems shifting from anarchy to hierarchy and back again, and equally many instances of unlike dominant units persisting for very long periods despite the operation of strong forces of socialization and competition. If neorealists want to maintain their claim to possess a universal theory, then they need both to reopen the second tier of their structural model (differentiation of units) and find some way of dealing with the fact that deep structure transformations from anarchy to hierarchy and back again have occurred as a regular feature of many international systems. The fact that the other two tiers of neorealist structure are active reduces the salience that neorealists have given to the third tier, distribution of power. Polarity does matter at the system level, but it does not define the really big changes, either within international systems, or when there are shifts of historical era which redefine international systems. Polarity is a shorter-term variable, and consequently has not featured much in our story. In large international systems it is also a variable at the regional level as well as at the global. One cannot understand regional security complexes without observing the effects of local balances of power such as those between India and Pakistan, Argentina and Brazil, or among Iran, Iraq, and Saudi Arabia, and neither can one understand the local effects of global polarity without seeing how they are mediated through local polarities (Buzan 1991: ch. 5; Buzan et al. 1998; Buzan and Wæver forthcoming).

If neorealists do not want to make these changes, then they have to drop their claim to universality, and accept that neorealism is a theory only of the modern era. Even then they need to deal with the constructivist anomaly of socialization lying at the heart of a supposedly materialist theory of like units. And if they do drop the claim to universality, they grievously weaken their claim to have anything decisive to say about the future.

Chapter 15 raised the question of how structures in different sectors relate to each other. Methodological monists usually deal with this problem by ignoring it, and simply assuming that useful theory can only be constructed within a single sector. Neorealists, for example, are unembarrassed by talking of political structure (anarchy-hierarchy, polarity) as *the* system structure, without asking whether there are other structural forces in play that might affect the operation of the international system. Methodological pluralists cannot ignore this issue, and we looked briefly at the main attempts to think about multiple structural effects working at the same time. We have not had the space in this book to dig deeper into this question, but it is clear that trying to understand the interplay of structures across sectors must rank high on the research agenda of those who accept that a methodological pluralist approach is the only sensible way to approach the study of a phenomenon as vast and as complex as international systems.

# 6. CONCLUSIONS

On the basis of these points, it seems safe to say that IR theory cannot develop properly unless it is rooted in a full-scale world history, and not just the European/world history of the last 500 or even the last 1,000 years. We have demonstrated that a wide range of IR concepts are relevant to premodern history, and can fruitfully be applied to analysis of the ancient and classical era. But even on the basis of this first attempt, we have also been able to demonstrate a whole set of major weaknesses in IR theory that stem from taking a short historical view. In sum, these are:

- The very idea of international system itself is under-theorized and under-specified because the concept has been hinged only to post-Westphalian history.
- The idea that the biggest type of system change is in the deep structure is shown to be false, and again an artefact of the focus on post-Westphalian history. In world historical terms, change of dominant unit type is the key to changes of era.
- The neorealist closure of the second tier of structure because of the effects of anarchy in creating like units is wrong. Unlike units can exist and have existed within anarchic structures.
- Neither process nor structure can be properly theorized without taking into account interaction capacity.
- Process and process formations are relevant and applicable concepts for at least 5,000 years of world history.
- Process and structure have to be differentiated by sector, and doing so reveals important differences in the way different types of interaction relate to interaction capacity. In particular, economic process seems always to outpace military-political in both scale and intensity of development at any given point in time.
- Neorealist claims that anarchic structures are stable rest only on post-Westphalian history and are not supportable as a universal claim.

Taken together, these points are a damning indictment of much of IR theory. For us, they confirm that linking IR and world history is not just a marginal luxury that IR theorists can take or leave as they wish. It is an essential act, without which IR theory can never hope to capture its subject. And as we argued in the Introduction, we also think that without the link to world history, IR will never break out of its own ghetto, and thus never develop its role as the integrating macro-discipline of the social sciences.

# Chapter 18

# WHAT INTERNATIONAL RELATIONS THEORY TELLS US ABOUT WORLD HISTORY

Having seen what world history has to offer IR theory, it is now time to turn the tables and see what IR theory has to offer world history. The most obvious answer to that question is the idea of international system itself. As we hope we have demonstrated, this idea, and its associated concepts of dominant units, scale, interaction capacity, process, and structure, provide an extraordinarily useful theoretical framework for studying world history. These concepts can produce a 'thick' conception of international system that has the potential to provide a rich and distinctive account of world history that captures main features that are missed or obscured by existing approaches. The concepts in our toolkit are well suited to the broad-brush approach that world history requires, and offer as much as, if not more than, any of the available alternatives.

We cannot do more here than we have already done in Parts II–IV to set out what this IR world history looks like. What we can do is to show how it relates to the debates about periodization, which lie at the heart of any world historical analysis. Periodization is about the criteria for defining what constitute major continuities and major changes in any story that evolves over time. Periodization of history is necessarily a product of theory, and the purpose of this chapter is to compare the arguments on this arising from IR theory with those arising out of mainstream world history, historical sociology, and other approaches that have attempted a macro-historical perspective. First we look at the nature and implications of periodization. Second we examine briefly how mainstream IR theory deals with the periodization of world history. Third, we reassess some of the dominant theoretical frameworks in the literature on the periodization of world history. And fourth, we summarize the resultant chronology.

## 1. PERIODIZATION AND WORLD HISTORY

Green (1992: 13; 1998) claims that periodization is among 'the most prominent and least scrutinised theoretical properties of history', and Bentley (1996: 749) suggests that as interest in world history has increased, so 'questions of periodization

present themselves with increasing insistence'. Historians experience an inevitable tension between the idea that the past represents a seamless web and the
practical need to divide the past into manageable chunks that can be investigated.
The dominant strategy for dealing with this dilemma is to divide and subdivide
the past into distinct periods. Over the past 200 years, there has emerged an
almost universal tendency in History to accept a tripartite primary division of the
past, which distinguishes ancient, medieval, and modern history. Within these
broad divisions, of course, there are secondary and tertiary subdivisions, the
bottom line being the analysis of any given historical decade or century.

The intellectual tension between the seamless web and schemes of periodization reflects the difference in reality between times marked by a high degree of
continuity and times when change seems to be in the driving seat. There is always
a mixture between the two, always room for debate about which is dominant.
Inevitably there is much dispute about what things should be thought important
in the assessment of continuity and change. The orthodox historical periodization
assumes that there is something that binds the ancient world together in a way
that is different from the way that either the medieval world or the modern world
are bound together. The danger inherent in periodization is that it encourages
people to lose sight of the past as a seamless web and become institutionalized
into thinking of the past as falling into distinct and readily dividable periods.
Instead of seeing the strong lines of continuity between the medieval and modern
periods, historians can easily fall into focusing exclusively on those features that
have been used to distinguish the modern from the medieval.

According to Green, very little thought has been given by historians to what
periodizing involves. But if we accept that periodizing history requires drawing a
distinction between continuity and change, then it has to be accepted that the
process is necessarily a theoretical activity. Two approaches to the task of dividing
history are distinguished by Green. The first identifies points in time when a
series of historical developments have converged so that, in aggregate, the world
looks very different before and after that moment in time. Green suggests, for
example, that there was a host of developments that occurred around AD 1500—
religious upheavals, scientific discoveries, political reconfigurations, and geographical discoveries—which, when taken together, warrant seeing this date as a
major historical turning point. The second approach to periodizing history
involves the identification of a specific event, for example, European contact with
the Americas, that in and of itself generated a whole series of subsequent changes
that led to the emergence of a new period in world history.

The tripartite division was initiated by historians who established the breaks on
a very impressionistic basis. But as historians have increasingly turned to social
science methodologies that focus more specifically on the processes of historical
change, these divisions have not been abandoned. These methodologies have
long historical antecedents, with the idea of a trade-based division of labour

precipitating change, for example, tracing back to Adam Smith, and cyclical demographic pressure as a source of change going back to Malthus. The other major force for change, associated with the idea of evolving modes of production, advanced by Marx, certainly endorses the tripartite division. Marx distinguished a slave mode of production that prevailed during antiquity; which gave way to a feudal mode of production during the Middle Ages, with feudalism giving way in turn to the capitalist mode of production associated with the modern period.

When we turn to periodization in world history it immediately becomes apparent that it is necessary to bring space as well as time into the equation. The metaphor of history as a seamless web is almost invariably used to summon up the temporal dimension of world history. But there is obviously a spatial dimension which poses identical problems. History does not move at the same speed all across the planet. Writing, for example, is 5,000 years old in some places, 2,000 in others, and less than 200 in others. In addition to chunking time, historians also need to chunk space, focusing on specific areas of the world as well as on specific periods. The two dimensions have, in practice, been conflated when we come to look at the conventional periodization of world history, because there is a clear Eurocentric bias to the familiar tripartite periodization: the medieval period is relevant almost exclusively to Europe, and not at all to the Americas, Africa, and most of Asia. Yet Green insists that most university texts on world history in the United States continue to rely implicitly or explicitly on this division. Our text also relies on a tripartite division, but not the orthodox one. We focus, first, on pre-international systems; we then depict a second period when international systems began to form and later became interlinked; and finally we turn to the establishment and evolution of a global international system.

The dividing markers we use denote relatively short periods of intensive change giving way to very long periods of continuity. But it is important to note that our markers embrace a spatial as well as a temporal dimension. They denote staging posts that come into play at different points in time across the globe. If we think of world history as a time–space matrix, during our second period, for example, what we observe is an increasing proportion of the globe moving out of pre-international systemic arenas and into international systemic ones. This process continues into the third phase, but it is overtaken by a new set of processes that generate a single global system which continues to evolve.

We think that this mode of periodization derived from our theoretical framework offers ways to overcome some of the serious problems that can be encountered in trying to provide an account of world history. We attach importance to pre-international systems because they continue to persist through the next two periods. Moreover, we have endeavoured to demonstrate that the existence of these systems continued to have an important effect after the emergence of international systems. It is not possible to understand how international systems operated or expanded if it is not acknowledged that they existed in the context of pre-international systems. This insight remains true even though the percentage of the globe occupied by pre-international systems steadily shrinks over time. By simply focusing on the relationship between international and pre-international systems, it is possible to chunk the time–space dimensions of world history into a single period, extending over five millennia, during which international systems steadily expanded at the expense of the long-established pre-international systems (see Fig. 18.1).

This formulation certainly overcomes the difficulty of how to think about the relationship between Eurasia and the Americas. Green (1992: 51–2) argues that 'the time warp between the two hemispheres creates a problem in achieving meaningful universal periodisation'. But this is not a problem for our approach. What we observe, during the second period, is an increasing number of international systems coming into existence, with the percentage of global territory occupied by international systems undergoing an increase around the time of Christ, when international systems began to consolidate in Central and South America. But this assessment is premised on the assumption that international systems can be traced back to the fourth millennium BC. If we accept the more conventional view that the contemporary international system is a product of the Treaty of Westphalia, then IR theory has relatively little to offer the study of world history. But if it is accepted that international systems have a long history, then, as we shall show in the third section of this chapter, IR theory has a significant contribution to make to the debates on periodization.

## 2. PERIODIZATION AND IR THEORY

A first glance at mainstream IR theory suggests that it can tell us little about how to periodize world history. It is possible to argue that there is either a strong resistance or a high degree of indifference amongst IR theorists to using the idea of the international system to periodize world history. Most IR theorists are simply too preoccupied with the contemporary international system to elicit any concern with world history. The tendency to raid the past in search of particular systems from world history that share common features with the European international system also militates against an interest in large-scale periodization. So also does neorealism, with Waltz asserting that his theory of the international system covers any historical period, thus eliminating the need for periodization.

Within IR there have been only a few attempts to periodize world history. Gilpin (1981: 29) sees 1648 as dividing the history of the international system into periods of hegemonic international systems that have prevailed throughout premodern world history, and post-Westphalian times, when international systems generally took a bipolar or multipolar form. Wight (1977: ch. 5) chooses the Council of Constance (1494) to mark the origins of the European states-system, and sees

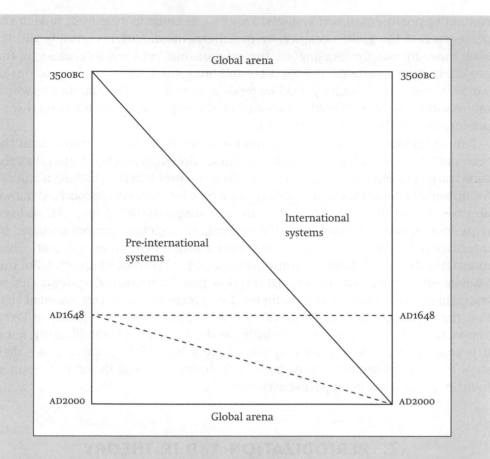

*Note:* The figure indicates very schematically that, over the last 5,000 years, international systems have overtaken pre-international systems, and the same picture emerges if we start the international clock ticking in 1648. At this juncture we are unable to provide even a rough indication of the actual contour of the diagonal line separating international and pre-international systems.

*Figure 18.1 Pre-international and international systems in world history*

Westphalia as its coming of age. Ruggie (1983) uses a critique of neorealist theory to postulate the existence of a distinctive medieval period, with different structural characteristics from the modern one. This view tends to reinforce the traditional tripartite scheme of historians. Watson (1992) confronts a five-millennium span, but his scheme only chunks time in a loose sense, identifying three overlapping types of international society: ancient states-systems, the European international society, and the global international society. Aside from these exceptions, the general assumption is that ever since the formation of states it is possible to trace the history of their relationships in terms of the shifting distribution of power. Although 1648, perhaps the best-known date in an IR timechart, is frequently used to mark the moment in European history when the modern international system finally emerged, it remains unclear how to characterize the preceding period. There is no universal agreement, moreover, that 1648 represents the appropriate moment to date the emergence of the modern international system (Krasner 1993, 1995–6; Wight 1977: ch. 5). The date has often been pushed back to 1500 and Tilly even starts the historical clock ticking around AD 1000.

Within the confines of post-Westphalian time, there is probably a near consensus amongst realists that the international system can be periodized as multipolar up to 1945, and then bipolar up to 1989. Unfortunately the assessment of polarity has become problematic since the end of the Cold War, so it is not clear how this sequence continues. An alternative is to try to characterize the system as alternating between periods of concert and conflict. But the fact remains that mainstream IR theory has made little headway in this area. It does not generally consider premodern periodization to be an important question, and most of the IR international history literature focuses on periodizing the twentieth century, largely following the conventional division into: pre-1914, inter-war years, Cold War, and post-Cold War.

But it is not just mainstream IR theorists who have failed to take world history on board. More surprisingly, the same criticism can be levelled at postpositivists who are deeply suspicious of mainstream IR theory, especially Waltzian neorealism, because of its lack of historicity. The postpositivists have done much to undermine many of the familiar certainties within the discipline. Central theoretical concepts, like sovereignty and anarchy, are now no longer taken for granted as foundational features of the international system. Postpositivists have depicted them instead as discursive practices that are imposed on a fluid and ambiguous reality. Implicit in much of the postpositivist literature is a very clear periodization which distinguishes between the premodern, the modern, and the postmodern. Within this periodization, there is a deep-seated criticism of modernity and those philosophies of history associated with modernity that describe the past in terms of progress, or which view the Enlightenment as a step forward in human history. Such meta-narratives are regarded as a feature of modernity and inherently flawed. Like mainstream IR theorists, the postpositivists have paid very little attention to the premodern period. But in contrast to most mainstream IR theorists there has also been a preoccupation with thinking about postmodernity and time–space relations. Much of this literature is full of insight. But as yet these IR theorists, while highly sensitive to the anachronisms of much mainstream thinking about the past in IR, have not displayed much interest in extending their ideas to the problems of periodizing world history from an IR perspective.

This assessment can be extended to virtually all IR theorizing, with the result that it lacks historical depth. By focusing on how a political system of states developed within Europe over the last 350 years, in the wake of the 1648 Treaty of Westphalia, and then using this understanding as a template for what constitutes international relations, the discipline has unnecessarily hampered itself. IR, therefore, like the blind man in the well-known fable who catches hold of an elephant's trunk, confronts insuperable problems trying to provide a description of the complex whole under investigation. More disturbing, without some overall understanding of the complex whole, it is all too easy to misinterpret that bit of the whole that has been grasped. Because IR theory currently fails to grapple with a world historical perspective it can neither understand the world history of international relations nor see the development of European international relations from a world historical perspective. So while the global reach encompassed by world history is beyond the current concerns of IR, at the same time, its finger is not even securely placed on the European historical pulse that forms the body of most IR theory.

The temptation is, of course, to throw out the theoretical baby with the historical bathwater and to assume that established IR theory is unable to help us to develop a world historical perspective on international relations. This would be a mistake. IR theory has, in fact, got a good deal to offer the analysis of world history. But it is worth noting that in contrast to IR, Wallerstein has provided a periodization for world history even though his primary interest is in world history since 1500. Even more important, his theoretical framework has been picked up and used by world historians as well as by sociologists, archaeologists, and anthropologists who are interested in earlier historical eras.

Without doubt there are ontological, epistemological, and methodological problems with the approach that we have followed. The danger of adopting a pluralistic stance is that you become vulnerable to attacks from all sides. But we think that the search by positivists for epistemological precision and certainty, and the insistence by postpositivists that we live in a world of ontological ambiguity and uncertainty—both schools seeming to work on the dangerous and erroneous assumption that in the land of the blind, the one-eyed man is king—is likely to stand in the way of saying anything new or interesting about the past, present, or future. We have tried quite self-consciously to provide a novel way of thinking about world history, but we could not have done so without recourse to the rich vein of IR theory that has so far remained, for this purpose, largely untapped.

# 3. COMPETING APPROACHES TO THE PERIODIZATION OF WORLD HISTORY

In this section we re-examine the periodization generated by our framework in the context of other periodizations for world history. This exercise has four purposes:

- to set out how we think the international systems approach should affect thinking about historical periodization;
- to raise awareness of how important periodization is to IR, and to highlight the limitations of Westphalia-bound theory in thinking about system change;
- in some places to challenge, and in others to support, conventional ideas of periodization; and
- to attempt a synthetic, comprehensive approach that pulls together the main lines of thinking about how to periodize world history.

As already noted, the main boundary points in our scheme differ from those of mainstream History. We postulate three major turning points in world history. One around 60,000–40,000 years ago with the emergence of pre-international systems, another, around 3500 BC, with the formation of the first international systems, and a final point of transformation around AD 1500 when the modern global international system first began to take shape. Our differences with historians on the first turning point simply reflects the fact that they are prevented by their methodology from dealing with times before writing. They leave those times to archaeologists. We agree with mainstream history that 3500 BC represents a major turning point, and we have new arguments to explain why. We also agree that there is a distinction to be made between the ancient and modern worlds, though we disagree that the medieval period sits between the two as a world historical era in its own right. From our perspective, the medieval period is a secondary matter of largely local concern. Rather than defining it as an interim period between the ancient and the modern, which is true only for European history, we see the world historical boundary between those two as direct, and we locate it at *c.* AD 1500. There is much debate about the nature and proper location of this boundary, on which more below.

In periodizing world history there is a strong consensus on two points. First is that all kinds of important transformations took place *c.*3500 BC with the rise of city-states, civilizations, and international systems. The reasons for identifying this as a clear primary turning point in world history are numerous and strong, and there is even quite broad agreement on the date. Second is that the rise of what might most generally be called 'modernity' constitutes an event of equal world historical importance to what occurred in 3500 BC. Perhaps because it is much closer to us in time, and much more richly attended with historical

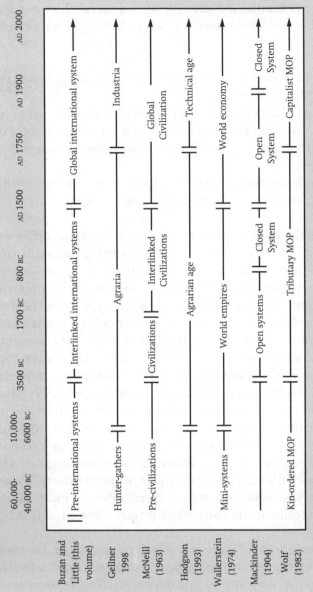

*Figure 18.2 Comparative periodization: primary turning points in world history*

Note: The figure compares the primary turning points that have emerged in this text with those identified by some of the key twentieth century world historians discussed in Chapter 3. The differences identified here would, of course, be further accentuated if secondary and tertiary turning points were brought into the picture.

evidence, there is still much debate about what was important in defining this transformation, and therefore about when it took place. All the other debates about periodization concern turning points of less weight than these two. We will therefore organize our discussion around these two primary points as follows:

- secondary turning points in prehistory;
- understanding the 3500 BC transformation point;
- secondary turning points in the ancient and classical era;
- the debate about the boundary between the ancient and classical and the modern eras;
- secondary turning points in the modern era;
- the question of a third primary transformation.

## WHERE TO START? TURNING POINTS IN PREHISTORY

Before we can identify any turning points, it is necessary to establish a starting point. It is universally acknowledged that the existence of mobile, egalitarian hunter-gatherer bands extends back to the dawn of human history, and it is generally acknowledged that modern human beings first emerged around 100,000 years ago in Africa. There is, however, a fierce debate about whether these modern human beings originated in Africa and then spent the next 80,000 years colonizing the rest of the globe, or whether modern human beings evolved from earlier forms of human beings in various regions around Eurasia. But this is not a debate that can be resolved by world historians, and there is no particular reason for us to accord it significance in our scheme.

For us, the key starting point lies within the long history of hunter-gatherer bands, and comes at the moment in time when the effects of human interaction began to extend across long distances. This marks the beginning of what we have called pre-international systems. Anthropologists and archaeologists now accept that some step-level change occurred around 40,000 to 60,000 years ago which ensured that HGBs became locked together like a vast jigsaw, with the consequence that although individuals may have operated locally, exotic goods could travel long distances (Diamond 1992; Gamble 1995). Giving a precise date for this turning point is impossible, because new research is constantly pushing it back in time. But the crucial point is that at some time after 60,000 BC, human beings began to exchange goods that could travel 'down the line' over hundreds of miles. Evidence from Australia and North America indicates that eventually these exchange links between HGBs extended across continents. Although there is still no agreed explanation for this development, the evidence certainly justifies our decision to use this event as the point in time when pre-international systems first came into existence.

It is worth noting that our framework is compatible with the argument developed by Gamble, that an unintended consequence of hunter-gatherer bands being able to maintain contact over a distance was that human beings were able to move into areas that had previously resisted colonization. One consequence of this development was that humans were able to colonize the Americas. Just as important as acknowledging the origins of these systems, is the recognition that they have persisted, right up to the present day. Despite the obvious importance attached to the subsequent emergence of international systems the continuing significance of pre-international systems must not be overlooked. By stressing that hunter-gatherer bands have always been capable of generating very extensive systems, it becomes much less easy to allow them to fade into the background, as happens with most other approaches with the exception of Wolf's. Our approach contrasts strongly with that of Wallerstein who argues that hunter-gatherer bands operated as autonomous and self-sufficient mini-systems until such time as they were absorbed into more developed economic systems.

The next turning point falls somewhere between 10,000 and 6,000 BC. Many analysts define this point in terms of the emergence of agriculture (Mann 1986: 40–1, ch. 3). Gellner (1988: 275) even claims this moment as the 'starting point' for an analysis of human history, and both he and Hodgson (1993) argue that the agricultural revolution inaugurated an historical period that extended to the industrial revolution. Stavrianos (1990: 45–51) uses a similar scheme, though he poses it as a transition from kinship to tributary societies beginning around 10,000 BC. Without the development of agriculture, it is argued, the emergence of civilization would have been impossible. It was often thought in the past that human beings developed agriculture in order to cope with population growth which could not be accommodated on the basis of hunting and gathering. But it is now recognized that teleological theories of this kind are not plausible. For many millennia after the emergence of agriculture, there were large parts of the world where the population remained stable and hunter-gatherer bands persisted. It is now recognized that the population only began to rise as a consequence of human beings living settled lives which then allowed them to breed more rapidly. Agriculture was a cause not a consequence of population growth. Indeed, the whole idea of an agricultural revolution is now regarded as highly suspect. What was viewed as an agricultural revolution is now seen to be the end of a long process that went on for many millennia.

From the perspective of our theoretical framework, there is no doubt that from around 10,000 BC there were various parts of the world where the social organization of hunter-gatherer bands did start to alter. Mobility gave way in some areas to a more sedentary way of life and hierarchy began to take the place of egalitarianism in the domestic political structure of units. Both of these developments can occur independently of the development of agriculture, but our framework suggests that both of them began to have a substantial impact on the nature of the systems within which hunter-gatherer bands operated. Humans began to operate in tribal villages around 8000 BC and, from our perspective, this development represents an important date for subdividing pre-international systems. At very different points in time over the subsequent millennia, villages in a limited number of areas across the globe became structurally and functionally differentiated with the emergence of chiefdoms, where chiefs occupied heavily fortified central villages and held sway over subordinate villages. These sedentary, hierarchical units are the precursors to more fully state-like entities, and unlike mobile HGBs begin to display behaviours characteristic of 'international' relations.

There is no doubt that the development of agriculture profoundly affected the emergence of sedentary and hierarchical groups. But as we demonstrated in Chapter 7, it is only one element in the much longer story of complex and far-reaching processes that eventually resulted in the complete transformation of hunter-gatherer bands. At least as important as agriculture, if not more so, are the long-established links amongst these groups that become more dynamic and complex as the groups become more sedentary and hierarchical. Although our analysis provides no more than a sketch of a very complex process, it goes much further than any of the other approaches which focus on the emergence of agriculture as a turning point.

## UNDERSTANDING THE 3500 BC TRANSFORMATION POINT

For many, although not all analysts, the period around 3500 BC marks a crucial turning point, although the nature of the turning point is characterized in rather different theoretical terms. Conventionally, this date is considered to mark the onset of civilization, or in Bentley's (1996: 756) terms, 'early complex societies'. But only McNeill (1963: 32) unequivocally draws on this formulation. For the next five millennia McNeill observes a sharp spatial distinction between barbarians and civilized communities. He sees the barbarians as living a nomadic existence and posing a constant threat to the civilized and sedentary communities. Civilization is closely associated with the formation of the city-state and a political and religious urban elite, the development of writing and accounting techniques, and the emergence of an artisan class which produced sophisticated craft products. None of this would have been possible without the development of agriculture and the capacity to produce a surplus of food that could be supplied to a sector of the population that was no longer responsible for feeding itself.

For theorists like Wolf, therefore, it is the production and redistribution of agricultural surplus as tribute that crucially defines the nature of the turning point. Civilization, however this term is defined, has to be seen as a by-product of this transformation in the mode of production. It is for this reason that theorists like Gellner, Hodgson, and Wallerstein, despite their radically different intellectual orientations, argue that the turning point associated with the development of agriculture has to be seen as one of the most important developments in world history. The problem with this formulation is that there were many areas across the globe where the development of agriculture did not give rise to tributary systems and urban civilizations. From this perspective, then, the slow emergence of civilizations around the world, first in Sumeria, Egypt, and India, and then a millennium or so later in what are now Turkey, Greece, and China, and after a similar period in Central and South America, does represent a distinct turning point that needs to be seen as quite separate from the development of agriculture, even though dependent on it.

From our perspective, it is the institutionalization of political power and social hierarchy, and the consolidation of the premodern state to embody these, that marks the most salient turning point. In our framework, the rise of these new units is the juncture at which pre-international systems give way to economic and full international systems. On the pre-international side of the dividing line, political systems remain extraordinarily fluid. Because power rested mainly on the success and charisma of chiefs, chiefdoms were unstable. The city-states and kingdoms constituting the first international systems, on the other hand, were much more stable and enduring. These new units represented the end points of many different political trajectories. At one end of the spectrum lie groups of city-states that stabilized as the result of the intense competition among them, as in Sumeria. At the other end lie very stable but non-urbanized states that emerged as the result of the steady accumulation of territory by a chiefdom that proved more stable and enduring than its neighbours, as in Egypt. These units related to each other in clearly 'international' ways: trade, diplomacy, alliance, military competition, war.

But one must not allow the drama of this temporal turning point to conceal the fact that it was initially, and for a long time, quite limited in space. Whatever the nature of the states that constituted these newly formed international systems, they developed, and continued to function, in the context of long-established pre-international systems. Indeed, it is not possible to understand some of the central features of these international systems, particularly their trading patterns, without taking the pre-international systems into account. So the date 3500 marks only the beginning of the long process extending almost up to the present, in which civilizations and their international systems steadily encroached upon, and absorbed, the territory of pre-international systems. In China, the same process took place more than 1,000 years later than its first appearance in Mesopotamia, and in the Americas, 3,000 years later. In Britain it did not begin until the Roman invasion, and in parts of Africa and the Americas not until the European invasions.

## SECONDARY TURNING POINTS IN THE ANCIENT AND CLASSICAL ERA

By far the biggest debate about secondary turning points during the ancient and classical era concerns the point at which one can begin to think about some sort of Eurasian system. The vagaries of what is held to constitute a system explain much of the uncertainty about how to date this event. There is not much dispute over the idea that around 1700 BC the various civilizations in the Middle East began to coalesce to form first a single economic system and later a military-political one. This system developed economic, but not military-political, links with the city-state system in the Indus valley. Bentley (1996) sets the date a little earlier, at 2000 BC, and casts it as a boundary between 'early complex societies' and 'ancient civilisations' taking imperial form. McNeill (1991) now sees the 1700 BC date as signifying the beginning of a general process in which civilizations came into increasing contact with each other eventually forming one Eurasian system. In his earlier work (1963) he identified 500 BC as the crucial historical moment when the four major Eurasian civilizations could all be seen to be in contact with each other. But when he reassessed his work twenty-five years later, he argued for pushing this turning point back in time. On reflection, he felt that the crucial point was when divergent civilizations first began to interact and that this juncture was more important than the point when there was contact amongst civilizations across Eurasia. This whole debate hinges on how much interaction, and of what type, is thought necessary to constitute a system, and here our framework provides some useful tools.

Given our argument that all early international systems operated within pre-international systems that operated over long distances, it follows that these international systems may well have been in contact, albeit indirect, via the pre-international systems, from the moment that they came into existence. Lapis lazuli, for example, was not only used extensively in Sumeria, but also in Egypt (Payne 1968). So there must have been some form of contact between these civilizations, if only indirect, from a very early stage in their existence. This means that 'first contact' is not a useful approach to trying to date the formation of a Eurasian international system.

One possible candidate for a date is the period 1,000–800 BC, when horse-riding steppe nomads began to have a significant impact across Eurasia. At this point, drawing on Mackinder's terminology, it could be argued that Eurasia formed a single closed system. Very little is known about this process, except that once horse-breeding had produced sturdy enough mounts to carry a rider (as opposed to pulling a chariot or cart) the horse-riding culture spread around Eurasia very rapidly. The absence of indigenous horses in the Americas, before the Europeans imported them after 1500, means, of course, that this development cannot be considered as a turning point from a global perspective. In Eurasia, the consequence was that the 'barbarians' beyond the boundaries of civilization that had posed no more than an inconvenience to their sedentary neighbours now became a major threat. Karl Jaspers (1953) linked this threat to the major spiritual and intellectual breakthroughs that occurred in the four major regions of civilization across Eurasia. He identified this period as the 'axial age' and this idea was picked up by Hodgson (1993), who viewed this period of intellectual and spiritual development as a crucial era within the agrarian age.

Our theoretical framework also acknowledges the significance of the steppe nomads, seeing them as forming a new kind of political unit with the potential to expand into empires. The evolution of horse-riding also constitutes a notable development in physical interaction capacity. But we stress the fact that the nomads developed a parasitic relationship with the sedentary states. A complex balance of power formed between these two very different types of unit that persisted for more than two millennia. The balance depended upon the fact that both units developed effective strategies for dealing with the other, so that neither unit was able to overcome the other (Barfield 1989; Christian 1998). While these events are significant in our framework, they do not qualify as making a Eurasian international system. The barbarians did pose a common threat to all of the Eurasian agrarian civilizations, and to that extent they became part of the various international systems in Eurasia. But the barbarians were never a coherent whole, and their high degree of fragmentation meant that they did not weld Eurasia together into a single international system, either economic of military-political. Although they represented a single phenomenon, the actual impact of the barbarians at this time is best understood as a series of separate developments affecting existing international systems without connecting them in any coherent way.

In our perspective, a much more plausible date for the making of a Eurasian (economic) international system is McNeill's original choice of c.500 BC. By this time, the expansion of the Persian Empire was linking the Mediterranean, the Middle East, and South and Central Asia, and joining up with similar developments in East, South-East, South, and Central Asia, and, a bit later, northern Africa. By 200 BC pastoralist states formed a link across Eurasia (Christian 1998: 183), and the Silk Roads trading system connecting China and the Mediterranean was already flourishing. Eurasia never became a full international system during the ancient and classical era, but its economic system flourished, albeit with waxings and wanings, for two millennia, carrying enough cultural baggage with it to justify McNeill's term 'Eurasian Ecumene'.

In some minds (McNeill 1963; Mann 1986: ch. 7, p. 292; Bentley 1996) 500 BC also marks a boundary between ancient and classical eras. There are two ideas in play here. First is that 'axial age' cultural developments stretching from Greece to China marked a significant step in the level of Eurasian civilization. Around this time there was undoubtedly a burst of religious and philosophical ideas: Socrates, Plato, Aristotle, and others in Greece (especially Athens), Zoroaster in Persia, Buddha in India, and Confucius and Lao-tzu in China. Second is that political developments, most notably democracy and citizenship in classical Greece, mark a step-level change in unit type between ancient and classical. Both of these ideas look problematic in our scheme. The problem with the axial age notion is that there were major developments of a similar type both before and after the period around 500 BC. Hinduism, Judaism, and monotheistic religions in Egypt all started well before 1000 BC, Christianity started half a millennium later than the axial period, and Islam more than a millennium later. In this perspective, the generation of major religions and philosophies looks more like a general feature of the ancient and classical world rather than a point-in-time development. The problem with the idea of breakthrough political developments is that by our criteria we see no transformation of units substantial enough to justify a historical boundary. We are suspicious that use of this date for that purpose simply reflects Eurocentric attempts to privilege Greek and Roman developments in relation to the rest of the ancient and classical world. We see a steady development in the art of government as a feature of the whole of the ancient and classical era, of which Greek and Roman developments were merely one expression.

We also reject as Eurocentric the setting of a secondary boundary at c.AD 500 (Frank 1990: 165; Bentley 1996). We do so on the grounds that in a world historical perspective, or even just a Eurasian one, this date privileges both the fall of Rome and the beginning of the medieval period, elevating them to a significance that they do not warrant. It is one of the keystones of Eurocentric world history. One has to remember that only the Western Roman Empire fell, with the Byzantine Empire continuing on in the East for another thousand years. Such events were not without parallels in Chinese history. And while the medieval development certainly loomed large in European history, and so eventually in world history, in and of itself it was mostly of local consequence. One cannot reinforce this story by attaching the rise of Islam to it, because, as argued above, that was part of another pattern distributed across the ancient and classical era. Taking all this into consideration, AD 500 represents a boundary of only tertiary significance.

## THE DEBATE ABOUT THE BOUNDARY BETWEEN THE ANCIENT AND CLASSICAL AND THE MODERN ERAS

While there is no disagreement that a primary world historical boundary does exist between the modern era and what came before it, there is sharp disagreement about where to place this boundary. From our perspective, AD 1500 is by far the best date for identifying this historical landmark. Not only did a new historical unit, the modern state, emerge at this time, but also a major development in interaction capacity, the ocean-going sailing ship, triggered the rapid creation of the first global-scale international system. There is a considerable weight of opinion gathered around this date. Like us, Jones (1987) and Bentley (1996: 768–9) put a lot of emphasis on the importance of linking the Americas to the Eurasian system, thus reinforcing the AD 1500 marker. From McNeill's perspective, prior to AD 1500 there was a rough balance maintained amongst the four major civilizations across Eurasia because of the lines of mutual influence that connected them. But after AD 1500, he argues, the 'grain' of world history began to run one way from Europe and the West to the rest of the world (McNeill 1963: 253). Kennedy (1989) similarly chooses 1500, and Wallerstein has constantly reiterated that after AD 1500 the nature of the world system underwent a dramatic transformation. In place of the largely autonomous world empires that dominated the globe prior to AD 1500, a world economy emerged that slowly but surely encompassed the many political units that covered the globe. Tilly (1990: 38–45) supports 1490 as the beginning of the era of the modern (or as he calls it 'national') state, and Wight (1977: ch. 5) chooses 1494. Mann (1986: ch. 14) offers 1477 as the boundary of the modern, and Frank (1990: 165) also takes this view. Stavrianos (1990: 95) dates the beginning of capitalism from 1500. And although less theoretically sophisticated, Mackinder (1904) also argued that after AD 1500, the Europeans were able to escape the Eurasian landmass and to transform the closed Eurasian system into an open system.

But there are dissenting voices. Nobody disputes the significance of 1500 for the dramatic leap to a global-scale international system. But some put the emergence of the modern state earlier: Anderson (1974b) for example puts it in the fourteenth century. Others pick different signifiers for the boundary, and therefore arrive at different dates. In mainstream IR, and particularly the English school (Watson 1992: ch. 17), 1648 is the key date, when the Treaty of Westphalia marks the emergence and self-definition of the distinctive international system and international society that went on to impose itself on the rest of the planet.

Another group of writers want to define the turning point to modernism as hinging on the industrial revolution and/or the onset of capitalism, seeing this as the key shift away from the agrarian political economy that underpinned the ancient and classical era. Opinion is divided on how to date both capitalism and the industrial revolution. Wallerstein and Stavrianos conveniently (from our point of view) defend 1500 for capitalism. But Hodgson (1993: chs. 4–6) dates modernity from 1600, with the arrival of 'technicalized' societies. Gellner (1988) and Wolf (1982) both consider that this capitalist/industrial turning point occurred towards the end of the eighteenth century. Not one of these three writers agrees with Wallerstein that capitalism can be extended back to 1500. From their perspectives, capitalism is intimately bound up with the industrial revolution which they all date significantly later than 1500. From their perspective, the link established between Eurasia and the Americas is not seen to have precipitated any change in the basic nature of world economics which continued to operate as it always had done on agrarian and mercantilist principles. They discount the issue of expanding scale, and focus on the underlying organizing principles of political economy. From our perspective, however, this assessment underestimates the extent to which international trade had always operated partially on the basis of market principles from a very early stage in the history of the international system. What the nineteenth-century industrial revolution did was to inject huge improvements in interaction capacity into an already globalized system, thereby greatly intensifying process and structure. Neither is there agreement on when to date the industrial revolution. Some historians, for example Jones (1987: ch. 3), Bautier (1971: 246–56), and Mann (1986: chs. 12–13), argue that the familiar European industrial revolution of the eighteenth and nineteenth centuries was preceded by a first industrial revolution in late medieval times, based on a variety of wind- and water-powered machines (including the famous ocean-going sailing ships, as well as mills), printing, metallurgy, and suchlike. This view could be taken as strengthening the case for c.1500, with the eighteenth- and nineteenth-century developments then being seen as later stages in something that started earlier.

Taking all this into account, the case for 1500 looks pretty firm, if not entirely uncontested.

## SECONDARY TURNING POINTS IN THE MODERN ERA

The modern era encompasses the main focus of work in IR, and there are consequently many possible contenders for significant dates. There are also two problems in assessing these. First is that identifying even secondary turning points gets more difficult as one has less historical perspective against which to judge them. Second is that placing dates within the modern era depends somewhat on when one thinks that era began. If we take 1500 as its start date, then there are five prime candidates for secondary turning points: 1648, c.1850, c.1900, 1945, and 1989. That there are so many in such a relatively short period (compared to only one for the five millennia of the ancient and classical era!) is grounds for suspicion even if one accepts, as we do, that history moves a lot faster in the modern era. Briefly put, the case for each of these turning points is as follows:

1. The year 1648 is when the Treaty of Westphalia crystallized the form of European international society, and its dominant units, which subsequently used their power to remake the global international system in their own image.
2. Circa 1850 is when the industrial revolution created major advances in interaction capacity; when liberal ideology began to break down the mercantilist obstruction to the development of social interaction capacity; and when a full, military-political international system reached global scale, and thus geographical closure, with the defeats of China and Japan by the Western powers.
3. Circa 1900 is when theorists such as Mackinder and Lenin observed a different kind of closure, namely that the great powers had occupied all of the colonizable territory in the system, with the consequence that their rivalries became more interlinked and more intense as their expansion shifted from a positive- to a zero-sum game. The First World War—or more broadly the three world wars (First, Second, and Cold) of the twentieth century—can be seen as consequences of this event. Some writers (Barraclough 1967: 9–42) also see this time as the beginning of the transition from European to world history, not least because of the arrival of Japan as the first non-Western great power.
4. The year 1945 has weight because of a conjuncture of three events: the shift

from a long-standing multipolar structure to a bipolar one (Kennedy 1989); the advent of nuclear weapons, and the consequent growth of strong pressure to avoid great power wars; and the beginnings of the wholesale decolonization that was to dismantle all the great power empires, and replace them with an international system and society made (often badly) in Europe's image. Another candidate for reinforcing this boundary is the reassertion of liberal economic norms and rules after their abandonment during the inter-war years. Some theorists such as Morgenthau (1973), Toynbee (1954), and Dehio (1963) also argued that from 1945 the balance of power had moved from the European arena onto the global arena, thereby transforming the nature of world politics, though it is also possible to place this idea *c.*1900, or after 1989.

5. The year 1989 is when bipolarity ended; the possibility arose that there would be no more great power wars; and the so-called 'ending of history' occurred, with the apparent conclusion of the great ideological conflicts that dominated the twentieth century over whether monarchy, liberal democracy, fascism, or communism would shape the future of industrial society. The rise of Asia seemed to underline the shift away from Western domination begun by decolonization.

Reviewing these claims in the light of our framework produces the following assessment. The year 1648 represents a transformation of societal structure, and has a strong claim. *Circa* 1850 is a transformation of physical and social interaction capacity, and a (not directly related) completion of the making of a full global-scale international system, and also has a strong claim. *Circa* 1900 is harder to place specifically within our framework, but clearly fits with its spirit. It seems to suggest the need for more thinking about the meanings of 'open' and 'closed' international systems. Our relatively simple ideas of geographical openness or closure as a function of interaction capacity and process do not capture the whole importance of this concept. This has at least a claim to tertiary status, maybe more. The year 1945 does not, on the face of it, seem to have more than a tertiary claim. Its change of structure is interesting but short lived. Nuclear weapons, while interesting for many reasons, do not fundamentally change the inter-national system or the behaviour of its units in any marked way. Their main effect is to amplify fear, and thereby to reinforce an aversion to war already created by the experiences of 1914–18 and 1939–45. Decolonization has more weight because it represents a substantial expansion of international society, though not a change in its structure.

Finally, there is the question of 1989. Being closest to us in time it is in some ways the most difficult to judge. The ending of bipolarity will probably not carry much long-term significance despite how important it seemed during the Cold War. But 1989 will almost certainly win a place in orthodox accounts of world history as marking the end of the short twentieth century (1914–89). It may also come to mark the end of the period of direct Western domination of world history, and the shift to a more truly global distribution of power not seen for 500 years. Perhaps it will also mark the end of the process begun over 5,000 years ago when international systems began to absorb pre-international ones. But as mooted in Chapter 16, this date may come to signify not just a secondary turning point within the modern era. It is not impossible that 1989 will come to be seen as a primary turning point, signifying the beginning of the transformation from the modern to the postmodern (or some other label) era, in which the defining features of the international system came to be determined more by economic processes and units than by military-political ones. Even to speculate about such a turn invites the charge of absurdly over-privileging current events just because we are close to them. But such a classification fits with the logic of our framework, and it would be remiss not to note it as a possibility.

## 4. SUMMARY OF THE CHRONOLOGY OF WORLD HISTORY DERIVED FROM OUR FRAMEWORK

(Placement towards the left increases world historical significance, towards the right decreases it. 1=primary, 2=secondary, 3=tertiary.)

**1**—60,000–40,000 BC: beginning of pre-international systems with the emergence of long-distance exchange networks amongst HGBs.

    **2**—10,000–6000 BC: emergence of sedentary, hierarchical units beginning to display some signs of characteristic 'international' behaviour.

**1**—3500 BC: emergence of durable, state-like units, and economic and full international systems. Beginning of the erosion and absorption of pre-international systems.

        **3**—2000–1700 BC: emergence of empires, and of international economic systems linking full international systems in the Middle East and South Asia.

        **3**—1000–800 BC: increase of interaction capacity in Eurasia with horse-riding, and consequent emergence of the steppe nomads as a major player in international systems.

    **2**—500 BC: emergence of a Eurasian economic international system (but not axial age religious and philosophical developments, or the emergence of a new type of unit in the classical empire).

        **3**—AD 500: fall of the Western Roman Empire and the rise of medievalism in Europe.

**1**—AD 1500: the emergence of a new dominant unit, the modern state, and a leap in interaction capacity with ocean-going sailing ships leading to the making of a nearly global international system by the linkage of Eurasia and the Americas. More arguably, the beginnings of capitalism and industrialism.

2—1648: emergence of new international societal structure.

2—*c.*1850: transformations of interaction capacity and closure of full global-scale international system.

**2?  3?**—*c.*1900: 'closure' of the system in terms of great power competition.

3—1945: bipolar structure, beginning of extension of international society to the whole system.

**1?**—1989: sectoral shift away from military-political towards political-economic interaction as the defining process of the system?

# Chapter 19
# REFLECTIONS

## 1. WORLD HISTORY AND INTERNATIONAL SYSTEMS

In writing this book we have worked on the basis of two fundamental and inter-related assumptions: first, that international relations theory has the potential to provide a framework that will foster a coherent and intelligible approach to the task of writing world history, and, second, that world history provides the most appropriate setting for developing and testing international relations theory. The book is intended to make a contribution both to world history and international relations and our aim has been to show that harnessing international relations theory and world history has mutually beneficial and synergistic consequences.

World historians have regularly acknowledged the need for a stronger and more inclusive framework than is available to them at this juncture. Although Waller-stein's conception of world systems is still seen by McNeill (1998: 26–7), and others, as the 'leading candidate', it is far from being generally acknowledged as providing a satisfactory framework for the analysis of world history; indeed, McNeill has noted that world historians are 'still fumbling around in search of a more adequate conceptualisation of human history'. And according to Green (1998: 62), 'debate on this matter is just beginning'. We are anxious to ensure that IR theorists make a contribution to this debate.

At the heart of our project is the belief that the theory surrounding the idea of an international system provides the basis for an effective, although obviously not the only possible, framework for examining world history. In making this claim we wish to challenge the widespread assumption inside and outside the discipline that IR must be a retarded social science. While we agree that IR has so far failed to make much of an intellectual impact outside its own borders (except perhaps in its popularity as a teaching subject), we argue strongly that it has both the potential and the obligation to do so. Our approach forms a direct challenge to the view of the philosopher Alan Ryan (1998: 27) who has noted 'the feebleness of theor-izing in international relations and the superiority of good narrative history to what is passed off as "theory"'. As the search for an effective conceptual frame-work by world historians amply demonstrates, the distinction between history and theory drawn by Ryan is false.

From our perspective, IR theory has been sold short on two main counts. First, there has been a widespread failure to look for ways of integrating the rich and divergent areas of theory that have been developed across the discipline over many years. Second, the attention of IR theorists has too often been restricted either to the contemporary international system or to an earlier system made up of European states. We take these two deficiencies as being largely responsible for the failure of IR thinking to make any significant impact on either history or the other social sciences, and in this book, we have made a concerted effort to rectify them.

Our attempt to link international relations theory to world history is not without precedent, and in some ways can be seen as extending the work of the English school. Some of the school's early members, Martin Wight in particular, were profoundly influenced by Toynbee's attempt to develop world history. But unlike Toynbee, the members of the English school wanted to advance the study of world history within an international setting—although Toynbee (perhaps as the result of his close contact with Wight) also came to see the need to examine relations between civilizations. Furthermore, as we discussed in Part I, members of the English school, in particular Wight, and later Bull, were drawn to a pluralistic approach to theorizing. They acknowledged that any attempt to analyse the international system from a single perspective would fail to capture the complexity of both international relations and world history.

Our framework is more eclectic than any advanced by the English school, though our use of sectors running in parallel does bear both substantive and methodological resemblance to its 'three traditions' (Hobbes, Kant, and Grotius) and the distinction drawn between international systems, world societies, and international societies. We have also provided a more systematic account of world history than any put forward by members of the English school. We have endeavoured to tell the story of how international systems and societies developed across world history by formally and systematically tracking each element of our framework across space and time. In some senses, what we have done could be read as an attempt to reformulate the English school by setting it onto firmer historical and theoretical foundations, and giving equal theoretical weight to each of its traditions. In pursuing a world historical context for IR theory we have specifically rejected the familiar strategy of trawling through world history texts in order to find elements that illustrate the central features of our framework. Doing that would have made the framework into a straitjacket that predetermined our account of world history. Instead we have tried to give a full account of world history (albeit at a high level of generalization), letting the different elements of the framework find their own balance for different times and places.

In looking forward as to where we take this research project from here, the centrality of the English school's idea of parallel 'traditions' (or in our terminology, multiple sectors) becomes increasingly apparent. Particularly noteworthy is the argument underlined in Chapters 14–18 that increases in interaction capacity and the strength of process were generating ever more powerful and penetrative structural effects, whether for the global market or international society. The balance of these structural effects was shifting away from the long-standing dominance of neorealist-type military-political structure towards other sectors. This line of thinking not only points strongly towards the English school ideas of international society and world society, it also takes us back to the 'two worlds' argument in Chapter 16, with its suggestion that at least for the weaker states in the system, the overall balance of power between the system level (in terms of structural effects and process formations) and the units might be changing rather strongly in favour of the system. It is worth trying to think about this in somewhat more theoretical terms than was done in Chapter 16.

## 2. WEAK AND STRONG INTERNATIONAL SYSTEMS

What lessons does our long historical perspective offer about the relationship between units and international systems? That this is *the* crucial relationship in understanding international systems is implicit in all the mainstream approaches to the subject. The materialist logic of neorealism supposes that units come first, that their coaction makes a structured system, and that structural effects then shove and shape the units into 'like' form and behaviour. This pattern also applies to economic logic, where products and labour might become specialized, but the structural pressures of market competition forces firms into 'like' form and 'efficient' behaviour. Constructivists, whom we have located in the societal sector, take a different view. They see units and systems in a mutually constitutive, circular, relationship, with each both feeding into the making of the other, and being affected by it. But regardless of whether the approach is materialist or constructivist, the relationship between units and system lies at the core of theory. What seems clear from our long look is that this relationship is not constant, and the question is how to begin bringing the changes in it into theoretical focus.

One possible entry point into this task is that the idea of *weak* and *strong* states (defined in terms of their degree of socio-political cohesion (Buzan 1991: 96–107)) is paralleled by an idea of *weak* and *strong* international systems, also defined in terms of their degree of socio-political cohesion. In principle one could use this matrix to set up comparative typologies of how units and systems relate: weak units in a weak system, weak units in a strong system, mixture of weak and strong units in a strong system, and so forth. Such typologies might serve as the basis for hypotheses about the interplay between units and systems. In a more ambitious perspective, they might have the potential to serve as the basis for some kind of grand theory of international systems.

The problem, as always, would be how to operationalize such an idea. Like power, the variable weak/strong is not easy to measure, even though the basic idea underlying it is clear enough. Indeed, and again parallel with power, it is not even easy to say whether comparisons in terms of weak/strong are on an absolute scale or a relative one. There must be absolute scales for both, and while we might imagine what the bottom ends of them look like (for power, complete helplessness to influence one's environment; for cohesion, chaotic lack of socio-political integration) it is almost impossible to guess what the top ends might be (for power, omnipotence, for cohesion, total integration). Omnipotence puts one in the realm of God(s); total integration in the realm of science fiction creations such as the 'Borg' (of 'Star Trek' fame), where all the 'individuals' in a civilization are wired into a single consciousness. Against such a scale, the current achievements of humankind would all rank well down in the bottom half. *De facto*, then, scales of power and weak/strong must be relative, with the top end defined by the best current performance (clearly the USA, for power; and less clearly, say, the Scandinavian countries for socio-political cohesion), and the bottom by the worst current performance (something like Haiti or the Maldives for power; and take your pick of Cyprus, Afghanistan, Somalia, Liberia, Congo, and several other failed states for socio-political cohesion). It is the degree of difference between them that counts, and this degree cannot but have both absolute and relative qualities. As with power, the more one thinks about how to measure the weak/strong variable, the more problematic the task seems.

Yet despite the difficulty of measurement, it is not all that hard to think through what the weak/strong variable means. At the unit level, socio-political cohesion describes the degree of consensual integration between civil society and government. It is a measure of the extent to which coercion has been removed from the relationship between a citizenry and its governing institutions. Weak states may have their actor quality in the system constrained by the fact of their internal incoherence, and they will certainly be more vulnerable to a wider range of threats, societal and political, as well as military and economic. Whether a state is weak or strong tells you about its existential quality as a member of the group of entities that we call states. Weak states have fragile claims to be counted as member of the class of states, failed states no claim at all unless other states want to keep the fiction of their international existence in being (as was done with Liberia, Lebanon, and Somalia). Since the quality of 'stateness' can be assessed against the criterion of sovereignty there are some clear benchmarks against which to judge where a state stands on the contemporary scale of weak/strong. Strong states will project influence into the system as well as being penetrated by it. Weak states will be penetrated more than penetrating, and their internal affairs may well lose autonomy to outside interaction or intervention. Indeed, with weak states, it may be extremely difficult to distinguish between interaction and intervention.

Shifting the weak/strong idea upwards to the system level looks at first to be fairly straightforward. It is not difficult, using the ideas of the English school, to think about international systems in terms of degree of socio-political cohesion. It is clear that a system with an international society in which all of the main units accept each other as legal equals has more socio-political cohesion than one in which the units do not accept each other as legal equals. If such a society has developed a thick layer of norms and institutions restraining the use of force in relations amongst the units, and standardizing their behaviour in various ways, then in parallel with the logic of low-coercion, consensual political relations within states, it seems reasonable to call such an international system 'strong' in terms of socio-political cohesion. Much the same line of argument might apply using the idea of 'world society'. If all, or most, human beings accept each other as legally and morally equal in terms of human rights, and practices such as slavery are illegal, then this is a 'stronger' international system than one in which they do not. This line of thinking runs closely parallel to Buzan's (1991, 1995b) idea of 'mature and immature anarchies'.

The spoiler in this seemingly neat constructivist scheme is that international systems, unlike states, do not have actor quality, and therefore there is no benchmark such as sovereignty against which to assess their degree of cohesion, and thus their weakness or strength (or 'failure'). Even worse is that there exists a whole other sense in which international systems might be considered strong or weak. As much of the discussion in this book about interaction capacity, process, and structure has made clear, the weakness–strength of international systems also varies according to the intensity and type of interaction, which as a rule will correlate directly with the intensity of structural effects. Here the conception of weak/strong in relation to systems focuses on the more mechanical aspect of the intensity of process, and the benchmark for weakness and strength is the extent to which structural forces penetrate the units and shape their behaviour. These two aspects (i.e. the mechanical and the social) of weak/strong in relation to international systems might coincide in a mutually reinforcing way, as they would for a highly institutionalized international society that had organized itself around a global market economy. But they might not coincide. In classical Westphalian warfare systems, such as that represented by modern Europe up to 1945, or by the Greek city-states, or Chinese 'warring states', of classical times, interaction might be intense, and structural pressures strong, even when parochial identities overwhelm collective ones, and political relations are dominated by coercion and war. In other words, international systems dominated by warfare in which the units seek simply to exterminate each other might have little or no international society, but still be 'strong' systems in terms of intensity of interaction and strength of structural effects. These examples suggest that the spectrum of weakness and strength in relation to international systems might differ according to what sector of interaction one is examining.

Nevertheless, it is still fairly easy to construct abstract examples that illustrate the difference between weak and strong international systems. A weak system, at one extreme, is in Kaplan's term 'subsystem dominant'—and in Waltz's view is probably not a system at all (Waltz 1979: 58). In such a system, the processes and structures generated within the state are much stronger than those between states, and the domestic life of units is dominated by what goes on inside them. It may be that physical interaction capacity is significantly higher within the state than outside it, though this does not have to be the case (one would expect social interaction capacity always to be higher within states than between them: if it was not it is hard to see how the state could exist). The economy in such a system is relatively localized, or else largely autarkic at the national level. The culture is relatively self-contained, perhaps insulated by a distinctive language. The state is relatively insulated from its neighbours, perhaps by difficult geography or water. There will be some trade and diplomacy, and perhaps quite a bit of societal inter-play with a wider civilization or religion. There may even be occasional wars, but most states will be able to defend their frontiers against invaders. As a rule, the unit will be able to maintain quite hard boundaries, within which it will be able to cultivate and defend a distinctive cultural, economic, and political life. Like Japan in the seventeenth century, China in the eighteenth, and the USA in the nine-teenth, a strong state in a weak system might well be able to close itself off from much foreign contact.

At the other extreme is a strong international system. Here interstate processes and system structures are powerful and penetrative. Because the technologies that carry them are hard to block, many kinds of cultural influences, including political propaganda, styles and fashions, and commercial advertising, will be carried across borders whether they are wanted or not. It will be hard to maintain any kind of cultural isolation, and virtually impossible to escape the pressures of an international culture. Similar circumstances obtain in the military and economic sectors. The state may be unable to block attacks with certain kinds of weapons (stealth bombers, terrorists, missiles), or unable to defend its territory without participating in an extensive alliance. It may have the choice in principle to culti-vate economic self-reliance, but be able to do so only by accepting severe relative impoverishment and technological backwardness compared to the more open economies around it (e.g. Myanmar, North Korea). Over time, the erosion of wealth and technological prowess that comes with pursuing mercantilism in the midst of a liberalized global economy could undermine both the power of the state compared to others, and the legitimacy of the governing ideology in the eyes of its citizens. Participation in the global economy offers the enticement of access to wider markets for goods and capital, but only at the cost of being forced to compete within a global division of labour, and of having foreign capital penetrate deeply into the political, societal, and economic life of the local community. For-eign capital will be stronger than local; foreign culture will be available as a chal-lenge to local values, styles, customs, and social hierarchies; and external sources of information will act as a counterpoint to any attempt by local elites to shape or maintain an indigenous social project.

These two images of course represent locations on a spectrum. At the bottom end of the spectrum is something like the neorealist image of units existing before they begin to co-act: i.e. all unit and no system. At the top end is an integration so total that units cease to have much in the way of independent identity or function. But if, for purposes of illustration, we stick with the two images given, then the question is how weak and strong international systems interplay with weak and strong states.

Since this is a concluding section rather than an introductory one, it is obvious that we do not have the space to unfold this line of thinking in much detail. All we are trying to do here is to think forward about a macro-approach to the study of international systems, and to offer some suggestions as to what a follow-on research agenda in IR theory might look like. It seems pretty clear that in this light, the story of the ancient and classical era is largely one of weak units in weak systems. Although military-political interaction was sometimes strong, international economic processes tended to be weak as compared with local ones, and international society, to the extent that it existed at all, remained pretty basic and thin. It might be argued that tribes were sometimes strong units in terms of socio-political cohesion, but they achieved this only by remaining small, and low in power. Tribal structures, unlike state ones, never managed to combine large scale with high cohesion. At best they could be temporarily united by charismatic warlords.

The story of the modern era is about the rise of strong units, and the making of a strong system first locally, then globally. The process of globalization proceeded at different speeds/times according to sector. The basic framework of a global economic system linking Eurasia, Africa, and the Americas was in place by the late sixteenth century. A full military-political international system was not really in place until the middle of the nineteenth century. A global international society did not really emerge until after the Second World War. Thus the structural pressures in the different sectors came on stream in quite widely separated times. A structured global international system in the neorealist sense only came into being about 150 years ago, and in the English school sense less than 50 years ago. While this full global international system was being constructed, the spectacular breakthroughs in interaction capacity starting during the nineteenth century transformed the relationship between units and system. Both became absolutely stronger, but the international system steadily became relatively stronger not only in relation to weak states but also in relation to strong ones.

Thinking about this story suggests the possibility of pursuing research into international systems around the following ideas.

- *Hypothesis 1.* In weak systems, weak states will be sustainable. (Case: empires during the ancient and classical era.)

- *Hypothesis 1a*. Weak states in weak systems will establish weak international societies based on hierarchies of political inequality. (Case: diplomatic systems in the ancient Middle East and elsewhere.)
- *Hypothesis 2*. Strong states in a weak system will have huge advantages, especially on first manifestation. (Case: the rise of Europe. Link: neorealism.)
- *Hypothesis 3*. In the long run, strong states (especially when they are also strong powers) will generate strong systems by projecting their domestic dynamics outward. (Cases: Greek city-states, rise of Europe. Link: the 'lateral pressure' idea of Choucri and North (1975).)
- *Hypothesis 4*. Weak states in a strong system will either be colonized or marginalized. A mixture of weak and strong states in a strong system will generate some version of a centre–periphery process formation. (Case: Third World. Links: dependency theory, IPE, world-system theory.)
- *Hypothesis 5*. Strong states in strong systems dominated by military-political interaction will establish international societies based on mutual recognition as political equals. (Cases: modern Europe, classical Greek subsystem.)
- *Hypothesis 6*. Strong units in strong systems dominated by economic interaction will establish international societies based on principles of functional differentiation amongst the units, and the rights and responsibilities of different types of unit in relation to both each other and other types. (Case: twenty-first century.)

## 3. AN END AND A BEGINNING

The idea of weak and strong systems requires an important modification to the theoretical framework presented in Part I, and the hypotheses provide the basis for a substantial new research agenda. Rather than return to the framework and rework it at this stage, however, we prefer to leave the task of reformulation to a later occasion. There are two interrelated reasons for adopting this tactic. First, it helps to expose more clearly the provisional character of our framework, and, second, in doing so, it simultaneously draws attention to the methodology that underpins our approach. That methodology combines inductive and deductive procedures and has been identified as retroductive inference (Hanson 1958). It presupposes a constant feedback process between theory-building and observation and it therefore postulates that the same body of data can be used to derive and test an evolving theoretical approach.

The current project represents an extension of an earlier project that was presented in *The Logic of Anarchy* (written with Charles Jones), but it also modifies it along a number of crucial dimensions. To avoid making endless modifications and extensions to the framework, and, even more important, to maintain its coherence, one of our key methodological rules has been to extend the framework only if absolutely necessary. When initially attempting in *The Logic of Anarchy* to expand

Waltz's neorealist framework, we acknowledged the legitimacy of his concern for parsimony. We only moved beyond the very tight limitations imposed by his framework when the move was dictated by or compatible with the underlying logic of neorealism. The introduction of interaction capacity was dictated by the logic, whereas the addition of sectoral analysis was designed to enrich neorealism while remaining compatible with its logic.

The enrichment process in this book has been heavily influenced by our contact with the English school. Although the English school approached the study of international relations from a systemic perspective, it was a very different perspective, with a very different pedigree, from the one being adopted at the same time in the United States. In Hollis and Smith's (1990) terms, the Americans were wanting to tell the story of international systems from the outside whereas the English school were wanting to tell the story from the inside—a positivist as opposed to a historicist approach. The emerging historiography of the discipline is making it clear that the English school, and in particular Hedley Bull, recognized the need to establish a synthesis between the American and English approaches to systems thinking (Dunne 1998: 125). The synthesis was achieved by drawing an analytical distinction between 'international system' and 'international society'. But the full methodological implications of the distinction were never worked out. We have endeavoured to make progress by associating the former with the military-political sector and the latter with the socio-cultural sector. The constructivists have also tried to find a mode of reconciliation. But in doing so, they have tended to elide the problem by viewing systems and societies as different possible ways of constructing international reality rather than as different elements of the same reality.

A central feature of our project, therefore, is to find ways of drawing together the mode of systems thinking associated most closely with Waltz, to the mode of systems thinking most closely associated with the English school. Although Waltz may have provided the starting point for our theoretical framework, the English school has undoubtedly been inextricably linked to the way that the project has developed. In particular, the attempt to ground the theoretical framework in a world historical setting reflects the influence of the English school. After working closely alongside Toynbee when he was writing *The Study of History*, Wight acknowledged the importance of world history (Dunne 1998: 49–50). His research reflected a passionate interest in world history and a recognition that theory could not be developed without the benefit of a comparative world historical perspective. Although his work on historical systems has been acknowledged in terms of 'inspired trail-blazing' (Yost 1979), and has been followed up by Watson (1992), the surface of world history has still barely been scratched by IR theorists. By setting down a future research agenda, as we draw this book to a close, therefore, we are mindful of T. S. Eliot's (1963: 221) observation that 'to make an end is to make a beginning. The end is where we start from.'

# REFERENCES

ABRAMS, PHILIP (1982), *Historical Sociology*, London: Open Books.

ABU-LUGHOD, JANET L. (1989), *Before European Hegemony: The World System AD 1230–1350*, Oxford: Oxford University Press.

ADAS, MICHAEL (1998), 'Bringing Ideas and Agency Back in: Representation and the Comparative Approach to World History', in P. Pomper, R. H. Elphick, and R. T. Vann, *World History: Ideologies, Structures and Identity*, Oxford: Blackwell Publishers Ltd.

ADCOCK, FRANK, and MOSLEY, D. J. (1974), *Diplomacy in Ancient Greece*, London: Thames & Hudson.

ADSHEAD, S. A. M. (1988), *China in World History*, London: Macmillan Press.

ALBERT, MATHIAS, and BROCK, LOTHAR, (1995), 'Debordering the World of States: New Spaces in International Relations', *Working Paper 2*, Frankfurt.

ALEXANDER, JOHN (1993), 'The Salt Industries of West Africa' in Thurstan Shaw et al. (eds.), *The Archaeology of Africa: Food, Metals, and Towns*, London: Routledge.

ALEXANDROWICZ, C. H. (1967), *An Introduction to the History of the Law of Nations in the East Indies (16th, 17th, and 18th Centuries)*, London: Oxford University Press.

—— (1973), *The European–African Confrontation*, Leiden: A. W. Sijthoff.

ALGAZE, GUILLERMO (1993), *The Uruk World System: The Dynamics of Expansion of Early Mesopotamian Civilization*, Chicago: University of Chicago Press.

ALLCHIN, F. R. (1995), *The Archaeology of Early Historic South Asia: The Emergence of Cities and States*, Cambridge: Cambridge University Press.

ALLISON, GRAHAM T. (1971), *Essence of Decision*, New York: Little, Brown.

ALLPORT, GORDON W. (1954), *The Nature of Prejudice*, Cambridge: Allison Wesley.

AMMERMAN, A. J., MATESSI, C., and CAVALLI-SFORZA, L. L. (1978), 'Some New Approaches to the Study of the Obsidian Trade in the Mediterranean and Adjacent Areas', in I. Hodder (ed.), *The Spatial Organisation of Culture*, London: Duckworth.

ANDERSON, BENEDICT (1983), *Imagined Communities: Reflections on the Origin and Spread of Nationalism*, London: Verso.

ANDERSON, JAMES (ed.) (1986), *The Rise of the Modern State*, London: Wheatsheaf.

ANDERSON, PERRY (1974a), *Passages from Antiquity to Feudalism*, London: Verso.

—— (1974b), *Lineages of the Absolutist State*, London: Verso.

ANGELL, NORMAN (1912), *The Great Illusion*, London: William Heinemann.

ARCHER, CLIVE (1983), *International Organizations*, London: George Allen & Unwin.

ARCHER, MARGARET (1988), *Culture and Agency: The Place of Culture in Social Theory*, Cambridge: Cambridge University Press.

ARON, RAYMOND (1966), *Peace and War: A Theory of International Relations*, New York: Doubleday & Co.

ASCHERSON, NEAL (1996), *Black Sea*, London: Vintage.

AUSTEN, RALPH A. (1988): 'The 19th Century Islamic Slave Trade from East Africa (Swahili and Red Sea Coasts): A Tentative Census', in William Gervase Clarence-Smith, (ed.), *The Economics of the Indian Ocean Slave Trade in the Nineteenth Century*, special issue of *Slavery and Abolition*, 9/3: 21–44.

—— (1996), "The Mediterranean Islamic Slave Trade out of Africa: A Tentative Census" in Patrick

Manning (ed.), *Slave Trade, 1500–1800: Globalization of Forced Labour*, An Expanding World: The European Impact on World History 15, Aldershot: Variorum.

AZZAROLI, A. (1985), *An Early History of Horsemanship*, Leiden: E. J. Brill.

BAECHLER, JEAN, HALL, JOHN A., and MANN, MICHAEL (eds.), (1988), *Europe and the Rise of Capitalism*, Oxford: Basil Blackwell.

BAIROCH, PAUL (1981), 'The Main Trends in National Economic Disparities since the Industrial Revolution', in Paul Bairoch and Maurice Lévy-Leboyer (eds.), *Disparities in Economic Development since the Industrial Revolution*, London: Macmillan.

—— (1982), 'International Industrialization Levels from 1750–1980', *Journal of International Economic History*, 11/2: 269–333.

—— (1988), *Cities and Economic Development: From the Dawn of History to the Present*, trans. by Christopher Braider, London: Mansell.

—— (1993), *Economics and World History: Myths and Paradoxes*, New York: Harvester Wheatsheaf.

BARFIELD, THOMAS (1989), *The Perilous Frontier: Nomadic Empires and China*, Cambridge, Mass: Basil Blackwell.

BARRACLOUGH, GEOFFREY (1967), *An Introduction to Contemporary History*, Harmondsworth: Penguin.

—— (ed.) (1978), *The Times Atlas of World History*, London: Times Books.

BARRETT, WARD (1990), 'World Bullion Flows 1450–1800' in James D. Tracy (ed.), *The Rise of Merchant Empires*, Cambridge: Cambridge University Press.

BARTH, FREDERIK (1964), *Nomads of South Persia: The Basseri of the Khamseh Confederacy*, London: Allen & Unwin.

BARTLETT, ROBERT (1994), *The Making of Europe: Conquest, Colonisation and Cultural Change 950–1350*, Harmondsworth: Penguin.

BAR-YOSEF, OFER (1998), 'On the Nature of Transitions: The Middle to Upper Paleolithic and the Neolithic Revolution', *Cambridge Archaeological Journal*, 8/2: 141–63.

BAUGH, TIMOTHY G., and ERICSON, JONATHAN E. (eds.) (1994), *Prehistoric Exchange Systems in North America*, New York: Plenum Press.

BAUTIER, ROBERT HENRI (1971), *The Economic Development of Mediaeval Europe*, London: Thames & Hudson.

BECK, CURT, and SHENNAN, STEPHEN (1991), *Amber in Prehistoric Britain*, Oxford: Oxbow Books.

BEGLEY, VIMALA, and DE PUMA, RICHARD DANIEL (eds.) (1992), *Rome and India: The Ancient Sea Trade*, Madison: University of Wisconsin Press.

BENTLEY, JERRY H. (1993), *Old World Encounters: Cross-Cultural Contacts and Exchanges in Pre-Modern Times*, Oxford: Oxford University Press.

—— (1996), 'Cross-Cultural Interaction and Periodization in World History', *American Historical Review*, 101/3: 749–70.

BERNDT, RONALD, M. (1976), 'Territoriality and the Problem of Demarcating Sociocultural Space', in Nicolas Peterson (ed.), *Tribes and Boundaries in Australia*, Canberra, Social Anthropology Series 10, Australian Institute of Aboriginal Studies, Atlantic Highlands, Humanities Press.

BLANTON, RICHARD E., KOWALEWSKI, S. A., FEINMAN, G. A., and FINSTEN, L. A. (1993), *Ancient Mesoamerica*, 2nd edn., Cambridge: Cambridge University Press.

BLAUT, JAMES M. (1993), *The Colonizer's Model of the World: Geographical Diffusionism and Eurocentric History*, New York: Guilford Press.

BLOCKLEY, R. C. (1992), *East Roman Foreign Policy*, Leeds: Francis Cairns.

BOULNOIS, LUCE (1966), *The Silk Road*, trans. Dennis Chamberlin, London: Allen & Unwin.

BOWERSOCK, G. W. (1991), 'The Dissolution of the Roman Empire', in Yoffee and Cowgill (1991).

BOZEMAN, ADDA B. (1960), *Politics and Culture in International History*, Princeton: Princeton University Press.

BRADLEY, RICHARD (1993), *Altering the Earth: The Origins of Monuments in Britain and Continental Europe* Edinburgh: Society of Antiquaries of Scotland.

BRAUDEL, FERNAND (1985), *The Perspective of the World: Civilization and Capitalism 15th–18th Century*, vol. iii, London: Fontana Press.

BRAUN, DAVID P., and PLOG, STEPHEN (1982), 'Evolution of "Tribal" Networks: Theory and Prehistoric North American Evidence', *American Antiquity*, 47: 504–25.

BRENNER, ROBERT (1977), 'The Origins of Capitalist Development: A Critique of Neo-Smithian Marxism', *New Left Review*, 104: 25–92.

BRUN, PATRICIA (1995), 'From Chiefdom to State Organization in Celtic Europe', in Bettina Arnold and D. Blair Gibson, *Celtic Chiefdom, Celtic State: The Evolution of Complex Social Systems in Prehistoric Europe*, Cambridge: Cambridge University Press.

BRUNN, STANLEY D., and LEINBACH, THOMAS R. (1991), *Collapsing Space and Time: Geographic Aspects of Communications and Information*, London: Harper Collins.

BULL, HEDLEY (1969), 'International Theory: The Case for a Classical Approach' in K. Knorr and J. N. Rosenau (eds.), *Contending Approaches to International Relations*, Princeton: Princeton University Press.

—— (1977), *The Anarchical Society*, London: Macmillan.

—— (1984a), *Justice in International Relations*, 1983–4 Hagey Lectures, University of Waterloo.

—— (ed.) (1984b), *Intervention in World Politics*, Oxford: Oxford University Press.

—— and WATSON, ADAM (eds.) (1984), *The Expansion of International Society*, Oxford: Oxford University Press.

BULLIET, RICHARD W. (1990), *The Camel and the Wheel*, Repr., with new preface, Cambridge: Mass.: Harvard University Press (1st pub. 1975).

BURKE, EDMUND III (1993), 'Introduction: Marshall G. S. Hodgson and World History' in Marshall G. S. Hodgson, *Rethinking World History: Essays on Europe, Islam and World History*, Cambridge: Cambridge University Press.

BURKERT, WALTER (1996), *Creation of the Sacred: Tracks of Biology in Early Religions*, Cambridge, Mass: Harvard University Press.

BURTON, JOHN W. (1968), *Systems, States, Diplomacy and Rules*, Cambridge: Cambridge University Press.

—— (1972), *World Society*, Cambridge: Cambridge University Press.

BUTTERFIELD, HERBERT (1949), *The Whig Interpretation of History*, London: Bell.

—— (1966), 'The Balance of Power', in Butterfield and Wight (1966).

—— and WIGHT, MARTIN (eds.) (1966), *Diplomatic Investigations: Essays in the Theory of International Politics*, London: Allen & Unwin.

BUZAN, BARRY (1984), 'Economic Structure and International Security: The Limits of the Liberal Case', *International Organization*, 38/4: 597–624.

—— (1987), *An Introduction to Strategic Studies: Military Technology and International Relations*, London: Macmillan; New York: St Martin's Press, for the International Institute for Strategic Studies.

—— (1991), *People, States and Fear: An Agenda for International Security Studies in the Post-Cold War Era*, Hemel Hempstead: Harvester-Wheatsheaf.

—— (1993), 'From International System to International Society: Structual Realism and Regime Theory Meet the English School', *International Organization*, 47/3: 327–52.

—— (1994), 'The Level of Analysis Problem in International Relations Reconsidered', in Ken Booth and Steve Smith (eds.), *International Political Theory Today*, London: Polity Press.

BUZAN, BARRY (1995a), 'Focus on: The Present as a Historic Turning Point?', *Journal of Peace Research*, 32/4: 385–98.

—— (1995b), 'Security, the State and the New World Order, and Beyond', in Ronnie Lipschutz (ed.), *On Security*, New York: Columbia University Press.

—— (1996), 'International Society and International Security', in Rick Fawn and Jeremy Larkin (eds.), *International Society after the Cold War*, London: Macmillan.

—— (1998), 'Conclusions: System versus Units in Theorizing about the Third World', in Stephanie Neuman (ed.), *International Relations Theory and the Third World*, New York: St. Martin's Press.

—— and HERRING, ERIC (1998), *The Arms Dynamic in World Politics*, London: Lynne Rienner.

—— JONES, CHARLES, and LITTLE, RICHARD (1993), *The Logic of Anarchy: Neorealism to Structural Realism*, New York: Columbia University Press.

—— and LITTLE, RICHARD (1994), 'The Idea of "International System": Theory Meets History', *International Political Science Review* 15/3: 231–55.

—— —— (1996), 'Reconceptualising Anarchy: Structural Realism Meets World History', *European Journal of International Relations* 2/4: 403–38.

—— SEGAL, GERALD (1998a), 'A Western Theme', *Prospect*, 27: 18–23.

—— —— (1998b), *Anticipating the Future: Twenty Millennia of Human Progress*, London: Simon & Schuster.

—— and WÆVER, OLE (1998), *Liberalism and Security: The Contradictions of the Liberal Leviathan*, Working Paper 23, Copenhagen: COPRI.

—— —— (forthcoming), *Regions Set Free*.

—— —— and WILDE, JAAP DE (1998), *Security: A New Framework for Analysis*, Boulder, Colo: Lynne Rienner.

CALLEO, DAVID P. (1996), 'Restarting the Marxist Clock? The Economic Fragility of the West', *World Policy Journal*, 13/2: 57–64.

CALLINICOS, ALEX (1995), *Theories and Narratives: Reflections on the Philosophy of History*, Cambridge: Polity.

CALVOCORESSI, PETER (1996), *World Politics since 1945*, 7th edn., London: Longman.

CAMILLERI, JOSEPH A., and FALK, JIM (1992), *The End of Sovereignty: The Politics of a Shrinking and Fragmenting World*, Aldershot: Edward Elgar.

CARNEIRO, ROBERT L. (1978), 'Political Expansion of the Principle of Political Exclusion', in R. Cohen and E. R. Service, *Origins of the State*, Philadelphia: Institute for the Study of Human Issues.

CARR, E. H. (1946), *The Twenty Years Crisis*, 2nd edn., London: Macmillan.

CASSON, LIONEL (1994), *Ships and Seafaring in Ancient Times*, London: British Museum Press.

CASTLES, STEPHEN, and MILLER, MARK J. (1993), *The Age of Migration: International Population Movements in the Modern World*, London: Macmillan.

Central Bank Survey of Foreign Exchange and Derivatives Market Activity (1995), Basle: Bank for International Settlements.

CERNY, PHILIP G. (1995), 'Globalization and the Changing Logic of Collective Action', *International Organization*, 49/4: 595–625.

—— (1996), 'Globalisation and Other Stories: The Search for a New Paradigm for International Relations', *International Journal*, 51: 617–37.

CHAGNON, NAPOLEON A. (1977), *Yanomamo: The Fierce People*, New York: Holt, Rinehard & Winston.

CHAN, STEVE (ed.) (1993), 'Democracy and War: Research and Reflections', special issue of *International Interactions*, 18/3.

CHASE DUNN, CHRISTOPHER, (1994), 'Technology and the Logic of World Systems', in Ronen P.

Palan and Barry Gills (eds.), *Transcending the State–Global Divide: A Neostructuralist Agenda in International Relations*, Boulder, Colo.: Lynne Rienner.

—— and HALL, THOMAS D. (1997), *Rise and Demise: Comparing World-Systems*, Boulder, Colo.: Westview Press.

CHATWIN, BRUCE (1987), *The Songlines*, London: Jonathan Cape.

CHAUDHURI, K. (1990), *Asia before Europe: Economy and Civilisation of the Indian Ocean from the Rise of Islam to 1750*, Cambridge: Cambridge University Press.

CHAY, JONGSUK (1990), *Culture and International Relations*, New York: Praeger.

CHERRY, COLIN (1971), *World Communication: Threat or Promise. A Socio-technical Approach*, London: Wiley.

CHIROT, DANIEL (1985), 'The Rise of the West', *American Sociological Review*, 50: 181–95.

CHOUCRI, NAZLI, and NORTH, ROBERT C. (1975), *Nations in Conflict: National Growth and International Violence*, San Francisco: W. H. Freeman & Co.

CHOWNING, ANN (1983), 'Wealth and Exchange among the Molima of Ferguson Island', in Leach and Leach (1983).

CHRISTENSEN, JENS (1998), 'Internettets verden' [The world of the internet], *Samvirke*, 4 (Apr.): 106–12.

CHRISTIAN, DAVID (1998), *A History of Russia, Central Asia and Mongolia*, i: *Inner Eurasia from Prehistory to the Mongol Empire*, Oxford: Blackwells.

CIPOLLA, C. M. (1981), *Before the Industrial Revolution: European Society and Economy, 1000–1700*, 2nd edn., London: Methuen.

CLAPHAM, CHRISTOPHER (1996), *Africa and the International System: The Politics of State Survival*, Cambridge: Cambridge University Press.

—— (1998), 'Degrees of Statehood', *Review of International Studies*, 24/2: 143–57.

CLAUDE, INNIS L. (1962), *Power and International Relations*, New York: Random House.

CLAUSEWITZ, CARL VON (1976), *On War*, ed. and trans. Michael Howard and Peter Paret, Princeton: Princeton University Press, 1976.

CLUTTON-BROCK, JULIET (1992), *Horse Power: A History of the Horse and the Donkey in Human Societies*, London: Natural History Museum Publications.

COHEN, RAYMOND (1995a), 'In the Beginning: Diplomatic Negotiation in the Ancient Near East', paper presented to the ECPR-SGIR Conference, Paris, Sep.

—— (1995b), 'Diplomacy 2000 BC–2000 AD', paper presented to British International Studies Association Conference, Southampton, Dec.

—— (1998), 'The Great Tradition: The Spread of Diplomacy in the Ancient World', paper presented at the Hebrew University, Jerusalem, Jul.

COLE, DONALD POWELL (1975), *Nomads of the Nomads: The Al Murrah Bedouin of the Empty Quarter*, Chicago: Aldine Pub. Co.

COLE, DAME MARGARET (1923), *An Introduction to World History for Classes and Study Circles*, London: Labour Research Department.

COLLEDGE, MALCOLM A. R. (1967), *The Parthians*, London: Thames & Hudson.

COMAROFF, JOHN (1992), 'Of Totemism and Ethnicity', in John and Jean Comaroff, *Ethnography and the Historical Imagination*, Boulder, Colo.: Westview Press.

CONNAH, GRAHAM (1987), *African Civilizations: Precolonial Cities and States in Tropical Africa: An Archaeological Perspective*, Cambridge: Cambridge University Press.

COOK, HELENA (1996), 'Amnesty International at the United Nations' in P. Willetts (ed.), *'The Conscience of the World': The Influence of Non-governmental Organisations in the UN System*, London: C. Hurst.

COOPER, ROBERT (1996), *The Postmodern State and the World Order*, London: Demos, Paper 19.

COORNAERT, E. L. J. (1967), 'European Economic Institutions and the New World: The Chartered Companies', in E. E. Rich and E. H. Wilson (eds.), *The Cambridge Economic History of Europe*, vol. iv, Cambridge: Cambridge University Press.

COX, R. W. (1976), 'On Thinking about Future World Order', *World Politics*, 28/2: 175–96.

CRAWFORD, HARRIET (1991), *Sumer and the Sumerians*, Cambridge: Cambridge University Press.

CROFT-COOKE, and COTES, PETER (1976), *Circus: A World History*, London: Elek.

CRONE, PATRICIA (1980), *Slaves on Horseback: The Evolution of the Islam Polity*, London: Cambridge University Press.

—— (1987), *Meccan Trade and the Rise of Islam*, Princeton: Princeton University Press.

CROSBY, ALFRED W. (1986), *Ecological Imperialism: The Biological Expansion of Europe, 900–1900*, Cambridge: Cambridge University Press.

CUNLIFFE, B. (1988), *Greeks, Romans and Barbarians*, London: B. T. Batsford.

CURTIN, PHILIP D. (1969), *The Atlantic Slave Trade: A Census*, Madison: University of Wisconsin Press.

—— (1984), *Cross-Cultural Trade in World History*, Cambridge: Cambridge University Press.

CUTLER, CLAIRE A. (1991), 'The "Grotian tradition" in International Relations', *Review of International Studies*, 17/1: 41–65.

DAVIES, H. A. (1968), *An Outline History of the World*, 5th edn. rev. C. H. C. Blount, London: Oxford University Press.

DAVIS, JOHN P. (1971), *Corporations: A Study of the Origin and Development of Great Business Combinations and of their Relation to the Authority of the State*, 2 vols., New York: Burt Franklin (1st pub. 1905).

DAVIS, R. E. G. (1964), *The World's Airlines*, London: Oxford University Press.

DE BARY, THEODORE (1988), *East Asian Civilizations: A Dialogue in Five Stages*, Cambridge, Mass.: Harvard University Press.

DEHIO, LUDWIG (1963), *The Precarious Balance*, London: Chatto & Windus.

DE LIGT, L. (1993), *Fairs and Markets in the Roman Empire: Economic and Social Aspects of Periodic Trade in a Pre-industrial Society*, Amsterdam: J. C. Gieben.

DE LUPIS, INGRID DETTER (1987), *International Law and the Independent State*, Aldershot: Gower.

DEUDNEY, DANIEL (1995), 'The Philadelphia System: Sovereignty, Arms Control and Balance of Power in the American State Union 1787–1861', *International Organization*, 49/2: 191–228.

DEUTSCH, KARL, et al. (1957), *Political Community and the North Atlantic Area*, Princeton: Princeton University Press.

DIAMOND, JARED (1992), *The Rise and Fall of the Third Chimpanzee*, London: Vintage.

—— (1997), *Guns, Germs and Steel: The Fates of Human Societies*, New York: W. W. Norton.

DICKEN, PETER (1986), *Global Shift: Industrial Change in a Turbulent World*, London: Harper & Row, 2nd edn.

—— (1992), *Global Shift: The Internationalization of Economic Activity*, 2nd edn. London: Paul Chapman.

DICKINSON, O. T. P. K. (1994), *The Aegean Bronze Age*, Cambridge: Cambridge University Press.

DIEHL, PAUL F., and GOERTZ, GEORGE (1991), 'Entering International Society', *Comparative Political Studies*, 23/4: 497–518.

DOYLE, MICHAEL (1983a) 'Kant, Liberal Legacies and Foreign Affairs, Part 1', *Philosophy and Public Affairs* 12: 205–35.

—— (1983b), 'Kant, Liberal Legacies and Foreign Affairs, Part 2', *Philosophy and Public Affairs*, 12: 323–53.

—— (1986), *Empires* Ithaca, NY: Cornell University Press.

DUNNE, TIM (1998), *Inventing International Society: A History of the English School*, Basingstoke: Macmillan.

DUNNING, J. H. (1983), 'Changes in the Level and Structure of International Production: The Last One Hundred Years', in Mark Casson, (ed.), *The Growth of International Business*, London: George Allen & Unwin.

—— (1993), *Multinational Enterprises and the Global Economy*, Wokingham: Addison-Wesley.

—— (ed.) (1997), *Governments, Globalization, and International Business*, Oxford: Oxford University Press.

EARLE, TIMOTHY (1991), 'The Evolution of Chiefdoms', in T. Earle (ed.), *Chiefdoms: Power, Economy and Ideology*, Cambridge: Cambridge University Press.

EASTON, DAVID (1953), *The Political System: An Inquiry into the State of Political Science*, New York: Alfred A. Knopf.

—— (1981), 'The Political System Besieged by the State', *Political Theory*, 9: 305–25.

ELIOT, T. S. (1963), *Collected Poems 1909–1962*, London: Faber & Faber.

ELVIN, MARK (1973), *The Pattern of the Chinese Past*, Stanford, Calif.: Stanford University Press.

FAGAN, BRIAN, M. (1991), *Ancient North America: The Archaeology of a Continent*, London: Thames & Hudson.

—— (1993), *World Prehistory: A Brief Introduction*, 2nd edn., New York: Harper Collins.

FALLDING, HAROLD (1974), *The Sociology of Religion: An Explanation of the Unity and Diversity in Religion*, New York: McGraw Hill.

FARB, PETER (1969), *Man's Rise to Civilization*, London: Secker & Warburg.

FEIL, D. K. (1987), *The Evolution of Highland Papua New Guinea Societies*, Cambridge: Cambridge University Press.

FERGUSON, R. and WHITEHEAD, N (eds.) (1992), *War in the Tribal Zone*, Santa Fe, Calif.: School of American Research Press.

FERGUSON, YALE, and MANSBACH, RICHARD (1996), *Polities: Authority, Identities and Change*, Columbia: University of South Carolina Press.

FERNANDEZ-ARMESTO, FILIPE (1996), *Millennium: A History of our Last Thousand Years*, London: Black Swan.

FINLEY, M. I. (1973), *The Ancient Economy*, Berkeley and Los Angeles: University of California Press.

FISCHER, MARKUS (1992), 'Feudal Europe, 800–1300: Communal Discourses and Conflictual Practices' *International Organization* 46/2: 427–66.

FLANNERY, KENT V. (1999), 'Process and Agency in Early State Formation', *Cambridge Archaeological Journal*, 9/1: 3–21.

FLOOD, JOSEPHINE (1995), *Archaeology of the Dreamtime: The Story of Prehistoric Australia and its People*, 3rd edn., Sydney: Angus & Robertson.

—— (1996), 'Culture in Early Aboriginal Australia', *Cambridge Archaeological Journal*, 6/1: 3–38.

FORBES, R. J. (1955), *Studies in Ancient Technology*, vol. ii, Leiden: E. J. Brill.

FORGE, A. (1972), 'Normative Factors in the Settlement Size of Neolithic Cultivators', in P. J. Ucko, R. Tringham, and G. W. Dimbleby, (eds.), *Man, Settlement and Urbanism*, Duckworth: London.

FORTUNE, REO FRANKLIN (1932), *Sorcerers of Dobu: The Social Anthropology of the Dobu Islanders of the Western Pacific*, London: Routledge.

FOX, EDWARD WHITING (1971), *History in Geographic Perspective: The Other France*, New York: Norton.

—— (1991), *The Emergence of the Modern European World*, Oxford: Blackwell.

FOX, WILLIAM T. R. (1970), 'After International Relations, What?', in Norman D. Palmer (ed.), *A*

*Design for International Relations Research: Scope, Theory, Methods, and Relevance*, Philadelphia: American Academy of Political and Social Sciences.

—— (1975), 'Pluralism, the Science of Politics and the World System', *World Politics*, 27: 597–611.

FRANK, ANDRE GUNDER (1990), 'A Theoretical Introduction to 5000 Years of World System History', *Review*, 13/2: 155–248.

—— (1995), 'The Modern World System Revisited: Rereading Braudel and Wallerstein', in Stephen K. Sanderson (ed.), *Civilizations and World Systems: Studying World Historical Change*, Wallnut Creek: Altamira.

—— and GILLS, BARRY K. (1993), *The World System: Five Hundred Years or Five Thousand?*, London: Routledge.

FREEMAN, MICHAEL (1991), *Atlas of the World Economy*, London: Routledge.

FRIED, M. H. (1967), *The Evolution of Political Society*, New York: Random House.

FUKUYAMA, FRANCIS (1992), *The End of History and the Last Man*, London: Penguin.

—— (1998), 'Reflections on *The End of History*, Five Years Later', in P. Pomper, R. H. Elphick, and R. T. Vann, *World History: Ideologies, Structures and Identity*, Oxford: Blackwell Publishers.

GALLAGHER, JOHN and ROBINSON, RONALD (1953) ' The Imperialism of Free Trade, *Economic History Review*, 2nd series, 6:1–15.

GAMBLE, CLIVE (1982), 'Interaction and Alliance in Palaeolithic Society', *Man* 17: 92–107.

—— (1986), *The Palaeolithic Settlement of Europe*, Cambridge: Cambridge University Press.

—— (1995), *Timewalkers*, London: Penguin.

GAUR, ALBERTINE (1992), *A History of Writing*, rev. edn., London: The British Library.

GELLMAN, PETER (1988), 'Hans J. Morgenthau and the Legacy of Political Realism', *Review of International Studies*, 14/4: 247–66.

GELLNER, ERNEST (1983), *Nations and Nationalism*, Oxford: Blackwell.

—— (1988), *Plough, Book and Sword: The Structure of Human History*, London: Paladin.

GIDDENS, ANTHONY (1979), *Central Problems in Social Theory*, London: Macmillan.

—— (1985), *The Nation-State and Violence*, Cambridge: Polity.

GILLS, BARRY K., and FRANK, ANDRE GUNDER (1992), 'World System Cycles, Crises and Hegemonial Shifts, 1700 BC to 1700 AD', *Review*, 15/4: 621–87.

GILPIN, ROBERT (1981), *War and Change in World Politics*, Cambridge: Cambridge University Press.

—— (1987), *The Political Economy of International Relations*, Princeton: Princeton University Press.

GOLDGEIER, JAMES M., and McFAUL, MICHAEL (1992), 'A Tale of Two Worlds: Core and Periphery in the Post-Cold War Era', *International Organization*, 46/2: 467–91.

GOLDSTEIN, JOSHUA S. (1988), *Long Cycles: Prosperity and War in the Modern Age*, New Haven: Yale University Press.

GONG, GERRIT W. (1984), *The Standard of 'Civilisation' in International Society*, Oxford: Clarendon Press.

GORDENKER, LEON and WEISS, THOMAS G. (1996), 'Pluralizing Global Governance' in Thomas G. Weiss and Leon Gordenker (eds.), *NGOs, the UN and Global Governance*, Boulder, Colo.: Lynne Rienner Publishers.

GOULD, J. D. (1972), *Economic Growth in History*, London: Methuen & Co. Ltd.

GOULD, R. A. (1980), *Living Archaeology*, Cambridge: Cambridge University Press.

GRAHAM, GORDON (1997), *The Shape of the Past: A Philosophical Approach to History*, Oxford: Oxford University Press.

GREEN, WILLIAM A. (1992), 'Periodization in European and World History', *Journal of World History* 3: 13–53.

—— (1998), 'Periodising World History', in P. Pomper, R. H. Elphick and R. T. Vann, *World History: Ideologies, Structures and Identity*, Oxford: Blackwell Publishers.

GRUNER, ROLF (1985), *Philosophies of History*, Aldershot: Gower.

GUZZINI, STEFANO (1998), *Realism in International Relations and International Political Economy: The Continuing Story of a Death Foretold*, London: Routledge.

HALL, EDITH (1989) *Inventing the Barbarian: Greek Self-Definition through Tragedy*, Oxford: Clarendon Press.

HALL, JOHN (1996), *International Orders*, Cambridge: Polity.

—— and IKENBERRY, G. J. (1989), *The State*, Milton Keynes: Open University Press.

HALL, JOHN A. (1985), *Powers and Liberties: The Causes and Consequences of the Rise of the West*, London: Penguin.

HALL, RICHARD (1996), *Empires of the Monsoon: A History of the Indian Ocean and its Invaders*, London: HarperCollins.

HALL, RODNEY BRUCE (1997), 'Moral Authority as a Power Resource', *International Organization*, 51/4: 590–622.

—— and KRATOCHWIL, FRIEDRICH V. (1993), 'Medieval Tales: Neorealist "Science" and the Abuse of History', *International Organization*, 47/3: 479–91.

HALLIDAY, FRED (1974), *Arabia without Sultans*, Harmondsworth: Penguin (3rd edn. 1979).

HAMMOND, MASON (1972), *The City in the Ancient World*, Cambridge, Mass.: Harvard University Press.

HANSON, NORWOOD RUSSELL (1958) *Patterns of Discovery: An Inquiry into the Conceptual Foundations of Science*, Cambridge: Cambridge University Press.

HARRIES, OWEN (1993), 'The Collapse of "the West" ', *Foreign Affairs*, 72/4: 41–53.

HARRIS, ROY (1986), *The Origins of Writing*, London: Duckworth.

HARRISON, S. (1993), *The Mask of War: Violence, Ritual and the Self in Melanesia*, Manchester: Manchester University Press.

HART, K. (1986), 'Heads or Tails? Two Sides of the Coin', *Man*, 21: 637–56.

HARTZOG, FRANÇOIS (1988), *The Mirror of Herodotus*, trans. Janet Lloyd, Berkeley and Los Angeles: University of California Press.

HASSIG, ROSS (1985), *Trade, Tribute and Transportation: The 16th Century Political Economy of the Valley of Mexico*, Norman: University of Oklahoma Press.

HAYASHI, RYOICHI (1975), *The Silk Road and the Shoso-in*, Tokyo: Weatherhill/Heibonsha.

HAYDEN, B. (1993), *Archaeology: The Science of Once and Future Things*, New York: Freeman.

HEADRICK, DANIEL R. (1988), *The Tentacles of Progress: Technology Transfer in the Age of Imperialism*, Oxford University Press.

HEEREN, A. H. L. (1857), *A Manuel of the History of the Political System of Europe and its Colonies*, trans. from 5th edn., London: Henry G. Bohn (1st pub. 1809).

HELLEINER, ERIC (1994), 'Regionalization in the International Political Economy: A Comparative Perspective', *East Asian Policy Papers*, University of Toronto–University of York Joint Centre for Asia Pacific Studies.

HELMS, MARY (1988), *Ulysses' Sail*, Princeton: Princeton University Press.

HEMMING, JOHN (1998) 'Do these People Need our Twentieth Century?', *Independent*, 6 July 1998, p. 8.

HERRMANN, GEORGINA (1968), 'Lapis Lazuli: The Early Phases of its Trade', *Iraq*, 30: 21–57.

HERZ, JOHN H. (1968), 'The Territorial State Revisited', *Polity*, 1/1: 12–34.

HEXTER, J. H. (1971), *The History Primer*, New York: Basic Books.

—— (1979), *On Historians: Reappraisals of some of the Makers of Modern History*, Cambridge, Mass.: Harvard University Press.

HIGHAM, CHARLES (1989), *The Archaeology of Mainland Southeast Asia*, Cambridge: Cambridge University Press.

HIRST, PAUL, and THOMPSON, GRAHAM (1996), *Globalization in Question: The International Economy and the Possibilities of Governance*, Oxford: Polity Press.

HOBDEN, STEVE (1998), *International Relations and Historical Sociology: Breaking down Boundaries*, London: Routledge.

HOBSBAWM, ERIC JOHN (1994), *Age of Extremes: The Short Twentieth Century 1914–1991*, London: Michael Joseph.

HOBSON, J. A. (1938), *Imperialism: A Study*, London: Allen & Unwin, (1st pub. 1902).

HOBSON, JOHN M. (1997), *The Wealth of States: A Comparative Sociology of International and Political Change*, Cambridge: Cambridge University Press.

—— (1999), 'The Two Waves of Weberian Historical Sociology: Beyond Neorealist State-Centrism', paper prepared for the conference 'Bringing Historical Sociologies into International Relations', Aberystwyth.

HODDER, IAN (ed.) (1978), *The Spatial Organisation of Culture*, London: Duckworth.

HODGES, RICHARD (1988), *Primitive and Peasant Markets*, Oxford: Basil Blackwell.

HODGSON, MARSHALL G. S. (1993), *Rethinking World History: Essays on Europe, Islam and World History*, Cambridge: Cambridge University Press.

HOFFMANN, STANLEY (1977) 'An American Social Science: International Relations', *Daedalus*, 106/3: 41–60.

HOFMAN, JACK L. (1994), 'Paleoindian Aggregations on the Great Plains', *Journal of Anthropological Archaeology*, 13: 341–70.

HOLLIS, MARTIN, and SMITH, STEVE (1990), *Explaining and Understanding International Relations*, Oxford: Clarendon Press.

HOLLIST, W. L. and ROSENAU, JAMES N. (eds.) (1981), 'World Systems Debates', special issue of *International Studies Quarterly* 2/1: 5–17.

HOLSTI, KALEVI J. (1967), *International Politics: A Framework for Analysis*, Englewood Cliffs, NJ: Prentice-Hall.

—— (1991), *Peace and War: Armed Conflict and International Order, 1648–1989*, Cambridge: Cambridge University Press.

HOLT, FRANK I. (1988), *Alexander the Great and Bactria: The Formation of a Greek Frontier in Asia*, Leiden: Brill.

HORSMAN, MATHEW, and MARSHALL, ANDREW (1995), *After the Nation-State: Citizens, Tribalism and the New World Disorder*, London: HarperCollins.

HOURANI, GEORGE F. (1995), *Arab Seafaring in the Indian Ocean in Ancient and Early Medieval Times*, rev. and expanded edn., by John Carswell, Princeton: Princeton University Press (1st pub.1951).

HOWARD, MICHAEL (1976), *War in European History*, Oxford: Oxford University Press.

HUDSON, G. F. (1931), *Europe and China: A Survey of their Earliest Times to 1800*, London: Edward Arnold.

HUGILL, P. J. (1993), *World Trade since 1431: Geography, Technology and Capitalism*, Baltimore: Johns Hopkins University Press.

HUNT, EDWIN S. (1994), *The Medieval Super-Companies: A Study of the Peruzzi Company of Florence*, Cambridge: Cambridge University Press.

HUNTINGTON, SAMUEL P. (1993), 'The Clash of Civilizations?', *Foreign Affairs*, 72/3: 22–49.

—— (1996), *The Clash of Civilizations and the Remaking of World Order*, New York: Simon & Schuster.

IBRAHIM, MAHMOOD (1990), *Merchant Capital and Islam*, Austin: University of Texas Press.

INTERNATIONAL AIR TRANSPORT ASSOCIATION (IATA) (1993), *World Air Transport Statistics, 37*.

IRWIN, GEOFFREY (1992), *The Prehistoric Exploration and Colonisation of the Pacific*, Cambridge: Cambridge University Press.

JACKSON, ROBERT H. (1990), *Quasi-States: Sovereignty, International Relations and the Third World*, Cambridge: Cambridge University Press.

—— and Zacher, MARK W. (1997), 'The Territorial Covenant: International Society and the Stabilization of Boundaries', paper presented to PIPES, University of Chicago, May.

JAFFE, A. J. (1992), *The First Immigrants from Asia: A Population History of the North American Indians*, New York: Plenum Press.

JAMES, ALAN (1992), 'The Equality of States: Contemporary Manifestations of an Ancient Doctrine', *Review of International Studies*, 18/4: 377–92.

JASPERS, KARL (1953), *The Origin and Goal of History*, trans. M. Bullock, New Haven: Yale University Press.

JONES, E. L. (1987), *The European Miracle: Environment, Economies and Geopolitics in the History of Europe and Asia*, 2nd edn., Cambridge: Cambridge University Press.

—— (1988), *Growth Recurring: Economic Change in World History*, Oxford: Clarendon Press.

JONES, ERIC, FROST, LIONEL, and WHITE, COLIN (1993), *Coming Full Circle: An Economic History of the Pacific Rim*, Boulder, Colo.: Westview Press.

JUDT, TONY (1994), 'Nineteen Eighty-Nine: The End of Which European Era?', *Daedalus*, 123/3: 1–19.

KANTNER, J. (1996), 'Political Competition among the Chaco Anasazi of the American Southwest', *Journal of Anthropological Archaeology*, 15: 41–105.

KAPLAN, M. A. (1957), *System and Process in International Politics*, New York: John Wiley & Sons.

KAPLAN, ROBERT (1994), 'The Coming Anarchy', *Atlantic Monthly*, (Feb.), 44–76.

KAUFMAN, STUART J. (1997), 'The Fragmentation and Consolidation of International Systems', *International Organization*, 51/2: 173–208.

KEELEY, LAWRENCE, H. (1996), *War before Civilization: The Myth of the Peaceful Savage*, New York: Oxford University Press.

KEGLEY, CHARLES W., and WITTKOPF, EUGENE R. (1987), *American Foreign Policy: Pattern and Process*, 3rd edn., Basingstoke: Macmillan Education,.

KENNEDY, PAUL (1989), *The Rise and Fall of the Great Powers: Economic Change and Military Conflict from 1500–2000*, London: Fontana.

KEOHANE, ROBERT O. (1984), *After Hegemony: Cooperation and Discord in the World Political Economy*, Princeton: Princeton University Press.

—— (1995), 'Hobbes' Dilemma and Institutional Change in World Politics: Sovereignty in International Society', in Hans-Henrik Holm and Georg Sørensen (eds.), *Whose World Order*, Boulder, Colo.: Westview Press.

KEOHANE, ROBERT O., and NYE, JOSEPH (1973) *Transnational Relations and World Politics*, Princeton: Princeton University Press.

—— —— (1977), *Power and Interdependence*, Boston: Little-Brown.

—— —— (1987), '*Power and Interdependence* Revisited', *International Organisation*, 421/4: 725–53.

KEYLOR, WILLIAM R. (1984), *The Twentieth Century World: An International History*, New York: Oxford University Press.

KHAZANOV, ANATOLY M. (1984), *Nomads and the Outside World*, trans. Julia Crookenden; with a foreword by Ernest Gellner, Cambridge: Cambridge University Press.

KINDLEBERGER, CHARLES P. (1981), *International Money: A Collection of Essays*, London: Allen & Unwin.

—— (1984) *A Financial History of Western Europe*, London: Allen & Unwin.

—— (1986), *The World in Depression, 1929–1939*, rev. edn. Berkeley and Los Angeles: University of California Press.

KLEINKNECHT, ALFRED, MANDEL, ERNEST, and WALLERSTEIN, IMMANUEL eds. (1992), *New Findings in Long Wave Research*, New York: St Martin's Press.

KNAUFT, BRUCE M. (1991), 'Violence and Sociality in Human Evolution', *Current Anthropology*, 32/4: 391–428.

KOSSE, KRISZTINA (1994), 'The Evolution of Large, Complex Groups: A Hypothesis', *Journal of Anthropological Archaeology*, 13: 35–50.

KRASNER, STEPHEN D. (1976), 'State Power and the Structure of International Trade', *World Politics*, 28/3: 317–47.

—— (1985), *Structural Conflict: The Third World against Global Liberalism*, Berkeley and Los Angeles: University of California Press.

—— (1993), 'Westphalia and All That', in Judith Goldstein and Robert O. Keohane (eds.), *Ideas and Foreign Policy: Beliefs, Institutions, and Political Change*, Ithaca, NY: Cornell University Press.

—— (1995-6), 'Compromising Westphalia', *International Security*, 20/3: 115–51.

KRATOCHWIL, FRIEDRICH (1986), 'Of Systems, Boundaries, and Territoriality: An Inquiry into the Formation of the State System', *World Politics*, 39/1: 27–52.

KWANTEN, LUC (1979), *Imperial Nomads: A History of Central Asia, 500–1500*, Leicester: Leicester University Press.

LANDES, DAVID S. (1969), *The Unbound Prometheus: Technological Change and Industrial Development in Western Europe from 1750 to the Present*, London: Cambridge University Press.

LANE, FREDERICK C. (1966), *Venice and History*, Baltimore: Johns Hopkins University Press.

LANNING, EDWARD P. (1974*a*), 'Eastern South America', in Shirley Gorenstein et al., *Prehispanic America*, London: Thames & Hudson.

—— (1974*b*), 'The Transformation to Civilization', in Shirley Gorenstein et al., *Prehispanic America*, London: Thames & Hudson.

LARSEN, MOGENS T. (1976) *The Old Assyrian City-State and its Colonies*, Copenhagen: Akademisk Forlag.

—— (1979), *Power and Propaganda: A Symposium on Ancient Empires*, Copenhagen: Akademisk Forlag.

LEACH, E. R. (1983), 'The Kula: An Alternative View', in Jerry W. Leach and Edmund Leach, *The Kula: New Perspectives on Massim Exchange*, Cambridge: Cambridge University Press.

LEACH, JERRY W., and LEACH, EDMUND (1983), *The Kula: New Perspectives on Massim Exchange*, Cambridge: Cambridge University Press.

LENIN, V. I. (1996), *Imperialism: The Highest Stage of Capitalism*, London: Pluto Press.

LEVINE, MARSHA A. (1999), 'Botai and the Origins of Horse Domestication', *Journal of Anthropological Archaeology*, 18/1: 29–78.

LEWIS, BERNARD (1966), *The Arabs in History*, 4th edn., London: Hutchinson.

LEWIS, NORMAN, and MALONE, JAMES (1996), 'Introduction' to V. I. Lenin, *Imperialism: The Highest Stage of Capitalism. A Popular Outline*, London: Pluto Press.

LIND, Michael (1996), 'Pax Atlantica: The Case for Euroamerica', *World Policy Journal*, 13/1: 1–7.

LINKLATER, ANDREW (1981), 'Men and Citizens in International Relations', *Review of International Studies*, 7/1: 23–38.

LITTLE, RICHARD (1985), 'The Systems Approach', in Steve Smith (ed.), *International Relations: British and American Approaches*, Oxford: Blackwell.

—— (1991), 'Liberal Hegemony and the Realist Assault Competing Ideological Theories of the State', in Michael Banks and Martin Shaw (eds.), *State and Society in International Relations*, Hemel Hempstead: Harvester Wheatsheaf.

—— (1994), 'International Relations and Large-Scale Historical Change', in A. J. R. Groom and Margot Light, *Contemporary International Relations: A Guide to Theory*, London: Pinter Publishing.

—— (1995), 'Neorealism and the English School: A Methodological, Ontological and Theoretical Reassessment', *European Journal of International Relations*, 1/1: 9–34.

—— (1996), 'The Growing Relevance of Pluralism', in S. Smith, K. Booth and M. Zalewski, *International Theory: Positivism and Beyond*, Cambridge: Cambridge University Press.

—— (1997), 'International Regimes', in J. Baylis and S. Smith, (eds.), *The Globalisation of International Politics*, Oxford: Oxford University Press.

LIU, LI (1996), 'Settlement Patterns, Chiefdom Variability, and the Development of Early States in North China', *Journal of Anthropological Archaeology*, 15: 237–88.

LOVEJOY, PAUL E. (1996), 'The Volume of the Atlantic Slave Trade: A Synthesis', in Patrick Manning, (ed.), *Slave Trade, 1500–1800: Globalization of Forced Labour*, An Expanding World: The European Impact on World History, 15, Aldershot: Variorum.

LUTTWAK, E. (1990), 'From Geopolitics to Geo-economics', *National Interest*, 20: 17–24.

LYOTARD, JEAN-FRANÇOIS (1984), *The Postmodern Condition: a Report on Knowledge*, trans. Geoff Bennington and Brian Massumi; foreword by Fredric Jameson, Manchester: Manchester University Press.

McCARTHY, F. D. (1938–9), ' "Trade" in Aboriginal Australia and "Trade" Relations with Torres Strait, New Guinea and Malaya', *Oceania*, 9/4: 404–38.

—— (1939–40*a*), ' "Trade" in Aboriginal Australia and "Trade" Relations with Torres Strait, New Guinea and Malaya', *Oceania*, 10/1: 80–104.

—— (1939–40*b*), ' "Trade" in Aboriginal Australia and "Trade" Relations with Torres Strait, New Guinea and Malaya', *Oceania*, 10/2: 171–93.

McCLELLAND, CHARLES A. (1958), 'Systems and History in International Relations', *General Systems Yearbook*, 3: 221–47.

MacCORMACK, CAROL P. (1981) 'Exchange and Hierarchy', in Alan Sheridan and Geoff Bailey, *Economic Archaeology: Towards an Integration of Ecological and Social Approaches*, Oxford: BAR International Series 96.

MacKENZIE, JOHN M. (1995), *Orientalism: History, Theory and the Arts*, Manchester: Manchester University Press.

MACKINDER, HALFORD J. (1904), 'The Geographical Pivot of History', *Geographical Journal*, 13: 421–37.

—— (1919), *Democratic Ideals and Reality*, London: Constable.

McNEILL, WILLIAM H. (1963), *The Rise of the West: A History of the Human Community*, Chicago: University of Chicago Press.

—— (1976), *Plagues and Peoples*, London: Penguin.

—— (1979), *A World History*, Oxford: Oxford University Press.

—— (1982), *The Pursuit of Power: Technology, Armed Force and Society since AD 1000*, Chicago: University of Chicago Press.

—— (1986), *Mythohistory and Other Essays*, Chicago: University of Chicago Press.

—— (1991), 'The Rise of the West after Twenty-five Years', in *The Rise of the West: A History of the Human Community*, 2nd edn., Chicago: University of Chicago Press.

—— (1993), 'Foreword' in A. G. Frank and B. K. Gills, *The World System: Five Hundred Years or Five Thousand*, London: Routledge.

—— (1994), 'The Fall of Great Powers: An Historical Commentary', *Review*, 17/2: 123–43.

—— (1997) 'Territorial States Buried Too Soon', *Mershon International Studies Review*, 41/2: 269–74.

—— (1998), 'The Changing Shape of World History', in P. Pomper, R. H. Elphick, and R. T. Vann, *World History: Ideologies, Structures and Identity*, Oxford: Blackwell Publishers Ltd.

McRAE, HAMISH (1994), *The World in 2020*, London: HarperCollins.

MADDEN, MARCIE (1983), 'Social Network Systems amongst Hunter-Gatherers Considered within

Southern Norway', in Geoff Bailey, *Hunter-Gatherer Economy in Prehistory*, Cambridge: Cambridge University Press.

MAGER, NATHAN H. (1987), *The Kondratieff Waves*, New York: Praeger.

MAISELS, CHARLES KEITH (1990), *The Emergence of Civilisation: From Hunting and Gathering to Agriculture, Cities and the State in the Near East*, London: Routledge.

—— (1993) *The Near East: Archaeology in the Cradle of Civilization*, London: Routledge.

MALLORY, J. P. (1989), *In Search of the Indo-Europeans: Language, Archaeology and Myth*, London: Thames & Hudson.

MANDEL, ERNEST (1978) *Late Capitalism*, trans. Joris De Bres, rev. edn., London: Verso.

MANN, MICHAEL (1986), *The Sources of Social Power, i: A History of Power from the Beginning to AD 1760*, Cambridge: Cambridge University Press.

—— (1993), *The Sources of Social Power, ii: The Rise of Classes and Nation-States, 1760–1940*, Cambridge: Cambridge University Press.

—— (1995), 'Review of Rosenberg's *The Empire of Civil Society*', *British Journal of Sociology*, 46/3: 554–5.

MANNING, C. A. W. (1954), *The University Teaching of Social Sciences: International Relations*, Paris: UNESCO.

—— (1962), *The Nature of International Society*, London: LSE.

MANNING, PATRICK (1996), 'The Problem of Interaction in World History', *American Historical Review*, 101/3: 771–82.

MARCUS, JOYCE (1992), *Mesoamerican Writing Systems: Propaganda, Myth and History in Four Ancient Civilizations*, Princeton: Princeton University Press.

MAYALL, JAMES (1990), *Nationalism and International Society*, Cambridge: Cambridge University Press.

MEAD, WALTER RUSSELL (1995–6), 'Trains, Planes and Automobiles: The End of the Postmodern Movement', *World Policy Journal*, 12/4: 13–31.

MEARSHEIMER, JOHN J. (1990), 'Back to the Future: Instability in Europe after the Cold War', *International Security*, 15/1: 5–56.

MEEHAN, E. H. (1968), *Explanation in Social Science: A System Paradigm*, Homewood,Ill.: Dorsey Press.

MEIJER, FIK, and VAN NIJF, ONNO (1992), *Trade, Transport and Society in the Ancient World*, London: Routledge.

MESCHNER, HERBERT D.G. and MESCHNER, KATHERINE L. REEDY (1998), 'Raid, Retreat, Defeat (Repeat), The Archeology and Ethnology of Warfare on the North Pacific Rim', *Journal of Anthropological Archaeology*, 17: 19–51.

MILLER, J. INNES (1969), *The Spice Trade of the Roman Empire 29 B.C. to A.D. 641*, Oxford: Clarendon Press.

MILNER, HELEN (1991), 'The Assumption of Anarchy in International Relations Theory', *Review of International Studies*, 17/1: 67–85.

MITCHELL, B. R. (1975), *European Historical Statistics, 1750–1970*, London: Macmillan.

—— (1982), *International Historical Statistics: Africa and Asia*, London: Macmillan.

—— (1983), *International Historical Statistics: The Americas and Australasia*, London: Macmillan.

MODELSKI, GEORGE (1972), *Principles of World Politics*, New York: Free Press.

—— (1987), *Long Cycles in World Politics*, Seattle: University of Washington Press.

MOORE, JAMES A. (1981), 'The Effects of Information Networks in Hunter-Gatherer Societies', in B. Winterhalder and E. A. Smith, *Hunter-Gatherer Foraging Strategies: Ethnographic and Archaeological Analyses*, Chicago: University of Chicago Press.

MOORE, R. I. (1993), 'World History: World-Economy or a Set of Sets?', *Journal of the Royal Asiatic Society*, 3rd series, 3/1: 99–105.

—— (1997), 'World History', in Michael Bentley (ed.), *Companion to Historiography*, London: Routledge.

MORENZ, SIEGFRIED (1973), *Egyptian Religion*, trans. Ann E. Keep, London: Methuen.

MORGAN, E. VICTOR (1965), *A History of Money*, Harmondsworth: Penguin.

MORGENTHAU, HANS J. (1970), ' International Relations: Quantitative and Qualitative', in Norman D. Palmer (ed.), *A Design for International Relations Research: Scope, Theory, Methods, and Relevance*, Philadelphia: American Academy of Political and Social Sciences.

—— (1971), 'The Commitments of Political Science', in *Politics in the Twentieth Century*, Chicago: Chicago University Press.

—— (1973), *Politics among Nations*, 5th edn., New York: Knopf.

MORPHET, SALLY (1996), 'NGOs and the Environment' in P. Willetts (ed.), *'The Conscience of the World': The Influence of Non-governmental Organisations in the UN System*, London: C. Hurst.

MORPHY, HOWARD (1990), 'Myth, Totemism and the Creation of Clans', *Oceania* 60: 312–28.

MOSLER, HERMANN (1980), *The International Society as a Legal Community*, Alphen aan den Rijn: Sijthoff & Noordhoff.

MOSLEY, D. J. (1973), *Envoys and Diplomacy in Ancient Greece*, Historia 22, Wiesbaden: Franz Steiner.

MOURITZEN, HANS (1980), 'Selecting Explanatory Levels in International Politics: Evaluating a Set of Criteria', *Cooperation and Conflict*, 15: 169–82.

—— (1995), 'A Fallacy of IR Theory: Reflections on a Collective Repression', unpublished MS, Copenhagen, Centre for Peace and Conflict Research.

—— (1997), 'Kenneth Waltz: A Critical Rationalist between International Politics and Foreign Policy', in Iver B. Neumann and Ole Wæver (eds.), *The Future of International Relations: Masters in the Making?*, London: Routledge.

NASH, RONALD H. (1984), *Christianity and the Hellenisitic World*, Grand Rapids, Mich.: Zondervan Pub. House.

NEAL, LARRY (1990), *The Rise of Financial Capitalism: International Capital Markets in the Age of Reason*, Cambridge: Cambridge University Press.

NETTLE, DANIEL (1996), 'Language Diversity in West Africa: An Ecological Approach', *Journal of Anthropological Archaeology*, 15: 403–38.

—— (1998), 'Explaining Global Patterns of Language Diversity', *Journal of Anthropological Archaeology*, 17: 354–74.

NEUBURGER, ALBERT (1930), *The Technical Arts and Sciences of the Ancients*, London: Methuen.

NICHOLS, J. (1990), 'Linguisitic Diversity and the First Settlement of the New World', *Language* 66: 475–521.

—— (1992), *Linguistic Diversity in Space and Time*, Chicago: University of Chicago Press.

NISSEN, HANS J. (1988), *The Early History of the Ancient Near East: 9000–2000 BC*, Chicago: University of Chicago Press.

NUMELIN, RAGNAR (1950), *The Beginnings of Diplomacy: A Sociological Study of Intertribal and International Relations*, London: Oxford University Press.

—— (1967), *Native Contacts and Diplomacy: The History of Intertribal Relations in Australia and Oceania*, Helsinki: Helsingfors.

NYE, JOSEPH S. (1990), *Bound to Lead: The Changing Nature of American Power*, New York: Basic Books.

O'DEA, THOMAS F., and O'DEA AVIAD, JANET (1983), *The Sociology of Religion*, Englewood Cliffs, NJ: Prentice Hall (1st pub. 1966).

OLIVER, ROLAND, and ATMORE, ANTHONY (1994), *Africa since 1800*, 4th edn., Cambridge: Cambridge University Press.

O'NEILL, J. (ed.) (1973), *Models of Individualism and Collectivism*, London: Heinemann.

ONUF, NICHOLAS (1995), 'Levels', *European Journal of International Relations*, 1/1: 35–58.

O'SHEA, JOHN (1981), 'Coping with Scarcity: Exchange and Social Storage', in Alan Sheridan and Geoff Bailey, *Economic Archaeology: Towards an Integration of Ecological and Social Approaches*, Oxford: BAR International Series 96.

PARK, CHRIS C. (1994), *Sacred Worlds: An Introduction to Geography and Religion*, London: Routledge.

PAYNE, JOAN CROWFOOT (1968), 'Lapis Lazuli in Early Egypt', *Iraq*, 30: 58–61.

PERSSON, J. (1983), 'Cyclical Change and Circular Exchange: A Re-examination of the Kula Ring', *Oceania*, 54: 32–47.

PETERSON, NICOLAS (1976), 'The Natural and Cultural Areas of Aboriginal Australia: A Preliminary Analysis of Population Groupings with Adaptive Significance', in Nicolas Peterson, (ed.), *Tribes and Boundaries in Australia*, Canberra, Social Anthropology Series 10, Australian Institute of Aboriginal Studies, Atlantic Highlands, Humanities Press.

PHILLIPS, E. D. (1965), *The Royal Hordes: Nomad Peoples of the Steppes*, London: Thames & Hudson.

PISCATORI, JAMES P. (1986), *Islam in a World of Nation-States*, Cambridge: Cambridge University Press in association with the Royal Institute of International Affairs.

POLANYI, KARL (1957), *The Great Transformation*, Boston: Beacon Press (1st pub. 1944).

—— (1971), *Primitive, Archaic, and Modern Economics: Essays of Karl Polanyi*, ed. George Dalton, Boston: Beacon Press.

—— (1977), *The Livelihood of Man*, New York: Academic Press.

POPPER, SIR KARL (1957), *The Poverty of Historicism*, London: Routledge & Kegan Paul.

—— (1966), *The Open Society and its Enemies*, 5th edn. (rev.), ii: *The High Tide of Prophecy: Hegel, Marx, and the Aftermath*, London: Routledge & Kegan Paul.

POSTGATE, J. N. (1992), *Early Mesopotamia: Society and Economy at the Dawn of History*, London: Routledge.

POUNDS, N. J. G. (1994), *An Economic History of Medieval Europe*, 2nd edn., London: Longman.

POWELSON, JOHN P. (1994), *Centuries of Economic Endeavour*, Ann Arbor: University of Michigan Press.

PRICE, T. DOUGLAS, and BROWN, JAMES A. (eds.) (1985), *Prehistoric Hunter-Gatherers: The Emergence of Cultural Complexity*, London: Academic Press.

RANA, A. P. (1993), 'The New Northern Concert of Powers in a World of Multiple Independencies', in K. Ajhua, H. Coppens, and H. van der Wusten (eds.), *Regime Transformation in Global Realignments*, London: Sage.

RASLER, KAREN A. (1989), *War and State Making: The Shaping of the Global Powers*, London: Unwin Hyman.

RAUTMAN, ALISON E. (1993), 'Resource Variability, Risk, and the Structure of Social Networks: An Example from the Prehistoric Southwest', *American Antiquity*, 58/3: 403–24.

REDMOND, ELSA, M. (1994) 'External Warfare and Internal Politics of Northern South American Tribes and Chiefdoms', in E. M. Brumfiel and John W. Fox, *Factional Competition and Political Development in the New World*, Cambridge: Cambridge University Press.

RENFREW, COLIN (1987), *Archaeology and Language: The Puzzle of the Indo-European Origins*, London: Jonathan Cape.

—— (1993), 'Trade beyond the Material', in Chris Scarre and Francis Healey, *Trade and Exchange in Prehistoric Europe*, Oxford: Oxbow Books.

—— and CHERRY, J. F. (eds.) (1986), *Peer Polity Interaction and Socio-political Change*, Cambridge: Cambridge University Press.

RENGGER, NICK (1999), *Beyond International Relations Theory? International Relations, Political Theory and the Problem of Order*, London: Routledge.

REUS-SMIT, CHRISTIAN (1997), 'The Constitutional Structure of International Society and the Nature of Fundamental Institutions', *International Organization*, 51/4: 555–89.

REYNOLDS, PHILIP A. (1994), *An Introduction to International Relations*, 3rd edn., London: Longmans.

REYNOLDS, SUSAN (1997), 'The Historiography of the Medieval State', in M. Bentley (ed.), *Companion to Historiography*, London: Routledge.

RICE, DAVID TALBOT (1976), *The Illustrations to the World History of Rashid al-Din*, Edinburgh: Edinburgh University Press.

RICE, TAMARA TALBOT (1957), *The Scythians*, London: Thames & Hudson.

RICHARDSON, J. L. (1988), 'New Perspectives on Appeasement: Some Implications for International Relations', *World Politics*, 40: 284–316.

ROAF, MICHAEL (1990), *Cultural Atlas of Mesopotamia and the Ancient Near East*, Oxford: Facts on File.

ROBB, JOHN (1993), 'A Social Prehistory of European Languages', *Antiquity*, 67: 747–60.

ROBERTS, J. M. (1993), *History of the World*, London: BCA.

ROBINSON, WILLIAM S. (1950), 'Ecological Correlations and the Behaviour of Individuals', *American Sociological Review*, 15: 351–7.

RODSETH, LARS, et al. (1991), 'The Human Community as a Primate Society', *Current Anthropology*, 32/3: 221–54.

ROEBROEKS, W., KOLEN, J., and RENSINK, E. (1988), 'Planning Depth, Anticipation and the Organization of Middle Palaeolithic Technology: The "Archaic Natives" Meet Eve's Descendants', *Helinium*, 28: 17–34.

ROLLE, RENATE (1989), *The World of the Scythians*, trans. Gayna Walls, London: B. T. Batsford (1st pub. 1980).

ROSCOE, PAUL R. (1996), 'War and Society in Sepic New Guinea', *Journal of the Royal Anthropological Institute*, 2/4: 645–66.

ROSECRANCE, RICHARD (1963), *Action and Reaction in International Politics*, Boston: Little, Brown.

—— (1986), *The Rise of the Trading State: Commerce and Conquest in the Modern World*, New York: Basic Books.

—— (1996), 'The Rise of the Virtual State', *Foreign Affairs*, 75/4: 45–61.

ROSENAU, JAMES N. (1990), *Turbulence in World Politics: A Theory of Change and Continuity*, London: Harvester Wheatsheaf.

ROSENBERG, JUSTIN (1994), *The Empire of Civil Society: A Critique of the Realist Theory of International Relations*, London: Verso.

—— (1995), 'Habermas' Century', *Monthly Review*, 43/3: 139–57.

ROSS, M. C., DONALDSON, T., and WILD, J. A. (1987) (eds.), *Songs of Aboriginal Australia*, Oceania Monograph: 32, Sydney: University of Sydney.

ROSSABI, MORRIS (1992), *Voyager from Xanadu: Rabban Sauma and the First Journey from China to the West*, Tokyo: Kodansha International.

ROSTOW, W. W. (1978), *The World Economy: History and Prospect*, London: Macmillan.

RUGGIE, JOHN GERRARD (1982), 'International Regimes, Transactions, and Change: Embedded Liberalism in the Postwar Economic Order', *International Organization*, 36/2: 379–415.

—— (1983), 'Continuity and Transformation in the World Polity: Towards a Neo-realist Synthesis', *World Politics*, 35/2: 261–85.

RUGGIE, JOHN GERRARD (1993), 'Territoriality and Beyond: Problematizing Modernity in International Relations', *International Organization*, 47/1: 139–74.

—— (1998), *Constructing the World Polity: Essays on International Institutionalisation*, London: Routledge.

RUNNELS, C. and VAN ANDEL, T. H. (1988), 'Trade and the Origins of Agriculture in the Eastern Mediterranean', *Journal of Mediterranean Archaeology*, 1: 83–109.

RUSI, ALPO M. (1997), *Dangerous Peace: New Rivalry in World Politics*, Boulder, Colo.: Westview Press.

RUSSETT, BRUCE (1993), *Grasping the Democratic Peace: Principles for a Post-Cold War World*, Princeton: Princeton University Press.

—— and STARR, HARVEY (1996), *World Politics: The Menu for Choice*, 5th edn., New York: W. H. Freeman & Co.

RYAN, ALAN (1998), ' "A Theory of Growing Concerns", review of F. Zakaria: *From Wealth to Power*', *Times Higher Educational Supplement*, 27 Nov. 1998, p. 27.

SAID, EDWARD W. (1995), *Orientalism*, new edn., London: Penguin (1st pub.) New York: Pantheon, 1978).

SANDERSON, STEPHEN K. (ed.) (1995), *Civilizations and World Systems: Studying World-Historical Change*, Wallnut Creek: Altamira Press.

SARDAR, ZIA, NANDY, ASHIS, and WYN DAVIES, MERRYL (1993), *Barbarian Others: A Manifesto on Western Racism*, London: Pluto Press.

SAVAGE, STEPHEN (1997), 'Descent Group Competition and Economic Strategies in Predynastic Egypt', *Journal of Anthropological Archaeology*, 16: 226–68.

SCAMMELL, G. V. ( 1981), *The World Encompassed: The First European Maritime Empires c.800–1650*, London: Routledge.

SCHMIDT, BRIAN C. (1998), *The Political Discourse of Anarchy: A Disciplinary History of International Relations*, Albany: State University of New York.

SCHNEIDER, LOUIS (1970), *Sociological Approach to Religion*, New York: John Wiley.

SCHROEDER, PAUL W. (1994), 'Historical Reality versus Neorealist Theory', *International Security*, 19/1: 108–48.

SCHWARTZ, GLEN M. (1995), 'Pastoral Nomadism in Ancient Western Asia', *Civilizations of the Ancient Near East*, vol. iv, gen. ed. Jack M. Sasson, New York: Scribner.

SEARY, BILL (1996), 'The Early History: From the Congress of Vienna to the San Francisco Conference', in Willetts (1996).

SECOY, FRANK RAYMOND (1953), *Changing Military Patterns on the Great Plains*, Seattle: University of Washington Press.

SEGAL, AARON (1993), *Atlas of International Migration*, London: Hans Zell.

SEN, DEBABRATA (1975), *Basic Principles of Geopolitics and History*, Delhi: Concept Publishing House.

SERVICE, ELMAN, R. (1979), *The Hunters*, 2nd edn., Englewood Cliffs, NJ: Prentice-Hall Inc.

SHENNAN, STEPHEN (1986), 'Interaction and Change in Third Millennium BC Western and Central Europe', in Renfrew and Cherry (1986).

SHERRATT, ANDREW G. (1995), 'Reviving the Grand Narrative: Archaeology and Long-Term Change', *Journal of European Archaeology*, 3/1: 1–32.

SILVER, MORRIS (1985), *Economic Structures of the Ancient Near East*, London: Croom Helm.

SIMKIN, C. G. F. (1968), *The Traditional Trade of Asia*, London: Oxford University Press.

SINGER, CHARLES, HOLMYARD, E. J., HALL, A. R., and WILLIAMS, TREVOR I. (1954), *A History of Technology, i: From Early Times to the Fall of Ancient Empires*, Oxford: Clarendon Press.

—— —— —— —— (1956), *A History of Technology, ii: The Mediterranean Civilizations and the Middle Ages c.700 B.C. to c. A.D. 1500*, Oxford: Clarendon Press.

SINGER, J. DAVID (1960), 'International Conflict: Three Levels of Analysis', *World Politics*, 12/3: 453–61.

—— (1961), 'The Level-of-Analysis Problem', *World Politics*, 14/1: 77–92.

—— and SMALL, MELVIN (1966), 'The Composition and Status Ordering of the International System 1815–1940', *World Politics*, 18: 236–82.

—— —— (1972), *The Wages of War, 1816–1965: A Statistical Handbook*, New York: Wiley.

—— BREMER, STUART, and STUCKEY, JOHN (1972), 'Capability Distribution, Uncertainty, and Major Power War, 1920–1965', in *Peace, War, and Numbers*, Beverly Hills, Calif.: Sage Publications.

SINGER, MAX, and WILDAVSKY, AARON (1993), *The Real World Order*, Chatham, NJ: Chatham House Publishers.

SKOCPOL, T. (1979), *States and Social Revolutions: A Comparative Analysis of France, Russia and China*, Cambridge: Cambridge University Press.

SMIL, VACLAV (1994), *Energy in World History*, Boulder, Colo.: Westview Press.

SMITH, ANTHONY D. (1991), *National Identity*, London: Penguin.

SMITH, DENNIS (1991), *The Rise of Historical Sociology*, Cambridge: Cambridge University Press.

SMITH, TONY (1981), *The Pattern of Imperialism: the United States, Great Britain and the Late-Industrializing World since 1815*, Cambridge: Cambridge University Press.

SOPEMI (1995), *Trends in International Migration: Continuous Reporting System on Migration: Annual Report 1994*, Paris: OECD.

SPENCER, CHARLES (1991), 'Factional Ascendance, Dimensions of Leadership and the Development of Centralized Authority', in T. Earle (ed.), *Chiefdoms: Power, Economy and Ideology*, Cambridge: Cambridge University Press.

SPRUYT, HENDRIK (1994a), 'Institutional Selection in International Relations: State Anarchy as Order', *International Organization*, 48/4: 527–58.

—— (1994b), *The Sovereign State and its Competitors: An Analysis of Systems Change*, Princeton: Princeton University Press.

STAVRIANOS, L. S. (1970), *The World to 1500: A Global History*, Englewood Cliffs, NJ: Prentice-Hall.

—— (1990), *Lifelines from our Past*, London: I. B. Tauris.

STEENSGAARD, NIELS (1972), *Carracks, Caravans and Companies: The Structural Crisis in the European–Asian Trade in the Early Seventeenth Century*, Scandinavian Institute of Asian Studies Monograph Series 17, Odense: Studentlitteratur.

—— (1987), 'The Indian Ocean Network and the Emerging World Economy, c. 1500–1750', in Satish Chandra, (ed.), *The Indian Ocean Explorations in History, Commerce and Politics*, New Delhi: Sage Publications.

STONE, ELIZABETH (1995), 'The Development of Cities in Ancient Mesopotamia', in *Civilizations of the Ancient Near East*, vol. iv, gen. ed. Jack M. Sasson, New York: Scribner.

STOPFORD, JOHN M., STRANGE, SUSAN, with HENLEY, JOHN S. (1991), *Rival States, Rival Firms: Competition for World Market Shares*, Cambridge: Cambridge University Press.

STRANG, DAVID (1991) 'Anomaly and Commonplace in European Political Expansion: Realist and Institutional Accounts', *International Organization*, 45/2: 143–62.

STRANGE, SUSAN (1988),'Defending Benign Mercantilism', *Journal of Peace Research*, 25/3: 273–7.

—— (1997), *Casino Capitalism*, Manchester: Manchester University Press (1st pub. 1986).

—— (1998), *Mad Money*, Manchester: Manchester University Press.

STRATEGIC SURVEY 1991–2 (1992), London: International Institute for Strategic Studies.

STREHLOW, T. G. H. (1970), 'Geography and the Totemic Landscape in Central Australia: A

Functional Study', in R. M. Berndt (ed.), *Australian Aboriginal Anthropology*, Nedlands: University of Western Australian Press.

SUGANAMI, H. (1978), 'A Note on the Origins of the Word "International"', *British Journal of International Studies*, 4: 226–32.

SWAIN, TONY (1993), *A Place for Strangers: Towards a History of Australian Aboriginal Being*, Cambridge: Cambridge University Press.

TAMBIAH, S. J. (1976), *World Conqueror and World Renouncer: A Study of Buddhism and Polity in Thailand against a Historical Background*, Cambridge: Cambridge University Press.

TAYLOR, PETER J. (1985), *Political Geography: World-Economy, Nation-State and Locality*, London: Longman.

TERRELL, J. E., HUNT, T. L., and GOSDEN, C. (1997), 'The Dimensions of Social Life in the Pacific: Human Diversity and the Myth of the Primitive Isolate', *Current Anthropology*, 38/2: 155–96.

TESCHKE, BENNO (1998), 'Geopolitical Relations in the European Middle Ages', *International Organization*, 52/2: 325–58.

THOMPSON, E. P. (1978), *The Poverty of Theory and Other Essays*, London: Merlin Press.

THOMSON, JANICE E. (1994), *Mercenaries, Pirates, and Sovereigns: State-Building and Extraterritorial Violence in Early Modern Europe*, Princeton: Princeton University Press.

—— (1995), 'State Sovereignty in International Relations: Bridging the Gap between Theory and Empirical Research', *International Studies Quarterly*, 39/2: 213–34.

TIBI, BASSIM (1993), *Conflict and War in the Middle East 1967–91*, London: Macmillan.

TILLY, CHARLES (1985), 'War Making and State Making as Organised Crime', in P. Evans, D. Rueschemeyer, and T. Skocpol, *Bringing States back in*, Cambridge: Cambridge University Press.

—— (1990), *Coercion, Capital and European States AD 990–1990*, Oxford: Basil Blackwell.

—— (1995), 'Entanglements of European Cities and States', in Charles Tilly and Wim P. Blockmans (eds.), *Cities and the Rise of States in Europe, A.D. 1000–1800*, Boulder, Colo.: Westview Press.

TOYNBEE, ARNOLD (1954), *A Study of History*, vol. ix, Oxford: Oxford University Press.

—— (1972), *A Study of History*, Oxford: Oxford University Press and London: Thames & Hudson Ltd.

—— (1958), *Civilization on Trial and the World and the West*, Cleveland: Meridian.

TRIGGER, BRUCE (1993), *Early Civilizations: Ancient Egypt in Context*, Cairo: American University in Cairo Press.

UBEROI, J. P. SINGH (1962), *The Politics of the Kula Ring*, Manchester: Manchester University Press.

UNCTAD (1993), *World Development Report*, New York: United Nations Conference on Trade and Development.

—— (1994), *World Development Report*, New York: United Nations Conference on Trade and Development.

—— (1996), *World Development Report*, New York: United Nations Conference on Trade and Development.

UNDESA (1973), *The Determinants and Consequences of Population Trends: New Summary of Findings on Interaction of Demographic, Economic and Social Factors*, vol. i, UN Dept. of Economic and Social Affairs, Population Study 50, New York: United Nations.

UNITED NATIONS (1965), *Statistical Yearbook 1964*, New York: United Nations.

—— (1983), *The United Nations Statistical Yearbook*, New York: United Nations.

—— (1988), *Statistical Yearbook 1987*, New York: United Nations.

—— (1996), *Statistical Yearbook 1994*, New York: United Nations.

VAJNSHTEJN, S. I. (1978), 'The Problem of Origin and Formation of the Economic and Cultural Type of Pastoral Nomads in the Moderate Belt of Eurasia', in Wolfgang Weisleder (ed.), *The Nomadic Alternative: Modes and Models of Interaction in the African-Asian Deserts and Steppes*, The Hague: Mouton Publishers.

VAN CREVELD, MARTIN (1991), *Technology and War from 2000 BC to the Present*, London: Brassey's.

VILAR, PIERRE (1976), *A History of Gold and Money 1450–1920*, trans. Judith White, London: NLB.

VINCENT, R. JOHN (1974), *Nonintervention and International Order*, Princeton: Princeton University Press.

—— (1986), *Human Rights and International Relations*, Cambridge: Cambridge University Press.

VON LAUE, THEODORE (1987), *The World Revolution of Westernization: The Twentieth Century in Global Perspective*, Oxford: Oxford University Press.

—— (1989), 'Toynbee Amended and Updated', in C. T. McIntire and Marvin Perry (eds.), *Toynbee: Reappraisals*, Toronto: University of Toronto Press.

WÆVER, OLE (1992), 'International Society: Theoretical Promises Unfulfilled?', *Cooperation and Conflict*, 27/1: 97–128.

—— (1994), 'After the Fourth Debate: Patterns of International Relations Theory in the 1990s', Copenhagen: Centre for Peace and Conflict Research.

—— (1996), 'Europe's Three Empires: A Watsonian Interpretation of Post-Wall European Security', in Rick Fawn and Jeremy Larkins (eds.), *International Society after the Cold War*, Basingstoke: Macmillan.

—— (1997), 'Regional Realism: A Mildly Constructivist Interpretation of European Security with Implications for "World Order"', paper presented to the 'New World Order: Contrasting Theories' Conference, Copenhagen, Danish Institute of International Affairs, 21–2 Nov.

—— (1998), 'Four Meanings of International Society: A Trans Atlantic Dialogue', in B.A. Roberson (ed.), *International Society and the Development of International Relations*, London: Pinter.

—— BUZAN, BARRY, KELSTRUP, MORTEN, and LEMAITRE, PIERRE (1993), *Identity, Migration and the New Security Agenda in Europe*, London: Pinter.

WALBANK, F. W. (1993), *The Hellenistic World*, Cambridge, Mass.: Harvard University Press.

WALKER, R. B. J. (1988), 'Genealogy, Geopolitics and the Political Community: Richard K. Ashley and the Critical Social Theory of International Politics', *Alternatives*, 13: 84–8.

—— (1993), *Inside/Outside: International Relations as Political Theory*, Cambridge: Cambridge University Press.

WALLERSTEIN, IMMANUEL (1974), *The Modern World-System*, New York: Academic Press.

—— (1984), *The Politics of the World Economy: The States, the Movements and the Civilizations*, Cambridge: Cambridge University Press.

—— (1991), *Geopolitics and Geoculture: Essays on the Changing World System*, Cambridge: Cambridge University Press.

—— (1993), 'The World System after the Cold War', *Journal of Peace Research*, 30/1: 1–6.

WALTZ, KENNETH N. (1959), *Man, the State, and War: A Theoretical Analysis*, New York: Columbia University Press.

—— (1979), *Theory of International Politics*, Reading, Mass.: Addison-Wesley.

—— (1986), 'Reflections on *Theory of International Politics*: A Response to my Critics', in Robert O. Keohane (ed.), *Neorealism and its Critics*, New York: Columbia University Press.

—— (1993), 'The New World Order', *Millennium*, 22/2: 187–95.

WARMINGTON, B. H. (1964), *Carthage*, Harmondsworth: Pelican Books.

WATSON, ADAM (1987), 'Hedley Bull, State Systems and International Studies', *Review of International Studies*, 13/2: 147–53.

WATSON, ADAM (1990), 'Systems of States', *Review of International Studies*, 16/2: 99–109.

—— (1992), *The Evolution of International Society*, London: Routledge.

—— (1997), *The Limits of Independence: Relations between States in the Modern World*, London: Routledge.

WEBER, MAX (1947), *The Theory of Social and Economic Organization*, ed. with introd. by Talcott Parsons, trans. A. M. Henderson and Talcott Parsons, New York: Free Press.

WELLS, H. G. (1925), *The Outline of History: Being a Plain History of Life and Mankind*, with maps and plans by J. F. Horrabin, rev. edn. London: Cassell.

WELTMAN, J. J. (1973), *Systems Theory in International Relations: A Study in Metaphoric Hypertrophy*, Lexington, Ky.: Lexington Books.

WENDT, ALEXANDER (1992), 'Anarchy is What States Make of it: The Social Construction of Power Politics', *International Organization*, 46/2: 391–425.

WESSON, CAMERON B. (1999), 'Chiefly Power and Food Storage in Southeastern North America', *World Archaeology*, 31/1: 145–164.

WHITTAKER, C. R. (1978), 'Carthaginian Imperialism in the Fifth and Fourth Centuries', in P. A. Garnsey and C. R. Whittaker (eds.), *Imperialism in the Ancient World*, Cambridge: Cambridge University Press.

WIESEHOFER, JOSEF (1996), *Ancient Persia*, trans. Azizeh Azodi, London: I. B. Tauris.

WIGHT, GABRIELE, and PORTER, BRIAN (eds.) (1991), *International Theory: The Three Traditions—Martin Wight*, Leicester: Leicester University Press.

WIGHT, MARTIN (1966a), 'Western Values in International Relations', in Herbert Butterfield and Martin Wight (eds.), *Diplomatic Investigations*, London: Allen & Unwin.

—— (1966b), 'Why is There no International Theory?', in Herbert Butterfield and Martin Wight (eds.), *Diplomatic Investigations*, London: Allen & Unwin.

—— (1977), *Systems of States*, Leicester: Leicester University Press.

—— (1979), *Power Politics*, Harmondsworth: Penguin.

WILDE, JAAP H. de (1991), *Saved from Oblivion: Interdependence Theory in the First Half of the 20th Century*, Aldershot: Darmouth Publishing Ltd.

WILLETTS, PETER, (ed.) (1982), *Pressure Groups in the Global System: The Transnational Relations Issue-Orientated Non-governmental Organizations*, London: Pinter.

—— (1996), *'The Conscience of the World': The Influence of Non-governmental Organisations in the UN System*, London: C. Hurst.

WOBST, H. MARTIN (1974), 'Boundary Conditions for Paleolithic Social Systems: A Sociological Approach', *American Antiquity*, 39: 147–78.

—— (1976), 'Locational Relationships in Paleolithic Society', *Journal of Human Evolution*, 5: 49–58.

WOLF, ERIC, R. (1982), *Europe and the People without History*, Berkeley and Los Angeles: University of California Press.

WOLFERS, ARNOLD (1962), *Discord and Collaboration*, Baltimore: Johns Hopkins University Press.

WOOD, ELLEN MEIKSINS (1995), 'What is the "Postmodern" Agenda?', *Monthly Review*, 47/3: 1–12.

WOODRUFF, WILLIAM (1966), *Impact of Western Man: A Study of Europe's Role in the World Economy 1750–1960*, London: Macmillan.

WOYTINSKY, W. L. (1927), *Die Welt in Zählen*, v: *Handel and Verkehr*, Berlin: Rudolf Mosse.

WOYTINSKY, W. S., and WOYTINSKY, E. S. (1953), *World Population and Production: Trends and Outlook*, New York: Twentieth Century Fund.

—— —— (1955), *World Commerce and Governments: Trends and Outlook*, New York: Twentieth Century Fund.

YEARBOOK of INTERNATIONAL ORGANIZATIONS (1994–5), *Yearbook of International Organizations*, iii: *Subject Volume*, 12th edn., Munich: K. G. Saur.

YOFFEE, NORMAN (1991), 'The Collapse of Ancient Mesopotamian States and Civilization', in Yoffee and Cowgill (1991).

—— and COWGILL, GEORGE L. (eds.) (1991), *The Collapse of Ancient States and Civilizations*, Tucson: University of Arizona Press.

YOST, D. S. (1979), 'New Perspectives on Historical States-Systems', *World Politics* 32/1: 151–68.

ZHANG, YONGJIN (1991), 'China's Entry into International Society: Beyond the Standard of Civilization', *Review of International Studies*, 17/1: 3–16.

# GLOSSARY

**ahistoricism,** the view that it is in principle possible to apply social theories to all times and places because similarities of structure underlie apparent historical differences.

**anarchophilia,** the disposition to assume that the structure of the international system has always been anarchic, that this is natural, and (more selectively) that this is a desirable thing.

**anarchy,** a political structure where units are not subject to any overarching authority. The opposite of hierarchy.

**behaviouralism,** the idea, and the movement to implement it, that the positivist methods of the natural sciences were the best way to approach the study of the social sciences.

**constructivism,** the idea, mostly in opposition to behaviouralism and materialist theories, that social realities are best understood as being intersubjective constructions of understanding that are continuously being created, reproduced, and dismantled within the processes that define society.

**defence dilemma,** in which fear of war begins to outweigh fear of defeat, and weapons begin to be seen as a problem in themselves rather than just as a problem when in the hands of others (Buzan 1991: ch. 7).

**empiricism,** the view that all knowledge of matters of fact derives from direct experience of the physical and social environment.

**English school,** a body of thought stemming from the work of Martin Wight and Hedley Bull, focusing on the concepts of international society and world society, and rooted in the view that international systems will always display anarchic, societal, and transnational elements simultaneously.

**epistemology,** concerning the nature of knowledge, and how claims to knowledge are validated.

**Eurocentrism,** the propensity to understand world history and international politics past and present as if they were merely offshoots of European history and Westphalian forms of international relations.

**functional differentiation,** the second tier of Waltz's definition of political structure. If units are functionally differentiated, they each take on different, specialized, elements of the function of government. If they are not differentiated each unit performs the same tasks as all the others. A system of sovereign states is functionally undifferentiated and in Waltz's view (and ours) constitutes an anarchic structure. In Waltz's view (but not ours) a system of functionally differentiated units must be a hierarchy.

**Grotianism,** the distinctive third path within the English school, separating realism and idealism, and emphasizing the centrality of states, the possibility of co-operation, and the importance of shared identity, international law, and institutions.

**heuristic,** something which helps one to learn or explore understanding without itself constituting a general rule or law.

**hierarchy,** a political structure in which units relate in a subordinate–superordinate relationship. The opposite of anarchy.

**historicism,** the view that events cannot be understood independently of the particular historical contexts in which they take place, and that any comparison across historical time and space that fails to accommodate this view is deeply problematic.

**holism,** pursuing understanding on the premiss that the whole is more than the sum of its parts, and that the behaviour and even construction of the parts is shaped and moulded by structural forces within the systems that contain them. Contrasts with methodological individualism.

**ideology,** the sets of ideas around which states, groups, or individuals (try to) organize their political, economic, and societal life.

**interaction capacity,** the level of transportation, communication, and organization capability in the unit/system that determines what types and levels of interaction are possible.

**interdependence,** activities or events in one place having significant effects on people in other places, whether good or bad, wanted or unwanted, intended or unintended.

**international society,** exists when states are conscious of certain common interests and common values, conceive of themselves to be bound by a common set of rules, and share in the working of common institutions (Bull 1977: 13).

**levels of analysis,** units of analysis organized on the principle of spatial scale (small to large, individual to system), and serving as the locations where both outcomes and sources of explanation can be located.

**liberalism,** one of the main paradigms in International Relations, emphasizing the possibility of change, the centrality of economic relations and markets, individualism, human rights, and the achievability of international co-operation.

**Marxism,** one of the main paradigms in International Relations, emphasizing class and class conflict rather than the state, privileging the economic and societal sectors, focusing on the political use of language, and mixing liberal-type optimism about change with realist-type pessimism about power and conflict.

**methodological individualism,** the view, contrary to holism, that explanations of social behaviour must be couched at the level of the individual rather than at the level of collective units, or systems, such as families, states, or societies.

**methodological monism,** the idea that subjects can only be approached from a single theoretical perspective.

**methodological pluralism,** the position that subjects can and should be viewed simultaneously from more than one theoretical perspective.

**methodology,** to do with the prevailing theories, principles, and analytical methods in a given discipline.

**most favoured nation agreements,** trade agreements in which parties extend the agreed tariff concession to others participating in the reciprocal system.

**nationalism,** the idea that shared ethnicity, culture, history, and particularly language, should provide the legitimate basis for claims to self-government.

**neorealism,** stems from the work of Kenneth Waltz, and attempts to put realism onto a more scientific basis by deriving the logic of power politics from the structure of the system rather than from human nature. Notable for its definition of structure and for its promotion of stricter distinctions between unit and system levels of explanation.

**normative,** to do with, or reflecting, preferred values.

**ontology,** to do with what actually exists, as opposed to ideas or theoretical constructs.

**paradigm,** a general conception of how a subject should be studied, including its appropriate theory and methodology.

**pluralism,** closely linked to liberalism, the word stressing the contrast with realism's emphasis on the state as the system-defining unit.

**positive- and zero-sum games.** A zero-sum game is one in which wins plus losses=0, i.e. what one person wins, another must lose. A positive-sum game is one in which wins plus losses=more than 0, meaning that everyone can win without anyone having to lose.

**positivism,** a strong form of empiricism, asserting that experiment and observation are the only forms of valid knowledge.

**process,** the interactions that actually take place amongst units.

**process formations,** durable or recurrent patterns in interactions among units.

**realism,** one of the main paradigms in International Relations, emphasizing state actors, permanent principles, pessimism, power politics, protectionism, and the need for actors to deal pragmatically with the system as they find it on a basis of self-interest and survival.

**reductionism,** the traditional methodology of the natural sciences, understanding how systems operate by looking at the nature of their constituent units and how they interrelate.

**sectors,** views of the whole system through an analytical lens which selects one particular type of relationship and highlights the types of unit, interaction, and structure most closely associated with it.

**security community,** a group of states or other actors whose members neither expect nor prepare for the use of force in relations with each other.

**sources of explanation,** variables that explain behaviour on any given level of analysis (in this book, structure, process, interaction capacity).

**sovereignty,** the claim, and its recognition by other actors, of exclusive right to self-government (respectively internal, or empirical sovereignty; and external or juridical sovereignty).

**state,** any form of post-kinship, territorially based, politically centralized, self-governing entity capable of generating an inside/outside structure. This broad category contains several different historical types, and where necessary we will differentiate by referring generally to *premodern* or *modern* states, or more specifically to city-states and empires.

**structural differentiation,** the issue of whether units have similar or different institutional arrangements.

**structure,** the principles by which units in a system are arranged.

**synchronic,** comparisons within a single time period.

**system,** the composite formed by a structured set of interacting units.

**systemic,** concerning the whole system.

**teleology,** more narrowly, the idea that human affairs can be understood as moving towards some predetermined end; more broadly, the idea that there is evidence of design and purpose in the universe.

**unit,** entities composed of various sub groups, organizations, communities, and many individuals, sufficiently cohesive to have actor quality (i.e. to be capable of conscious decision-making), and sufficiently independent to be differentiated from others and to have standing at the higher levels (e.g. states, nations, transnational firms).

**world society,** is made up of individuals who accept the existence of a world common good defined in terms of the common ends or values of the universal society of all mankind (Bull 1977: 84).

# INDEX

Note: Page numbers followed by an '*f*,' refer to figures and page numbers followed by an '*m*,' to maps.